TYRANNY

A New Interpretation

WALLER R. NEWELL
Carleton University

W0010051

CAMBRIDGE
UNIVERSITY PRESS

CAMBRIDGE UNIVERSITY PRESS
Cambridge, New York, Melbourne, Madrid, Cape Town,
Singapore, São Paulo, Delhi, Mexico City

Cambridge University Press
32 Avenue of the Americas, New York, NY 10013-2473, USA

www.cambridge.org
Information on this title: www.cambridge.org/9781107610736

First published 2013

Printed in the United States of America

A catalogue record for this publication is available from the British Library.

Library of Congress Cataloguing in Publication Data
Newell, Waller Randy.
Tyranny : a new interpretation / Waller R. Newell, Carleton University.
pages cm
Includes bibliographical references and index.
ISBN 978-1-107-01032-1 (hardback)
1. Despotism. I. Title.
JC381.N43   2012
321.9–dc23   2012028449

ISBN 978-1-107-01032-1 Hardback
ISBN 978-1-107-61073-6 Paperback

CONTENTS

CONTENTS

ACKNOWLEDGMENTS

As I was nearing the completion of this book, the world was being inspired by the struggle for freedom unfolding across the Arab lands. During that same period and for some time preceding it, according to Freedom House, the world's democracies had been in retreat while tyrannical forces were on the rise. We seem to be living through an era in which expectations for freedom and the proliferation of tyranny are intensifying simultaneously. More than ever, then, it is incumbent on us to study tyranny, attempt to identify its varieties, and try to anticipate its emergence and hostility to the forces of freedom. Tyranny is generally an unpleasant subject, but one does not think about tyranny because one wants to think about unpleasant things. Rather, if one wants to think, it must be about both pleasant and unpleasant things.

This book grew out of many years of reflection, and some of the chapters (1, 3, 4, 5, and a portion of 6) contain greatly transformed and lengthened versions of earlier articles. The Introduction, Chapters 2 and 7, and the Conclusion are entirely new. None of the chapters, however, simply duplicates the content of the earlier articles, because I only arrived at the central thesis of this book through writing them. They have now been reshaped in light of that thesis, which I set forth in the Introduction. This book can be read entirely on its own, independent of my other writings. At the same time, it does draw on, and is the scholarly culmination of, my earlier books on Plato, the manly virtues, and political leadership.

Earlier versions of some of the chapters were presented at Peterhouse College Cambridge, Yale University, and the University of Toronto. I gratefully acknowledge the stimulation and the hospitality I received on those occasions. I also have the pleasure and the honor of acknowledging the critical insight and support that I have received from many colleagues over the years. Although they share no responsibility for the book's shortcomings, they have contributed to whatever of value readers may find in it. They include, in no special order, the following: Charles H. Fairbanks, Thomas L. Pangle, Lorraine Pangle, Clifford Orwin, Ryan Balot, Nalin Ranasinghe, Stanley Rosen, Catherine Zuckert, Barry Strauss, Paul Rahe, Robert Sibley, Steven Smith, Travis Smith, Graham Howell, Jarrett Carty, Geoffrey Kellow, Peter Ahrensdorf, Harvey C. Mansfield, Lynette Mitchell, Jeff Sikkenga, Norman Doidge, Kenneth Green, Michael Zuckert, Gregory MacIsaac, Peter Emberley, Tom Darby, Samuel Abraham, H. D. Forbes, Edward Andrew, and Gary McDowell. I also have the especially gratifying obligation to acknowledge the insights I derived from discussing the political philosophies examined in this book with students past and present, some of whom are now embarked on their own careers. Finally, I owe special thanks to my editor at Cambridge University Press, Robert Dreesen, and to the anonymous reviewers for the original proposal, who prompted me to address many important issues in advance that I had neglected.

This book is dedicated to my best friend and collaborator, my wife Jacqueline Etherington Newell.

INTRODUCTION

The Conquest of Eros

Tyranny is elusive. Although everyone wants to be known as just, especially when they are not, no one wants to be known as a tyrant, especially when they are. Yet this most elusive of political phenomena is one of the most widespread and shockingly real. From the innermost sanctum of the household to the politics of nations and empires, there are victims and there are oppressors. Civil war, revolution, terrorism, superpower conflict – in all these spheres of human violence, the pursuit of power over others is accompanied by the furious or heartrending demand for justice, whose first act must be to expose the aggressor for what he or it truly is. The dilemma is only complicated by the fact that, as students of politics from Aristotle to Abraham Lincoln have observed, the would-be tyrant may appear in the guise of a liberator. More extraordinary still, in the modern age, our potential oppressors are sometimes not necessarily human at all – technology is a faceless, impersonal power that nevertheless could destroy the entire planet or, some have argued, terrify us into peace and moderation. Hence one of the oldest themes in political philosophy and one of the most lastingly relevant: Who and what is the tyrant?

The word *tyrannos* in ancient Greek meant a ruler without ancestral descent from a lawful king, a *basileus*. A *basileus* was sometimes a semisacerdotal figure, sometimes, as in the Spartan dual monarchy, exercising military command. Often a king was seen as a kind of father of his people, a link to the ancestors and the womb of the country, and to the gods themselves, who were the fathers of the fathers.[1] By contrast,

---

1 Consider Aristotle *Politics* 1252b15–27, 1285b3–1285b20. In the first lines of *Oedipus the Tyrant*, Oedipus tries to assert his status by addressing the Thebans as "children."

a tyrant was often a "new man," someone who seized or usurped exclusive power, whether over a formerly free people or by taking the place of a lawful king. Sometimes their rule was violent or began in violence, but tyrants could also be recognized as benevolent, better at the art of ruling than a legitimate king, and so successful that their position might become hereditary for a time. However, they never entirely escaped the taint of illegitimacy. Hence Max Weber derived his famous category of "charisma" from Sophocles' *Oedipus the Tyrant*. Because he came to power by ridding Thebes of the sphinx and labors under mutterings about how the legitimate king Laius had been murdered, a crime that he must also solve to remove a famine, Oedipus must compensate for his lack of hereditary royal authority and sanctity by proving his intellectual prowess and boldness, which of course leads to his undoing as he is exposed as his father's murderer and in an incestuous relationship with his mother. Throughout the play, one senses the uneasiness of Oedipus' hold on the throne, how even in the opening lines, the priests seem unwilling to recognize his claim to authority (30–35), and his vexation with his behind-the-scenes power-sharing deal with Kreon, the representative of the nobility from which a legitimate king would normally be drawn (575–584). In another variation of the problem posed by absolute rule, for the Romans, a king (*rex*) was himself tantamount to a tyrant, hence the Latin translation of Sophocles' title as *Oedipus Rex*. The Romans' hatred of their original Etruscan kings was so intense that even men who later wielded what amounted to royal power such as Julius Caesar and, above all, his serpentine successor Augustus dared not claim this title openly but had to sheath it in the constitutional garb of "first citizen" or "commander" (*imperator*), even though Augustus was openly hailed in the Greek provinces as a monarch.[2]

There are so many ways we can use this term "tyranny" that it is difficult to isolate a common definition. At a minimum, we could define it as the use of coercive or violent force to treat others unjustly through the exercise of political supremacy. But is this not a matter of perspective? As Hobbes sourly observed, if someone does us good, we praise him; if someone harms our interests, we call him a tyrant.[3] There is

---

2 For the classic account of how the usurper Octavian sheathed himself in the outward garb of the restorer of the Republic, see Syme (2002).
3 Hobbes (1971) p. 722.

some truth to this observation. The tyrant's injustice is inevitably to an extent a perception held by some but not by others, although the perception of tyranny itself, valid or otherwise, is a palpably and universally observable political phenomenon. Hitler and Stalin were venerated by many of their own countrymen, despite their millions of victims. Disturbingly, they combined their projects for genocide with ordinary and needed agendas for economic and technological modernization. Indeed, the deeply paradoxical prospect of the tyrant as a political *reformer* – entertained circumspectly by the ancients and openly extolled by moderns like Machiavelli – will be a central theme of this study. However, we use the condemnatory term "tyranny" in many other ways as well – the tyranny of petty bureaucrats, vindictive high school principals, parents over their children, spouses over their partners. If the power to destroy millions, or even the entire human race, is a characteristic of tyranny, then we could even assign it to purely impersonal forces such as nuclear weapons or the devastation of the environment. Another central theme of this study is the contention that the transition from ancient tyranny to modern tyranny involves just such a shift from personal to impersonal oppression.

Sometimes tyrants are purely secular. There have been modernizing state-builders like Kemal Ataturk who used dictatorial methods to try to establish a democratic culture in a country that had never before had one. Abraham Lincoln was decried as a tyrant for provoking the civil war by endangering states' rights and for suspending habeas corpus. Franklin Roosevelt arguably acted tyrannically by interring innocent Japanese Americans because of their race. Religious zealots can also rule tyrannically, as in Iran or wherever the Taliban gain local control in Afghanistan. Finally, there are what I term "garden variety" tyrannies, the oldest and most enduring variety. These are regimes ruled by one man or clan and an extended network of cronies who exploit an entire country as if it were their private property, a network of venality sometimes laced with religious or modernizing ideology, sometimes not. Here one can think of Spain's General Franco, whose government was conflated with his personal household and whose followers were enriched with contracts and privileges, under a veneer of protecting traditional morality and the Church. More recently, we witnessed the collapse of the shambling oligarchy that was Mubarak's Egypt, with its baksheesh-run economy, purloined billions of American foreign aid for more lavish villas for the elite, headed by a canny old mafioso survivor. Even religiously fanatical regimes such as the rule of the Ayatollahs in Iran can combine their zealotry with old-fashioned greed and graft of this kind: the mullahs are said to have stolen millions in public funds for their personal fortunes. Dictatorships like the former Soviet Union claiming to be bent on modernization also created a *nomenklatura* system of special privilege and purloined wealth for the party elite. When the regime fell, they simply stole the state's property and thereby became "entrepreneurs," a feat imitated more successfully and without a full-blown regime change by China, a mercantilist oligarchy still claiming to be Marxist. The list goes on and on.

The psychology of tyranny is also a rich vein for speculation. We all sense that there are different psychological types among tyrants – the voluptuary, the sadist, the puritan, the coldly efficient manager. Hitler was a vegetarian and teetotaler as he ordered the deaths of millions. Stalin issued similar orders while indulging in a gluttonous appetite for food and booze. Indeed, as we see at length in this study, Aristotle's identification in the *Politics* of despotism with a form of "household" authority, in which the ruler treats the country as an extension of his own property, has endured throughout history. In addition to the example of Franco, both Hitler and Stalin conducted their most important state business from their private households and dinner tables, with a blurry line at best between state official and personal retainer. Although Hitler himself was not a gourmand, the household pattern of authority was extended from his getaway home in the Alps to daily lunches in Berlin where the top paladins of the regime – Speer, Goebbels, Goering, and others – would discuss policy and monitor each other's status while sharing a common meal. According to Albert Speer, these daily lunches were the heart of the Nazi government.[4]

Two psychological types have assumed special prominence in the tradition coming from the classics – the erotic voluptuary and what we might term the rational or benevolent despot. The first of these is clearly a tyrant in a blatant way recognizable by all. Think of the mad and depraved Caligula and Nero with their endless rounds of cruelty and debauchery. The status of the second type, however – the rational despot – is much more ambiguous. Everyone has this contrast

---

4 See the accounts in Speer (1997) and Montefiore (2005).

encoded as a part of our cultural heritage, including popular entertainment culture. Think of Joaquin Phoenix's marvelous turn as the emperor Commodus in *Gladiator*. Besotted with pleasure, he is also gloomy, suspicious, and thin-skinned in a way that makes him lethally dangerous to those around him. Wandering his palaces sleeplessly at night, searching for a new pleasure, a new hatred, to fill his coruscating inner emptiness with a spasm of feeling, he finally provokes his own murder by outraged subjects who would rather risk death a single time than live in unremitting terror. Commodus in this film is much like the figure of the Master in Hegel's famous master-slave encounter in the *Phenomenology of Spirit*. The Master has achieved independence by dominating his slaves, but he has no sense of personal achievement or self-worth and can only despise the honors he receives from those who fear and curry to him. Hegel's Master in turn recalls Socrates' portrait of the tyrant in Book 9 of the *Republic*, probably the single most famous denunciation of tyranny in the canon, Hegel's version being laced with a further strain of Lutheran contempt for such witless immersion in the tinsel of worldly pleasure and renown.

In contrast to this gloomy and paranoid monster typified by Commodus, think, on the other hand, of Julius Caesar as portrayed by Ciaran Hinds in the television series *Rome*. It will be difficult to visualize Caesar in the future without recalling this Irish actor's thoroughly convincing portrayal. In all the historical accounts of him, Caesar is erotic, a famous womanizer whose own soldiers sung ribald lyrics about his unquenchable thirst for both sexes. However, he was also a well-educated and cultivated man with refined tastes in literature and a great prose stylist himself. He took a huge interest in public business, including the construction of great public works, making taxation more fair, securing land distribution for his troops, and trying in general to improve Roman life as against the purblind, stubbornly reactionary resistance of his own fellow aristocrats. Above all, he was urbane. He preferred being your friend to being your enemy. He forgave almost anyone who crossed him once but then repented. All in all, he was a magnificent figure, reviled by those who regarded him as a demagogue and traitor to his class, revered by his beneficiaries and his comrades in arms. Even Cicero could not resist his charm, although he regarded him as the very death of republican liberty. As Cicero wrote to a friend after Caesar had arrived uninvited for dinner one day at Cicero's villa with an entourage of hundreds, he found Caesar a charming and witty conversationalist at table as always, but not the sort of person with whom you would end the visit by saying, "Come again soon!"[5]

These preliminary contours add force to our original question: Who and what is the tyrant? Many books have been written on this theme. This book is concerned with a specific dimension of it: How does the modern conception of tyranny differ from the ancient one as a theme in the history of political philosophy? The core of its approach is to draw a contrast between the Platonic understanding of tyranny as a misguided longing for erotic satisfaction that can be corrected by the education of eros toward civic virtue and the modern identification of tyranny with terror deployed in the service of political reconstruction. Although Hegel is not discussed at length, my approach is very much influenced by his analysis of the French Revolution in *The Phenomenology of Spirit*.[6] Hegel locates a change in the meaning of tyranny in modern politics from the tyrant's pursuit of pleasure to an impersonal, self-abnegating, and therefore seemingly "idealistic" destruction of all premodern ties to family, class, and region in the name of a contentless vision of a unified community or state. Thus, whereas Plato considered tyrants to be fundamentally venal, what is so frightening about modern terroristic rulers such as Robespierre, Stalin, Hitler, or Pol Pot is precisely their apparent imperviousness to ordinary greed and hedonistic pleasure in their rigorous dedication to a "historical mission" of destruction and reconstruction. Their savagery becomes a duty that cannot be "compromised" by their own self-interest or love of a noble reputation, which arguably puts them outside of the Platonic starting point for the diagnosis and treatment of the tyrannical personality. Their eros cannot be rehabilitated because it is absent in the first place, rooted out by an act of will.

The studies that follow concentrate on a specific hinge of the shift from personal to impersonal tyranny suggested by Hegel: the transition from the classical teachings on statecraft to the modern science of politics inaugurated by Machiavelli and his successors. Machiavelli's formulation of the relationship of princely *virtu* to Fortuna is, it is argued

5 Amusingly retold by Everitt (2003). For a masterful account of Julius Caesar as animated by a love of Greek heroism, see Meier (1997).
6 Hegel (1979) sections 582–595.

here, at the origin of an ontological shift in the meaning of tyranny, transferring to the secular prince a transformative power of creation ex nihilo formerly reserved for God. For Plato, tyranny is a misunderstanding of the true meaning of human satisfaction whose cure is the sublimation of the passions in the pursuit of moral and intellectual virtues grounded in the natural order of the cosmos. The Machiavellian prince, by contrast, stands radically apart from nature construed as a field of hostile happenstance, so as the more effectively to focus his will on attacking and subduing it. Mastering Fortuna includes the prince's mastering that part of his *own* nature – eros specifically – vulnerable to believing in the Platonic cosmology with (what Machiavelli takes to be) its unwarranted, delusory hopefulness about the success of morality, nobility, and reason in the world. In this sense, central to the conquest of Fortune is the conquest of eros. The result is a new kind of power seeking that is at once passionately selfish and cold-bloodedly methodical – a mixture arguably not accounted for in the Platonic psychology of tyranny. With Machiavelli, we encounter a new view of princely vigor according to which terror can be a catalyst for social and political reconstruction. As we will see, this places the diagnosis of tyranny on a new basis, including the grounds on which it is to be condemned. For Plato and the ancients, the tyrant is a monster of desire who plunders and ravishes his subjects. Beginning with Machiavelli, the "prince" is envisioned as dispensing terror in a disciplined and dispassionate manner to purge society of its bloated desires and corrupt "humors," thereby laying the foundations for a stable and productive social order.[7]

Using eros as a prism, my aim is to explore the extent to which tyranny possesses an ontological basis and how that basis changes between ancient and modern thought, contributing, it is hoped, to an

---

7 Readers of Harvey Mansfield will recognize my debt to his exploration of these themes in *Machiavelli's Virtue* (1998), *Machiavelli's New Modes and Orders* (2001), and *Taming the Prince* (1993), although I do place more emphasis on explicitly metaphysical themes in my readings. Mansfield's works are discussed in the chapters to follow. For the development of my thesis about the contrast between the personal character of ancient rule and the impersonal character of modern authority, I am also indebted to Mansfield's seminal essay on Hobbes and the "science of indirect government" (1971). Other important approaches to Machiavelli and his legacy are considered in due course, including Rahe (1992, 2005, 2008) and Sullivan (1996, 2004). The identification of modern state authority with the transition to impersonal authority is also a theme of the recent book by Fukuyama (2011).

important debate in the history of political ideas that is discussed a little later in this introduction. My premise is that, interesting and salutary as it may appear to do so, one cannot posit a single psychology of tyranny that explains its ancient and modern types. The theme of tyranny is intrinsically connected to the relationship between human beings and nature. As the meaning of tyranny alters, so does the relationship of reason, virtue, will, and technical prowess to nature. The reverse is equally true: as the content of reason, virtue, will, and technical capacity undergoes a fundamental change, so does the meaning of tyranny. Tyranny thus emerges as a crucial avenue for thinking through the shift from classical political theory to that of modernity altogether, crystallized as the conquest of eros.

Now one might argue that classical and modern political theory differ most importantly in their practical, moral, and psychological implications for statesmanship. Given the richness of that debate, do we need to think about it in more purely theoretical or ontological terms? Are not the human things enough? I hope to show that, rich as those practical and psychological dimensions of statesmanship are – and this book treats them at length – they are always intertwined with more purely theoretical speculations about the ultimate character of reality, and that these streams cannot be treated in complete separation from one another.[8] That is to say, the psychological and practical dimensions of statecraft derive from a particular view of nature – because human nature is a part of nature as a whole – and in turn furnish evidence in the human realm of day-to-day civic experience for those larger cosmologies themselves.[9]

8 In this sense, Weiss's interesting book would be on a different page from mine because she argues that Socrates in the *Meno* is defending the possibility of adequate moral virtue bereft of metaphysical inquiry (2001). As Stauffer argues, Socrates in his rhetoric stresses the tension between philosophy and the city while arguing that, at the same time and for this very reason, philosophy is "the moral conscience of the city" (2006, p. 179).
9 This is why I cannot go all the way with Hadot (1995), interesting as his argument is, in seeing Socratic or Platonic philosophizing as "spiritual exercises" akin to personal therapy or mystical techniques or as if Socrates simply embodied a vague "way of life" alongside other ways of life. The Platonic Socrates does not base his argument solely on the best *askesis* for the individual but on what is objectively true and real about the cosmos, and philosophy is not presented merely as a "way of life" but as *the* magisterial guide to the truth about the cosmos, or at least the pursuit of it, and therefore as the most suitable *governor* for other "ways of life" including politics and poetry. Admirable as the postmodernist reading of Plato is in some respects as a way of freeing it from the dead

The studies that follow are much concerned with the problem posed by excessive ambition spurred by an eros for glory and for possession of the city, a problem exemplified in different ways by Sophocles' Oedipus, Homer's Achilles, and Socrates' companion Alcibiades. Plato begins a tradition of suggesting that those aberrant erotic longings for victory and possession might be rechanneled toward serving the common good guided by philosophy. Unlike modern thinkers such as Hobbes, the classics take it as given that these aberrant erotic passions cannot be wholly suppressed or extirpated but must be reshaped and redirected through civic *paideia*. As the examples of Oedipus, Achilles, and Alcibiades variously illustrate, the energy and vigor of the ambitious, although potentially dangerous, are sometimes needed by the political community in situations of extreme peril, war, or national emergency. For the classics, the challenge is to shape such men's characters in a way that will make them prefer the honor of vigorous citizenship in cooperation with their fellow citizens to the excesses of tyranny. However, this rehabilitation of eros on a psychological level to become the ally of sound statesmanship is indivisibly connected to a view of the cosmos as balanced and moderate so as to ground and justify on the transhuman level the desired human and civic therapy. If the cosmos is characterized by violent impulse and disorder, the human soul will mirror those dangerous qualities. If, however, the cosmos is harmonious and balanced, civic education can aspire to inculcate those same virtuous qualities in the citizenry. This link between soul and cosmos, this balance between mind and passions, is crystalized in such famous Platonic images as the Chariot of the Soul and Diotima's Ladder, just as later classical statements of this need for balance such as Cicero's depiction of the Dream of Scipio the Younger tie the correct balance of active and contemplative virtues in the soul to a vision of the celestial order. That is why for Plato, as we consider in this book, the reform of political psychology and statesmanship is indivisible from a critical encounter with the pre-Socratics' and Sophists' radically opposed understanding of nature as motion and its concomitant endorsement of tyrannical aggression (as in Book 10 of the *Laws*).[10]

hand of utilitarian and analytical rationality, it often leads to an even more misleading reduction of ancient philosophy to mere personal "care of the self."

10 Plato, the *Laws* 888–890. On the ontological arguments of the pre-Socratics and Sophists, consider Newell (2000) ch. 2.

As the modern understanding of princely authority is launched with Machiavelli, there emerges a parallel set of arguments linking the moral and practical dimensions of political life to the transhuman and cosmological. On the most massive level, whereas the ancients stigmatize tyranny in favor of virtuous citizenship or envision how a potential young tyrant might be guided by philosophy to become a good statesman (as in the fourth book of the *Laws*),[11] the moderns argue that princes should abandon the distinction between tyranny and civic virtue and do whatever it takes to achieve "effectual" power, stability, and prosperity for themselves and their subjects.[12] As Hobbes bluntly argues, the worst imaginable tyranny, if it creates stability and order, is preferable to the absence of any rule at all with its inevitably resulting war of all against all.[13] Accompanying this practical advice is a psychological argument claiming that by nature men are driven by the pursuit of power to preserve their lives, with no intrinsic openness to virtue. The ambition for mastery driven by a love of personal glory or a profession of nobility, once exposed as nothing grander than an impulse for survival, can be extirpated by indoctrination or terror. However, these practical and psychological tenets, just like the classical precedents they aim to reverse, all go to the meaning of nature. In the modern view, nature is matter in motion, and its human equivalent is every individual's pursuit of continued motion through self-preservation. Moreover, as matter in motion devoid of objective teleological purpose, nature can be mastered and reconstructed to save us from our own violent passions and make nature serve our material needs.

Accordingly, in the studies that follow, I explore my main theme along two parallel and equally necessary tracks, the psychological and the cosmological. One level discusses character and soul-craft – how the ancients stressed education as the deterrent to potentially tyrannical souls (as in the education of the Auxiliaries in Plato's *Republic*), whereas the moderns focus more on disciplined methods of rule (as in Machiavelli's recipe for alternating between "the lion and the fox"). Another level discusses the different ways in which ancients and moderns conceive of, and relate to, nature – not only human nature but the wider

11 Plato, the *Laws* 709–712.
12 Machiavelli, *The Prince* ch. 15.
13 Hobbes *Ibid*.

natural world with which human nature is connected and from which it seeks its bearings. For the ancients, both the danger of the tyrannical soul arising and the possibility of a therapy for it emerge *within* the order of nature, so that the correct treatment for aberrant erotic passions is to redirect them toward their proper natural fulfillments – civic virtue and the contemplative life. For the moderns, by contrast, starting with Machiavelli, the possibility is explored that through an effort of will, we can master Fortuna, striving to step outside of nature's limitations altogether. As we will see, this involves a complex dyadic movement in which the prince achieves control over Fortuna by, paradoxically, channeling "her" impulsiveness to empower his own daring. The Platonic orientation by which eros leads the soul on a hierarchical ascent from the outward beauties of visible reality to the imperishable beauty of the Good is replaced in Machiavelli's new psychology by the prince's interior and invisible modulation of the rhythms of Fortune's subrational impulses within the inward reaches of his own solitude. This contrast is explored through studies of Plato, Aristotle, Xenophon, Machiavelli, and Hobbes treating different aspects of this overarching theme. I conclude with a general discussion suggesting the wider implications of the new conception of princely rule launched by Machiavelli including, for example, a discussion of Shakespeare's history plays. I also try to show how the sometimes bewilderingly various interpretations of Machiavelli, as well as his multidimensional influence on the various streams of modern political thought, all derive from his fundamental project for the mastery of fortune.

Let us dwell for a moment more specifically on why eros can be considered the prism for clarifying some important aspects of the general shift away from the classical emphasis on our reconciliation with nature to the modern project for subduing it. For Plato, eros, if left unguided, can be the source of spontaneous tyrannical ambition. However, as he presents it, eros also contains the potential for its own redirection toward a love of the beautiful and the good, entailing the rehabilitation and sublimation of those aggressive passions in the service of philosophy and a devotion to the common good. That is to say, erotic longing can be rehabilitated by being directed toward a love of the balance and harmony that are superordinate over chance and impulse in the cosmos as a whole. Eros, in other words, is the key to an orientation toward the beneficence of the natural order. That is why, for Machiavelli, eros must be extirpated from the heart of the prince. The kind of erotic longing for the beautiful and the good set forth in Plato's *Symposium* is, as we will see, the most dangerous psychological example of what Machiavelli means by "relying on Fortuna," that is to say, entertaining a deluded hopefulness about nature's friendliness toward our needs, aspirations, and desire for an honorable life. Therefore, Machiavelli is not merely endorsing tyranny of the kind that Plato opposed. On the contrary: he is arguing that the entire Platonic starting point, which sees eros both as the source of aberrant tyrannical passions and as the source of their rehabilitation, must be abandoned. Instead, the prince must aspire to step outside of nature altogether, face the harsh truth that Fortuna is entirely indifferent to if not outright hostile to human hopes, and, emboldened by that sense of alienation, turn back on nature and master it. The key to this revaluation of values is that, before the prince can master Fortuna outwardly, he must first conquer within himself the allure of eros and its vision of a beautiful cosmos. The first victory of the prince must be over his own latently Platonic soul. In this book's inter- pretation, then, modern tyranny is launched on the premise that eros can be extirpated and that nature, thereby reduced to sheer hostile and purposeless happenstance, can be mastered by an act of cold-minded will.

THE DEBATE ABOUT ANCIENT AND MODERN TYRANNY

Let me dwell momentarily on how this book might contribute to some wider debates about ancient and modern political philosophy. The debate about whether and to what extent the modern concept of tyranny differs from the classical concept has a long pedigree continuing down to the present. Some – most notably Sir Karl Popper – have argued that modern totalitarianism was a direct repercussion of Plato's *Republic* and its utopian model for the complete subordination of the individual to the community.[14] Thus, whereas Plato would have us believe that the rule of reason (the philosopher-king) is the only sure antidote to tyranny and other vices, Popper believes that the rule of reason itself is a different and more dangerous, all-controlling form of despotism. Others have maintained, however, that there is a distinct break between

14 Popper (1971).

the ancient condemnation of tyranny and the modern tolerance for it as an engine of political power and prosperity and that this ethical break was paralleled by a new view of nature. Max Horkheimer, for example, explored the underlying connections between the emergence of modern natural science and Machiavelli's new science of politics, seeing in the *Discourses* a new "physics" of clashing political "bodies."[15] Closer to the beginning of the modern age, Bacon and Spinoza acknowledged their indebtedness to Machiavelli's new political science with its emphasis on power seeking, stability, and prosperity.[16]

In more recent years, Leo Strauss and Alexandre Kojeve famously debated the difference between ancient and modern tyranny in their discussion of Xenophon's *Hiero*.[17] For Kojeve, to some degree following Hegel, modern tyranny or totalitarianism is a project for the universal actualization of reason originating in the classics. Today's emergent "universal homogeneous state" is but the working out of a blueprint for rational politics offered by Simonides in the *Hiero* or by Plato's *Republic*. Strauss argues, by contrast, that the creation of a rational world order may be the aim of modernity, or a certain dimension of modernity, and of a certain kind of modernizing tyranny, but not of ancient political philosophy, because the philosophic life can never be entirely assimilated to any project for a rational politics. However, Strauss's position could thereby be taken to imply that modern tyranny cannot be fully comprehended or anticipated within the classical premises; that it has radically altered its character inasmuch as modern political science obliterates the distinction between the active life and the contemplative life and enlists reason in the service of the former. This poses a conundrum: If the classics cannot fully explain or anticipate modern tyranny, then how can Strauss argue that the classical view of politics is preferable to the modern view, specifically preferable to the modern project embraced by Kojeve for the actualization of reason, and preferable

---

15 Horkheimer (1995) (2007).

16 As Bacon writes in *The Advancement of Learning* in a gloss on chapter 15 of *The Prince*: "We are much beholden to Machiavelli and others, that write what men do, and not what they ought to do. . . . As for the philosophers, they make imaginary laws for imaginary commonwealths, and their discourses are as the stars, which give little light, because they are so high." Quoted in Kennington (2005). For Spinoza's view of Machiavelli, see Spinoza (1997) 5.7, 10.1.

17 Strauss (1968).

in general for distinguishing sound from unsound statecraft? I hope to shed light on this unresolved issue by suggesting that the meaning of reason itself, and its relationship to authority, changes between the classical and modern paradigm shifts in the understanding of nature.

Strauss's rejoinder is that, whereas modern tyranny is distinctive, the classics provide the best starting point for thinking that distinctiveness through. He grants that "'the conquest of nature'... made possible by natural science" at least arguably differentiates the modern conception of tyranny from the classical. Hence his willingness to entertain (without ultimately embracing) Eric Voegelin's view that the distinctively modern tyrant, exemplified by Machiavelli's Prince, is an apocalyptic or "postconstitutional" ruler whose millenarian aspirations to step outside of the boundaries of nature comprise a key ingredient of modernity.[18] By using eros, and especially the Platonic understanding of eros, as a touchstone for drawing out important contrasts between the classical and modern understandings of tyranny, I share with Strauss the view that the classics provide the best starting point for thinking those differences through. At the same time, as will already be evident, I am also partial to Voegelin's emphasis on the distinctively millenarian and apocalyptic quality of modern tyranny at its most radical. Thus, although my approach has been considerably influenced by Strauss, my particular interpretation of Machiavelli as a post-Christian and in some ways "apocalyptic" thinker owes something to Voegelin, although I am less inclined than him to see a generally seamless continuity between Platonic and Christian transcendentalism as together grounding the "metaxy" or middle ground of sound practice. Instead, I am more inclined to view the Augustinian revaluation of political honor as "dominion" in *The City of God* as constituting an irreparable break with the Platonic understanding of the erotic ascent set forth in the *Symposium*. Indeed, this book tries to show (especially in Chapters 6 and 7) that there are grounds for reading Machiavelli's new science of politics as the secularization of certain key Augustinian tenets, part of an original path that rejects both classical and Christian transcendence on post-Christian grounds. I would also argue that the broadness of Voegelin's contrast between the traditional tyrant and

---

18 Voegelin's review of *On Tyranny* first appeared in *The Review of Politics* (1949), and Strauss's response appeared in later editions of *On Tyranny*.

the postconstitutional prince, although stimulating, can undermine the precise psychological and ethical content of the shift from personal to impersonal tyranny, including specific changes in the meaning of regime types and institutions. By concentrating specifically on eros – by taking my bearings from the Platonic understanding of eros as the fundamental phenomenological link between the human soul, the political community, and the world at large – I hope to invest the broadness of Voegelin's approach with the psychological finesse encouraged by Strauss's exegeses.[19]

In exploring modernity in one of its fundamental dimensions as a project for the conquest of eros, and therefore (at least at its most radical) an incipiently totalitarian assertion of man's absolute power to master and reconstruct nature, this book radiates out toward a number of other major debates in contemporary political thought. Martin Heidegger famously argued that modern global technology originates in Platonic metaphysics itself. Whereas for Plato, reason is the cure for tyranny, according to Heidegger, Plato's metaphysics – the "all-dominating" agenda to bring all that exists under the "yoke of the Idea" – is working itself out as "technology," the complete rational mastery of nature (one of Kojeve's sources of insight).[20] Here, too, however, I would argue that the meaning of reason itself has undergone a profound alteration between ancients and moderns and that the conquest of eros presupposes a shift from the Platonic cosmology of the world as endowed with purpose, moderation, and goodness to the Machiavellian and Hobbesian view of nature as purposeless flux. If that is so, then global technology is a hallmark of modernity alone, not of the classical view of the world. Platonic cosmology invites us to reconcile ourselves to the supervening beneficence of nature and the cosmos, the highest fulfillment of our own erotic longing for completion. The new physics of matter in motion, by contrast, invites us to master nature and reshape it to serve our material needs.

Hannah Arendt, developing while modifying some of Heidegger's themes, sees totalitarianism as a deformation (beginning with Hobbes)

19 A further consideration of the differing positions of Strauss and Voegelin unfolds in Chapters 1, 6, 7, and the Conclusion.
20 Martin Heidegger, "The Letter on Humanism" and "The Question Concerning Technology" (1993). See also "Plato's Doctrine of Truth" (1998) and "Uberwindung der Metaphysik" (1954).

of the classical teachings, in which the technical and materialistic imperatives of the household are released from, and soon overwhelm, the
ethical guidance of the political community.[21] I agree with this as a
general thesis, but we also need to stress that the meaning of these
terms – household and city – undergoes a profound change owing to
the modern project for the conquest of nature. For the conquest of
nature requires that the household *itself* be drained of Aristotelian teleology every bit as much as the city, depriving it of its own contribution
to the community (the ethical rearing of future citizens). Once the teleological connection traced by Aristotle between reason and the cosmos
is hollowed out by the new physics, what remains is a project in which
political reason becomes a purely anthropocentric project for project-
ing rational control over nature as matter in motion. Aristotle's "art of
household management," with its potential for both ethical and uneth-
ical usages in the maintenance of private and family life, now drained
of its own teleological purpose, is employed as a mere methodological
means for the Machiavellian mastery of nature.

This profound shift in the meaning of terms sheds further light on
Heidegger's argument that modernity has been entirely assimilated to
the project for global technology, the "working out" of metaphysics
reaching all the way back to Plato. In my view, Plato's evocation of eros
as the longing for the beautiful and the good, first experienced through
human longing but orienting us toward the transcendental harmony,
moderation, and unity of the cosmos, stands in the way of Heidegger's
attempt to assimilate classical metaphysics to the continuous unfolding
of modernity into technology.[22] On the other hand, if, as Heidegger
remarks, the precise historical juncture at which modern technology
comes into its own is "unknown" but is connected to the rise of modern
physics as a "calculable coherence of forces," I suggest that in Hobbes's
thought we might see the beginning of this project for technical mastery
based on the new physics, an early synthesis of the political and scientific
dimensions of modernity behind the rise of what Heidegger means by
technology.[23]

21 Arendt (1996) pp. 28–38.
22 Consider Newell (2000) ch. 5.
23 Heidegger (1998) p. 303.

Mark Lilla, in his interesting book, has tried to locate in eros a way of exploring a continuity between the ancient and modern understanding and experience of tyranny.[24] In this view, Heidegger's notorious commitment to National Socialism would be a variation on Plato's flirtation with educating the tyrant Dionysius, both stemming from an immoderation born of excessive eros. Attractive as this thesis may be to establish a link between ancients and moderns that might validate the classical starting point and typologies, I argue in this book that eros is not a constant psychological or ontological category throughout these ancient and modern examples of philosophic immoderation on behalf of tyranny. Although one might concede that, broadly speaking, Heidegger and Plato were both under the sway of passion, as were their respective tyrants of choice, it is not the *same* passion of eros in the original classical meaning. To put it briefly but not misleadingly, Plato believed that tyranny might be cured by moving the soul away from spontaneous impulse toward what is metaphysically highest – and mistook Dionysius for an eligible candidate – whereas Heidegger chose as his "hero" the leader whose "resolve" he believed would shatter the grip of metaphysics over the sheer spontaneity of existence. The Leader was, indeed, the candidate of Being.[25]

As this book argues, the depiction and evaluation of eros changes between the classical and modern approaches to statesmanship, as does the role of nature. For the ancients, eros lies within the order of nature, and the therapy for its spontaneous natural proneness to immoderation lies in its redirection through education toward its naturally highest fulfillments, civic virtue and the contemplative life – an ascent that entails moderation. In sharp contrast, for the moderns beginning with Machiavelli, the erotic link between human nature and the cosmos is shattered by our fundamental experience of alienation from the "malignity of Fortuna." We must step outside of nature to master it, which entails purging ourselves of our own erotic hopes for cosmically grounded repose. To reiterate an earlier point: For Machiavelli, it is not simply a matter of endorsing the kind of tyranny that the classics condemned, but of

24 Lilla (2001).
25 On the intrinsic connections between Heidegger's philosophy of the 1920s and 1930s and his commitment to National Socialism, consider Newell (1984, 1988a, 1988b, 1988c).

evading their whole starting point for comprehending the excesses of princely rule, in which both diagnosis and therapy are rooted in eros. Just as the prince must subdue unstable Fortuna, the scientist, according to Bacon, must torture her to make her yield her secrets so as to maximize our power over nature "for the relief of man's estate."[26] Modern tyranny, including the commitment to the people's destiny evoked by the Nazis that Heidegger found so attractive, is hence more fundamentally characterized by an act of will than it is by an eros for magnificence and honor, more akin to a "secular saint" than to Alexander the Great or Julius Caesar.[27] To the extent that one *can* employ Platonic psychology to approximate the modern phenomenon of tyranny, it is arguably much closer to the passion of thumos than to eros, although even that parallel is not precise. In my view, eros is the fundamental passion in Plato's account of the soul, from which thumos itself is derived. Unlike some authors, who have suggested a continuity between Plato's evocation of thumos and will-based modern moralities like Kantianism, I believe that this continuity is highly questionable. Indeed, I argue that for Plato, strictly speaking, there is no equivalent for the modern, Kantian conception of the will.[28]

Moreover, to be as precise as possible, when I argue that modern tyranny, including totalitarian systems like National Socialism, are more fundamentally to be viewed as a deformity of will than of eros, I am making this judgment within the parameters of the massive contrast

---

26 Bacon (1937) p. 214.

27 Still worth pondering in this regard is Walzer (1982).

28 My emphasis on the centrality of eros to understanding the classical approach is cognate with recent books by Ahrensdorf (2009) and especially Ludwig (2006), although I examine a different set of authors and focus on the character of the shift from ancients to moderns. I share with Stauffer (2006) an interest in reading Plato to explore the possibility of a philosophically reformed rhetoric for shaping citizens but lay more emphasis on the cosmological hypothesis to which this "noble rhetoric" is connected. I share with Ranasinghe (2000) a broad assumption that Plato's erotic psychology is the key to his cosmological and metaphysical speculations and the limitations imposed on them by our human finitude, a premise of my own previous book on Plato. I share with Craig (1994) and Zuckert (1988) an interest in thumos as one of the keys to Platonic political psychology and the prospect for reconciling the pursuit of honor with service to the common good. I try to show, however, that eros is the fundamental passion in Plato's account of the soul, from which thumos itself is derived. Unlike some authors – for example, Shell (1996) – who have suggested a continuity between Plato's evocation of thumos and will-based modern moralities like Kantianism, I believe that this continuity is highly questionable.

between ancients and moderns that this book is devoted to uncovering – the conquest of nature. As I argue in the Conclusion, however, although some dimensions of modern tyranny and totalitarianism can indeed by illuminated by the rubric of the conquest of nature, the fuller understanding of collectivist or *Volkish* tyrannies such as National Socialism must carry us beyond those parameters altogether, thereby amplifying my view that one cannot, as Lilla does, treat the relationship between philosophy and tyranny as a set of constants. This book, by focusing strictly on the project for the conquest of nature characteristic of an intellectual phase of early modernity, will bring us to the cusp of that new collectivist politics of the General Will whose originator is Rousseau and without which we cannot fully account for totalitarianism.

To return to our overarching question: Is modern tyranny a continuation of the ancient concept? Is modernization, especially its totalitarian version, the attempt to actualize classical utopias such as Plato's *Republic*? Or is it something fundamentally different? This book argues for the latter alternative. My approach is to show how the moral and psychological issues surrounding the tyrannical character that sharply distinguish the ancient and modern views are inextricably bound up with, and illuminated by, the ontological shift in man's relationship to nature. In other words, to understand how the psychology of statecraft changes between ancients and moderns, we must consider how the entire relationship of reason to nature and to rule, and all of its cognate terms, changes between ancients and moderns. It is not enough to offer a judgment that either the classical or the modern understanding of political life is more or less natural or reasonable, because nature, reason, and the art of ruling all alter their meanings between Plato and Machiavelli, with eros at the core of the debate. These issues are held in play through a close comparison of some highly relevant classical and modern texts. In this way, I believe that my exploration of the conquest of eros can be a touchstone for these larger issues in the history of political ideas.

It should be made clear from the outset that I am far from arguing in this book that the *entire* meaning of modern political philosophy, even of early modern political philosophy, is exhausted by the Machiavellian project for the conquest of nature. I readily concede that Machiavelli's *Discourses*, for example, contain a defense of republicanism whose roots are in the tradition of the *zoon politikon* going back to Aristotle, although I also maintain that Machiavelli almost entirely subverts and transvaluates their meaning. What we might term the Promethean vision of the prince as the potential master of Fortune is more sharply etched in *The Prince*, whereas the approach of the *Discourses* is both more communal and more explicitly reflective about the existential limits placed by external reality and human psychology on our exercise of will.[29] Nevertheless, as we will see, the Promethean vigor of the ideal prince is, according to Machiavelli, also an important element in the founding and institutional makeup of republics. Altogether, then, in focusing on that strain of modernity pursuing the conquest of nature, I am abstracting what Max Horkheimer termed the "dark" dimension of the modern project (typified in his view by Machiavelli and Hobbes) from modernity as a whole, an undertow that weaves in and out of its more benign enterprise typified by such thinkers as Spinoza and Locke for the establishment of communities of rights bearing, tolerant, free, and fulfilled individuals. How and to what extent this darker current vitiates the more benign dimensions of liberalism is a question to which I hope my focus on extracting this more strictly Promethean strain might contribute. In other words, is Heidegger right to claim that, in our age, the benign face of the Enlightenment has been unmasked to reveal nothing but this underlying darker project for global technological mastery?

REMARKS ON METHOD

Because the word "ontology" can be used in different ways, my particular use of it in the studies that follow should be clarified. An ontology is a characterization of the fundamental status of all reality, beyond which or behind which there is no further basis or ground. Accordingly, all the

---

29 *The Prince* and the *Discourses* deserve pride of place among Machiavelli's writings because they are the only books in which he claims to have presented everything he knows (Mansfield [2001] p. 9. I hope I will be forgiven, as a political theorist, for not engaging the crowded field of Machiavelli biographers. Among many fine entries, I lean to Sebastian de Grazia (1994). The burden of his biography, to me convincing, is that Machiavelli, in inventing *Realpolitik*, was recommending the use of conventionally immoral means to bring about arguably sound political ends – greater stability and prosperity for the state and its inhabitants.

more proximal experiences of human life – the everyday phenomena of human psychology, morality, politics, and even philosophizing itself – are derived from this ontological ground, and it to some degree shapes in advance the specific content that those more proximal experiences contain for us. When Aristotle, for example, proclaims that we should approach what is "first by nature" only by way of what is "first for us," questions of ethics and political authority, he is to some extent presupposing a view of the cosmos as an ordered teleological hierarchy within which what is "first for us" already receives its rank and substance (*Nicomachean Ethics* 1095a17–b6).

In this book, beginning in the first chapter, a contrast is drawn between what I term primordialist and transcendentalist ontologies as a basis for speculating about tyranny. In the case of transcendentalist ontologies, the supreme expression of which is Plato's speculative metaphysics, life is preeminently characterized by a cosmic structure of orderliness, moderation, harmony, friendliness, and benevolence, all radiating from the Idea of the Good. By contrast, primordialist ontologies such as those of the pre-Socratics and Sophists stress that life is fundamentally characterized by strife, chance, and motion, the concomitant human behavior for which would elevate selfish impulse and the quest for domination over others as the most "natural" behavior. As we will see, the Platonic therapy for tyranny is squarely directed at repudiating this primordialist ontology that gives despotic and aggressive impulses the sanction of nature itself. Machiavelli's political thought is in some measure a return to the view of the Sophists, but only to a limited degree. As I argue, Machiavelli's adaptation to secular human rule of the Abrahamic concept of a God who can stand entirely outside of nature and reshape it places his new science of politics beyond the parameters of even the most open endorsement of tyranny by the Sophists and pre-Socratics, none of whom believe man possesses this degree of power to reshape his existence.

Why insist on introducing these rather freighted terms? After all, it is possible to read the history of political philosophy entirely on the level of moral experience. Seen in that light, we can find writers as diverse as Plato, Kant, and Nietzsche all endorsing self-control, virtue, honesty, and justice, often in similar if not identical-sounding terms. Who, indeed, among the great thinkers is *not* in favor of being just to oneself and others, of living honestly, of being true to oneself, of not compromising with baseness? The problem with this approach is that it risks reducing the history of thought to an undifferentiated mass in which everyone is the same as everyone else and in which there are no sharp and possibly irreconcilable differences among their philosophies and worldviews.

Only when one connects the moral evaluations of different political philosophies to their respective ontological foregrounds does one understand how the content and derivation of words such as "justice" or "moderation" are fundamentally different from one philosophy to another. The lesson of Sophocles' *Oedipus Tyrannus* – that one should aspire, allegorically speaking, to the blindness of Teresias and not tempt the gods with one's hubristic belief in one's own intellectual prowess – presupposes the tragic and Heracleitean view of life as motion and flux, what Seth Benardette termed "the Homeric-Heracleitean doctrine" of the pre-Socratics.[30] It is thus derived from a different basis than that of Platonic ethics, in which sight is the primary metaphor for the soul's openness to knowledge and in which the capacity for virtue is derived from and supported by a view of the cosmos in which rest and unity are always superordinate over chance and necessity, and hence the opposite of the tragic worldview. To take another such case, when Gorgias argues in one of the fragments attributed to him that "prudence" is one of the city's two most important virtues along with courage, he means something very different from Socrates' use of it in the dialogue devoted to Gorgias. Because Gorgias shares the Heracleitean and Empedoclean view of *physis* as motion, "prudence" is the hale and manly prowess by which rulers assert their power and achieve fame and prosperity.[31] For Plato's Socrates, by contrast, prudence leads (in the *Gorgias*) to the complete subordination of bodily passion and the manly contest for distinction through pre-eminence to a cosmos of pure orderliness, harmony, and rest. Similarly, to take a final example, to derive moral virtue as Kant does from the will to overcome our natural inclinations as the drag on us of a natural world driven by material necessity is diametrically opposed to Aristotle's view of virtue as the fullest flowering *of* our natural inclinations guided by teleological purpose. On a certain level, Kant may sound like Aristotle or the Stoics in his exhortations

---

30 Benardette in Plato (1984) p. 117.
31 Gorgias 8. In Freeman (1948). Consider also Newell (2000) pp. 17–20.

to overcome base and witless pleasures, but at bottom the content and derivation of these accounts of moral virtue are at odds with one another.

For reasons beyond the scope of this study, we political theorists have sometimes lost sight of the fact that the history of political ideas is one of fundamental alternatives, not a happy chorus in which all the great ones agree with each other. The sidelining of the metaphysical and onto-logical dimensions of political philosophy now in vogue enables one to evade the likelihood that it may not be possible to agree with all the great ones at the same time. We should avoid committing the fallacy of concluding from the fact that we understandably and justifiably admire both Nietzsche *and* Plato that Nietzsche *is* Plato. Once we grasp that Plato's cosmology and Nietzsche's teaching on the will to power, or Plato's approach to Being and that of Heidegger, are opposed and anti-thetical concepts, we will be liberated from this fallacy, and understand far better, moreover, why Nietzsche and Heidegger themselves regarded Plato as their antipodal opposite and chief antagonist.[32]

I will tax the reader further with one brief methodological considera-tion. To the extent that I have worked out a hermeneutic for interpreting political theory, I try to avoid a stage-theory of history in which one philosophy "causes" another one in a direct linear development. To my mind, the meaning of a political philosophy is not most fully grasped as its next measurable impact on another thinker chronologically in time. Hence, the meaning of Machiavelli is not reducible to his influ-ence on Hobbes, who some would argue is his most immediate and compatible successor. As I argue in the Conclusion, the meaning of Machiavelli is comparable to many spokes radiating outward from a single wheel, the full significance of which is an ongoing exploration for the interpreter down to the present. I do not view the history of political thought as primarily linear at all, but rather as a mutating and dynamic whole within which many views contend and out of which one can abstract for purposes of examination one of those complexes in contrast with others. Much less do I accept the still-prevalent notion that political theory concerns the realm of the "ought" or the normative in contrast with the realm of the "is" or the empirical. Why would any sensible adult spend his life studying an "ought" that is divorced from

32 This argument is explicated at further length in Newell (2010).

what is real? To my mind, political theory is a *way* of studying politics. Arguably, political theory may not be the primary cause of great historical events. Although I am inclined to believe that it is, and find compelling, for example, Richard Kennington's characterization of the seventeenth century's religious wars over the Reformation as in effect wars launched by Machiavelli, Bacon, and Hobbes against the Catholic, Aristotelian, and feudal conglomerate of the old politics, I cannot prove it. At a minimum, however, by separating out from the warp and woof of historical causality in its limitless overlapping layers the motif of a distinct set of political ideas, we are unquestionably lighting up one *way* of explaining what causes great historical events.[33]

For reasons such as these, I am sympathetic to Hegel's view that education is not the rote learning of given data from a chronological sequence, but the "recollection" of moral, spiritual, and theoretical energies that may have taken place in the distant past but none of which have been simply outmoded by the march of time and all of which are dwelling with us right now as modern men and women as latent energies that can be "raised to consciousness" through an interaction in which both the interpreter and the text are transformed.[34] Hence, for example, by considering how Sophocles' Oedipus could not possibly be "guilty" from a modern Kantian perspective that assumes we can take autonomous responsibility for our actions in full awareness of them, we learn more about both the ancient and the modern view of life through what each of them lacks and may need from the other – how Sophocles downplays the importance of autonomy as the key to ethics and how Kant downplays the extent to which unmerited, unintended, and hidden fate can undermine our pursuit of virtue. Gadamer's hermeneutic of the "fusion of horizons" is in my view the direct successor to Hegel's pedagogy of recollection, in which precisely the irreconcilable contradictions between, say, Aristotle's *Physics* and Bacon's *Novum Organum* disclose the meaning of both in a sharper and richer way than if we had access only to one or the other.[35] This is not progress but dialogue.

33 Kennington (2005). Consider Manent's subtle yet trenchant defense of the need to recognize in the ideas of modern political philosophy the animating spirit of modern liberal civilization as a whole (1995).
34 Consider Newell (2009a, 2006).
35 Gadamer (1975) p. 273.

Accordingly, the essays in this book are not written as a chronological sequence in which I try to show, step by step, how Plato influenced Aristotle and how Machiavelli influenced Hobbes. I am indeed clustering these studies around a break between ancients and moderns that I argue is fundamental, the modern project for the conquest of nature. Each study, however, as the reader will discover, is a more-or-less self-contained reflection in which classical texts are paired with modern texts in the hope of opening up a deeper vein of insight into how moderns differ from ancients.

I

IS THERE AN ONTOLOGY
OF TYRANNY?

In this chapter, I set forth the main premise of this book – that the classical understanding of tyranny viewed it as a deformed and excessive version of eros, the cure for which lay in the proper redirection of eros toward civic virtue and philosophy. In contrast, I argue, modern political thought, beginning with Machiavelli, understands statecraft as originating in an act of will that attempts to master nature, and above all to master the passions expressed through eros. Thus, whereas for the ancients, both the problem of and the therapy for tyranny take place within the natural order and man's place in it, for the moderns, tyranny is assimilated to a project for the rational conquest and control of nature, including and especially human nature, starting with the prince's own.

Because I am proceeding at a certain level of abstraction, let me furnish some preliminary content by beginning with a specific set of contrasts between Machiavelli and his closest point of contact among the ancients, Xenophon, a linkage to which we return a number of times throughout the studies that follow. The most important difference between them is the extent to which Xenophon's writings on princely rule (culminating in the *Education of Cyrus*) explore a kind of high political hedonism. Cyrus's motivation as Xenophon depicts him in the *Education of Cyrus* is not only the pursuit of honor but also the pursuit of pleasure from the successful arrangement of his life and tastes. More importantly, he is consumed by an eros to gratify "all men" (1.1.5) without their being in a position to gratify him in return. In this respect, Xenophon's presentation of his rise to empire is a riposte to the Aristotelian contention that liberality could be confined within the boundaries of the polis and republican self-government. The perfection of this virtue of character, Xenophon maintains, requires an imperial politics. Xenophon's exploration of political honor seeking as hedonistically motivated is further revealed by the fact that Cyrus's empire is the attempt to actualize the teaching about the Good explored by the Xenophontic Socrates, a teaching that (in contrast to Plato's *Republic*) is not only not necessarily connected to a polis but in fact cannot be reconciled with republican government. Ruling on behalf of the Socratic Good, Cyrus builds a cosmopolitan multinational empire based on the architectonic division of labor (to this extent alone like the *Republic*) and the ability of individuals to actualize their respective capacities and enjoy the rewards of their merit.

Cyrus's own fulfillment as an individual at the peak of this vast multinational household crowns the ranked satisfactions available to the meritocracy that serves him. His rule is the working out of Aristotle's definition of monarchy strictly speaking in Book 3 of the *Politics* as the rule of a prudent man according to the proper art of household management and capable of extension over many cities and nations (1285b20–33). In keeping with this teaching about political hedonism, which implies a rank ordering of respective human satisfactions, Xenophon – in contrast to Machiavelli – evinces serious reservations about man's capacity to interfere with or reshape the order of nature and of the soul's satisfactions. For example, Cyrus's father Cambyses (a Socrates stand-in) warns the ambitious young conqueror that the variability of fortune (*tuche*) and the inscrutability of the gods' favor set limits on what we can impose on nature through art (*techne*). To this we should add Xenophon's comparative assessment of Cyrus as a "good" man who practices the art of ruling vis-à-vis the gentleman or "beautiful" character pointed to by Ischomachus and the example of the Spartan Lysander in the *Oeconomicus*. These distinctions are also given in the order of the soul's natural satisfactions, and the possibility that even Cyrus's meritocratic empire cannot encompass all of them (particularly the *kalos kagathos*) reflects a natural limitation on the capacity of even the best regime to foster every form of human excellence (*Cyropaedia* 1.6; 2.3.4; *Oeconomicus* 11.8; 4.4–16; 4.17–25; *Memorabilia* 3.9.10–13).

From this perspective, as we will see at length in the studies that follow, Machiavelli's differences stand out starkly. The capacity to transform nature that Machiavelli attributes to the virtuous prince goes much further than anything entertained by Xenophon. Machiavelli has no teaching about political hedonism in the high sense of showing how the virtues of the statesman par excellence are also the key to the soul's happiness. That Machiavelli (in chapter 9 of *The Prince*) promotes the gratification of pedestrian desires in "the people" as a bond between them and the prince does not contradict this assertion, because those desires are limited to physical survival and material well-being – in other words, limited, from the classical perspective, to the realm of mere *epithumia* as opposed to eros. Machiavelli cannot have a teaching about high political hedonism incentivized by an eros for honor and a love of the noble because he does not share Xenophon's or the other classical thinkers' view that there is an order of nature and of the soul's natural satisfactions. This lack of a high political hedonism in Machiavelli's thought is connected to his view of the world as Fortuna, as clashing and hostile motions or "bodies." The radical elevation of motion over rest characteristic of Machiavelli's new science of politics, reversing the priority of classical philosophy and political philosophy, is the source of a series of paradoxical assertions that stand the classical teachings (including Xenophon's) on their head – to wit, that "disunity" and "chance" were the source of Rome's greatness (*Discourses* 1: 2,4). By contrast, it is as true for Xenophon as it is for Plato or Aristotle that only unity or rest could be the source of the best regime and the art of ruling. For, again, Cyrus's cosmopolitan empire is the proper art of household management writ large, a reflection of the natural order.

In this connection we should note at the outset the continual privileging throughout *The Prince* of touch and sensation over sight. As he advises the prince in chapter 18 about how to manipulate his externally perceived reputation for virtue, "everyone sees you, few touch what you are." The distrust of the visible phenomena of everyday politics – the preference for the hidden, the subterranean, the unproclaimed – goes together with the rejection of classical metaphysics, the most famous Socratic metaphor for which is the eye of the soul, implying an initial trust in how the visible "looks" of political life present themselves to the eye and are clarified through logos. This reversal of the classical priority of sight over touch is summed up in Machiavelli's maxim that it is better for the prince to be feared than loved (*The Prince*, chapter 17). Love orients us to the world of the visible. The loving prince (Machiavelli's example is Scipio Africanus the Elder, disciple of Xenophon's *Education of Cyrus* and immortalized in Cicero's *Dream of Scipio* as the ancestor who comes in a dream to Scipio the Younger) believes he can trust his subjects' love for him as he stands revealed in his splendor for having successfully ascended the ladder of the soul from lower to higher virtues, from battlefield courage to the civic virtues to the life of the mind in its access to the eternity of the divinely ordered cosmos. He is in turn for his followers a visible object of their own erotic longing for the noble and good, the embodiment of the longing for immortality through lasting fame. Fear, by contrast, cuts underneath the world of the visible and touches us in our innermost passions of base survival, and for Machiavelli it is therefore more reliable, because opinions about the noble can change, while our fear of death is constant. For Xenophon, however, although Cyrus's status as a noble ruler and an object for his subjects' admiration is certainly open to suspicion and undercut by many of his own hidden actions, it is by no means a pure illusion or manipulation of appearances. In Machiavelli's new science of politics, the first step in the conquest of human nature is to strip it of its noble pretensions and bring it face to face with its fear of extinction.

As we consider at length in Chapter 3, Aristotle argues in Book 1 of the *Politics* that there is certainly room for the art of political construction and fabrication – what Machiavelli comprehends as the mastery of Fortuna – in statesmanship. In Aristotle's view, however, the constructivist dimension of statecraft based on habituation through coercion and fear must be severely circumscribed, or politics (whether republican or monarchical) would collapse into mastery, and the political realm would disappear. Hence, Aristotle continues, we must believe that, just as nature provides us with a sufficient wherewithal for economic survival such that nature need not be radically transformed by *techne*, so it is also true that nature provides statesmanship with people whose natures possess a sufficient degree of virtue that they do not have to be "made" into citizens from scratch (*Politics* 1258a20–30). For all the greater latitude that Xenophon gives to imperial politics, and notwithstanding his comparative diminution of the claims of republican government, he is in agreement with this argument of Aristotle's, and the limitations his political theory places on the constructivist dimension of statecraft are, at bottom, the fundamental philosophical difference between him and Machiavelli. A telling sign of this is that in the *Hiero*, the work of Xenophon's that is most candid about transforming a tyrant into a benevolent "leader," it is not a philosopher who dispenses the advice but a poet (literally a "maker"). Evidently Xenophon wishes to separate the philosopher from the teaching that suggests nature (in this case, a human nature) can be transformed or refabricated. Machiavelli, by contrast, simply merges himself as thinker with the poet, assuming the same transformative role with respect to the addressee of *The Prince* that Xenophon has Simonides assume with respect to Hiero. We explore these nuances at length in Chapters 4 and 5.

Now, to be sure, as Chapters 6 and 7 show in detail, Machiavelli also believes there are limits on our capacity to master Fortuna, providing a philosophical point of contact with the classics. Still, Machiavelli's optimism about the extent of our capacity to master Fortuna far exceeds, I argue, anything to be found even in Xenophon, the classical thinker most open to a politics of imperialism, individualism, and acquisition. One need only mention the contention in chapter 6 of *The Prince* that the most outstanding exemplars of virtue were able to "introduce into matter whatever form they pleased." This is a familiar scholastic formula for describing God's power to transform nature ex nihilo.[1] That Machiavelli appears to transfer this capacity for open-ended transformation to a human ruler speaks for itself – its radicalism can hardly be exaggerated. It goes together with the assertion that Fortuna provides such men with nothing more than the "opportunity" to test themselves, in the form of dismally unpromising, obscure, dangerous, and hostile origins and circumstances. By contrast, as we see in Chapters 4 and 5, Xenophon's Cyrus was highly favored by nature and circumstance – his innate character and talents, the civic education he receives under the Persian Republic, and his grandfather's preference for Cyrus as his heir to the throne of Media. For Machiavelli, by contrast, the only favor nature does us is to goad us to strike back and make a stand. Understanding Fortuna leads to radical alienation and dissociation from nature, an experience that equips us with the strength of will to turn back against nature so as to subdue and transform it.

---

1 Consider Thomas, *Summa Theologica*, Questions 44 and 93 *The Principles of Natural Science*, Book II, Lecture 14, No. 268. See also Cornoldi (1893) ch. 7. A fuller discussion of this issue is undertaken in Chapter 6.

In this connection, let me turn in a general and preliminary way to Xenophon's *Hiero* and Machiavelli's rejoinder to it, a relationship taken up at length in Chapters 4 and 5. Similar to some of Socrates' criticisms of the tyrant's life in Book 9 of the *Republic*, Simonides as Xenophon depicts him in the *Hiero* tries in part to convince Hiero that he will not only be more secure in his rule but he will also be a happier man, to the extent that the passion of unbridled eros for honor and pleasure gives way to the more moderate sentiment of friendship (*philia*) in his soul. Because neither his personal nor his public relations will be exploitive, Simonides assures him, he will be able to trust the friendship others profess for him. For his own part, Hiero is undoubtedly dissimulating about the degree to which he really wants friendship as opposed to the power to possess both the city and other people as a lover. Nevertheless, he is not *simply* lying, I think, when he says that he would prefer voluntary and trusting friends to minions who are afraid of him and secretly hate him. In other words, although Hiero may not be a promising candidate for reform from a tyrant into a benevolent "leader" (*hegemon*), it is plausible that the moderating of eros urged by Simonides into philia both personally and politically is meant seriously as a possible way of reforming a tyrant into a statesman (similar, as we will see in due course, to the Platonic Socrates' argument to Callicles in the *Gorgias*).

For Machiavelli, by contrast, the problem is with the whole assumption that eros exists in the first place and can therefore at least be plausibly discussed as the basis for understanding tyranny and perhaps moderating it. Machiavelli is not simply saying the ancients were naive to think that a tyrant will give up his erotic pleasures for the calmer pleasures of friendship. What he objects to is the whole characterization of the tyrant as erotic, the whole psychological category of eros, precisely because it *does* contain the possibility for reforming the tyrant, however great the difficulties may be. It is the very belief in the existence of eros, of the longing for beauty and nobility, that corrupts. This is the problem with Scipio, who spoiled the soldiers with his love and undermined the austere virtue of the Roman Republic (*The Prince*, chapter 17), as we consider at length in Chapter 5. This is why, again, properly understanding Fortuna jolts you into realizing that there are no objects in the world in which your erotic longing can fulfill itself, only alienation, dissociation, and the need to fight back. Plato and the ancients ask: which way of life is erotically more satisfying, philosophy or tyranny? For Machiavelli, it is the very posing of the question in this way that obscures clear thinking. The methodical alternation within oneself of caution and impetuosity – of the fox and the lion – takes the place of the soul's openness to transcendence through the longing for the beautiful.

THE PRIMORDIAL AND THE TRANSCENDENTAL AS FUNDAMENTAL PERSPECTIVES ON POLITICAL EXISTENCE

Having made these preliminary comparisons between Machiavelli and the classical thinker most congenial to his project as an initial way of disclosing what precisely is modern about Machiavelli's teaching on tyranny, and by way of sketching the architecture of this book, I now want to broaden the argument into a more general contrast between the classical and modern approaches to statecraft. To this end, I suggest looking at politics as a tension between the primordial and the transcendental, a tension revealed by the psychology of *thumos* and *eros*, the two fundamental passions in the Platonic account of the soul. By primordial, I mean not only the idea that politics serves the passions but also the ontology that establishes the primacy of the passions: the sense that man is burdened with a consciousness of his finitude, mortality, individuality, and alienation (an emphasis on anxiety stretching from Hobbes to Heidegger). In this view, the origins are fundamental. By transcendental, on the other hand, I mean the view of politics as directed toward a common end that lifts man above his passions and orients him toward permanence and eternity. Whereas primordial politics has as its extreme the abstract homogeneity of the passions (what Hobbes termed the "similitude of the passions"),[2] the extreme of transcendental politics is the abstract homogeneity of pure self-identity and the One (exemplified by Socrates' argument in the *Republic* that the citizens of the *kallipolis* should be united like the limbs of a single body [420b–421c]). The reform of tyranny emerges as the attempt to actualize these extremes of transcendental or primordial homogeneity as a political project, corresponding respectively to the ancient and modern paradigms. The two ways of reforming tyranny differ crucially. For the

2 Hobbes (1971) pp. 82–83.

classics, tyranny, once reformed into a rational despotism like that of the herdsman of "featherless bipeds" in the *Statesman* (266–267) or Aristotle's model of the best monarch, attempts to bring political life into closer conformity with the unchanging One, and the pattern of cosmological reason within which human nature finds its place. For the moderns, by contrast, reason *itself* is assimilated to the will, while the substantive content of reason articulated through the cosmologies of the ancients becomes the purely anthropocentric capacity for the methodical imposition of formalistic order on nature through an act of will. The classical way of reason in politics becomes the modern way of political rationality.

Let us begin with the psychological dimension of the classical and modern approaches to see how the passions of the soul might connect with the wider world. In Plato, aggressiveness derives primarily from the psychology of spiritedness (*thumos*) – not psychology in the behavioral sense but as an intimation of the link between the soul and the world. The spirited man is the revealer of the gods, whom he calls into being to lend his own suffering or frustration the significance of a cosmic opponent (as when Achilles challenges the river god; *Republic* 391a–b). This man also invokes the gods as allies in punishing others, avenging himself for the deprivation he suffers. The spirited man can be subversive of the city when, like Leontius, he is drawn to dwell obsessively on the crimes and violence on which even lawful societies are founded (439e–440b). Like Polus, he may feel he has to become a tyrant out of fear that he will otherwise be tyrannized over (*Gorgias* 469–470). What is common to these manifestations of thumos is that the disjunction between man's longings for happiness, dignity, and repose and the achievement of their goal hurls him back on himself, with increased feelings of fear and vulnerability or anger and belligerence. Thumos is revealed in this tension (one of its etymologies relates it to rushing like the wind), calling on the gods from the depths of the soul not to forsake us. As the embodiment of thumos for Plato, Achilles is either a mad hero or in a paralyzing funk.

The complement of thumos is eros, the longing for completion through union with the beautiful or noble. Spiritedness comes to the fore when eros is thwarted. Callicles, who loves the boy Demos and the Athenian people (*demos*), loses his temper when Socrates likens his position (both personally and politically) to a catamite (*Gorgias* 494e).

As Socrates prods him into seeing the chasm between his longing for nobility and the putatively pandering character of his relationships in both private and public life, his eros collapses into his thumos. Before that, his mood is one of sublime confidence in his own capacities and of admiration for the even greater "natural master" who tramples over all convention (*Gorgias* 482–486). After Socrates deflates his eros, his generosity and good humor give way to sullen resentment. As we will consider in Chapter 2, the most potent figure in political life, capable of either the noblest or the basest actions, is the man whose thumos is absorbed into his eros, who sails above anxiety in his urge to consummate his union with the city, his "beloved." This is the type of nature Socrates most hopes to save for philosophy, and his closest embodiment in the dialogues is Alcibiades. For Plato, the root psychological motivation behind tyranny is an erotic longing to possess the city in the same way that ordinary men would long to possess another human being. In such a deformed soul, the zeal and aggressiveness of thumos become the allies of an eros for tyrannical possession of the city. The aim of Platonic civic pedagogy is to reorient eros toward the love of the Good glimpsed through philosophizing, so that thumos can act instead as the ally of wisdom and the civic virtues.[3]

Thus, in my view, and as I argue throughout this book, of these two fundamental passions that can lead us either toward tyranny or toward an openness to the eternal Good, eros entails and has primacy over thumos. In its spontaneous emergence, prior to philosophic and pedagogical shaping, eros strikes out for whatever it desires, summoning forth the aggressive energy of thumos as its ally. Left on its own, thumos by itself, without the leadership of eros, wallows in gloomy ruminations, fear or anger – only erotic longing gives it a purpose. The same holds after these passions are sublimated in the service of philosophy and the common good: eros unifies the soul in the pursuit of the Good, assigning thumos its subordinate role as ally.[4] To see how Platonic civic pedagogy tries to effect this sublimation, let us consider some of Plato's famous images of the soul.

3 Newell (2000) pp. 1–5.
4 On interpreting thumos as an existential stance toward the world, consider Ricoeur (1965) pp. 161–163m, 184–185. On the interrelatedness of thumos and eros, see Pangle (1976) pp. 1059–1077.

EDUCATION AND IMITATION: IMAGES OF THE SOUL IN PLATO'S DIALOGUES

If one accepts (as I do) the grouping of the Platonic dialogues according to their intrinsic content as early, middle and late, then one of the hallmarks of Platonic political philosophy is the transition from the early protreptic dialogues, which are mainly based on the Socratic elenchus of the short question and answer, to the middle dialogues, in which there is a sudden flowering not only of more rounded human portraits but of Socrates' interest in the passions of the soul, especially eros and thumos.[5] To this period belong as well the dialogues most famous for their myths and images – the *Republic*, *Phaedrus*, and *Symposium* notable among them. Whereas the early dialogues show Socrates attempting in the main to convince his interlocutors strictly according to reasonable argument, in the middle period, Socrates is shown as being aware that the intellect must also be reached through the passions and emotions. In other words, people will not necessarily act reasonably even if persuaded of the truth by reasoned argument. Their characters must be put into a proper condition to receive this truth, and

---

5 To a degree, then, I differ from the emphasis of Zuckert (2009), whose study of the dialogues has rightly been termed "magisterial." Zuckert's approach, similar to another recent book by Lampert (2010), argues that we should arrive at the order of the dialogues by examining the internal biography of Socrates that they present. Although I agree that this is a fruitful approach, in my own view, the internal biography of Socrates presented by Plato is only one among a number of useful perspectives one might take on the dialogues. Another is to group them thematically as dealing with a) the short question-and-answer "protreptic" approach of the Socratic *elenchus* characteristic of, say, the *Euthyphro*; b) Socrates' extensive use of myths, images, and rhetoric as ways of appealing to the intellect through the affects typified by the *Symposium* and *Republic*; c) a concern with more purely metaphysical issues characteristic of the *Theaetetus* and *Sophist*. To be sure, one could assent to this thematic division into three groups without necessarily buying into any theory about the order in which the dialogues were composed – for example, the fact that the *Euthyphro* is more of a protreptic dialogue does not in itself entitle one to conclude that it was composed at an earlier date than, say, the *Symposium*. Still, against the exclusive reliance on the internal biography, I maintain that Plato viewed his teacher from these three different although not unrelated perspectives as his own meditation on the life of Socrates unfolded over time. In his edition of the *Gorgias*, Dodds claims that Plato deliberately blurs the internal chronology of the dialogues, juxtaposing events and personalities that could not have been together at the same time, to prevent us from viewing the dialogues, even internally, as unfolding in unilinear time according to the stages of Socrates' life. There is a sense, Dodds remarks, in which they take place "any time" because Platonic philosophy itself is concerned with truths that are not time bound. Dodds in Plato (1979) pp. 17–18.

they must also be convinced of the emotional and aesthetic satisfaction that is entailed by the pursuit of philosophical insight. Accordingly, these middle-period dialogues also introduce a new stress on education, rhetoric, and the reform of poetry as mediums through which the wisdom sought by philosophy, and the value of the philosophic life, can be shaped for reception by a variety of psychological types and audiences.[6] The passions of eros and thumos are the gateways to transcendence; pathways, through their own progressive self-understanding and redirection, up toward the sunlight of what truly is. Of course, we must not push this periodization of early, middle, and late too far: Ostensibly early dialogues such as the *Alcibiades 1* do supplement argument with long speeches (the royal myth extolling the Persian and Spartan constitutions), while middle dialogues such as the *Gorgias* contain long exchanges of refutational reasoning (such as the exchange with Polus) that are relatively barren of imagery. Even so, the trove of great myths and images including the Chariot of the Soul, the three images of philosophy in the *Republic* (the Sun, the Line, and the Cave), the myths of judgment in the afterlife that conclude the *Gorgias* and the *Republic*, and Socrates' long speech about eros in the *Symposium* – these do appear to set off the middle-period dialogues in their distinctive concern with appealing to reason through the affects.

Although the Platonic Socrates' intellectual adversaries, that group we now call the Sophists, are sometimes understood as appealing to passion in contrast with Socrates' appeal to reason, a more nuanced consideration would show that, although the Sophists' understanding of passion remains fairly sketchy and minimal, often reducing to a mere desire for "getting the better" of others, the Platonic Socrates has a vastly more subtle and probing diagnosis of the affects. To take but

6 Blondell (2002) has persuasively argued for the need to reconcile the dramatic or psychological reading of the Platonic dialogues with the analytical, to see how seemingly impersonal metaphysical speculations emerge from psychological portraits of literary genius, in such a way that the dramatic reading should only further illuminate the analytical. Annas (1981) also argues that, for Plato, making the right intellectual choice about just action is inseparable from the character development required for embracing that choice. I make a similar argument, against a Kantian approach to Plato, that Plato cannot be understood exclusively in terms of either moral duty or perfectionism (Newell 2000, ch. 3). Arguing specifically with respect to shame and Socrates' employment of certain varieties of it to bolster civic virtue, Tarnopolsky (2010) also argues that there can be no strict dichotomy between emotion and reason in Platonic political psychology.

one example, where in any of the surviving pre-Socratic or Sophists' writings would we encounter a figure as darkly brilliant, ambivalent, saturnine, and glimmering as Alcibiades in the *Symposium*? As a literary portrait, it ranks with anything to be found in Shakespeare or Flaubert. Yet it is also a vehicle for considering the meaning of the philosophic life and its satisfactions by ranging Socrates' independence from the Athenian demos alongside the frustration experienced by its greatest living statesman. He appears in the *Symposium* on the eve of the disastrous military expedition to Sicily, which he more than any other leader provoked the Athenians to undertake and which will bring him down, the final political consequence of his tortured careening between wooing the many and wooing Socrates – the man who starts out, as Alcibiades bitterly complains, as your lover but who always transforms himself into the beloved (222b–d). Moreover, whereas for the Sophists, passions and desires could never be more than local coloration for whatever set of conventions happened to prevail in a given city and are therefore, as we would now say, culturally conditioned, the Platonic Socrates takes seriously the universality of the passions as a constant in human nature everywhere, a path to tyranny and violence but also potentially the path to a transcendence that would also be universally valid and not merely a feature of some local code, custom, or prejudice. The Socrates parodied in Aristophanes' *Clouds* naively believed that, as a Sophist, he could protect himself from the passions of the many by using his intellect to erect a buffer of rhetorical self-coloration between himself and them. While studying natural science, he could insulate himself from the ignorant many by teaching the art of tricky rhetoric for pay. As Aristophanes' depiction suggests, the Sophists at their most venal saw rhetoric as mere camouflage, a bag of tricks for manipulating local prejudices that had no connection with the universality of real knowledge such as the study of nonhuman nature through mathematics or astronomy. But the angry revenge taken against Socrates in the *Clouds* by Strepsiades, the country bumpkin who has married up, for corrupting his wastrel son shows how impossible it is to protect reason from its influence on the nonphilosophic – and that passions of family honor, familial attachments, and outraged indignation at the alienation of sons from their fathers by corrupt mentors are constitutive of human life everywhere.

In contrast with Aristophanes' lampoon of him, the Socrates we encounter in the Platonic dialogues, especially the middle dialogues, has fully absorbed the need to fashion rhetorically and psychologically subtle appeals to the emotions that will lead them toward philosophy or at least a respect and friendship for it. In this sense, he leans far away from the reductive utilitarian rationalism of the Sophists and is more interested in learning from, while rehabilitating, the depth of the emotional landscape uncovered by the poets and tragedians.[7] While Socrates certainly does call for the censoring of poetry, this does not imply its complete suppression, but rather its redirection.[8] As he argues in the *Republic*, one must expose oneself to the charm of the vices lionized and made dulcet by the poets in order to be able to distinguish virtue from vice and praise it in verse (409b–d). His final word on the poets is that the "sweetness" of their verses might well be an ally in charming the impressionable young to prefer virtue over vice, as long as heroes like Achilles are shown for the spoiled and insubordinate whiners that they frequently are (like bawling children who go around holding the part that hurts until they get some attention [604c–d]). Most of Socrates' own tales and images – the Chariot of the Soul, the story of Leontius, the myths of Er and Rhadamanthys, the Ship of State, Diotima's Ladder – contain recognizable elements from widely known poetry, tragedy, comedy and folk-lore that would make them automatic "hooks" for his listeners, even as he massages their content away from the teaching attributed by Socrates to his predecessors that nature is strife and motion – and that, therefore, a life of impulse and domination is more truly reflective of nature at large – toward the Platonic cosmological hypotheses that "soul came first"; that stability

---

7 For the background of Socrates' relationship to tragedy, consider Eliade (1978) pp. 259–264 and Dodds (1984) pp. 29–50.
8 Socrates on the dangers of poetry: "For my dear Adeimantus, if our young should seriously hear such things and not laugh scornfully at them as unworthy speeches, it's not very likely that any one of them would believe these things to be unworthy of himself, and would reproach himself if it should enter into his head to say or do any such thing. Rather, with neither shame nor endurance, he would chant many dirges and laments at the slightest sufferings... We'll beg Homer and the other poets not to be harsh if we strike out these and all similar things. It's not that they are not poetic and sweet for the many to hear, but the more poetic they are, the less should they be heard by boys and men who must be free and accustomed to fearing slavery more than death" (*Republic* 388d, 387b).

and moderation are super-ordinate over motion and strife both in the world and in a properly attuned soul (*Laws* 892).

Viewed in this light, Socratic philosophizing can be seen as an alternation between refutation and integration – between elenchus and image. On one level, the *Republic* as a whole can be seen as Socrates' exploration of a new, reasoned poetry that would replace the manipulators of the "images" carried along the ramp at the rear of the Cave, the unseen source of the shadow play that the prisoners chained below mistake for reality. Socrates' new images will still be only a reflection of the truth, but they will contain a kernel of philosophic transcendence that might induce their viewers to turn around and look for the light of true being, the Idea of the Good, in which those partial truths participate – not mere seeming, but "correct" seeming or opinion. The elenchus is the rough handling that Socrates says the prisoner in the cave first needs to force him to turn around and look up toward the light (515d–516a). Its negative refutation serves to dissect and expose as inadequate the opinions of Socrates' interlocutors about the virtues they profess to know about and seek, while Socrates' images gather the fragments of this negative dialectic and re-integrate them into a more satisfying account on the basis of what has been learned. For instance, the image of the Ship of State (488) beautifully integrates the proposition that there is an art of ruling properly informed by the philosopher's desire for knowledge of the Good, and that the nonphilosophic will benefit, like the passengers of a well-steered ship, if political life is guided by this true pilot. Yet the actual content of this art, and of the philosophic life itself, as well as its precise benefits for the city, are merely sketched rather than filled out in the image. For up to this point in the *Republic*, Socrates has merely asserted that there is an art of ruling analogous to the other crafts, and that it is synonymous with philosophy, but the content of which has not yet been filled in, merely assigned a place to hold in the tri-partite hierarchy of the city and the soul.[9] It is no more than a supposition at this point that there is an art of ruling comparable to

---

9 Socrates' introduction of the philosophic Guardians rests on the most flimsy of analogies conceivable, that between the loyal guard-dog Auxillaries' knowledge of how to distinguish between citizen and non-citizen and the philosopher's search for the distinction between knowledge and lack of knowledge in general: "Does the man who will be a fit guardian need, in addition to spiritedness, also to be a philosopher in his nature? . . . since (this soul) defines what's its own and what's alien by knowledge and ignorance . . . So

the other crafts in the precision of its knowledge and its criterion for the distribution of a solid benefit to a specific clientele. We know what those other arts are – we do not yet know what justice is.[10] The assimilation of statesmanship to philosophy is lent a solidity by the Ship of State image that is not actually manifest in the discussion itself at that point in the *Republic*, but whose very ambivalence and incompleteness invites further reflection while outwardly preserving the vision of a politics guided by selfless moderation grounded in a knowledge of the starry cosmos.

Socrates depicts his intellectual autobiography in the *Phaedo* as turning away from the attempt to give the direct speech about being – the pre-Socratics' tendency to identify nature with one force such as motion, strife, or a simple dyadic alternation between love and strife as principles regnant throughout the cosmos – and toward conversing about different opinions regarding the virtues (95a–107d). As Aristotle was later to put it, the only approach to what is "first by nature" – that is, metaphysical truth – is by way of what is "first for us" – political life and morality (*Nicomachean Ethics* 1095a17–b6). For Socrates, the debate about what justice, moderation, piety, and so on might mean pointed to the fact that there must be an "idea" or "form" of each virtue that solicited the debate and disagreement. Since the form was entirely consistent with itself, stable and permanent, then by considering how an opinion held about a virtue failed to be free of contradiction or instability, we would know in the case of each such opinion what virtue was not, and thereby make progress, through excluding mere seeming, toward what virtue truly is. If opinions about a virtue could be sifted through, retained, or cast aside to the extent that they were consistent or inconsistent with the "form" of virtue "in itself," then progress toward the truth could be made, not through the direct characterization of being, but intermediately through the clarification of these heterogeneous human qualities. Thus, when Socrates asks Euthyprho to define the holy, and Euthyprho proceeds to give a series of examples of pious behavior, Socrates tells him that he does not want a mere list of arguably pious

shall we be bold and assert that . . . the man who's going to be a fine and good guardian of the city will in his nature be philosophic, spirited, swift and strong" (375d–376c).

10 As Zeigler notes, we need a skilled craftsman to pursue the good because it is not a matter of subjective preference, but instead is grounded in the objective ordering of the whole (1979) pp. 124–125.

actions, but to know what the form of the pious is unchangingly "in itself" (6e).

The focus on the Ideas as the beginning of the Socratic "turn" comports with Socrates' famous claim in the *Apology*, another attempt at an intellectual autobiography, that he knows that he knows nothing (21d; *Republic* 354c).[11] While Socrates' claim is ostensibly humbly advanced, the ability to know in the case of every important human endeavor what the limits of our knowledge are amounts to a powerful theoretical claim. For the clarification of the virtues guided by the search for, in each case, a permanent, unvarying and universally valid Idea, amounts to parsing opinion to show in each case how justice is *not* this, is *not* that, is *not* this either, until one has demolished most conventional and authoritative opinions and is left with mere fragments.[12] For instance, in the very first pages of the *Republic*, by considering the customary opinion that justice is paying what is owed, and comparing that with the question of whether it would be good to return a borrowed weapon to someone of unsound mind, Socrates' companions learn that justice is not necessarily synonymous with property rights, a powerful negative insight that almost requires in itself, then and there, that a just regime will be communistic, though the implications are not spelled out for several more books.[13] Knowing that we know nothing amounts to knowing how any given opinion or phenomenon falls short of the consistency and non-contradictory permanence of the Idea in which it participates. Socrates' myths and images, accordingly, are ways of restoring a sense of the wholeness that our opinions about the virtues seemingly possess before they are deflated by the elenchus, re-integrating what refutation has shattered by fashioning an emotionally appealing symbol of the progress in knowledge that has been made. Hence, the growing awareness in the middle dialogues of Socrates' need to enlist allies in making

---

11 For a discussion of the Delphic Quest in the *Apology* as another version of the Socratic "turn," consider Strauss (1983).

12 In his elegantly argued discussion of Socrates and his successors, Villa (2001) stresses the skeptical, questioning side of the Socratic dialectic, more intent on exposing the inadequate conceptions of his fellow citizens than in bolstering their moral attachments. In this sense, Villa argues, he was a "bad" citizen. As Annas observes of the *Republic*, it is "*meant* to startle and shock" (1981) p. 2.

13 As Blitz observes about this passage, "legal force" in the defense of property right is valid only to the degree to which it is guided by a knowledge of what is truly good for the individual and for the common good (2010) p. 167.

philosophy more palatable and accessible to the emotions – the need to reform rhetoric, perhaps to enlist rhetoricians like Gorgias or Protagoras in a new, philosophically grounded art of oratory; the need to provide poets with new models of the soul and cosmos, which Socrates tries to do with Phaedrus in the dialogue with him and with Agathon in the *Symposium*, where Diotima's alleged speech about eros reported by Socrates is, I will argue, meant to provide Agathon with a model for the new poetry of love he aspires to create in place of Homer's poetry of tragic necessity and strife.

Socrates' encounter with Callicles in the *Gorgias* brings a number of these elements together. In his great set piece extolling injustice, Callicles draws upon a number of familiar views attributed to the Sophists and pre-Socratics, doubtless a reflection of his esteem for Gorgias himself, the eminent visiting rhetorician, grammarian, and ambassador for hire. In particular, Callicles distinguishes between what is just and noble merely by convention – the morality of equality – and what is just and noble by nature – the sway of the "natural master" who tramples over all such pusillanimous democratic moralizing (483e–484a).[14] In this, he hopes to rescue Gorgias and Polus from their earlier encounters with Socrates, where, Callicles maintains, they were tricked by Socrates into confusing natural justice and nobility with the merely conventional kind, forcing them to admit that what was just by nature was shameful by convention, with Socrates unscrupulously flitting back and forth between one criterion and the other without saying so. In responding, however, rather than tackle Callicles' position head on through refutation, as he did with Gorgias and Polus, Socrates instead begins by engaging his position through the emotions, especially through

---

14 Callicles uses language akin to a religious revelation when he proclaims that "nature herself" manifests the "shining" truth that it is "just" and a "law of nature" for the better and more powerful to rule over the worse and weaker and to "get the better" of them, building up to a crescendo of anti-egalitarianism: "I think these men are acting in accordance with natural justice when they do such things, and, by God, in accordance with the law, too, the law of nature – though not, indeed, the laws we frame. For we mold the natures of the best and strongest among us, raising them from infancy by the incantation of a charmed voice, as men do lion cubs. We enslave them by saying that they must be equal and that only this is noble and justice. Yet I think that if a real man appears, of capacity sufficient to shake off and break through our mass of written rules, spells and charms – all against nature – our erstwhile slave will stand forth revealed as the master, and thus natural justice will shine forth!" On the character of the Greek, see Dodds in Plato (1979) p. 267.

eros.[15] The ensuing refutation is grounded in a psychological diagnosis by Socrates that claims Callicles is a "double man" because of his erotic confusion (482). Callicles believes that he can become, or at least approximate in his impending political career, the natural master he extols in his speech by becoming the conventionally powerful leader of Athens. In this, Socrates predicts, he will find that his role of master quickly reverses itself into the role of slave and pander. Just as he is at the beck and call of the fickle boy Demos, whom he wants to possess, so he will be at the beck and call of the fickle Athenian democracy (481). His erotic longing for complete satisfaction and independence is natural, but it cannot be satisfied, Socrates tell him, through tyranny or any kind of merely political pre-eminence. He needs to replace his passion for erotic victory over the Athenian Demos and the boy Demos with a more moderate desire for friendship (*philia*) with them. Just as he should be Demos' friend in order to lead him to virtue rather than his ravisher, he should, in his upcoming political career, seek to turn the Athenian demos away from empire and the erotic excesses it feeds and instead turn Athenian politics inward into purely internal self-government with limited material needs and external entanglements. In this way, the city led by Callicles might, along with his love life, mirror the orderliness, balance, friendliness, and geometrical proportionality characteristic of the cosmos as a whole (504–508).

It is arguable that Socrates is also addressing Gorgias himself through his fiery young follower, appealing to the older teacher to re-calibrate his own teaching of rhetoric to serve these more moderate ends. As Socrates warns Callicles – and therefore perhaps also Gorgias, who is listening to the exchange along with the other participants – Callicles' belief that mastering others is the natural life while the democratic morality of equality is merely a convention is as likely to get *him* into trouble with the Athenian democracy as is Socrates' philosophizing, especially if he is one of their leaders when the empire falls (519). A moderate rhetoric might both prevent anti-democratic hot-heads like Polus from being associated with Gorgias (who is adamant in disavowing responsibility for how certain of his students turn out [457]) and shield Gorgias

---

15 On how Socrates enlists Callicles' passions in order to play on his longing for wholeness to turn him away from tyranny, and not by an appeal to reason alone, consider Klosko (1983).

himself from the imputation of endorsing tyranny. The appeal of this prescription for Callicles, however, is left in doubt by his silence at the end of the dialogue, and by his refusal to engage in open discussion with Socrates after Socrates compares him to a catamite (494). In so rigorously suppressing eros and subordinating all the passions to a rather contentless, proto-Stoic creed of austere self-overcoming both in politics and private life, Socrates ends up forbidding Callicles the erotic inducement both to philosophizing and to political honor with which he began his own psychiatric diagnosis of Callicles and his hope that Callicles might change his ways. Given a choice between witless eros and passionless reason as Socrates poses the stark alternatives here, grounded in an exaggeratedly absolute distinction between body and soul, Callicles truculently embraces the former. He is a stunning example of how a man can be persuaded by Socrates' arguments on the level of reason, but deliberately resist them in order to preserve his dignity and pursue the life he desires.

In other dialogues, however, such as the *Symposium, Republic* and *Phaedrus*, Socrates is able to achieve a more convincing and appealing balance and symbiosis between intellect and passion through his great images of the soul. While the *Gorgias* ends up positing a division between the body and the soul so dichotomous that it anticipates Stoicism and even Christianity, in the *Symposium*, in a compensating move toward the middle realm, eros is depicted as the vehicle for a continuous, seamless ascent from bodily passion through the nobility of civic virtue to the highest level of contemplating the eternally beautiful in itself – an ascent that is simultaneously rational, aesthetic, character-forming, and erotically therapeutic.[16] As Socrates depicts it, Diotima had upbraided him at some unspecified earlier period for not being "willing" to examine the "human beings' eros for honour." Were he to do so, she told him, "you would be amazed at their irrationality, unless you bear in mind what I have said and reflect on how uncannily

---

16 Eros is a "demon" between the divine and the human, an intermediary that "binds together the whole" (202e–203a). As for the Beautiful itself, Diotima says: "(It) is always being and neither comes into being nor passes away...It is by itself and with itself, always being of a single form...For this is what it is to proceed correctly in erotics, or to be led by another – beginning with the beautiful things around us, always to proceed on up for the sake of beauty itself, ending at that study which is the study of nothing other than the beautiful itself" (211a–c).

they are affected by their love of renown . . . for the sake of immortality, virtue and an illustrious reputation" (208c–d). His initiation by her into the rites of eros constitutes another version of the Socratic "turn" from cosmology and natural science to the human things variously depicted in the *Apology* (through the Delphic Quest) and the *Phaedo* (the turn from the direct speech about being to the clarification of political and moral opinions through the Ideas). While initially unwilling to examine the eros of humans for honor because it was "irrational," Socrates' "wonder" at this eros at length incentivized him to "reflect" on the honor-seekers' psychology, just as Diotima adjured him to do. The *Gorgias, Symposium*, and *Republic*, taken together, explore the reaches of this eros for honor, including the attraction to tyranny, and try to re-direct this energy away from such excess to a robust service of the common good, hopefully accompanied by at least a respect for philosophy if not an outright pursuit of it. All of the most famous images are therefore aimed at enlisting while moderating a love of honor that is potentially tyrannical, using visual symbolism to extol a life guided by reason in which the erotic and spirited passions would achieve their greatest emotional satisfaction precisely through being sublimated by an orientation toward the eternal truth.

Let us look more closely at how these images are fashioned to sublimate and re-direct the eros for political honor away from tyranny toward civic virtue and philosophy. I want to begin with the general observation that even most contemporary exponents of artificial intelligence would concede that there is something about the soul or the self that cannot be expressed in propositional terms; that even if all human knowledge and experience could be digitalized or expressed algorithmically, it would not constitute a self-conscious personality. In other words, the super-computer Big Blue may be able to defeat a Grand Master at chess, but Big Blue is not playing chess – it is merely solving a problem, and could as well be operating a desalination plant or the space shuttle. A computer can simulate Bach by sampling all information about his music to a degree that might fool all but a seasoned musicologist – but would it occur to a computer to compose music of its own? The motivation to create is strictly human.

What cannot be expressed logically about the soul and its relationship to the world might be expressed symbolically as a myth, such as Freud's

Oedipus complex. As Sophocles' original depiction of Oedipus would have it, destiny and fate always play a role, perhaps more powerful than the intellect and freedom of choice, in determining our conduct. Oedipus begins by imagining he is the favorite of Apollo, the god of the sunlight, patron of beauty, mind and the art of ruling. But he goes down to his doom in a Dionysian unraveling as his destiny destroys his claims to be a beneficent ruler: From a tyrant aspiring to legitimize himself into a king, he is exposed as a parricide in an incestuous relationship with his mother. By gouging out his own eyes, he not only punishes himself, but exacts vengeance on himself for his trust in the shining image of his own superiority, literally duplicating the blindness of Teresias, whose advice is to lay low, not probe too deeply into life's secrets, and not tempt the gods with one's hubris (315–320; 375–380; 1330–1335).[17]

In the tragic view of life, something about the world and especially about ourselves will always elude complete clarity: We are in the grip of forces larger than ourselves. Poetic imagery is a way of showing how man might relate to and cope with these forces; how they might operate on us through our desires, hopes, fears, and passions. Religious ethnographers like Eliade (1978) have argued that mythic archetypes are embedded in our subconscious way of grasping the world at a tacit, prereflexive level. We continually act out these cycles of heroic despair and triumph, the knight's longing to serve a chivalrous cause and rescue a damsel in distress, a heroism often requiring a long night of the soul and inner purification, like Tamino in Mozart's *Magic Flute*. Plato's use of myth and images most definitely probes these archetypes. Think of Glaucon's Ring of Gyges tale in the *Republic* (359c–360b). It blends the philosopher's prying into things under the earth (as Socrates claims people charge him with doing in the *Apology*) with archaic heroism

---

17 As Euben notes, at the beginning of the play, Oedipus thinks he is the child of *tuche* or fortune, independent of *nomos* or convention (1990) p. 98, n.8. On the greater affinity of the *Republic* with comedy than with tragedy, consider Euben (1990) p. 241 and Saxonhouse (1978). See also the illuminating study of Sophocles by Ahrensdorf (2009). As against Nietzsche's critique of Socrates for destroying the tragic age with his hypertrophic rationalism, Ahrensdorf argues that Sophocles does promote a role, although not an excessive one, for reason in good government, as opposed to the hubristic reliance on reason of Sophocles' Oedipus. He also argues, against Nietzsche, that the political philosophy of Plato evinces a profound awareness of the tragic dimension in life and political life, a view with which I very much concur in my interpretation of Plato's myths and images, and especially in the disjunction between the erotic longing to possess the beautiful forever and our human incapacity to do so.

promising a secret source of strength. Gyges descends into a womblike cave in which he finds the naked body of some larger than life hero within a windowed bronze horse. He takes the hero's ring of invisibility (it is unclear whether it conferred that power on the archaic hero, or only on Gyges for uncovering the secret of his existence) and uses it to steal of Queen of Lydia and usurp the throne. As a shepherd, Gyges stands outside of society like other famous rustic usurpers including Romulus and the Cyrus of Herodotus' account (unlike that of Xenophon), who rise from rural obscurity to great power. Through such myths, Plato concedes that an existential experience of "wonder" (*thaumazein*) at life's buried mysteries might be needed to explain what incentivizes us to seek knowledge.[18] (Just as Diotima told Socrates that men's eros for honor and its apparent irrationality would strike him as "wondrous" were he willing to examine their love of honor more closely.) Indeed, Socrates explains his own study of the Ideas as rooted in an erotic longing for completion, a longing for union with the beautiful and the good – or, as Diotima puts it, a longing to possess the Good as one's own forever – and he can probe the souls of his interlocutors to unlock this same longing for completion. That all said, however, we must never cross all the way over into identifying Platonic myth and imagery with a purely intuitive, existential, or pre-rational experience. What might begin as an erotic intuition of neediness leads, when properly clarified, toward the study of the Good, the objective reality that informs both a reasonably structured cosmos and a well-ordered soul. Diotima's account of eros as the lean and hungry off-spring of Resource and Poverty (203b–d) may begin with a level of prereflexive experience analogous to that explored by Freud and Jung. But her Ladder of Love reaches its highest rung in the same pursuit of permanent knowledge about the whole as that sought by Newton or Einstein.

If the *Apology* is the most public of Plato's depictions of Socrates, the *Symposium* is the most personal, ensconced *Rashoman*-like within five layers of surrounding narrative, boxes within boxes. Not coincidentally, it is also the most complete portrait of Alcibiades, who, after his first encounter with Socrates in the *Alcibiades 1*, reappears like

---

18 Euben makes an intriguing argument for returning to a Nietzschean view of the Greek polis as providing a context for the rise of classical philosophy, liberating us from intervening attempts at historical teleology (2003) ch. 2.

one of Balzac's recurring characters in cameo roles until the *Symposium*, where we finally see how central he and Socrates have been to each other's lives. Alcibiades' appearance may well be on the eve of his departure on the Sicilian Expedition, the zenith of Athenian imperial overextension whose chief instigator, according to Thucydides, was Alcibiades himself.[19] Chosen by the Athenians as the man likeliest to be victorious, they shortly recalled him because they feared he would tyrannize over them on the speed of that success, guaranteeing the expedition's doom by placing it under Nicias, the leader most opposed to the venture, extremely reluctant to expand the war while Athens had not yet beaten Sparta. All in all, Alcibiades is the paradigm of the young man described in the *Republic* as having both the greatest potential for philosophy and the greatest potential for being de-railed into excessive ambition and tyranny (491d–492a), and Socrates' intimate relationship with Alcibiades – in his detractors' eyes, a licentious and war-mongering demagogue – is a touchstone for his efforts to re-direct those energies toward philosophy and the common good.

But to what degree is Socrates responsible for the way his protégé turns out? That is not easy to determine. In Aristophanes' parody of their relationship in the *Clouds*, Pheidippides, the Alcibiades stand-in, begins, prior to any exposure to the "sophist" Socrates, as an unthinking libertine and spoiled rich kid. Once exposed to Socrates, when he reemerges from the "thinkery" (*phrontisterion*) of Socrates' pale-faced crew, he begins to justify his vices with the theoretical language of the distinction between nature and convention, thereby suggesting the possibility that the Aristophanean Socrates may have deepened Pheidippides' corruption by giving it a philosophical basis. The Platonic Socrates' first encounter with Alcibiades contains a kindred ambiguity. Socrates prods Alcibiades into confessing that he has a passion to rule not merely in Athens but over the whole world (104–105). But it is not clear how precisely or self-consciously the youth had formed this ambition for himself beforehand.[20] Socrates wants to expand the horizons of this promising young aristocrat beyond Athens, using the two paradigmatic and superior regimes of Sparta and Persia to convince Alcibiades that he needs to make a study of the art of ruling, inasmuch

19 See the fuller discussion in Chapter 4 and in Newell (2009) Part III.
20 On Socrates' seduction of Alcibiades, consider Zuckert (2009) p. 230.

as they embody the best republic and the best monarchy, respectively (121–124). But by stimulating Alcibiades' ambition to soar above the local level to the universal so as to engage him in pursuing knowledge about the whole, including or through the medium of *politike*, it is not inconceivable that Alcibiades retained the global ambition to which Socrates inspired him without fully cultivating the longing for universally valid knowledge which Socrates hoped would be its final aim, just as in Diotima's Ladder, the longing for immortality through political honor is the way station to the philosophic life.

By enflaming Alcibiades' eros for honor, Socrates may have been making one of his first efforts at turning away from the direct speculation about cosmology (as limned in the *Phaedo*) to probing the souls of his interlocutors, responding to what he depicts in the *Symposium* as Diotima's criticism of him at some point much further back in time when he was still the Socrates who studied nature rather than human affairs, for failing to pay attention to the "amazing" eros of men for honor. But if the *Alcibiades 1* can be seen as a first step down this highway from the Socrates depicted in the *Clouds* to the Socrates of the Platonic dialogues, with Socrates testing his new insight into the eros for honor on one of the city's most promising young aspiring politicians, the dialogue leaves it in some doubt whether the erotic diagnostician was successful in this early attempt to use philosophy as a therapy for the ambitious soul, or whether philosophy did not merely deepen whatever tendency to tyranny was present in Alcibiades in the first place, just as in the presentation of Socrates' effect on Pheidippides in the *Clouds* behind the closed doors of the thinkery. Alcibiades' lament decades later in the *Symposium* that he wants Socrates when he courts the Demos and wants the Demos when he is with Socrates may be in part self-serving, presenting as an agonizing and tragically moving failure what in fact is his own strong preference for politics over philosophy. But it may also suggest that the universality of Athenian imperialism, whose main exponent he was – according to Thucydides, after Sicily he planned to conquer Carthage, telling the people that there was no natural limit on their empire (6.18.5–16) – substituted for the universality of philosophy's search for wisdom that was only partially successfully implanted by Socrates in his soul. If so, Socrates may have soured both alternatives for Alcibiades, dooming him to act on his stronger impulses for political action while cursed with knowing that life to be second rate. Was he a magnificent abortion in Socrates' art of midwifery, compelling Socrates to search ceaselessly for new and improved products like Glaucon and Theaetetus?[21]

In turning specifically to Diotima's teaching about the Ladder of Love, an image fashioned by Socrates through his long speech in the *Symposium*, let us recall the setting of the dialogue. The purpose of the dinner party is to praise eros on the grounds that it has not received sufficient praise to date. Puzzling on the face of it, given the poets' accounts of Aphrodite as the goddess of eros (she appears, for instance, in Book 3 of the *Iliad* to facilitate an amorous encounter between Paris and Helen), this claim suggests that the participants in the dialogue are searching into eros for a natural grounding for both personal happiness and public excellence to replace the fading traditions of the poets. This is especially likely given that the winner of the contest in whose honor the dinner is being held, Agathon, wants to replace the old Homeric and Hesiodic poetry of titanic strife and necessity with a new, more optimistic and forward-looking celebration of the Age of Love. (In one of his surviving fragments, Gorgias, who is a preceptor for Agathon, claims that the new elite of wise rhetoricians headed by himself will replace the authority of the older poets through their capacity to make any image they wish seem to come into being [13–14].) Because the ground rule is that each guest will give a long speech praising eros, there is far less dialectical refutation than in other dialogues. The speakers build on each other's accounts cumulatively, and Socrates' speech attributed to the teachings of Diotima draws on (while modifying) all the preceding ones.

Like Pausanias, Socrates' Diotima distinguishes between base, merely bodily eros, and the noble kind whereby the lover cultivates the beloved's capacity for excellence. Like Eryximachos, she identifies eros as being constitutive of the entire cosmos, the link (she maintains)

---

21 Alcibiades says that Socrates' "philosophical speeches" are like the bites of a "painful viper." Further: "He conquers all human beings by speeches . . . He compels me to agree that, although I myself am still in need of much, I neglect myself while instead I deal with the affairs of the Athenians. I feel only shame before him. For I know within myself that I do not have the capacity to contradict him when he says what I must do; yet, whenever I leave him, I succumb to the honor of the many" (213e, 216a–c). While Alcibiades does not conquer all human beings through politics, Socrates does conquer all human beings through speeches. Alcibiades recognizes the superiority of Socrates' empire to his own semi-successful attempt.

between the human and the divine, and between seeming and being – unlike Aristophanes, who depicted eros solely as a human trait on a purely anthropological level. Further, while Aristophanes had somewhat democratically recognized the existence of eros in all kinds of people, not merely the agonistic and pederastic *kaloi kagathoi*, even ordinary husbands and wives, along with homosexuals and lesbians, Diotima preserves from Agathon's speech the depiction of eros as hierarchical, reserved for the best natures, the soft and cultured few, in ascending rank. She does, however, preserve from Aristophanes the crucial distinction between eros and the good for which it longs, identifying this good, not with the forever lost bodily unity of now split genders (as in Aristophanes' myth), but with the over-arching and eternally present Idea of the Beautiful. Eros is drawn upwards by this pre-eminent cosmic orderliness and wholeness, and is not, as Agathon depicted it, a sheer force or impulse of graciousness. Eros is not the good itself, but, in Diotima's phrase, "wants the Good to be one's own forever" (206a).

As earlier observed, Diotima's speech is another account of the Socratic "turn," analogous to the Delphic Quest or the *Phaedo*. Common to all the accounts is the implication that philosophy of the kind Socrates practices in the Platonic dialogues emerges from a dawning awareness of the divine in human life, the boundedness of the human by the divine, and the search for a demonic link between the human and the godlike.[22] All the dialogues may be said to abstract from the Idea of the Good, the superordinate reality that is unvarying throughout Socrates' metaphysical speculations. The dialogues are different paths to that same end, depending on the psychological leanings and situations in life of the chief interlocutors. Socrates' therapy for Callicles' erotic doubleness ends up with a cosmology that abstracts from eros altogether. The *Symposium*, by contrast, attempts to derive all virtue from it, showing how thumotic aggression might be assimilated and guided by eros itself. In further contrast, the *Republic* strikes a balance: The civic virtue of the Auxillaries is purged of eros in its primordial manifestations (the love of one's own including wealth and the family)

---

22 Voegelin's key concept of "metaxy" is closely connected to Diotima's presentation of eros as a spirit in between the human and the divine (1999) vol. 3. In Zuckert's formulation, eros mediates between the sensible and the intelligible (2009) pp. 193–198.

and is grounded primarily in thumos as the psychological basis for cosmologically guided honor-seeking through the reform of theology and poetry. Eros is re-introduced in Book 5, but only as the incentive to philosophize. This may be Socrates' considered judgment, given in his own voice, on the attempt he attributed to Diotima to derive all virtue from eros. The denouement of Diotima's teaching, the drunken and belligerent entry of Alcibiades, and his semicomical, semiserious vying with Socrates for the love of Agathon, calls into serious question the seamless ascent of Diotima's Ladder of Love, according to which the eros for political honor is continuously subordinated to, and guided by, the philosophic eros for the Beautiful itself. It is far from clear that Alcibiades ever has been or ever will be governed by his wise counsellor. On the other hand, the *Republic*, by grounding civic virtue in a code of austere collective honor whose psychological mainspring is thumos, while reserving erotic longing for the philosopher alone, strikes a balance between these two fundamental passions, albeit at the price of introducing a fatal psychological contradiction between the Guardians and the Auxillariues and their respective purchases on the world. For while the former are guided by a direct study of the Idea of the Good, the latter are guided by a mere set of opinions about it whose theoretical basis they are by definition incapable of grasping. Little wonder that Socrates is concerned lest these thumotic men become "angry" if their beliefs are ever exposed as mere beliefs and not the unshakeable truth (480a). Just as Strepsiades burns down the thinkery, these moralistic warriors may one day overthrow the rule of Guardians who turn out to lack conviction.[23]

All in all, Diotima's Ladder of Love is arguably the single most dazzling attempt by Plato to show eros as the unitary passion of the soul harmonizing ordinary family life, civic virtue, and philosophy in a continuous ascent. The soul progresses simultaneously toward intellectual enlightenment and emotional and aesthetic satisfaction.[24] That is why

23 On the incompatibility between the erotic incompleteness of Socratic philosophizing and the fact that the Guardian class of the *Republic* would have to have achieved at least a degree of settled wisdom about the art of ruling, see Hyland (1990). On the good and bad potentialities of civic honor and its connection to the theme of education in the *Republic*, see Gadamer (1980) pp. 54–59.

24 As Nussbaum notes, "a central feature of the ascent is that the lover escapes, gradually, from his bondage to luck . . . (The philosopher's) contemplative love for all beauty carries no risk of loss, rejection, even frustration" (2001) p. 181.

it is such a compelling crystallization of the Platonic Socrates' search for an appeal to the intellect through the affects. The temptation to tyrannize is the limit test case of the capacity of the philosophic life to establish order in the city and the soul. Only if these ambitious men can be soothed and satisfied and rendered friendly to learning can this project for establishing the optimal *politeia*, at least in discourse if not in real life, have any prospect of success. Throughout these middle period dialogues, we see Socrates embarked on the search for possible interme-diaries – new rhetoricians, educators, and poets – who might assist in this enterprise, while Socrates himself of course has a prodigious talent for fashioning such images (*Republic* 487e–488b). In the *Symposium*, where Socrates' brief attempt to use the elenchus in getting Agathon to grasp the distinction between eros and the object of its longing ends in the poet's befuddlement, the ensuing long speech attributed to Diotima's inspiration might be seen as Socrates' way of appealing to the poet in a more explicitly poetic (as opposed to dialectical) vein, providing him with a guide for the new poetry he aspires to create (199c–201d). Dio-tima is a seer from an unspecified time in the past, shrouded in mystery, enigmatic and even terrifying. She is Socrates' guide in somewhat the same way as Athena is that of Odysseus or Telemachus. The previous speakers in the dinner conversation tended to view eros as an agonis-tic relationship in which an older man possessed a younger beloved, endowing him with advice about how to succeed in life in exchange for enjoying his beauty – a one-sided possessiveness mirroring the view of politics itself as the manly pursuit of distinction in the agora. In sharp contrast to this agonistic ethos, Socrates, by attributing his knowledge about eros to a woman, stresses a more androgynous conception of the soul and a more mutual, fertile kind of friendship, in which both lover and beloved are united in their common service of the Good, rather than the victory of one over the other (lover over the beloved, ruler over the ruled). A part of the implied therapy for the tyrannically inclined man is that his harsh and aggressive "manliness" (*andreia*) will, in his soul's ascent upward, be tempered and softened by the philosopher's "love of the human" (*philanthropia*).

With the preceding considerations in mind, we should now turn to the three images of philosophy provided by Socrates in the *Republic* to see how they bear on our theme of the sublimation of tyrannical and aggressive impulses. The three images provide different although linked perspectives on the philosopher's quest for wisdom. The image of the Sun is an erotic image about nature's wholeness in which the sun's warming power, analogous to the Idea of the Good, solicits all natures toward their respective fulfillments and enables them to be known. The image of the Divided Line is another rendition of this ascent toward the Good, now mapped as a theory of cognition, in which we ascend from unclarified experience through the concrete entities of the everyday world, themselves clarified by the mathematical properties we abstract from them, guided at the highest level by the permanent Ideas under which families of phenomena are grouped.[25] The third and most famous image, that of the Cave, integrates the erotic and the epistemological ascent of the previous two into the fuller context of moral psychology and the exigencies of political life. Now we learn that the ascent toward the sunlight of the Good is not an effortless rise, like the opening of a flower in the sunlight implied in the first image, or a dash up the Divided Line, because we are bound in place by our prejudices and attachment to convention. Bound in place and facing away from the sunlight, we mistake for reality what is actually a series of images shaped by the poets and Sophists casting shadows on the rear wall of the cave from atop a ramp partway up the ascent.

Socrates' own trove of images and myths, his speeches about eros, his reforms of theology and poetry, are meant to replace these image-bearers (plausibly identified with the old poets and their successors, the Sophists, but also with the tragedians of Socrates' era) with a new, philosophically grounded poetry and ethics.[26] For example, the story of Leontius in Book 4 of the *Republic* and his attempt to make war on his illicit thumotic absorption in violent death on behalf of the governor within him of reason is one that Socrates says he "trusts" (439e). In other words, this tale corresponds to the level of "trust" (*pistis*) on the Divided Line, the level of the solid reality of the world around

---

25 As Rosen comments, "the first image is primarily ontological while the second is epistemological. What is missing from these two images is human life. Nor does this seem unusual, since we are discussing the most difficult abstractions of philosophy" (2006) p. 269.

26 Both the Sophists themselves and the Platonic Socrates regarded the old poets including Homer, Hesiod, and Pindar as the Sophists' forbears. See, e.g., Plato *Protagoras* 316D–E; Jaeger (1965) pp. 289–296; and the discussion of Machiavelli's relationship to the Sophists in Chapter 2.

us, because it reveals some elementary components of morality and its relationship to reason purged of the Dionysian obfuscation, tragic self-pity and reveling in the passions characteristic of the old poetry. By distinguishing among the three states of the soul (reason, thumos, and desire) and the arrangement whereby reason rules desire with thumos as its ally, the story crystallizes in a vivid, semi-comical anecdote (Leontius, initially covering his eyes, runs toward the pit of corpses while screaming at his eyes for their evil wish to gaze at them; 440a) the analytical rigor by which, in comparing virtue to an art, Socrates was able to compartmentalize the soul and the city as characterized by three distinct "jobs." Establishing the permanent self-sameness of each such nature served as an introduction to the "forms" and the reform of the gods as similarly stable, unchanging, and purged of Dionysian whimsicality or passion. Above all, the conversion of young Glaucon to the dazzling vision of the splendors of philosophy presented in the Cave image is aimed at equipping him with a respect for the philosophic life while also equipping him with a moral compass – the best regime as a "pattern in the sky" (592b) – that will enable him to live responsibly in the imperfect city of reality in the here and now, his leanings toward tyranny assimilated by the more pure and lasting pleasures of philosophy.[27] Nevertheless, as Socrates warns, grave danger may await the man who returns to the shadow-play at the bottom of the Cave. Blinded by his time gazing straight into the sunlight and unable to make out the shadows regarded by the chained prisoners as the truth, he may incur their resentment for his seeming neglect of conventional decency and piety – the fate of Socrates himself. And as we recall, this backlash could even take place among the Auxillaries of the best regime itself if they find their piety and morality exposed as shadows: Even the best regime, while an improved cave where morality is to an extent illumined by the Idea of the Good, is still a cave with most people living according to the prejudices instilled in them by (in this case philosophically shaped) convention.

Finally, let us note the image of the Chariot of the Soul in the *Phaedrus*, put forward, like Socrates' revelation of Diotima, as a model for

---

27 Consider Roochnick's interesting proposition that Books 8 to 10 of the *Republic* represent a dialectical advancement over the previous books' argument because they are equipped with the insights about justice derived from the image of the Cave (2003).

how eros, properly understood, might guide poetry (247–254). While the images in the *Republic* cumulatively stress the difficulties of the soul's transcendence from the transient toward the eternal, the image of the Chariot suggests a more harmonious, holistic approach that is the direct antecedent of later prescriptions for the balanced soul like Cicero's *Dream of Scipio*.[28] In Plato's image, the soul is likened to a chariot, the charioteer representing the mind (*nous*), while the two powerful horses he steers represent the passions of spirit and desire, both vying for power over the soul. As long as the charioteer is able to steer the horses, the soul's chariot enacts a celestial journey of calm and moderation. If the charioteer loses control of the horses, either one or both of them can plunge the chariot from the heavens down into the realm of chaos, corresponding to the sheer impulsiveness of the passions. Yet, lest we too quickly see in this analogy a Kantian prescription for the repression of the inclinations by an act of will, we should remember that the Platonic notion of happiness analogized by the image is one of balance, harmony, and symbiotic combination – not the repression of nature, but its fulfillment. For, while the chariot must be guided by the charioteer, just as the mind must guide the passions, the chariot is not going anywhere without the power of those steeds, just as the intellect cannot on its own achieve virtue without the energy of the passions. The passions must be sublimated and redirected away from the frenzy of spontaneous impulse so that they might energize the intellect and, through their shaping by philosophically guided education, rhetoric, poetry and theology, integrate mind and body in a satisfying

---

28 Cicero's *On the Commonwealth* is the consummation of the Platonic-Aristotelian approach to the proper balance of mind and passion, and of a duty to serve the common good under the guidance of philosophy. That Cicero somewhat elevates the claims of civic virtue to being on a par with philosophy, or even as enriching it, may be evidence of how the gentlemen Plato and Aristotle were trying to enlist in a friendship for philosophy might have tweaked the balance of elements to favor politics a little more, something which Aristotle, if not Plato, would have found satisfactory: "Let us count those who treat the philosophy of life as great men . . . But at the same time let us admit the existence of an art . . . which comprises the theory of politics and the government of peoples . . . What indeed can be more glorious than the union of practical experience in great affairs with an intelligent enthusiasm for the liberal arts? . . . Hence I hold that a man who has been able and willing to combine these two interests and has disciplined himself both in the ways of his ancestors and in liberal culture, has attained everything that entitles a man to praise." Quoted in Newell (2001) p. 304.

emotional and aesthetic middle ground. Virtue cannot be divorced from happiness.[29]

It should be stressed that these images do not only serve to appeal to reason through the affects, but that, by reasoning through the images, we actualize philosophizing itself. For their surface sheen quickly yields many ambiguities that prompt the refutational analysis whose fragmenting of opinion they were meant to heal in the first place: The dyad between refutation and holism is at the nerve of the images themselves, calisthenics for the soul. In every image, there are subtle variations which are not exactly contradictions, but rather show how the soul can be viewed from different perspectives depending on the conversational context and different psychological types requiring different kinds of educational therapy. To sum up: Plato's images of the soul point to a fundamental contrast between the ancient and modern understandings of tyranny and statecraft that will recur throughout this book. For the classics, freedom (*eleutheria*) flows from a harmonious balance between the passions and the mind. It is the experience of a well-tempered wholeness and dignity that flowers naturally when our desires and our intellect are integrated by the vision of a beautiful and beneficent cosmos. Freedom in this perspective is not a will that we impose on nature. It is not so much a matter of self-assertion and autonomy but of reconciliation, both within ourselves and with other people, especially our fellow citizens. Whereas the modern conception of freedom is based on self-hood, what Plato means by eros – the longing for union with the eternally beautiful and good – leads to self-forgetting and self-transcendence, a falling away of bellicosity. With Machiavelli, we encounter a fundamental shift in the meaning of freedom to our capacity to oppose

---

29 On the incompatibility of virtue and happiness, see Kant (1956) pp. 42ff. Many contemporary approaches to Plato are grounded in Kantian distinctions between freedom and nature, autonomy and heteronomy, altruism and egoism, and treating others well for their own sake as opposed to for the sake of perfecting oneself. See, for example, the discussion in Kraut (1973) pp. 330–334 and Vlastos (1981). I share the reservations expressed by other scholars about this Kantian approach. See, for example, Griswold (1986), Kossman (1976), and Nussbaum (1983) pp. 4–6, 285–287. Zeigler (1979) argues against interpreting the Platonic Socrates as a psychological egoist, pp. 123–133. Kraut (1973) argues for attributing a much broader conception of self-interest to Plato than is implied by the notion of egoism.

ourselves to nature and bend nature to our own purposes, extracting the power we need from it to create political security and well-being. In place of Socrates' majestic prophetess Diotima, his guide into the rites of Love, Machiavelli will present Fortuna, who in her boundless caprice and malignity, must be forcibly subdued by the hot-blooded young.

Having given some consideration to the psychological dimensions of tyranny in the classical tradition and the use of Platonic imagery as a therapy for it, let us return to the more foursquare political dimensions of tyrannical ambition. Much of Platonic and Aristotelian political psychology is concerned with elaborating the tyrannical longing to possess the city with a view to disarming it and converting the energies of tyrannical eros and thumos to the service of republican citizenship and, in the best instance, philosophy. But uncovering the treatment requires a certain hermeneutical attentiveness because as much is stated by silence as by asseveration. The union of eros and thumos in the tyrannical longing to possess the city like a lover is treated with a good deal of circumspection, lest painting it too vividly might make it more appealing than its corrective therapy. This is most notable through the virtual disappearance (aside from a few mentions and a cameo appearance in the *Protagoras*) of Alcibiades, who fully embodies the alliance of thumos with eros in tyrannical longing, after the *Alcibiades I*, reemerging in whole only in the magnificently ambivalent portrait of him many years later buried deep within five layers of recollection in the *Symposium*. In the *Laws*, it is suggested that a young man possessed of "an eros for the city" might be the one who could found a regime in accordance with the mores elaborated by the Athenian Stranger (709–712). Yet, while as we will see in Chapter 2, this hint of a Promethean human founder is by far the frankest discussion in the dialogues of the prospect for harnessing tyrannical eros to the establishment of a just regime, it is no more than a brief sketch, rapidly submerged by a theological discussion of "the god" who is to be seen as the source of the city's belief in these laws after the founding (however that may take place). Similarly in Aristotle's *Politics*, a founder is mentioned briefly in connection with the admission that human nature does not "grow" seamlessly into a city but requires a degree of "making" (*poiesis* 1253a29) – the beginning, as we will see in Chapter 3, of a constant alternation in the *Politics* between Aristotle's massive foreground preference for the self-governing republic and the more muted claim of the "best man" to absolute authority that is continually breaking through to the surface.

Symptomatic of this circumspection, as I will try to show, political eros is never fully or adequately elaborated in Plato's *Republic*. In the civic psychology of the Auxillary class (the bulk of the citizenry) in Book 4, thumos is presented mainly as the master or slave of physical or (in the case of Leontius) morbid desires, and as distinct from calculation (*logismos*). Later on, in Books 6 and 7, when the education in philosophy strictly speaking is discussed – as distinct from the civic education of the Auxillaries – eros comes to the fore, but in a context largely abstracted from politics. The fullness of longing for and development toward the Good is evoked by the analogy to the nourishing, warming qualities of the Sun, or schematized as an epistemological ascent up the Divided Line. Politics, by contrast, is depicted as a cave where the sunlight (therefore, allegorically speaking, philosophical enlightenment) does not penetrate or only in a dim form. Life there is an imprisonment. The wall along which the masters of simulation walk recalls the wall of the city that Leontius followed to the execution pit (439e). The moral psychology of the thumotic Auxillaries, which the story of Leontius is meant to verify, exists in the realm of "trust" and "correct opinion." But it is also barred by a wall from the complete truth – that the philosophic life, not the moral life of the citizen, is the only sure source of all prudence (476d–478c; 480a; 517c).

The tri-partite psychology of the *Republic* has the effect of depicting politics as a realm where eros cannot be satisfied, and where thumos is present only in its compulsive and anxious manifestations unless it is educated to become the ally of justice. Only philosophy can channel eros toward its satisfaction. Hence, when the three parts of the soul are reinterpreted in Book 9 as forms of desire, Glaucon has long since been ready to reject tyranny as a life of aimless, degrading pleasures. But he rejects it in favor of the philosophic life – not, strictly speaking, in favor of the just life considered as distinct from the philosophic life. Only in the ostensibly more personal, less political milieu of the *Symposium* does Plato find it safe to present an eros for the city's honor as being *on the route* to the satisfaction which philosophy more nearly approaches. But even in Diotima's sketch of a continuous ascent from lower to higher forms of eros entailing political virtue along the way, the potential for clashing ambitions among the lovers of the city is largely occluded. Diotima does not stress or perhaps does not realize that too many brilliant competitors in the service of the common good will almost unavoidably turn on each other. There cannot be a republic full of Julius Caesars. Alcibiades' belligerent entrance after Diotima's revelation provides, through the dramatic action of the dialogue, a tacit emendation of her assimilation of eros to civic virtue in an untroubled ascent to philosophy. The dilemma is summed up by Diotima's own remark, earlier mentioned, that eros is the longing to possess the beautiful or noble "as one's own forever." The deepest problem surrounding Platonic civic paideia is this explosive contradiction between the love of one's own and the eternal good.[30] Diotima's formulation expresses the dubious paradox that a virtuous citizen could somehow "possess" forever a truth that transcends all local political virtues, attachments, patriotism, family ties, and the love of one's own. The truth is ownerless. But justice requires a commitment that says: "This is mine – my city, my family, my god – and I will defend it." One of the major complexities in thinking through the connection in Platonic philosophy between the philosopher's direct pursuit of what is immortally lasting through the longing for the beautiful and the good and the citizen's indirect pursuit of it through virtuous citizenship is considering whether the prospective ascent outlined by Diotima from civic virtue to philosophic virtue is indeed continuous and relatively untroubled, or problematic to a degree requiring considerable rhetorical embellishment and artistry. That complexity will loom large throughout the chapters that follow.

In Plato, the ambiguity of the attempt to reconcile eros, whether tyrannical or philosophic, to the city is evident to the attentive reader,

---

30 Like Ranasinghe (2000), with whose approach I am in broad concurrence, I am not suggesting that eros is a kind of pre-established, disembodied cosmic force that antecedently informs every thought and action in the Platonic dialogues. On the contrary, eros opens up the inscrutable and agonizing disjunction between the longing for immortality and our own inescapable immurement in a world of finitude and impermanence. Eros lights up that longing, and so discloses a new envisioning of the soul in relation to the cosmos, linked by philosophic longing. By the same token, of course, the prospect for success in achieving union with the beautiful and the good is always present, however elusive, fleeting, or unlikely. The longing does not, as it does for modern existentialism, condemn us to permanent absurdity, man as "the great stupidity" to use Nietzsche's language. See also Nelson (1986) pp. 203–204.

which invites an ongoing dialectical rejoinder to the starting points. Socrates' attempt in the *Gorgias* to convert Callicles to moderate citizenship does not meet with evident success, while the cause of the best regime's downfall in the *Republic* is the rebellion of the Auxillaries, the thumotic warrior class, suggesting that thumos is an element of the soul which makes the reordering of political life "according to reason" highly problematic.[31] Most muted of all, though, is a full elaboration of the man whose eros for the city could convert his thumotic energies to the creation of the conditions for transcendental politics. That is to say, a tyranny on behalf of the Idea of the Good. For to unleash this possibility would be to court the danger of a tyranny much worse than the sot of pleasure presented in Book 9 of the *Republic*, not a Nero or Commodus but (to analogize somewhat broadly) a Napoleon or Stalin who conquers on the basis of a universalistic conception of the state. This possibility is not muted only out of considerations of prudence and the philosopher's need to be "politic," but because to court it would be to embrace a fundamentally different view of man's place in the whole, that is to say, the primordialist ontology of the pre-Socratics and the Sophists or "motion-men" according to which the originating power of nature as genesis fuels the tyrant's mighty impulses (*Laws* 888e890a; *Theaetetus* 152e, 179e, 180d). That primordialist ontology, as we have already suggested and as the rest of this book will explore at length, takes on the potential for truly earth-shaking transformations when it is hitched to the modern conception of the will to master nature altogether that emerges with Machiavelli. For Plato, as the culmination of the defense of justice in Book 9 of the *Republic* demonstrates, the tyrannical urge is to be assimilated directly by an eros for philosophy, because the superior satisfactions of the philosopher on an erotic level are so manifest in their contrast with the inferior erotic satisfactions of tyranny. More muted, however, is the direct evaluation of philosophic eros in comparison, not with tyrannical excess, degradation and demagoguery, but with the honor that might accrue to a tyranny guided by reasonable political aims. As we will consider at length in Chapters 4

---

31 See the article by Skemp on how the psychology of thumos epitomized by Leontius in Book 4, and especially his failure to master his desires, prefigures the rebellion of the Auxillaries in Book 8. As Skemp puts it, "we forget Leontius" after Book 4 until the rebellion of the thumotic class. Skemp (1982) p. 91.

and 5, Xenophon, by contrast, presents in full form the possibility that Plato occludes. His idealized Cyrus is driven by an eros for the love of all human beings, and by placing his thumotic aggressiveness at the service of this erotic but non-philosophic motive, Cyrus creates a cosmopolis whose universality and meritocracy mirror philosophic truth in as direct a manner as is possible for any regime, by dispensing altogether with the polis. To reiterate our introductory comparison between Xenophon and Machiavelli, the Xenophontic Cyrus's world household is Machiavellian statecraft minus the secularization of the will of the Abrahamic God to conquer nature. Its ruler's motivation is a hedonism higher and nobler than the witless excesses of the wastrel tyrant of Book 9 of the *Republic*, the fulfillment of nature rather than its conquest.

In Aristotle, as Chapter 3 treats in detail, the Platonic psychology of eros and thumos virtually disappears as politics is categorically separated from philosophy with a clarity never found in Plato, and therefore separated from the fullest human satisfaction. In Plato's dialogues, the life of philosophy is always directly present in the character of Socrates to surpass in excellence all political longings. At the same time, at least the possibility is sketched that, through the rule of philosopher-kings, or of citizens educated toward philosophically guided correct opinion, politics could bask more or less directly in the light of the Good. Aristotle, however, rigorously divides the two realms of life, endowing politics with greater stability and self-sufficiency by blanking out the superior competing alternative of philosophy. If, for Plato, the light of the sun makes its way down into the cave in only a dim form, or as a mixture of sunlight and the light of a man-made fire, one might say that Aristotle virtually bricks up the opening at the top, leaving nothing but a chink. As Aristotle argues (1251a1–24), there cannot be a single apodictic "science" (*episteme*) that would enable a monarch to grasp faultlessly all political problems, as Plato had depicted in the *Statesman* (258e, ff.). Instead, flesh and blood rulers and citizens must try to develop prudence in assessing how far particular events and variable circumstances can measure up to natural right. Although there is some question whether the great-souled man of the *Nicomachean Ethics* would really be satisfied with the austere aristocratic republic outlined in the last two books of the *Politics* (as opposed to becoming Cyrus), the contradiction is much less glaring than that between, for example,

Callicles and the Auxiliaries of the *Republic*. While for Aristotle the highest moral virtue is fenced off from true happiness (the contemplative life), for that very reason it can flourish on its own, unafflicted by the unflattering contrast always manifest in Plato between the splendor of philosophy and the rather robotic civic virtue of the best regime. In Aristotelian political psychology, thumos becomes a mere subdivision of courage (albeit the "most natural" form of it [*Nicomachean Ethics* 1116a20–1117a10]), rather than (as for Plato) the part of the soul which is the source of this political virtue as well as of religious revelation and theology (the theology of Books 2 and 3 of the *Republic* is specifically fashioned for the thumotic part of the soul and city). Although, as we will see, there are cryptic references in Aristotle to a god-like ruler whose claim supersedes all others (*Politics* 1288a25–30), the competition implied is not, as it is in Plato, between philosophy and all merely political virtue, but between monarchical and aristocratic political virtue. The philosophic life is indeed superior to both, but it does not and should not rule. The psychology of thumos and eros fades from view in Aristotle's political philosophy in the same measure as the politics of transcendence are conventionalized and fenced off from philosophy: The code of the *kalos kagathos* can stand improvement, but need not be shattered by an exposure to the highest truth. By the same token, Aristotle's great-souled man arguably participates more directly in the repose for which eros longs than do Plato's Auxillaries, and would be a more appealing prospect for a Callicles otherwise drawn to tyranny.

THE MODERN POINT OF DEPARTURE FOR
THE NEW SCIENCE OF POLITICS

The overwhelming practical aim of classical political philosophy was, as it were, to make Coriolanus content with Rome. Plato is more revealing than Aristotle about the full spectrum of possibilities because he concedes that the longing for satisfaction from politics may, in rare instances such as Alicibiades or Callicles, be open to a philosophic eros for knowledge of the whole. Still, common to both Plato and Aristotle is the conviction that philosophy is a superior way of life, both in dignity and pleasure, to any kind of politics, even the best. A useful way of taxonomizing subsequent political thought is to see how this assumption is challenged by the moderns through a reinterpretation of the psychology of political ambition and its primary passions of eros and thumos. For Plato, the gods revealed by thumos are not a human projection. They are an "enthusiasm" issuing *through us by way of thumos*, a revelation further clouded by the needs and passions men bring to their piety. Hence, the gods are not inventions, but both approximations and distortions of the divine *nous* that orders the world and is the source of wisdom. As Book 10 of the *Laws* argues, the spirited man's resentment and despair over the gods' indifference or malevolence toward the human situation can be an invaluable propaedeutic, if not to philosophy, at least to a philosophical theology that grounds republican citizenship (899–904).[32] Eros can also be a bridge between the primordial and the transcendental – sexual passion is a low but real intimation of a beauty that objectively graces nature's most perfect beings.

I will argue that the modern tradition – if one attempts a direct interpretation of the moderns on the basis of the categories provided by the ancients – is characterized by the ontological priority of thumos over eros, the reversal of what I have argued is the Platonic priority of eros over thumos. In other words, the time-bound, anxious, individualistic side of human longing is radicalized and separated from an openness to its objective satisfaction guided by eros – union with the beautiful. In keeping with this severance of thumos from the beautiful is the transformation of transcendental politics from the approximation by political life of the objective *nous* that orders the cosmos into a self-conscious human construct fashioned in opposition to a nature devoid of purpose. Looked at in Platonic terms, in other words, modern political philosophy is dominated by thumos: the thumotic man comes into his own virtually unchallenged – anxious, self-conscious, alternately fearful and arrogant, ready to storm the heavens in order to get three meals a day. What is more remarkable, however, is that precisely as thumos is liberated from its classical restraints, modern political psychology loses sight of thumos as a phenomenon about which it can give a reasonable and rounded account. When everything is thumos, thumos disappears.

---

32 Plato writes sympathetically about how thoughtful young men are often led by their pride to gloomy ruminations about life's meaning. They are aware of how often injustice goes unpunished, how some men enjoy enormous wealth and glory at the expense of others and die peacefully in their beds of old age. It makes them doubt whether a rational and beneficent order governs the world. *Laws* 899–900. Consider Pangle (1976).

Not being limited by anything, it cannot be defined and compared. This occlusion of eros, I argue, is crystallized by Hobbes.

At this juncture, it should be emphasized that when I characterize the shift to modernity as the ontological priority of thumos over eros, I am making this characterization still largely from within the classical horizon itself. In other words, the priority of thumos over eros is the closest way of expressing modern political psychology in terms of classical psychology. But we cannot leave it at that. The classics were already aware of what it would mean for thumos to lead the soul. The story of Leontius in Book 4 of the *Republic* is a cautionary tale about the difficulty of containing the soul's thumotic capacities for zealotry, fury, and morbid ruminations even while attempting to sublimate and re-direct those passionate energies toward a vigorous civic-spiritedness. Indeed, the *denouement* of the kallipolis as a whole comes when the spirited men throw off the rule of the philosophers and institute a regime based on honor. That is to say, even *after* the elaborate civic pedagogy of the first four books of the *Republic*, the "correct opinion" instilled in the Auxillaries – which might have been thought sufficient to forestall Leontius' only very shaky mastery of his passion, since he had not been the beneficiary of such an education – does not prove a sufficient insulation against thumotic indignation even among those who *have* received, at least within the fiction of the dialogue, this philosophically guided civic paideia.

Beginning with Machiavelli, however, modern political psychology alters the whole relationship between reason and passion. While the thumotic, honor-seeking dimension of the soul certainly *is* privileged by Machiavelli over the erotic dimension (a love of the beautiful or noble being for Machiavelli, as I will argue in Chapters 5 and 6, the most profound source of a prince's delusional "reliance on Fortune"), thumos is also diminished and displaced, although not altogether snuffed out. By being sundered from its connection, through eros, its proper guide, to a longing for the beautiful and the good, thumos is diminished from an openness to divine transcendence and reduced to mere human aggression, the "lion" side of the lion and the fox, Machiavelli's somatic metaphor in which the traditional alliance in the soul between the divine and the animal is replaced by an alliance between two animals, the cunning and the forceful. Having been severed from its connection to the beautiful and good, thumos is further and more fundamentally displaced by the will to master Fortuna, to master nature, whose project thumos will now serve. It is well to remember that in Platonic psychology, thumos is not itself the source of volition. Thumos is not the Platonic equivalent of the will.[33] Thumos is a passion, a kind of moral depth charge in the soul which, properly shaped by the correct civic education, can produce a burst of zealous energy to set the levers of volition in motion so as to serve the leadership of reason, both within the individual soul and within the tri-partite best regime. In both the classical and modern psychologies, in other words, thumos is the ally of volition,

33 As Zeigler observes, the seat of volition in the Platonic account of the soul is *boulesis*, from the verb *boulomai*, meaning deliberative resolve. *Boulesis* does not mean "will" in the modern sense. It is more akin to a reasoned wish or a wish arising from deliberation. It entails a particular end or counsel advantageous to the situation. Zeigler (1979) pp. 126–127. Evidence of this is that *boulesis* is cognate with the word *boule*, a council of citizens appointed to deliberate upon the daily affairs of the polis. For reasons such as these, Platonic volition cannot be equated, in my view, with the modern Kantian concept of "autonomy," the striving to exert a pure will unmediated by empirical correlates, which I trace to the Abrahamic conception of a God who stands outside of nature and exerts his will to transform it. See also Hyland (1981) pp. 7ff. Of course these issues can admittedly never be resolved through etymologies alone, but etymologies are helpful. Along with *boulomai*, there are several other verbs that connote wishing, wanting or resolving, with varying nuances of impulse, instinct, unconscious and conscious desire, or deliberative choice, including *ethelein* and *epithumein*. I will provide here for readers' interest a note on the debate about their precise meanings, but stress in advance that none of these verbs, however one assesses their bearing on volition, has the modern connotation of the will to strive to stand outside of nature and master it. Indeed, the very uncertainty about the precise connotation of these different words for volition testifies to the lack of a single term possessing the clarity that the term "will" does for us, at least philosophically. Gottlob Schrenk comments as follows on the difference in meaning between *ethelo* and *boulomai*: "The original difference in meaning between *boulomai* and *ethelo* is disputed in philological investigation. Two diametrically opposing views confront one another. The one finds in *ethelein* impulsive and unconscious desire and in *boulomai* rational and conscious choice. *Ethelein* thus signifies volition by inclination or natural instinct... while *boulomai* denotes a decision of will based on deliberate resolve... On the other hand, *ethelein* is understood to mean the resolution of the spirit, and *boulesthai* as desire or inclination, as the wish of the soul. The first view is supported by the fact that *boulesthai* is related to *boule*, *bouleuein*, *bouleuesthai*. The second view argues amongst other things that it is often used synonymously with *epithumein*. It is difficult to decide between them because at a very early date the two groups overlap. Hence the only course is to study the usage in different periods. The following results accrue from such historical investigation. In Homer there are 38 instances of *boulomai* and 294 of *ethelo*. *Boulomai* always has here the sense of 'to prefer,' 'to choose,' whereas *ethelo* is used for all the other nuances of volition. Thus *ethelo* is the older and more comprehensive term. It is particularly loved by the poets, whereas *boulomai* is preferred by the prose writers and predominates from the time of Herodotus." Quoted in Halloran (1973).

which is seated in reason. What changes so profoundly is the status of reason.

For the classics, the soul seeks, through the intellect, union with the eternal truth. The soul governed by the intellect mirrors and instantiates the harmony and unity of the cosmos itself. Volition is at the service of, and solicited by, this erotic longing for completion. Beginning with Machiavelli, by contrast, reason is assimilated *into* the will to master nature. Reason is no longer the guide to the whole, but an anthropocentric pattern of rationality – of formal order and control – imposed *on* nature by the "virtue" of the new prince. A part of the leonine ferocity of the traditional meaning of thumos is, to be sure, incorporated into the steely resolve of Machiavelli's new prince. However, the representation of princely calculation as "the fox" endows it with an entirely somatic and animalistic spirit, just as the metaphor of the lion and the fox as a whole collapses the classical distinction between the purely animal and the divine spark of the soul – mediated by the in-between realm of the passions shaped by the virtues – into a thoroughly reanimalized understanding of the human. While a certain dimension of thumos can still be found in Machiavelli's new princely psychology, this passion must be methodically disciplined to pursue the goal of dispassionate mastery, never allowing its hopes for transcendence, its perplexity about the gods, or its openness to tragic gloominess to distract the new prince from the ongoing project for the mastery of Fortuna. For shorthand purposes, one could contrast Achilles, the ancient prince of untutored thumos, with Shakespeare's presentation of Henry Bolingbroke, the modern methodist of power seeking. The untamed passion of Achilles, leading him to career between tragic despair and mad daring, is, in Platonic psychology, to be reshaped and moderated by the education of the Auxillaries, governed by a philosophic cosmology of eternal stability, mediated by the "tales" making up their education. Henry Bolingbroke, by contrast, has mastered his unruly passions through his own silent resolve to overcome all obstacles placed in his path by Fortuna, summed up in the flawed Christian monarch and Augustinian poet of the soul's deepest despair, Richard the Second. Bolingbroke's career is not *reasoned*, but it is *rational*. The content of reason – the longing for union with the beautiful and good – is replaced by method. In this way, Shakespeare's Bolingbroke reflects Machiavelli's maxim, which I explore in the next chapter, that the classical prescription whereby philosophy provides a prince with a guide to prudence must be replaced in such a way that the prince is the source of his *own* prudence, with no need for a philosophical governor (or, therefore, a potential rival). We revisit the "stage Machiavel" in the Conclusion.

As I will argue throughout this book, and most thematically in Chapter 6, of paramount significance to the modern approach is the change in the interpretation of political ambition effected by certain strains of Christianity. In St. Augustine, for example, the happiness that Aristotle believed could only be achieved within the political community becomes the preserve of the City of God. Political life, what Augustine terms the City of Man, is separated and reduced from this happiness to the merely negative police function of restraining human sinfulness after the Fall so as to maintain order and the Church as the City of God's earthly outpost. Virtue, a term used by Plato and Aristotle to describe various kinds of human excellence ranging from the statesmanship of Pericles to the talents of generals, poets and ordinary artisans, and not necessarily or exclusively synonymous with law-abidingness or self-restraint, is now narrowed to mean the suppression of all worldly desires. Classical political virtues like pride and magnificence (fueled by an eros for honor) are now proclaimed not to be virtues at all; indeed, they are depicted as caricatures of their classical originals.

Since true happiness has been banished to a spiritualized Beyond, political ambition is drained of its erotic character (the longing for happiness, immortality, the noble and the good) and, thus deontologized, is depicted as a gray and compulsive drive toward "dominion," "power," and "vainglory." In Aristotelian terms, politics is reduced from the good life to mere life, while the good life departs the natural realm. Paralleling this transformation, the word used predominantly for soul or spirit in the New Testament is not, as it would have been for the ancients, *psyche* or thumos, but *pneuma*, a more disembodied and immaterial concept with connotations of escaping the evil world of fallen nature. Whereas soul (*psyche*) had originally meant undifferentiated life, the holism of *psyche* is now dichotomized as bodily *animo* versus spiritual *anima*.[34] To be certain, this dichotomy is already present in the more

---

34 For an illuminating explanation of how ancient accounts of the soul differ from those of Christianity, see Davis (2011). He sees in the soul of Achilles the archetypal struggle between immortality and mortal life, a tension I trace to Diotima's presentation of eros

proto-Stoic of Platonic dialogues such as the *Gorgias*. But not only is that dichotomy but one perspective among others in the dialogues, whose foil is the unification of the soul by eros in a continuous ascent from the passions of the body to the passions of the mind by way of the passion for honor; more important, in all versions of Platonic psychology the aim is the fulfillment of our natural longings within the sphere of nature. Augustinian Christianity's diminution of nature to the corporeal, lustful, irrational, and perishable helps explain the hardening of the two dimensions limned earlier of primordial and transcendental politics into a metaphysical cleavage. To be sure, not every version of Christian theology promotes this cleavage as sharply as does Augustine. St. Thomas, for example, tries to bridge the chasm between the two worlds and preserve a place for human nature in its own right, to be filled with large swaths of Aristotle's philosophy. But he no less than Augustine makes God the efficient cause, the creator who imposes final and formal causes on matter, thus elevating the lowest cause in the *Physics* to the highest. Nature can only hold up under the sustaining impact of God's will. For Aristotle, by contrast, efficient cause has been, along with material cause, solicited into movement by the self-movement of substantive Being most clearly manifest in formal and final cause. The Unmoved Mover informs the world but does not create it.

Machiavelli is taken by many to be among the chief founders of modernity. But his transformation of political philosophy could not have taken place, in my view, without an engagement with Christianity, especially in its Augustinian variant. Some, like Voegelin, see Machiavelli as an apocalyptic thinker. Others see him as reversing the classical priority of the community over the individual, and therefore as a harbinger of liberalism and commercialism. Still others see him as reviving classical republicanism as against the excessive other-worldliness of Christianity in a way that was used by later figures like Harrington to resist Hobbesian absolute monarchy. All of these interpretations shed light on Machiavelli, and I will discuss them at some length in the Conclusion. My main point for now is that they are all compatible with, and flow from, the characterization I am making here of Machiavelli as a post-Christian thinker. By viewing Machiavelli in light of the tension

as the contradictory and self-vitiating longing "to possess the beautiful as one's own forever." This theme is also central to the fine book by Ranasinghe (2000).

between the primordial and transcendental, I want to argue, the following new synthesis emerges: Machiavelli accepts the Augustinian reduction of politics to "dominion" while rejecting the City of God. He urges the return to classical praxis (embodied by the history of the Roman Republic), but also urges the rejection of classical philosophy, which he groups with Christianity (the "imagined republics" of Plato and Augustine). This is an original and unprecedented synthesis. In some sense, Machiavelli liberates from Augustinian reductionism the phenomenological richness that we find in Plato's and Aristotle's political theories, the full-blooded and nuanced depictions of rule, virtue, honor, and ambition. Yet he interprets these phenomena in post-Christian terms, as mediations and epiphenomena of dominion. In urging, for example, that man forsake the allegiance of his soul (*anima*) to the City of God so as to recover the commitment of his spirit (*animo*) to the earthly fatherland, Machiavelli, even in repudiating Christian other-worldliness, accepts its mundane interpretation of political virtue. Nowhere, I maintain, does Machiavelli account for political eros in its original and full Platonic sense. His heroes have lusts and rages which occasionally distract them from the frigid "glory" of mastery, but none of them are "lovers of the city": A passion for honor is never the route to an eros for transcendence. In this respect, one may contrast the helpless admiration which Socrates playfully evinces in the presence of beautiful bodies and souls, or how much he learned from the priestess of love, Diotima, with the cold-minded rape of Fortuna urged by Machiavelli.[35]

Machiavelli accepts the primordialist view of politics as a field of passions entirely severed from an erotic orientation toward the eternal Good and raises this cleavage to a metaphysical certainty, as had Christianity. While rejecting the Christian God, Machiavelli accepts the Christian view of nature as forces that issue out of a void and return to it. Fortuna, like God, is what/that it is. In this sense, God is assimilated by Being, or, put another way, nature is collapsed into existence subject to time. Hence, as Strauss writes (1969, p. 214), Machiavelli's meditations on Fortune bear a resemblance to meditating on the will of God, an issue we will treat at length in Chapter 6. While for Christianity,

---

35 Bruell (1977) observes that Socrates' attraction to the beauty of Charmides enables him to contemplate the effects of eros on the others present while not succumbing wholly to it himself.

nature so conceived was perishable and corrupt unless held up by God's supernatural will, for Machiavelli it is the source of all vitality, spontaneity, and energy. Whereas for the classics, Fortuna was a subsidiary dimension of the whole within its supervening beneficent orderliness, Machiavelli identifies it with Being *tout court*. By recognizing the overwhelming singularity that is Fortuna, we recognize that nature does not support either classical or Christian hopes for virtue and offers no prospect for lasting peace, justice, and decency. This awful truth, however, liberates us to face the world without illusion and bend it to our will, making it as productive and livable as we can. This requires a politics in which acquisitiveness is liberated and served by the new art of government.

The spontaneity and willfulness of Fortuna well up into each of us as our passions, the "lion" of human psychology. By releasing this chunk of Fortuna within ourselves, we can adjust ourselves to Fortuna and anticipate her treacherous reversals. Being at home with our selfishness, we build dams to prevent the world from upsetting our plans (chapter 25 of *The Prince*). This requires, of course, that we purge ourselves ruthlessly of any lingering disposition to reify Fortuna as the objective support for our human longings for peace, order, and justice – the "imagined republics" of the great classical-Christian conglomerate. Paradoxically, the full release of the primordial in human nature requires the dispassionate mastery of the "fox" – the wary manipulator of his own and other people's passions – so as to construct a self-consciously human project for an entirely this-worldly transcendence, the imposition of order on nature through political fiat. As I will argue in Chapters 6 and 7 as well as in the Conclusion, Machiavelli's new conception of the self anticipates the Cartesian ego, purged of all received tradition, purged of what Machiavelli's admirer Bacon called "the idols of the tribe," his term for Machiavelli's "imagined republics." The radical opposition Machiavelli posits between the prince's virtues – meaning his strength of will – and the hostility of Fortune also anticipates that aspect of Hegel's philosophy according to which striving against the necessity of nature establishes our freedom.

Fortuna is so unreliable that she cannot be relied upon to be unreliable: Dealing with her may equally require the impetuosity of "the young" or the caution of Fabius the Delayer. Neither principalities nor republics have a privileged place in Machiavelli's political science, but republics are arguably more inclusive since they can accommodate princely natures in the appropriate camouflage of dictators and leaders who must periodically re-found the republic and extirpate its malign "humors." Fortuna generates "bodies" and republics and principalities are characteristic modes in which these bodies clash, repel, and coalesce. An expansionist republic whose masses are alternately unleashed and restrained as foreign and domestic conditions require by an elite enlightened as to the truth about Fortuna seems to anticipate all the possible manifestations of Fortuna, immanentizing them in a cosmopolitan empire composed of "men of many nations" that is progressively perfected by "chance" and "the aid of events" (*The Prince* chapter 17; *Discourses* 1.2). Since the cosmos is not ordered by *nous*, there can be no Aristotelian "middle way" in the destiny of regimes or in the moral life of individuals. Liberality, for instance, is not a mean between parsimony and extravagance. Exposed to the clashes and reversals of Fortuna, you must either be parsimonious so as to avoid financial ruin or liberal with other people's possessions.

In these ways, I want to argue, Machiavelli recaptures the phenomenological *range* of classical political philosophy but on post-Christian principles. Viewed from within the classical horizon, thumos becomes the chief trait of the soul for Machiavelli because the primordialist view of politics entirely displaces the transcendental view oriented through eros, which is easier to get rid of because it has already been drained out of politics by Augustinian Christianity. Eros has already been split into mere appetitive lust within the confines of nature and the incorporeal love of God. But precisely because the transcendental object of eros has disappeared – the ascent up Diotima's Ladder from civic virtue to the eternally beautiful – the nature of thumos is also occluded. It is no longer understood in the complexity of its relations with eros, philosophy, and the gods. It has become neutral "power," the engine for the reconstruction of nature. Even tyrannical eros, which Plato saw as the basis for the critique of the tyrant, is too moral a category for Machiavelli because it harbors the possibility of reformation: it is already a part of Plato's solution. What Machiavelli means by *gloria* is something colder, subjective, self-made, and containing no intimation of transcendence or immortality. It is *reputazione*, the ruler's external image based on the awe, fear, and gratitude of his subjects, stemming from his successful mastery of Fortuna. It is at most the nimbus, the surface sheen of eros, bereft of the immanent potentiality for nature's development toward perfection. This diminishing of eros, and therefore of thumos, begins the evasion of the classical starting point for understanding tyranny. If my argument is plausible, it follows that Machiavelli cannot be comprehended, as Strauss would have it, solely in terms of how his philosophy contrasts with classical thought without regard to his engagement with Christianity. At the same time, Voegelin arguably underestimates Machiavelli's originality by interpreting him as an epigone of the Joachite stream of millenarian Christianity.[36] As I will argue throughout this book, Machiavelli is after much bigger stakes – the imposition of the eidetic quality of classical rationalism *on* Fortuna through an act of will, the rational re-shaping of the natural world, a starting point that makes his project irreducible either to the

36 See the discussion of Voegelin and Strauss in Schram (1987). It is difficult to summarize the complexity of the debate between Strauss and Voegelin over the meaning of Machiavelli. Broad strokes must suffice. Voegelin saw Machiavelli as a continuation of the apocalyptic millenarianism of Joachim of Fiore, who preached the dawning of a new age, a third age, based on the Book of Revelation, in which the Church would no longer be necessary because all men would be in direct contact with God, the message of the Gospels and universal love would reign everywhere, and Christians would unite with Moslems. In other contexts, Voegelin saw Machiavelli as a continuation of Gnosticism, the rejection of the current world in favor of a new epoch where man would be totally liberated from the constraints of bodily and material necessity. Strauss, by contrast, viewed Machiavelli almost wholly within the framework of Machiavelli's debate with, and attempted repudiation of, classical political philosophy. Rejecting (or bypassing) Voegelin's suggestion of religious or pseudo-religious and millenarian motifs in Machiavelli's thought, Strauss believed it was more accurate to see him as being influenced by Latin Averroism. I have a difficulty with this view because, as I discuss in detail in Chapters 2, 6, and 7, I see Machiavelli's focus on man's freedom of will to oppose and re-fashion nature to be a secularized version of the Abrahamic God, which argues for a more intimate connection between Machiavelli and certain strains, predominantly Augustinian, of Christian theology. At the same time, by suggesting (as I interpret him) that man might master nature by stepping outside of it, Machiavelli does not entirely comport with the Averroists who, as followers of Aristotle and classical thought, believed that human nature, virtue, and the soul fell *within* the ambit of nature, to be clarified by philosophy. Averroism wanted to restore classical philosophy and elevate it over the authority of revelation. Machiavelli, by contrast, wants to assimilate reason to the will-power to master nature, a secularization of God's will. The side of Machiavelli that encourages the progressive mastery of nature does not comport with the Averroists' wish to restore the natural philosophy of the ancients as permanently valid. For his part, Voegelin believed that Averroism itself, through its attempt to sunder reason entirely from revelation and establish reason's supreme authority, bore a resemblance to Gnosticism, and paved the way for the hypertrophic rationalism and urge to reconstruct the world in conformity with abstract reason culminating in twentieth-century totalitarianism, aided by Joachite-Machiavellian millenarianism.

classical or Christian horizons, or to a mere reversal of them, or to the horizon of the Sophists.

In rejecting the City of God, Machiavelli immerses himself in the City of Man in order to offer his own elaboration of the same phenomena which Plato and Aristotle explore. His synthesis of classicism (the centrality of honor) with Christianity (the centrality of the will) has the universal scope of both: the phenomenological richness of classicism freed of Christian otherworldly moral restraints and the creative, anti-natural willpower of Christian revelation delivered from God, the chief artificer, into the hands of man. Owing to the broadness of this synthesis, Machiavelli, I argue in the Conclusion, cannot be reduced to liberalism, though he offers a recipe for some of its features. In light of the narrowing of Machiavelli's teaching effected by Bacon and Hobbes as they founded the new physics and the political physics of the social contract deriving from it, one can readily and even eagerly look behind them to Machiavelli for far more of the scope, substance, and historical variability of political existence, including an awareness of the limits of what material self-interest and commerce alone can achieve for a sound political order. When Burke, for example, counters the narrow appetitiveness promoted by certain strains of modernity as the chief aim of the social contract with a historically more robust and rounded account of the traditional "powers" of the English constitution, his understanding owes more to Machiavelli's view of the equilibrium of powers in the Roman Republic as modalities of the self-originating motions of Fortuna than to Aristotle's discussion of the classification of regimes under the aspect of eternity.

For the classics, human nature is capable of fulfilling its own natural potential for excellence within a civic community. For Augustine, by contrast, human perfection is not possible within the limitations of nature – no human virtue is possible without faith in God. This leads to a radical diminishing of political life, in which civic virtue is reduced to mere dominion or power-seeking. It is paralleled by Augustine's view of nature as intrinsically fallen, incapable on its own of sustaining happiness or excellence, held up only by the will of God. Machiavelli in effect agrees that human virtue is reducible to power-seeking while jettisoning Augustine's concern with the divine, and also accepts his view of nature as random, incoherent happenstance. He speculatively transfers from God to man to capacity to order nature through a sustained act of will, although the full radicalization of this speculative project as the basis for modern physics and the social contract only comes with Bacon and Hobbes. By accepting the Augustinian view of nature as random, purposeless motion – but now stripped of its divine external ordering – Machiavelli arrives at a view of *Fortuna* which differs fundamentally from that of the ancients, whether we are referring to classical philosophy, tragedy, or sophistry. In all three of the ancient versions, fortune or chance is not unambiguously hostile to man and most definitely cannot be mastered from without. The prospect for transferring from God to man a capacity to re-fashion nature broached by Machiavelli is therefore not intelligible without the intervening concept of the Abrahamic God's capacity to stand outside of nature altogether and re-shape it. I will bring these contrasts into relief through a detailed comparison in Chapter 6 between Diotima's Ladder in the *Symposium*, where human nature's capacity for excellence leads continuously toward trans-human repose, and Augustine's dichotomous contrast between the City of Man and the City of God, where nature and transcendence are almost entirely sundered.

THE HOBBESIAN NARROWING OF MACHIAVELLI'S NEW SCIENCE OF POLITICS

With Machiavelli, then, transcendental politics is reduced to an epiphenomenon of primordialist politics, not its fulfillment but its constructed product. Thumos comes to the fore but loses clarity because it is no longer limited, bounded by, and contrasted with eros. Future political philosophy tries instead to clarify the ways in which freedom becomes conscious of itself through the opposition of nature. The outward manifestation of the pursuit of freedom is the will to re-shape nature transferred from God to man. Thumos, stripped of its transcendental orientation to the immortal Good by way of eros, reduces to an existential undertow of anxiety, alienation and rage, psychological fuel for the will's negation of nature.

Beginning with Hobbes, liberal political philosophy can be seen as an attempt to curb the potentially Promethean excess of Machiavelli's summons to master nature by achieving an equilibrium between primordialist politics and the transcendental politics that man now artificially constructs to serve the passions. As I will argue in the Conclusion,

Hobbes's theory of the social contract and the Sovereign is the juncture at which the dark and light corridors of modernity intersect before heading in different directions – the endless reconstruction of nature through revolutionary will *versus* the establishment of communities of rights-bearing individuals living in peace and tolerance.

Just as for Machiavelli, for Hobbes man's rationality is not given from an objectively reasonable world, but instead dawns on him as he struggles not to be destroyed by nature's purposeless chaos and the grip of that chaos on him through the passions. Hence, the criterion for rationality is what the passions require for their own safe and efficient pursuit. This symmetry between passion and rationality requires that the passions move even further in the direction of abstract homogeneity than was the case in Machiavelli. Starting as he did with the full range of political phenomena, the same broad canvas of war, peace, honor, and domestic faction surveyed by Aristotle, Machiavelli recognized that glory could plausibly be more worth pursuing than self-preservation, and in rare spirits constitutes an independent source of human motivation. He in effect preserves the distinction made by Xenophon's Simonides – whose advice to the tyrant Hiero is one of the models, as we will see in Chapter 4, for Machiavelli's art of princely rule – between the "real men" (*andres*) who aim for mastery and the common run of "humans" (*anthropoi*) who are content with self-preservation (*Hiero* 2.1; 7.3). Since, for Machiavelli, domestic politics are inevitably connected to foreign policy – indeed, a republic that does not wish to atrophy and die must have an expansionist dynamic – the pursuit of glory through conquest is an irreducible necessity for healthy political bodies. Because Hobbes, by contrast, confines himself to the internal ordering of the polity, and begins with an a priori method – the "similitude of the passions" – even these Machiavellian approximations of eros (as the glory attendant upon successful imperialism) fade away, replaced by the abstract and contentless *summum malum* of non-existence, the fear of violent death. This reduction of the passions to the desire for self-preservation makes it possible to make the state synonymous with what Aristotle had called the art of household management. But for Hobbes, unlike Aristotle, there is no distinction between good and bad, noble and ignoble usages, for household management and property. Whereas Aristotle had argued for an economics of sufficiency to enable citizens to devote themselves to politics and philosophy, and for wives and children to cultivate the virtues appropriate to their potentials, in contrast with open-ended economic maximization and despotic authority, Hobbes opted for the latter alone, draining the teleological substance of Aristotle's distinctions and turning household management into a pure method of management and productivity.

Since, as he argues in the *Leviathan*, the "objects" of the passions – what we want from, and how we relate to, the political community and the world – are too diverse and changeable (as are we ourselves) for us ever to be able to agree on what they are and whether they are good or bad (and even if we agreed for a time, we would change and no longer agree with our own selves), we should turn away from the world and look inward to the "similitude" of the passions themselves (Hobbes [1971] pp. 82–83). Severed from their objects in the world (and opinions about them), the passions of every individual are universally reducible to such simple modes of self-preservation as fear and desire. Aristotle had argued that humans fulfill their natures by living in a polis and offering reasoned opinions about the just and the unjust, the noble and the base, and the advantageous and the disadvantageous. These reasoned opinions correspond to what Hobbes terms the "objects" of the passions. By denying that these opinions possess any rank order or even stability, Hobbes in effect demolishes the Aristotelian understanding of the common good. Every man becomes a pedestrian tyrant motivated by the desire to stay alive and avoid violent death. By orienting ourselves by the similitude of the passions rather than their objects, we also deny from the outset the existence of intrinsic natural differences among human beings of virtue, "wit," and prudence, as well as the classical assumption that there is an independent capacity in the souls of some men to seek honor for its own sake, as opposed to mere self-preservation. Every one who introspects and understands his true motive will realize that he seeks power to remain alive. In Xenophontic language, there are no "real men," only "humans." And this, I maintain, is the fatal flaw in Hobbes's theory.

Why? Let us reiterate that the similitude of the passions stripped of their objects is a rationality of the origins, not of the end. Like the Cartesian ego, it is an abstraction of the conditions for pure selfhood from all mediating traditions and social practices. Machiavelli's delicate interplay between Fortuna and man, embodied in the cycles of history and the rise and decline of republics and principalities, becomes in Hobbes a frozen dichotomy between nature as a field of random happenstance and the anthropocentric power to re-fashion it so as to maximize survival. The great puzzle that Hobbes cannot explain is: Why would anyone want to become the Sovereign? Since the toils and dangers of attempting to rise to supreme power are by definition an insane goal for every human *qua* human – since we are compelled by nature to seek survival and avoid danger – how does the Sovereign achieve power in the first place? Hobbes seems to assume that these tyrants emerge like spontaneous natural forces. He envisions them as supplying the institutionalized terror that, by simulating the terror of the state of nature where the absence of government exposes us all to the daily danger of violent death, will remind every subject that no advantage to be gained from breaking the contract and attempting to tyrannize could possibly outweigh the dangers involved ([1971] p. 202). At least one "real man" is needed to keep the "human beings" in line.[37] But Hobbes's theory cannot account for the possibility of such a man.

Clearly this tyrant, re-cast in functional value-neutral language as "the sovereign," will be a man of thumos. In a tacit revision of Plato's three states of the soul and city, Hobbes argues in chapter 19 of *The Citizen* that it is not the highest part, the "head" and the seat of "counsel" that will rule, but the middle part – which Plato identifies as thumos, and which Hobbes identifies altogether with the "soul" and the seat of "will" and "command" in contrast with "counsel," thus joining Machiavelli in preferring *animo* to *anima* ([1972]). But, on his own principles, Hobbes cannot elaborate this psychology in any rich detail. It is apparent only through the most cryptic inferences – for example, Hobbes's claim that although Sovereignty by institution (consent) can be distinguished analytically from Sovereignty by acquisition (conquest), "the (Sovereign's) rights are the same in both," because both are based on fear ([1971] pp. 252–253). Tyrannical thumos lurks unseen behind this dry parsing of the modes of order. The lacuna is further illustrated by the famous conundrum as to whether Hobbes believed that man's natural power-seeking is limitless in everyone or only in the "vainglorious" few.[38] If it is limitless by nature in everyone, then politics as a

---

37 Consider Habermas (1973) p. 57: the political absolutism of Hobbes's Sovereign is
  necessary to bring about the utopia of social peace envisioned by Thomas More.
38 Consider Strauss (1952).

universally applicable, deductively rigorous science of the kind Hobbes professes to have created is impossible, since people cannot be relied upon (even when terrorized) to prefer safety to vainglory. If, however (as Hobbes mostly seems to suggest), it is limitless by nature only in a troublesome few (war-like young men fired up by reading the ancients on honor), this would suggest that the majority of human beings are by nature intrinsically capable of moderating their desires for the sake of peace – that is, in the state of nature, prior to the construction of the compact. This conclusion would undermine what Hobbes argues is the self-evidently necessary transition from the state of nature to the compact and its conflation with the Sovereign, preferably a monarchy, because it would be possible in principle for men to reach a peace treaty among themselves in the state of nature prior to such despotic coercion.

I think there is no consistent solution to this conundrum on Hobbes's terms. Whether and how often these Sovereign natures would arise is literally a matter of accident; they would emerge spontaneously from Fortuna. Reason, being an anthropocentric faculty with no intrinsic connection to the world, can supply no account of these unfathomable upsurges; no psychology of statesmanship in which ambition is understood (as in Plato) as a mode of the longing for union with the immortally Beautiful and Good, thereby both dangerous and capable of rehabilitation. The link between the anthropocentric ratiocination that, for Hobbes, demonstrates the necessity of the Sovereign and the spontaneous appearance of such natures is, at bottom, fated. This is a corollary of the larger and central ambiguity of Hobbes's philosophy. Humans are able to make sense of nature by assigning it causality, and to remedy its deficiencies by re-constructing it. (The compact, for example, supplies an artificial supplement and improvement to humans' natural inability to pursue their rights without degenerating into the war of all against all, contradicting their ability to pursue their rights.) But this human capacity is at bottom unfathomable, since nature itself is not objectively ordered so as to render itself intelligible to human reason. Accordingly, the possibility of Sovereign natures emerging can only be inferred from the primordialist and Machiavellian undertow of Hobbesian methodology, the self-emergence of Fortuna as what/that it is.

Because of Locke's liberal democratic emendation of Hobbes, and through the historical evolution of liberalism in practice, this theoretical lacuna has not been glaringly evident in the world of events. Indeed, within the liberal democracies, the taming of eros and thumos is one of the most striking indications that Hobbes may have been right to believe that these traits, the psychological core of classical statecraft, could be ignored, suppressed, or gradually bourgeoisified by the promulgation of a psychology of pedestrian hedonism and appetitive self-interest "in the universities," successfully actualized through the rise of commercial economies ([1971] p. 728).

However, looking at the pace of modernization in the non-Western world (Mao, Pol Pot) or in Western regimes hostile to the West (Stalin, Hitler), one may wonder whether the Hobbesian Sovereign has not in fact haunted the modern project all along. In these cases, terror has been used all too literally to reduce people to the "similitude of the passions" and strip them of all religious, family, and national traditions so as to convert them into human integers who are interchangeable with one another as units of a unified and contentless compact. Perhaps nowhere is the poverty of the liberal psychology of pedestrian power-seeking more apparent than here. When, as in Hobbes's theory, a tyrant is needed to re-shape human nature through terror to make it conform to a psychology which by definition dismisses such tyrannical natures as impossible or absurd from the outset, then one invites the emergence of a tyrannical project which exceeds the worst prognostications of the classics while at the same time sacrificing the classics' capacity for identifying the tyrannical nature as a deformed version of the erotic longing for immortality by contrasting it with the healthy pursuit of civic honor and an ambition to serve the common good. When everything is thumos, thumos disappears, becoming the ghost in the machine of modernization.

II

THE TYRANT AND THE STATESMAN IN PLATO'S POLITICAL PHILOSOPHY AND MACHIAVELLI'S REJOINDER

This chapter centers on Plato's most explicit discussion of the possibility that a young tyrant's "eros" for the city might be harnessed to the Athenian Stranger's prescription in the *Laws* for founding a just regime (709–712).[1] This is the classic statement of the relationship between an ambitious young ruler and the philosopher who should act as his mentor, a relationship echoed in many later works such as Cicero's depiction of Scipio the Younger and in his own real-life (and unsuccessful) attempts to govern the young Octavian Caesar. I then proceed to present Machiavelli's very different interpretation of this rubric in chapter 23 of *The Prince* on the need to avoid "flatterers," in order to show how, in his evaluation, a prince's methodical exercise of will can do away with the need for this philosophical governor, in effect enabling the prince to become the source of his *own* prudence.

Before turning to the *Laws*, I begin with some general observations about the theme of tyranny in classical political thought. The ancient understanding of tyranny involves both psychological and theoretical dimensions, as well as considerations of pragmatic statecraft, and all three dimensions must be kept in play if we are to penetrate it. At bottom, the ancients, as I suggested in the Introduction, distinguish between two types of tyranny. The first is ordinary "garden variety" tyranny based on selfish passion and excess; its need for condemnation

---

[1] "The possibility," as the Athenian Stranger puts it, "that a divine erotic passion for moderate and just practices should arise in some of the great and all-powerful rulers" (711d).

is straightforward, and its correction lies in the proper education of eros and thumos within a harmonious soul grounded in a cosmology of balance and moderation.

In addition, however, the ancients explore the prospects for reforming tyrannical power into virtuous monarchy or statesmanship through an alliance between the tyrant's or potential tyrant's ambition and a philosophically guided pattern for a justly or at least beneficently ordered regime (exemplified, as we consider in this chapter, by Book 4 of the *Laws* and, as we consider in Chapter 4, by Xenophon's *Hiero* and the *Education of Cyrus*). This case is far more complex because it involves some relaxation of the moral condemnation of tyranny if it can be rehabilitated to serve philosophy's vision of a just regime. As Plato, Aristotle, and Xenophon were aware, this speculative tangent was playing with fire, and, as we see throughout this chapter and the ones to follow, it had to be treated with great circumspection lest it backfire, undermining the condemnation of tyranny essential to the ethos of a republic *without* producing the desired transition of the tyrant into a benevolent ruler. As I argue with respect to Xenophon in particular, to the extent that the ancients do entertain the reform of tyranny, they nevertheless do sometimes come quite close – although not all the way – to being "Machiavellian."

As we observed in the Introduction, closer to real-world Greek and Roman practice, a tyrant was fundamentally distinguished from a *basileus*, a king by lawful hereditary descent. However, tyrannies could be relatively beneficent, even hereditary. Sophocles' Oedipus is the exemplar of how a charismatic and brilliant usurper, bedeviled by underlying resentment of his illegitimate status on the part of the old nobility, is driven to prove himself by ever more brilliant deeds in the service of the city, sealing his own doom. The Romans had a deep-rooted abhorrence for tyrants (or "kings") as monsters of arrogant passion like the Tarquins, the enemies of free peoples. Yet the Augustan principate actualized the notion, first entertained by the Greek philosophers, that a certain kind of tyranny, now decked out in seemly constitutional garb, might bring about a rational world of peace and order. Hence the Antonine emperors' claims to embody the high moral standards of Greco-Roman culture, Stoicism, and philosophy in the *Pax Romana*. In general, going back to the political philosophies of Plato and Aristotle, tyranny was coeval with "despotism," the rule of a master over slaves as opposed to free citizens, and, as Aristotle and Thucydides both observed, entire cities could act as collective tyrannies toward the peoples they conquered (Thucydides 2.64–65; Aristotle *Politics* 1324a–b22). In this respect, the categories of tyranny and despotism, when applied to one city's relationship to others, were ways in which the ancients conceptualized what we would now more likely term "imperialism." Again, however, a straightforward moral condemnation of tyranny, whether the tyranny of individuals within cities or of cities over other peoples, was complicated by the possibility – explored in varying ways and degrees by Plato, Aristotle, and especially Xenophon – of a universal rational monarchy ruling over many peoples in conformity with the beneficent art of household management. With these preliminary considerations in mind, let us turn to the specifically Platonic teaching.

THE LOVER OF THE CITY

It can hardly be said of the Platonic dialogues that they are squeamish or unworldly about the existence of tyranny and of tyrannical longings for pleasure and mastery. In modern political philosophy, the tyrannical longing tends either to be reasoned down to a misunderstanding of a more primordial impulse for self-preservation and pedestrian gratification in the Hobbesian manner, or, in the Kantian manner, banished altogether to a realm of equally compulsive inclinations to be repressed by the metaphysics of morals that establishes the identification of moral freedom with the will's striving to be unconditioned by natural determinations. By contrast, in Plato's evocation of the phenomena of political life, people are quite open about their ambition to gain a degree of prestige, wealth, and power that exceeds that of their fellow citizens. As Callicles puts it, to "fare like a real man" means to win distinction in the agora (*Gorgias* 485). Success in politics was often identified with "getting the better" of or "having more than" one's competitors (*pleonexia*).

With some prodding by Socrates, some of these ambitious young men (Alcibiades, Polus, and Theages to mention three) confess that they admire and wish to emulate the despots and tyrants of nonpopular regimes. Socrates often enflames this interest in mastery precisely because he wishes to redirect it toward philosophically moderated statesmanship and some degree of friendliness for philosophy itself. Hence, in the *Theages*, he encourages an ambitious young man to conflate thinking about being the master of a household (*oikos*) with thinking about what it would be like to rule an entire country as if it were one's personal household (138c–d). The limit test case of despotic fantasy in the Platonic dialogues is usually the Great King of Persia, who, with his multinational empire of millions of subjects and his vast standing army, represented for the ancient Greeks the very apogee of human might – and a political stability that, increasingly in the years following Socrates' generation, the Greeks could only compare ruefully with their own fractious city-states. For the Greeks, the *oikos*, whether private or encompassing an entire regime, was a human association that, much more than the civic association, articulated itself naturally in terms of a ranked division of labor and required moderation and loyalty from its members. So when Socrates encourages his young interlocutors' fantasies of mastery, he simultaneously channels that inchoate adolescent longing toward the ensemble of specific disciplines with their objects in the world laid down by the ordering of the household – an architectonic rationality that in turn must be grounded in the self-control of a virtuous character. As we observed in Chapter 1, Alicibades is educated toward this self-reflection by the royal myth of the two paradigmatic regimes, the monarchy of Cyrus as the embodiment of household management and Sparta as the model for virtuous self-government by the "beautiful and good ones" (*kaloi kagathoi*). In an analogous manner, in Xenophon's *Oeconomicus*, his Socrates points to the Persian king and the Spartan king as the two poles of gentlemanliness, corresponding respectively to reasonable monarchical management according to the Good and the nobility of the citizen among a free people.

Yet for all this frankness about the natural wish of some people to rule over others, whether for the fame of political honor or for simple exploitation, the Platonic dialogues have almost nothing to say about the role of a tyrannical personality in the founding of new political orders. Throughout political history, for better or worse, constitutions have often been preceded by the figure Hobbes terms "the Sovereign" and Rousseau calls "the Legislator" – the founder who effects the necessarily tumultuous transition from disorder to order, from the old constitution to the new. Sometimes they use a blend of persuasion and force to knit together a previously scattered people. Sometimes they are the objects of religious veneration. Often they use force to such a terrible degree that the constitutional arrangement they establish finds it must bury the memory of the enormities of the founding, lest they make it impossible to believe in the decency of the order thereby established.[2] This ambiguity was encoded in the Romans' contradictory accounts of their own founders, the pious and heroic Aeneas versus the criminal gang of Romulus. Yet in all the Platonic dialogues, the references to this phenomenon of the entirely new founding are so scant as to number no more than a few pages. There is the notorious but brief passage in the *Republic* in which Socrates mentions, almost as an aside, that for the education prescribed for the citizenry to take root from an early age, it would be best if they could somehow start with a fresh generation of children (541a). The reader is left to wonder momentarily what would happen to their parents on being driven away but not encouraged to pursue the thought. The other, more pragmatic reference – but still only several Stephanus pages long – is the discussion we focus on in this chapter in Book 4 of the *Laws* of how a young tyrant with an "eros" for the affairs of the *polis* might be the best means for quickly founding the constitution of Magnesia, setting its laws and institutions in place all at once.

The reasons for this peculiar reticence become clear if we bear in mind that the chief purpose of Socrates' investigations of tyranny and statesmanship is not to provide an agenda for actual reform but to provoke his interlocutors to self-reflection through exploring the meaning of the virtues. Before turning in detail to Book 4 of the *Laws* to see how its frankness about the tyrannical founder is the exception that proves the rule, let us pause to consider what is by all accounts the most exhaustive defense of philosophically grounded justice against the injustice of the tyrant, Plato's *Republic*. Although it culminates in the seemingly resounding critique of the tyrant's life in Book 9, the grounds on which that critique is mounted are carefully qualified and not the entire story. For the *Republic* itself is very far from being a wholesale

---

2 This is hinted at in the *Republic* in the shameful indecency of Leontius' morbid desire to gaze into an execution pit full of corpses. At bottom, the laws and the regime presuppose the use of deadly force, both in the founding and in continuing to enforce the law. However, healthy-minded citizens will not dwell on this underside of political life lest it sap their capacity for loyalty to the city's ways and encourage them to identify with its foes.

defense of republican self-government in contrast with the mastery of a single man. On the contrary, from the outset, its identification of virtue with knowledge – with an "expert" (*technikos*) – carries a profoundly antidemocratic undertone. The *Republic* does not so much defend republican self-government against arbitrary rule as it explores a kind of rational absolutism – the rule of the philosopher-king – in contrast with irrational absolutism. However, for the very reason that Socrates wishes to make the superiority of the philosophic way of life paramount over all merely political alternatives, even the best pattern of authority that is the *kallipolis*, he must adopt a strategy that occludes the appeal of rational tyranny in comparison with irrational tyranny and, by reducing the meaning of tyranny to the most monstrous excesses of erotic dissipation flowing directly from the vulgarity of democracy (562a–d, 565d–e), establish the philosophic life as the much more reliable path to happiness on a personal level in the here and now, rather than as a superior form of rule meant literally to be implemented. He wants Glaucon to internalize the rule of reason over eros and thumos within himself, not attempt literally to found the rule of reason, which now simultaneously floats off into a "pattern in the sky" and is buried as an irrecoverable golden age in the most distant past (546a–547b, 592a–b).

This concealment of the appeal of rational tyranny is evident from the earliest pages of the dialogue. When Socrates first proposes that justice be considered on the analogy of an art, he is already implicitly identifying the art of ruling with expert knowledge, as opposed to the opinion of the many, especially of the democracy. The first result of this analogy, however, is the disappearance of politics altogether, because Polemarchus is driven by Socrates to conclude that, insofar as justice is an art, it can do no harm, for the arts only improve what they work on and never harm them. This would appear to make both external warfare against enemies of the city and coercion and punishment directed at malefactors within the city impossible (335e).

Thrasymachus' angry interjection at this point is not only based on his offended sense of realism, but because he wants to restore the focus on the question of the regime and how it is ordered. His formula that "justice is the advantage of the stronger" applies a universal definition that allows for all possible regime types. He starts out, therefore, in the pose of the bluff defender of the status quo, of established power, as against Socrates' ineffectual and subversive pacifism (336b–338c). However, in a key admission, Thrasymachus agrees with Socrates that it is possible for rulers to make mistakes about what is to their own advantage. The true ruler will be – or be guided by – an expert, a technician of injustice who knows how to take advantage most efficiently of others in all circumstances. Socrates and Thrasymachus agree that the ruler is the *technikos* – the superlatively accomplished craftsman of authority. What they disagree over is the meaning of the most advantageous way of life. When Socrates tries again to show that, insofar as the ruler's advantage is practiced as an art, it can do no harm to the ruled, Thrasymachus distinguishes more explicitly between those who happen to be in power and those who understand that, by nature, the best of way of life is untrammeled selfishness resulting, in the most successful instances, in tyranny (341a, 343b–344d). Those who merely happen to be in power may actually believe in the conventions promoting justice. The true *technikos* of rule, by contrast, is like a shepherd who does benefit his flock by fattening them up, but only for their eventual shearing and slaughter. In other words, the true technician of rule could abide by certain conventions of morality and benevolent rule outwardly and provisionally, as means toward making the people he wishes to master more prosperous and therefore riper for exploitation and profit. Yet by making this distinction between the tyrant who is fully enlightened as to the best way of life by nature and not under the spell of conventional morality and those who are merely powerful through convention but may not pursue their self-interest with clarity or consistency, Thrasymachus can no longer pose as the bluff defender of the status quo, particularly of regimes with popular rule like Athens, where democratic government introduces the greatest possible tension between the morality of the many and the claims of the expert few.

In Book 2, Glaucon restores Thrasymachus' defense of tyranny as the most natural way of life, in contrast with the pusillanimous morality of the majority, by tactfully casting it as the opinion of others, which he is merely summarizing. He also places *techne* squarely in the camp of the tyrant, refining Thrasymachus' thesis that the ruler by nature will practice the art of flawlessly pursued injustice, an art so perfect that it will make its practitioner seem outwardly just in the eyes of the gullible many. He also demands that if Socrates is to defend the just life as superior to the tyrant's life, the defense must not be tainted by any "wages" for the just man, because that would suggest a utilitarian motive other than justice itself. In fact, Glaucon claims, the only way we could be sure a man was being just purely for its own sake would be if he was stripped of every ordinary benefit of conforming to conventional morality and, furthermore, was perceived by others as unjust, suffering horrific punishments as a consequence (361a–362b). In answering Glaucon's challenge to show what justice is "all alone in the soul" and prove that it is more worth possessing than the life of the tyrant who successfully camouflages himself as just and gains all the benefits of a just reputation as well as enormous wealth, pleasure, and power on top, Socrates implicitly denies that he can defend justice as an entirely inward-directed virtue bereft of any role in relation to others. The proposal to trace the "city writ large" implies that justice must first be found as the ordering pattern of the city, then traced back to the individual. Justice, according to Socrates, can be satisfying both for its own sake and for the benefits it brings (368d–369a).

Continuing to pursue the analogy of justice to an art, Socrates proposes that each nature in the city will be best suited for one job or deed (370c–d). Those functions are then internalized as the three components of the individual soul. Although initially the transition from the bucolic "city of sows" based on simple survival is sparked by Glaucon's longing for erotic refinements, excess wealth, and luxuries, which will require a foreign policy of imperial aggression, Socrates proposes that a class of soldiers will be needed whose main character trait is not erotic passion but thumotic bellicosity (372c–374a). Paradoxically, even though the warrior class is summoned into being by the imaginary city's erotic excesses demanded by Glaucon, eros is driven underground in the political psychology of the unfolding best regime in favor of the thumotic capacity for loyalty to one's fellow citizens and inflicting harm on the city's foes. On the basis of the threadbare comparison of the warrior's capacity to distinguish, like a guardian dog, between friend and enemy with the philosopher's capacity to distinguish between what is and what is not, a ruling class of Guardians, the future philosopher-kings, is cemented into place in the tripartite relationship between the city and the soul (376b–c).[3]

---

3 For a subtle consideration of the soul-city parallel and its complexities, consider Ferrari (2003).

Because thumos does not equate with a single job like material desire (*epthumia*) and the lowly crafts that serve it but is dangerously "double" in its capacity for both friendliness and ferocity, education is needed to make sure it reserves its friendliness for fellow citizens. The civic education of Books 2, 3, and 4 of the *Republic* fashions a cosmology that will redirect the combative and bellicose excesses of untamed thumos into disciplined civic-spiritedness and honorable service to the common good. The story of Leontius, who tries unsuccessfully through self-castigation to master his morbid longing to look at the corpses of executed criminals, proves, Socrates says, that thumos, properly reared and habituated, could at least "sometimes" be the ally of reason in ruling over aberrant impulse (440a).[4] Insofar as the *Republic* is Socrates' extended attempt to defend justice against injustice, as Glaucon first demanded, Socrates appears to believe that the thumotic side of the soul could best be rehabilitated by a devotion to public service and honor, as if to suggest that the belligerence of thumos has a collective leaning toward moral indignation on behalf of the "we." But this would appear to skirt the possibility of a supremely ambitious individual's capacity for thumotic rage and zeal being the fuel for a purely individual, tyrannical claim to rule – indeed, even an aspiration to use that absolute power to establish justice in the city. This is the possibility, to which we presently turn, briefly explored in Book 4 of the *Laws*, where the ambitious young man's eros for the *polis* directs his thumotic energies toward the pursuit of tyranny, a drive that the Athenian Stranger suggests might be amenable to redirection by a wise advisor so that the tyrant would find honor from founding a city that would be just in the future. Instead of, as in the *Republic*, thumos acting as the enforcer of reason on behalf of the common good against tyranny, for these few pages of the *Laws*, thumos, guided by an eros for the city, might cooperate with reason to found a just city by tyrannical means.

This alternative is not openly discussed even briefly in the *Republic*, where the argument is skewed in another direction. In Book 5, having earlier suppressed the erotic side of human psychology in the education of the Auxiliaries, Socrates now reintroduces it, but only to characterize the philosophic soul. A second education ensues, that of the philosophic

---

4 This equivocation parallels Socrates' earlier remark that it "is possible" that thumos might be educated to be gentle toward friends and harsh toward enemies (375d).

Guardian class per se, whose virtue is not grounded in the mere "correct opinion" inculcated in the Auxiliaries by seemly "tales" about the gods but by their direct, unvarnished longing to study the Idea of the Good. Studying the Idea of the Good is now said to be the surest source of all prudence (505a–c, 536a–b, 539c–540a, 485c–486a). This argument precisely prepares us for Aristotle's objection that by failing to distinguish between wisdom and prudence, Socrates assimilates all virtue, including civic virtue, to the single type of the philosopher and robs the virtue of the nonphilosophic citizens of any independent dignity or self-sufficiency (*Politics* 1260a, 1261a10–22; *Nicomachean Ethics* 1141b). Consequently, when Socrates finally turns to the long-anticipated showdown in Book 9 between the philosopher and the tyrant – the ultimate version of Glaucon's original contrast between the truly just man reviled for being unjust and the truly unjust but convincingly outwardly just man – the basis for the contest is primarily erotic rather than thumotic, philosophy (like tyranny) being chiefly erotic in its motivation, whereas civic virtue is chiefly grounded in thumos. Moreover, by depicting the tyrant in Book 8 as emerging from the debased hedonism of the democratic regime, Socrates makes tyrannical eros appear vulgar, low, and contemptible in contrast with the elevated pleasure of philosophy, while at the same time stigmatizing it by appealing to an aristocratic disdain for the mob.

The tyrant who emerges from democracy in Book 8, setting up the showdown in Book 9 between the tyrant and the philosopher, is a pleasure-ridden demagogue and libertine, a Cataline or a Nero. This derivation of tyranny from the vulgarity of democracy omits the at least equally plausible hypothesis that another kind of tyrant – austere and warlike – could emerge *directly* from timocracy, the second worst (or best) regime type in the typology of regimes in Book 8. Only the formal agreement among the interlocutors to trace the decline of the city in speech as a decline in which each successively worse regime – timocracy, oligarchy, and democracy – represents a widening gap between the good of the individual and the good of the whole, which had been absolutely harmonious in the *kallipolis*, allows Socrates to ignore the objection that *another kind* of tyranny – zealous, austere, self-disciplined, and warlike – could have emerged (544e–545d). For the argument pulls in the direction of the tyrant as the most extreme instance of the contradiction between the common good and the selfish individual, the radicalization of the witless pleasure seeking already attributed to democracy, where even the animals stagger around drunk (562e). Yet history and common sense both prompt us to recognize that there are ambitious tyrants who act cold-bloodedly to refound the community in what they perceive to be a more efficient and even just manner, undistracted by the excesses of pleasure seeking. Socrates' way of setting up the critique of tyranny accounts for a Caligula or a Commodus, but not for Cyrus, Alexander, and Caesar, Machiavelli's favored trio of "princely" rulers in chapter 14 of *The Prince*. Even within the *Republic* and the way the decline of the regimes is set up, whereby the thumotic Auxiliaries overthrow the rule of reason to institute a regime based on honor, it can easily be envisioned that such a rebellion might be led by an outstandingly ambitious and honor-driven individual, just as Xenophon (as we consider in Chapter 4) depicts the young Cyrus as leading a rebellion of his fellow peers against the quasi-philosophically grounded Persian Republic so as to liberate their ambitions through imperialism. Socrates' insistence that the timocrats would collectively and immediately decline into greedy oligarchs is unwarranted, at best only one possibility among others. Indeed, Socrates' own description of timocracy undermines this claim. For it is clear that a tyrant or aspiring tyrant could emerge directly from such men as these. They have, Socrates says, fire, magnificence, and quickness, "but such natures don't willingly grow together with understandings that choose orderly lives which are quiet and steady. Rather, the men who possess them are carried away by their quickness, wherever chance leads and all steadiness goes out of them" (503c1–7). Surely a class of men so described is likelier to produce a Julius Caesar than a Uriah Heep. Only in the *Laws* is this proto-Machiavellian ruler, whose ambition disciplines his eros so as to instill self-mastery, briefly allowed to emerge.

In Book 9 of the *Republic*, Socrates tries to establish the superiority of the philosophic life to the tyrant's life depicted as a purely personal obsession with one's own indiscriminate pleasures. Even in this context, it is tacitly conceded that eros *is* the main candidate for the leader of the soul, whether directed toward tyranny or wisdom. Eros leads thumos, whether for good or for ill (572e–573e). However, tyrannical eros as depicted here is divorced from the context of a more honor-driven longing for prestige through great public accomplishments. The tyrant of Book 9 is a pleasure-besotted monster of excess, tormented by jealousy, possessiveness, fear of those he has injured through his outrages, driven from one empty and fruitless spasm of delight to another, haunted by his inner emptiness (579b). Socrates' proof of the philosopher's superiority hinges on the fact that his eros pursues a lasting object – the Idea of the Good – whereas the tyrant's eros pursues pleasures that are bodily, hence transient and perishable. Only the pursuit of the lasting object makes one truly independent, with a satisfaction that is lasting, not fleeting (582a–d, 583a–b, 585a–c). In emphasizing the philosopher's eros for the eternally lasting Good, Socrates draws on the cosmology of the earlier civic education of the Auxiliaries to show how only philosophy can defeat with complete certainty the claims of tyranny. The crucial difference, however, is that whereas the education of the Auxiliaries treated the honor of exercising the moral virtues as intrinsically choice-worthy in its own right, Socrates' defense of the philosopher's superiority to the tyrant is primarily hedonistic: because the philosopher's eros is overwhelmingly absorbed in the pursuit of wisdom, passions that in the nonphilosopher might lead to aberrant impulses of pleasure seeking and domination are completely assimilated to the longing for the Good, thereby entailing a morally virtuous life as a second-order consequence of a life devoted to the highest and most satisfying pleasure (485d–e). At bottom, in other words, the philosopher does not choose justice for its own sake alone, as Glaucon had originally demanded.

The tyrant of Book 9 is not a man whose limitless lust for glory might incentivize him to discipline himself to undergo every hardship and privation on the road to his goal of immortal fame. To this extent, Socrates' critique of tyranny in the *Republic* is compelling but incomplete. It is still possible, on the basis of the dialogue's own arguments, to envision a *technikos* of rule, an aspiring tyrant whose motivation is not philosophy strictly speaking but superlative honor and who, in rationally pusuring that goal, is capable of a steely self-control, abstinence from pleasure, and self-overcoming that is a reflection of the philosophic life, a figure more like (as we consider in Chapters 4 and 5) Xenophon's Cyrus. The *Republic* itself largely glides over the issue of whether and to what extent such a man would, in his lust for glory, be wholly unswayed by the claims of reason in their own right – the imperative to establish a regime that was reasonably ordered and beneficent – or might, on the other hand, be amenable to a partnership with those philosophical principles, just as Xenophon's Simonides tries to convert the tyrant Hiero into becoming a benevolent "leader" or as his Cyrus conquers the world out of a zeal to bring the art of good government perfected by the Persian Republic to his millions of new subjects. These principles of good government, as we see in Chapter 4, are partly reflected in the education provided for Cyrus by the Persian Republic and partly conveyed to Cyrus by his father, the Persian King Cambyses, whose attempt to imprint on his son the need for just government has clearly identifiable similarities to arguments made by the Xenophontic Socrates. Elsewhere, Plato himself (in the *Statesman*) sketches the model for a rational despotism, although he does not discuss the specific issue of how such a regime would be founded (258e, 300c–e, 307e, 309d).[5]

The *Republic* itself contains the seed of the destruction of any kind of neighborly city-state once its contradictions are exposed to the full glare of the universality of reason. For the division of labor on which the tripartite division of the soul and the city is based – that each nature best performs one job – is inherently universalistic. That is to say, an architectonic meritocracy could not possibly be confined within the boundaries of a single *polis*. For, very simply, the best people for the best jobs are universally distributed, requiring some kind of cosmopolitan regime. In this respect, one could say that what is "noble" about the "noble lie" is that it takes a universalistic principle of meritocracy based on the division of labor and grafts it onto a single, autochthonous *polis*, embedding its natural hierarchy in the earth of a single city's most ancient past (the "myth of the metals" according to which each class springs from the earth their souls mixed, in ascending order, with iron, silver, and gold [415a–d]). To clarify the lie would mean the doom of the *polis*. (As a mixture of myth and reason that invites its own dissolution through reasoning itself, the Noble Lie illustrates my characterization of Socratic images in the last chapter as a holistic perspective that invites analytical refutation while preserving a surface integrity that promotes the virtues.)

In other words, the very notion of a city ruled by philosophy is arguably inevitably a way station to some kind of cosmopolitan order.

---

5 See also the *Lovers*, where Socrates equates the king, tyrant, statesman, household manager, master, the just man and the moderate man: all possess a single *techne* of ruling (138c–d).

As we see in Chapter 4, this is the alternative Xenophon explores through his life of Cyrus the Great, and, as we have already observed, this household pattern of rule recurs throughout many of the Platonic dialogues themselves. Indeed, Aristotle in his critique of the *Republic* argues that it automatically turns into the rule of one man (the philosopher-king) over a city that becomes his personal *oikos*, and, as Aristotle tells us elsewhere in a passage sometimes thought to be a harbinger of Alexander the Great, the art of household management as a regime principle can be extended to many "cities and peoples" (*Politics* 1261a10–20, 1285b20–33). That Plato's Socrates tries to conceal the inevitable universality of the division of labor within the confines of a harmonious and autochthonous *polis* likely stems from two sources – a disinclination for philosophy to be distracted from its truest concern, the love of wisdom, by a real-world project for a more rational politics through benevolent despotism, along with the Socratic philosopher's own preference for a neighborly *polis* in which freewheeling and spontaneous conversations about virtue provide his eros with the psychological loam for the art of midwifery that he practices on his mostly younger fellow conversationalists.[6]

THE HIDDEN TYRANT

In arguing that Socrates' chief purpose in investigating tyranny and how it contrasts with both philosophy and sound statesmanship is not to provide a blueprint for actual reform, I am not arguing that the optimal arrangements set forth in the *Republic* have no bearing at all on actual government or that they represent an "ideal" in opposition to the "reality" of political practice. The categorical distinction between the real and the ideal, or between the is and the ought, is unknown to Platonic and classical thought. What is highest, noblest, and most lasting is also what is most naturally real. The Idea of the Good and the other Ideas are the stable archetypes of perfection in which phenomena participate, and therefore, to the extent that a phenomenon is connected to what is immortal and unchanging and entirely reasonable, it is also in its most natural condition. As Diotima puts it in the *Symposium*

6 Consider Newell (2000) pp. 89–100.

in describing the Idea of the Beautiful toward which all erotic longing ought properly to be directed:

[It] is always being and neither comes into being nor passes away.... It is by itself and with itself, always being of a single form.... For this is what it is to proceed correctly in erotics, or to be led by another – beginning with the beautiful things around us, always to proceed on up for the sake of beauty itself, ending at that study which is the study of nothing other than the beautiful itself. (211a–c)

To the extent that the "beautiful city" of the *Republic* is governed by reason, by a meritocracy based on the division of labor, and by a cosmology of eidetic stability and oneness that provides a guide for properly fashioned poetry to inculcate in the souls of the citizens the repose and orderliness that are characteristic of the cosmos as a whole – to this extent, the *kallipolis* is the most *real* of cities, even if the necessities of human vice and circumstance make it virtually impossible that it will ever coincide with an observable city in our lifetimes.

What I mean to say is that Socrates' *chief* purpose in exploring the prospects for a just political community is to clarify the longings of the soul. The *Republic* is a thought experiment about what it would mean to think through the ultimate object of most political reforms – what it would mean, that is, to resolve the contradiction between self-interest and the common good. The dialogue deliberately offers an extreme hypothesis for investigation – that a certain set of local political conventions might be coterminous with reason itself, such that obedience to its authority would be to the degree humanly possible voluntary and based on rational assent, rather than, as is much more frequently the case in political life, coerced or a matter of customary and unreflective loyalty. By extrapolating from the parts of the soul what the proper objects of the soul's activities would be in a just community, Socrates is able to offer an articulation of a well-ordered soul that is in harmony with just behavior toward others (435e, 464c–e). The fact that the optimal city is unlikely ever to come into existence – dependent as it is on the extraordinary chance of a philosopher willing to govern coinciding with a king who is genuinely philosophic (472d) – and unlikely to last even if it did come into being, takes nothing away from the fact that the soul of the individual in its relations with others should be patterned to the degree possible on this city arranged according to the Good.

For whether or not this city is possible and whether or not it is desirable from every plausible perspective on human happiness (given its demands for the abolition of family life, property, and every other version of the love of one's own), it is the paradigm for what it would mean for political arrangements to be naturally good. It is the only pattern of authority, in other words, that would enable human nature to develop toward its fullness and completion within the constraints of political convention, to the degree that any political convention might fulfill human nature. Indeed, when turning to the education of the philosophic Guardian class in Book 7, Socrates argues that even the philosophers actually existing in the world today are in some measure deformed because they have not had the experience of an education in governing and the experience of governing itself (539e–540a, 520d–e, 534d, 536a–d). That there might be private pursuits, or blends of private pursuits and civic engagement, that might as well or better fulfill the fullest range of natural human potentialities for the good life than could an optimally ordered city is a question that remains open, of course, throughout the Platonic dialogues, which are not exclusively concerned with politics even in the broad sense discussed here. The purpose of elaborating the city in speech is, in short, as a propaedeutic for the education of the soul, regardless of the likelihood of those arrangements coming fully into existence. In the *Republic*, the soul's erotic ascent to philosophy proceeds by way of the question of justice. The ascent to philosophy entails the moral virtues, just as the cosmology guiding the Auxiliaries' education flows from the Ideas, although the ascent to philosophy ultimately does not account for those moral virtues as good in themselves but as consequences of the philosopher's absorption in studying the Idea of the Good. Nevertheless, the philosopher will *also* possess the character traits of the Auxiliaries: moderation, steadfastness, and self-control, even if they derive from a source other than the Auxiliaries' civic education. So in a sense, the moral life of civic virtue will imitate the life of the philosopher.[7] In the education of the Auxiliaries, Socrates' own quality of steadfastness (*karteria*, a virtue of Socrates praised by Alcibiades in the *Symposium* 219d–221c) becomes a standard for the citizenry (*Republic* 399a).

---

7 See the argument in Pangle (1985) p. 14.

These themes are crystallized in a crucial exchange between Socrates and Glaucon (472c–e):

"It was therefore for the sake of a pattern," I said, "that we were seeking both for what justice by itself is like, and for the perfectly just man, if he should come into being, and what he would be like once he came into being; and, in their turns, for injustice and the most unjust man.... We were not seeking them for the sake of proving that it's possible for these things to come into being."

"What you say is true," he said.

"Do you suppose that a painter is any less good who draws a pattern of what the fairest human being would be like and renders everything in this picture adequately, but can't prove that it's also possible that such a man can come into being?"

"No, by Zeus, I don't," he said.

"Then what about this? Weren't we, as we assert, also making a pattern in speech of a good city?"

"Certainly."

"Do you suppose that what we say is any less good on account of our not being able to prove that it is possible to found a city the same as the one in speech?"

"Surely not," he said.

Socrates' analogy to painting here suggests that the optimal city is an imitation of a beauty found in nature. At the same time, the fact that painting is a mere semblance of natural beauty delicately reminds us that the best regime is no more than an approximation of what reason unconstrained by any concern with political life might discover about nature and how best to live. However, the optimal city is at least patterned on nature, if only ambiguously so. It is not an "ideal" in the sense of being a construct of reason meant to highlight the deficiencies of a merely naturalistic conception of political motivation, whether rooted in the utilitarianism of Hobbes or the ethical imperative of Kant aimed at striving to overcome that utilitarianism. Again, the very use of the term "ideal" to describe the *kallipolis* distorts Plato's thought by freighting it with a modern distinction between nature as matter in motion and reason as an anthropocentric capacity for utilitarian calculation or ethical formalism that it does not recognize. For Plato, as a matter of practicality and circumstance, and given the prevalence of the love of one's own, the best city may be vastly less likely ever to come into being than the flawed democracies, oligarchies, timocracies, and tyrannies we usually encounter. Yet because the *kallipolis* is the *best* city, it is, however rare, more *real* than they are.

As Glaucon comes to see, then, the main practical purpose of the optimal city is that one can "found it" in one's own soul regardless of what kind of regime one actually lives in. This does not, it must be emphasized, imply a kind of withdrawal into the self, because what one "founds" in the well-educated soul is a series of virtues elaborated precisely *through* a reflection on our involvement with other people in accordance with the common good (the search for the soul "writ large" as the *polis*, yielding the tripartite parallel between the soul and the city). Moreover, although democracy is ranked very low by Socrates because of its wide divergence between the self-interest of the individual and the common good, democracy is, due to this very lack of communal cohesiveness and uniformity, the regime in which all the *other* latent regime types and their accompanying psychologies can be found and explored (557b–e). In other words, the democracy is bustling with real or would-be timocrats, oligarchs, and tyrants, so that it is possible to compare them with one another, whereas in each of those other regimes, one type of soul would predominate to the exclusion of the others. Hence, as Socrates says in Book 10 when returning to the theme of the reform of poetry, we first have to grasp the "forms" of all the souls as a guide for poetic imitation, an inventory that has been filled by the examination of the defective regimes in Book 8 in their falling away from the best regime, an inventory that democracy possesses in its fullest variety (595a).

Moreover, Socrates is not suggesting in the *Republic* that nothing is ever to be hoped for from actual political reform guided by philosophical reflection. This is how I would interpret the otherwise seemingly absurd assertion by the politically powerless Socrates in the *Gorgias:* "I think I am one of the few Athenians, not to say the only one, attempting the true art of statesmanship [*politike techne*]; nowadays, I alone am handling political affairs [*prattein ta politika*]" (521d). A person who has founded the *kallipolis* within himself – or, it must follow from the reforms of Book 5, herself – will look for opportunities to achieve whatever reforms are possible, to a relative degree in the given circumstances, in the direction of the optimal conditions revealed through the city in speech. In other words, a citizen will look for opportunities to decrease, comparatively speaking, the influence of private property over public affairs, if not to abolish private property altogether; to decrease divisions and inequalities between men and women, if not to make men and women identical; to educate children to become citizens who care for the public good rather than identify themselves unthinkingly with ancestry, family, and clan, if not to abolish family and clan. The practical message is one of conservative reformism, Burkean in temperament if not in theoretical principle. At the same time, the *Republic* offers no encouragement whatsoever for setting about actually to create the conditions for founding the best regime. Only if a *basileus* – meaning to say a lawfully established king, not a usurper or revolutionary – should also "chance" to philosophize "genuinely" might the optimal city come into being. This is such a big "if," such an extraordinary coincidence (*sumbebikos*) of qualities rarely observed to coincide, that one might as well pray for an endless summer of blue skies in San Francisco. As my analogy suggests, of course, that coincidence would still be a natural occurrence, however incredibly rare – not an ideal reconstruction of nature's parts to remedy the limitations of nature, a hallmark of modern political rationality characteristic of Machiavelli and Hobbes.

What the *Republic* precludes from consideration by the lack of any hint of its possibility is that a nonphilosophic political genius – a Cyrus the Great, Alexander the Great, or Augustus Caesar – might make the rule of philosophy, or of its reflection, his practical agenda, in the sense of patterning an actual regime, a multinational cosmopolitan empire, on the universality and unity characteristic of reason. Indeed, as Hegel argues, the very emergence of Socratic philosophy may have sounded the death knell of the *polis*, for, however much the universality of reason may have been sheathed in the preference for the aristocratic republic, its dynamism was bound to bore through the confines of the neighborly *polis* and lead to the great cosmopolitan empires of Alexander and Rome.[8] In the case of these ancient imperial masters, it should be

8 More generally, as Hegel observes, Socrates' claim to be guided by a demonic sign, tantamount to the introduction of new gods for which he was indicted, really was subversive of established Athenian religion, public life, and family life: "Is it then to be

noted, they still attempted to legitimize their rule as falling within the bounds, and actualizing the highest potential, of nature. Not for nothing did Augustus very deliberately promote the philosophical school of Stoicism as encouraging the kind of civic character he claimed to embody in himself and to whose imitation he morally exhorted his fellow Romans in the ruling classes.[9] Or consider Trajan's Forum, the architectural embodiment of the Augustan Principate in its finest flowering under the Good Emperors – the great library encircles and is higher than the column illustrating Trajan's military victories, reminding every citizen that the life of the mind in its contemplation of the eternal truth must always transcend civic and martial virtue even at their most glorious.[10] It must wait for the modern summons, first sounded by Machiavelli, to stand outside nature and master it before the conditions can be planted for the totalitarian project of literally and fully removing, by untrammeled violence, every normal human tie that prevents the political community from coinciding with the universality of pure reason, extirpating private possessions, faith, patriotic and family ties, and any erotic bonds that might interfere with the complete submergence of the individual in the community. More about that in due course.

Even without the prospect of this modern project for the mastery of nature, one can infer readily enough Socrates' reticence about the rehabilitation of tyranny as a means for founding a just regime. To encourage such a project would be to invite, in the greatest conceivable magnitude, the aggressive and erotic passions for victory that it is Socrates' overriding concern to moderate, sublimate, and redirect toward philosophy. Attempting to institute literally the rule of wisdom, or of the one universally valid philosophic teaching, entailing the eradication of all substantive and customary human ties that interfere with conformity to the common good (the prescription for the communism of property and the family set forth in Books 3, 4, and 5) is a project that might well afford tyrannical ambition with a vast agenda for the destruction of tradition and conventional decencies, and for the

wondered at that Socrates was found guilty? We might say that it had to be so." Hegel (1962) pp. 388–389.
9 Syme (1982) remains the classic analysis of Octavian propaganda.
10 See the splendid study by Carcopino (1960).

concentration of power. It could provide a fair pretext for the grossest acts of violence and plunder. Thus, the *Republic* largely masks the possibility that tyrannical force might play a constructive role in political reform. The dangers it would be likely to unleash through the nonphilosophic master's ambition would far outweigh the prospect of benevolent change. Only with Xenophon, as we will presently consider at some length, do the classics provide us with another route, a prescription for a rational multinational despotism as a derivation from the art of household management patterned on Socrates' own understanding of the Good.

In Plato, the same elements of an analysis of tyranny that we encounter in Xenophon are present, but distributed in a much different way and given a much different emphasis. For Plato, tyranny is fundamentally the rule of one man unconstrained by law. However, to recall our taxonomy from Chapter 1, that definition of tyranny pulls in two very different directions, the primordial and the transcendental. The primordial tyrant is the monster of passion and excess whose deformed character parallels the Sophists' and pre-Socratics' view of the world as a chance flux issuing in "great motions," an upsurge of unfathomable force mirrored in the tyrant's own bellicosity, impulsiveness, and lust (*Laws* 888–890). This is the tyrant famously excoriated in Book 9 of the *Republic*, a denunciation that was transmitted to posterity down through the Renaissance humanists and beyond. However, lawless rule can also move in the other direction, beyond the restraints of convention to the despotic imposition of a rational and architectonic art of ruling, the "art of herding featherless bipeds" limned in the *Statesman*, in which citizens are stripped of any responsibility for their own political deliberation and assigned their role by the *politikos* in the architectonic division of labor (*Statesman* 266e). This transcendentalist despotism is a mirror of the orderly and hierarchical unity of the whole. Whereas the denunciation of the primordialist version of tyranny is front and center as one of the culminating peaks of the *Republic*, the depiction of the rational despot concludes a trilogy of works generally characterized by their immersion in questions of epistemology and the theory of knowledge, and relatively (although not completely) unconcerned with discussions about political life in the everyday meaning of the term, in which the characters openly debate the meaning of justice and the other virtues.

The rational despot of the *Statesman*, moreover, is not a Socratic philosopher. Rather, he corresponds to the second of two types of philosopher between whom Socrates distinguishes in the *Republic*. The first philosopher is one like himself who, through his love of sights and variety, is able to clarify through his erotic longing for wisdom how the heterogeneous world of experience in which we are enveloped proves to "participate" in the Ideas that crown the various families of phenomena as stable archetypes. But there is another kind of philosopher, Socrates observes, who is able to *directly* intuit the Idea of the Good without needing to tarry in a love of spectacles (476b–d). This kind of philosopher closely parallels the rational despot of the *Statesman*, more Parmenidean than Socratic, able to leap over the middle realm of participation and access the Good through direct noetic intuition and apply it directly to political affairs as the art of human herdsmanship. It has plausibly been argued, moreover, that even the philosopher-king of the *Republic*, a regime that, unlike the architectonic art of ruling in the *Statesman*, is supposed to permit an independent dignity for civic life and a degree of reasonable participation in public affairs by the Auxiliaries, more closely resembles the transcendentalist Parmenidean ruler of the *Statesman* than the Socratic philosopher. Socrates, whose ceaseless thirst for wisdom through his immersion in the variety of daily experience also incentivizes him to ceaseless skepticism as he interrogates appearances and opinions in the quest for what *is*, would arguably be unable to live as a conformist even in the *kallipolis*, where, despite its reasonableness, there must be a large degree of doctrinal fixity to the institutions and education of the best regime, a fixity perhaps better guarded over by the unerotic Parmenidean statesman with his indifference to spectacles or to a thirst for variety.[11] Finally, in addition to the two types of lawless rulers sketched so far (primordial and transcendental), there is yet a third variety explored by Plato, that of a tyrant who is erotic, and therefore primordialist, in his spontaneous psychology, but whose primordial passion might be educated to serve the

---

11 As Zuckert observes (2009), the Eleatic philosopher Parmenides is depicted by Plato as unerotic because he already possesses wisdom and does not need or long for it like Socrates. This unerotic stance toward philosophy also informs the Eleatic Stranger's science of ruling in the *Statesman*. On the acceptance by "young Socrates" of the Eleatic Stranger's reduction of the art of ruling to a technique of management with no regard for eros or human psychology, consider Griswold (1989) pp. 141–167.

transcendentalist aim of founding a just regime guided by the correct, anti-Heracleitean cosmology of orderliness and eternal oneness. This third variety, even more than the alternative presented in the *Statesman*, receives the very scantiest of treatments, in Book 4 of the *Laws*. By contrast, as we see in Chapter 4, the rational despot, incentivized by an eros for universal honor, grafted onto the historical personage of Cyrus the Great and the multinational empire he founds according to the art of household management, is the theme of Xenophon's magnum opus, the *Education of Cyrus*, the parallel work in his corpus to Plato's *Republic*. What is most muted in Plato is most explicit in Xenophon.

In the Platonic dialogues generally, tyranny is depicted not primarily as an agent of political change but as an inclination or temptation on the part of an ambitious young man who is ready to embark on a public career within a city that already has an established constitutional authority of a more or less popular tincture. The dialogues, in other words, take place in a setting of "normal" constitutionality. The dangers of war, violence, usurpation, and revolution darken the edges of these discussions as Athens' imperial rise and decline unfolds behind the conversations, and through them as well. However, the conversations themselves open up havens of discursive leisure in which it is always "now"; in which it is possible, at least for a time, to discuss justice and the other virtues without being compelled to make a decision and act. Indeed, it is of great importance to the whole Socratic enterprise of redirecting tyrannical longings toward philosophy and the common good that they not present themselves in the context of an "emergency" or "postconstitutional" situation in which excessive daring and revolutionary aggressiveness might be publicly sanctioned and find the excuse to act in the dire need to stave off collapse from internal strife or external conquest. For to the extent that it is, to use Thucydides' terms, normal and desirable for the city to be at rest rather than in motion – looking inward to the responsibilities of daily self-government rather than launched outward on the seas of imperialism – to that extent also, tyrannical longings not only distort the soul but harm the *polis*.[12] When Socrates enflames Alcibiades' ambition so as to make him transcend the limitations of Athens and reflect on his soul by way of the

---

[12] For a discussion of rest and motion in Thucydides, see Kleinhaus (2001).

two archetypal regimes, Sparta and Persia, it is in the hope that, for Alcibiades, the universality of his ambition will be but a way station to the universality of reason and the Idea of the Good. When Socrates tries to moderate Callicles' eros into friendship, that psychological therapy serves a prescription for self-government that looks inward to its own domestic affairs and avoids the external entanglements prompted by an eros for ever-increasing wealth and glory abroad, summoning the most ambitious and potentially tyrannical men to the forefront of public affairs.

Plato's circumspection about the possibility of a constructive role for tyranny in public life is closely connected, in my view, to his emphasis on eros as the key to the tyrannical character. For Plato, the desire for political mastery stems from a misguided eros, and the therapy for it lies in the redirection of this longing for wholeness and completion. According to Socrates, Callicles is a "double" man because he is confused about the objects of his erotic longing – the Athenian Demos and the boy Demos. That the names of these objects of longing are identical suggests that Callicles believes he can gain the same kind of satisfaction from success in public life as he would from a personal love affair – that he can possess the city and be loved by her just as he wants to possess and be loved by the boy. In reality, according to Socrates, he will end up pandering to the city just as he panders to the boy, servant rather than master (513, 519). Socrates, by contrast, has distinct but ranked objects of eros – Philosophy and Alcibiades (482). By keeping these two loves distinct, with an eros for political excellence clearly subordinate to an eros for wisdom, Socrates claims his love life is ordered in a way that, in contrast with the divided Callicles, unifies his soul.

In considering the Platonic approach to tyranny, however, we should beware of making too hard and fast a distinction between diagnosis and therapy. For when we return to the political phenomena that such a distinction helps to clarify, it may well be that the Socratic diagnosis of the tyrannical longings of an erotic would-be politician such as Callicles *already* entails a large part of the therapy. By emphasizing the extent to which tyranny is primarily a consequence of the aberrations of eros in its spontaneous, untutored, primordial manifestations, Socrates encourages Callicles to interpret his own experiences in this way. Because Socrates consistently defines the art of ruling on the analogy of a selfless managerial *techne*, Callicles is driven to articulate his dissatisfaction with this mundane interpretation of civic eminence by reaffirming the erotic scope of passion that Socrates is trying to subdue and redirect. When Socrates engages Callicles in dialogue after both men have given their speeches about what makes a man happy, the definition of the "best" man, the man most entitled to rule, is quickly refined as the most "prudent" man (489). Socrates then pushes Callicles to identify prudence with art and with the expert. Yet while Callicles sees *techne* as a means to the skilled acquisition of power, Socrates characteristically presents it as leading to beneficence and self-forgetting, incapable of taking advantage of others. Callicles tries to prevent this drift by adding courage to the definition of the best man.[13] For Callicles, both prudence and courage are means to be employed in the contest for honor at the service of Athens' recovery of her faded Themistoclean and Periclean imperial glory.[14] For Socrates, by contrast, the orderliness and benevolence of the arts intimate a cosmos of harmonious proportionality mirrored in a moderate political community that looks inward and avoids excessive wealth and empire – a transition that increasingly alienates Callicles from the discussion. Whatever the success of Socrates' diagnosis and therapy for Callicles, by psychoanalyzing him from the outset as a man whose "doubleness" stems from a lack of clarity about the rank ordering of the objects of eros – a clarity that Socrates claims to

13 It is because he wishes to reopen the gap between nature and convention that Callicles responds so eagerly ("Yes, by Zeus!") when Socrates suggests that a "better" man be defined as an intelligent and prudent man (*phronimos*, 490a). Prudence or practical wisdom (*phronesis*) generally meant an understanding earned from a wide experience of human and especially political affairs. In what proves to be a key move in the dialogue, Socrates narrows the meaning of prudence to the expertise of a craftsman (*technikos*) and defines rule on the analogy of craftsmanship (490b). Callicles lets this narrowing of prudence slip by. His receptiveness to the notion of an art of skillful ruling doubtless reflects the fact that a number of professional teachers of rhetoric, including Gorgias, stressed the manipulative might of the *techne* of rhetoric that their instruction could impart to the politically ambitious. Socrates offers a very different conception of art, however – art as a reflection of the regularity and form that characterized nature, not the human capacity to mold and shape nature's formless becoming. Socrates wants to convince Callicles (in a clear repudiation of the ontology of the motion-men) that "excellence" of soul is "present" and "most nobly" effected by an arrangement of art, not through chance becoming (506d–e): "Surely the virtue of each thing, whether of an implement or a body or a soul or any living being, does not come about in the noblest way through a mere accident, but by an order, a correctness, and an art that is apportioned to each one specifically."

14 As Irwin observes, "Callicles cannot both reject all restraint and advocate a way of life which requires courage" (1977) p. 121.

embody in his own love life – Socrates tries to prepare him for precisely
the sort of refutation of tyranny that he sets forth at length in Book 9
of the *Republic*. There, Socrates presents tyranny as a kind of eros that
is less satisfying than the eros of the philosopher. The tyrant's pleasures
are manifestly connected with his power to plunder and ravish his subjects. Yet by having the tyrant compared with the philosopher, whose
life is presented as one of superior personal happiness, the effect of
Socrates' refutation is to present tyranny mainly as a form of personal
satisfaction and to expose its deficiencies on those grounds. Tyranny as
a form of actual political authority, let alone as the foundation of the
best regime, receives scant attention.

In other words, the chief Socratic refutation of tyranny abstracts from
the full-blown context of governance in which we ordinarily encounter
tyranny in the political world. The main treatment of tyranny as a constitution occurs, as we have seen, in the typology of regimes in Book 8,
but the discussion is summary, and it too is mainly in personal terms,
concentrating on how defective the tyrant's way of life is as opposed
to how tyrannies differ from each other and operate in practice. As
we have noted, the whole discussion of regimes in Book 8 ranks them
in descending order according to how far the individual interest strays
from the common good. The decline from one constitution to another is
depicted as a series of revolts by less worthy sons against more worthy
fathers, the sons being given over increasingly to the nonphilosophic
love of one's own. Hence, the timocrats rebel against the philosophers
because they feel their honor as warriors has been slighted. Their sons,
in turn, find that public honor is too frail a guarantee of success and
influence and so turn to moneymaking. The sons of the oligarchs want
to spend the money earned by the diligence of their fathers on feverish
luxuries, a relaxation of standards that ushers in democracy as a society
of hedonistic *laissez-aller* in which even the animals are corrupted. The
tyrant emerges from the democracy as the hedonist with the biggest
appetites. By ranking the constitutions in this way, Socrates is able to
impart to timocracy, the constitution of the spirited honor seekers, a
dignity second only to that of philosophy, for the Auxiliaries are educated and habituated to practice the moderation that the philosopher's
own overwhelming passion for wisdom automatically entails (by draining off the erotic energies that might normally expend themselves in
pleasure seeking). Because the tyrant is depicted here as a monster of

erotic dissipation, he drops to the bottom of the list of human types – a radicalization of the sloth and self-indulgence characteristic, in Socrates' depiction, of the open rule of the demos. Because tyranny is ranked in terms of the dignity of one's personal life, there is no hint in Books 8 or 9 that some tyrants might be seriously interested in upholding or even improving orderly government for the good of the populace and might achieve this as readily as or even more ably than the ostensibly superior timocrats or oligarchs.

There are, of course, examples from history of "democratic despots" who largely fit the depiction of tyranny in the *Republic*, rulers who first emerge as tribunes of the people and who increase their power by pandering to the baser passions of the majority, freeing them from the responsibility of governing themselves so that they can devote themselves to moneymaking and pleasure. Tocqueville regarded this as a danger peculiar to democracy and believed it was confirmed in practice by the rise of Napoleon III from the presidency of the Second Republic.[15] This is plainly not the whole story about despotism, however, for there have been at least as many examples of individual and collective despotism motivated by martial honor (Napoleon III wanted that too), aristocratic pride, and religious zealotry. Tyranny is as likely to emerge, as it were, among the Auxiliaries – among the Junkers, or the colonels, or the Mujahadeen – as it is among the populist demagogues and shameless libertines of democracy, but by ranking timocracy well above tyranny and by stigmatizing tyranny through tracing its origins to the basest aspects of the most vulgar constitution, Socrates appeals to an aristocratic inclination among his listeners not to identify themselves with such a low type. We can see the seed of this aristocratic rhetoric in the *Gorgias* when Socrates goads Callicles into declaring that the strength of a superior mind and character was worth "ten thousand" of the many with their mere strength of numbers (490). Socrates elaborates the typology of constitutions ranking timocracy above hedonistic democracy and tyranny both as a description and a prescription, just as he consistently tries to enlist the pride Callicles invests in his hopes from a public career in the service of contempt for hedonistic self-indulgence.

---

15 See the discussion of Tocqueville's fears regarding the "democratic despot" in Newell (2009) Part II.

Altogether, then, Socrates' refutation in the *Republic* of tyranny as base in comparison with timocracy and as erotically unsatisfying in comparison with philosophy abstracts from the dangerous but all-too-real potential that despotic authority can possess in some circumstances for restructuring the political order and getting worthy things done. Julius Caesar, for instance, was reviled as a tyrant and usurper, a king in false constitutional clothing, by his Senatorial opponents, but he could rightly reply that their generational paralysis and incapacity to make the slightest concessions to public need rather than lose an iota of their exclusive supremacy had made the Republic unworkable and that only dictatorial means could salvage it.[16] Caesar was erotic, but his ambition to be admired for doing good displaced his eros from hedonistic self-indulgence to the longing for political immortality and safely confined it from committing outrages on those around him based on spontaneous lust. His violence was purposeful and limited, deployed against inveterate foes, never whimsical or prompted by jealousy and cruelty. This type of despotism is absent from Socrates' treatment in the *Republic*. By identifying tyranny primarily with ungoverned eros, an immersion in personal pleasure that is the very negation, Socrates argues, of any regime principle, Socrates is better able to reduce it to a strictly personal sphere. He presents it largely as a debased and unfulfilling individual alternative within a constitutionally normal situation in which civic virtue is manifestly the only respectable and useful form of political activity, a normalcy that also harbors the pursuit of friendship and philosophic intercourse about the meaning of human excellence. Socrates' circle is in effect a philosophic *polis* within the larger Athenian *polis*, one whose members share a common good of reflecting on the very virtues of justice, moderation, courage, and wisdom that all sound-minded Athenians would agree are indispensable to the political community, disagree as they might on what precisely they mean.

THE HIDDEN FOUNDING

In Book 4 of the *Laws*, however, Plato draws the curtain back ever so briefly from the constitutionally normal situation. The Athenian

16 This is the burden of Meier's argument in his to my mind unsurpassed biography of Caesar (1997).

Stranger takes us, if only for a few minutes, to a place where Socrates will not go – to the dangerous, violent underpinnings of the established order; to the moment when the foundations were laid upon which the normal order could grow. Readers of the *Republic* will recall that Socrates will not grant the premise of Glaucon's rehearsal of the Sophists' account of justice, according to which the "nature" of politics resides in its prepolitical origins, so that law and convention are but artificial constructs through which the pusillanimous minimize their suffering in the competition among selfish individuals for survival and well-being. As Socrates describes the first city, the "city of sows," nature comes into being already articulated according to the division of labor among the banausic arts, and those arts simultaneously serve a community based on the simplest needs (370d–372a). Contrary to the Sophists' teaching, the city precedes the individual. In Book 8, the city "according to speech" is transported to the most distant past, both because what is oldest and ancestral is best, and because, according to Socrates, the natural origins of justice are not the strife, violence, and motion ascribed to nature by the pre-Socratics and Sophists but an already long-established harmony and community.

Unlike Socrates (who does no more than hint at it), the Athenian Stranger does concede that even a virtuous political order must begin at a specific historical juncture and that the energy and ambition of a naturally masterful individual might have a constructive role to play in instituting it properly and all at once. In the Athenian Stranger's description of this personality, we encounter a variant of the relationship between eros and thumos that is rather different from the variants we encounter in the *Republic*, *Symposium*, and *Gorgias*. In the *Symposium*, well-directed eros entails civic virtue on its way to philosophizing: The immortal fame gained through engendering virtue for the city is a comparatively more lasting object of erotic longing than the mere physical immortality perpetuated through reproduction, and is a way station on the ascent to the philosopher's apprehension of the truly eternal and imperishable Good. In the *Republic*, as we earlier observed, eros is repressed within civic life on behalf of the civic virtue of the Auxiliaries, rooted in the thumotic part of the soul, then rehabilitated as a motive for philosophy. Common to both paths to a moderate and orderly soul is the notion that eros cannot be thought to satisfy itself in the proper way through political glory and mastery alone.

The young tyrant briefly described in the *Laws*, however, combines qualities of both the erotic and thumotic dimensions of the soul, and they are directed neither toward civic virtue strictly speaking nor philosophy. Instead, the Athenian Stranger is more receptive than Socrates to the spontaneous passion to possess the *polis* as a lover that Socrates diagnoses as the public pole of Callicles' confused longing for the boy Demos and the Athenian Demos. Callicles delusionally longs for a pre-eminence in political life that would have the same direct satisfaction of possessing the beloved in a personal love affair, a delusion that, Socrates forecasts, will compel him to pander to the many just as he panders to the boy. However, the Athenian Stranger takes a different tack. He implies that the founder of an entirely new order is likely to be motivated by this dangerous erotic passion for the regime he is fashioning. To find the motivation and energy to face the dangers of rearing this city into being, he must want to own it for himself, to possess it in its entirety like a lover possesses the beloved. For Plato, this is the root of tyranny in the soul – the longing to "own" the city like a jealous lover; the inability to distinguish the public good from the object of a private passion. Socrates strives to correct this deformity in Callicles and the other ambitious young men among his interlocutors, assimilating this erotic longing for completion to the noble restraint of citizenship or to philosophy itself. In this one situation in the *Laws*, however, Plato concedes that this dangerous passion might have to be given a looser rein, prior to any attempt at its rehabilitation; that it might have an indispensable role to play in a form closer to its spontaneous first impulse. For although Socrates ordinarily tries to redirect and sublimate his interlocutors' eros through the pursuit of public honor in serving a moderate common good and through philosophy, in the situation of the founding, there is as yet no common good to which ambition could be redirected, and the foundations for the community can most efficiently be constructed by the very type of personality it will later try to educate out of existence, or forestall from ever arising. Here, in other words, if we were to take the *Republic* literally, is the kind of man who might drive out everyone over the age of ten so that the citizens of the *kallipolis* could be reared free of taint. But in order to be capable of acting in this tyrannical way, he could not possibly have received that rearing in citizen virtue himself. Moreover, how would one get rid of him when the job was done?

I will return to the passage in the *Laws* momentarily with some detailed observations. For the moment, I want to elaborate on the general point that the Socratic diagnosis of tyranny tends to cover over and direct our attention away from a kind of eros that is purely and properly political – a "pleasure" that cannot be dismissed as sheer personal self-indulgence (like Socrates' comparison of Callicles to a catamite) and yet is at the same time not assimilable to civic virtue either, since it is needed to found the constitution under which civic virtue might later flourish. Just as Socrates generally discourages the erotic passion to possess the city, he is equally circumspect about the possibility of a constructive political purpose for the thumotic side of the personality in its spontaneous, untutored, and primordial manifestations prior to civic and philosophic education. One of Socrates' rhetorical and pedagogical purposes in presenting tyranny chiefly in terms of misguided eros, it seems plausible to argue, is to obscure the sheer savagery of the thumotic side of the soul – its pathological defensiveness, combativeness, fury toward competitors, moralistic zeal, and taste for death and destruction. In other words, by getting the tyranically inclined individual to understand himself primarily in terms of erotic longing rather than thumotic rage, Socrates already begins to tame the tyrant even before suggesting a new direction for this eros, for to the extent that the tyrant is a hedonist absorbed in his pleasures, he is less absorbed in the fury and vengefulness characteristic of thumos. Consider again in this context the story of Leontius in Book 4 of the *Republic*. The morbid characteristics of thumos – the desire to gaze on the corpses of criminals, thus savoring the violence and perhaps arbitrary injustice underlying every established order, perhaps thereby putting oneself in that criminal's place and summoning up dark currents of alienation and a wish to be oppressed so that one can lash back – are softened by the somewhat comedic light in which the story is cast. Leontius castigates his eyes for wanting to look at the foul sight while simultaneously running toward the pit (440a). By affecting to "punish" his eyes by forcing them to revel in the very sights for which he is castigating them, like a perfect Tartuffe, he is able to gratify his passion while affecting a stance of moral probity. It is as if someone with a weakness for wine grabbed a bottle and before downing it, shouted, "There you go, you wretched throat! You wanted wine? Well, go ahead and drown in it!"

Upon reflection, the rather Basil Fawlty–like comic touch of Socrates' depiction of Leontius' rage puts into the background two dangers the story illustrates. One is that although Leontius is morally outraged at the rebelliousness of his own senses, he *fails* to stop gazing at the corpses. Thus, as Socrates carefully puts it (and to reiterate an earlier observation), the story does no more than prove it is "possible" that thumos might be the ally of reason in governing the desires in the soul and in the city. The other danger, however, is that even when thumos *has* been properly educated in the mode of the Auxiliaries (as Leontius has not) to become the fierce guardian of civic justice, it must never be allowed to become *too* harsh an enforcer of morality. The danger that the enforcer of morality could become a bloodthirsty fanatic is muted, however, because the bearing of the discussion shifts midway through the *Republic* from a comparison of the unjust and unjust lives first broached in Book 2 to a comparison of the pleasures of the philosopher vis-à-vis the pleasures of the tyrant. The danger does not disappear, however: Indeed, the indignation of the Auxiliaries toward their philosophic Guardians for being too wan in their defense of the city's code of honor is arguably what prompts the overthrow of the best regime by the timocrats.

Much of the Socratic therapy for tyranny is devoted to preventing an alliance of erotic wantonness with thumotic belligerence, zeal, and fury – in the *Symposium* by assimilating aggressive impulses to a ranked hierarchy of the virtuous objects of erotic longing; in the *Republic*, by extirpating eros from the political psychology of the Auxiliaries and attempting to educate thumos to a communal moderation and steadfastness grounded in a taste for the orderly harmony of the cosmos. Alongside the danger that thumos might align itself with eros to serve its untrammeled desires lurks another, possibly even greater danger – that spiritedness might feed on its own bellicosity, self-righteous zealotry, and gloomy fixation on the stark alternatives of mastery or defeat. Although our theme in this book is tyranny, it is not irrelevant to bear in mind that Socrates himself was to suffer from the zeal of Meletus and his other accusers and their indignation that Socrates alone corrupted the city, rejected the gods, and alienated sons from their fathers. As brought back to life by Plato, Socrates has a compelling personal reason to want to avoid rule by the zealots. It is not surprising when, on the eve of his trial for impiety, Socrates remarks to Euthyphro, who complains that the Athenians laugh at his soothsaying, that he would be only too pleased if the Athenians were merely laughing at him rather than aroused in their angry thumos (*Euthyphro* 2 c–e). Under certain circumstances, one can wish for a ruler whose ambitions are exhausted by gluttony or lust rather than someone who enjoys the spectacle of death, like Leontius' peculiar fixation on the mangled bodies in the executioner's pit. Even more dangerous than an erotic but self-controlled reformist tyrant like Julius Caesar, or even a monster of eros like Caligula whose depradations are confined to those in the ruling classes unfortunate enough to live nearby, is a Robespierre or Himmler, the joyless executioner and fanatic. Socrates' story of Leontius partly disarms our perception of this danger by casting it in a humorous vein. But we are made discretely aware of the disturbing and subversive pathology evinced by his lust to look at disfigured corpses. The danger of regarding the founding situation as the most natural and revealing situation in political life – the danger, in other words, of viewing the emergency situation as if it were in fact the normal one – is that this taste for destruction, which can ordinarily be stigmatized as dangerous, destabilizing and indecent, is offered a legitimate scope for action. Although it is no longer fashionable to do so, it is not so many years since Stalin's campaigns of forced collectivization with their millions of victims were defended by some as regrettable but necessary "start-up costs" for building a stable and rationally planned socialist order where the public good would always prevail over private self-interest.

Of course, while we are peeling away the decent surface of everyday political life and probing its dark underpinnings, we are also constrained to observe that never to use force in the defense of authority can be as harmful as a constant reliance on it. At this juncture, I want to begin bringing Machiavelli into the discussion, since, as we will see, the discussion of a tyrannical founder guided by a wise man in Book 4 of the *Laws* is a *locus classicus* for Machiavelli's advice in chapters 22 and 23 of *The Prince* on what kind of counsellors the prince should have. Whereas Plato gingerly concedes for a few Stephanus pages of the *Laws* that sometimes the emergency situation will have to take priority over the normal situation, for Machiavelli, the emergency situation *is* the normal situation: All politics is a series of continual re-foundings. As Machiavelli puts it, sometimes it is cruel to be compassionate, especially if a ruler's reluctance to use the force at his disposal to suppress riot and subversion ends up by bringing on collapse and hence ruining the lives of his law-abiding subjects (*The Prince* chapter 17). It is always better, Machiavelli observes, to be ready to go to war today against a minor foe than to wait until that foe is so strong that one is forced to go to war to survive, and at a much greater cost (*The Prince* chapter 3). This wisdom Machiavelli attributes, not to "the writers" among the ancients like Plato and Aristotle, but to the reality of ancient political practice, above all that of the Romans. As much as it would be, in some circumstances, an insane and paranoiac foreign policy always to launch pre-emptive wars against potential future foes, in other circumstances it arguably lessens human suffering. One need only think of the thirty thousand lightly armed troops Hitler possessed when he occupied the Rhineland in a daring bluff, as against France's one hundred divisions. By failing to knock out Hitler then when he was at his weakest, the Allies swelled his prestige and seeming infallibility in Germany, and convinced him they would not fight back, bringing about a war killing tens of millions.

Plato, however, is not willing to go down this road. He insists that tyranny be deplored in general and that even at its arguably most constructive, it never be allowed to displace the priority of the political community as a pattern of nature. Hence, as we will presently consider in more detail, although in Book 4 of the *Laws* the Athenian Stranger briefly entertains a constructive role for the tyrannical founder, he quickly qualifies it by adding that the danger that such a ruler will lack moderation – and will therefore not limit his tyranny to the necessary measures for founding a good constitution but will continue to tyrannize over the newly founded city as if he were its jealous lover – probably outweighs anything positive to be achieved from considering this alternative further. (Not every Cincinnatus will be content to return to his plough after tasting the powers of a dictator.) The Athenian Stranger then promptly covers over the whole violent substratum of the founding by invoking "the god" and beseeching Kleinias to act as if the conditions for the founding had sprung into being in answer to a prayer. This has the same effect of grounding the just regime in nature while discouraging its creation by force majeure as Socrates' placing the *kallipolis* in the venerable past, proving that it is still the best life for man in principle but irrecoverable due to our own failings and the inevitable decay of all things partnered with man. In neither dialogue can the best regime be brought about by human action. After this invocation of the god, the *Laws* resumes its proper topic, which is not how an entirely new order is to be founded but how the common good might best be ordered in normal times.

In striking contrast, Machiavelli's main theme in *The Prince* and, in a less obvious way, the *Discourses* is founding, which he regards as indispensable not only to making sure that the constitution is securely and properly ordered but to keeping it so. For at bottom, Machiavelli argues, there is no normalcy, no "middle way," only emergencies kept at bay or creatively deployed against each other to generate a dynamic equilibrium of selfish interests, "each power checking the other" (*Discourses* 1.2.6). Machiavelli in effect therefore asks: Might we dispense with the Platonic concerns and reservations over the tyrannical founding in order to think through how the act of founding might unfold and perpetuate itself in the working of the constitution? Might there be a founder who did *not* require the moderate character said by the Athenian Stranger to be necessary for even considering this alternative, and so unlikely to exist among potential young tyrants as therefore to make it unwise to consider it at length or too explicitly? Machiavelli's answer is that, in a sense, the founder's possession of this moderate character is immaterial, so long as the founding is carried out in a way that is both methodical and in the service of the founder's and the citizens' interests. In making this argument, though, Machiavelli also means to say that the whole Socratic diagnosis of tyrannical ambition and the reticence it entails is both false as a description of the phenomenon of rule and harmful to the prospects for stable, prosperous, and well-governed political orders. As we will see, Machiavelli's teaching is not simply a negation of the Platonic one. He is not simply saying: Tyrants and would-be tyrants, go ahead and indulge your passions to the fullest, including your longing for mastery. What he is saying is something more akin to the following: Do not commit the error encouraged by ancient "writers" such as Plato of understanding yourself to *be* erotic – and therefore of longing for the "offspring" of noble deeds and immortal honor through the cultivation of justice, moderation, and humaneness; of longing for transcendental repose in union with the beautiful and the good through the ascent up Diotima's Ladder. For the Platonic characterization of the ruling passion as erotic, even in its spontaneous, untutored, and therefore dangerous manifestations, already implies the possibility of the transcendence of princely ambition and therefore, according to Machiavelli, the abandonment of the prospects for real success in politics.

For Machiavelli, it is not simply that Plato's strictures against misguided erotic longings are in error, as if it would be enough simply to liberate those unvarnished longings and dispense with the rehabilitation. More fundamentally, it is Plato's understanding of the ruling passion in erotic terms altogether that is the flawed starting point. For Machiavelli, not only does the attempt to redirect eros toward civic virtue frequently fail to convince anyone to do so, but, worse, to the extent that it *does* succeed, this rehabilitation and sublimation of eros actually does more to undermine political order and republican virtue than if the effort had never been made. Encouraging a prince to win the "love" of his fellow citizens by making himself the object of their affection and admiration subverts the republic by offering an impossible combination – a preeminence of fame and honor that can in truth only be monarchical, allegedly put at the service of a constitution that regards citizens as equals. As we see in Chapter 5, this is the brunt of Machiavelli's critique of Scipio, shining exemplar of the classical mirror of princes, and his preference for the cruelty of Hannibal or Manlius Torquatus. To take a clear case of what Machiavelli views as the fundamental Platonic flaw, Socrates attempts in the *Gorgias* to persuade Callicles that the combination of natural independence and the political mastery he longs for can only be combined at the expense of the former. For to woo the Athenian Demos and become its possessor, Callicles will have to pander to it and be at its beck and call, just as he is with the boy Demos. Only by subordinating his personal erotic longings to a civic order that mirrors the transcendental order of the cosmos can he exchange pandering for citizenship devoted to the common good. Machiavelli, by contrast, is saying that the pursuit of transcendence in the Platonic sense by citizens and statesmen can only come at the expense of the civic order, robust citizenship, and the common good. For Machiavelli, it is the Platonic teaching that corrupts.

As Leo Strauss famously observed, for a proper appreciation of Machiavelli's originality and boldness, we need to begin with the perception of him held in his own time and later by adherents of traditional political morality – the imposing civilizational conglomerate of classical and Christian teachings that was at the heart of the meaning of the

West – that he was a teacher of evil.[17] It is equally important, however, having begun with this view, that we not rest with it. For what might be regarded, from the viewpoint of the Platonic tradition, as Machiavelli's immoralism in deriding the naiveté of thinking that the traditional strictures on pleasure and power seeking could ever persuade – or had ever persuaded – real-world political actors is only the first stage in his critique of the classics. Although a part of Machiavelli's charm is to invite his readers to smile at the foolishness of the old teachings for thinking that people ever really subordinate their self-interest to the common good, at bottom Machiavelli no more encourages unrestrained erotic passion than does Plato – indeed, far less so. For, at bottom, Machiavelli's conception of the art of princely rule is one in which the prince methodically represses eros in himself and obviates its connection with thumos and the other passions within an overall economy and harmony of the soul. The tripartite Platonic soul, in which reason, that part of us closest to the immortality of the truth governing the cosmos, enlists spiritedness to wage moral war over the lower desires is collapsed and transformed by Machiavelli into the psychology of the lion and the fox. Rage and bellicosity are to be selectively released by the cunning of the fox, an animalized, carnalized, and desacralized wisdom. It is a somatic and anthropocentric wisdom, unconnected with what Machiavelli takes to be the delusions caused by relying on Fortuna in the guise of the "imagined republics" of classical and Christian transcendentalism. The lion and the fox symbolize the vital worldly intelligence that is the parallel in the individual self of the collective devotion to the this-worldly "fatherland" which Machiavelli exhorts us to prefer over the heavenly Kingdom of God (*Discourses* 2.1). Not only does Machiavelli deny that the princely nature is characterized by the spontaneous unfolding of erotic longing prior to rehabilitation that Socrates diagnoses in Callicles, but, by denying the centrality of eros, Machiavelli obscures the character of thumos as well – again, it must be emphasized, not merely the reformed version of that passion once it has been educated Platonically, but the character of the passion at its immediate, pristine, and spontaneous emergence, including its openness to the gods and the mysteries of the whole. Machiavelli is not merely reversing the Platonic ranking of the transcendental over the primordial and urging

---

17 Strauss (1969) p. 9.

the liberation of the latter. He is fundamentally reorienting our under-standing of the primordial realm itself, which, in its Platonic evocation, even at its most spontaneous, still contains the *potential* for education toward transcendence and is therefore in Machiavelli's view a source of delusion.

In the Platonic understanding, the natures of eros and thumos are delineated and clarified by abstracting them from each other, as we observed earlier about the relationship of the *Symposium* to the *Republic*. Eros is at its purest when its sheer absorption in the beautiful object of longing causes jealousy and anger to subside. Thumos is at its purest when its possession of that object is threatened, such that the prospect of pleasure does not relax the passion for honor and victory. The inca-pacity of either passion to make us entirely satisfied demonstrates the need to reintegrate their capacities within an overall harmony of the soul. For Machiavelli, however, the de-eroticization of statecraft that his new science of politics envisions dissipates the distinctions among this ensemble of affects. There is nothing to harmonize and no need for an elaborate phenomenology of the passions or an elaborate ped-agogy that might restrain them while satisfying them. Because eros is forgotten, so too is thumos, which is sundered from its Platonic well-spring of an openness to the divine, holy awe, ruminations on our place within the whole, whether or not the gods care for us, and so on and begins to collapse into the abstractions of "power" and "domination" that attempt to say everything and so say very little about how political life observably unfolds. This truncation is necessary for the methodical concentration on the achievement of "effectual" rule.

To understand how the passions, which for Plato possess their own substantive natural articulation and can be harmonized by the virtues to achieve a concretely satisfying way of life, begin with Machiavelli to devolve into a series of uniformly compulsive inclinations, we must also consider Machiavelli's relationship to Christianity and how it places the meaning of rule and statecraft on a new ontological basis. If my inter-pretation is plausible, we would have to see Machiavelli as not merely returning to the focus of the Sophists on material acquisition and power seeking, important as that dissident tradition may be for Machiavelli's own approach. I will argue that Christianity both makes it impossi-ble fully to revive that alternative ancient tradition and at the same time offers a much more dramatic scope for the transformative power of princely rule, far exceeding anything envisioned by the Sophists. Before turning to that theme, however, I want to draw together some of the preceding observations about Machiavelli's relation to the classical tradition by looking more closely at the discussion of the tyrannical founder in the *Laws*.

PARADOXES OF THE TYRANNICAL FOUNDING

The Athenian Stranger begins with a reflection on the power of fortune over human affairs that at first sight seems almost despairing:

I was going to say now that man never legislates at all. Accidents and calamities occur in a thousand different ways, and it is they that are the universal legislators of the world. If it isn't pressures of war that overturn a constitution and re-write the laws, it's the distress of grinding poverty, and disease too forces us to make a great many innovations.... Realizing all these possibilities, you may ... say what I said just now, that ... human affairs are almost entirely at the mercy of chance. (709)

In these few lines, Plato anticipates and evokes the full force of the primordialist ontology of the pre-Socratics and Sophists that the Athenian Stranger summarizes later on in Book 10 and with which this chapter concludes. Stated briefly for now, the identification of nature with motion and strife led to the view that law and government are as chaff before the wind compared with the awesome, underlying motions of *tuche* – the power of fortune to overturn human plans both in the obvious sense of disease and bad weather and in the subtler sense that chance is operative on human nature through the necessity of passion, prompting the struggle for mastery within and between nations, so that the turmoil of class warfare, hunger, and ambition are always seething behind the settled pattern of the laws.

But the Athenian Stranger just as quickly rejects the view that *tuche* is what chiefly characterizes human nature and the world at large. Instead, he goes on to maintain, the supreme element of control over life comes from (the) god. As we learn elsewhere in the *Laws*, for the Athenian Stranger, the god is not the interventionary deity of revealed religion whose acts of mercy or punishment are ultimately unfathomable within the limitations of reason. Instead, this is a god of *nous* – an overarching divine presence that upholds the prevalence of order and reason in the cosmos over chance and strife. By practicing virtue, human beings can make themselves the "allies" of this god and help the Good supervene in human affairs progressively throughout the ages, so that justice increasingly becomes the normal human condition rather than unbridled passion (just as, by analogy, clement weather is more ordinarily representative of the cosmos than storms or hurricanes [896–897, 903]). As the Athenian Stranger puts it here, chance and opportunity are mere ancillaries to the noetic rule of (the) god, temporary lapses from a more superordinate unity. As such, they are openings in the current of events for human beings to assist the power of *nous* to supervene over disorder and licentiousness. Chance and disorder are, in other words, temporary rifts in a more typical orderliness in the world that human beings may, paradoxically, seize upon so as to work actively for the continuing influence of that cosmic orderliness on human cities and affairs.[18]

Techne is the chief exemplar of the way in which human beings can minimize the reversals of fortune by laying hold of and introducing into their own affairs a portion of the orderly beneficence governing the cosmos. Characteristically, in Plato's use of *techne*, it is not aimed at a human being's control of nature. Instead, the arts tap into the orderliness of the cosmos through their various aims, and, through their bodies of knowledge and technique, introduce a degree of that orderliness directly into human affairs. Furthermore, just as the disciplined routine of the arts helps us in all manner of practical affairs, the Athenian Stranger goes on, the same pursuit of skill in statecraft will help found and maintain a virtuous political community:

For instance, in a storm the steersman may or may not use his skill to seize any favourable opportunity that may offer itself.... So the same will apply in the other cases too, and legislation in particular must be allowed to play the same role.

The craftsman of the founding will be a tyrant – young, with a good memory, quick to learn, courageous, and possessed of a natural eros for the city (709). The description of this young founder combines a

---

18 Cropsey's meditations on seven of Plato's dialogues vividly evoke the disjunction between the vision of an orderly and just cosmos adumbrated by philosophy and the world of contingency – of injustice and absurdity – within which we all find ourselves placed. Improvement is possible but far from guaranteed and can often be undermined by character flaws, bad luck, and even good intentions. Cropsey (1995).

number of the traits attributed elsewhere in the dialogues to thumos and eros: Socrates' characterization of the spirited part of the soul in Book 2 of the *Republic* as quick, tenacious, and courageous, his attribution to Glaucon of courage as the energizer of his boldness in learning (357a, 374e), and the tendency of the erotic politician as exemplified by Callicles to conflate the satisfaction he looks for in personal love affairs with the wish to possess the city as a whole like a lover.

Kleinias, the Athenian Stranger's interlocutor, doubts that people could readily be expected to obey a ruler who claims such an absolute latitude for persuasion and compulsion. In effect, he is raising an objection to the tyrannical founder from the viewpoint of a republican constitution before the conditions for such a constitution have been established. For the Athenian Stranger, however, given the absence of any competing communal loyalty in the founding situation, it will be easy for the tyrant to mold the people in whatever way he chooses:

When a tyrant wants to change the habitual ways of a city, he doesn't need to exert himself very much or spend a lot of time on the job. He simply has to be the first to set out on the road along which he wishes to urge the citizens – whether to the practice of virtue or vice – and give them a complete model by setting his own example; he must praise and commend some courses of action and censure others, and in every field of conduct he must see to it that anyone who disobeys is disgraced. (711)

On the face of it, the Athenian Stranger's language is not unlike Machiavelli's description in chapter 6 of *The Prince* of princes of the most "outstanding virtue," those who, like Cyrus or Moses, create "entirely new modes and orders" through violence and persuasion. But there is a crucial difference. For the Athenian Stranger, the challenge is distinguishing successfully ahead of time between a virtuous founding and a vicious one. For Machiavelli, by contrast, as we see in Chapter 6, the challenge is making the new beliefs stick, regardless of whatever specific kind of order is created.

The "hard" part of the founding, the Athenian continues, is to ensure that the blueprint will be in conformity with virtue rather than vice. Here, two conditions are indispensable. The first is that the young tyrant have a natural leaning toward moderation, the kind that "flowers early in life... and in some cases succeeds in imposing a certain restraint in the search for pleasure, but fails in others." The other condition is that the young tyrant have the good fortune to be instructed by a wise lawgiver. As the Athenian Stranger puts it: "When supreme power in a man joins hands with wise judgement and moderation, there you have the birth of the best political order with laws to match; you'll never achieve it otherwise. So much for my somewhat oracular fiction." In other words, you have to take a chance on picking the right young man. As Socrates says in the *Republic*, the best natures are so delicate that they can turn into the worst natures if they are not well reared (491a–492d). As we see in the next chapter, Aristotle warns that what appears to be the man best suited to rule may be a tyrant disguised as a benefactor, or may even be a genuine benefactor who nevertheless will display flashes of tyrannical violence and indignation over having his opinions challenged. As Machiavelli will argue, however, if you get rid of the requirement of a natural leaning toward moderation, you quite simply dispense with taking that chance, because you are not dependent on such a virtuous character arising in the first place. Mastering the situation of the founding requires the correct method, in which both prince and people are made secure and prosperous, not relying on hopes that a good man will arise. Here we have a precise and revealing locus for the contrast between the classical and modern approaches. The classical approach is to pin one's hopes on what Hobbes terms the "wit" of the prince: his putative virtues of character and mind. The modern approach, inaugurated by Machiavelli, is to avoid relying on those hopes, to assume the worst about the nature of the prince, and to compensate for those deficiencies with a straightforward appeal to everyone's self-interest and the methods needed for the aggrandizement of both prince and people.

The Athenian Stranger began by denying that despair over fortune's power to thwart man's aims is justified if we properly understand the cosmos. He then introduced the heady prospect that a tyrannical *technikos*, a craftsman of politics, could "easily" establish the sound basis for a good constitution. Yet although this prospect is possible according to nature and reason, it quickly transpires that the conditions that must be met for it to unfold are extraordinarily rare to the point of being, as he himself concedes, "oracular." It requires a young man whose leaning toward moderation is so strong that it innately directs his political ambition in such a way that he fulfills his love for the *polis* and exercises his ambitions by guiding the city toward virtue rather than using the city to gratify his passions. As the *Republic* makes clear, in Socrates' view, the most typical sort of politically ambitious person will require the education fomented by an already well-established constitution in order for this self-restraint to be inculcated. Moreover, the innate moderation of the young founder cannot come to constructive fruition unless he is guided by a wise lawgiver. The chances of this happening are, in the end, almost as rare as the coinciding of the philosopher and *basileus* in the *Republic*. Indeed, the Athenian's wording here ("my oracular fiction") reminds us of Socrates' claim that only the extraordinarily unlikely conjunction of these two "jobs" will establish the optimal constitution and bring an end to "the ills of the cities" (473d).

The most one can say in favor of the greater practicality of the discussion of founding in the *Laws* is that the coincidence of a young lover of the city joining up with a wise advisor is *somewhat* less unlikely to happen than the coincidence of wisdom and power in the *Republic*. For whereas Socrates maintains that the king and the philosopher must actually be the same person, the Athenian only requires that the city be founded by a ruler of potentially extraordinary natural moderation who is closely guided by a wise lawgiver. Moreover, whereas the philosopher-king would have to truly philosophize, the young founder presumably need mainly be guided by the correct opinions provided by his advisor (perhaps like the advice Cyrus receives, with mixed results, from his Socrates-like father Cambyses in the *Education of Cyrus*, an encounter we discuss in Chapter 4). Even so, the unlikelihood of this partnership between political genius and wise statesmanship, combined with the danger that a founder possessing the tyrannical power to change everything might well choose to imbue the new city with thoroughgoing viciousness, quickly leads the Athenian Stranger to abandon further reflection on the practical exigencies of the emergency situation and return to a concern with how the citizens of a republic somehow always already founded ought best to be educated and governed. "The god" comes to the fore at this juncture as a symbol of Platonic circumspection as the young tyrant recedes from the discussion. "The god," heralded by the Athenian's "oracular" prelude, in effect replaces the young tyrant as the founder, obscuring the original measures in a haze of pious custom. The tyrant's withdrawal and replacement by the god is evocative of the fact that it would take a partnership between wisdom and authority so rare as almost to be miraculous to found the new constitution from scratch. It is also evocative of the fact that there is a certain impiety and hubris attached to going on at length about a mere human being wielding such godlike powers of transformation. Certainly it would not do for the type of spirited young men who will form the bulk of the citizenry of Magnesia to dwell on the founder's superhuman achievements, lest they seek a similar field of action.[19] Thus, the emergency situation is discreetly covered over by the Athenian's pious hope that they will be able to act as if the founding has already been taken care of: "Let us therefore summon the god to attend to the foundation of the city. May he hear our prayers, and having heard, come graciously and benevolently to help us settle our city and its laws."

This brief segment is Plato at his most candid about the emergency situation of the founding. I will try to show through my interpretation of *The Prince* and the *Discourses* that Machiavelli reverses this Platonic circumspection over tyranny and the founding, just as he reverses the Platonic ontology that reduces fortune to a mere privative mode of true being.[20] A few preliminary observations will help to establish this

19 For a discussion of this rubric in the history of political thought leading up to Abraham Lincoln's great *Lyceum* speech, see Newell (2009).

20 Did Machiavelli read Plato? Blanchard (1996) writes: "Machiavelli tells us, in his famous letter to Francesco Vettori, that he invested in his *Prince* the capital accumulated from numerous nocturnal conversations with ancient men." More specifically, as Blanchard notes, the first paragraph of chapter 25 of *The Prince* is a gloss on parts of the passage from Book 4 of the *Laws* discussed earlier, although, in contrast with Blanchard, I conclude that Machiavelli's understanding of the connections among chance, art, and prudence is diametrically opposed to that of Plato. Blanchard is not claiming that Machiavelli's engagement with Plato is necessarily conscious, but the gloss on the *Laws* in *The Prince* is compelling evidence that it was, along with his own insightful contrast between Machiavelli's preference for "touch" and the Platonic epistemology of "sight," which I examine in Chapter 6. For a detailed treatment of the reception of Plato among civic humanists of the Renaissance in Italy, see Hankins (1990) vol. 1: pp. 58–81. As for Machiavelli's specific references to Plato and Aristotle, their paucity is, I argue beginning in Chapter 5, strategic. Plato is mentioned by name only once, and quite dismissively, in *Discourses* 3.6.16 as a mentor for conspirators. Aside from alluding to an unnamed Aristotle when discussing the regime types in *Discourses* I, Machiavelli mentions him by name but once in 3.26.2, referring to his depiction of tyrants in the *Politics* as prompting their own overthrow because they plunder and outrage their subjects. Is this perhaps Aristotle's best moment in Machiavelli's view? He may also be alluding to Aristotle among others, but not by name, when he mentions "philosophers who believe in the eternity of the world" (*Discourses* 2.5.1).

contrast. As we have just considered, Plato treats the theme of founding with circumspection. Looking at *The Prince*, we might say that it treats the constitutionally normal situation with circumspection, as if it is dwelling upon it, rather than its opposite, that impedes sound statecraft. Scant paragraphs are devoted to the "hereditary" principality and republic in *The Prince*. There is little to say about them because nothing much happens to them. In discussing hereditary principalities in chapter 2, Machiavelli may deliberately run together the identities of two Dukes of Ferrara, as if drolly to suggest that these rulers, required to do so little and displaying such minimal talents, are hard to tell apart. "It is with new principalities," he announces at the beginning of chapter 3, "that the difficulties begin," setting the theme for the rest of the book. It transpires in both *The Prince* and the *Discourses* that constitutions always face these kinds of difficulties, so that prudent statesmanship consists of a capacity for recurrent refoundings – a knowledge of how to preempt the disasters that will naturally occur because of ambition and class strife and tap into them, revitalizing the constitution with new elements and projects. Indeed, Machiavelli is not merely maintaining that one must know how to restore stable conditions (the ancients would have agreed with this, and, as we consider at length in Chapters 3, 4, and 5, even with the occasional need for coercive measures), but that, as an ontological matter, there *is* no order and normalcy in the world. To hope and plan on the basis of this putative normalcy, then, is an error of thought as likely in Machiavelli's outlook to result in bad political practice as it is in Plato's outlook to minimize it. So far is Machiavelli from arguing merely that disorder is a defect of the constitution that can be remedied by reorienting its laws toward the *nous* that supervenes over chance in the cosmos that he explains how the Roman Republic was "perfected" by "chance" and how the "disunion" between rulers and ruled there made that republic stronger, more virtuous, and more free (*Discourses* 1.2).

The difference between Machiavelli's approach to the founding and Plato's is brought out especially well by Machiavelli's discussion of how the young tyrant might create "new modes and orders" from the bottom up. Like the Athenian, he sees this founder as having the opportunity to impose a constitutional blueprint on a people whose latitude no subsequent civic leaders will be able to duplicate, because they will be bound by its provisions. However, whereas the Athenian specifically mentions the young tyrant's power only to persuade and punish by disgrace, circumspectly downplaying his capacity for violence and leaving it for Kleinias to mention at all (711), Machiavelli is explicit that force is even more crucial to the founder's success than his ability to persuade:

Whence it comes to pass that all armed prophets conquer and the unarmed ones are ruined. For . . . the nature of the people is variable, and it is easy to persuade them of a thing, but difficult to keep them firm in that persuasion. Therefore it is needful to order such matters in such a mode that when the people do not believe any more, one is able to make them believe by force. Moses, Cyrus, Theseus and Romulus, had they been unarmed, would have been unable to make them long observe their constitutions, as in our times happened to Fra Girolamo Savanarola. . . . Therefore such men as these have great difficulty in the conduct, and all their perils are on the way, and they must with their virtue surmount them; but having surmounted them, and commencing to be held in veneration, having extinguished those who were envious of their qualities, they remain powerful, secure, honoured, happy. (*The Prince* chapter 6)

The Athenian had observed that the "easy" part of the founding would be the young tyrant's ability to shape the new constitution, brushing aside Kleinias's doubt that people would readily obey someone claiming such titanic authority over them. The hard part would be that such a tyrant should be naturally moderate and fortunate enough to have associated with a wise legislator. For Machiavelli, however, the hard part of the prince's path is to establish his absolute authority in the first place, such that he is in a position to implement reforms ("all their perils are on the way"). Although Machiavelli is thus more informative than the Athenian Stranger about the actual dangers of becoming the master of the state, he says nothing about what for the Athenian was truly the hardest part: the alliance between wisdom and a naturally moderate character. Furthermore, in discussing the greatest founders, Machiavelli makes no distinction between the use of the founding power for virtuous as opposed to exploitive ends. Instead, he mentions historical examples of successful princes such as Cyrus, Romulus, Theseus, and Moses and derives from the fact that they succeeded the judgment that they must have been outstanding in virtue. If a prince is successful in founding new modes and orders on the magnitude of such great precedents as these, this is a sufficient criterion for calling him virtuous, regardless of whether he was a prophet of God or founder of a pagan empire.

It is thus not necessary to wait – or pray – for the coinciding of a naturally moderate character in a lover of the city with guidance by a wise lawgiver. Machiavelli does not believe that a virtuous prince requires the rare natural disposition of an innate leaning toward moderation, or the rare good fortune to have been brought together with a wise counsellor. Nor does a prince require some elaborate pedagogy of character formation to direct his passions toward their proper ends and away from their spontaneous first inclinations. In chapter 17 of *The Prince*, Machiavelli goes out of his way to contrast Hannibal, with his rude, untutored belligerence and "inhuman" cruelty, favorably with the Roman gentleman-statesman Scipio, ancestor of the Scipio idealized by the statesman-philosopher Cicero, an admirer of Socrates and of Xenophon's the *Education of Cyrus*, and the conscious imitator of the qualities of generosity, humaneness, and honesty praised by the "writers" of antiquity. For a prince to be successful, Machiavelli says, it is only necessary to pursue "the natural desire to acquire" with sufficient vigor and skill (*The Prince* chapter 3). For whereas innate moderation and receptivity to wise guidance are rare qualities, the desire to acquire is "perfectly ordinary." Because, as Machiavelli might contend, both he and Plato would agree with this latter observation, why not think this aspect of human behavior through to the conclusion that the universal desire for "security and well-being" is the only sound basis for political success and stability? Echoing Thrasymachus and other Sophists, Machiavelli observes that people only blame the ambitious for their vices when they fail to achieve mastery; when they succeed, people sing their praises and attribute the traditional moral virtues to them anyway, out of fear of offending them or in the hope that such a man will protect their own interests. (As we will see in the final part of this chapter, however, Machiavelli differs profoundly from the Sophists in the key aspects of his new political science.)

Thus, no especially virtuous character or education of the kind sketched in Plato's great images of the soul that we considered in Chapter 1 are necessary for princely virtue, only an intense desire to acquire and master – although, as we see in Chapter 5, this wantonness of impulse paradoxically requires a new kind of discipline for its effective functioning that may well be aided by a reading of past writers on the exploits of great men, carefully guided by Machiavelli's editorial control of these sources. It follows that the optimal founding need not wait upon the rare coinciding of power with wisdom, or of ambition with wise counsel. As he does so often with the rubrics of traditional political philosophy, Machiavelli begins his discussion of the advisors to princes with what sounds like a Platonic formulation, only to subvert it from within: "For this is a general rule that never fails; that a prince who is not wise by himself cannot be counselled well, unless indeed by chance he should submit himself to one person alone to govern him in everything, who is a very prudent man" (*The Prince* chapter 23). For Plato, as we have seen, the difficulty is that this chance is so unlikely to occur that it would be tantamount to an answer to a prayer, while experimenting with reformist tyranny in the absence of real certainty that it was indeed wisely guided would only encourage a tyrannical blueprint of the vicious kind, Thrasymachus' shepherd who manages the flock efficiently so as to fatten it up (*Republic* 343b). For Machiavelli, however, the difficulty is not merely that the coincidence of princely power with wise counsel is unlikely but that hoping for it at all is undesirable. For, as he mordantly remarks, if it did chance to happen that the prince submitted himself to a "very prudent man," that prince would indeed be well counseled, "but it would not last long, because that governor would in a short time take away his state."

In order that a prince not be dependent on a counsellor and thereby in time lose his power to that counsellor, Machiavelli concludes, "good counsel, wherever it comes, must arise from the prudence of the prince, and not the prudence of the prince from good counsel." Yet that is to collapse altogether the classical distinction between wisdom and power. Beginning with what sounds like an endorsement of Plato – the need for wise counsel and power to coincide by "chance" as the only hope for sound politics, reiterated in both the *Laws* and in the famous discussion of philosopher kings in the *Republic* – Machiavelli ends by completely overturning it. If the prince is the source of his *own* prudence, his reliance on the "chance" connection with a wise counsellor is obviated, a particularly revealing illustration of the prince's need to avoid relying on fortune or chance in general and to master it instead. In this trenchant reformulation of a Platonic maxim, Machiavelli uproots the whole Platonic conception of the relationship between the art of governing and the soul of the ruler. Socrates had defined prudence in the *Gorgias* as a variant of *techne* – the expert (*technikos*) on the art of ruling – and had argued from the structured beneficence of *techne* to the geometrical proportionality of the cosmos approached through philosophizing. At bottom, then, for Plato, the "prudence of the prince" must and can only arise from the "good counsel" of the wise man – whether through their direct association or indirectly through a civic education that inculcates, through the twilight medium of correct opinion, those tenets of philosophical cosmology that best ensure an orderly soul in the citizen. Machiavelli's way of dealing with the tension between wisdom and rule, however, is not to attempt to subordinate rule to wise counsel but to break down the distinction between prudence and what a prince must do to gain and maintain his state.

To a certain extent, Machiavelli as it were takes the side of the Auxiliaries in the *Republic* in their rebellion on behalf of martial prowess and honor against the rule of philosophy. Given that, even on Plato's argument the Auxiliaries are incapable of grasping with theoretical clarity the grounds for their submission to the good counsel of the Guardians, we might view Machiavelli's solution as a radically simple one to the quandaries that torture the political psychology of the *Republic* as it attempts to ameliorate the tension between ambition and reason. To put it another way, Machiavelli supports Callicles' side of the argument with Socrates over the meaning of the art of ruling, encouraging us to share Callicles' indignation and amazement when Socrates tries to separate the meaning of *phronesis* and statecraft from what Callicles regarded as the concern of a sensible man of affairs with expanding the city's power and honor, along with his own, emulating the great imperialists of the past, Themistocles and Pericles. As we will see, crucial to this inversion is Machiavelli's way of looking at the relation of *techne* to the art of ruling. For the Athenian Stranger just as for the Platonic Socrates, the art of ruling is, like the other arts, in conformity with an orderliness that intimates the supervening stability of *nous* and *eidos* over disarray and perishability – a propaedeutic for the soul's reconciliation to the larger natural order within which human nature also finds its place. For Machiavelli, by contrast, the art of ruling is a power that a prince achieves over natural conditions, enabling him to "introduce any form" he pleases into the "matter" provided by the adversity that challenges him (*The Prince* chapter 6).

We can now sum up the contrast between Machiavelli's and Plato's understandings of the relationship between virtue and fortune as brought out by the situation of the founding. For Plato, opportunity and chance are openings in the flux of events whereby we may, by practicing the arts that intimate the *nous* governing the whole, move human events closer in the direction of that eidetic stability and virtue and further away from their potential for vice and decline. Politically, this means that the art of ruling is above all dedicated to educating citizens to be virtuous, which will impart to them as much of the orderly repose of the cosmos as it is in human nature to receive and which will, by fortifying their souls against the primordial pull of the passions, enable them to rise above their dependence on external goods, hence above (to the degree possible) the reversals of fortune. The art of ruling has its place within the natural whole. For Machiavelli, however, nature is a field of hostile happenstance. It provides princes and aspiring princes with an "opportunity" to achieve power and glory – nothing more. It does not provide any innate, substantive leaning toward moderation of the sort that the Athenian Stranger says the founder should possess. There is no need for a prince to cultivate such virtues of soul in himself or in his subjects, although, as we will see in Chapters 5, 6, and 7, the reputation for them can be a considerable source of power.

For Machiavelli and the moderns, then, art is not a reflection of the rationality that governs the world as a whole, in cultivating which the soul learns one way of surmounting the disorder that tugs it down through the passions. Instead, art is the means whereby people of spontaneously bold and vigorous ambitions can impose their will on the world, reshaping events so as to maximize their strength. Whereas Plato and the other classics believed one might transcend the reversals of fortune to some degree by minimizing one's dependence on the external and perishable objects of the passions through cultivating the soul's inner harmony, Machiavelli argues that a methodically deployed art can conquer nature's impediments in a very different way – through aggression rather than reconciliation – and in this sense conquer chance. As we will see, for Machiavelli, to "rely on one's own arms and virtue" and to avoid relying on "fortune and the arms of others" (*The Prince* chapter 1) is not at bottom or in the first instance a matter of the crude power struggle to disarm and defeat one's competitors. The transformation Machiavelli has in mind, although it entails actual power struggles and domination, is a more profound reorientation of human longing toward the world, centering on the subtlest inward psychological treacheries of the reliance on Fortuna. It is a transformation that in the first instance requires that princes or potential princes (including, as we will later consider, princes of thought who write about politics) liberate themselves from the belief that the world is predominantly orderly and beneficent, a world in which it would make sense to believe that philosophy and rule could conceivably in principle – and perhaps aided by our prayers – coincide.

MACHIAVELLI AND THE SOPHISTS

Machiavelli is sometimes interpreted as returning behind the mainstream tradition of classical natural right established by Plato and Aristotle and reviving the dissident stream known to us now as "the Sophists," reanimating their original defense of selfish individualism, materialism, and the pursuit of political mastery as against the classics' emphasis on a virtuous common good and the elevation of duty over self-interest. Before entering further into Machiavelli's new science of politics, it will be useful to consider this relationship. There are indeed parallels. For instance, Machiavelli writes in chapter 3 of *The Prince*: "Truly it is a very natural and ordinary thing to desire to acquire, and always, when men do it who can they will be praised or not blamed, but when they cannot and want to do it anyway, here lie the error and the blame." Thrasymachus argues similarly in Book 1 of the *Republic* that taking advantage of others is the most natural way of life, culminating in tyranny, and that when a man attempts to become a tyrant and fails, he will be condemned and punished, but should he succeed, all will praise him and attribute to him the conventional moral virtues. Similarly, when Machiavelli argues in chapter 18 that the prince should "appear all mercy, all faith, all honesty, all religion" while never actually practicing those virtues for their own sake as opposed to mounting the appearance of them for the sake of enhancing his power, one is reminded of Glaucon's contention in the *Republic* that the perfectly unjust man will be outwardly perceived as possessing all the virtues while never practicing them for their own sake, whereas the truly just man who practices the virtues for their own sake without regard to profit not only will not achieve the wealth and power of the unjust man but will actually be condemned and executed for being unjust. Owing to such parallels, not only is Machiavelli sometimes seen as the successor to the Sophists, but, conversely, the Sophists are sometimes viewed as direct precursors of modern political rationalism and utilitarianism, as for instance when Lessing in *Laocoon* describes Simonides as "the Greek Voltaire." Finally, one can detect a resemblance between the view of the pre-Socratics and Sophists that nature is fundamentally to be characterized as motion, chance, and necessity and Hobbes's view of nature as matter in motion, itself derived from Bacon, who attributed this view of the external world to Machiavelli, more poetically expressed as Fortuna.

These are valid parallels, but they are also limited in important ways. For, in my view, there is no direct parallel among the pre-Socratics and Sophists for Machiavelli's radical summons to the new prince to conquer nature or chance and introduce into matter "whatever form he pleases." Moreover, when they identify nature with motion, the pre-Socratics and Sophists do not mean precisely that nature is a field of sheer random and empty happenstance, of clashing particles, as in Hobbes's version. The closest parallel among the ancient schools to Hobbes's Baconian physics is that of Lucretius. Even in Lucretius' atomism, however, the atoms evolve continuously through ever more complex concatenations into entire worlds and civilizations, whereas for Hobbes matter in motion always stands across a barrier from artificially constructed political convention, a secularized version of Augustine's categorical distinction between the City of Man and the City of God in which the City of God is replaced by man's own power to reshape the chaotic realm of human and nonhuman nature. More fundamentally, whereas for Lucretius the understanding of nature as the clash of atoms should predispose us to eschew the irrationality of political life with its toils and dangers and cultivate our private pleasures, for Hobbes, it is precisely the way in which matter in motion individuates us by acting upon us through our fear of violent death and desire for continued life that should motivate us to join the social contract.

For the pre-Socratics and Sophists as they are depicted by Plato and as their views survive in the fragments attributed to them, nature's originary power as "chance motion" has a substantial content and a direct bearing on how we understand the human realm of politics, justice, and morality. For "motion" is not necessarily merely atomistic but is more fundamentally a wellspring of primordial myth and passion, which is why Socrates in the *Theaetetus* includes Homer and the poets along with cosmologists such as Heracleitus and the other "motion men," arguing that, in their eyes, Homer's poems taught esoterically and through myth and allegory what the natural philosophers taught openly – the ontology of primordialism.[21] Socrates' characterization of Homer as the hidden founder of the ontology of motion is paralleled by the fragments of Gorgias (8–13) in which he claims that those like him who possess expertise in the art of rhetoric have now replaced the poets because of their power to make any appearance seem utterly real in the minds of their audience:

Speech is a great power, which achieves the most divine works by means of the smallest and least visible form.... The power of the incantations uniting with the feeling in the soul soothes and persuades and transports by means of its wizardry. [This] can be shown firstly from the arguments of the cosmologists, who by removing one opinion and implanting another, cause what is incredible and invisible to appear before the eyes of the mind, and from legal contests, in which a speech can sway and persuade a crowd by the skill of its composition, not by the truth of its statements.[22]

In Book 10 of the *Laws*, the Athenian Stranger gives a succinct and telescoped summary of this pre-Socratic ontology of primordialism (what the Gorgias fragment terms "the arguments of the cosmologists"). Nature issues in "great motions," emerging "according to chance" and "out of necessity" (889). The first beings, such as the heavenly bodies, are the "greatest" and "noblest" because of their temporal priority and huge scale. They generate numberless smaller combinations of "chance powers" down to the appearance of the settled world as we experience it in daily life. These concatenations come into being bereft of "mind" or "art," which came "late" in the generation of phenomena and which exist in the "mortal" realm alone, the world of convention, including politics and morality. In a sense, therefore, nature for the pre-Socratics is akin to revelation, an unfathomable matrix of origination in which

---

21 The poets were commonly included among "the wise." As Jaeger observes, the Sophists "were the heirs of the educational tradition of the poets; they were the successors of Homer and Hesiod, Solon and Theognis, Simonides and Pindar. Jaeger (1965) pp. 289–296.
22 All references to the pre-Socratics and Sophists are from Freeman (1948).

the gods are replaced by the alternation between chance and necessity. As one of the Heracleitus fragments (30) puts it: "This cosmos, which is the same for all, was not created by any one of the gods or of mankind, but it was ever and is and ever shall be ever-living Fire, kindled in measure and quenched in measure."

The arts are "mortal" and "paltry" because they are short-lived fabrications of man in contrast with the great primordial motions of nature. Certain arts like "music" (tragic and lyric poetry) are utterly paltry. (This judgment probably reflects the claim of Gorgias and other rhetoricians to have replaced the role of the old poets in shaping opinion.) Some arts, however, like medicine, farming, and gymnastic, are relatively "serious" because they share their power "in common" with the life forces of nature. We can tap into the potency of nature through agriculture and through the care of the body. The realm of convention, by contrast, is utterly artificial and opposed to nature, even more so than the arts. *Nomos* adjures us to be pious, just, to seek peace and respect the lives and property of others. However, to live naturally is to allow the impulsive motions of nature to well up in ourselves as the passion to maintain our lives and gratify our desires. The "correct" life "according to nature" is to "dominate the rest," to "get the better" of others. The natural man's passions will impel him to strive spontaneously for "victory" over others, "by force" if need be, shattering the artificial dictates of conventional morality and equality. Echoing Callicles' speech in the *Gorgias* extolling the natural master, the pre-Socratics' and Sophists' view as summarized in the *Laws* stresses that, although the laws say we must reject the natural life as unjust and impious, for a real man to accept these dictates is to live like "a slave." It may be just and noble by convention to treat others as equals, but it is just and noble by nature (another echo of Callicles) to tyrannize over others whenever one can. Finally, the whole subject matter of statecraft and legislation is held to be purely by art, and therefore entirely unnatural – except for a "small part" of the art of ruling which is in "partnership with nature" like the other "serious" arts of medicine, gymnastic, and farming. That "small part" is in my view the art of rhetoric, which for the Sophists is tantamount to everything meaningful about statecraft, a point I will enlarge on subsequently.

Although a "small" part of art is connected to nature, according to the Athenian Stranger's rehearsal of the ontology of the motion-men, the realm of convention including justice, piety, and moderation has no basis in nature as an underlying matrix of origination at all. Nature as origination does well up *into* the realm of nomos, however. Each city evolves from its unique and unfathomable origins in local "motions" to embody its own special "way." The realm of convention is "authoritative" (*kurios*) for as long as it lasts. In other words, although motions issue out of chance, whatever settled form they eventually achieve must exist according to necessity, because it cannot be other than it is until the temporary concatenation of motions making it up dissolve back into the flux of becoming.[23] The city's way is authoritative while it lasts, because no conventional view of justice can be transcended in the direction of the eternal and universal truth, inasmuch as justice possesses a wholly phenomenal and local existence confined to the realm of temporal mutability. Accordingly, as Socrates has Protagoras put it in the *Theaetetus*, the characterization of a city's way of life including its view of morality is not "true" – because the truth about nature is that "nothing is" – but an assessment of that way of life can be "correct," inasmuch as it is rooted in that city's unique historical way of life. As an advisor (like Protagoras was to Pericles), the Sophist can help a city better and more clearly pursue its own given way, whatever that has turned out to be.[24]

Some of the motion-men such as Protagoras tried to defend the realm of convention by arguing that, precisely because its natural underpinnings are in violent strife, we should cling all the more dearly to whatever bulwark of order the city has achieved over time (this is the implication of his myth in the *Protagoras* [320c–323c]). As a fragment attributed to Antiphon put it: "Nothing is worse for mankind than anarchy. Hence

---

23 Anaximander: "Whence things have their origin, there they must also pass away according to necessity; for they must pay the penalty and be judged for their injustice, according to the ordinance of time." Quoted in Heidegger (1984) p. 13.

24 Dodds translates *nomos* as "the conglomerate," a web of interlocking social, religious, legal, and customary prohibitions against vice and impiety. He also argues that not only those whom we now term the Sophists but the earlier natural philosophers and cosmologists including Heracleitus had been deeply subversive of traditional and conventional morality. Dodds (1984) pp. 21ff. For an impressive interweaving of historical, cultural, and theoretical contexts for the emergence of the pre-Socratics and the Socratic school, see Balot (2006), especially "Archaic Greece and the Centrality of Justice," pp. 21ff. Kerferd (1981) makes an insightful and detailed case for the philosophical and intellectual coherence of the pre-Socratics and Sophists, rescuing the latter from the charge that they were mere charlatans. See also Newell (2000) chapter 2.

our forefathers instilled obedience into their children, so that when they grow up they might not be overcome by any great change of fortune (61)." Others, however, used the primordialist ontology as the basis for a direct assault on all conventional morality in the name of selfish individualism and, taken to its logical extreme, tyranny. According to the Athenian Stranger, the most consistent implication of the view of nature as motion is indeed the praise of "getting the better" of others as the only truly natural way of life. This does not mean that the Sophists were what we would now term moral relativists, however. They had a definite view of natural human excellence and fulfillment that could be defended on reasoned grounds. Because, as they would have it, nature originates in strife and impulse, those "great and noble motions" can well up as the ruling passion of individuals and cities, meaning that, although treating people well and as equals may be just and noble by convention, tyrannical mastery, whether achieved by individuals or by cities, is just and noble by nature.[25]

The successful tyrant, reveling openly in his glory, is arguably the most direct human counterpart of those great and noble motions at the heart of becoming, a sheer spontaneous impulse to rule. There is an echo of this implication in the *Gorgias* in Callicles' professed admiration for Hercules as the pattern of the natural master, a Bronze Age cattle thief, brute, and killer who, Callicles somewhat fancifully relishes, might return and smash through the placid and pusillanimous egalitarianism of the Athenian democracy. Callicles also echoes the view just noted, attributed by the Athenian Stranger to the pre-Socratics and Sophists, that there is a distinction between what is just and noble by convention (equality) and what is just and noble by nature (manly victory) [483]). All in all, then, the motion-men do recognize certain natural and substantive human excellences as rooted in, and flowing from, the primordialist view of nature. Gorgias, for example, in another fragment attributed to him, regards courage and prudence as the two natural virtues most important to any city (8; 11.1). By "prudence" he means the real-world sagacity of experienced and powerful leaders,

---

25 Heracleitus' fragment number 80 could thus be read on both a nonhuman and a human level: "One should know that war is universal and jurisdiction is strife, and everything comes about by way of strife and necessity." Freeman (1948) p. 30.

not the Socratic derivation of prudence from philosophical contemplation of the Good. For Hobbes, by contrast, illustrating the differences between ancient and modern conventionalism, all virtues exist solely by convention, created by human compact in the wholly artificial realm of the state.[26]

As for that "small" part of art said by the primordialist ontology as presented in the *Laws* to be connected to the underlying motions of nature, I have suggested that it can most plausibly be identified as the art of rhetoric, the possession of which is claimed by Socrates' most prominent Sophistical interlocutors including Gorgias, Protagoras, and Thrasymachus. The rhetorician can manipulate conventional appearances for his own sake or that of his clients. Finding himself in a given city, he can adapt himself to the coloration of the local circumstances like a chameleon. He can defend that city's justice in his speeches or undermine it, depending on the client's needs. Protagoras argues that any given city's conventions about virtue can be "picked up" by an exposure to the locality, like children pick up language, denying Socrates' attempt to connect a knowledge of virtue to a rigorous and universally valid standard of reason of the kind prefigured by the arts, one that does not change from place to place.[27] In a similar manner, when Gorgias says in reply to Socrates' question about whether he teaches justice that he can indeed teach justice if asked to do so, he too means that he can give a plausible defense of however the city he happens to be in understands its morality (460). He does not fathom Socrates' implication that there could a universally valid knowledge of *politike* that, like geometry or astronomy, would transcend mere local custom and prejudice, showing genuine perplexity for the first time when Socrates introduces this notion to Polus (463). For Gorgias, as a student of the primordialist ontology, local custom and

26 As Hobbes writes in chapter 10 of the *Leviathan*: "Nobility is power, not in all places, but only in those Commonwealths where it has Privileges; for in such privileges consisteth their power.... The public worth of a man, which is the value set on him by the Commonwealth, is that which men commonly call dignity. And this value of him by the Commonwealth is understood, by offices of Command, Judicature, public employment; or by Names and Titles, introduced for distinction of such Value.... So that, of Civil Honour, the Fountain is in the person of the Commonwealth, and dependeth on the Will of the Sovereign, and is therefore temporary."
27 Consider the analysis by Nussbaum (1983) p. 105.

prejudice is all justice could ever mean as a phenomenon. For these reasons, both the Athenian Stranger and Socrates argue that the ontology of motion leads most consistently to tyranny as the most natural way of life and can offer no binding argument based on its own principles of reasoning to prefer justice to tyranny. Still, as we have observed, some of the Sophists like Protagoras did regard themselves as the guardians of conventional morality – only some, like Thrasymachus, assailed it openly. Moreover, as the Gorgias fragment praising courage and prudence as natural virtues suggests, the haleness and energy of nature as great and noble motions could be seen as imparting manly vigor and boldness to the city living in accordance with nature, and that is a *kind* of moral standard or standard of excellence, if radically different from the Socratic one. Hence, Callicles echoes Gorgias in agreeing with Socrates that Athens needs both courage and the prudence of successful statesman, while omitting any agreement with Socrates about the need for justice and moderation.

Now, it might be argued that the Sophists sometimes come close, in the claims they make for the power of rhetoric, to Machiavelli's exhortation that fortune can be mastered. A fragment attributed to Empedocles, the teacher of Gorgias, is apt here: "You shall check the force of the unwearying winds which rush upon the earth and lay waste the cultivated fields. And again, if you wish, you shall conduct the breezes back again. And you shall bring out of Hades a dead man restored to strength (111)." Control over nature is certainly implied. But I would take this to mean that rhetoric cannot literally refashion nature in the ways the fragment details but instead, as in the Gorgias fragment about the power of rhetorical persuasion, can produce the appearance of such transformations in the minds of the audience – not so much create a storm as create one on stage. Yet even if we take their claims more literally, I would argue that the Sophists thought of controlling nature mainly in the sense of *managing* its shifts and eddies, of surfing its waves, of using the protective coloration of whatever arbitrary conventions locally obtained in order to disguise their own pursuit of *pleonexia*. Even Empedocles' fanciful talk of "summoning" this power is more like a shamanistic incantation or a spell (to echo the language about "wizardry" in the Gorgias fragment quoted earlier), a way of tapping into and releasing the potent energies residing under the surfaces of life in the primordial wellsprings of *physis*. Machiavelli's play *The Mandragola* may point to a similar taproot of fecundity in nature as one way of gaining power over it. However, managing nature by cultivating its potencies is different in principle, I would argue, from Machiavelli's larger and more distinctively modern claim that a prince might exercise the radical capacity to stand entirely outside of nature and impose rationality on it through an act of sheer willpower.

To sum up: the pre-Socratics and Sophists do differ profoundly from the Platonic Socrates over man's relation to nature and what way of life is naturally best by nature, but their dissent remains within the boundaries of nature and the debate about its character. Whereas I am arguing that what is distinctively new and modern about Machiavelli's political science is the prospect it offers of standing outside of nature altogether. Analogously, the pre-Socratics' and Sophists' concession of the need to recognize that nature's motions do well up into and ground in historical existence the authoritative "way" of the city differs radically from Hobbes's argument, based on Bacon's narrowing of Machiavelli's project for the conquest of nature, that man as *homo faber* can replicate the ordering of the cosmos like a clockwork and remake the social contract into a perfect mechanism of self-regulation. This enormous expansion of the prospects for mastering nature, outstripping anything to be found in the dissident strain of the Sophists and pre-Socratics within classical thought, requires, I will try to demonstrate, the concept of an antinatural will borrowed from the Abrahamic God and the diminution of nature into random and empty motion already implied in Augustine's understanding of the world when it is bereft of God's sustaining will to uphold all phenomena.

For the ancient primordialist ontology, to reiterate, nature is a fecund force to which one can adapt oneself, a wave one can ride, a power for *pleonexia* that a "real man" can tap into. In this sense, as we earlier observed, the story of Gyges' Ring in the *Republic* symbolizes both an investigation into nature and the unlocking of mythical subterranean powers and Bronze Age heroism, the joint pedigree of cosmology and poetry that Socrates attributes to the motion-men in the *Theaetetus*. When Protagoras famously remarks that "man is the measure of all things," he is not, like Hobbes, Hume, or Kant, arguing that man assigns causality to matter in motion through an act of will. The Greek phrasing has, on the contrary, the connotation that this is a truth that man must "bear" (*Theaetetus* 152a). In other words, in the ontology of the motion-men, there is something uncanny and disturbing about how the great motions of nature press in on us, threatening to overwhelm us through life's unfathomable reversals and the chaotic promptings of our own passions. The tragedians reacted to this ontology of chance and necessity by suggesting that the very attempt to master it must lead to destruction. Sophocles' Oedipus begins with the confidence of a Sophist in his power as a "child of chance" to navigate its eddies with his Apollonian powers of reason and boldness. However, he is ultimately ground down by the "breakers" of these titanic clashing forces of chance and necessity (1080, 1525–1530). In contrast to the tragic teaching of Sophocles, the Sophists are generally more confident that, through the art of rhetoric, they can continue to tack and trim against the overwhelming power of nature. Even so, at bottom, they do share with the tragedians a sense of how much of life is beyond our control; how much we are the playthings of destiny, and why we should cling to convention as the bulwark built up by civilization to protect us from our own savage and hubristic natures, from the strife at the heart of existence. This cautionary stance is exemplified by Aristophanes' myth in the *Symposium*, where the laws of the city constrain us to moderation and protect us from reverting to the heavens-storming hubris that led Zeus to split us all in half. Never do the Sophists suggest, as will Machiavelli and his successors, that man can remake his own political condition from the ground up. That requires a distinctively modern, and post-Christian, conception of the will.

III

SUPERLATIVE VIRTUE,
MONARCHY, AND
POLITICAL COMMUNITY
IN ARISTOTLE'S *POLITICS*

In this chapter, I look at an important ambiguity in Aristotle's political philosophy – the issue of whether the "best regime" is a self-governing republican aristocracy (the theme of Books 7 and 8 of the *Politics*) or the much more muted claim that there may be a single ruler of superlative virtue and prudence who might rule over many "cities and peoples" according to the art of household management, a rational monarchy of the kind sometimes associated with Alexander the Great but also with Xenophon's idealization of Cyrus the Great. I argue that Aristotle mutes the claim because, while true, it would undermine the integrity and claim to merit of the self-governing political community that is at the forefront of his political philosophy. Although arguably more rational, the monarchy of the "best man" is a regime in which citizenship vanishes altogether under the architectonic art of household management conducted by an all-powerful ruler. Hence, what is true, strictly speaking, according to reason may have to retract its claims in order that the political community of shared civic deliberation can flourish in its own right. This, as we will see, is the context for Aristotle's well-known and forthright critique of what he takes to be Plato's insistence on excessive unity for the city, the Platonic Socrates' failure to distinguish theory from prudence, and his belief in the unity of virtue. Yet Aristotle's own analysis of political authority cannot entirely exclude his partiality toward precisely the kind of rational monarchy for which he takes Plato and the Platonic Socrates to task.[1]

---

1 Although I have used the familiar translation of *arete* as "virtue," one should bear in mind that the Greek word has a broader range of meanings than its English equivalent. Literally, it means "excellence." Hence, it can make perfect sense in ancient Greek to

By way of conclusion, I compare Aristotle's notion of the "architectonic" monarchy of the man of "superlative virtue" with Hobbes's prescription for monarchy to show that, despite some surface resemblances, the Hobbesian Sovereign is a fundamental departure from Aristotle's rational monarch. Whereas Aristotle's monarch exercises his superlative virtue as the fulfillment of his nature within a cosmos that is itself architectonically and teleologically ordered, Hobbes's Sovereign harnesses the art of household management in the service of an explicitly modern project, inspired by Machiavelli and Bacon, for the conquest of nature. Hence, whereas for Aristotle monarchy requires the highest degree of virtue *within* the natural order, for Hobbes, sovereignty is entirely a matter of the correctly applied method for reconstructing nature, especially human nature.

Before proceeding, we should bear in mind that Aristotle's critique of the doctrine of the unity of virtue that he attributes to the Platonic Socrates and which forms the basis for his critique of the *Republic* is underlain by a deeper shift in the relationship between reason and political virtue that we first broached in Chapter 1. For Aristotle's capacity to criticize Socrates for failing to distinguish clearly between prudence and wisdom flows from his own disinclination to embrace a single passion, whether it be eros or thumos, as the unifying dimension in political psychology.[2] There is no equivalent in Aristotle's political philosophy of Diotima's Ladder or the Image of the Cave, in which a philosophic eros for the truth entails the moral and civic virtues along the path of the soul's ascent. In terms of the ontological framework outlined in

---

speak of the "virtue" of a carpenter, doctor, orator, or general, meaning their talent for what they do. This can strike a modern reader as odd because we usually take "virtue" to mean something disinterested, the capacity to rise above our own desires and preferences for the sake of the general good. We therefore might think that a general's talent to kill and conquer people, or an orator's talent at persuading someone to believe that a lie is the truth, are too prone to deceit and self-interest to be considered properly virtuous. The Greek *arete* certainly can have the connotation of self-denial and a preference for the common good above one's own self-interest, but its meaning is not restricted to this kind of moral purity, and virtue is never categorically defined in this way to the exclusion of all other meanings.

2 For an interesting history of *thumos*, see Koziak (2000). She draws attention to the fact that, for Aristotle, thumos represents a general capacity for all manner of emotions and desires. To me, this means that Aristotle deliberately strips it of its Platonic status as one of *the* primordial passions that open us to the question of the gods and the transcendence of our mortal limitations.

Chapter 1, Aristotle moves to fence off the transcendental much more firmly from the primordial than does Plato. Whereas Plato explores how the primordial longings of eros and thumos might, if properly clarified and educated, lead continuously upward through the virtues of character required by a just regime toward the study of the Good, Aristotle is more bent on compartmentalizing the levels of this ascent. This means that philosophy changes from an erotic longing for wisdom about the whole to a more formally resolved doctrine on how to study the whole, such that, whereas for Plato the knowledge of all phenomena leads us toward the Good which is the source of their being and of their completion, including knowledge itself, Aristotle is able to separate out formal categories for the study of Being itself as an object of knowledge.[3] More central to our concerns, it also means that Aristotle denies that transcendence can only be approached by way of the study of the city or that only the philosopher is the perfect guardian of the just and the source of all prudence, including civic virtue. Instead, there is a body of knowledge appropriate to *politike* and another body of knowledge appropriate to *theoria*. By the same token, however, precisely by compartmentalizing the political virtues and setting them apart in their own right, Aristotle can be seen as portraying the realm of civic virtue as self-sufficiently noble in its own right, saving it from vanishing, as it arguably does in the Platonic dialogues, into the overwhelmingly superior claim of philosophy, with the consequence that its own satisfaction and the status of the knowledge grounding it are radically dubious, the mere twilight of Platonic "correct seeming." These larger considerations inform my specific treatment of the theme of monarchy and superlative virtue, and their relationship to tyranny, in what follows.

MONARCHY AND THE POLITICAL COMMUNITY

My aim is to demonstrate the importance of the monarchical dimension of Aristotle's political thought for understanding the character and limits of his preference for political community by examining the problem of what Aristotle calls "superlative virtue" in the *Politics* (1284a–b, 1286a5–10). In Aristotle's presentation, the public claims of the "best

---

3 On the relationship between the Idea of the Good and the other Ideas in Plato's metaphysics, consider Newell (2010).

man" to rule monarchically constitute an especially revealing test case for the political community's claims to be able to govern itself. For here the community's aims are at loggerheads not merely with selfish desires – which Aristotle of course has no difficulty in repudiating – but with the highest degree of virtue itself. As I argue in this chapter, Aristotle has a way of resolving this problem in favor of what he takes to be the requirements of politics and the political community. Yet although the cumulative message of the *Politics* is Aristotle's endorsement of an aristocratic political community as the preferred regime, the claim of superlative virtue to rule monarchically continues to undulate throughout it, leaving this endorsement a nuanced and conditional one.

The problem of superlative virtue in the *Politics* comes clearly to light in Aristotle's equivocal definition of the best claim to rule. In the sixfold classification of constitutions presented in Book 3, the "correct" constitutions are monarchy, aristocracy, and polity, and the "deviations" are tyranny, oligarchy, and democracy. Aristocracy means, literally, "rule of the best" with respect to virtue, making it the "best constitution" (1279a–b, 1278a15–20, 1284b20–30, 1293b1–10). Aristotle also argues in Book 3, however, that the rule of the best could be monarchical. In fact, if the "best man," a man of "superlative virtue," were to appear, even an aristocracy – indeed, especially an aristocracy – should give him complete authority, because virtue is its principle of justice. Strictly speaking, then, it appears that the rule of the best – aristocracy – is monarchy, rather than the self-governing community that bears this name in the sixfold classification. Some commentators regard this aspect of Book 3 as a rather puzzling relapse into Platonism, as if Aristotle had suddenly conceded the possibility of the Platonic philosopher-king and of the assimilation of the political association to the "royal" art of ruling so roundly trounced in Books 1 and 2. It is all the more puzzling because when Aristotle turns, in Books 7 and 8, to the full analysis of the "best constitution," he proceeds to describe an aristocratic *community* – as if he had never admitted that, strictly speaking, the most virtuous form of rule was monarchical (1252b30–40, 1326b9).

We can make sense of this apparent inconsistency by relating it to some broader issues in the *Politics*. The case of the individual possessing "superlative" virtue is part of an extended discussion of the meaning of justice in Book 3. The core of this argument is the section on ostracism, in which Aristotle says that to exclude the man of superlative virtue from monarchical authority bespeaks "a certain political justice" but would not conform to the "absolutely just" (1284b17, 1284b25). However, to understand the full bearing of Aristotle's distinction between "absolute" justice and "political" justice, we should first consider more closely what he means by "political." I begin, therefore, by examining Aristotle's way of distinguishing between political and other kinds of authority. As we will see, this turns out to be a distinction between a political community whose members possess enough virtue to be able to govern themselves and a prudent monarch whose virtue is so outstanding that he deserves to rule the city with the same kind of authority that a master exercises over a household. However, the claim of superlative virtue to exercise this kind of authority leads to the destruction of the city understood as a community of diverse contributions and interests. Having shown the tension between political community and monarchy, I then turn to Aristotle's consideration of what happens when the claim to possess superlative virtue rears its head in the midst of the political community itself.

The association that aims at the supreme good, according to Book 1 of the *Politics*, is the political community (*koinonia politike*).[4] A member of this community is a citizen who holds office in alternation with other citizens. A political community, in other words, is one where, by natural endowment and condition of life, people are equal – or, at least, no one is sufficiently superior to the others to be entitled to hold office permanently. The other kinds of rule, although they are associations, are thus not *political* associations, but varieties of monarchical rule: the king or royal ruler, household manager, and master. Aristotle is at pains to point this out become "some" hold the view that these forms of rule do not differ in kind, but only in number. If this were so, Aristotle argues, it would mean that statesmanship, kingship, mastery, and household management could be conflated. However, the three types of one-man rule do have more in common with each other than they do, taken together, with the political community. As we soon learn,

---

4 The political community is Aristotle's most general term for a community of shared rule in contrast with monarchy. The "constitution" (*politeia*) is the more specific ordering of the city, and the distribution of offices and authority within it, in accordance with a correct or deviant interpretation of justice. "Constitution" is also the name of *one* of the six "constitutions." I translate it in the familiar way as "polity" to avoid confusion.

household management and the mastery of slaves are both required by the household (*oikos*) to secure the necessities of life. As for kingship, some have evidently thought that the city itself could be ruled like a household – a view that, in Book 2, Aristotle attributes to Plato's *Republic* (1261a10–22). From the very outset of the *Politics*, then, and with Plato's *Republic* as well as the *Statesman* likely in mind, Aristotle is disputing the argument that all human associations, public and private, could be organized by a single royal "science" (*episteme*) of governing (Plato *Statesman* 259; Xenophon *Memorabilia* 3.4.12, 3.6.14). A city ruled like a household in which the monarch's subjects do not participate in rule but passively carry out the tasks assigned to them is the alternative that Aristotle is concerned to prevent from overwhelming the validity of deliberative self-government by the citizens of a political community.

The distinction between political and monarchical rule sheds light on the long discussion of the household that completes Book 1 (1253b–1260b). Many commentators see the aim of this discussion as establishing the superiority of public, communal existence over the private household's concerns with material necessities and comfort. This is one of its aims, but focusing on this aim alone misses what for Aristotle is the more problematic and extended part of the investigation: can the household's forms of rule be applied not only to managing one's private affairs but to entire cities? When Aristotle poses the question of whether the art of household management is identical with the acquisition of wealth, he is concerned not only with private households. This question is one of his ways of exploring more fully the possibility that there is a "science" of mastery that would swallow up not only the management of private households but the spheres of statesmanship and kingship as well – an error, he points out, "which we raised at the beginning" (1253b15–20). The discussion of the household and its place vis-à-vis the city thus doubles back to that alluring prospect of a single monarchical science of government. Moreover, whereas Aristotle is certain that the life of citizenship is better for a human being than absorption in private moneymaking and acquisition, he is not nearly so categorical in asserting the superiority of the "political community" to a certain version of the household as a pattern for government.

The analysis of the household begins with the rule of a master over slaves. According to Aristotle, the tools, including slaves, that the master employs are either for production (*poiesis*) or action (*praxis*). The epitome of productivity is the "architectonic" rule of a master-craftsman (*architekton*) over a ranked division of labor, his slaves being "tool[s] serving tools." Optimally, Aristotle suggests, tools would direct themselves automatically to fulfill their part of the master-craftsman's plan. The fanciful comparison of such tools to the legendary self-moving statues of Daedalus implies that, just as the most productive tools would be animate, the most productive slaves would be inanimate, or as close to automatons as human beings could become. Perfect productivity, in other words, would abstract from all action. However, a slave, rightly considered, is an instrument for action rather than production (1254a1–10). It is like a bed, which provides nothing beyond its use, rather than like a shuttle, which produces a commodity. A slave is thus someone who by nature belongs to a master as an instrument of action. In this way, Aristotle tries to prevent the identification of mastery with the open-ended acquisition and production of wealth.

As to the question of whether the authority of master over slave can be justified quite apart from the question of its economic consequences, Aristotle argues that this is a matter of distinguishing natural slavery from merely conventional or legal slavery.[5] Despite the attention this particular passage has understandably received from commentators, we should bear in mind that Aristotle is not only or even mainly concerned with the frequent injustice of conventional slavery (which he admits), but to distinguish political rule over naturally equal citizens from the rule of a master over slaves even when the latter would be just. Although some details of the argument justifying natural slavery are drawn from private life, in its conclusion we are reminded once again that its main target is that error discussed during the initial distinction between political and other kinds of authority: "all [forms of] rule are not [the same], although some say they are" (1235b15–20).

In order to come to grips with Aristotle's assessment of the role of property and the economy within the political community, we must avoid imposing on it an inappropriate set of modern distinctions.

---

5 The degree to which Aristotle believed that conventional slavery coincided with natural slavery – or whether he believed such a coincidence ever occurred – is a much argued question. See, for example, Ross (1960) pp. 241–242; Strauss (1977) pp. 22–23; Nichols (1983); Mulgen (1977) pp. 42–45; Smith (1983); Fortenbraugh (1977).

Aristotle is not making a rigid distinction between something like our modern "bourgeois" or "nuclear" private family and a political community selflessly dedicated to the common good, with the implication that the household is an entirely negative realm of materialism, self-interest, and apathy in contrast with an entirely communitarian realm of idealistic civic dialogue. The reality is a good deal more complicated.

It is true that the first discussion of the household reduces it to the level of necessity, thereby denying it entry into the realm of ethical choice, because it is restricted to the drives of physical survival and reproduction (1252a24–1252b27). However, this is the family only in its most primitive version, isolated or part of loose and scattered settlements. When the household is incorporated within a fully evolved city, its status is also ennobled, such that, in Aristotle's second discussion of its virtues, the household and its members dwell within the properly ethical realm of deliberative choice and education (1259a37–1260b20). As such, it is the first source of the city's future citizens.

Moreover, although the city, fully evolved, is devoted to the "good life" as opposed to the "mere life" of material survival, it does not entirely transcend that realm of material necessity nor, therefore, the economic realm of the household. The city "is" for the good life but "becomes" for material life (1252b25–1253a30). Its *telos* is deliberative communal citizenship (the realm through which the city participates in what truly is). But that highest aim is always coeval with the economic wherewithal guaranteeing the leisure for its pursuit (the lower realm of becoming). Moreover, to the extent that the telos of deliberative citizenship is fulfilled, the good life is actualized not only for cities, but also "for households," an addition often overlooked in discussions of Aristotle's famous definition of man as being by nature a political animal. Again, its proper integration within the political community ennobles household life as well as the civic life whose participants the household provides.

More than this: For Aristotle, the household is not primarily a private sub-political association at all. Allowed to unfold to its fullest degree, it is a regime-level principle of monarchical rule, the most widespread and in some ways most compelling alternative to republican self-government altogether. The main theme of Book 1, accordingly, is the contrast between these two fundamental variants of authority, the political community and some form of *oikonomia*, the art of household management. Therefore, when we turn to the discussion of the latter, we must always bear in mind that Aristotle, in discussing the art of household management and the proper limits of acquisition, is always simultaneously discussing both a regime-level pattern of authority *and* a pattern of authority within private households belonging to a *polis*. The household manager can mean the citizen of a *polis* in his capacity as head of a family and its economic concerns, or the chief overseer and steward for that family head. But it can also mean the single monarchical ruler of an entire society organized according to the household paradigm. The four main themes in the rest of Book 1 are components of this over-arching paradigm: 1) the authority of masters over slaves; 2) the proper art of household management; 3) how much the natural environment will provide for man's material needs; and 4) the virtues that subordinate members of the household, when it is properly ordered within a city, might contribute to the family, and thereby to the political community at large.

As we have seen, the discussion of "mastery" over slaves and servants introduces the fundamental criterion by which Aristotle will assess all forms of economic acquisition and production as either proper or improper – the distinction between making (*poiesis*) and doing (*praxis*). To the extent that pure untrammeled making is the goal of household management, the best slave would be like a machine programed for ceaseless fabrication within the architectonic division of labor required for maximized productivity (1253b23–1254a8). However, the proper use of slaves and servants is as a means for doing, to provide masters and household heads in their roles as citizens with the wherewithal for a devotion to "politics or philosophy" (1255b30–1256a1). Public life is the end, moneymaking only the means. The proper purpose of economics is to furnish the *chremata*, the equipment, for actualizing the virtues. For example, you cannot be liberal toward the deserving if you do not possess an adequate income beyond what is needed for your own self-preservation (1263a40–1263b7). Intending to reward the meritorious without the means to do so is not fully virtuous, for virtue is above all a deed, not merely a leaning, temperament or aspiration (*Nicomachean Ethics* 1098b30–1099a5, 1176b1–5). Hence, although someone born into a position of wealth may have done nothing to earn it, while someone born into straitened circumstances will be compelled to labor for a living regardless of his potential merit, only the wealthier man can practice the virtue of liberality, however good may be the intentions of the poorer man (*Nicomachean Ethics* 1120a4–15).

As to whether slavery or servitude is ever just, Aristotle argues that nature as a whole is characterized by the pairing of ruling over ruled, such as the soul over the body and the intellect over the appetites. To be just by nature, the master's rule over a slave would have to be as beneficial to the slave as the rule of the soul over the body or the intellect over the appetites within a single man (1254a17–1254b32). By implication, this natural standard, in which the slave is the chief beneficiary of the arrangement because he could no more take care of himself than could a body without a mind, rarely if ever coincides with the conventional institution of slavery, as evidenced by the fact that those who are masters by convention feel compelled to seek a natural justification for what is almost inevitably their arbitrary and unmerited power over other human beings (1254b32–1255a3, 1255a20–1255b16).

To maintain the distinction between the proper use of the art of household management in the service of doing and its improper use in the service of making, Aristotle argues that there are limitations on the degree to which acquisition is natural to human beings and necessary for meeting their natural needs. We need only acquire what is sufficient for life, not luxury. Wealth should primarily be based on agriculture and livestock, not commercial exchange and liquid assets. Commercial exchange, when unavoidable, should be limited to procuring the basic necessities of life, not for the sake of luxury or surplus income (1256a1–18, 1256a40–1256b7, 1257a5–1257b40). Of course, these parameters are imprecise, meant only as general guidelines, because some level of surplus between the means for self-preservation and superfluous luxury will be required to practice virtues such as liberality that are impossible to actualize without some extra wealth.

If, to argue the contrary, household management *were* synonymous with open-ended acquisition, then all the virtues would have to be viewed as means to moneymaking and material pleasures (1257b40–1258a15). Someone who is unable to fulfill his desires in private life may seek to do so "by other means" such as "courage" or "generalship" – that is, by political and martial daring (1258a5–15). Aristotle's examples of virtue in this passage remind us again that the art of household management can be employed at the regime level, and not only by the private family within the city. Courage and generalship are public virtues that, properly directed, are employed by citizens in defense of the political community's internal way of life from external aggression. If, however, the political community is swallowed up by a project for limitless economic acquisition, then these virtues could be perverted into means for launching imperialistic expansion and exploitation abroad. The improper use of household management, in other words, is coeval with tyranny, whether of a ruler tyrannizing over his own city or of a city tyrannizing over other peoples as a conqueror. The tyrant, Aristotle remarks, is in many ways like the personal owner of an enormous household made up of his subjects, someone who disposes of an entire city as his private property and business enterprise (1259a23–37), echoing the Platonic diagnosis of this political disorder. As we recall from the discussion of the proper end of the *polis*, the good life and mere life are copresent in the city. The good life outranks mere life, just as "being" (the mode in which the good life is) outranks "becoming" (the mode in which mere life is [1252b28–30]). The household, as the sphere of mere life, must be limited and circumscribed by the city, by the good life that can only be actualized in the public deliberations of the citizenry. Otherwise, it is possible that the economic aims of the household pattern of authority may slip its bonds and absorb the city itself, so that the *polis* becomes a monarchical household or even an empire.

The tenability of Aristotle's distinction between the proper and improper employment of *oikonomia* hinges, at bottom, on the ontological relationship between human nature and nature as a whole. For what if, as Machiavelli will argue, nature is in truth unremittingly hostile to human efforts to survive and prosper? In order to maintain the distinction between proper and improper *oikonomia*, according to Aristotle, we need to envision nature as providing for our basic needs without an excessive emphasis on transforming nature through human productive techniques. Only in this way can we stress doing (*praxis*) over making (*poiesis*) and circumscribe the latter by the former, which is tantamount to circumscribing the household by the *polis*. If, on the contrary, nature were to prove inherently too poor, sterile, or hostile to provide for those basic needs, we would be driven to remake nature and force it to yield the material for our survival – to "master Fortuna," as Machiavelli will put it, or as Bacon, following upon this fundamental shift in the meaning of *politike*, will argue, to convert science into the power for "the relief of man's estate."

The first conclusion Aristotle draws, then, about the art of household management is that it should not be identified with productivity. Were this identification to be made, the inflated desires such productive arts would serve in private life could, Aristotle observes, fuel an ambition for power, wealth, and status in public life or even abroad through the pursuit of empire. The productivity of the private household must therefore be circumscribed by the requirements of the common good. The proper use of wealth is to enable the heads of households to pursue public affairs and philosophy within the city.

Although this argument might seem to dispose of the claim of the household as a model for good government, it is far from the whole story. For the question remains as to whether some form of one-man authority besides the exploitive, tyrannical kind might be more beneficial for the city than the "political community." This leads to the more complex level of Aristotle's investigation. If there are not enough people in any given city who are sufficiently naturally talented to be able to pool their abilities and govern their own affairs, might not a monarch who organized them into their respective functions be a superior alternative to a self-governing community? Anticipating this objection, Aristotle argues that "nature" will provide "human beings" fit for citizenship just as she can be expected to provide both household managers and statesmen with the material necessities. Statesmanship, therefore, does not have to "make" or produce (*poiein*) human beings fit to live in a city, just as weaving does not produce wool but "uses" wool already provided for it (1258a20–30). At most, statesmanship must be able to distinguish between the good and bad people already present. The derogation of "making" in favor of "using" what has already been provided recalls Aristotle's earlier criticism of the household devoted wholly to productivity, epitomized by the rule of a master-craftsman over a ranked division of labor. Just as the household does not need to be wholly given over to the "architectonic" organization of the arts, Aristotle implies, neither does the city.

In light of what has preceded, Aristotle goes on to make the rather startling remark that "the ruler must have complete moral virtue, for the work [he does] is, taken absolutely, that of a master-craftsman, and reason (*logos*) is a master-craftsman" (*architechton*; 1260a10–20). Until now we have received the impression that Aristotle prefers shared rule to monarchical rule and that the monarch's skill in "producing" people fit to live in a city need not override the community's claim to be able to govern itself. Has Aristotle now reversed himself to endorse the "architectonic" pattern of rule? This question must be pondered on several levels. As we have observed, Aristotle makes a direct connection between the proper stance toward nature as the source of the where-withal for economic sufficiency and the proper relationship between technical fabrication and the political community. For, just as there should be no project for the conquest of nature, there should be no project for the conquest of human nature. We do not have to intervene radically in nature with our powers of fabrication because nature provides a sufficiency of wealth on hand through the cycles of agriculture and herdsmanship. Because a sufficiency of wealth is on hand from the start, we can stress the good life over mere life and need not be preoccupied with scarcity and survival. Similarly, we do not need to re-create or radically recraft human nature to achieve political order. Nature provides a sufficiency of sound human material on hand from the start, a widespread parity among human beings in their receptivity to an education in or habituation to virtue. This allows us to stress the actualization of our potential for moral and intellectual virtue through the political community – to stress the good life for citizens over a project for sheer political coercion. The parallel is clear and compelling. If nature at large is too poor, we will have to stress economic productivity over purposeful use. If human nature is too vicious from the outset, if its psychological material is too poor or intractable, statecraft will have to stress compulsion based on fear and coercion over relying on people to be capable of virtue if properly educated in an environment where the laws support virtue.

Aristotle is not unaware of the need for coercion in political life. As he puts it in the *Nicomachean Ethics*, for base natures, or for noble natures who occasionally lapse into baseness, education and noble rhetoric may require the supplement of punishment and the dread it instills (*Nicomachean Ethics* 1179b1–30). However, if politics is assimilated into a project for the rational reconstruction of human nature to coerce it to behave in an orderly way, then the very prospect of a virtuous political community vanishes into the Gulag and the reeducation camp. *Poiesis* would entirely displace *praxis*. We would be brought to the Hobbesian model of sovereignty, where both of Aristotle's criteria for the relationship of nature to human nature are reversed: 1) nature is inherently hostile to human hopes for survival and must therefore be remade in order to yield material wealth; 2) human nature inherently lacks a sufficiency of excellence for the capacity for a voluntary acceptance of virtue and must therefore be reconstructed by a Sovereign who employs terror openly as the only alternative to disobedience leading to anarchy.

Paradoxes abound here. Do we need to conceive of nature in the way Aristotle recommends *because* that will encourage us to behave properly? Or is it that understanding nature properly in this way would *lead* directly to that behavior? Is it possible that Aristotle is rhetorically exaggerating nature's friendliness, downplaying the degree to which we do have to labor for survival all the time, because otherwise the leisure time we need for philosophy and political deliberation would be undermined by our preoccupation with mere life? At the same time, we also know that, in Aristotle's view, human nature does not unfold automatically like a flower from its seed. It requires a *degree* of poiesis, like the sculpture carved from the stone: the lawgiver must "make" laws that foment correct opinion and education (*Nicomachean Ethics* 1179b–1180a10, 1180b20–1181a10). So it might be necessary for Aristotle to rhetorically exaggerate to some degree nature's beneficence as an element in the climate of opinion surrounding the "making" of character through law, habit, and pedagogy that will nudge the nature of citizens into unfolding correctly.

The *Nicomachean Ethics* and the *Politics* together might be seen as guides for statesmen of the greatest prudence in their fashioning of the education, habits, and opinions that citizens of lesser virtue require. If so, then the seed of or predisposition toward virtue must really be in human nature and nature as a whole, even if human nature needs some assistance or nudging from political craftsmanship. Otherwise, the account of nature as supportive of virtue would be a purely salutary fiction made up to disguise nature's emptiness of purpose or even its hostility toward man. For how could people be habituated to behave virtuously in Aristotle's way unless at least the seed, the potential, for it existed in nature? If the account of nature is entirely a fiction, how would Aristotle be different from a modern like Hobbes, who argues that nature is a purposeless flux that can and must be reshaped to serve man's material needs and buttress social peace? Why make up this particular story? Why not tell the truth about nature openly, like Machiavelli or Hobbes? At bottom, in however qualified or attenuated a sense, Aristotle does believe that nature will provide. The closest analogy for understanding nature, Aristotle tells us in the *Physics*, is a physician who heals himself. Similarly, a statesman must employ the art of governing to encourage the healthy flourishing of the human potential for virtue – in which statesmen themselves share – with which nature furnishes *politike*. We return to this analogy when looking at some broader differences at the end of this chapter between the classical and modern ontologies of tyranny.

For Aristotle, the danger posed by the art of household management and its household paradigm of rule to the political community is not merely the danger that the *polis* might be usurped by a tyrant or a tyrant city. Although every decent person would surely agree that the political community should not be swallowed up by the improper use of the art of household management, what about the possibility that it might be assimilated by the *proper* use of that art? The deeper difficulty is that there is something inherently reasonable about the division of labor itself. Human nature is fulfilled, Aristotle has told us, by citizens employing *logos* to deliberate about what is just, noble, and advantageous (1253a10–20). Yet now he tells us (to reemphasize this arresting phrase) that "logos is an *architechton*" – reason itself is a master-craftsman, the architectonic art (1260a13–18; *Nicomachean Ethics* 1094a25–30). In other words, the search for reasoned clarity about the meaning of justice, nobility, and the advantageous may lead ineluctably away from shared deliberation toward the hierarchical distinctions uncovered by unhindered reason, because, as we recall, the cosmos as a whole is constituted by hierarchy (1254a17–1254b2). There is thus a very real sense in which the political community's shared deliberations must, if left untrammeled, transcend themselves in the direction of a rational *oikonomia* and the rule of "one or a few" statesman of "superlative" prudence (1277a15–25, 1277b25–32, 1278a40–b6). This is why Aristotle will eventually tell us that "the whole of justice" must occasionally be sacrificed to preserve the "political justice" of the city (as in the ostracism of the best man [1284b1–30]), and why the best regime per se may not be a self-governing aristocracy so much as a rational monarchy that exercises prudence and rules over "cities and

peoples" according to the paradigm of the art of household management (1285b20–35). The fullest employment of reason in politics may
threaten the very existence of politics.

THE CLAIM OF SUPERLATIVE VIRTUE IN THE DEBATE ABOUT JUSTICE

So far we have considered the rule of the "best man" in the context of
oikonomia and its own regime principle of monarchy. Now we examine the claim of superlative virtue as one being advanced *within* the
political community itself. I will begin with a general observation about
Aristotle's notion of *politike*, a word that means both the study and
the practice of statesmanship. Aristotle's ambiguity about the role of
monarchy at its best vis-à-vis the claim of the political community at its
best mirrors his general injunction that statesmanship cannot aspire to
the deductive necessity of mathematics (*Nicomachean Ethics* 1094b12–
1095a6). Its irregularities and messiness are intrinsic to its character as
a field of study. In this, he is at odds both with other classical attempts
and with certain modern attempts to make *politike* more closely akin
to mathematics and rigorous science.

Among the ancients, the Platonic approach, at least in the dimensions of it on which Aristotle focuses his criticism, and chiefly characterized by the *Statesman* and the *Republic*, attempts to derive the
science of ruling directly from the Idea of the Good. Consequently,
Aristotle argues, because the virtues are commensurable like number,
all the virtues of character are directly assimilable to the virtue of the
philosopher (1260a–b; *Nicomachean Ethics* 1144b–1145a). Among the
moderns, as the mirror-image opposite of this Platonic science of ruling, Hobbes argues that "the similitude of the passions" provides a
formal universal from which the structure of the social contract can
be deduced with the logical necessity of geometry. In the Platonic case,
statecraft is informed by the geometrical proportionality that informs
the whole. In the Hobbesian case, geometry is an anthropocentric faculty that enables us to impose rational causation on nature understood
as matter in motion. In this respect, Aristotle thus occupies a middle
ground between the cosmological transcendentalism of Plato and the
anthropocentric transcendentalism, the project for the manmade reconstruction of nature, of Hobbes.

In Book 3 of the *Politics*, we learn that although rulers and ruled may share certain virtues of character in common, one virtue is peculiar to rulers alone. This is prudence or practical wisdom (*phronesis*). Prudence therefore demonstrates why the virtue of the good citizen rarely coincides with that of the good man (the prudent man) per se, because prudence cannot be exercised by citizens who do not themselves govern. Prudence is at all events uncommon, characteristically exercised by "one" or "one with others." Aristotle emphasizes its rareness with two illustrations. First, the ruled do not need prudence for understanding political affairs but can get by with "true opinion." This presumably enables them to understand and carry out the prudent judgments of their rulers without sharing the capacity to make them. Aristotle likens this relationship between ruler and ruled to that between a pipe player and his pipes. Second, Aristotle's example of the prudent ruler here is Jason, who could not bear to retire from tyranny into private life because he had such a "hunger" to rule. All in all, a large gulf separates the virtue of the ruler from that of the citizen (1277a15–25, 1277b25–32).

The virtue of the "best man," Aristotle observes later in Book 3, is "superlative" specifically with respect to "political capacity" (1284a10). Prudence is similarly characterized in Book 6 of the *Nicomachean Ethics*, and the discussion there clarifies a number of the terms we have encountered (1180b25–1181a10). Prudence is both the chief intellectual virtue apart from wisdom and the condition for the possession of the moral virtues in their entirety. The rare individual who possesses prudence will therefore also possess such virtues as greatness of soul, liberality, moderation, and courage, whereas people possessing one or more of these lesser virtues will not necessarily achieve prudence. Prudence is not an art (*techne*) because it does not "make" or "produce" (*poiein*) things. It is not a science (*episteme*) like geometry because it does not deal with permanent conditions but with variable ones (1140a25–1140b10). However, prudence is something considerably more precise and skillful than instinct, improvisation, or even debate among informed citizens. For prudence must be guided by an "architectonic" faculty for "statesmanship," applying this faculty according to "correct reason" (1141b10–30, 1144b10–25). Aristotle's example of prudent statesmanship in the *Ethics* is Pericles, whose predominance over the Athenian democracy Hobbes, in a comment on his translation of Thucydides, compares to a monarchy in all but name.[6] Whereas Socrates in the *Gorgias* would not, to Callicles' indignant amazement, deign to include Pericles among the ranks of prudent rulers, Aristotle's use of him as the exemplar of the highest practical virtue reflects his critique of Socrates for failing to distinguish that crowning virtue of the statesman from philosophical contemplation.[7] By opening up a realm for political genius and even (as the example of Pericles implies) a kind of measured imperial ambition between the empyrean heights of philosophy and the arguably robotic conformism of the Auxiliaries in the *Republic*, Aristotle is trolling for men like Callicles who fit into neither extreme. He is promising them a life of political preeminence that is noble and satisfying in its own right.

The characterization of prudent statesmanship as an "architectonic" faculty guided by correct reason also suggests that the gap between technical and scientific reasoning on the one hand and prudence on the other is not as wide as it might at first appear. As we have observed in Book 1 of the *Politics*, Aristotle regards the architectonic organization of the arts as the optimal one for technically skilled production (*poiesis*). Moreover, although "intelligence" (*nous*) is initially characterized in the *Ethics* as the source from which "science" intuits the first principles of deductive proofs, Aristotle later suggests that "intelligence" also furnishes prudence with an intuition of the particulars with which *it* must deal (1143b1–10). In Book 10 of the *Ethics*, when Aristotle discusses the transition from ethics to government, the distinction between art and science on the one hand and prudence on the other is relaxed further still. This appears to parallel Aristotle's contention that we must turn from ethics to government because persuasion is not enough to make most human beings prefer virtue to vice: for most people, "force" and law are also required. The prudent ruler is now said to have to know "statesmanship" with the same acuity as scientists know science and artisans know art, so as to be able to "make (*poiein*) people better." In other words, the transition from questions of ethics to questions of government and rule leads to less emphasis on

---

6 In Schlatter (1975) p. 14.
7 See the fascinating study by Burger (2008), who argues that the *Nicomachean Ethics* may be read as the dialogue that Plato never wrote, a dialogue between two philosophers, in which Aristotle is directly engaging Socrates.

persuasion and the voluntary aspect of citizens' habituation to virtue and to more emphasis on the need to supplement persuasion with regulation and punishment. As this transition occurs, prudence moves correspondingly closer to (although it never fully coincides with) *poiesis* and *episteme*.

These modulations in the meaning of prudent statesmanship take us back to the underlying debate between Aristotle and Plato. Aristotle will not abandon the distinction between prudence as a kind of skilled and seasoned judgment of political experience and the pure expertise of scientific and technical knowledge. In contrast with what he takes to be the teaching of Plato, Aristotle will not allow the sphere of practical statesmanship to be assimilated entirely to a monarchical science of rule. This parallels his unwillingness to see the sphere of public life obliterated by the monarchical science of household management. His examples of prudent statesmen, although individuals of rare ability, are flesh-and-blood actual rulers such as Jason and Pericles (warts and all) rather than the totally disinterested and intellectually pure prototype of Platonic monarchy. On the other hand, however, Aristotle is willing to modify the distinction between prudent statesmanship and technical reasoning as he moves from the formation of a gentlemanly character in the *Ethics* to the frequent need in wider political practice for more direct and coercive modes of habituation.

Let us return to the passage in the *Politics* from which this excursus began (1260a10–20). If the ruler in the "absolute" sense, who rules according to "reason" and "complete moral virtue," is to pattern his rule on that of the master-craftsman, then it would seem that politics ought indeed to be organized according to the ranked division of labor. For this is the master-craftsman's way of organizing the household. In Book 2, we learn that Aristotle interprets Plato's *Republic* – the city, as the Platonic Socrates put it, "according to reason" (*Republic* 369a) – as functioning according to just such a division of labor. In this context, Aristotle observes that just as it is more productive for shoemakers always to do the same job rather than rotating their jobs for others, so would it be "better" if the rulers of the political community were "always . . . the same" (1261a30–1261b10). When consulting the criterion of the good, in other words (*beltion* [better] being the comparative of *agathos* [good]), Aristotle seems to be at one with Plato on the best form of rule. Where that is not possible because "all are naturally equal," he continues, the members of the community should rule and be ruled in turn.

Yet even if the ranked division of labor between ruling and ruled were possible, it is difficult to reconcile Aristotle's approval of it in the context just cited with the main drift of his arguments in favor of shared participation in ruling. The way to make sense of this, however, is to keep before us the fundamental distinction he makes between political and nonpolitical associations. The *Republic*, Aristotle argues, is so unified owing to its hierarchy of labor that it is like a single household rather than a city. For the nature of the city is differentiation. Diverse contributions, selfish interests, and conflicting opinions about justice comprise its fragile unity. According to Aristotle, Socrates' demand for the total unity of the city turns it into an *oikos*, a household ruled by its "owner," the philosopher-king. The *polis* is entirely swallowed by the "economy." Perfect unity, Aristotle maintains, is not appropriate for the plural, composite nature of the city. The more the city tends toward complete unity, the more it moves in the direction of household management and royal rule with its architectonic division of labor. Human nature is a composite of intellect and appetite. These can be well arranged but not made unitary, nor can classes be sorted out on the basis of only one character trait or the other (as Plato does with the Guardians and Auxiliaries). The division of labor is not practicable in political communities, where freezing the ruling element permanently in place will cause "outrage," especially among the spirited Achillean kind of men whom the *Republic* is meant most particularly to assuage (1264b6–10).

This outrage is precisely what does lead in the *Republic* itself to the overthrow of the Guardians by the honor-loving Auxiliaries, a revolution which, as we discussed in the last chapter, might just as plausibly take the form of an individual tyrant coming to power as a timocratic class. As we will see in the next chapter, something roughly akin to this happens in Xenophon's *Education of Cyrus*, where the young Cyrus leads a revolution of the other young aristocrats of military age in the Persian Republic (a self-governing regime partly patterned on Platonic prescriptions) against the gerontocracy that rules the republic and its unchanging laws and institutions, including its avoidance of foreign conflict as a source of internal disorder through overweening military ambition and its concentration on purely inward-looking self-government. In one of his many interesting variations on Plato and Aristotle, whereas Plato believes wisdom should rule and Aristotle believes this will be intolerable to the nonphilosophic honor-loving citizenry, Xenophon's Cyrus is motivated by his love of honor to lead a revolution of the honor-loving citizenry issuing in a world-state based on the Xenophontic Socrates' art of *oikonomia*.

To return to Aristotle: the division of labor, as Aristotle concedes in Book 2, is natural to the arts. No rotation is needed because each artisan is an expert and is assigned his most efficient place. In cities, however, offices must rotate because citizens are equal, or if not entirely equal, sufficiently on a level with each other so as to not need to be ruled over permanently (1261a30–1261b10). In this connection, we might recall from Book 1 Aristotle's argument that nature will provide sufficiently sound human material for statesmanship from the outset. There as well, Aristotle criticizes Socrates for having held virtue to be the same in every soul, differing only in the amount of it that each soul possesses. Instead, Aristotle continues, different kinds of virtue are distributed in varying degrees among men, women, and children, depending on which virtue, and how much of it, is needed for their tasks as slaves, servants, family members, or citizens – tasks that will vary further with the particular kind of constitution under which they live (1260a–b). Aristotle here and elsewhere speaks of "absolute" or "whole" virtue, but by this he means something very different from the prospect that, as in the *Symposium*, for example, eros might lead us on a continuous ascent from family life through civic virtue toward the highest good, contemplative virtue, of which the lower rungs are but approximations, with a single passion acting as the soul's leader. Instead, in keeping with what Aristotle takes to be the composite character of the soul, the wholeness of virtue comes from the harmonious actualization of its respective parts. Prudence, the highest of the active virtues, actualizes and brings to completion the other virtues of character like greatness of soul and magnificence, which, nevertheless, are self-sufficient and noble in their own right. For Aristotle, although it is doubtless better to climb all the way to the top of the ladder ascending from family life to civic virtue to contemplation, you can stop off on one of the lower rungs and still be entitled to be regarded (and regard yourself) as virtuous. Man's fulfillment of his telos as the member of a political community is without qualification noble and even "godlike" in itself (*Nicomachean Ethics* 1094a19–b12).

Let us sum up the results so far of this analysis of Aristotle's distinction between political and monarchical rule. Aristotle argues that, although there is such a thing as a good form of household rule, it is not a city, and that although there is such a thing as the rule of the "best man" employing "superlative virtue," it need not assimilate the lesser and diverse varieties of virtue which make the city go.[8] Thus, while the prudent ruler may indeed be the ruler in the "absolute" sense, reason need not assert its claim to rule where nature has supplied people of sufficient, diverse virtues to govern themselves. Where human nature is not deficient, the "architectonic" rule of reason would be unnecessarily and unjustly coercive. Even where human nature were so deficient as to require this kind of rule, however, it would still be *unpolitical* rule, destructive of the city and citizenship. With these arguments in mind, we can now consider how Aristotle treats the claim of superlative virtue to monarchical authority when it presents itself among the other claims to authority that contend in actual political life. What happens, in other words, when the man of "superlative virtue" rears his head in the midst of the community of shared rule and strides forward to claim his place?

A GODLIKE MAN IN THE CITY?

The claim of the "best man" to supreme authority is taken up in the midst of a discussion of the meaning of justice in political argument. According to Book 3 of the *Politics*, justice is equal treatment for people in those respects in which they are equal, and unequal treatment in those respects in which they are unequal. Yet while there is widespread agreement on the comparative value of things, there is serious disagreement over who really deserves which things. Our own interests are inextricably involved when we argue about what constitutes just treatment. Hence, for example, partisans of oligarchy mistake their superiority in wealth for superiority in all contributions to the political community. The partisans of democracy mistake their equality in free birth for the

---

8 On the difficulties of reconciling the civic friendship that ought to take place among citizens with the conflicting claims to rule made in political deliberation, as well as the difficulties of reconciling civic friendship with the higher claims of friendship per se, best actualized through philosophic friendship, see the fine study by Lorraine Pangle (2000).

equality of human beings in every respect. Thus, Aristotle says, "all adhere to a kind of justice, but they only proceed so far, and do not discuss the whole of justice" (1280a5–15). The decision about the meaning of justice, commonly a blend of the contending party's self-interest and a "part" of justice, generates the distinctions among constitutions. Roughly but not intolerably imprecisely put, Aristotle's approach to political argument is a blend of Marx and Kant.[9]

In Book 3, however, Aristotle raises doubts about the adequacy of his own sixfold classification of constitutions. In effect, he asks: Is not even this variety of possible decisions about how to constitute the political community too limiting of the possible meanings of equality and inequality, each one too exclusive and narrowly based within itself? Does not each of these regime principles, even the good ones, contain an element of tyranny? For there are other qualities (for instance, ancestry and family background) that contribute to the city's survival and pursuit of the good life besides those contained in the six principles. How, then, can we judge precisely a person's equality or inequality in comparison with other people so as to know who is entitled to "offices"? Distinguishing equality from inequality in a politically relevant way, it transpires, is a problem for which we need "political philosophy" (1282b).

Aristotle offers an illustration of the problem (1282b20–1283a30). Some would argue that if people are equal in other respects, any remaining superiority will suffice to justify the unequal distribution of offices. To this, he responds that not all forms of superiority justify superior *political* authority. Using an analogy, Aristotle argues that a superior pipe player will always deserve the best pipes. This will be the case even where another person is superior to the pipe player in birth or good looks in a greater proportion than the pipe player is superior to that other person in pipe playing, and even supposing looks and birth to be greater goods than pipe playing. In other words, the diverse contributions that people make to the city are not commensurable.[10] They

---

9 See the detailed and probing exegesis of Aristotle with respect to economics and redistributive justice by Balot (2001).

10 In Book 4, where the most inclusive constitution, polity, is discussed in detail, Aristotle observes that not only are there many claims to virtue, but they may coexist in the same people, making it even more difficult to decide precisely who is equal and unequal in a politically relevant way: "the same people (may be) soldiers, farmers and artisans, as

cannot be super-added to arrive at a ranked hierarchy of who deserves what. This is in keeping with Aristotle's criticism, earlier noted, of the Socratic argument for the unity of virtue – the notion that virtue is the same for all people, varying only by the amount each person possesses. If this were the case, it would be possible to conclude that the second man was more entitled to the best pipes than the best pipe player, because his superior birth and looks added up to more "superiority" than the pipe player's musical talent.

Of course, in another sense, the analogy *does* point toward the unity of virtue and monarchical rule. For even though the contributions of different types of people cannot be added up into one overriding claim to rule, apparently *one* person could possess enough virtue to make this claim from the outset. After all, the best pipe player does unambiguously deserve the best pipes. Earlier in Book 3, as we observed, Aristotle makes this point more explicitly by comparing the relationship between an outstandingly virtuous ruler and his subjects to that between a pipe player and his pipes (1277b25–30). Here, though, the drift of the argument is toward inclusiveness. Hence, returning from the analogy to the problem of justly distributing political authority, Aristotle concludes that the well born, the free, the wealthy, the educated, and the virtuous – taken together, in combinations of two or more, or separately – cannot claim *all* political honors and influence, although they are certainly entitled to a share of them.

The specific mention of "education and virtue," the concomitants of aristocracy (1283a35–1288b), makes it clear that Aristotle is not just speaking of virtue in the relative sense of the many talents which keep the city going. While allowing that education and virtue have the "most just" claim to political authority, he maintains that even these do not deserve "inequality in all" (1283a20–25). It therefore transpires that "all such constitutions," including aristocracy, are "deviant" because in each case the ruling part mistakes superiority in one quality for superiority in all. We are not surprised to learn this about the regimes previously described as deviant because they do not rule for the common good but only for the ruling part's advantage. It is surprising, however,

---

well as councillors and judges, and indeed everyone thinks they are capable of holding most of the offices" (1291b1–10).

to learn that virtue *itself* can push its claim to authority too far – that virtue can be "overbearing," even tyrannical, in its claims.[11]

But this is just what Aristotle means, and his reason for it is "political" in the sense discussed earlier. Here we should bear in mind that the most inclusive of the correct constitutions – most conveniently translated as "polity" – is both specifically distinguished from rule according to virtue (aristocracy) and given as its own particular name the name common to all six principles of rule (*politeia* – "constitution," 1279a35–1279b). Although it is the least virtuous of the correct constitutions, polity is evidently closer to what Aristotle takes to be the practical aim of "constitutional" government as such – the inclusion within the political community of as many diverse and conflicting interests and abilities as possible.[12] For a city that excludes too many people from rule will be "full of enemies," and hence unstable, making both mere life and the good life impossible to sustain (1281v25–35). The derogation in this context of the politics of virtue in favor of the "constitutional" politics of inclusiveness helps to explain Aristotle's remark that we have to consider what will happen when all six claims to rule "are present in one city." This appears to mean that the sixfold schema, although useful as a heuristic device, is too abstract; that there will seldom if ever be a precise fit between real cities and the six principles of rule. Cities as we observe them in practice are more likely to be a kind of political cauldron in which all the claims are contending for power at once. Even in cities that do fit closely to one of the classifications, other claims are seething beneath the surface, waiting for their opportunity. Far from being able to stabilize the political community, therefore, each of the constitutions (with the probable exception of polity) is likely to be felt as a tyrannical imposition by those whom it excludes. Aristotle underscores this deficiency by arguing that, pushed to its extreme, each

---

11 As Newman notes, the problem cannot be solved by assuming that "all such constitutions" refers only to tyranny, oligarchy, and democracy or to ones in which authority is claimed on the basis of something other than virtue. Aristotle is clearly referring to the correct regimes as well as the deviant ones. Newman in Aristotle (1950) vol. 3 pp. xxii–xxiii.

12 Polity is the most inclusive and stable of constitutions because it blends the principles of democracy and oligarchy that, between them, include the most people and are the source of the most explosive and prevalent conflict: rich versus poor. Consider Clark (1975) pp. 104–105; Randall (1968) pp. 263–264.

principle of rule, as it were, self-destructs, ruining the self-interest and authority of its very claimants, necessitating a more inclusive approach to power sharing. Thus, the oligarchs, in order to live up to their own principle, must give way to the one or few richest in their midst or to the common people if they are collectively richer than the oligarchy. Those claiming to be equal by free birth will have to yield to the freest-born by background and ancestry. Those who claim to rule through virtue will have to yield to the one or few most virtuous in their midst (1283b5–1284a).

Up to this point, Aristotle's argument seems strongly to favor a broad definition of contributions to the city and a broad claim to public authority. In a rather abrupt shift, however, he goes on to argue that there may be "one" whose virtue is so outstandingly superior to all other virtues as to make him a "god" among "human beings," and who cannot even be considered "a part of the city" (1284I–15). The sudden transition to this godlike ruler is in keeping with the preceding discussion of the self-shattering of the other regime types, which might appear to deny anyone this supreme status, if one bears in mind that Aristotle's denial of supremacy to any one virtue, and the overall derogation of virtue in favor of "constitutional" rule, was made squarely within a "political" context as that term was discussed earlier. The point here, by contrast, is that the man of "superlative virtue" is literally *not* political, not "a part of the city." Here, then, we are getting the other conclusion from the pipe player analogy that Aristotle did not draw when stressing the limited claims of various kinds of virtue to order the political community. Although the diverse contributions in any given political community cannot be ranked so as to establish an entitlement to exclusive authority, some rare individuals possess a degree of virtue so overwhelming that it cannot be included within this balancing and blending of claims in the first place. This is the "best man" with that rare kind of prudence that sets him apart from the rest.

Although Aristotle recognizes the force of this claim to rule, we should note that he does not present superlative virtue as an exclusively or self-evidently beneficent quality from the perspective of the political community. Superlative virtue certainly can be taken to mean rule in the "absolute" sense, rule according to reason by one who possesses complete moral virtue, but even a reasonable or prudent ruler, Aristotle implies here, could be partly motivated by an ambition for honor and perhaps even by desire, appearing to his subjects like a predatory lion among the hares. We recall that the exemplars of prudence offered in Book 3 and in the *Nicomachean Ethics* (Hercules, Jason, and Pericles) were men scarcely devoid of grand ambition and accustomed to having things done their way. They are easily classifiable within the tribe of what the Athenian Stranger termed those with an erotic longing for the city. Whether purely benevolent or willing to rule benevolently in exchange for certain advantages, such a ruler will in any case be hard for the "equals" making up a political community to bear, just as the Argonauts found Hercules too heavy for their ship to stay afloat (1284a15–25). For precisely the reason that Aristotle abandons the Platonic Socrates' argument that, in principle, prudent statesmanship could be directly derived from philosophical moderation, his "best man" is not a philosopher or even the philosophical governor advising the young tyrant envisioned in Book 4 of the *Laws*, but a man whose chief drive is for supreme honor through a life of great action.

The questionable desirability of superlative virtue from the perspective of the political community – the question of whether such a ruler's talents and beneficence could ever outweigh the overbearing quality of his authority – is emphasized by Aristotle's initial discussion of it in the context of ostracism. In Aristotle's presentation, ostracism is a typically democratic practice because the claim of superlative virtue to absolute authority exists in a starker contradiction with democracy, whose principle is absolute equality, than with any other regime. However, the question of how to accommodate such a claim is a problem for all regimes, according to Aristotle, the correct as well as the deviant. Ostracism is in fact analogous to the practice of tyrants in "lopping off," like the tallest blades of grass, the leading citizens who might rival them. Despite his usually strong condemnation of tyranny, in this connection Aristotle does not consider the critics of tyranny to be "absolutely correct" (1284a25–40). For the other regimes – "even the correct ones" – must likewise lop off the outstandingly virtuous. (One is put in mind of how Alcibiades was driven into exile by the democracy of Athens, despite, according to Thucydides, his faultless conduct of the Sicilian expedition.)[13] Once again, any partial embodiment of justice in a regime principle contains an element of coercion and exclusion.

---

13 Consider the discussion in Newell (2009) part 3.

In this sense, he implies, all regimes contain an element of tyranny, including an uncompromising suppression of the best title to rule, and in this they are adhering to "a certain political justice," although not to "absolute justice." The community as political community, as a differentiated unity, cannot tolerate the unified authority of the "best man" except at the price of its own being – any more than a painter can allow one part of his painting to be disproportionately large, or a chorus-master can allow a performer whose voice is "nobler and more powerful" than all the rest (1284b1–30).

However, when the constitution's own principle of rule is "the best," there appears to be an insurmountable problem in principle. For neither the deviant constitutions (which are nakedly based on the rulers' self-interest) nor polity (which aims at a blend of diverse interests and contributions) espouse virtue as their exclusive and undiluted claim to authority. Yet how can an aristocracy consistently reject the rule of one who is "surpassingly virtuous"? For it to do this, Aristotle argues, would be like "claiming to rule over Zeus." In an important qualification of his claim in Book 1 that statesmen need not "make" human beings because nature will provide sufficient numbers of them capable of governing themselves, Aristotle now adds that superlative virtue and its claim to authority also flow from nature (1284b20–35). In the case of this one constitution (that is, aristocracy) one-man rule over-rides "political" rule strictly in keeping with a correct principle of "political" rule itself. In other words, the aristocrats' claim to authority over the political community lays bare, in an especially revealing way, the inability of "political justice" altogether to live up to the requirements of "absolute justice." Thus, while allowing that other constitutions may need to ostracize individuals of superlative virtue, Aristotle depicts the claims of the "best man" as being particularly embarrassing for an aristocracy. Within the sixfold classification, aristocracy is a peculiar sort of halfway house between the deservingness of superlative virtue and the necessity for inclusiveness. On the one hand, aristocracy is likely to exclude too many people in comparison with polity. On the other hand, because aristocracy recognizes virtue as the only claim to rule, its failure to embody the highest degree of virtue is more glaringly unjust than in the case of constitutions which judge people's contributions and interests less rigorously and with a greater view to stability. Thus, Aristotle concludes in what sounds almost like a quotation from Plato' *Republic*

(473d), "it remains for all to obey such a man gladly, so that men of this sort are kings in the cities forever."

MONARCHY, REASON, AND NATURE

The discussion of monarchy that completes Book 3 is a recapitulation of the problem of how to reconcile competing claims for authority – how to judge between the equal and the unequal – in light of the admitted possibility of superlative virtue. Aristotle's presentation of virtuous monarchy as a regime principle recalls his discussion in Book 1 of rule in the "absolute" sense, the "architectonic" rule of reason. For this monarchy of the "best man" is a form of household management (1285b20–1286a). Moreover, alone of the correct constitutions, monarchy is in principle lawless because knowledge always trumps convention or law and because its ruler "acts in all things according to his own will" (1287a1–10, 1287a30–40; Plato *Statesman* 292b–303c).

In presenting the case here for a regime that is beneficent but lawless, Aristotle rather sharply qualifies his earlier-stated preference in Book 2 for law over innovation. Stable laws, he there argues, are the element of any regime hoping to promote virtue. Yet, Aristotle concedes, many laws and conventions are silly or outmoded, whereas improvements in the arts, such as medicine, have tangibly improved the human condition. People naturally want the good, and prefer it to convention if the two conflict. Mankind has evolved since its most primitive beginnings in large part because of technical progress. In earliest times, Aristotle observes, the entire human race was like the most foolish individuals are today. Laws have to change, and statesmanship must admit the possibility of progress. No set of laws can anticipate everything – room must be left for modification. However, not implementing a reform, especially if it is not momentous and clearly needed (the "if it ain't broke, don't fix it" rule), may well be preferable to encouraging people to habitually question the law in their addiction to innovation (1268b22–1269a29). Lawfulness requires habit, so there is no easy harmony between law and technical advancement or between political community and *oikonomia*. It must wait for modern thinkers like Hegel to argue that human community and technique progress harmoniously together. For Aristotle, they remain in a permanent tension.

Having earlier cautioned against technical innovation in favor of the stability of law, Aristotle now, when turning to monarchy, concedes the full weight of the opposite argument, also made in Plato's *Statesman* (which he had criticized by implication in the first lines of the *Politics* for conflating royal rule with all other kinds), that the monarch strictly speaking must rule without the constraints of law because he possesses knowledge. It is an emphatically "unpolitical" form of rule, that is, incompatible with any notion of civic community. Because the view of justice it embodies – the outstanding merit of one person – can in no way be shared or participated in by the members of a local community, it is also universalistic in principle and so capable of swallowing up whole cities and "nations," a passage often linked with Aristotle's semilegendary tutorship of Alexander the Great but that could as readily apply, as we will see in the next chapter, to Xenophon's Cyrus the Great.

Aristotle proceeds to raise some possible objections to virtuous monarchy from the "constitutional" perspective on the city as an association "composed of many (people)" (1286a25–35). Thus, he suggests that the "multitude," by pooling its judgments, may frequently be a better judge of public affairs than the expert, in the sense that a banquet provided by many hands will be superior to one provided by a single individual. Whereas one man – even, apparently, a virtuous ruler – can be corrupted by "anger" or some "other such passion," it is more difficult for everyone in a crowd to be led astray at once. If the "majority" – relative to the monarch – are actually of "sound soul," that is to say, an aristocracy, then they will resist the tendency of a "multitude" to split into factions and will therefore be altogether preferable to the rule of one (1286a35–1286b10).

Some would argue, moreover, that it is simply "against nature" that one man should rule because the city is composed of equals. Thus, a community where law rules and offices are rotated is preferable to monarchy. For although man is a political animal possessing reason (1253a1–10), he is an animal nonetheless, and to allow even the "best man" absolute power unconstrained by law may offer too much temptation to the "wild beast" (*therion*) within him of desire and spiritedness (*thumos*; 1287a25–40). Thus, we are reminded again that – at least from the perspective of the political community – the "best man" may mix his benevolent expertise with the leonine qualities of a lord and master. We might add that the potentially overweening thumotic qualities of the genius-statesman are all the more evident given Aristotle's unwillingness to concede Socrates' argument that the philosophic life is ultimately the source of the moderation needed in statesmen, if only through the intermediary of civic education. By allowing political ambition its freedom from contemplative virtue, Aristotle also risks unleashing its innate aggressiveness, although to nothing like the degree explored by Xenophon in the *Education of Cyrus*, let alone Machiavelli. The rule of law, by contrast (he goes on), is like intelligence devoid of such passions. Moreover, although experts admittedly must sometimes override the law (just as a doctor must sometimes depart from prescribed treatment), expertise can be used for unjust ends (just as a doctor knows best how to kill a fit patient). Thus, the rule of law is on the whole preferable to the rule of an expert, a "mean" between (apparently) absolute monarchy and the spontaneous impulses of the multitude (1287a40–1287b).

Still, it is important to note that these are not so much Aristotle's own arguments as hypothetical objections presented for our consideration. He concludes by stating that, when men are equal, monarchy is neither just nor advantageous, even if the monarch is (relatively) "superior in virtue" – "except in a certain case." This is the case, as at the outset, of the man of "superlative" virtue who should not rule "in alternation" like citizens but "absolutely." For, having rehearsed the objections, Aristotle does not find them sufficient. Although an absolute monarch should not rule over equals, if he is "outstandingly" unequal, they are plainly no longer (even relatively) equal (1288a1–30).

Aristotle brings us full circle to the problem of distinguishing equality from inequality and argues, somewhat startlingly, that this problem is solved by the claim of superlative virtue to monarchical authority. We are reminded that all the other constitutions, including aristocracy, make claims to authority based on different kinds of inequality. However, although they all urge the justice of these claims, only monarchy meets the requirements of "the whole of justice," of justice in the "absolute" sense. Whereas the partiality and exclusiveness of the other claims led Aristotle earlier to back away from the sixfold classification and to stress the need to blend as many competing claims as possible, in the case of superlative virtue, he appears to regard the equal and the unequal as reconcilable through the rule of the one best man. This claim is commensurable with all the others if only in the negative sense that all the other claims are incommensurable with it. However, this kind of monarchy, based on the principle of household management, is, in accordance with the distinctions between kinds of rule made at the beginning of the *Politics*, unpolitical. The one constitution that meets the requirements of justice is not itself a political community. Thus, although we are reminded in conclusion that to ostracize such a man would never be in accordance with "absolute justice," we remember that it is in a sense "politically just" to do just that.

Although Aristotle continues to include monarchical rule among the possible meanings of aristocracy (the "rule of the best"), throughout the rest of the *Politics* aristocracy has mainly the meaning of a political community of the virtuous (1289a26–38, 1293a35–1293b7, 1294a9–29). In Books 7 and 8, where the "best constitution" is prescribed in detail, it has exclusively this meaning. On the basis of the preceding analysis, several reasons can be suggested for this ambiguity. First of all, aristocracy in the latter sense, although extremely rare, is in Aristotle's view relatively closer to practical possibilities, and thus more easily emulated, than the rule of a "godlike" monarch. Oligarchies, for instance, can sometimes qualify as "loose" aristocracies, a blend of wealth and virtue (1249a9–29). Polity, the correct regime that Aristotle believes has the best chance of setting a standard for actual practice, can encourage the awarding of offices on the basis of virtue, the aristocratic principle of distribution (1294a35–1294b14).

The other reason for Aristotle's equivocal definition of aristocracy (mostly as a republic, occasionally as a monarchy), I would suggest, lies in the danger that he believes is posed to public life by the advancement of a merely presumptive claim to superlative virtue. As we saw in Book 1, Aristotle cautions against perverting the proper use of the household or monarchical form of rule into a tyrannical exploitation of the city. In real life, Aristotle later remarks, most people are not even aware of the distinction between monarchy and tyranny but tend to identify all government with "mastery" – the exploitation of the ruled by the ruler (1324b22–41).[14] Thus, the claim to possess superior virtue could be used as a powerful rhetorical camouflage by those who aim at

14 See the discussion in Lord (1982) pp. 190–191.

tyranny – the thin edge of the wedge for Hobbes's critique of Aristotle. As Aristotle concedes, even someone who really does possess the knowledge to govern may also be prone to a desire for a monopoly on all honor, excessive anger, and an intolerance for even a reasonable and well-intentioned airing of views by others.

In this respect, we might defend the Platonic Socrates against Aristotle's critique of him for conflating *sophia* with *phronesis* as follows: the philosopher-king, at least in principle, removes the danger of an excessively honor-seeking and anger-prone statesman of genius of the kind explored by Aristotle, because those dangerous passions would be absorbed by the eros for wisdom. So perhaps it was not so unreasonable after all to hold the criterion for the proper exercise of the art of ruling to such a high standard that even the genius-statesman (but also imperialist) Pericles did not qualify, as Socrates argued in the *Gorgias*. But, in defense of Aristotle, we might observe in turn that Plato, when he has his Athenian Stranger entertain the possibility that just such a genius-statesman, a young tyrant with an eros for the city, might found a just regime, is so sensitive to the danger that this tyrant's claim to serve justice might only be putative, or might be mixed with a desire for limitless honor, or end up not being reined in by a philosophic advisor, as to abandon the prospect after only a few pages and treat the just founding as the object of a prayer. Given that danger, Aristotle might say, why not cooperate with the ambition for supreme honor on its own terms, appealing to the gentleman's own innate preference for virtuous over disgraceful conduct and sidelining the need for philosophical mentoring? At any rate, while Aristotle arguably defines the *phronimos* more realistically than does Plato, both their political philosophies are dependent on the coinciding of supreme political virtue and actual power in the same leader. As we saw in the last chapter, it is this dependence on chance, on Fortuna, as Machiavelli will put it, that takes us to the heart of Machiavelli's critique of the classical orientation.

In this light, we can see Hobbes as arguing that Aristotle did not go nearly far enough in his warning that a prospective ruler claiming to possess superlative prudence could turn out to be a would-be tyrant in disguise. Hobbes's solution, ingeniously, is to dispense with the distinction between superlative virtue and tyranny altogether while maximizing the total authority of the "sovereign," now liberated from the opprobrious comparison to a tyrant. For Hobbes, admitting even the possibility of superlative virtue promotes political instability. For the presumptive claim, once admitted as a possibility, is always open to recognition and acceptance, meaning that the "vainglorious" (enflamed by their reading of Aristotle and the other ancients who flatter them into supposing themselves great men) have a convenient pretext for their ambition. The solution to the threat to civil order posed by these would-be tyrants camouflaged as men of superlative virtue is to conscript one of their number, suitably disabused of the misunderstanding of his own motivation as some kind of eros for an immortal reputation for nobility and justice, to crush the others.

Hobbes's presentation of the state of nature is meant to convince us that no claim to superior virtue can outweigh our fundamental equality in vulnerability to violent death. Paradoxically, this argument for a low egalitarianism ends up entailing a sovereign with powers far outstripping any that Aristotle would have attributed to virtuous monarchy. For Hobbes, even fear of violent death at the whim of the Sovereign, let alone resentment at his failure to recognize merit or rule beneficently, is preferable to a state of open contention for power based on competing claims to virtue, the war of all against all that maximizes each individual's peril. If the protection of life, rather than the possession of virtue, is the only admissible claim to absolute authority, the result is a Sovereign who cannot, in practice or principle, be distinguished from a tyrant. Hobbes's frontal and parodistic assault in the *Leviathan* on Aristotle's argument for virtuous monarchy, which we return to in the Conclusion, flows from his own adaptation of Machiavelli's view that man can stand outside of nature and reconstruct it through an act of will, presupposing a view of nature as purposeless motion grounded in the physics of Bacon, who in turn acknowledged the inspiration of Machiavelli's teaching about virtue and fortune. Viewed from this perspective, Aristotle's tortuous ambiguities about superlative virtue vis-à-vis the political community are replaced by the application of the correct method for the maximization of power, such that, as Machiavelli puts it in *The Prince*, a ruler can be the source of his own prudence without recourse to such ambiguous and convoluted philosophical guidance.

For the very reasons that Aristotle is willing to mute the claim of superlative virtue, it might be asked whether we cannot push Aristotle further in this direction by abandoning his concern with superlative

virtue while exclusively retaining his endorsement of political community. This is the brunt of the communitarian reading undertaken
by Arendt, Gadamer, and Beiner, among others. (I examine Arendt's
momentarily.) However, a conception of political community that
excluded superlative virtue, whatever the merits of that conception
might be, would not be an *Aristotelian* conception of political community. This is because Aristotle's understanding of politics, while trying
to give inclusiveness and diversity their fair weight, is inegalitarian in
principle. According to Aristotle, man fulfills his nature in political life
by pursuing virtue. What Aristotle means by virtue, as we have seen,
is on a kind of sliding scale between monarchy and slavery. Between
these extremes of excellence and helplessness, the degree of virtue to be
expected from people will vary with the circumstances. The "constitutional" politics of inclusiveness, and even an aristocratic community,
require only a degree of virtue as close to the monarchical end of the
scale as the differentiated unity of the city can withstand. The fact that
"constitutional" virtue does not measure up to the monarchical standard – the fact that citizens, for example, may only be able to understand
prudent judgments while not being able to make them for themselves –
does not rob it of its relative worth in Aristotle's eyes. However, such
worth as it has derives from its ranking in comparison with that higher
standard. Thus, although Aristotle is tolerant of the looser approximations of virtue achieved by most political communities, he cannot
embrace the notion that there is no higher order of virtue in principle
than that of which every human being is capable. He does not regard
prudence, for example, as the faculty of man *qua* man but only of the
rarest statesmen. Aristotle's endorsement of political community cannot
be severed from his concern with superlative virtue because superlative
virtue is the absolute standard from which the relative worth of political
community is derived.

For Aristotle, *both* the political community *and* monarchical rule are
sanctioned by nature. That is, both shared participation in ruling and
the exclusive rule of one are natural. The reasoning behind this understanding of the nature of political life is supplied by Aristotle's *Physics*,
where nature is understood both in terms of spontaneous self-movement
and as being analogous to the rational precision by which an artisan
produces things. In other words, natural phenomena are a mixture of
the spontaneous and the rationally constructed. Nature is characterized

not only by self-movement but by *techne* and *poiesis*. Extending this understanding of nature to political life, the natural realm of politics is accordingly a mixture of the self-government of political communities and the skills of monarchical statecraft through which prudent rulers "make people better." I have suggested how Aristotle, in contrast to Plato, resists the assimilation of political community to monarchical rule. But although Aristotle's argument cannot be driven to a purely monarchical outcome, it cannot be driven to a purely communitarian outcome either, because his conception of the naturalness of politics requires a mixture of the spontaneous and the technical dimensions (*Physics* 193a5–193b20).

Aristotle rejects the pre-Socratic understanding of nature as pure spontaneity or chance becoming because it cannot account for the forms and purposes of visible beings. Aristotle's discussion of nature tries to take account of both the rational causality typified by production (*poiesis*) according to art (*techne*) and the self-movement of living beings. He believes that a full account of nature must embrace both aspects. The danger of separating them, according to Aristotle, is illustrated by Sophists like Antiphon, who believe that nature (in keeping with our discussion of the pre-Socratics in the last chapter) is to be understood as the generative origin of visible beings. As Aristotle relates it, Antiphon illustrates the power and primacy of this invisible substratum over the visible forms it generates by depicting a bed left out of doors being overgrown by roots and ferns, back into which it slowly dissolves. The illustration suggests that nature as origination produces phenomena like artisans produce artifacts. Both products are equally conventional, a form stamped temporarily on the flux of becoming. Nature creates these forms like an artisan but also reabsorbs them into the flux, whence new forms temporarily emerge. The underlying irrationality of nature as becoming, extended to politics, encourages us to view statesmanship as the equally temporary stamping of conventional forms on the underlying instability of natural life.

Aristotle, by contrast, maintains that nature reveals itself in a way that is *analogous* to the arts but not quite so precisely as the stages of productive technique (*Physics* 199a10–20). For this reason, it is easier to envision the four causes (efficient, material, formal, and final) as being operative in, for example, carpentry, than in the growth of a flower.

In strictly natural growth, efficient cause is harder to separate out, and formal and final cause are harder to distinguish from each other. Moreover, whereas art has a perhaps limitless freedom to create new forms of production, nature is somehow held back from doing so. His riposte to Antiphon's bed being overgrown and reclaimed by the earth is that trees do not transmute into entirely new flora or into animals but recur permanently as trees; nor does a bed ever grow back from the earth. Nature, in other words, is not reducible to sheer becoming but is a blend of rest and motion, of body and form. So Aristotle resists the pre-Socratics' ontology of origination while at the same time he resists the opposite extreme of making nature synonymous with the rationally constructed. This latter point is perhaps less obvious because of the influence of Christian Aristotelians led by Thomas Aquinas, who, in Aristotle's name but in a fundamental distortion of his philosophy, erroneously assimilates final and formal cause to the efficient cause of God, the master artificer,[15] an assimilation of classical teleology to a fabricating act of divine will that, as I have earlier suggested, is then transferred by Machiavelli to the secular prince's conquest of nature and by Hobbes to the artificer of the social contract who remedies the defects of human nature. Although Aristotle likens nature to art in some respects in order to refute the pre-Socratics' emphasis on becoming, his analogy for nature in all respects, as I observed earlier, is that of a "doctor who heals himself" – an irreducible equipoise of generational substratum (the patient's sick body with its potential for health) and art (the doctor's medical expertise; [*Physics* 199b27–35]). Exactly the same equipoise informs his discussion of the comparative merits of community and monarchy: nature provides the human material with a sufficient capacity for virtue, while statecraft assists in its cultivation and shaping.

Beginning with Machiavelli and Hobbes, this Aristotelian equipoise falls apart. In terms of the *Physics*, one might say that the Antiphonian view of nature reemerges – and Antiphon also held a view of the city as a social contract based on self-interest often invoked as a precursor of Hobbes. In making this observation, of course, we must bear in mind the arguments made in Chapter 2 to the effect that modern materialism is not simply a revival of the pre-Socratics and Sophists, at least in terms

15 Thomas (1963) p. 124.

of how Plato and Aristotle understood them. For the modern Baconian, Hobbesian, and Newtonian conception of matter in motion cannot be precisely mapped with the primordialist ontology of the pre-Socratics and Sophists, where the "great motions" of nature's originary upsurges have the substantive content of a certain view of human excellence and one's natural entitlement to rule (the distinction made by the unnamed pre-Socratics in Book 10 of the *Laws*, echoed by Callicles, between what is just and noble by nature and what is just and noble merely by convention). The pre-Socratics' ontology also has direct implications for the city itself as a hale outgrowth of this underlying matrix of origination (echoed in Gorgias' endorsement of the somatic virtues of courage and manly prudence, as against the merely conventional virtues of justice and moderation), and even for the content of the works of the poets, led by Homer, whom Socrates regards as the founder of the other "motion-men," with his whole rich psychology of manly virtue, tragic fate, and agonistic nobility.

This whole substantive alternative account of human excellence is excluded from the modern physics of matter in motion, which reflects the fact that the material world has already been drained of its substantive qualities of enchantment, nobility, and glory by Augustinian Christianity's reduction of nature to sheer fallen matter. To reiterate an earlier observation: if there is a close precedent for the physics of matter in motion among the ancients, it would be the stricter atomism of Lucretius, in which there are no immanent qualities of grandeur and heroism of the kind I have attributed to the pre-Socratics' understanding of nature, and for whom the visible world is generated by the sheer, accidental "swerve" of one contentless atom into another. For Lucretius, the hedonism stemming from his materialistic view of life meant that a man should cultivate his pleasures in private and avoid the pain, violence, and stupidity of politics. The genius of liberalism beginning with Hobbes might be characterized as erecting a new theory of the just society on the very basis of this individuating ontology of motion. For Hobbes, nature is now conceived of as a field of forces whose accidental clashes generate visible phenomena. Human reason has no immanent connection with nature so conceived; it is a uniquely human tool whereby man can reconstruct his environment so as to tame it and secure himself from its treacherous reverses. Precisely the empty irrationality of nature makes it malleable to the structures that man's will imposes on it. For Hobbesian man as *homo faber*, to make something is to know it.[16]

Liberal political philosophers such as Hobbes upset the Aristotelian equipoise by reducing the understanding of nature to spontaneous self-movement alone and asserting man's capacity, transferred from the Abrahamic God, to turn against nature so conceived of and reconstruct this purposeless flux. Rousseau reacts against this purely technical mode of statecraft by evoking the spontaneous freedom and wholeness of the natural life, in contrast with the artificiality and alienation brought about by the modern bourgeois project with its burgeoning economic and scientific apparatus. This return to nature from civilization is developed by Hegel and the historical school as the return from the state as an artificially crafted contract to society as an underlying historical community. Now nature is seen as developing in history as the immanent mores, traditions, and contexts of agreement that precede the artificial, alienating, and atomizing imperatives of the bourgeois era with its social contract. On the face of it, the return to nature launched by Rousseau as the search for an individual and communal wholeness from which we can resist the juggernaut of materialistic modernity bears a general resemblance to Aristotle's preference for political community over the unrestrained productivity of the art of household management, and serves to recall that dimension of nature that is simply given and self-renewing and not reducible to mere material for human technique. By the same token, however, this return bypasses the whole dimension of Aristotle's account of nature stressing its resemblance to the causality most clearly exemplified by *poiesis* and *techne*, not only in physics but in politics. The communitarian reading of Aristotle echoes the Rousseauan conviction that, were man to be released from the bonds of the state and the technical reasoning that upholds it, his happiness would be free to flower. The point, however, is that not only the Hobbesian emphasis on technique cut adrift from its natural mooring but the Rousseauan emphasis on spontaneity bereft of rational construction are *both* distortions of what Aristotle meant by the naturalness of political life.[17]

16 Hobbes (1971) pp. 81–82, 115.
17 For attempts to adapt Aristotelianism to a broadened conception of contemporary community, consider Beiner (1983) pp. xiv–xv, 72–101; Gadamer (1975, 1976, 1983); Galstone (1980); and MacIntyre (1981). For a bracing dissent, see Yack (1984).

In Aristotle's view, although man inclines naturally toward virtue and cooperation, he does not do so spontaneously or automatically, or merely through the removal of external constraint. On the contrary, laws and punishments are required to force recalcitrant people away from their equivalently powerful inclination toward vice. Education is also required, promoted by the regime, to further condition a receptive human nature in the direction of virtue, analogous to how a sculptor or a gardener both bring out the inner potential of the natural material they work with. Virtuous statecraft is therefore a kind of "making" or construction that fulfills human nature's potential by enabling it to resist its lower impulses and pursue its higher end. For Aristotle, then, although politics cannot be assimilated to production and art, neither are the latter simply alienating and restrictive. Politics are "natural" in the Aristotelian sense because they are always moving, in response to circumstances prudently assessed, between the freedom of self-government and the authority of statesmanship.

ARENDT ON THE HOUSEHOLD AND THE COMMUNITY

I am arguing in this book that modernity's emphasis on individualism and acquisition is not simply the reversal of the classical preference for community and virtue or a return to the dissident ancient tradition of Sophistry and materialism, but the regrounding of statecraft in a new ontology. An example of this misunderstanding is Hannah Arendt's well-known argument in *The Human Condition* in which modernity as typified by thinkers including Hobbes and Adam Smith is to be seen as reversing Aristotle's priority of the *polis* over the household – of the community over economic productivity and private life – leading to the replacement of the political by the social and the conversion of government into economic management and the promotion of private property.[18] Although unexceptionable in broad outline, and only one aspect of a book of considerable brilliance, her argument with respect to Aristotle misses the nuances that go to the heart of what is distinctive about the new science of politics.

In the first place, Arendt makes too sharp a distinction between the *polis* as the source of all communality, deliberation, and civic virtue

18 Arendt (1996) pp. 32–33.

and the *oikos* as the sole preserve of economic productivity and private individualism.[19] When Aristotle famously argues that man is by nature a political animal who fulfills himself through deliberation about the meaning of the just, the noble and the advantageous, he says that this teleological activity takes place "in cities *and households*" (my emphasis), a detail often overlooked in the communitarian reading (1257a17–18). As we earlier observed, only in Aristotle's first presentation of the household as one of the archaic and subpolitical associations that go to make up the fully evolved *polis* is its role reduced to material and reproductive necessity. Once the household is considered as a part of the city, it too is ennobled. In the second presentation, the relationship between father, mother, and children is based more on deliberation than on compulsion or the mere assertion of patrimonial authority, and the virtues of character that the family enshrines and cultivates in children pass straight on to the role of family members as citizens deliberating on the common good. To be sure, Aristotle does present the second version of the family ennobled by its membership in the city as analogous to a small community that is a blend of the republican and the monarchical. The husband is to persuade his wife as to the correctness of his opinions, rather than simply force her obedience, and the same is true of the relationship between parents and children. In both cases, the subordinate partners only need to acquire correct opinion, not rigorous knowledge (1259a37–1260b8). Nevertheless, the husband's persuasion of his wife and the parents' persuasion of their children is an appeal to their capacity for reasoned assent, not the simple exertion of force. The family is like a political community in which the offices do not rotate. However, this patriarchal monarchy of the household, based on the capacity of women and children to actualize their own potentiality for virtue, is diametrically opposed to the bad version of household management that is tantamount to a master's rule over the household's members as if they were mere slaves. The family has its own teleology. It is not reducible to the realm of mere life – the life of material necessity – as opposed to the good life of the *polis unless* it is perverted by being given over to the aim of open-ended productivity and acquisition, although Aristotle is clear that a modicum of material wealth is

19 Arendt (1996) pp. 12–13, 24–29.

necessary if citizens are to have the leisure for their two highest ends of politics and philosophy.

In addition to overlooking the teleology of the *oikos*, Arendt also overlooks Aristotle's argument that *oikonomia* is not merely a subpolitical unit – our private bourgeois or nuclear family – but, more important, a regime-level principle whose claim to teleological primacy over the *polis* is, as we have seen, no simple matter to displace in unequivocal favor of the *koinonia politike*. Finally, in her excessive dichotomization of the household and the community, Arendt imports into her vision of the ancient *polis* a Heideggerian existential stance of "risk." For Aristotle, however, politics is not about seeking authenticity through making a resolute stand amidst Being. It is, at its best, a rational conversation about how to make the proper choices among the ranked ends of the moral and intellectual virtues. Its primary aim is not community for its own sake, the prediscursive being-with-one-another-in-the-world of Heidegger's existential anthropology of Dasein that he locates in the archaic, prephilosophic *polis*. On the contrary: for Aristotle, political deliberation is inherently controversial, always potentially divisive, and capable of boiling over from heated argument into violence and insurrection. Only gregarious animals like bees (1253a) have the kind of sheer immanent communality romantically read back into the *polis* by Arendt from Heidegger.

Hobbes does indeed, on a massive level, invert Aristotle's priority of the city over the household and apply the art of household management to society through the construction of the social contract and the leeway that it grants to individual self-enrichment. However, it is not Aristotle's art of household management that Hobbes erects – not even Aristotle's view of the incorrect art of household management, which he identifies with the excesses of hedonism and which can culminate in tyranny, either within a city or by a city over other cities. For Hobbes, by contrast, the art of economic productivity entailed by a properly constructed social contract has been totally drained of Aristotelian teleological content. It is a contentless method, stemming from the priority of efficient cause over all the other causes, for the imposition of effectuating will on the purposeless fodder of nature, inherited from Machiavelli by way of Bacon. As for the virtues Aristotle argues might first be nurtured in family life, they are fine with Hobbes, but politically irrelevant, mere private avocations. People may enjoy private life and property however they wish in "recompense" for the Sovereign's absolute authority,[20] as long as they do not presume to be entitled to a role in public deliberation, the exclusive purview of the Sovereign, the de-eroticized tyrant who methodically crushes the vainglorious.

Whereas Heidegger and Arendt romanticize "the Greeks" by conflating Aristotle's view of the *polis* with sheer, spontaneous historical communality, Hobbes knowingly and deliberately attributes to Aristotle the view that Aristotle explicitly repudiates, that men *are* gregarious animals like bees, so as to deny Aristotle's frank recognition of the dangers of political deliberation boiling over into violent strife and thereby present him as naive, the better to arrogate to Hobbes's own political science the claim of unique insight into man's natural contentiousness. Aristotle wants to guide civic deliberation away from violence by the promotion of reason as the arbiter of debate.[21] Hobbes wants to crush civic deliberation altogether on the grounds that in reality it always leads to violence, especially when the ambitious can dress up their power seeking in the meretricious garb of Aristotelian claims to superior prudence, "wit," and nobility of character.

THE GLOBAL HOUSEHOLD

Do Aristotle's reflections on the tension between the monarchical principle, including the art of household management, and the political community resonate with us today? I would argue that the competition between them first explored by Aristotle has never vanished from human affairs and lives on unabated or even intensifying in the twenty-first century. The thinkers and statesmen of liberal democracy at its inception – including Locke, Montesquieu, and the American founders – tried to follow Aristotle's prescription for a "mixed regime" steering a middle way between the extremes of tyranny and mob rule, although as we consider at length in Chapter 7, that classical republican prescription was heavily filtrated and transformed through Machiavelli's new political science. At the same time, however, the age-old pattern of patrimonial authority has remained vibrant in many regions of the world. Its power has been compounded by the nondemocratic version

---

20 Hobbes (1971) p. 202.
21 I discuss Hobbes's knowing distortion of Aristotle in detail in the Conclusion.

of modernization launched by Hobbes, which harnesses Machiavelli's call for the conquest of nature to an authoritarian and rationalistic monarchy that gives its subjects the right to acquire property and prosper through commerce in exchange for yielding all political authority to the Sovereign, in effect a modernizing version of the art of household management.

Although frequently endangered by war, civil strife, and economic reversals, the Enlightenment's best child, liberal democracy, inaugurated by America and spreading throughout North America, the Old World, and outposts beyond, has endured with impressive success. Although it did not, strictly speaking, endorse Aristotle's contention that economic wealth should be employed wholly for the pursuit of the highest human excellences ("politics and philosophy"), it did at least agree that a virtuous character was required both for economic success and sound democratic politics. In its noblest version, liberal democracy never viewed the purpose of individual rights as the exclusive and limitless pursuit of property. Instead, our natural freedom as individuals was viewed as the basis for a number of rights and opportunities including religious tolerance, liberal education, political participation, family life, aesthetic cultivation, and freedom of speech. Property rights were but one tangible dividend of this underlying emphasis on our natural liberties as citizens of self-governing communities.

In the postcommunist and globalizing age through which we are now living, however, the household pattern of authority appears to have made a roaring comeback at the regime level. Large-scale multinational and geographic empires like China and Russia appear to be employing the art of household management to create enormous centralized and repressive security regimes "owned" by dictatorial and oligopolistic elites which at the same time generate open-ended economic maximization that in some cases rivals the West. These emerging world powers are surrounded by a constellation of more or less illiberal, authoritarian oligarchies in which "sovereign wealth funds" comprise one of the largest sources of capital in the global economy. The disturbing implication, its final outcome too distant to forecast, is that it may be possible to combine economic maximization with an illiberal regime, or, what is saying the same thing, that the connection between economic prosperity and the civic virtue of free self-governing peoples may be tenuous, historically fragile, and only one possible combination among others.[22] Perhaps now more than ever, therefore, Aristotle's warning that *oikonomia* and its hierarchical structure of despotic technical management might swallow up the political community should engage our most sober reflection.

22 On this traditional connection, consider Newell (1994) and (2004).

IV

TYRANNY AND THE SCIENCE OF RULING IN XENOPHON'S POLITICAL THOUGHT

Before properly entering into the complex relationship between Machiavelli's modernism and a certain dimension of Christianity limned in previous chapters, we need to complete our examination of his relationship to the classical tradition in its own right by turning to the one classical thinker and Socratic who perhaps comes closest to anticipating the modern project launched by Machiavelli. This chapter examines Xenophon's lengthy and explicit exploration of the possibility that the best regime might be that of a monarch possessing what Aristotle terms "superlative virtue," undertaken through his pseudo-history of Cyrus the Great.[1] Whereas, as we have seen in the previous chapters, this monarchical claim is muted by Plato and Aristotle for the sake of the political community, Xenophon goes much further than either of them in jettisoning the claims of republican self-government in favor of an open endorsement of rational, benevolent absolutism. Hence, Xenophon's *Education of Cyrus* can be regarded as his monarchical utopia, a direct riposte (as noted by later Hellenistic, Roman, and Renaissance commentators) to Plato's republican utopia, the *Republic*.[2] As I argue, the *Education of Cyrus* is the full elaboration, in the form of a utopian historical narrative, of the prescription for reforming tyranny into "leadership" set forth by Simonides as he is depicted by Xenophon in the *Hiero*.

---

1 For a discussion of Xenophon's pseudo-historical method, consider Tatum (1989); Breitenbach (1966) pp. 1708–1718; Barker (1951) p. 99; Delebecque (1957) pp. 384–385; Higgins (1977) p. 44.
2 See Athenaeus *Deipnosophists* 504F–505A; Aulus Gellius *Attic* Nights 14.3.2–4. See also the discussion by J. S. Watson in his "Bibliographical Notice of Xenophon" prefacing his translation of *The Cyropaedia or Institution of Cyrus* (1880) p. xvi.

ROADS TO THE *EDUCATION OF CYRUS*:
THE DISTINCTIVENESS OF XENOPHON'S
POLITICAL THOUGHT

It is a commonplace regarding ancient political philosophy that it has no relevance for us today because the Greeks had no experience of large-scale societies and governments like our own. According to this view, because the ancient Greeks lived in small city-states, they idealized this particular kind of government as the best one in principle for all places and times.

A passing familiarity with ancient Greek philosophy and history dispels this assumption. In the first place, even the smaller of the city-states were probably too large to match the prescriptions for the best regime elaborated by Plato or Aristotle – to say nothing of their political, educational, economic, and religious practices. Plato's and Aristotle's contemporaries in Athens generally thought pretty well of their city's military and cultural achievements past and present, but it is far from clear that the philosophers shared this view. The Platonic Socrates rather starchily refuses to concede that the great Pericles knew the art of ruling as well as Socrates himself – a seeming absurdity that has his interlocutor Callicles spluttering with incredulous indignation – while praise for Athens is conspicuously absent from Aristotle's *Politics* when it comes to discussing even relatively virtuous regimes (as opposed to a segment devoted to Sparta).[3]

Even more significant, however, is the fact that the ancient Greeks were entirely familiar with large-scale alternatives to the polis. In Book 3 of the *Politics*, for instance, Aristotle mentions commercial leagues that had been formed by various peoples for the purpose of promoting and regulating trade. Aristotle's rejection of such large-scale authorities as a proper regime principle stems not from a lack of awareness that they existed but from the fact that commerce is one of the concerns of the household – the sphere of life including family relations and the

---

3 Although naming Pericles as an example of a prudent statesman in the *Nicomachean Ethics* (1140b6–40), in general he views the Athenian democracy as a decline from the laws framed by Solon. The Athenians' empire, he writes, "gave them a great opinion of themselves, and they chose inferior men as popular leaders when respectable men pursued policies not to their liking" (*Politics* 1274a11–20). This assessment is rather close to that of Thucydides, who viewed Pericles' successors as placing their own self-interest ahead of what was best for the city. See the discussion of Thucydides later in the chapter.

production of material goods (hence our term "economics"). As we considered in Chapter 3, however valuable and necessary, the concerns of the household must be circumscribed by, and subordinate to, the nobler and more important concerns of the political community. If that is the case, then even the private relations within the household itself will be raised and ennobled beyond mere material survival and reproduction and act as an incubator for the virtues needed by citizens. For Aristotle, therefore, a commercial league or trading alliance is not a *political* authority, even if it is physically far larger and more populous than any actual city-state, because its justice, being confined to acquiring economic wealth, is merely contractual (*Politics* 1280a34–1280b29).

The Greeks were also aware of a far more imposing and successful example of large-scale political authority, however, one that was no mere trade association but had apparently worked out complex institutional arrangements for every aspect of human association. This was the Persian Empire, an enormous regime embracing millions of people from dozens of different nationalities. The Greeks had fought off the Persian kings' attempts to add them to that empire, and this victory began the Greeks' own rise to the greatness of the classical era, but the thoughtful among them were far from despising the Persian alternative. On the contrary, they had frequent occasion to rue the comparison between their own fractious, small, and unstable regimes and what struck them as the awesome power and efficiency of the great multinational monarchy to the east. Xenophon begins the *Education of Cyrus* with this reflection (1.1–5).

Indeed, both the Platonic and the Xenophontic Socrates point to the Persian king as a kind of paradigm for what it would mean to know the art of ruling. Yet whereas Plato ultimately prefers some form of neighborly republic, Xenophon carries this exploration much further. The *Education of Cyrus* is a utopianized version of the Persian monarchy. Its main purpose is not historical accuracy, but rather to use the real-life example of an apparently successful large-scale political system to flesh out the precepts of good government on the level of principle. As presented by Xenophon, Cyrus takes the principle of the *oikos* – the household with its private and economic concerns – and expands it until it becomes the basis of the regime itself, swallowing up the polis. His empire is a gigantic household ruled by him, embracing the millions of households of his lieutenants and subjects.

According to Castiglione, whereas Plato is the authority on the perfect republic and Cicero the authority on oratory, Xenophon is the authority on the perfect monarch.[4] What distinguishes Xenophon from the other classical writers on government, and what Machiavelli (as I argue) found so congenial about his writings, is his lengthy and candid exploration of princely ambition as the vehicle for founding stable and prosperous political orders.[5] Xenophon's distinctive approach to princely ambition and rule is clear in a general way from the division between those of his works that focus on Socrates and those that focus on Cyrus. For Xenophon, Socrates and Cyrus are the exemplars, respectively, of the philosophic life and the excellence attainable by statesmanship. This is not an absolute distinction. The Socratic writings certainly concern politics, and philosophy is not wholly absent from the "princely" writings. However, the division can be made in the following sense, and it is characteristic of Xenophon's way of presenting the relationship between politics and philosophy. In Plato's dialogues, the figure of Socrates dominates the investigation of the meaning and satisfactions of political virtue. Whereas Socrates is most often depicted conversing with well-born youths and political aspirants, even well-known politicians like Critias and Alcibiades are shown that Socrates' own way of life might clarify their yearnings and deficiencies. As we observed in Chapter 2, in the *Republic*, Socrates never actually meets Glaucon's challenge to prove that justice pursued entirely for its own sake is preferable to tyranny, but he does make a convincing case that philosophy is. Because, according to Socrates, a devotion to philosophy assimilates the passions leading to injustice, an education in philosophy is thus shown to perform a signal service to civic virtue.

Xenophon, by contrast, wishes to allow political excellence – the talent of extraordinary statesmen and generals – to unfold in its own dimension, unencumbered by the philosophic alternative. An episode from the *Education of Cyrus* illustrates this difference. There, the archetypal ruler Cyrus encounters the archetypal philosopher Socrates only by the shadow of the latter's absence. Tigranes, a young Armenian who had once been "intimate" with a Socrates-like "sophist," transfers his affections to the great conqueror Cyrus when Armenia falls to his

4 Castiglione (1959) p. xi.
5 Consider Wood (1964) pp. 42–47, 50–60.

forces. Cyrus punishes the young man's father, the king of Armenia, who had executed this sophist for alienating his son's affections from their household, by stripping the father of his autonomous authority. In this way, Cyrus's monarchy effects a reform of the tyrannical kind of politics that allows a philosopher to be put to death (3.1.14, 3.1.23–24, 3.1.39–43). (A tyrannical action of which democracy is also capable, because the actual Socrates was also condemned in part for alienating sons from their fathers.) We do not know from Xenophon's narrative, however, whom Tigranes would have preferred between Cyrus and the sophist if the sophist had lived. Socrates and Cyrus and the ways of life they embody touch. They never – like the two components of the Platonic philosopher-king – coincide. Nor is it obvious whom Xenophon himself prefers between Socrates and Cyrus.

Indeed, if there is a single premise that explains the distinctiveness of Xenophon's political thought, it is his doubt whether the peaks of human achievement can coexist in a single person. In other words, he doubts the doctrine of the unity of virtue often associated with the Platonic Socrates.[6] Like Aristotle and in contrast to Plato, Xenophon appears to believe that the virtues – particularly political excellence – cannot be assimilated to philosophic virtue but should be explored and accounted for in their heterogeneity. For Aristotle, however, and notwithstanding his tortuous acknowledgment of the claims of superlative virtue that we traced in the last chapter, the heterogeneity of the virtues has the primary political consequence of bolstering the claims of republican communities to be able to govern themselves and resist the assimilation of citizen virtue to the Platonic science of monarchy. For Xenophon, by contrast, the political virtues appear to reach their fullest development in a supremely able – but honor-loving, nonphilosophic – monarch. Monarchy without philosophy and heterogeneity without republicanism: this, broadly formulated, is what makes Xenophon's point of departure for assessing the varieties of rule so distinctive, although, as we will see, his assessments are not inflexible.

The *Education of Cyrus* is Xenophon's most sustained investigation of princely rule, a monarchical utopia as opposed to the republican utopias of Plato and Aristotle. It can be situated within Xenophon's writings by considering two other works, each of which provides a sort

6 Irwin (1977) pp. 86–90.

of prologomenon to it – the *Hiero* and the *Oeconomicus*. I will begin
with the *Hiero*. It depicts a dialogue between the "wise man" Simonides
and Hiero, tyrant of Syracuse. On the face of it, the *Hiero* provides a
more convincing critique of tyranny than Book 9 of the *Republic* (with
which it has a number of parallel passages). For although the *Republic*
presents a philosopher trying to persuade a politically inexperienced
young man of the evils of a life which the philosopher has never experienced, in the *Hiero* the tyrant himself tells a knowledgeable man of
the world – as it were, from the horse's mouth – how wretched tyrants
are. As it transpires, however, Hiero begins by depicting a tyrant of
what I have earlier termed the garden variety – a devotee of bodily
hedonism (*Hiero* 1.10). Hiero believes this is how the average person
thinks of tyranny, and perhaps he thinks, therefore, that this rather
vulgar satisfaction can be made to seem unattractive to a sensible and
accomplished man like Simonides. For Hiero is wary of Simonides as
a critic or possibly even as a rival. He respects Simonides not only
for being wise but for being a "real man" (*aner*) – an honor seeker –
and suggests that Simonides may not remain in private life forever (1.3).
Hiero also believes that Simonides envies his ability to gratify his friends
and harm his enemies. In general, Hiero distrusts "the wise . . . lest they
plot something" threatening to his rule, a danger also noted by Machiavelli, as we saw in Chapter 2, in his discussion of the advisors to princes
with his suggestion that a prince who is dependent on a counsellor may
lose his throne to that advisor. Upon consideration, therefore, the *Hiero*
may prove to be less persuasive than the *Republic* about the undesir-
ability of tyranny, because Hiero is so unwilling to endanger or part
with it that he will mount an elaborate stratagem to conceal its full
satisfactions.

In characterizing the tyrant as a hedonist, Hiero aims to convince
Simonides that there is no pleasure the private citizen does not enjoy
more successfully than the tyrant. A private citizen, he argues, can
enjoy the pleasures of sight, sound, smell, and taste without the tyrant's
burdens of ruling and the tyrant's risk that overindulgence will dull
his future appetites. Simonides is skeptical of these arguments, but
Hiero more or less holds his own (1.11–12). However, when Hiero
tries to apply the latter argument to sexual pleasure – the tyrant gets so
much sexual satisfaction that he loses the keenness of erotic longing –
Simonides laughs in open mockery (1.27–31). For tyrants, Simonides

retorts, have a manifest advantage over private citizens in "having intercourse with the fairest they see" – their power to get their own way.
Now that the distinct advantages of tyranny are beginning to come to
light, Simonides reveals that he has known all along that tyrants do
not care much about bodily hedonism but do care about "honor" and
the capacity to execute "great enterprises." It is these masterful qualities that distinguish the few "real men" (*andres*) from the multitude of
"human beings" (*anthropoi*) who live like "beasts" for the satisfaction
of bodily desire (2.1, 7.3). Whereas Plato has the wise man Socrates
protect Glaucon from the allure of tyrannical "great enterprises" by
reducing the depiction of tyranny to a life of debauchery, Xenophon
has the wise man Simonides force the tyrant, who has adopted the same
depiction of the tyrant as we encounter in Book 9 of the *Republic* as
protective camouflage, to come clean about tyranny's real allure.

Simonides' accurate characterization of the tyrant's motives forces
Hiero to be more candid about the truly troubling aspects of his life. His
omissions of the compensating advantages are correspondingly more
revealing. The most revealing thing Hiero does is to compare his erotic
relationships with his relationship to the city as a whole. Having failed
to convince Simonides that his passionate longing (*eros*) was dulled by
too much gratification, Hiero now says that what he really wants is
friendship (*philia*) from a "willing" partner. Put another way, he pur-
ports voluntarily to enlist in precisely that effort to moderate eros into
philia that the Platonic Socrates urges on the utterly skeptical Callicles.
Whereas the *Gorgias* depicts the wise man urging a therapy for moderating eros to a skeptical proto-tyrant, the *Hiero* depicts a tyrant prone
to embrace this therapy before a skeptical wise man. Hiero claims that
he would like to be loved in return not only by his beloved but by his
subjects (1.33–38, 7.5–8, 8.1, 4.1). However, because they fear him or
want to curry favor, he can never trust their profession of friendship.
The tyrant can never know whether he is loved for himself and must
be ever on his guard against the flatterers and conspirators who sur-
round him. (Again, Hiero's depiction of his own lot closely parallels
the Platonic Socrates' depiction of the tyrant's misery in the *Republic*.)
The life of "citizens" in "the cities" is thus far preferable, Hiero argues,
to tyranny. For "even the cities," he observes, "do not fail to notice
that friendship is the greatest good." What is more, the city's laws provide every man with security – with a "bodyguard" of laws – because

the laws forbid everyone equally from harming anyone else (3.3, 4.3, 6.10). As for the poor tyrant, unloved and unsafe, he might as well hang himself.

As Simonides wryly notes, the fact that Hiero has achieved and maintained this, by his own argument, most dangerous of stations is convincing evidence that he prizes the honor it bestows more than he fears the dangers and difficulties it entails (7.1–2). Plainly Hiero has omitted some compensating advantages likely to postpone his suicide indefinitely. Hiero had remarked that taking something from an "unwilling" enemy was to him "the most pleasant of all things." Although he meant to contrast this with the friendship of a "willing" partner, in the course of describing the reciprocity of friendship, he admits that the "most pleasant" moments of erotic pleasure come during the "fights and quarrels" on the beloved's part (1.34–35). It is not so clear, therefore, that Hiero would really prefer the reciprocity of friendship with his lovers and subjects to the unqualified possession of them to do with as he pleases or even to the struggle he may face in getting his way (1.32–33).

Moreover, the tyrant possesses additional advantages over the citizen in pursuing erotic fulfillment. When Hiero says that "even the cities do not fail to notice" the value of friendship, we sense that, in his view, the life of citizenship is by no means more conductive to making friends than the tyrant's life, if as much so. There are two reasons for this. First, even family ties, which Hiero considers to be the "firmest" friendships, must, he says, be "compelled by law" to follow the "inclination of nature" (3.7.9). For example, cities protect the right of husbands to slay adulterers (3.3). If, as this suggests, even the strongest natural ties require a degree of political – nay, tyrannical – enforcement, the tyrant with his absolute authority is much better equipped than a private citizen to keep his friends and relatives in line. The need to enforce even private erotic and familial ties is illustrated in the *Education of Cyrus* when Tigranes' father, in justifying his execution of the Socrates-like sophist for alienating his son's affections, compares it to a husband justly killing his wife's seducer (3.1.39). If even ordinary family life in a city where the laws provide all men with a "bodyguard" can only be maintained through such draconian incursions, how much in accordance with nature are civic and family life at all? Second and more important, Hiero omits to mention the vastly superior resources that a tyrant possesses compared with a citizen to gratify his friends and win their loyalty by benefits and honors. After all, his rule can draw on the resources of an entire city to maintain his personal household. Socrates argues in the *Republic* that the tyrant's limitless power to reward his friends and harm his enemies irrespective of their virtue, extolled by Glaucon in his evocation of the perfectly unjust man, is one of his central character flaws. The *Education of Cyrus*, however, shows that this tyrannical power might also be used to reward merit. Cyrus's grandfather Astyages, although the king of Media by hereditary descent, rules as a tyrant and "master" without legal restrictions (1.3.18). He is thus able to lavish gifts and honors on his grandson and, in his affection for Cyrus and recognition of his talents, raises Cyrus above his own son and legitimate heir (1.3.13–14). In this way, it would seem that not only a political community but a tyrant can rise above the love of one's own – in the case of Astyages, a father's ordinary attachment to his son – fuelled by an appreciation of the superior merit of a youth he loves more. Capricious? Yes. Unjust? Not necessarily. Cyrus learns from this egregious favoritism, which would have been promptly suppressed in his Persian homeland with its strict code of republican equality, how to win his subjects' friendship with a skillful mixture of a "master's" generosity and recognition of merit with his capacity to inspire fear.

It is not that Hiero is lying, then, when he enumerates the drawbacks of tyranny. They certainly exist. However, in omitting the compensations of tyranny and the drawbacks of citizenship, he gives a very one-sided diagnosis. Hiero's belief that Simonides is "jealous" specifically of his "supreme power" to benefit his friends and crush his enemies confirms our impression of Hiero's reluctance to expound fully these advantages of tyranny to a potential critic or competitor (*Hiero* 6.12).

Notwithstanding these omissions, Simonides gives Hiero some advice on how he "might" convert his unwilling subjects into "willing" ones and "friends." To clarify this advice, we should pause to note the distinctions between kinds of rule that Socrates makes in the *Memorabilia*. Monarchy is rule over willing subjects according to law, whereas tyranny is lawless rule over unwilling subjects (*Memorabilia* 4.6.12–13). However, when Socrates considers whether "knowledge" (*episteme*) might not be a more efficient and beneficent title to authority than conformity to law, an extra category is introduced – rule over willing subjects transcending the law. As Socrates presents it, knowledgeable rule pulls away from the republican standard of a community of shared rule under law and points instead toward a "household" where the monarch rules according to his own will over a ranked division of labor, every class doing the jobs for which its members are naturally best suited. This is the model of rule which Simonides recommends to Hiero.[7] If Hiero follows his advice, Simonides argues, his subjects will become loyal and happy members of a good master's household. Relieved of any need to concern themselves with public affairs, cared for, protected, and rewarded by the "leader" (Simonides delicately avoids conferring on this reformed tyrant the fully legitimate title of king [*basileus*]), they will be productive workers increasing their own wealth and the city's (*Hiero* 9.6.7,8; 10.3; 11.4,11,12,14). Whereas, as we saw in the previous chapter, Aristotle oscillates between the claims of law and the claims of knowledge because of his reluctance to endorse the monarchical art unreservedly, Xenophon has his Simonides prescribe it without reservation.

The dialogue ends, however, with no evident success on Simonides' part in persuading Hiero to undertake this reform. Although Hiero can doubtless see the advantages of a plan that would bolster his authority without constraining him with laws, we have the feeling that he does not quite want to renounce his unqualified possession of the city even if he would be better off doing so. Hiero's revelation of his own psychology and motives as a ruler suggest two explanations for this reluctance. Hiero may enjoy his recurrent triumph over the "fights and quarrels" of his subjects too much to allow their discontent to evaporate. He may prefer the recurrent sensations of risk and victory to the tranquillity of efficient political management. In this sense, his eros and thumos may enjoy their vital bellicosity too much to curtail themselves even for the sake of more secure power. (In a similar mood, Callicles tells Socrates that only a corpse would be content with being moderate [*Gorgias* 492].) Moreover, Simonides did not claim that the "real men" would be reconciled to the tyrant's rule by his advice, only the "human beings" (11.8,11,14). Since the "real men" are likely to provide, because of their ambition, the greatest threat to Hiero's power and, because of their love of honor, the kind of friends he would deem most worth having,

---

7 Thus, as Luccioni remarks, the *Hiero* is Xenophon's "development of an idea dear to Socrates" – that rule in the optimal sense should be based on knowledge, not law or custom (1947) p. 77. See also Strauss (1968) pp. 70, 75–79, and Wood (1964) p. 63.

Hiero may have concluded that Simonides' omission of them vitiates the rest of his advice. What honor or safety comes from dominating a herd?

The other route to the *Education of Cyrus* is provided by the *Oeconomicus*, which investigates the correct art of household management. Broadly cognate with Aristotle's discussion of the art of household management, the conclusions are rather different. How a gentleman – a "beautiful and good" man (*kalos kagathos*) – ought to manage his household is Xenophon's way of investigating the question: What is a gentleman? His life includes the responsibilities and honors of citizenship, and the responsibilities and pleasures of private or family life. Is one of these pursuits more important, or do they have a common aim? The perfection of the art of household management points to the example of Cyrus, who ruled a vast empire like a household divided into classes of farmers, artisans, and soldiers (*Oeconomicus* 4.4–16). Because of his extraordinary talent, courage, and splendor, Cyrus appears to be the exemplar not only of the life according to the good (in this context, the useful and pleasant) but of the beautiful or noble. Socrates, however, casts some doubt on identifying Cyrus with the perfection of gentlemanliness by recalling a visit to Cyrus made by the Spartan gentleman Lysander, who praised Cyrus as a "good" man (particularly with respect to his talents as a farmer) while omitting any comment on his nobility (4.17–25). The dialogue raises the question, in other words, whether the art of household management – employed in private life or as a monarchical replacement for the political community – can achieve the nobility of citizen life. This may help to explain why Kritoboulos seems initially surprised by Socrates' suggestion that so great a man as the king of Persia concerns himself with farming as opposed to an exclusive focus on the art of war. It suggests a lack of manly nobility (4.4).

But what exactly is the nobility of the life of citizenship? This side of the problem is taken up in Socrates' recounting of his conversation with the Athenian gentleman Ischomachus. Socrates appeared to have acquired from Ischomachus his interest in the art of farming as a guide for understanding gentlemanliness (7.2–3, 15.2–4). However, Ischomachus is also strongly attracted to the life of royal authority over "willing" subjects that Cyrus exemplifies (21.12). It is not clear, however, what the "noble" part of gentlemanliness would consist of either in monarchy or in a private household. For instance, Ischomachus compares his wife's supervisory position over his household with that of the "queen bee," apparently without reflecting that this suggests he has no specific function there himself and may, in effect, be a drone (7.32–40).[8] Moreover, Ischomachus describes his housekeeper in a way strongly reminiscent of Cyrus's characteristics in the *Education of Cyrus*. Like the housekeeper, Cyrus is continent about food, drink, and sex and aims at gratifying the rest of the household to win their honor (*Education of Cyrus* 1.3.9–14). Unlike the caricature of the tyrant in the *Republic* as a monster of Neronian excess, and much more like the disciplined and methodical prince Machiavelli will extol, Cyrus has a straitlaced aversion to overeating, drunkenness, and sexual passion. His eagerness to win people's honor by ministering to pleasures he himself does not share is prefigured in the *Education of Cyrus* when, as a precocious boy visiting his grandfather's court in Media, he cheekily takes over the duties of Astyages' steward at table, thrusting out the servant so that he can serve his grandfather himself (1.2.1, 1.3.4–5, 1.3.10, 1.4.1, 5.2.5–6,14, 5.1.12). Is the greatest king then nothing more than a kind of glorified housekeeper? Ischomachus resists this conclusion when he amends the view stated by Socrates in the *Memorabilia* that royal rule is indeed simply the extension of household management to larger numbers. Although he agrees with Socrates that ruling is the architectonic art – the knowledge "common to all actions" – he claims that to be a *royal* ruler requires in addition "education" and a "good nature" (*Oeconomicus* 21.2,5,8,11–12). The king cannot learn how to rule solely through instruction from an expert – as is the case with arts such as farming and smithing – but must possess a good natural character that has been well educated from early life. Royal rule, in other words, cannot entirely be assimilated to rule according to knowledge but requires an ethics of character development. Ischomachus' resistance to the complete identification of royal rule with household management throws his perplexity about the meaning of gentlemanliness into sharper relief: the gentleman is drawn to being something more than a citizen or the head of a private household, but the knowledgeable monarch toward whom his aspirations are drawn may not be a gentleman.

8 See Strauss (1970) p. 139.

The *Education of Cyrus* brings together and further develops the approaches to princely government explored by the *Hiero* and *Oeconomicus*. It uses an idealized, pseudo-historical account of the great Persian monarch to depict *ad seriatem* the formation and education of the perfect king's character, his rise to imperial power, and his administration of an empire that is a gigantic household embracing the millions of individual households of its subjects. As a king who transcends the law and rules according to "knowledge" (1.1.3), Cyrus perfects the model of rule that Simonides recommended to Hiero.

In this work, Xenophon also endorses the view he attributes to Ischomachus in the *Oeconomicus* that the monarch cannot learn how to rule through expert instruction alone but must also possess a good character and education. The meticulous education in civic virtue that the Persian youths receive under the republic enables Cyrus's natural love of honor and learning to flourish. At the same time, however, Xenophon confirms the low opinion of the republican way of life he attributes to Hiero by showing that even the best republic imaginable fails to satisfy the natures of its most talented and energetic citizens. Unlike "most cities" (1.2.2–3) – including even the comparatively virtuous example of Sparta – the Persian republic tries to supplement the protection provided for every citizen by the laws and the courage inculcated in the citizens to make them able to defend their country with a feeling of genuine friendship (*philia*) developed by their deliberations on and participation in public affairs. In Xenophon's pseudo-historical narrative, accordingly, the Persians have long ago abandoned the Spartan practices of teaching the boys to steal and discouraging them from conversing or expressing their opinions, lest these severities prevent a sentiment of civic friendship from taking root in their characters (1.6.27–34). The Persian Republic is Xenophon's rendition of the neighborly homogeneous republic recommended by Plato and Aristotle. It is ruled by a small, self-governing aristocracy whose citizens are rigorously educated to place the common good above the private, and it discourages economic productivity. On Cyrus's return from Media, however, where he spent his adolescence at the luxurious court of his grandfather, Cyrus subverts the Persian education by convincing his own generation of young citizens to cease pursuing virtue as an end in itself and instead use it as a means of acquisition through imperial expansion. Cyrus blasts the virtuous republic apart by throwing open the opportunity to rise in life to all its inhabitants, eventually even including the large mass of toiling commoners hitherto excluded from any kind of civic education or citizen participation (rather as if the Auxiliaries in Plato's *Republic* invited the Artisans to join them as comrades in the common cause of empire). In this way, Xenophon explores the possibility that an imperial monarchy could democratize opportunity and allow individual merit to override any injunctions to prefer the common good to one's own. The lesson Cyrus has learned in Media is that the individualism characteristic of the Median king and his privatized subjects can, by employing the skill and courage of the Persian education, acquire for each Persian of all classes "great wealth, happiness and honor" that they would otherwise never experience (1.5.8–12). We can already anticipate Machiavelli's partiality toward Xenophon among the ancients: an alliance between a prince and the common people based on material self-interest, a project for turning republican virtue outward as the fuel for imperial expansion and prosperity – these, as we will see, are hallmarks of *The Prince* and the *Discourses*, and references to "Xenophon's Cyrus" are woven by Machiavelli throughout his exploration of them.

CYRUS'S IMPERIALISTIC REVOLUTION

The action of the *Education of Cyrus* expands dramatically as foreign policy comes to the fore. Upon returning to Persia from his visit to his grandfather's court, Cyrus resumes the regular curriculum and reaches the age of military service. Years pass, and the Assyrian king forms a coalition of nations for war against Media. The Medes call on Persia to help defend their common region and, remembering Cyrus's precocious talents at his grandfather's court, ask to have him command the Persian army. The need for a strong commander to organize Persia's defenses enables Cyrus to assume a personal authority over the peers that would never be permitted during peacetime. For a decade, Cyrus has patiently resubmitted himself to the civic education, quietly waiting for just such an opportunity for his ambition. He seizes it to convince the other young men in the citizen class of the deficiencies he discovered in the Persian regime during his formative years at a tyrant's court (1.5.7–14).

Like Plato and Aristotle, Xenophon connects the transition from an inward-looking political community to an expansionist foreign policy with the stimulation of unbounded personal ambition at home, including the danger of tyranny. As Thucydides relates it in *The Peloponnesian War*, Athenian imperialism provided ambitious young men, above all Alcibiades, with the opportunity to thrust themselves to the forefront of democratic politics as the proponents of imperial expansion. Plato and Aristotle respond to this dilemma by prescribing a regime that forestalls such thrusting ambition by forestalling imperial expansion. Xenophon, by contrast, is posing the question: Instead of repressing the longing for mastery at home through an isolationist foreign policy, why not, on the contrary, discipline that tyrannical longing precisely *by* turning it outward, where it can seek a release through empire, enriching everyone back home regardless of class? In this sense, Cyrus is like an Alcibiades who receives a proper education from his earliest youth in republican virtue *before* embarking on the quest for empire, whereas the Platonic Socrates was compelled to work with the real Alcibiades' already corrupted longings and try to redirect them toward moderation of the kind one would find in a well-ordered regime other than Athens. In Plato's *Republic*, the transition from the moderation of the "city of sows" to the "feverish city" of imperialism is sparked by Glaucon's eros for glory and pleasure, an eros that is crushed in the imaginary best city by the thumotic education of the Auxiliaries and an inward-looking common good that avoids foreign entanglements. Xenophon is arguing, by contrast, that the rebellion of the timocratic Auxiliaries that in Plato's presentation eventually undoes the best regime might be forestalled by turning it outward; that their virtue might be disciplined and enriched *by* the project of imperial expansion.

Calling the peers together for an address, Cyrus tells them that virtue should not be practiced for its own sake but as a means for getting good things – "great wealth, honor and happiness." He compares virtue to an art or technique whose reward lies in its result. Hitherto, he says, the Persians have trained in virtue without applying it, "growing old and feeble" before they can taste its benefits. This makes no more sense than for a farmer to sow and tend his crop but never reap it. Cyrus remembers how the Medes used their arts to cultivate prosperity. He now wants the Persians to focus their military prowess on this Median goal, cultivating wealth through conquest and thereby living more pleasurably (1.5.8–10).

There is a problem, however. If the peers are wholeheartedly convinced that virtue is merely a means to pleasure, they might abandon their painful discipline at once, preferring this immediate gain in comfort to the merely presumptive future pleasure attending successful conquest. Cyrus realizes that the peers must retain their austere virtue if they are to succeed in winning wealth and glory abroad, but that the explicit conversion of virtue into an acquisitive technique might sap their will to practice it. (It is as if the Auxiliaries of Plato's *Republic* were immediately freed to enjoy the fleshpots of the Artisans' prosperous free enterprise zone. Why go to war when wine, partners, and song await downtown?) Cyrus resolves this dilemma by deemphasizing the Median goal of wealth facilitating pleasure in favor of the more Persian goal of glory – a glory to be achieved in the dangerous exploits of conquest leading up to the acquisition of wealth (1.5.12). Cyrus had learned as his grandfather's favorite to look on self-exertion and self-discipline as means to preeminent personal prestige, whereas the Persian peers have been educated to believe that their honor is inherent in conforming to the laws and serving the common good. Encouraging the peers to become "lovers of praise," to have an eros for praise, Cyrus now instills them with some of his own open-ended ambition. In this way, he hopes to dull the peers' perception of the contradiction between present pain and distant pleasure, giving them a motive for continuing hardihood.

This speech represents the first phase of Cyrus's revolution. The threat of war would in any event have brought about a temporary priority of the military aim of the Persian education over its domestic aim. Cyrus uses the paramountcy of war to lay bare the contradiction between these aims. Applying to virtue the criterion of means-end rationality, he liberates the young Persians' hardy competitiveness from the peacetime constraints of Persian law, directing these energies outward toward the goals of acquisition and prestige. In the *Education of Cyrus*, the success of the traditional Persian education, with its resultant stable self-government, stands or falls by the correctness of the regime's assumption that its austere public-spiritedness is truly naturally more rewarding than the selfish passions that Cyrus has now summoned forth – the core teaching of classical republicanism altogether, including that of Plato and Aristotle. In other words, the regime assumes that its education does not merely coerce but rather guides human nature toward its own fullest satisfaction. The young peers shatter this assumption by unhesitatingly accepting Cyrus's proposals, overturning their years of painstaking civic education in a trice. That Cyrus can subvert the republican ethos with a fifteen-minute speech is Xenophon's tacit speculation about just how naturally choice-worthy the common good is for its own sake.

Although Cyrus in one sense corrupts the Persian education by arguing that virtue is not its own reward, in another sense he fulfills the aims of that education to produce citizens of "surpassing nobility" more successfully than the republic had ever been able to. We recall from Chapter 3 that at just the point where he fully and explicitly defines true monarchy as the multinational empire of a man of supreme prudence governing according to the architectonic art, Aristotle draws back from this claim so as to endorse instead a self-governing aristocratic republic. Xenophon's *Education of Cyrus* fills that lacuna, taking off from precisely where Aristotle ends, tracing what would happen if a man of Alcibiadean ambition but properly trained in civic virtue were to burst the boundaries of the aristocratic republic precisely by acting on its claim to favor meritocracy. If Hegel is correct that the universalism of Socratic philosophy spelled the death of the polis by making a cosmopolitan state inevitable, the *Education of Cyrus* would seem to provide the speculative blueprint. With Xenophon's opening lament of the Greek city-states' ills and his idealization of Cyrus's world state, political philosophy and history come close to touching. For what begins as a monarchical utopia in the *Education of Cyrus* becomes reality as Alexander of Macedon leads his fellow youths out of their backward polis to conquer Persia, assuming the Cyrean role of universal monarch, just as Julius Caesar and Augustus Caesar will do later in subverting the Roman polis – charismatic imperialists and populists who, like Xenophon's Cyrus, clad themselves in the outward form of republican legitimacy as its restorer and rejuvenator.

To reiterate: the Cyrean revolution encourages the "career open to talent" (to use Napoleon's famous phrase) that the old republican education had always claimed to be based on because it claimed to breed the rule of the best. First as imperial commanders and later as heads of splendid households encompassing the provinces and fiefs of the empire, Cyrus's comrades excel at the noble and good in ways that were not

possible under the republican rule of law with its restrictions on outstanding personal achievement. The *Education of Cyrus* may also be
taken as Xenophon's critique of the view he attributes to Simonides that
a tyrant can convert, well along in his career, to a more efficient and
beneficent method of governing. The influence of Cyrus's education on
his character remedies the crucial defect in Hiero that may have prevented him from profiting from Simonides' advice. Cyrus learned about
the household form of rule in Media *without* losing the immunity from
hedonism acquired during his austere Persian education. As a ruler,
consequently, Cyrus has no erotic passion for the literal possession and
consumption of his household and subjects. His relations with his subordinates are untinged with the jealousy or suspicion that arise from the
competition for pleasures. Cyrus can be ruthless, as we consider more
closely in our examination of Machiavelli's reading of him. However,
he takes no pleasure (as does Hiero) in "fights and quarrels" with his
subordinates for their own sake apart from the cold-blooded goal of
expanding his power. He is more Oliver Cromwell than Caligula.

By resisting the conflation of political authority with a lover's jealous possessiveness, the perfect monarch is, in Xenophon's presentation,
psychologically distinct from tyrants as we usually encounter them and
bears little if any resemblance to the tyrant excoriated in Book 9 of
the *Republic*. Whether he is truly a king, however, or a new kind of
tyrant cloaked as or merged with a monarch remains an open question.
Whereas Socrates says in the *Republic* that, in the tyrant's disrupted
soul, eros usurps the role of reason and becomes the "factional leader"
of the desires by enflaming them (572e–573e), Xenophon presents Cyrus
as a man whose eros for limitless honor, thoroughly drained of other
erotic desires, conquers others by helping them to gratify their pleasures, guided by the art of architectonic management. Whereas for
Plato, reason should govern eros and thumos, in Cyrus, an eros for
honor employs both "knowledge" (the science of ruling) and thumos in
its service. Cyrus might be likened to the "noble nature" described in
Book 6 of the *Republic*, capable of the best and worst actions. His education through an exposure to both Persia and Media parallels the royal
myth in Plato's *Alcibiades I*, in which Socrates exposes the young man
to the two mother regimes of republic and monarchy. The difference
is that the Platonic Socrates hoped philosophy would assimilate Alcibiades' ambition. He begins by stimulating Alcibiades with the vision of

world rule, then brings him back to the polis now seen in light of the universal. By contrast, the young Cyrus receives a quasi-theological education from his father Cambyses that is partly Socratic but not explicitly philosophic. Meant primarily to instill political moderation, it does not stimulate an openness to the contemplative life. In founding his world order, Cyrus eschews philosophy per se in order to actualize a Socratically rational politics in which the execution of a "Socrates in Armenia" is avenged.

Is Cyrus, then, an unequivocally successful example in Xenophon's eyes of the perfection of the gentlemanly life that citizenship under law may reach for but cannot fully attain? Is his career meant to show a way of transcending the perplexities of Ischomachus? It might well seem so. Ischomachus had said that royal rule was a "divine" life (*Oeconomicus* 21.5.11–12). At the penultimate stage of his conquests, Cyrus's allies present him with a captive queen as his war prize (4.6.11, 5.1.6). Reputed to be the most beautiful woman in Asia, her name – Pantheia – means, literally, the "wholly divine." Her award to Cyrus thus seems to symbolize his crowning achievement.

Yet as Xenophon presents it, the cumulative answer to these questions remains tentative. This can be illustrated with several further observations from the *Education of Cyrus*. Cyrus's rule is likened by one of his lieutenants to that of a "king-bee" (5.1.24). We recall that Ischomachus' praise of his wife as the "queen-bee" raised the possibility that the gentleman is useless to his own household. The merging of king and queen-bee in Cyrus suggests this problem could be avoided by the extension of household management to kingship, which requires the exercise of political and military as well as economic skills. It requires the hardy virtues of the "real men" to bring about a world of pleasure and safety for the "human beings." This remedy does not dispose altogether of the possibility that royal authority is still comparable to the rather mundane managerial skills of a housekeeper, however – especially after the period of conquests is over and there is no more glory to be won. The air of hedonistic dissipation and laxness that overtakes Cyrus's government in his waning years points to this difficulty. Moreover, while a republic can replicate its way of life through its institutions, Cyrus, being a perfect monarch, could not be replicated – his sons were mediocre. As the *Education of Cyrus* draws to a close, the crisis of the succession throws the virtuous small republic with its emphasis on a high average level of virtue among all citizens into a retrospectively better light.

Furthermore, Cyrus's means of acquiring power may be hard to reconcile with "beautiful and good" conduct. He "is said," as Xenophon equivocally puts it (1.2.1), to have been heir to the Persian throne. As we will see in the next chapter, Machiavelli sets aside this more seemly account of Cyrus's royal birth in favor of Herodotus' depiction of Cyrus as a semibarbarized usurper who rose from "base origins." Yet even if Cyrus's royal lineage was not in doubt, this did not entitle him to subvert the laws of Persia or to usurp the authority of Astyages' heir Cyaxares. Cyrus is practiced in many deceptions unknown to earlier generations of Persian gentlemen. Although he initially tells the Persian peers, for example, that he is only interested in a defensive war against the Assyrian empire, he continues his conquests long after Persia's security from external aggression has been guaranteed. Publicly, Cyrus tells the peers that justice will be on their side in the coming war because they are defenders rather than aggressors (1.5.1). Immediately after this, however, in private conversation with his father, Cyrus expresses his contempt not only for the Assyrians but for his supposed allies the Medes and for other peoples poorly governed in comparison with Persia. It would be a "disgrace," he says, not to fight them all and reform their slothful, inefficient governments (1.6.8–9). Persia's institutions had been designed to make its citizens content with internal self-government and serving the common good. For Cyrus, they have become a standard for reform that he wants to make his banner for imperial conquest. There is something of (again) a Cromwell or Napoleon in his zealotry, his conviction that his glory will also serve the triumph of righteousness and reason among all nations. It is as if, instead of the timocrats collectively overthrowing the rule of the philosopher-kings in the *Republic*, one of the timocrats arose and made the rule of reason the basis for revolutionary reform and imperial expansion. The *Education of Cyrus* is a ten-book elaboration on that logical lacuna in Plato's best regime that we discussed in Chapter 2, the Platonic Socrates' exclusion of the possibility of an honor-loving tyrant arising directly from timocracy in the typology of regimes in Book 8.

In Xenophon's presentation of Cyrus's charismatic rise, numerous threats, half-truths, executions, and transportations take place in the background of Cyrus's marvelous rhetoric of peaceful reconciliation and his magnanimity toward those ready to surrender without a fight (4.4.5–6). Eventually the "real men" making up Cyrus's top command are as much in terror of him as the "human beings" whom they have conquered. Xenophon's use of accounts of Cyrus that clearly came *after* his rise to greatness and his success in inspiring millions with "fear" of him (1.1.5) must cause us to wonder to what degree an extraordinary conqueror can influence the reputation he leaves behind. Who knows what other crimes and usurpations formed the basis for the immense prestige of Cyrus in the mature stage of his life, when the accounts Xenophon drew on were presumably gaining wide currency? Machiavelli states the implication openly in chapter 6 of *The Prince* when, partly in reference to Cyrus as a rare example of an "outstanding" prince, he says that a ruler who uses enough force in the beginning of founding a "new order" will silence his enemies, dazzle the half-hearted, and shape a glowing account of himself for posterity.

Finally, it is doubtful whether the distance between Cyrus and his lieutenants permits the reciprocity between them necessary for genuine friendship based on a shared dedication to virtue, a hallmark of the gentleman's code. Xenophon vividly illustrates this problem when Cyrus's friend from boyhood and high lieutenant Araspas falls passionately in love with Pantheia, Cyrus's prize of war, to whom Araspas has been assigned as protector. In a dialogue with Araspas inspired by the beauty of the captive queen, Cyrus reveals the motive for his coldness by likening eros to an enslavement that makes us neglect our practical interests. After assuring Cyrus in their dialogue about the pitfalls of eros that he will not succumb to Pantheia's beauty, Araspas makes a play for the captive queen, who, repulsing him and highly indignant over this disrespectful treatment, complains to his master. Although Cyrus is not possessed by an erotic longing for Pantheia himself and behaves with perfect chastity toward her, as a political matter, he must treat Araspas' passion for the captive queen as a threat to the external majesty of his authority, reducing this once proud associate to a paroxysm of fear (6.1.31–41). As we see in the next chapter, when guided in our reading of this episode by Machiavelli, particularly enigmatic is the "disappearance," under several layers of murky intrigue worthy of *Smiley's People*, of Cyrus's former favorite.

A number of parallels with the episode of Cyrus, Araspas, and Pantheia suggest themselves. As we discussed in Chapters 1 and 2, Plato's

Socrates, in turning away from natural philosophy and the direct speech about being, is inspired by what he depicts as Diotima's teaching about eros, and he hopes that Alcibiades' natural eros for the beautiful and good will lead him to philosophy by way of civic virtue. However, Alcibiades' late and disruptive entrance in the *Symposium* at the height of his political preeminence blocks that ascent and calls it into question through his rivalry with Socrates for the possession of Agathon ("[the] Good" [*to agathon*]), symbolic of a rivalry between wisdom and power. In this case, the beauty of Pantheia (the "wholly divine") inspires an erotic longing for the beautiful in a young man. But it is Cyrus himself, a ruler rather than a philosopher, who blocks the erotic ascent in the name of a prudence guided by the art of ruling, a prudence that disavows a love of the beautiful. The Xenophontic debate about eros also recalls Homer's *Iliad*. There, Agamemnon and his ally Achilles vie over a captive woman, the flashpoint for Achilles' wounded honor and insubordination toward the king who has slighted him by seizing his war prize. In the *Education of Cyrus*, by contrast, a self-controlled monarch resists the erotic battle for prestige over a captive woman with an Achillean subordinate, instead crushing his eros through fear. Whereas for Plato the prospect for curing the Achillean man lies in philosophically grounded eros, for Xenophon it lies in efficient rule by a ruler whose eros for honor is undistracted by a love of the beautiful.

Especially when considered in the light of his coldness and his friendlessness, there is something indiscriminate and egotistical about Cyrus's "thirst" for the gratitude and honor of millions of people whom he never lays eyes on and not one of whom is in a position to earn his gratitude or respect in return (5.1.1). Cyrus's coldness (noted jokingly by his innermost circle) toward any particular erotic attachment is not, after all, the moderation of a citizen subordinating his desires to the common good, but the psychological means he has devised in himself to devote his talents undistractedly to what could be characterized as shameless pandering to the material needs of the "human beings." Whereas for the Platonic Socrates, lower erotic passions are assimilated by an eros for the Good, for Xenophon's Cyrus, they are assimilated by an eros for the universal and demotic love of "all men." As we see in the next chapter, Machiavelli makes use of the Pantheia episode, in ways both approving and disapproving, to develop his argument that a prince must resist the allure of eros – not only as it relates to his own passions, but in the broader sense of longing for the love of his subjects by believing that his eros for supreme honor is compatible with the service of the common good. Machiavelli weaves a dense layering of associations in which Scipio Africanus the Elder, the greatest Roman admirer of Xenophon's Cyrus, becomes, through his desire to enact the erotic ascent up Diotima's Ladder, the corrupter of the Roman republic and a wholly negative standard for either princely or republican government, a tableau we explore in detail in Chapters 5 and 6.

Cyrus's lack of restraint with respect to his eros for universal honor is prefigured by his obliviousness as a young man to any sense of awe or shame before the gods. As he tells his father Cambyses, he cheerfully regards the gods as "friends" who unfailingly reward ambitious effort like his own with commensurate success (1.6.6–36, 2.3.4). By contrast, Cambyses tries to moderate his son's ambitions by stressing that there is an inscrutable disjunction between human virtue and the gods' favor that a prudent ruler should bear in mind before undertaking too ambitious an enterprise (1.6.18,23–24,26,44–46). Cambyses' exchanges have parallels in Xenophon's depiction of Socrates, and his stress on the role of chance in the prospects for the success of virtue and wise rule is, as we have seen in previous chapters, in keeping with Plato's presentation of Socrates as well. This private conversation between the constitutional monarch and his son might suggest that, behind the insistence of the regime on conformity to the law, there is a deeper theological justification for the moderation it instills, one that reaches beyond what service to the common good requires and says something about the world at large. Cyrus, however, is confident that *techne* can overcome *tuche*. He compares an energetic general to a productive farmer, as if every human virtue were a means to human procurement, and as if a general's marshalling of force to destroy a foe were comparable to a farmer's cultivation of nature to yield produce while caring for the soil (1.6.18, 2.2.24–26). Cambyses observes in reply that even an energetic general may be thwarted by "a god," while he greets the comparison of generalship to farming with silence. It is as if, in Cambyses' view, the relation between man and the earth illustrates the disjunction between the cultivation of virtue and the nonhuman order especially clearly, an irreducible complex of art, nature's potential, and the cultivation of an outcome beneficial to humans but leaving the fecundity of nature unexhausted. Despite his admiration for royal rule, Ischomachus likewise remarks in the *Oeconomicus* that the gods do not unfailingly reward the diligence that prudent human beings display through farming and the other branches of household management (11.8). Ischomachus' doubts about the power of human skill over nature are of a piece with his doubts that possessing the nature of a ruler is synonymous with acquiring a skill, without the supplement of education and a good nature. Something about nature – be it chance, necessity, or the gods' inscrutable will – eludes the human capacity for planning and control. A prudent or even pious regard for this disjunction appears to be one of the traits that, in Xenophon's treatment, distinguishes a gentleman from a ruler like Cyrus. Xenophon reinforces these reservations about Cyrus's gentlemanliness by frequently likening his knowledge of ruling to feeding pigs, gelding horses, and other aspects of the herdsman's art (*Education of Cyrus* 1.1.2, 2.1.28–29, 7.5.62–65).

As the preceding reveals, Xenophon's exploration of the advantages of an imperial monarchy through his pseudo-history of Cyrus the Great has mixed results from his own viewpoint. On the one hand, he allows the ambition for limitless rule to unfold in all its grandeur, appearing to overshadow republican virtue with its severe restrictions on personal achievement. When allowed to run its course, however, the pseudo-history of Cyrus's rational and benevolent despotism does not prove, in spite of its manifest advantages, to be preferable in every respect to the life of citizen virtue. Initially glorious and optimistic, the *Education of Cyrus* ends, as is widely noted, in a depressing atmosphere of corruption stemming from the avarice, dissipation, and self-absorption of Cyrus's subjects and lieutenants.[9] In this way, the imperial monarchy pays a price in the long run for its freedom from republican or philosophical moderation. Xenophon wishes to elaborate the optimal potentiality of princely virtue for stable and prosperous rule, but also its drawbacks. As we see in the next chapter, this open-minded but ambivalent assessment is what makes Xenophon both a suitable precedent and a suitable foil for Machiavelli's diagnosis of princely rule.

9 See the detailed discussion in Nadon (2001) as well as Breebart (1983) p. 126 and Higgins (1977) pp. 57–59.

THE PELOPONNESIAN WAR AND THE THUCYDIDEAN
CONTEXT

Before turning to Machiavelli and the beginning of the modern transvaluation of tyranny and statecraft, let us recall the central problem, according to the classics, of civic pedagogy as we have explored it in our consideration of Plato, Aristotle, and Xenophon: How is the potential tyrant to be converted to an ally of justice and good government? How do we make a clear distinction between encouraging a constructive ambition to serve the common good and giving leeway to tyrants to emerge, perhaps disguised in the first instance as benefactors? How might we find a middle ground whereby a man's belligerent impulses and love of fame might be educated, sublimated, and directed away from tyranny and unprovoked aggression into the honor that comes from serving one's fellow citizens in a republic of laws or as a virtuous monarch?

As we began to consider in Chapter 1, the Platonic and Aristotelian way of engaging this dilemma begins with – but also marks a considerable modification of and departure from – the poetic tradition, which was ambivalent about this very issue. For example, Homer in a sense holds out Achilles as the eternal model for Greek youth. However, Achilles was deeply insubordinate, withdrawing his services from his allies during the Trojan War out of a purely personal vendetta against their leader Agamemnon based on a fight over a woman and other perceived slights and insults. On the other hand, when Achilles does return to the fray, motivated by yet another personal bond, his desire to avenge the death of his best friend Patroclus, he is indispensable to the Trojans' defeat. Whether disloyal or loyal to his allies, his incentive is always a personal erotic tie and wounded pride (Homer *Iliad* 1.120–285; 18.20–30, 85–125, 145–154; 22.260–272, 244–360).[10]

Homer and the other poets take the view that, although tyranny and insubordinate ambition are dangerous, they cannot simply be dispensed with or in all cases disparaged. The problem with consistently denouncing tyrannical aggressiveness is that the tyrant and the leading citizen might, at bottom, share some of the same darkly hubristic, combative qualities. The chorus in Sophocles' play *Oedipus the Tyrant* give vent

---

10 For further discussion, see Newell (2003) pp. 63–69.

to this quandary when they pray that (the) God will protect them from tyrants while at the same time helping the man ambitious to serve his country. A part of the tragedy of the play is that, in their subconscious anxiety, the Thebans are not sure which category Oedipus himself falls into, tyrant or statesman – and neither is he. They begin:

> Insolence breeds the tyrant, insolence
> if it is glutted with a surfeit, unseasonable, unprofitable,
> climbs to the roof-top and plunges
> sheer down to the ruin that must be,
> and there its feet are no service.

They then, however, qualify their condemnation of such vaunting excess:

> But I pray that the God may never
> abolish the eager ambition that profits the state.
> For I shall never cease to hold the God as our protector (870–885).

Sophocles is suggesting that the difficulty of distinguishing between the self-professed protector of the state and its would-be tyrant is a permanent quandary of civic life, while hinting between the lines that his fellow Athenians face this same riddle with their own leaders right now. For although the drama concerns eternal themes, it is also first presented in the very midst of the cauldron of the Peloponnesian War, and has not implausibly been taken as an attempt to moderate Athenian imperialistic hubris through the cautionary tale of the rise, nemesis, and downfall of the tyrant Oedipus, perhaps a personification of Athenian imperialism or a stand-in for the great war-time Athenian leader Pericles.[11] If this is so, then just as the lesson of the tragedy is, as the blind wise man Teresias sums it up, to lie low and avoid tempting the gods' wrath through overweening ambition (*Oedipus the Tyrant* 315–360), the lesson for Athens would be that she should clip her own imperialistic wings and return to a more traditional conception of moderate, inward-looking politics (perhaps paralleling Thucydides' praise of the oligarchical regime of the Five Thousand that took power in the aftermath of Sparta's rise and Athens' decline following the Sicilian

---

11 See, for instance, Foster (2010) p. 133.

expedition, a moderate regime interested more in stability than expansion [*Peloponnesian War* 8.26.97]).

Oedipus' initial arrogant confidence in his intellectual power to reason his way out of the plague besetting Thebes and the mystery of the murder of Laius might also be taken to parallel the arrogance of the Athenian generals on Melos as Thucydides depicts them in a celebrated classic of *Realpolitik*, the so-called Melian Dialogue (5.17.84–116). Common to both is an excessive reliance on reason and its power to unlock the truth about nature. The generals on Melos echo the view held by a number of Sophists that the distinction between nature and convention establishes that "getting the better" of others wherever and whenever one can is the most natural and most reasonable way of life for any individual or city possessing the power to do so (5.17.105). Just as Oedipus' hubristic faith in his capacity to unriddle nature brought him down, so, in one interpretation of Thucydides, the arrogance of the generals in the Melian dialogue is met by the nemesis of the Sicilian expedition. As we recall from our discussion of the pre-Socratics and Sophists in the *Laws*, they believed that nature sprang from "chance" in alternation with "necessity." At one point in the play, when Oedipus comes to believe (mistakenly) that he is illegitimate, he revels (somewhat like Edmund in *King Lear*) in the fact that he is the "child of chance," a man who stands outside the conventions of legitimacy and lineage, the more effectively able to assert himself through his ambition and power of mind (*Oedipus the Tyrant* 1075–1090). In the denouement, however, he is ground down and brought low by necessity, becoming a Dionysian blood sacrifice to the regeneration of Apollonian order.

In Thucydides, we possess a real-life historical narrative of the struggle allegorized by Sophocles. An ancient tradition credits Xenophon with the discovery and safe-guarding of Thucydides' unknown manuscript about the Peloponnesian War and it is instructive, in concluding our first consideration of Xenophon's monarchical utopia, to view it in the context of Thucydides' account of the crisis of war and imperialism faced by Athens during the lifetimes of Socrates and his school. When Socrates in the *Republic* traces the development from the simple archaic and bucolic ways of the City of Sows to the erotic refinements, luxury, and imperialism of the "feverish city," on one level he is making a theoretical transition from simple desire (*epithumia*) organized by the division of labor to the erotic longing for honor and pleasure (including the pleasure of philosophy) and therewith to the need for thumos in a class of soldiers. On another level, he is telescoping Athens' own transition from its old-fashioned austerity and piety, flowering at Marathon and Salamis in the defeat of the hated Persian oppressor, to its newfound imperialism, sophistication, and hubris in which Athens, as Sparta and her other critics frequently charged, tries to take the place of the King of Kings – whom they had all fought to defeat – over the rest of Greece (*Peloponnesian War* 1.3.68–69, 1.4.97–100, 1.5.117–122, 124). This transition from the old-fashioned virtues that predated the war against Persia and enabled the Greeks to win it to the imperial pretensions of Athens herself is also paralleled in Aristophanes' depiction in the *Clouds* of the Just and Unjust Speeches (*Clouds* 889–1104). The Just Speech pines nostalgically over "the good old days" – a code of reverence for the ancestors, for modesty and piety, to some extent preserved by Sparta but, many felt, almost vanished in Athens. The Unjust Speech, by contrast, offers a brazen, flashy and shameless defense of unbridled hedonism, moral relativism, and materialism at home enabled by conquest abroad. Generally speaking, the City of Sows is to the Feverish City as the Just Speech is to the Unjust Speech.[12] This latter speech is the one that is embraced by Pheidippides, the stand-in for Alcibiades in the *Clouds*.

As we discussed in Chapter 1, the connection of Alcibiades with Socrates, on the one hand, and (as chronicled by Thucydides) with Athenian imperial expansion on the other is intimate and troubling. In the *Alcibiades I*, we observe Socrates enflaming the young Alcibiades' eros for honor (the key to understanding human nature, as he later claims Diotima had taught him in turning him away from natural to political philosophy [*Symposium* 208c–d]), by suggesting that he

---

12 See the discussion of the *Clouds* in Nicholls (1983a) pp. 35 ff. As Athenian power rose and waned during the Peloponnesian War, there was a widespread feeling that the old religious and moral codes were melting away, leaving a vacuum filled by the Sophists' morality of "getting the better." See Dodds in Plato (1979) p. 292, and Guthrie (1983) pp. 106–107. Shorey describes Callicles, whose defense of the natural master closely parallels that of the generals on Melos, as "the embodiment of the immoralist tendencies of the age" (1968) pp. 141, 146–147. Friedlander sees a connection between the debate over the two ways of life – tyranny and philosophy – in the *Gorgias*, *Republic*, and other dialogues and this surrounding climate of moral anxiety and further observes that Socrates' discussion with Callicles revolves around three intertwined issues: justice versus injustice, philosophy versus politics, and Socrates versus imperial Athens (1973) p. 261.

wants to rule the whole world (*Alcibiades I* 105c). The ambition to transcend Athens, kindled or at least crystallized by Socrates, in the scope of his honor-seeking is pedagogically employed by Socrates to provoke Alcibiades to transcend the limitations of Athenian education in political prudence – left largely to private instruction in rhetoric – and to think about statesmanship in terms of the two paradigmatically well-ordered regimes of Sparta and Persia. In the sequel, however, it might appear that, although Socrates did help Alcibiades crystallize the scope of his ambition onto a worldwide stage anticipating Alexander the Great (as Thucydides reports, in whipping up the Athenian demos to conquer Sicily, Alcibiades remarks that Carthage is next, and that there is no predictable limit to the future Athenian empire [6.18.19]), the transition from the universality of his ambition to the universality of philosophical transcendence is flawed or stillborn, to use the midwife imagery from the *Theatetus* (150B–151D). Torn between his love of Socrates and his love of the Demos, the mature Alcibiades' imperialism as it is depicted in the *Symposium* is indeed limitless but tinged with a bitter undertone of alienation and lost innocence, as if Socrates had spoiled political honor for him in contrast with philosophy while at the same time leaving him unable or unwilling to enter into philosophy wholeheartedly.

According to Thucydides, whereas the initial wartime leader of the democracy, Pericles, identified his own honor with what was best for Athens as a whole, his successors pursued their own self-interest at the expense of what was best for the city (2.7.65–67). Having always advised the city to match its foreign conquests to its real resources, he might well have opposed the Sicilian expedition as imprudent. It is important to note, however, that this would have been a utilitarian objection, not an ethical one. Pericles was wholeheartedly in favor of empire, only counseling a prudent scheduling of expansion. In this, he was in harmony with the more level-headed of the Sophists, who, although they counseled "getting the better" (*pleonexia*) as the most natural way to live for individuals and cities, would certainly have been against suicidal boldness and in favor of the proper amassing of military and economic strength to guarantee success. We recall from Chapter 2 that one of Gorgias' fragments maintains that courage and *phronesis* (in this utilitarian sense of how to get the better) are the two main virtues of the city (omitting any mention of justice and moderation). Pericles differed from more aggressive imperialists like his successors Cleon and Alcibiades only about the means to empire, not the end itself. Therefore, from Socrates' viewpoint in the *Gorgias*, he is not fit for inclusion in the ranks of truly prudent statesmen who would understand the need for the city's internal moderation to be matched by an external avoidance of the temptations to tyrannize over other cities abroad.

Although the Athenians did foolishly underestimate the size, wealth, and resources of Sicily before undertaking the invasion (6.18.1–3), Thucydides observes that the main reason for its failure stemmed from Athenian internal politics after Pericles' death. Alcibiades began as the leader of the invasion force, and his conduct "was as good as could be desired." It was his recall and replacement by Nicias that doomed the invasion (6.18.16, 2.7.65–67, 6.19.61–62).[13] Thucydides is a unique figure in the intellectual context surrounding the emergence of the Socratic school. He appears to share the Sophists' view of politics as a ceaseless struggle for individual and collective aggrandizement; that motion is the natural condition of politics rather than rest. At the same time, he keenly appreciates the perils that expansionism poses to the freedom and internal ordering of regimes that are embroiled in it. In the long run, the superpower conflict between Athens and Sparta, in part based on self-interest (Athens' desire for glory and wealth and Sparta's fear that Athens' rising power must be nipped in the bud before it becomes overwhelming) but also on what we might term an ideological struggle between two different regime principles, democracy and a timocratic oligarchy, reaches into and subverts the internal politics of all the

---

13 For a longer discussion of the Peloponnesian War and its significance for political philosophy, see Newell (2009), Orwin (1994), and Palmer (1992). On the relationship between political philosophy and the historical context of Athens' rise to empire, see the fine study by Balot (2001), a deft and sure-footed interdisciplinary cross-hatching of intellectual, political, and cultural history. It is part of a distinguished school of classical and historical scholarship including Kagan (2003), Ober (1998), and Strauss (2004) from which political theorists can learn much. On the pivotal role of Alcibiades in Thucydides' history, Balot writes: "Once Alcibiades is removed from a position of leadership, the centrifugal tendencies of the democracy spiral outward in an increasing display of civic mistrust and divisiveness. The democratic process can no longer coalesce successfully around Alcibiades' compelling personality and vision" (2001) p. 178. If I am warranted in describing Thucydides' history as a secular tragedy, Herodotus' history is arguably even more *sui generis* with a less clear connection to the pre-Socratics and Sophists. See Thompson (1996), who argues that, for Herodotus, the transmission of stories is crucial for the identity of a political community.

city-states, kindling domestic strife between partisans of the conflicting regime principles (3.81.2–84). The rise and fall of Athens through the overreaching ambition of the Sicilian expedition does savor of a tragic nemesis. Yet, as Thucydides relates it, the war is a real-world historical cycle, not a mythic one (1.1.6–11, 21–24), and, as distinct from the viewpoint of some of its actors (like the pious Spartans and their counterparts in Athens who hold to the old ways of the Just Speech [1.2.80–85]), Thucydides himself appears to assign no divine provenance to these events. If he is a tragedian, he is a secular or empirical tragedian.

As Thucydides sums up his career, Pericles was mistaken to think or hope that his successors would, like him, find more glory in serving Athens as a whole, especially through a prudential middle ground of expansion in keeping with resources, than in dominating the demos to pursue their private interests. Neither Alcibiades nor Nicias, the leaders of the war and peace parties respectively in the post-Periclean period, found that his personal interest coincided with that of the city as a whole. Alcibiades and Nicias, however, were more typical of Athens than was Pericles, who, as Hobbes concluded from his study of Thucydides, was a happy accident, a monarch in all but name masquerading as leading citizen, whose successors fragmented what he had held together. Alcibiades embodied youth, daring, hedonism, and a love of innovation and was tainted by the reputation for impiety (6.18.14–16, 27–30). He was the avatar of Athens' most sophisticated side, both culturally and in the more literal philosophical sense, paralleling Aristophanes' depiction of the Unjust Speech (sometimes and understandably translated as "Sophistry") in the *Clouds* and parodied there as the arrogant wastrel Pheidippides. The older Nicias, by contrast, wanted peace with Sparta and no further expansion of the empire. He was admired for his moderation, piety, and caution, paralleling the Just Speech in the *Clouds* (6.23.9–14, 21–24; 7.21.8–10; 7.22,48; 7.23.51–52, 86–87). The bifurcation of Athenian politics into these two representative figures reveals that, beneath the unity crafted by Pericles through his matchless rhetoric, a "silent majority" (as we might put it) of Athenians remained attached to "the good old days" extolled by the Just Speech. Less flashy than the imperialists and their foreign Sophist friends (Pericles was a friend of Protagoras, and Alcibiades, as we know, frequented Socrates' circle through which passed itinerant teachers of rhetoric), these people were shocked by the Plague into thinking the gods were punishing them for unjustly provoking war with Sparta and appalled by the desecration of their ancestral villages and tombs when the rural population was brought within the Long Walls to protect them from the invading Spartans.

Absent an accidental monarch in disguise like Pericles, Thucydides implies, the public and private interest in an imperialistic democracy may be irreconcilable. This is what led to the war expanding beyond the bounds set by Pericles . Alcibiades wanted glory and needed money to float his many extravagances. Leading the city to fresh conquests and plunder was the surest route. It also led to the failure of the Sicilian expedition and Sparta's subsequent rise to predominance, for Nicias was not the right kind of man to place in charge of carrying out so bold a scheme. After the death of Cleon, another bellicose leader of the war party who had dominated Athenian politics following the demise of Pericles' centrist policy, the way was open for Nicias to conclude a peace treaty with Sparta (5.15.17). Many were in favor, but others, whipped up by Alcibiades, felt themselves taken advantage of – the war was ending before they had a crack at the riches to come from further expansion (5.16.43,45–46; 6.18.1,8–9).

Nicias tries to dissuade the assembly from undertaking the new war against Sicily by detailing the enormous preparations they will have to make to carry it off (6.18.9–15). But his very assiduousness in listing these preparations convinces the demos that they have the prudent advice they need to make the invasion a success. Alcibiades seizes the moment to advance himself as Nicias' junior partner – he, the young and daring son, will carry out the invasion guided by his elder's sober logistical advice. In this way, he concludes, he and Nicias together, boldness tempered by prudence, will make success inevitable (6.18.15–20). Whereas Alcibiades believes in daring, innovation, and improvisation, Nicias (broadly speaking, more like Cambyses, cautious father of the daring Cyrus in the *Education of Cyrus*) relies on fortune and the ultimate wisdom of the gods, who discourage overweening human ambition. In contrast with the Athenian generals on Melos, Nicias believes that we must behave justly because the gods uphold justice. He represents a side of Athens that is attracted to the more traditional culture of their Spartan adversaries, who live archaically as if nothing had changed since the defeat of Persia and the rise of Athens. If one viewed the

Athenian common good as coeval with imperial expansion, then Nicias did not serve it. If one viewed the Athenian common good as peaceful and nonexpansionist, then Alcibiades did not serve it. Athens by this point, however, could not clearly embrace one alternative or the other. Although Pericles advised against overexpansion, he also told the Athenians they could not simply let their empire go. Their so-called allies regarded them as a "tyrant city" and would exact revenge if Athens' power slipped (2.7.64–65). The Athenians had a tiger by the tail.

Bearing in mind these different leaders and social strata in Athens after the death of Pericles, let us examine the famous "staged" dialogue between unnamed Athenian generals and the leaders of the small island city of Melos, whom the Athenians want to switch sides from the Spartans. The generals argue that the Melians, confronted by Athens' overwhelming strength, should put aside the issue of the justice of Athenian conquests and consult only their own self-interest and survival, thereby surrendering. Thucydides makes the Athenian generals express a compendium of views that we attribute to the Sophists, views paralleled in many Platonic depictions of them through Socrates' debates with Thrasymachus, Polus, Callicles, and Glaucon and also available from their surviving fragments. To the extent that the Melian dialogue is based on the real climate of opinion in Athens at the time, it suggests rather remarkably the extent to which this intellectual culture of Sophistry and *pleonexia* has permeated the upper strata of political actors bent on public fame and empire, providing their spontaneous desire for power, wealth, and glory with a philosophically derived rhetorical platform, the ontology of the "motion-men." The possibility that Athenian imperialism was already thoroughly interwoven with the primordialist view of nature adds a degree of clarity to our earlier suggestion that Socrates himself, in the *Gorgias* and *Symposium*, was looking for poetic, theoretical, and rhetorical intermediaries who might help shape his contrary message in favor of moderation and the eschewal of empire. It also sheds light on the Athenian Stranger's remark to Kleinias that, living off the beaten track in Crete, he does not understand that moral vice today is buttressed by philosophical arguments about the cosmos. Although writing for the ages, Plato also depicts Socrates as being, as he claims in the *Gorgias*, the only man truly practicing statecraft in the Athens of his day (521), interweaving his defense of moderation with his repudiation of the Heracleitean view of nature.[14]

The core of the generals' view is this: "Of gods we believe, of men we know, that by a necessary law of nature they rule wherever they can" (5.17.104–108). Their view has three elements. The first element echoes the skepticism expressed by Adeimantus in the *Republic* and by unnamed thumotic and gloomy young men in the *Laws* about the gods: they are either indifferent to human affairs and justice or side outright with the unjust who can give them greater honors. As tyrants themselves on a superhuman level, the gods do not condemn human tyranny or care about human virtue. The second element echoes the ontological premise of the pre-Socratics and Sophists summarized by the Athenian Stranger in Book 10 of the *Laws*. The city and its conventions issue unfathomably out of nature's "great motions" according to necessity and chance, achieving a completely time-bound and transitory authority for as long as they last. The city's conventions, although put forth as a defense of justice, piety, and decency, in reality serve only the desire of the ruling element to "get the better" of the ruled. One rules either by rhetorical stealth and wrapped in the garb of conventional morality or by open force, but everyone who understands the distinction between nature and convention, and has the guts and brains to do so, seeks rule (*Laws* 888–890). Finally, the generals' maxim is cast in the form of a universally valid anthropology similar to Thrasymachus' maxim that "justice is the advantage of the stronger" (*Republic* 338d) and that every regime, regardless of its professed principle of justice and its ruling element, is the same in pursuing its rulers' advantage. Again we recognize the connection between the pragmatic political teaching advanced by the Sophists and their underlying connection to the natural philosophy of the pre-Socratics: if nature is taken universally to be motion and genesis, then the universal human counterpart of nature

---

14 See the fine reading of the *Gorgias* by Ranasinghe (2009). He explores Socrates' claim that it is better to suffer evil than to do it, juxtaposed against the violent backdrop of the Peloponnesian War and its incitement to demagogic violence, calling into question the famous Socratic proposition that no one can willingly choose to do evil if he knows what virtue is. Arguing that the rhetorical arguments of the Sophists encountered by Socrates in the *Gorgias* are baser and more nihilistic than those treated in the *Republic*, Ranasinghe underscores the urgent need addressed by Socrates to find a noble rhetoric of justice to defeat the interweaving of the Sophists' and Athenian imperialism's demagoguery.

are those "motions" that upsurge into human beings as the impulse to master and exploit others. Regimes are local, happenstantial modal variants of this underlying universal urge.

The Sicilian expedition and its disastrous denouement, the destruction of the fleet and of the flower of the Athenian forces, dying slowly of starvation and exposure trapped in a marble quarry in Syracuse, follows closely on the Melian dialogue, suggesting in a massive way that it is a deserved comeuppance for the Athenian generals' position that men by nature "rule wherever they can" (*Peloponnesian War* 7.23). Appealing as we might find this interpretation of a historical drama echoing the tragic structure of hubris followed by nemesis, we should bear in mind that the Athenian "few" – the generals on Melos – may well not have spoken this way to the Athenian "many" back home. (The entire dialogue takes place behind closed doors between the elites of both sides.) Counseled by the Sophists, they likely concealed their unvarnished impiety and *pleonexia* behind a more seemly deference to convention. For, as Thucydides relates, the Athenian "silent majority" (as we have put it) are deeply concerned at this time over a defilement of the Hermes, a god dear to the common folk, widely suspected to have been carried out by Alcibiades on one of his drunken carouses (6.18.28–30). (Is it too much to wonder whether the defilement took place just before, and making him late for, his boozy arrival in the *Symposium*?) Still plagued by guilt over starting the war, these conservative Athenians have been consulting oracles about the gods' judgment (2.6.54). The generals, on the other hand, who believe the gods, if they exist at all (they say they "know" the truth about men but merely "believe" it about gods), are indifferent to justice either in their own sphere or the human sphere, represent the new Athens at its most extreme, the side that Alcibiades belongs to as well. The generals on Melos, however, have not as yet thought through or carried out the consequences for Athenian *domestic* politics of what they propose for foreign affairs: if, as a necessary law of nature, you must "have more" wherever you can, why not achieve this tyrannical power over your own people? The Athenian silent majority instinctively fear that Alcibiades, on the eve of being placed in command of an enormous armada and army, is on the verge of connecting these dots.

The Athenians continue to want power over others and the prosperity it brings. They continue to heed Pericles' advice, in his waning days, that their empire is a tiger by the tail and that, if they let it go, the peoples they have oppressed will turn on them savagely. Yet although the essence of Pericles' utilitarian moderation was that the empire should neither expand beyond its resources nor be abandoned, the majority of Athenians, whatever their misgivings, cannot resist the lure of further expansion and so launch the Sicilian expedition. At the same time, however, they are afraid that to give the man with enough daring to bring the invasion off the military power to do so – Alcibiades – will simultaneously allow him to have power over them. They want to tyrannize over others without being tyrannized over. This is why they recall Alcibiades from the expedition after it has embarked and place their confidence in Nicias, even though Nicias lacks the daring to carry it off and opposed it categorically as madly imprudent for opening another war front when the contest with Sparta was far from resolved (6.18.9–13). The demand for freedom from tyranny in democratic domestic politics, Thucydides teaches, contradicts the measures that need to be taken to achieve tyranny abroad. The expedition is a disaster because of the nature of democratic politics in particular and of the political community in general. Imperialistic democracy gives full flower to individual ambition, freedom, prosperity, innovation, public magnificence, and open-mindedness – all the things Pericles praised about Athens in his famous funeral oration at the outset of the conflict with Sparta (2.6.34–47). Imperialistic democracy also subverts the common good, however, creating an irreparable tension between the individual and the city, and gives those inclined to or tempted by the prospect of tyranny a licit scope for their ambition.

Although Plato's dialogues are of permanent significance, rising from the particular context of ancient Athens to elucidate truths that are universal and lasting, they do unfold quite explicitly against the backdrop of Athens' extraordinary rise and fall as narrated by Thucydides, and many events and characters from Thucydides' narrative (Alcibiades, Nicias, Laches) appear in Plato's dialogues. Moreover, the Alcibiades of history and of the Platonic dialogues do closely converge. For it was Alcibiades, the leader of the war party in Athens, who most certainly did think through the unspecified ramifications for internal Athenian politics of the thesis advanced by the generals on Melos that one rules wherever one can. He did connect the dots between empire abroad and tyranny at home. He was impious and recognized no legal or moral restraints on his ambition. After Sicily, he planned to go on to take Carthage (6.18.5–16). He was also the beloved of Socrates. It is clear from the Platonic dialogues that Socrates encouraged all of his interlocutors to distinguish between happiness by nature and happiness by convention, not in order to encourage them to identify the natural life with *pleonexia* but, on the contrary, to enable them to grasp that mastery was itself the aim of most conventional accounts of the good life, to be contrasted with the naturally superior happiness of philosophizing. In other words, contrary to the Sophists' depiction of a naturally enlightened few who pursued mastery and a pusillanimous majority who clung to conventional equality and safety, in Socrates' diagnosis of the ills of the cities, most people were conflicted about these aims. The desire for mastery was itself in a way vulgar and demotic. Hence, the inevitable dissatisfaction of Callicles who, as a prospective "best man," can in Socrates' judgment only assert his natural excellence by pandering to that same pusillanimous majority (*Gorgias* 513, 521). Socrates presents philosophy as a way of life that, in the devotion of all its passions to the love of wisdom, thereby sluicing eros and thumos off from the temptations of tyranny and *pleonexia*, entails the civic virtues of justice and moderation as well. In this way, he can plausibly present the philosophic life as the best guardian of justice, protecting it from the assaults of the Sophists and the "motion-men," as well as the best curative therapy for the proto-tyrant (*Republic* 485d–486b).

Nevertheless, the Platonic Socrates' defense of justice on philosophical grounds is not the same thing as believing in it out of custom, habit, and veneration for tradition, like the Just Argument in the *Clouds*. Before Socrates can defend justice as natural, he must concede, even stimulate, an awareness of the distinction between true justice or happiness and their merely conventional versions. However, while calling the desirability of tyranny into question, that probing into the difference between natural and conventional happiness also calls into question ordinary morality, patriotism, the love of family, and piety. As we earlier observed, the opening move in the *Republic* to examine justice on the analogy of an art subverts property rights almost instantly (including the usefulness of wealth in propitiating the gods through sacrifice). By the time the best regime is set in place, every source of ordinary human decency flowing from family affection and respect for tradition has been abolished (*Republic* 449c–d, 472c–e, 462c–d). Socrates must tempt the young to abandon conventional justice to a degree, so as to ground natural justice more firmly in their characters through a vision of the soul and of the whole that connects it to the transcendent truth. This means that, in some way, he *is* subverting the conventional decencies, just as a great teacher whom a student ends up loving more than his own father (like Xenophon's story of Tigranes and the "Armenian Socrates") *is* in some sense a corrupter of the youth.

Hence the dilemma of Callicles, who can readily join Socrates in criticizing Pericles' successors as unworthy for not knowing the art of ruling but who is genuinely shocked when Socrates defines Pericles himself out of the equation (*Gorgias* 503). Callicles wants someone to restore the manly and imperial expediential prudence of the great Pericles so as to restore the city to its former grandeur. Socrates, by contrast, identifies prudence with the reining in of eros by reason in the soul, both within each citizen and within the city collectively (504–508): It is a little as if Socrates dismissed any distinction between Winston Churchill and Jimmy Carter as leaders because neither of them truly understood the geometrical proportionality of the cosmos. And so, at the end of every corridor in the world of the dialogues, we encounter the remaining mystery of Socrates' influence on Alcibiades: Did he have to corrupt him a little further in order to salvage what was still incorruptible? Is the selfish, thoughtless wastrel who enters Socrates' *phrontisterion* in the *Clouds* – to emerge, after his unseen and unheard instruction, equipped with the theoretical distinction between nature and convention to justify his vices – better or worse off than he was before?[15]

The central dilemma of the Peloponnesian War, then, was the contradiction between democratic self-government at home and imperialism abroad. The Athenian demos feared the rule of a tyrant over themselves, but happily acted as a tyrant city over others. The transition from the archaic city to the feverish city opened up an avenue of ambition for the young that the old ways would have thoroughly suppressed, as do the Spartans still in their preference for collective discipline and ingrained custom over individual brilliance and innovation (*Peloponnesian War* 1.3.80–86). A psychological type like Alcibiades is solicited by the aggressive aims of empire, simultaneously opening up the danger of tyranny at home.

15 Consider also Newell (2000) pp. 185–195.

Viewed against the backdrop of this long imperial struggle, its zenith and denouement in Athenian defeat, the backlash at home of fear (8.24.1) and suspicion of would-be tyrants and their cronies and mentors (Socrates was eventually swept up in this post-Alcibiadean atmosphere of populist paranoia), the classics offer two solutions for resolving the contradiction between democracy and empire. They shared common ground with the poets in that they did not dispute the fact that exceptional ambition is a naturally recurrent and spontaneous variation in human psychology; that it could not be extirpated or entirely forestalled, and was sometimes necessary to aid the city. But, whereas the poets were resigned to ambition periodically arising and periodically being crushed by an inscrutable divine necessity, the classical political philosophers believed that this potentially tyrannical soul could be rehabilitated into the consistent service of justice. On the other hand, in contrast with modern Hobbesian statecraft, the aim was not to re-wire Alcibiades through behavior modification into a clockwork orange (like Anthony Burgess' character Alex), but to turn him into a steadfast and self-controlled Stoic warrior like (to take one important version) the Auxillaries in the *Republic*.

The mainstream classical tradition embodied by Plato and Aristotle tries as much as possible to insulate a self-governing republic from foreign entanglements, which involves discrediting democracy itself – with its licentiousness, individualism, love of variety, luxury and foreign fashion, and proneness to demagogues – in favor of an austere, inward-looking, aristocratic republic of the best men. A concentration on internal self-government and an avoidance of imperial ambition through a purely defensive foreign policy, according to the classical prescription, will prevent politics from soliciting the supremely ambitious proto-tyrant who can court the many and mask his rise as the indispensable servant of imperial expansion bringing the common people greater riches (*Republic* 422a–423b; *Politics* 1333b26–40; 1330b–1331a; 1324b22–41; 1325b23–33). These potential tyrants, the Alcibiadean men, must be forestalled from developing the erotic disorder that is the psychological root of their tyrannical longing by an education in civic virtue governed by philosophy. Alcibiades might have proven to be a magnificent half-birth, but if the "pattern in the sky" (*Republic* 592b) of the best regime is transmitted to posterity, it may re-shape the characters of future such men. Alcibiades will become Cicero's Scipio, subordinating the licit honor that comes from serving a republic of laws to his higher admiration for the life of the mind, thus submitting to the hierarchy of reason over honor in Diotima's Ladder in a way that the actual Alcibiades, beginning with his ribald and swaggering entrance to the dialogue and his semi-comic, semi-serious battle with Socrates to woo Agathon, refused to do (*Symposium* 212d–213e).

Thus, in the main, for Plato and Aristotle the rule of reason, to whatever degree practically possible, aided by an education that sublimates and re-directs tyrannical eros and thumos toward serving the common good, is at its best co-terminous with republican self-government. Even so, as we have seen at some length, Plato and Aristotle do admit the possibility of a tyranically founded just regime and a rational monarchy absolute in authority and multi-national in scope. In Xenophon, we find the fullest exploration of this alternative, whereby reason is co-terminous with the multi-national art of household management. It is hard not to see in Xenophon's re-creation of the young Cyrus a version of what Alcibiades might have become if a philosophically grounded education had taken hold in his character from early on, converting him, not into the citizen of a republic friendly to philosophy envisioned by Plato and Aristotle, but into a benign, efficient, moderate, and self-controlled universal ruler extending the pattern of the Good to all peoples under his sway while at the same time gratifying his eros for limitless prestige. In other words, instead of, as the Platonic Socrates does, leading Alcibiades to the universality of thought by way of his universal ambition so as to deliver him back to his city better equipped to govern in it, Xenophon in effect takes him from the universality of thought to the actualization of a universalistic government. Whereas Plato and Aristotle try to resolve the contradiction between democracy and empire by excluding empire and extolling the reform of republican self-government in accordance with reason, Xenophon resolves it (at least speculatively) by forsaking the *polis* and extolling the reform of empire in accordance with reason. My suggested identification of Xenophon's Cyrus with an Alcibiades transformed into an architectonically guided imperial statesman of genius is hinted at in Cyrus's indirect encounter with the "Armenian Socrates" whose unjust execution for allegedly alienating the sons from the fathers he posthumously avenges. This identification is even more strikingly evoked by Cyrus's dialogue with his father Cambyses, a republican limited monarch who apparently is guided privately, beyond the sphere of the Persian laws, by an understanding of the Good with many parallels to the Xenophontic Socrates.[16] It is as if, while by convention, Socrates cannot take the place of the biological father of Alcibiades, in a regime like the Persian Republic where the cultivation of justice and the rest of virtue in the soul is more natural than the accidents of birth, he could be Alcibiades' father by nature in the highest and fullest meaning of what is natural.

In this fictional makeover of Alcibiades, the flawed yet brilliant and preeminent democratic leader of his generation, Xenophon seems to take the tumultuous career of Alcibiades' friendship with Socrates and graft it onto a naturally virtuous political order, reimagining a world in which Socrates (Cambyses) could govern and in which Alcibiades (Cyrus) could be a good citizen and, later, a benevolent king. In this fantasy, Socrates goes from being the older man who seduced the younger man so as to draw him into philosophy – and thereby arguably undermined his attachment to conventional mores by enflaming his ambition as a propaedeutic to greater philosophical openness – to being the wise, grave, and responsible father of a brilliant boy, the intersection of whose naturally great intellect, bravery, and eros for honor with an education in republican moderation and justice flowers in a perfect ruler for all mankind. Socrates, the lover of Alcibiades in the wide-open democracy of Athens, becomes, through Xenophon's philosophical fantasy, his father as the king of a virtuous republic. In this sense, Xenophon's monarchical utopia, often hailed as the first mirror of princes, the *viade mecum* of Scipio the Elder, enabled Socrates, as it were, to father many ambitious young men posthumously and lead them from the temptations of tyranny toward excellence of soul, perhaps succeeding with them where he had failed with Alcibiades himself.

Indispensable to the rearing of this improved Alcibiades would be his initial exposure to the rigors and habituation of that republican education with which the life of Cyrus begins, a partial concession by Xenophon to the Platonic and Aristotelian understanding of the best regime. A tall order, one might think – rational and benevolent imperial authority rooted in republican virtue of character. Yet as we have already noted, as a first installment in the historical influence of this

16 See the very able discussion of "Cyrus' Socratic education" in Rasmussen (2009) ch. 5.

prescription, we might look to Alexander the Great, whose upbringing in a semi-Greek backwater of martial prowess led him eventually to take the real King of Kings' throne, aided by an education in Greek philosophy, perhaps even by Aristotle. That is to say, a crude and minimalist version of Plato's and Aristotle's republican prescription, of their preference for the neighborly and austere small polis over empire and even over the feverish polis Athens, yields at length the Xenophontic *pambasileus* in historical reality. As we see in the chapters to come, this derivation of successful imperialism from republican virtue is precisely Machiavelli's understanding of the success of the greatest empire ever known in reality, that vastly more stable and long-lived successor to the Alexandrian empire, "the Senate and People of Rome." Although in almost all respects Machiavelli must forsake the Platonic and Aristotelian accounts of virtue and the art of ruling, in Xenophon he finds a common stalk.

V

MACHIAVELLI, XENOPHON, AND XENOPHON'S CYRUS

Readers of Machiavelli might well be struck by the prominent place occupied in his works by Xenophon. To be sure, this is more puzzling to present-day readers than it would have been to Machiavelli's contemporaries. Castiglione and other contributors to the "mirror of princes" genre typically linked Xenophon with Plato, Aristotle, and Cicero as being among the chief ancient authorities on good government. Humanists including Poggio, Bruno, and Pontano – often discussed as components of the Renaissance context surrounding Machiavelli – were admirers of Xenophon's writings and influenced by them. As a successful general and arbiter of the affairs of Persia, Xenophon was particularly admired during classical antiquity and again during the Renaissance for his balance of active and contemplative virtues, of particular concern to the Renaissance humanists' wish to free a sphere for pragmatic statesmanship from the excessive restrictions of Christian otherworldliness.[1] Still, given the paucity of Machiavelli's explicit

---

[1] There is a distinguished strain of French classical scholarship on Xenophon's political thought. See especially Delebecque (1957), Luccioni (1947), and Hemardinquer (1872). Cicero described the *Education of Cyrus* as the "model of the just empire" and the constant guide of Scipio the Elder (*Tusculan Disputations* 2.26.62), descriptions that were echoed many times in humanist literature (see, e.g., Gallet-Guerne [1974] pp. 182–184]). Munscher provides a detailed summary of Xenophon's influence on Greek and Roman literature (1920) pp. 70–75. For the Renaissance and Enlightenment reception of Xenophon, see Anderson (1974) pp. 1–8. The *Education of Cyrus*, the *Hiero* and the *Oeconomicus*, all of which deal with princely rule, were among the first classical treatises to be translated when the knowledge of Greek was reintroduced to the West. Bruni translated the *Hiero* into Latin in 1400–1404 (Gallet-Guerne [1974] pp. 58–59; Baron [1955] pp. 117). Cardinal Tomaso Parentucelli, the future Pope Nicholas V and founder the Vatican Library, asked Poggio in 1403 to translate the *Education of Cyrus*. The Cardinal's other translation assignments included Herodotus, Thucydides, Plutarch, Polybius,

references to other classical authors in contrast with his contemporaries among the humanists, his emphasis on Xenophon stands out, especially in contexts in which Plato, Aristotle, and Cicero seem especially conspicuous by their absence. For example, Machiavelli's famous complaint in chapter 15 of *The Prince* that "many have imagined republics and principalities that have never been seen or known to exist in reality" would seem especially to evoke the *Republic* of Plato, a "nowhere" and "pattern in the sky" that St. Augustine had adapted to Christianity as the otherworldly City of God. This statement occurs, moreover, in the midst of Machiavelli's refutation of the traditional catalogue of virtues including liberality, compassion, and honesty, a refutation aimed at both their original classical sources and their adaptation by Christian and humanist authors. Here, of all places, one would expect Machiavelli to criticize Plato, Aristotle, Cicero, and the Stoics explicitly. Yet it is Xenophon whom Machiavelli offers as his sole example of traditional "writers" about the virtues.

Why, then, should Machiavelli have chosen as the chief representative of classical thought a figure who, although esteemed by his contemporaries, would probably not have been chosen as the one name most worth mentioning, to the exclusion of all the others, among the ancient authorities on good government? In this chapter, I argue that the explanation lies in Machiavelli's paradoxical need to refute, at what for him is exceptional length, the classical author whose views of politics most resembled his own prescription for princely government that encourages material prosperity through imperial expansion. In this chapter, Machiavelli's partiality toward Xenophon will be substantiated through a close reading of every reference to Xenophon in *The Prince* and *Discourses*. On the basis of those readings, we also consider why, at the end of the day, Machiavelli must part ways with even this most congenial of classical antecedents. The reason centers on what

---

Plato's *Republic*, Aristotle's *Metaphysics*, and Xenophon's *Memorabilia* (Gallet-Guerne [1974] pp. 60–63). According to Gilbert, Aristotle's *Politics* and Xenophon's *Education of Cyrus* were the main classical authorities for Bernaldus, Pontanus, Erasmus, and Pigua. Gilbert (1938) pp. 12–13, 236. See also Butterfield (1940) p. 56. Thus, Erasmus's *Education of a Christian Prince* was written with the *Education of Cyrus* in mind. In 1470, Vasco Fernandez translated Poggio's Latin *Education of Cyrus* for the young Duke of Burgundy, making it one of the first transmissions of Italian humanism to Burgundian humanism (Gallet-Guerne [1974] pp. xi–xvi, 27–32). Poggio's Latin version was translated into Italian by his son Iacoppo di Messer Poggio in 1521.

I am arguing throughout this book is the crucial distinction between classical and modern theories of statecraft altogether. For Xenophon, Cyrus's excellence unfolds within the natural order as the fulfillment of a human potentiality for virtue. For Machiavelli, by contrast, statecraft is a project for the external mastery of nature and human nature, including the prince's own inner psyche. Ultimately, as we consider here, Machiavelli is therefore critical of Xenophon for – like Plato – understanding the prince's longings in erotic terms. Although as we saw in Chapter 4, Cyrus is cold toward personal erotic attachments, he is consumed by an eros for the admiration of "all men" and eager to be their beloved without loving them in return. For Machiavelli, by contrast, these varieties of eros amount to a specious criterion of natural satisfaction that, especially as evidenced by Xenophon's influence on Scipio, can only lead to failure and the undermining of manly republican vigor. Along with my discussion of Machiavelli's deeroticization of princely psychology, in order to bring into relief what is new about Machiavelli's teaching, I also argue that Machiavelli's prescription for the mastery of Fortuna is at bottom and somewhat unexpectedly linked to a post-Augustinian understanding of nature and will and is therefore impossible without the precedent of the Abrahamic God's relationship to nature. This means that his new science of politics cannot be understood solely within the context of a debate with the classical teachings. A part of what is distinctively modern about Machiavelli, I try to show, is dependent on a variant of Christian ontology – albeit entirely secularized and desacralized – not found in any classical source.

"The life of Cyrus written by Xenophon," as we will see, is at the heart of Machiavelli's hermeneutical encounter with the ancients. As we have observed in previous chapters, Cyrus the Great haunted the imagination of the ancient Greeks not only because he was the founder of the empire that almost overwhelmed them, but – more intriguingly – as a model for their own statecraft. It is well known that the classical philosophers, chiefly represented by Plato and Aristotle, endorsed the neighborly small republic as their main prescription for virtuous government. Nevertheless, they also display considerable approbation for monarchy, particularly the kind represented by Cyrus. The Platonic Socrates uses the Great King as a paradigm for clear thinking about the art of ruling, and the Athenian Stranger in the *Laws* considers Cyrus's type of monarchy to be one of the two mother regime principles along with democracy (Plato *Laws* 694–697). As we saw in Chapter 3, Aristotle in his *Politics* defines virtuous kingship as the exercise of the art of household management over "cities and peoples" (Aristotle *Politics* 1285b20). Although this passage from Aristotle is sometimes taken to allude to Alexander the Great, we have observed that it could also serve as a brief summary of Xenophon's monarchical utopia, the *Education of Cyrus*. Among the classical writers on statecraft, Xenophon stands out for his interest in the model provided by Cyrus's monarchy, which he explores in greater depth and to a far greater extent than any of the others. As we noted earlier, according to an ancient tradition, the *Education of Cyrus* was widely regarded as Xenophon's central treatise on politics, a multinational monarchical ideal paralleling (and perhaps intended to rival) Plato's idealized polis in the *Republic*.[2]

Just as the interpretation of Cyrus teaches us something about how the Greeks evolved their own conceptions of monarchy, the way in which that classical complex of ideas was interpreted by Machiavelli can teach us something about how the modern conception of monarchy and of statecraft in general differs from its classical antecedents. As we saw in the last chapter, among the ancient thinkers, Xenophon gives considerably more latitude, through his reflections in the *Education of Cyrus*, to a rationally organized, expansionist, multinational monarchy premised on the glory seeking and material enrichment of its individual subjects, and correspondingly downplays the appeal of the small homogeneous republic with its nonexpansionist foreign policy and economic austerity. Xenophon's idealization of Cyrus's monarchy, in other words, is congenial with one major rubric of Machiavelli's own recommendations for a more realistic art of ruling expressly aimed at the maximization of power and economic well-being. Because Xenophon was widely admired during classical antiquity and the Renaissance as one of the best writers on monarchy, it is, I suggest, rhetorically convenient for Machiavelli to wrap himself in the venerable

---

[2] See, for example, Xenophon (1880) p. xvi. I have described these prescriptions as "ideal" because that term is immediately accessible. However, I remind the reader to bear in mind my earlier remarks on why the classical prescriptions for the best regime cannot strictly speaking be considered "ideals" in the modern Kantian sense.

Socratic's authority while otherwise undermining the overall classical preference for the nonexpansionist small republic.[3] At the same time, by carefully comparing what Machiavelli terms "the life of Cyrus written by Xenophon" in contradistinction to what Machiavelli would have us understand about the *real* Cyrus and how he rose to power, we will understand what is distinctively modern about Machiavelli's conception of monarchy, such that he must at the end of the day part ways with even this most congenial of classical precedents.

VIRTUE DEFINED AS THE MASTERY OF FORTUNA

In chapter 6 of Machiavelli's *Prince*, virtue is defined as the capacity not to rely on *Fortuna* but to assert one's mastery over it. In contrast with the ancients, who believed that we achieve virtue to the extent that we can reconcile ourselves to nature's patterns, virtue is now equated with the strength of will to oppose nature out and out. The traditional distinction between virtue and vice is therefore replaced by Machiavelli's distinction between relying on virtue and relying on fortune. As we will see, however, it is still useful for a ruler to *appear* virtuous in the traditional sense – that, too, is a source of power.

In his use of the word *virtu*, Machiavelli plays upon an ambiguity central to the concept of virtue. The Greek word for virtue, *arete*, meant more generally "excellence" in many different areas. It could possess the connotation that later came to predominate, through the influence of Stoicism and Christianity, of self-abnegation on behalf of the morally good, but it was originally far more elastic, extending to excellence in areas – for instance, the art of war – to which we would not ordinarily apply the term "virtue" in its more spiritualized version. Moreover, even when a thinker like Aristotle uses the term to connote the

---

[3] Most humanists read the *Education of Cyrus* as presenting a paragon of kingly goodness, although this was not always thought to be incompatible with martial prowess. See, for example, Poggio's dedication of his translation to Alphonso of Aragon (quoted in Gilbert [1938] p. 131) and Vasco Fernandez's preface to his translation (Gallet-Guerne [1974] pp. 182–184). Montaigne, although admiring the work, was "astonished" by "the great liberty allowed by Xenophon" in "his complete emperor" for deception. Montaigne (1952) p. 13. Sometimes we find Xenophon being read in a more starkly Machiavellian manner, as when, for example, James I in the *Basilikon Doron* refers to the *Education of Cyrus* to establish the maxim that a prince needs to begin his reign by being deliberately cruel so that he can then afford to be merciful. Gilbert (1938) p. 101.

proper balance of the intellect and the passions in pursuit of the good, a meaning of virtue that we would readily recognize, he does not exclude the possibility that excellence in civic life could encompass a longing for preeminence bordering on arrogance and a disregard for the views of others – such that his term "superlative virtue," which describes those few who possess prudence and are therefore best suited to govern, has a connotation of "overbearing" or "excessive" (*huperbole*) talent, when we would not ordinarily think it possible to have *too much* goodness of character. These ambiguities are heightened by the Latin translation of *arete* by the much narrower and specific term *virtus*, the root of which means a manly man, analogous to the term *aner* in Greek, such that *virtus* is very nearly synonymous with manly courage, especially in war. Hence, moral thinkers such as Cicero, and later Christian theologians such as St. Augustine, must continue to use this word originally connoting martial prowess as they transpose to it gentler virtues of moderation and an openness to philosophical or divine transcendence. While *virtus* comes to include these more sublime connotations, it never loses its original connotation of manly courage and honor in ordinary usage. Hence, when Machiavelli discusses the "virtues" of the prince and of statesmen, he can play upon this full range of meanings by pushing what he means by *virtu* back in the pagan direction of manly honor and victory as the basis for his even more radical assimilation of virtue to the will to master nature. Even the morally inclined reader finds it difficult to resist being drawn in, because even from the Christian perspective, it would not have been claimed that virtue had *no* connotation at all of political and military strength or of civic-spiritedness, even if faith ranked much higher. This is the thin edge of the wedge for Machiavelli slowly but surely divesting his use of *virtu* of any otherworldly or transcendental associations at all. Among the ancients, Xenophon is his closest ally in doing so, which is why it is so useful for Machiavelli, writing in an atmosphere of intense respect for classical antiquity, to invoke his venerable precedent.

Cyrus the Great is listed, along with Moses, Romulus, and Theseus, as princes of "outstanding virtue" because of their capacity to master fortune. Here the classical and Abrahamic codes of rule begin to be conflated, for not only is a prophet (Moses) equated with secular rulers (Cyrus, Romulus, and Theseus), thus anticipating Spinoza's presentation of him as creating Judaism to achieve social cohesion among the Hebrews, but the reverse is also true – extraordinarily successful secular rulers are implicitly equated with prophets. Such "princes," Machiavelli writes, receive nothing from fortune but "the opportunity, which gave them the matter enabling them to introduce any form they pleased." As we observed in Chapter 2, the capacity of God as chief artisan of the universe to introduce form into matter is a recognizable scholastic formulation. Through his use of this scholastic terminology, Machiavelli speculatively transfers this divine capacity to reshape nature to human princely agency, a stark repudiation of both the classical and Christian traditions. For Aristotle, we recall from Chapter 3, statesmanship should rely as much as possible on the breeding of character through education and on a favorable environment. As we saw, the recrafting of nature through economic productivity and of human nature through despotic reforms is severely discouraged (*Politics* 1258a). For St. Augustine, whatever degree of virtue humans are capable of achieving can come only through submission to God's grace – man's will can achieve nothing on its own ([1958] p. 116]).

Machiavelli's redefinition of virtue as antinatural willpower is squarely aimed at both traditions. To recall an argument from Chapter 2, for the classics generally – and on this point Christian theology would have been at one with them – the only way in which a man can decrease the influence of fortune over his life is to decrease his reliance on the external and perishable goods required to gratify his excessive pleasures. The mastery of fortune, to the extent that it is possible, comes through the transcendence of aberrant passion and the reform of the soul through its realignment with the moderation and orderliness that are superordinate over chance and impulse in the cosmos. For Machiavelli, by contrast, as we consider at length in this chapter and the next, the effective channeling of the passions into the maximization of power and wealth empowers the will to conquer the limiting conditions placed on us by nature; above all to conquer the delusion of that harmonious view of the cosmos that, in Machiavelli's view, retards honor seeking and vigorous princely action. The methodical or dispassionate harnessing of passion to energize the will – not the harmony of mind, soul, and passions prescribed by the classics and, suitably modified for religious purposes, by Christian theology – is the paradox at the core of Machiavelli's new prince.

Whereas both the classical and Christian authorities encourage us to rely on the beneficence of fortune (be it nature or providence), for Machiavelli, bad fortune is actually *preferable* to good fortune because it compels us to struggle and fight back:

It was necessary then for Moses to find the people of Israel in Egypt, enslaved by the Egyptians, so that they would be disposed to follow him in order to get out of their servitude. It was fitting that Romulus not be received in Alba, that he should have been exposed at birth, if he was to become king of Rome and founder of that fatherland. Cyrus needed to find the Persians malcontent with the empire of the Medes, and the Medes soft and effeminate because of a long peace.

This account of Cyrus as an adventurer of obscure origins who rallies a Persian people already under the yoke of the Medes clearly does not correspond with that of Xenophon but more closely resembles that of Herodotus. Why? Because in Xenophon's account, Cyrus relies on many gifts from fortune – the fact that he is born the son of the Persian king and grandson of the neighboring, largely benevolent tyrant of Media, who recognizes his merit and elevates him among the Medes at the expense of his own son and heir, and above all the superb education the young Cyrus receives from the Persian Republic, an idealization of the Spartan republic. In Xenophon's account, far from being unruly vassals of the Medes as Machiavelli presents them, the Persians have their own self-sufficient regime rigorously devoted to a civic education in serving the common good. As we saw in the last chapter, Xenophon's Cyrus sparks Persia's rise from republic to empire by appealing to the ambitions of the other young aristocrats for wider horizons for glory and wealth. It transpires that they are not content with the regime's austere internal *paidea*. Machiavelli, however, thrusts all of these nuances aside – Xenophon's complex interconnections between Cyrus's natural disposition, his educational character formation, and his inherited circumstances – and instead gives us Herodotus's unvarnished account of an obscure adventurer who leads a rebellion by a downtrodden people into ever expanding conquests. In the starkest imaginable contrast with Xenophon's portrayal of Cyrus's Median grandfather as a benign benefactor, Herodotus relates that he tried to have his infant grandson killed (*Histories* 1.102–130).

The main lesson of the chapter, according to Machiavelli, is that "armed prophets" succeed and "unarmed prophets" fail. Still, arms alone are not enough. A prince of truly outstanding virtue must also be perceived by the people as a prophet and "held in veneration." Both secular and religious rulers (for Machiavelli, a distinction without a difference) use their limitless power at the height of their achievements to shape the history of their own rise retroactively and leave behind an account that to the degree possible omits the bloodshed and illegitimacy of their origins and burnishes the ruler for posterity with the conventionally acclaimed moral virtues. Machiavelli's implication is that Moses decisively shaped the account we receive of him from the Torah, while Theseus and Romulus also enter received history as divinely inspired and mandated.[4] In a similar vein, we can envision the real Cyrus – the "armed prophet" who rose from nothing – passing himself off to posterity as the ennobling and edifying account we find of him in the *Education of Cyrus*.

CYRUS THE GREAT IN MACHIAVELLI'S *DISCOURSES*

The forgoing considerations will help us understand Machiavelli's further account of Cyrus in the *Discourses*, which will in turn prepare us for the extended critique of classical statecraft undertaken through the treatment of the traditional catalogue of the virtues in chapters 15 to 18 of *The Prince*, where both the real Cyrus uncovered by Machiavelli and Xenophon's Cyrus form a major leitmotif.

The first cluster of references to Cyrus is in Book 2, chapters 11 to 13, of the *Discourses*. The general theme of these chapters is the comparative merits of the use of force and fraud and how they contribute to the reputation of a prince. Chapter 11 argues that one should not make alliances with leaders who have a great reputation but lack the force to back it up. This is the transition to chapter 12, where Machiavelli considers the maxim that if you fear a potential enemy, you should go and assault him where he lives rather than wait to be attacked. If you wait to be attacked, even if you defeat the enemy inside your own borders, he will retain his kingdom intact to threaten you another day. If you strike him at home and win, the threat is removed. Referring to Herodotus's

---

[4] Still fascinating in this regard is the interpretation of Moses by Wildavsky (2005).

account of Cyrus, Machiavelli says that Croesus gave this advice to Cyrus with respect to attacking Queen Tamyris of the Massageti. Others, Machiavelli continues, say that Hannibal gave Antiochus the same advice – attack the Romans in their own Italian homeland. This pairing is probably deliberate, for, as we will consider, in chapter 17 of *The Prince*, Machiavelli again links Hannibal with the real Cyrus as opposed to Xenophon's Cyrus.

In chapter 13 of Book 2, Machiavelli proposes that "one comes from base to great fortune more through fraud than through force." Men of lowly and obscure origins can only come to greatness through force or fraud or a combination of the two, albeit with an emphasis on fraud. Left aside altogether from consideration are those whose "rank . . . may be given or left by inheritance to them." These latter are, in other words, favored by fortune by being born to their princely status, and so not compelled to rely sheerly on their virtue as defined in chapter 6 of *The Prince*. Xenophon's Cyrus, born the son of the Persian king Cambyses, firmly conforms to this latter pattern, whereas Herodotus's Cyrus, an adventurer of obscure origins, does not. Machiavelli's first line of argument is that one can rise from "obscure or base fortune" to empire through fraud alone but not through "open force alone." This would appear to imply that he could also rise to great fortune through a combination of force and fraud, or through the indirect (as opposed to "open") use of force. To illustrate the point, Machiavelli provides the longest discussion of Xenophon's Cyrus so far in the *Discourses*:

Xenophon in his life of Cyrus shows this necessity to deceive, considering that the first expedition that he has Cyrus make against the king of Armenia is full of fraud, and that he makes him seize his kingdom through deception and not through force. And he does not conclude otherwise from this action than that it is necessary for a prince who wishes to do great things to learn to deceive. Besides this, he makes him deceive Cyaxares, king of the Medes, his maternal uncle, in several modes; without which fraud he shows that Cyrus could not have attained that greatness he came to.

The reader must wonder just how apt this illustration is for Machiavelli's own theme of rising from base to great fortune. For Xenophon's Cyrus was, to reiterate, never a man of base or obscure origins. In fact, as the son of the Persian king and grandson of the Median king, he would appear to be squarely in the category that Machiavelli has excluded from consideration: "rank that another has attained may be given or left by inheritance to them." I suggest that what Machiavelli is doing here is to accept Xenophon's foreground account of Cyrus, but supplementing it with his own more realistic account of Cyrus's base origins (closer to the Herodotean version) in order to let the reader know how the real Cyrus might eventually have been in a position to leave to posterity Xenophon's account of him as a legitimate prince marked for great fortune from the very outset. To some extent, then, he relies on Xenophon's account for important evidence of Cyrus's statecraft but will not limit himself to a reliance on it. As a prince of thought, so to speak, Machiavelli's own virtue, the root of his own ability not to rely on fortune, emerges from his will not to rely on the classical political philosophers, enabling him to encourage princes and potential princes not to rely on their advice regarding practical statecraft.

As described here by Machiavelli, Xenophon clearly shows an understanding of the need for fraud: his Cyrus subverts and seizes the kingdom of Armenia through fraud and not through "open" force. Yet in the full account of Cyrus's conquest of Armenia in the *Education of Cyrus*, Cyrus's massing of forces on the Armenian border on the eve of the invasion under the pretense of a hunt is also a kind of force or at least a threat of force. The feigned hunt evolves seamlessly into war; fraud evolves seamlessly into force. In Book 3, chapter 39, the maxim of which is "that a Captain ought to be a knower of sites," Machiavelli further blurs the distinction between force and fraud in his final reference to Cyrus:

In the life of Cyrus, Xenophon shows that when Cyrus was going to assault the king of Armenia, in devising that struggle he reminded his men that this was none other than one of those hunts that they had often undertaken with him. He reminded those whom he sent in ambush on top of mountains that they were like those who went to hold the nets on the ridges, and those who rode the plains that they were like those who went to flush the beast from the cover so that when hunted it would trip into the nets.

Returning to Book 2, chapter 13, of the *Discourses*, Machiavelli, as we have seen, states rather bluntly that Xenophon "makes" Cyrus deceive his uncle Cyaxares repeatedly. However, this might not be so clear to someone reading the *Education of Cyrus* unaware of Machiavelli's interpretation. It is not so much that Cyrus ruthlessly deceives

Cyaxares, heir to the throne of Media, as that Cyrus's grandfather, the benign tyrant Astyages, is hugely taken with his grandson's talents and gradually allows the boy to displace his own hapless son and heir. Cyaxares reacts to his displacement more with resignation than with anger, and, later on, Cyrus reconciles him to his figurehead role by surrounding him with luxury. As Cyaxares says resignedly when Cyrus outshines him even as a young boy by being too daring on the hunt, "Do as you wish, for now it looks as if it were you who are our king" (1.4.9). In the *Education of Cyrus*, the principal cause of Cyrus's elevation to being the most prominent man in Media is not relentless deception, although deception is certainly involved, but his grandfather's natural affection and discernment of his grandson's natural merit. That is to say, Xenophon's Cyrus rises principally through reliance on the good fortune of his birth, his circumstances, and the capacity of an affectionate older patron to recognize his merits. On all of this, Machiavelli is completely silent.

Now we see more precisely the relationship of the *Education of Cyrus* to Machiavelli's overall conclusion that you cannot rise from "base fortune . . . to attain great empire" through "open" force alone, as opposed to a combination of fraud and force, indirect force, or the exercise of fraud as disguised force or the threat of force. Machiavelli's implication is that if we read Xenophon properly, guided by Machiavelli, we will find evidence for this maxim. This is true either because Machiavelli has interpreted the evidence about Cyrus presented by Xenophon more insightfully than Xenophon himself or because Xenophon consciously provides the reader with evidence of what he "makes" Cyrus do (for example, deceive Cyaxares repeatedly) beneath the generally more seemly surface of this first mirror of princes. Indeed, it is even possible, reading the *Education of Cyrus* from Machiavelli's perspective, that Xenophon stresses Cyrus's use of deception so as to bury more deeply his use of force. That is to say, the seemliest and surface level of Xenophon's account, where Cyrus is the paragon of the traditional virtues and the protégé of a patron who recognizes his merit, may on closer inspection yield a deeper stratum revealing his extensive use of fraud, itself concealing until thought through on the basis of Machiavelli's new conception of virtue as the mastery of *Fortuna* an even deeper stratum of outright violence and usurpation.

When Machiavelli says that Xenophon "makes" Cyrus perform certain actions, I detect an echo of what he says about princes of "outstanding virtue" in chapter 6 of *The Prince* – that they are free to introduce into matter "any form they pleased." Perhaps the real Cyrus re-created his origins, refashioned the account of his own life retroactively, so as to hand down to writers on statesmanship like Xenophon the materials for composing the seemlier account. Or perhaps Xenophon was a kind of prince himself, a prince of speculation like Machiavelli, a shaper of "new modes and orders" through his power to "make" Cyrus into a model for future statesmen. However this may be, in Machiavelli's presentation, the sober grounding for properly interpreting Xenophon's more seemly account of Cyrus as the paragon of monarchical virtue is Herodotus's unvarnished account of a ferociously ambitious and criminal usurper who rises from obscure fortune to imperial might through his relentless willpower.

To the extent that Machiavelli is persuasive, one might reread the *Education of Cyrus* with a more jaundiced, suspicious, and *Realpolitik* cast of mind. Let us take an example that Machiavelli does not raise (although, as I suggest later, he does allude to it), the famous episode discussed in the last chapter in which Cyrus assigns the captive queen Pantheia to the care of his trusted subordinate and friend since boyhood Araspas. We recall that, after claiming in a dialogue with Cyrus that he is capable of gazing upon the queen's beauty while firmly reining in his erotic longing in order to perform his duty as her guardian, Araspas in fact proves he cannot when he tries to violate her. After she throws herself on the protection of Cyrus, who is resolutely chaste and moderate toward her, the erotic young lieutenant Araspas falls from power and, shortly thereafter, is heard from no more. Does he simply exit the narrative when his role in the story ends? Or, looking at it in a Machiavellian frame of mind, is there something more sinister about his "disappearance" after failing in his duty to his master, like a former paladin of Stalin vanishing and being "airbrushed" from subsequent history?

Machiavelli points us toward some dark reaches in Xenophon's life of Cyrus. In a plot so devious that Machiavelli himself, not to mention John le Carré, could only relish it, Cyrus ostensibly forgives Araspas, who is terrified of his master's wrath. However, news of his fall spreads throughout the army just as if it were real and he had not been forgiven

in private. Cyrus then gives Araspas a secret mission. He is to defect –
ostensibly – to the Assyrian side, pretending to fear Cyrus's wrath while
knowing secretly that he has been forgiven, and, while playing the role
of defector, to spy on the disposition of the Assyrian forces and report
back to Cyrus. His reduction from a proud lieutenant of Cyrus's inner
circle to a spy in seeming disgrace at home, although ostensibly only a
deception concealing his secret rehabilitation, does strike one as a kind
of punishment and humiliation for failing in his commission to guard
Pantheia: under any interpretation, his life as a double agent is a lie.
After giving his report on the Assyrian forces to Cyrus and his inner
circle (Cyrus pointedly discourages them from showing Araspas too
much affection when, to their surprise, he returns ostensibly forgiven
and still trusted by Cyrus), Araspas simply *vanishes* from the narrative,
on the eve of the greatest battle of all, the victory over the Assyrian tyrant
that will secure the empire (*Education of Cyrus* 6.3.15–18). Given that,
in the eyes of the world at large, Araspas really *is* a traitor and a defector,
his disappearance would not have been hard to arrange and would not
have caused widespread shock or dissatisfaction. Indeed, Cyrus's odd
warning to his circle just before Araspas returns that they should avoid
showing him too much affection might be taken as a tacit warning
that his rehabilitation was not a sure thing. Had Cyrus ever intended
genuinely to forgive him? Or, having disgraced him, did he simply use
the fallen paladin like a tool, making practical good use of his disgrace
in the interval before his final fate by holding out the false hope of
his rehabilitation by sending him on the spy mission, pretending to
Araspas that he was merely pretending to disgrace him so as to deceive
the Assyrian, all the while deceiving both the Assyrian and his former
lieutenant (who, in the eyes of the world, confirmed his disloyalty to
Cyrus beyond any doubt by defecting)? Did Cyrus perhaps deliberately
expose Araspas to Pantheia in the first place, knowing this top paladin
would likely succumb to her beauty, giving Cyrus the opportunity to
exploit him as a tool before getting rid of him? These are the depths of
intrigue to which a Machiavellian reading of the *Education of Cyrus*
can take one. As Machiavelli says of the prince: "All see you, few touch
what you are."

Showing, as this episode does, how chaste and self-controlled Cyrus
was in erotic matters in contrast to a subordinate who fails this test and
subsequently falls from power and vanishes might indicate how a prince

like Cyrus could shape posterity's view of him by the choice of materials he passes down about his exploits. It might also demonstrate the power that a writer about princes like Xenophon has in shaping those same materials. The reader would be left to ponder whether the seemlier foreground account is likelier to be true – where Araspas simply exits the narrative when his role in the story ends – or the darker version implied by a Machiavellian reading of his fate. It is unclear whether Machiavelli is attributing this darker sensibility to Xenophon himself or merely inviting us to read in a darker perspective evidence amassed by Xenophon more benignly or innocently, a perspective grounded in Herodotus's more realistic view of Cyrus as a man who owed nothing to fortune or his obscure origins and had to fight for it all.

The next group of chapters dealing with Cyrus in the *Discourses* is in Book 3, chapters 20 to 23. The overarching theme here is the comparative benefits of a ruler displaying, on the one hand, clemency and humanity or, on the other, harshness and severity. These chapters include a comparison of Cyrus, Hannibal, and Scipio, thus more directly paralleling chapters 15 to 18 of *The Prince*, which we consider more closely in the next section of this chapter.

Machiavelli begins chapter 20 of Book 3 of the *Discourses* by offering for our consideration the observation "how much more a humane act full of charity is sometimes able to do in the spirits of men than a ferocious and violent act." We immediately note the qualification: sometimes – not always. His proof that humane behavior is sometimes more effective than ferocity is that Scipio's fame came less from conquering Carthage than from his chastity in having returned a wife to her husband unmolested, "which made all Spain friendly to him." Readers of the *Education of Cyrus* will likely recall here how Cyrus returned the captive queen Pantheia unmolested to her husband, reminding us again how Scipio modeled himself on his *viade mecum*.[5]

Machiavelli observes how greatly "peoples" desire this kind of moderation and capacity to refrain from tyranny in "great men," and how much it is "praised by writers, and by those who describe the life of princes, and by those who order how they ought to live." Given what we have seen of his own views, perhaps Machiavelli is suggesting that

---

[5] See, for example, Xenophon (1968a) introduction.

"the writers" of traditional political and moral philosophy side with the delusions and unwarranted hopes of the common people for ethical purity in their outstanding princes, or pander to their illusions so as to enhance their own safety and stature. Xenophon, he goes on, "toils very much to demonstrate how many honors, how many victories, how much good fame being humane and affable brought to Cyrus, and not giving any example of himself either as proud, or as cruel, or as lustful, or as having any other vice that stains the life of men." (The reference to Xenophon's Cyrus not being lustful suggests that Machiavelli is aware that Scipio's chastity toward the captive wife in Spain parallels, and was likely imitating, Cyrus's chastity toward Pantheia.)

For Machiavelli, such edifying accounts of a great prince as a paragon of moderation may be a screen inserted by "the writers" between the harsh reality of such men and what the common people long for in them. For, as he immediately observes, "Hannibal attained great fame and great victories with modes contrary to these." Just as in chapter 6 of *The Prince*, here, too, princes of outstanding "virtue" in the Machiavellian sense, and in contrast with what "the writers" claim, can impose their will through violence and deceit, and, having attained godlike positions of venerability, rewrite their own past to hand down to their future biographers. Hannibal, to be sure, is not to be compared with the greatest of the "armed prophets" like Moses. Yet in both *The Prince* and the *Discourses*, Machiavelli uses lower-level exemplars of open violence, treachery, and mass slaughter among second-tier princes such as Hiero and Agatholces of Syracuse to imply what he wants us to understand about the greatest princes as well, shrouded as they are in impenetrable sanctity. If you understand Machiavelli, you might be able to combine Moses' stature with Hannibal's methods. Machiavelli's Hannibal contradicts at every point what traditional sources such as Xenophon say about outstanding monarchs, but Hannibal may be far closer to the reality of Cyrus than the Cyrus of the *Education of Cyrus*. Of course, from Machiavelli's perspective, the *Education of Cyrus* might well be a useful model of how a prince should rewrite his history for posterity, useful as a model for propaganda as long as one does not take it literally. Whereas Xenophon writes as if Cyrus possessed the moral virtues suitable to a benign monarch from the outset, and as if they were the source of his success, Machiavelli is suggesting that he displayed the very opposite qualities, ones that would traditionally be considered vices, and thereby rose to a position of power that left him free to remake himself and endow himself retroactively with the traditional virtues.

Hannibal, then, is contrasted not with the real Cyrus – whom he resembles – but with Xenophon's Cyrus, a paragon of humanity and kindness that is "the very opposite" course. Scipio, on the other hand, we are told, practiced only the virtues of "humanity and benevolence" that he had learned from the *Education of Cyrus*. Either Hannibal's or Scipio's method is capable of success or failure, Machiavelli concedes, depending on the "virtue" of the one who employs it, but he definitely leans toward Hannibal's method as the more reliable. Scipio's generosity to his troops, Machiavelli maintains, inflamed their desires to the point where he could no longer satisfy them or maintain discipline. Hannibal, however, with his "inhuman cruelty and infinite virtue" terrified his soldiers into reconciliation to his rule and gratitude for whatever positive favors he chose to bestow (*The Prince* chapter 17). In other words, it is not enough for a prince to rely on his subjects' own assessment of their self-interest. By contrasting Scipio's failure at ruling with Hannibal's success, Machiavelli suggests that the imitator of the real Cyrus would inspire fear in his subjects so as to make it always in their minimal self-interest to obey him and to inspire their deeper gratitude for benefits beyond the minimum of survival – an anticipatory job description for Hobbes's Sovereign.

Chapter 22 again stresses Xenophon's importance in the history of the mirror of princes. For, as Machiavelli observes, the humanity of Cyrus praised by Xenophon "conforms very much with what Titus Livy says of Valerius." Nevertheless, according to Machiavelli, Livy himself is of two minds about whether humanity or hardness is the better way, for he "speaks honorably in the same way of Manlius, showing that his severity in the death of his son made the army so obedient to the consul that it was the cause of the victory that the Roman people had against the Latins." So, as Machiavelli concludes, "it would be difficult to judge" which course is better. But he does offer a judgment: the severity of Manlius is better for a republic of laws because it is impartial. As he explains: "By showing oneself always harsh to everyone and loving only the common good, one cannot acquire partisans; for whoever does this does not acquire particular friends for himself, which we call ... partisans." By contrast, the humane approach of Valerius, although it may produce some of the same benefits for a republic in its foreign policy, creates a "particular goodwill" among the soldiers, turning them into his personal adherents, and may thereby lead to "bad effects on freedom" in the long run. Machiavelli inclines toward Manlius on the grounds that his cruelty prevented him from becoming popular, which helped preserve the rule of law as opposed to parties loyal to the leading men. Machiavelli approves of more gentle rule and the qualities Xenophon attributes to Cyrus – or at least the appearance of them – when it comes to monarchies strictly speaking, as opposed to republics in which leading citizens like Scipio are tempted to imitate monarchical qualities and so undermine the republic's collective vigor. (Machiavelli's endorsement of Xenophon in this context is presumably the Xenophon whom he has told us earlier shows Cyrus to be a master of deception.) Interestingly, Manlius executed his son for killing an enemy in single combat, violating the orders of the consuls – in other words, he executed his son for seeking individual glory at the expense of the whole army. We might therefore note that Manlius's willingness to kill his own son to preserve the laws shows that such harshness and moral zealotry might be a more certain way of overcoming the love of one's own than the Platonic prescription in which our eros for honor overcomes base passions by transcending itself in the direction of the Idea of the Good. Perhaps the thumotic enforcers of honor are more reliable guardians of justice than the philosophically inclined.

To sum up Machiavelli's maxims in these chapters: humane behavior in a leader is conducive to his private ambition because it creates a client group that is personally loyal to that man. By contrast, uniformly exercised severity is disinterested and idealistic, serving only the common good. Even more significantly, each approach is appropriate to a specific regime, and those regimes are mutually exclusive. Humane leadership fits a monarchy like that of Cyrus, who is the source of everyone's happiness and the cynosure of all men's admiration, whereas a republic of equality under the laws must discourage the emergence of such leaders, who can only subvert its austere collective freedom. This crucial distinction prepares us for the thematic consideration of the traditional catalogue of civic virtues in *The Prince*. We now see more clearly why Machiavelli believes that the classical "writers" on statecraft can have a harmful, even subversive, influence on republican mores. The danger in republican leaders such as Scipio and Valerius using "Xenophon's Cyrus" as their guide is that it improperly encourages proto-monarchical behavior in the servants of a republic:

(I)f we have to consider a prince, as Xenophon is considering, we shall take the side altogether of Valerius, and leave Manlius, for a prince ought to seek obedience and love in soldiers and in subjects. Being an observer of the orders and being held virtuous give him obedience; affability, humanity, mercy and the other parts that were in Valerius – and that, Xenophon writes, were in Cyrus – give him love. For being a prince particularly well wished for and having the army as his partisan conform with all the other parts of his state. But in a citizen who has the army as his partisan, this part already does not conform with his other parts, which have to make him live under the laws and obey the magistrates.

Machiavelli's summation of this group of chapters parallels and prepares us for the discussion in chapter 17 of *The Prince*, to which we now turn, on whether it is better to be feared or loved, and here, too, we are offered a comparison of Cyrus, Xenophon's Cyrus, Scipio, and Hannibal. Here, too, the lesson is that the love that a monarch or aspiring monarch can obtain from the common people by making Xenophon's Cyrus his model will, if practiced by the servant of a republic, subvert its harsh equality and, by creating a faction loyal to that one man, court the dangers of demagoguery and tyranny.

SUBVERTING THE TRADITIONAL CATALOGUE OF THE VIRTUES

The textual relationship between Machiavelli and Xenophon is evident from the opening pages of *The Prince*. Whereas Plato has his Socrates discourage young men from becoming tyrants in the *Republic* and elsewhere, and Aristotle advises tyrants in Book 5 of the *Politics* to reform themselves as rapidly as possible into monarchs, Machiavelli openly advises princes and potential princes on how to acquire and maintain power regardless of whether they employ ethical means or not. He does not distinguish, as does Aristotle in Book 3 of the *Politics*, between the correct regime of monarchy and the defective regime of tyranny, but blurs them into the value-neutral term "princes."

Xenophon is Machiavelli's closest precedent among the ancient thinkers for this more pragmatic approach to the statecraft of one-man rule. Machiavelli adopts the same stance toward the advisee addressed by *The Prince* as Xenophon has Simonides adopt toward his potential advisee, the tyrant Hiero in the work of the same name. Moreover, there is a direct gloss on the *Hiero* at the end of chapter 21 of *The Prince*. Here, closely paralleling Xenophon's presentation of Simonides' advice to Hiero for transforming himself from an opprobrious tyrant into a benevolent "leader" (if not truly a "king"), Machiavelli advises the prince to encourage his subjects to prosper economically, to reward them for any technical innovations they contribute to the state's economy, to make sure they know their earnings are protected from arbitrary seizure, and to entertain the people with feasts and spectacles (*Hiero* 9.5–10, 10.5, 11.4).

We have already seen in our consideration of chapter 6 of *The Prince* how Cyrus the Great is an example of the rare princes of "outstanding virtue," but we also saw how the model provided by Cyrus there is not necessarily *Xenophon's* Cyrus, a distinction further confirmed by our subsequent examination of all the references to Cyrus in the *Discourses*. Fundamentally, Machiavelli invites us to reread the *Education of Cyrus* in a more jaundiced light, treating it as an account that can be grafted onto the far more realistic explanation of Cyrus as a self-made man who rose from base origins to high fortune through acts often criminal and bloody, but who was then able to rewrite history to leave a glowing account for posterity in which he is retroactively endowed with all the ethical virtues extolled by philosophers. This edifying account is summed up by the *Education of Cyrus*. The real Cyrus, Machiavelli leads us to envision, prepared the ennobled version of himself found in Xenophon's writings just as, by implication, Moses was able to transform himself through the Torah. Remaking themselves in this way for posterity is one of the chief ways in which princes of "outstanding virtue" can "introduce into matter whatever form they please." Machiavelli wants to unlock this secret of empire by provoking us to ground the surface, edifying Xenophontic Cyrus in the subterranean, darker account more accurately revealed by Herodotus.

The most serious discussion of Xenophon's Cyrus in contrast with the real Cyrus comes in the group of chapters in *The Prince*, 15 to 18, that deals with "those things for which men, and especially princes, are praised or blamed." Here we get a catalogue of the virtues and their corresponding vices from both classical and Christian sources: liberality versus parsimony, cruelty versus pity, being loved versus being feared. This theme is announced at the end of chapter 14, where Machiavelli tells us that a prince should study the exploits and actions of past great leaders, "as they say Alexander the Great imitated Achilles; Caesar [imitated] Alexander; Scipio [imitated] Cyrus." He continues: "And whoever reads the life of Cyrus written by Xenophon will then recognize in the life of Scipio how much glory that imitation brought him, how much in chastity, affability, humanity and liberality Scipio conformed to what had been written of Cyrus by Xenophon." In other words, whereas Alexander the Great imitated Achilles directly, and Caesar imitated Alexander directly, Scipio did not imitate Cyrus directly, but only *Xenophon's* Cyrus, an indirect imitation with which Machiavelli fairly clubs us over the head by twice mentioning Xenophon's authorship of the *Education of Cyrus* in the same sentence.

Let us note that when offering Achilles, Alexander, and Caesar as examples of princes who imitated other princes directly, as opposed to Scipio's reliance on Xenophon's account of Cyrus, Machiavelli omits the rather obvious detail that Alexander could arguably only have imitated the Achilles created by Homer, a "writer," since Homer's account of Achilles is certainly the fullest. It would seem as if Machiavelli exempts the ancient poet from the criticism he makes of the ancient philosophers, perhaps because Homer depicted Achilles in such a way as to minimize his own moral interference and so enable his daring hero to be directly imitated by real-life princes. Whereas Alexander could imitate Achilles directly because Homer does not intervene, Machiavelli is silent about the equally obvious tradition holding that Alexander was tutored by Aristotle, and, in creating his multinational empire, was arguably at least as much influenced by the cosmopolitanism of Greek philosophy (nowhere politically more explicit than in Xenophon's monarchical utopia) as by the tragic hero of the Trojan War. Machiavelli's silence about Homer's shaping of the model of Achilles for Alexander is a compliment to the poet's silent presence as its creator, while his omission of Aristotle is due to the screen of moralizing distortion the classical thinker interposes between princes and the "effectual truth" about statecraft, the reverse of Aristotle's entire political theory.

Machiavelli's partiality toward the ancient poets over the philosophers is evident elsewhere, as when, for example, he cites approvingly the fable of Chiron, the half-human, half-animal teacher of Achilles and other ancient princes for communicating the maxim that a prince must be able to use the bestial as well as the human side of his nature (*The Prince* chapter 18). Perhaps Machiavelli even prefers that Achilles be identified with this myth rather than explicitly with Homer, whose poetry was, after all, thought capable of a degree of moral rehabilitation by Plato. The semianimalized Chiron is the transition to the fully animalized psyche of what Machiavelli calls the lion and fox. The Chiron model (since it is not entirely somatic) is still too reliant on a transcendental conception of the soul, but less wholly given over to the transcendental than Aristotle's concept of the soul, which is virtually drained of anything somatic and makes no mention of moral virtues such as courage and prudence that are conducive to political success.[6] Machiavelli's preference for poetry in general over traditional philosophy with its transcendental metaphysics can further be seen in his invocation of Petrarch at the end of *The Prince* for stirring the patriot's love of the fatherland. Finally, there is the gloss on Xenophon's *Hiero* in *The Prince*. We observed in Chapter 2 that Xenophon distinguishes both himself as author and Socrates as a philosopher from the depiction of Simonides, a poet, giving the tyrant advice on how to reform, on the grounds that poets dwell in the realm of becoming and mutability, whereas philosophers are oriented to the eternal truth. By contrast, Machiavelli, in addressing the prince, merges himself with the roles of both author and advisor, a mutability that is also more in keeping with poetic "making" (*poiesis*) than with a love of the eternal and unchanging truth. (Homer also merges himself with his narrative as the silent conduit for the Muse [*Iliad* 1.1–5; *Odyssey* 1.1–10].)

These observations are of a piece with my earlier argument that Machiavelli is in part returning to the dissident strain of ancient thought, that of the pre-Socratics and Sophists, especially if we accept the Platonic Socrates' contention that the poets, led by Homer, already express

---

[6] See, for example, Aristotle *On the Soul* 414a30–b15, where thumos, for Plato the seat of courage in the soul and distinct from mere bodily desire (*epithumia*), is demoted to merely one variety of desire along with *epithumia*, and where intellect (*nous*) is discussed without any reference to *phronesis*, the highest virtue of the statesman in the *Politics* and *Nicomachean Ethics*.

through image, myth, and allegory the ontological argument made by their more prosaic successors, that nature is motion whose human upsurge is the life of mastery. Now as earlier, however, we must beware of taking this too far and depicting Machiavelli as a simple return to ancient materialism and hedonism. He is after much bigger game, as exemplified by the redefinition of virtue as the project for overcoming nature and chance. Socrates' inclusion of Homer – in his view the greatest tragedian – and the other poets among the motion-men reminds us that, far from believing that nature could be mastered from without, the core of tragedy was the need for man to reconcile himself to the reversals caused by the awesome alternation between chance and necessity (*Republic* 595b–c; *Theatetus* 152d–e). Even Zeus cannot overrule the Fates. Those who, like Achilles, aim high must expect to be brought down and can only look their doom in the face with noble resignation (Aeschylus *Prometheus Bound* 515–518; Homer *Iliad* 1.350–355, 510–530; Plato *Republic* 379b–380a). Even without Plato's censorship of Homer to make him more plainly into an advocate of justice, the *Iliad* itself is not uncritically enthusiastic about Achilles' violent passions and insubordination. A price will be paid, as Zeus warns Achilles' mother when acceding to her request to help Achilles show up Agamemnon by making his withdrawal from combat result in a Trojan victory. Zeus issues another warning to Thetis when her son exceeds the wrath appropriate to mere men and exacts a god's revenge on the corpse of Hector (*Iliad* 24.125–135). Machiavelli might well provisionally prefer the open ambition and dominating qualities of Achilles to the "effeminated" rulers of his own Christian era, but that is as far as it could go. He certainly could not approve of Achilles' overwhelming erotic attachments to Briseis and Patroclus, which robbed him of all judgment, just as he could not approve of that side of Alexander's imitation of Achilles that fueled his love of Hephaisteon and his unfortunate tendency to place that love above the demands of cool calculation as a commander. For Machiavelli, Achilles would know too much about the lion and not enough about the fox. Insofar as Machiavelli is arguing for the exertion of rational control over nature, first and foremost by the prince over his own nature, he is to this extent in the camp of reason rather than poetic and tragic revelation.

Machiavelli's fundamental argument in this group of chapters is that the traditional virtues should not be practiced for their own sake. For, although ancient writers such as Aristotle say we will be happy if we practice virtue for its own sake, how could a prince be happy if by doing so he loses his state? According to *The Prince*, the problem with the traditional-minded "writers" whom Machiavelli uses Xenophon to exemplify is that they misinterpret the virtues that people attribute after the fact to princes who have succeeded in bringing them peace and prosperity as the prior causes of their success. In other words, they "effeminate" virtue by trying to ground it in an "imagined" realm of eternal, preexistent ends of peace and justice. However, *appearing* to have the virtues can be a useful source of power in itself. Here, then, the intrinsic pursuit of virtue for its own sake recommended by both classical and Christian authorities is replaced by the manipulation of the appearance of virtue as propaganda to embellish a leader's reputation. At a phenomenological level, the virtues do contrast with the vices – they produce a different psychological impact on the ruled. However, both virtues and vices, traditionally regarded, can be either useful or harmful depending on how they are employed: "For if one considers everything well, one will find something appears to be a virtue which, if pursued, would be one's ruin, and something else appears to be a vice, which if pursued results in one's security and well-being" (*The Prince* chapter 15). Rather than being pursued or avoided for their own sake, the virtues and vices are now alike subjected to the common underlying aim of maximizing the security and well-being of both the prince and his subjects.

The really interesting twist in Machiavelli's discussion is that when the virtues are practiced for their own sake, not only do they fail to avoid their corresponding vices; they *guarantee* to bring them about. Liberality causes parsimony; pity leads to cruelty. If a prince is liberal toward the meritorious, as Aristotle recommends, he will, Machiavelli reasons, have to overtax his subjects to get the wherewithal, making him hateful to the majority. If he then makes economies, they will hate him for being stingy. People do not really admire a ruler's generosity because of the qualities it reveals in him but because of the benefits they derive from it. Hence it follows that, faced with the choice between impoverishing his subjects in order to have the wherewithal to practice generosity for its own sake and being stingy, the prince should choose stinginess as the course of action least likely to enrage his subjects by violating their interests. The best solution of all, however, is like "Cyrus,

Caesar, or Alexander," to despoil other peoples in order to be able to practice generosity toward one's own people at no cost to oneself or them: "Either the prince spends from what is his own and his subjects' or from what belongs to someone else. In the first case he should be sparing; in the other, he should not leave out any part of liberality." Whereas Aristotle argued that liberality could be practiced by citizens within a self-governing republic, in reality, Machiavelli argues, it can only be practiced by the monarch of a prosperous empire like that of Cyrus. The citizen of a republic who is liberal toward those he deems deserving will, as we saw in Machiavelli's discussion of the humane Valerius in the *Discourses*, in fact be creating a faction of clients personally loyal to him, undermining republican equality and courting the rise of a demagogue or tyrant.[7]

Machiavelli's examples here in chapter 16 of *The Prince* of the realistic practice of liberality through imperialism are "Cyrus, Caesar, and Alexander." The observant reader will note a change from the list of famous predecessors at the end of chapter 14. There, Machiavelli had Alexander directly imitating Achilles, Caesar directly imitating Alexander, but Scipio only indirectly imitating Cyrus through "the life of Cyrus written by Xenophon." At the end of chapter 16, by contrast, Machiavelli urges a prince to imitate "Cyrus, Caesar, and Alexander," tacitly moving Cyrus over to the list of princes who imitated the reality of their forbears, not a version filtered by the classical writers. Generosity on the basis of imperialism was the basis of the real Cyrus's success, which should be directly imitated, as opposed to Xenophon's interpretation, which Scipio imitated. Machiavelli's implication, I think, is that studying Xenophon's Cyrus would not make you sufficiently keenly aware that the only basis for liberality toward one's subjects is imperial conquest involving massive bloodshed and destruction. For it is true that, in the *Education of Cyrus*, we see relatively little of these darker dimensions of empire. Aside from a few major battles like the one against the Assyrian empire, most of Cyrus's subjects come to him voluntarily, and the peace and prosperity with which he reconciles his millions of

---

7 For an interesting discussion of Hume's interpretation of Machiavelli's understanding of the virtues (including liberality), how Hume traced their practice through the careers of English monarchs including Elizabeth, and how he drew on Machiavelli's criticism of the Aristotelian account of liberality to elaborate his own economic theory, see Whelan (2004).

subjects to his absolute authority seem to flow effortlessly from the fact that "all men were willing to obey him."

In chapter 17, Machiavelli debates whether a prince should practice pity or cruelty. Pity evokes both the classical virtue of clemency toward defeated foes practiced by great rulers like Cyrus, Alexander, and Caesar and the cardinal Christian virtue of compassion. As Machiavelli observes, it is traditionally held that a ruler who practices the virtue of compassion will be loved by his subjects, whereas the cruel ruler will be feared and hated. Hence, in the traditional view, compassion is both good for its own sake and contributes to a ruler's security. In stark contrast, Machiavelli argues that a ruler who is excessively compassionate will allow civil strife and foreign foes to gain the upper hand, leading to an increase in the violence and disorder suffered by the majority of his subjects, which is tantamount to subjecting them to enormous cruelty. Again, practicing the virtue for its own sake is guaranteed to bring about its opposite vice. Instead, Machiavelli argues, the judicious use of force to suppress incipient insurrection or preemptively knock out a foreign foe will, through a short and efficiently targeted interval of cruelty, guarantee long-term peace and prosperity for the people. Moreover, he maintains, it is quite possible in reality to be cruel in this efficient and utilitarian way without being hated, although one will be feared. So in this way, too, a prince's authority and hold on power will be more stable through his being cruel rather than compassionate. This is so long as the cruelty is, as he puts it in chapter 8, "well-used," which means for the sake of maximizing security and well-being for both princes and peoples, and not prompted by some spasm of personal lust or fury. He concludes: "A prince...so as to keep his subjects united and faithful should not care about the infamy of cruelty, because with very few examples he will be more merciful than those who for the sake of too much mercy allow disorders to continue" (*The Prince* chapter 17).[8]

---

[8] See the fine exegesis by Orwin (1978), especially his emphasis on how Machiavelli liberates pity from piety, and argues that "well-used" cruelty, applied judiciously and all at once, is in the long run more compassionate than abstaining from violence, because it saves everyone from the far worse cruelty of unrestrained civil strife, a point of contact between Machiavelli and Hobbes's unvarnished remark that the worst conceivable tyrant, if he maintains order, is preferable to relapsing into the state of nature and the war of all against all. On the need to use force methodically, see Wolin's discussion of how, for Machiavelli, politics is a "science of the controlled application of force" (2006) p. 221.

How can a prince manage to be feared without being hated? Here, in my view, we reach the core of Machiavelli's critique of the tradition: his preference for fear over eros as the psychological orientation for the relationship between princes and peoples. A prince may be able to gain the love of his subjects through treating them with compassion, but that love cannot be relied on, because love is a voluntary emotion and can be withdrawn on a whim: "For love is maintained by a chain of obligation which, because of men's wickedness, is broken on every occasion of their own utility." Fear, on the other hand, "is maintained by a dread of punishment which never abandons you." It is a more reliable basis for authority because, unlike love, it is involuntary: no one can *not* be afraid of punishment or death. However, as Machiavelli goes on, fear need not be accompanied by hatred if (in advice paralleling the gloss on the *Hiero* in chapter 21) a prince does not arbitrarily plunder or otherwise violate the families or possessions of his subjects: "Above all he must abstain from the property of others, because men forget the death of a father more quickly than the loss of a patrimony." They will put up with their fear of the prince in exchange for the tangible benefits of a peaceful economy and personal security. In return, all they need do is never contest the absolute political predominance of their ruler.

In this chapter, every traditional teaching about the preferability of either republican or monarchical virtue as opposed to tyrannical vice is turned on its head. Machiavelli's prince will be a tyrant in the sense of relying on force, fraud, and the capacity to instill terror. But he will not be a tyrant in the sense decried most particularly by the ancients in Book 9 of the *Republic* and elsewhere (and, at least on this point, Machiavelli agrees with them). The prince who governs according to Machiavelli's prescription will not be a Nero or Caligula, an erotic out-law and monster of excess constantly violating his subjects' lives and possessions. Neither, however, will the new Machiavellian prince strive to perfect those virtues of character that, according to the classics, can make the statesman an object of love and admiration among his companions and fellow citizens. For that can only be achieved through being excessively, ruinously clement. In this way, Machiavelli is attempting to extirpate root and branch the teaching of Diotima's Ladder in the *Symposium*, where rationally guided erotic longing is the key to both personal and civic excellence. Specifically, political ambition is ennobled by being placed on the second highest level of the Ladder, second only to philosophic eros. By living virtuously in the service of the common good, Diotima teaches, one can achieve the immortality of an illustrious reputation for posterity (like the account of Cyrus transmitted by Xenophon) and be the object of an erotic longing among one's fellow citizens who are attracted to the virtuous fulfillment that the best statesmen bring to fruition because it answers to their own longings for erotic completion in union with the beautiful and the good. We admire and love in a virtuous citizen or statesman the nobility that we at our best long for in ourselves, and those leaders, by participating in what is eternally noble more fully than we do, present us with models to look up to. All this, Machiavelli tells us, must go. Believing that the world is rationally ordered and harmonious in such a way as to favor this cultivation of virtue and the love it will inspire in others is the greatest possible example of the dangerous reliance on Fortuna, for it makes one face the world not only literally "unarmed," but, much more important, psychologically unarmed and deluded about what truly comprises "the most outstanding virtue."

We also encounter in Machiavelli's formulations about love and fear in this chapter of *The Prince* a sedulous and characteristic use of elements of Christian ontology in order to undermine both the classical and Christian moral teachings. By arguing that relying on love is too unstable because men will break their "chain of obligation" through their "wickedness," Machiavelli attributes this failing to an Augustinian-sounding evaluation of man's fallen nature. Yet whereas Augustine would have argued that our wickedness makes us incapable of virtue in the absence of God's grace, Machiavelli is arguing that we should abandon any effort to live according to this moral standard. We are simply incapable of it, God or no God. Our natures are indeed fallen, but with God left out of the equation. Moreover, our being too "wicked" to love the prince must also extend to our incapacity to love *the* Prince, the Prince of the Universe. In Chapters 6 and 7, we will see in greater detail how constantly Machiavelli employs the Augustinian view of nature and human nature as fallen in order to justify the exclusion of the City of God altogether, along with its classical antecedants, as being beyond the range of a possible and desirable politics.

Machiavelli's proof that it is better to rely on fear than love is the behavior of Scipio, who, as he has told us, modeled all his actions on "the life of Cyrus written by Xenophon." The mutiny of Scipio's troops in Spain demonstrated his failure of one of the chief tests of republican leadership, the exercise of military command in foreign wars:

(His) armies in Spain rebelled against him. This arose from nothing but his excessive mercy, which had allowed his soldiers more license than is fitting for military discipline. Scipio's mercy was reproved in the Senate by Fabius Maximus, who called him the corrupter of the Roman military.

The man who passed this test, the successful exemplar of leadership, is Hannibal, whose methods could not have been more diametrically opposed to the gentle approach of Scipio:

Among the admirable actions of Hannibal is numbered this one: that when he had a very large army, mixed with infinite races of men, and had led it to fight in alien lands, no dissension ever arose in it, neither among themselves nor against the prince, in bad as well as in good fortune. This could not have arisen from anything other than his inhuman cruelty which, together with his infinite virtues, always made him venerable in the sight of his soldiers; and without it, his other virtues would not have sufficed to bring about this effect. And the writers, having considered little on this, on the one hand admire this action of his but on the other condemn the principle cause of it.

Hannibal, who successfully united men of numerous nations in an imperial enterprise and reconciled them wholly to his rule, cannot help but remind us of Cyrus the Great, the model for Alexander and Caesar, but not the Cyrus written about by Xenophon – consistently affable, chaste, and humane – on whom Scipio modeled himself because he, in accordance with Diotima's presentation of the eros for immortal fame through civic virtue on the second level of her Ladder of Love, wanted to be loved and admired by his fellow Romans. Instead, Hannibal is like the real Cyrus, the Cyrus whom Machiavelli reveals by stripping away the veneer of moral virtue with which he was endowed by Socrates' companion Xenophon. As interpreted by Machiavelli, the *Education of Cyrus* emerges as a more or less self-consciously propagandistic rewriting of history to credit Cyrus retroactively with all those virtues of liberality and compassion praised ever afterward by the classical and Christian traditions of statesmanship, and whose materials might well have been supplied by the historical Cyrus himself as he, along with Moses and the other examples of the most "outstanding virtue," shaped the accounts of themselves to be handed down to posterity by religious, poetic, and philosophical filters. Machiavelli's Cyrus is the truly effective if terrifying reality, the man who rises through force and fraud from base origins by constantly fighting the malignity of Fortuna with his strength of will, so that he can, godlike, introduce into matter whatever form he pleases.

MACHIAVELLI'S RHETORICAL EMPLOYMENT OF XENOPHON IN THE APPEAL TO ANTIQUITY

In the history of the mirror of princes genre, Xenophon was recognized as one of the originals, along with Plato and Cicero. We have already noted Castiglione's praise of Xenophon in *The Book of the Courtier*. As we have seen in this chapter, Machiavelli made extensive use of Xenophon, and their kinship was recognized. This is evident, for example, from Francis Digby's 1685 translation of the *Education of Cyrus*, which he recommends to the reader on the grounds that it is "written, indeed, much like Machiavel's *Florentine Prince*." Yet as we have seen throughout this chapter, Machiavelli's approval of Xenophon is carefully qualified and limited. Much of what Xenophon tells us about Cyrus, Machiavelli implies, is useful for statecraft, but only so long as we see that account primarily as a successful example of propaganda after the fact, not the means by which such a man could actually rise to the kind of power he eventually possessed.

We are now in a better position to understand both Xenophon's particular appeal for Machiavelli among the classical authorities on princely government and Machiavelli's reservations about his political theory. To understand this appeal, we should step back for a moment from the more equivocal aspects of Xenophon's views and reemphasize what is most massively distinctive about his point of departure. Whereas Plato's *Republic* and Aristotle's *Politics* culminate in prescriptions for the best civic community, the *Education of Cyrus* sets aside this prescription at the outset in favor of an individual's ambition for empire. However, much as Machiavelli wishes to join Xenophon in commending the example of Cyrus's success, he also wishes to distinguish "the life of Cyrus written by Xenophon" from his own appraisal of what such a ruler would actually have had to do to succeed on this scale. Tracing this distinction brings the double-edged quality of Machiavelli's interpretation of Xenophon into focus. Moreover, Xenophon's reservations about the methods and character of a ruler like Cyrus help to explain Machiavelli's reservations about Xenophon as an analyst of princely success.

Let us begin with the issue of candor about the ingredients of political success. We must ask: is it a fair reading of Xenophon when Machiavelli suggests that Scipio was misled by the *Education of Cyrus* into the neglect of tough-minded governance for the pursuit of those gentle virtues admired by philosophers? For in the very first pages of Xenophon's life of Cyrus, we read that Cyrus inspired such "fear of himself that he struck all people with terror and no one tried to withstand him; and he was able to awaken in all so great a desire to please him that they always wished to be guided by his will." Thus, we receive from Xenophon himself the description of a prince capable, like Hannibal, of "inhuman cruelty" and whose success exceeded anything achieved by the Carthaginian. Moreover, Tigranes, the former intimate of the "sophist" whose execution by his father Cyrus avenges, advises Cyrus after his first military victory to make his new subjects "moderate" by inspiring them with "soul-crushing fear," a policy he follows with stunning success (3.1.23–25). In contrasting Machiavelli's diagnosis of princely rule with Xenophon's, then, it does not seem sufficient to say that Xenophon's version is candy-coated. On closer inspection, moreover, it proves that Machiavelli himself does not believe this, for, as we have seen, he states his view that Xenophon did not present Cyrus as succeeding solely through the "humanity and affability" admired by Scipio but through a "variety of deceptions."

In this respect, Machiavelli's interpretation of the *Education of Cyrus* is amply demonstrated by the smooth game through which Cyrus strips the pathetic Cyaxares of his power while affecting to do him homage. We noted other examples of Cyrus's deceit earlier. If Machiavelli is aware that Xenophon is aware of the darker side of a political success like that of Cyrus, why does he so strongly imply that Xenophon's version of Cyrus will lead an imitator to failure? The answer lies, I believe, in the very qualified sense in which Machiavelli concedes Xenophon's political realism. Machiavelli, as we saw in

Book 2 of the *Discourses*, uses the example of the Xenophontic Cyrus's practice of deception to illustrate the point that someone is likelier to rise to a high position through fraud alone than through force alone. He does not, however, rule out someone rising through force *and* fraud. On the contrary, he portrays the Romans as being adept at using both force of arms and the reputation consequent upon their victories to delude and intimidate their foes and their allies alike. In chapter 6 of *The Prince*, where Machiavelli discusses examples of truly rare virtue, force is given more emphasis. In this chapter, Cyrus – as distinct from Xenophon's Cyrus – is said to have led the downtrodden Persians in a rebellion against their Median suzerains and thereby begun his rise to empire. This contradicts Xenophon's more seemly account of how Cyrus, as heir to the throne of an autonomous Persian republic, was asked to lead the Persian part of an allied military force against Assyria by his kinsman the king of Media. As these chapters from the *Discourses* and *The Prince* illustrate, then, when Machiavelli wants to emphasize the need to use fraud, he buttresses his argument with Xenophon's version of Cyrus stressing his talents at deception. When he wants to emphasize the need to use force, however, he ignores Xenophon's version in favor of his own. The implication is that while Xenophon teaches well enough the need for fraud, he does not make his readers sufficiently aware of the need to use force. Xenophon shows how Cyrus took advantage of his status as heir to the Persian throne to pursue his ambition, but, Machiavelli implies, Xenophon does not make it clear enough that Cyrus's very legitimacy may have been a retroactive rewriting of history, consequent upon victories achieved at even deeper levels of violence, base origins, and usurpation.

That Xenophon downplays the need for force as opposed to fraud strikes me as being a plausible characterization of Xenophon's political science, certainly from Machiavelli's viewpoint. Whereas Cyrus's use of fraud in the *Education of Cyrus* can be established fairly easily by a comparison of his statements, his use of force lurks more in the background, as we saw with the "disappearance" of Araspas under a cone of silence. Its extent and degree can be inferred from how the foreground events are affected by it. Typically, in Xenophon's approach, "force" is the discreet background guarantee of the "fraud" consummated in the foreground by Cyrus's many lengthy speeches. Cyrus always waits until he has deployed his forces in such a way as to achieve overwhelming military superiority before completing, through rhetorical persuasiveness, the conversion of former enemies into "willing" allies and subjects (3.1.1–6; 4.2.32). He relies on persuasion, not merely on fear, and is a formidable "sophist" himself. His loquaciousness contrasts strikingly with the silent and subterranean maneuvering of Shakespeare's Henry Bolingbroke, an exemplar, as I argue in the Conclusion, of Machiavelli's new prince on the Elizabethan stage. For example, Cyrus's defense of his conduct to his uncle Cyaxares, whose position he has usurped, although based on well-constructed (if self-serving) arguments, is silently guaranteed success by the fact that Cyrus has already lured Cyaxares' troops away from him and reduced him to a powerless figurehead (4.2.11; 4.5.8–12). On another occasion, Cyrus deliberately lies in wait for some of his newer allies drawn from among his conquered subjects whom he suspects of wanting to sneak away at night with their possessions. Those who attempt it are summarily slaughtered without any chance of repentance. This slaughter follows immediately upon, and silently underscores, a speech in which Cyrus promises these new allies his friendship in exchange for their loyalty (4.4.9–13; 4.5.3–7). The *Education of Cyrus* does furnish illustrations of Machiavelli's point that a ruler should play on his subjects' fears in order to make them see their self-interest as being served by his supremacy. It is also true, however, that in the *Education of Cyrus* we see much more of Cyrus giving than taking, winning consent than coercing obedience, rewarding than punishing. The most charming and memorable aspect of Xenophon's narrative is made up of the speeches that establish Cyrus's reputation for benevolence and his subjects' loving gratitude. Machiavelli's critique of the *Education of Cyrus*, therefore, is not so much that it contains nothing about the need for force as that this lesson is buried too deeply – is too discreet and indirect – to be of practical use to real-life imitators of Cyrus.

From Machiavelli's viewpoint, then, it would appear that Xenophon wants to have it both ways, like the other ancient "writers." Although Xenophon explores the prospects of princely ambition for achieving political stability and prosperity much more extensively than Plato and Aristotle, in the last analysis he refuses to abandon the principled distinctions between monarchical and tyrannical authority and

between virtuous and vicious, noble and base, gentlemanly and unrestrained conduct. He sees in a ruler like Cyrus a high degree of excellence but also deficiencies that may be compensated for by the excellences of citizenship and philosophy. Cyrus's love of honor may be
too demotic and undiscriminating. He loves to gratify others but will
never allow himself to be put in the position of the beneficiary, which
calls into question his capacity for friendship. He is moderate but
also cold. By monopolizing all honor, he in the long run robs his
ruling elite of any serious responsibilities. His increasing reliance on
eunuchs symbolizes how his monopoly of honor has over the course
of time "effeminated," to use Machiavelli's term, his own once-proud
fellow aristocrats. He cannot provide a successor on his own level.
He truly benefits his peoples but is capable of ruthless violence. This
mixture of admiration for Cyrus and reservations about him makes
Xenophon unwilling to depict Cyrus either as an out-and-out tyrant or
as a paragon of virtue. For Machiavelli, as a consequence, Xenophon's
not inconsiderable value as a source of advice for princes is undermined by the ancient philosopher's ambivalence toward his own model
of princely success. Machiavelli would have us understand the unvarnished truth that successful princes act on their untutored impulses
for dominion, glory, and wealth. Xenophon, by contrast, holds up
the rare example of a monarch educated as far as possible like a
gentleman through the most elaborately wrought civic pedagogy – a
monarch who, although not exactly legitimate, especially beyond the
borders of Persia, is not exactly a tyrant either; who, although not
exactly noble, develops his talents and achieves many benefits for his
followers.

Xenophon's unusual and equivocal position – less republican than
Plato and Aristotle, less "princely" than Machiavelli – explains the
double-edged relationship of his political thought to that of Machiavelli. Because Xenophon possesses the venerable authority of a classical
author, it is convenient for Machiavelli to be able to play up Xenophon's
preference for princely rule and his elaboration of its advantages, and
so draw his readers' minds away from the strictures placed on political
and military belligerence by Plato and Aristotle. Thus, as I observed at
the beginning of this chapter, Plato and Aristotle are not so much as
mentioned when the context (for example, the criticism of those who

have "imagined republics") would seem especially to require it, and Xenophon is made to stand for all the nameless "writers" about the traditional catalogue of the virtues. On the other hand, if Xenophon is correct that a prince can achieve the most glorious success imaginable *and* embody to a high (if not to the highest) degree the classical virtues of liberality, moderation, and justice, then he poses a real obstacle to Machiavelli's desire to undermine the classical tradition as a whole. For this reason also, then, Xenophon's views must be dealt with at greater length than the more republican-minded classical authors. It is precisely because Xenophon comes so close among the ancient authorities to Machiavelli's idea of an "effectual" politics that it becomes especially important for Machiavelli to refute him on some grounds while embracing him on others.

There is another dimension to the rhetorical advantages Machiavelli gains from singling out Xenophon for attention, and it is a way of entering the issue of Machiavelli's relationship to classical and Christian transcendentalism, which will be the special focus of the final two chapters. Many of the Renaissance humanists cite classical authors such as Cicero to show that pagan philosophy already anticipated the truth of Christian revelation because of its orientation toward a vision of the cosmos as beneficent, rationally ordered, and guided by the eternal truth and through its adjurations to transcend bodily and temporal passions guided by the divine spark in the soul. By stressing the proto-Christian transcendentalism of the classics, the Renaissance humanists also hoped to show their contemporaries that one could still assign top priority to the concerns of the soul and eternal salvation through faith while combining those most important of concerns with a more robust commitment to this-worldly civic duties than was sometimes granted by the exponents of medieval Christianity.[9] Machiavelli, in sharp contrast,

---

[9] Consider, for example, Castiglione on the influence of the classics and their reputation during the Renaissance. His pantheon of heroes is similar to that of Machiavelli. This passage combines a desire for eternal glory through the love of honor from the *Symposium* with the superiority of the life of the mind from Cicero's *Dream of Scipio*, with the added insight that the immortality of great writers better enables one to understand, by analogy, the immortality of fame through noble deeds, hence the need for liberal education: "What soul is there so abject, timid and humble, that when he reads the deeds of Caesar, Alexander, Scipio, Hannibal and many others, is not enflamed by an ardent desire to be like them, and does not make small account of this frail two day's life, in order to win the almost eternal life of fame, which in spite of death makes him live in far

is *only* concerned with the extent to which the classical authors focus on this-worldly statecraft. He excludes any consideration of classical (much less Christian) transcendentalism from his understanding of statecraft. In contrast with many of his contemporaries who wrote about classical philosophy as well as statecraft and the way in which the former must provide a moral compass for the latter, there is virtually no discussion of this kind in either *The Prince* or the *Discourses*. Machiavelli almost always wears the garb of the historian, and when he does occasionally allude rather distantly to philosophical debates (as we consider in Chapter 7), it is never for the sake of a purely theoretical discussion but always directly connected to a concern with political practice. At all turns, he embraces the this-worldly "fatherland" (*Discourses* 2.2) to the exclusion of the otherworldliness of both the classical and Christian traditions, the "imagined republics," as he dismissively terms this joint conglomerate, without naming names, in chapter 15 of *The Prince* – a reference, we can be certain, not only to Plato's *Republic* but surely also to St. Augustine's *Civitas Dei*. Among the classical sources, Xenophon comes closest to matching not only Machiavelli's pragmatism, partiality to imperial expansionism, endorsement of economic prosperity, and high regard for political honor, but also his aversion for metaphysical transcendence. Not unreasonably, Xenophon's depiction of Socrates has been characterized as philosophy stripped of the Ideas.

To look preliminarily into the religious implications of Machiavelli's political philosophy that will bulk large in the remaining chapters of this book, let us recall that chapters 15 to 19 of *The Prince* are a critique not only of the classical catalogue of the virtues but also of their adaptations by Christian theologians and humanists. For instance, the question as to whether princes should "keep faith" – that is, be honest – can also be read as the extent to which they should "keep *the* faith." Similarly, the discussion of "compassion" refers both to the classical conception of *clementia*, a civic virtue famously invoked by Julius Caesar, and the cardinal Christian virtue of pity that is to some extent built on its classical antecedent, while ultimately pointing to the

---

greater glory than before? But he who does not feel the delight of letters, cannot either know how great is the glory they so long preserve, and measures it by the life of one man or two, because his memory runs no further." Quoted in Newell (2001) pp. 140–141.

very different basis of a compassion for man through one's pity for Christ crucified. Indeed, the very term "pity" (*pietas*) reminds us that so important was this virtue to Christian revelation that the word for "piety" in general was appropriated for its specific designation. To pity man for the sake of God was the sum and total of what it meant to be pious. The undercurrent of religious motifs in Machiavelli's discussion of virtue is also evident in the contrast made in chapter 6 of *The Prince* between "armed prophets" such as Cyrus, Moses, Romulus, and Theseus and rulers who are "unarmed" owing to Christianity and ancient moral philosophy. The description of pagan rulers as "prophets" would appear to invest them with an authority at least akin to that of religious revelation itself. Moreover, the equation of the prince with the prophet in chapter 6 reminds us that when Machiavelli later contrasts the real Cyrus on the one hand with Xenophon's Cyrus and Scipio on the other, he is still tacitly discussing different kinds of princely "prophets," with Scipio's excessive compassion as a pagan ruler doubling as an excess of proto-Christian mercy.[10]

In assessing Machiavelli's joint critique of pagan and Christian statecraft, it is well to remember that Christianity's assimilation of ancient moral philosophy had never been smooth or complete. Christian

---

[10] On Machiavelli's blurring of the distinction between prince and prophet, consider the fine formulation by Ruffo-Fiore (1985) p. 2: "Machiavelli's new Prince is unquestionably an ideal hero, an exceptional military and political role-model with remarkable capacities of intelligence, will, and character. He is a hero-leader who has mastered the techniques of *virtu* and understands the inevitability of *fortuna*. Although Machiavelli utilizes such classical sources as Theseus, Cyrus, and Romulus for the mold of his ideal leader and seems deliberately to exclude the relevance of traditional Christian virtues to his character and actions, the Prince does reflect a disciplined selflessness and dedication in his pursuit of national identity, stability, and glory. The persistent interest in the prince suggests that something in Machiavelli's treatment captures the human imagination and fulfills a universal need. In studying this problem for a number of years, I have concluded that much of this fascination with the prince derives from Machiavelli's allusive, pervading vision of the sacral nature of the national patriarch. As a leader the new prince embodies the biblical idea of the prophet-king who has received a special divine call, a covenant from God to guide the destiny of the nation toward an appointed goal. The force and authenticity of this princely image, at once supremely attractive and frightening, results from how Machiavelli metaphorically parodies the religious theme of divine election and applies it in a purely secular context. His intent is to show the redeeming, communal function of a trustworthy leader who will liberate the people from captivity, define their national and ethnic identity, and reinstitute political order in a time of crisis." This is strong corroboration for the thesis formulated by Voegelin according to which Joachite millenarianism is immanentized in the secular prince.

orthodoxy could not abide the more full-blooded evocations of civic and martial achievement found in the classics, but instead emphasized the classics' concern with transcending worldly politics in the direction of the eternal truth. Thus, Petrarch, for example, as a good Augustinian, abhorred Cicero's pragmatic advice on statesmanship while admiring his devotion to philosophy. Machiavelli's aim of criticizing Christianity in tandem with his criticism of the ancient philosophers is clear when we bear in mind that his critique of Scipio the Elder for his reliance on Xenophon's *Education of Cyrus* glides easily into a critique of Cicero, whose account of Scipio the Younger in the *Dream of Scipio* entered the mirror of princes genre alongside the elder Scipio's guide. In Cicero's depiction, the younger Scipio prefers the life of the mind and the fate of his eternal soul to the world of political action, although virtuous action in the civic sphere is the route to those higher kinds of fulfill-ment. In the *Dream of Scipio*, it is his adoptive grandfather, the elder Scipio who was the devotee of the *Education of Cyrus*, who imparts to his descendant the eternal truth about the order of the cosmos. Thus, the younger Scipio's subordination of political ambition to the life of the mind, admired by Cicero and enshrined in his dialogue, flows from an ancestor who was decisively shaped by the writings of the Socratic Xenophon. In the *Discourses*, as we will see, Machiavelli witheringly criticizes Cicero's crashing failure in real life to bring the ambitious young Octavian Caesar under his guidance, attempting to practice that sublimation of ambition by wise counsel idealized in his own portrait of the younger Scipio and its antecedents including the prescription in Book 4 of the *Laws* for the lover of the city to be governed by a wise counsellor. When we read of Machiavelli's critique of Scipio the Elder in *The Prince* and *Discourses*, therefore, we are permitted subliminally to think of the younger Scipio as well (especially given Machiavelli's penchant, earlier remarked upon, for treating two identically named men as one). Both Scipios, elder and younger, compass the deleteri-ous effects of Greek philosophy, in its unworldliness, on Roman vigor, including on Cicero himself.

Machiavelli's critique of Cicero is the reverse of Petrarch's: whereas Petrarch criticized Cicero for allowing his philosophical interest in the eternal truth to be undermined by his preoccupation with political life, Machiavelli's implicit critique is that Cicero allows his grasp of statesmanship to be undermined by his respect for philosophy. Cicero's admiration for philosophy was often cited as a pagan prefiguration of the life guided by Christian revelation. Machiavelli is criticizing both the tendency of the classics to elevate moral and philosophic virtue over the hard necessities of politics and Christianity's selective reading of the ancients to emphasize still further this transcendence of political action. Altogether then, Machiavelli's use of the *Education of Cyrus* illustrates especially well the ambivalent relationship between ancient political philosophy and Christian morality. Xenophon's relatively open-minded assessment of princely ambition made his works useful for Machiavelli when he wished to play upon his Renaissance readers' admiration for classical antiquity in general in order to advance his own anti-Christian views on statecraft. At the same time, for Machiavelli, Xenophon's embellishment of the real Cyrus's ruthless drive with the virtues of peace and justice is a prime example of how "thoughtless writers on the one hand admire" a successful ruler's actions, and "on the other condemn the principal cause of them."[11]

To pursue the religious undercurrent a step further: just as Xenophon's Cyrus and his imitation by Scipio illustrate for Machiavelli the dangers of being "unarmed" by philosophical and religious morality, Machiavelli implies that a biblical ruler like Moses, once stripped of the Bible's edifying camouflage, could be understood in much the same ruthless terms as other "armed prophets" like the real Cyrus. Conversely, Machiavelli implies, we could start to view great secular rulers like Cyrus as having the same epochal scope for the creation of "new modes and orders" – new peoples, states, and moralities – that the Bible reserves for a few of God's appointed. If the linkage of Cyrus and Moses in chapter 6 of *The Prince* deflates the claims of Christian

---

[11] Coby (1999) makes a persuasive case that Machiavelli's debt to classical Roman thought, especially that of Livy, has sometimes been overlooked by those eager to enshrine him as the founder of modernity and modern political science. He argues that Machiavelli is both returning to ancient Rome and anticipating the Enlightenment, which I certainly agree with. I would be more inclined, however, to make a sharp distinction between Machiavelli's endorsement of Roman practices and the content of Roman history and his repudiation of classical political philosophy, including its influence on Livy. Whereas, for instance, Livy is equivocal about whether harshness or gentleness are the best modes of republican statesmanship, Machiavelli, as I argue in this chapter, although initially echoing Livy's balanced assessment, upon consideration is shown to definitely endorse harshness within republics, reserving gentleness for monarchy, and implying that the misapplication of gentleness by, for example, Scipio within a republic tends to subvert its moral vigor.

revelation over secular political authority by placing the biblical prince on a level with the pagan one, it also expands the claims of secular authority to an epochal scope formerly reserved for the instruments of God, the beginning of the divinization of the political sometimes associated with modern political millenarianism and totalitarianism. By contrast, Xenophon, even at his most candid, never allows that princes could exercise this power to shape "matter . . . into whatever form they thought fit," to re-create altogether the conditions of political existence (if not of all existence per se). The contrast allows us to see how far Machiavelli departs from the classical tradition even at its most pragmatic and sympathetic to imperial ambition.

A final comparison of Machiavelli and Xenophon will illustrate the restrictions placed by classical political thought in all its variants on this view of princely rule as epoch-making and creative. We recall that Machiavelli adopts the same stance toward the addressee of *The Prince* as Xenophon has Simonides adopt toward Hiero. In both cases, the wise adviser professes his ignorance about the life of high political authority only to go on to reveal that he knows more about effective ruling than the actual ruler. As we observed earlier, the parallel between the two works is confirmed when Machiavelli, after criticizing the traditional account of the virtues, in chapter 21 offers a gloss on Simonides' advice to Hiero on how to reconcile his subjects to his rule. Machiavelli advises the prince to honor and reward the talented, innovative, and industrious, a direct contradiction of Aristotle's warning against innovation as undermining the habit of lawfulness. The prince should also "encourage his subjects to pursue their trades in tranquillity" by allaying their fears of being despoiled or defrauded, a pithy anticipation of the Hobbesian Sovereign as the umpire and enforcer of contract law. The people should also be kept occupied with "festivals and shows," and the prince should make periodic displays of his generosity to the city's various guilds and clans. All of these points, frequently similarly worded, are found in Simonides' advice to Hiero. Each work tells a prince how he might protect the humble interests of the common people and so win their loyalty against the ambitious maneuverings of the nobility. However, while Xenophon depicts a politically canny poet advising a tyrant, he does not depict Socrates as doing so. Aside from protecting Socrates' reputation, Xenophon may be, as I suggested earlier, implying that the poet's concern with "making" (*poiesis*) is more suitable for converting a bad ruler into a good one than is the philosopher's concern with what things permanently are. That is, Socrates may be reluctant to admit that nature is so plastic or given to becoming that a ruler can supersede his crimes and transform himself into what he was not before. By contrast, Machiavelli simply merges himself as the author of *The Prince* with this advisor. Ending the book with a poetic appeal to Italy's prospective liberator, Machiavelli conflates the roles of philosopher, poet, and advisor. Machiavelli also rejects the idea of nature as regular, orderly, and placing limitations on human ambition for the "poetic" idea that corrupt political "bodies" can be re-made into healthy ones by vigorous princely action.

Xenophon's reservations about committing philosophy to the reform of tyranny might be thought to enable him to identify tyranny more clearly for what it is than can Machiavelli. Still, Machiavelli is able to adapt Xenophon's writings to his own purposes by radicalizing their character in a way that Plato's and Aristotle's works do not permit. Whereas Xenophon divides the spheres of politics and philosophy so as not to confound their respective excellences, Machiavelli simply lops away the sphere of philosophy by adapting Xenophon's political writings without making any reference to the Socratic ones. He thus takes advantage of the greater latitude Xenophon offers for the separation of politics and philosophy to argue that philosophy as traditionally conceived has nothing to do with "effectual" government. Furthermore, as we begin to explore in the next chapter, Machiavelli's strongest ally in this bifurcation between political primordialism and banished transcendentalism is, strangely enough, the author of one of the greatest "imagined republics" of them all, St. Augustine with his *City of God*.

Still, in characterizing the originality of Machiavelli's new science of politics, it would not go far enough to say that Machiavelli is liberating from Xenophon's prudent reservations the capacity for *poiesis* that Xenophon himself admits, through his depiction of Simonides, might transform a tyrant into something he was not before. For, as I have argued in earlier chapters, the classical Greek notion of "making" is not tantamount to the Abrahamic notion of creation ex nihilo. As we observed in Chapter 2, for the pre-Socratics and Sophists, remaking nature has more the connotation of tapping into its vital rhythms and, equipped with the insight that there is no distinction between seeming and being, recombining appearances through rhetoric for their persuasive effect. In combatting this teaching, the Platonic Socrates disarms the constructivist power of *poiesis* even further by making the arts the intimation of the Ideas, such that the practice of the art of ruling can never lead to self-aggrandizement. Socrates' analogies for *poiesis* imply arrangement, design, breeding, and cultivation in accordance with the preexisting eternal Ideas, not creation out of nothing in the Abrahamic sense. So passive and noninterventionary is the demiurge in Socrates' conception that he compares it to someone who carries around a mirror and "makes" things by merely allowing this mirror to reflect them – "in such a manner, he will quickly make the sun and the things in heaven, and quickly the earth," including animals, tools, plants, "and everything else" (*Republic* 596d). In a fateful twist, Machiavelli is able to radicalize tremendously the power of political effectuation by embracing a feature of Christian ontology that is unique to it and incompatible with any philosophical school of the ancients. I mean the reshaping or even re-creation of nature by the will. He speculatively transfers this capacity from the Abrahamic God to the most outstanding of secular princes. He also accepts the Augustinian reduction of the classical account of this-worldly civic virtue to mere power seeking, dominion, and selfish glory, while jettisoning Augustine's and all religious concerns with otherworldly salvation. He says, in effect: Yes, there is no possibility of high civic virtue of the kind extolled by Plato and Aristotle; there is only power seeking – so embrace that reality. The last two chapters of this book attempt to trace this remarkable new synthesis.

Here, then, is another place where Machiavelli and Xenophon must part ways. Xenophon endorses monarchical honor seeking and the acquisition of empire to a far greater degree than Plato and Aristotle, and he also allows for a masterful exertion of personal will by such an imperial conqueror and multinational monarch of a kind that Plato and Aristotle generally decry or keep under wraps. To this extent, "the life of Cyrus written by Xenophon" is a useful cloak in which Machiavelli can wrap himself – given the widespread respect in which Xenophon was held – so as to appear superficially to be doing no more than, like the other Renaissance humanists, liberating a greater degree of civic virtue and this-worldliness to offset the widespread perception, especially in Italy, that a return to ancient virtue and statecraft was needed as an antidote to contemporary instability and an excess of Christian passivity.

However, at the end of the day, and notwithstanding the possibility of a darker account beneath the surface when the *Education of Cyrus* is read in a Machiavellian frame of mind, in my view Xenophon really does regard even imperial virtue as compatible with moderation, generosity, humanity, and justice, and it is in demonstrating these qualities that he believes the life of Cyrus has its chief value. Moreover, as much as any other classical thinker, Xenophon believes that the scope for human excellence and success falls entirely within the ambit of nature; that excellence and success come from more perfectly reconciling ourselves to the Great Chain of Being and the reflection in our own characters of the harmony of the cosmos through cultivating the virtues. Machiavelli's bold maxim that Fortuna can be conquered is therefore ultimately as alien to Xenophon's political thinking as it is to any other classical source. It is in this new project for the conquest of nature "for the relief of man's estate" – as Bacon was to describe his new physics – that we find an important distinguishing theoretical feature of modern as opposed to ancient monarchy and the exercise of state authority generally. For as Bacon generously acknowledges in *The Advancement of Learning* (with a gloss on Machiavelli's remark about "imagined republics" in chapter 15 of *The Prince*): "We are much beholden to Machiavelli and others, that write what men do, and not what they ought to do. ... As for the philosophers, they make imaginary laws for imaginary commonwealths; and their discourses are as the stars, which give little light, because they are so high."[12]

---

[12] Quoted in Kennington (2005).

VI

GLORY AND REPUTATION

The New Prince

A reader skeptical of my effort to draw a sharp line between ancients and moderns with respect to the understanding of tyranny and of statecraft in general (with Machiavelli inaugurating the modern approach) might well ask at this point: when Machiavelli offers to show how princes of "outstanding" virtue might achieve an immortal reputation for glory, does he not share a fairly large degree of common ground with the classical political philosophers? Is his prescription for princely honor so different from, say, Diotima's Ladder, whose second level promises great citizens and statesmen an immortal reputation, to be extolled by philosophically guided poets as Homer had earlier extolled Achilles, for the virtues they engender on behalf of the city? In this and the following chapter, I argue that, although on a certain level Machiavelli can be seen as continuing the promise of immortality to great statesmen offered by the classical thinkers, the *kind* of glory and immortality promised by Machiavelli are of a fundamentally different character.

That difference can be stated summarily as follows. Plato's political philosophy is offering the virtuous citizen immortality through the pursuit of traits of moderation and justice that are solicited by, and characteristic of, the cosmos in its immortal perdurance. Poets properly educated in this view of the cosmos – or suitably bowdlerized after the fact, like the re-writing of Homer prescribed by the *Republic* – will find artistic ways of extolling these recurrent demonstrations of virtue and passing them down to posterity for emulation by statesmen to come. In sum, for Plato, the statesman's prospects for immortality fall within nature through the statesman's actualization of his soul's potential for virtue in harmony with the whole.

Machiavelli, by contrast, is offering the prospect of a glory altogether colder, more artificial and conventional. Emotionally, it has more to do with Handel's *Music for Royal Fireworks* – pomp and magnificence drained of heart – than with Plutarch's judicious and sympathetic sifting of the shades of virtue and vice and how they contend for leadership in the soul of a statesman, or a statue by Praxiteles in which princely greatness and noble grace are indissolubly intertwined. Psychologically, Machiavellian glory has more to do with Shakespeare's coldly calculating Octavian Caesar, "the universal landlord," than with his superbly erotic, generous, humorous, and magnanimous uncle. For Machiavelli, founders of the greatest strength of will, daring, and fortitude might be able to shape events and mold human beings in such a way as to "satisfy and stupefy" the multitude, and thereby convey to the future their epic feats, retroactively endowing themselves with every admirable quality (*The Prince* chapter 6). The new Machiavellian prince's glory is entirely of his own creation, very far from the participation in a transhuman standard of the imperishable Good explored by Plato.

The expanded scope of the new prince's power to shape events is pointed to by Machiavelli's blurring of the distinction between a statesman who achieves immortality on classical grounds under the guidance of reason and the prophet who introduces "new modes and orders" with the supposed inspiration of God. Such princes must become the creators of their own reputations for posterity, whether directly (as in the authorship of the Torah traditionally ascribed to Moses) or indirectly (Virgil's *Aeneid*, which ascribes retroactively to his patron Augustus all the Stoic virtues and links him to Rome's first founder, the immortal hero Aeneas, or, with the qualifications we discussed in Chapter 5, Xenophon's *Education of Cyrus*). These examples remind us, it should be added, that Machiavelli frequently finds in the lives of statesmen from Greco-Roman antiquity the best examples of his own "modern" innovations. He is always careful to distinguish between the ancient "writers," whose views he rarely embraces and frequently rejects entirely, and the ancient practices, perfected by his true heroes, "the Romans" (although, for reasons we discuss in the next chapter, he has little to commend about Augustus).

More than even blurring the distinction between princes and prophets, for Machiavelli's new prince to be successful, our very notion of reason itself must undergo a profound reversal – to wit, the assimilation of virtue to the will, a watershed of modern thought altogether, presaged here and reemerging with increasing radicalization through Hobbes, Rousseau, Kant, and Ficthe. As we considered in Chapter 2, this transition is implied in chapter 22 of *The Prince*, where Machiavelli argues that a prince must be the source of his own wise counsel, and not, as the classics had urged, place himself under the tutelage of a philosophic governor. In order for the prince to be the source of his own prudence, wisdom must collapse into will, and the concept of the will, as I have argued and continue to try to substantiate in what follows, is one that is to be found only in the concept of the Abrahamic creator-god and has no precise parallel among the writings of the ancient thinkers. Only a prince bred to this insight will be able to go the limit in creating his own reputation for posterity through the use of fraud and violence. Or, to put it as succinctly as possible, the glory and reputation of the new prince will exist nowhere but historically – a politics of pure primordialism, immanentized within a world drained both of classical transcendence and Christian otherworldliness. Although all three Abrahamic faiths stress the concept of a will that can oppose nature, one way of explaining the particular connection of the Christian version to Machiavelli's new science of politics is to bear in mind that Christ, the true prince (*Il Principe*) of the world, also embodies, in his life as a man, the divine thoroughly immanentized within fallen nature, a synthesis akin to Machiavelli's prince in his inward existential encounter with Fortuna. However, whereas Christ is resurrected and rejoins the Father in heaven, Machiavelli's prince asserts his transformative will entirely within the fallen sphere of the world itself. His glory and reputation will be the consequence of stupendous, entirely earthly, somatic, and this-worldly struggles and a well-nigh miraculous reshaping of human mores, civilizations, and events. Such princes will not mirror an eternal hierarchy where, as in Diotima's Ladder, they will dwell on a second level below that of their governors, the philosophers. Instead, they will create such hierarchies on their own as forces of history, anticipating Nietzsche's conflation of the founder, thinker, and prophet in his Zarathustra.

The love of honor, then, certainly is a common theme shared by Machiavelli and the classical thinkers in their respective analyses of political existence. Yet as Machiavelli's repeated critique of "imagined republics," Aristotle's "middle way," and the whole conglomerate of classical-Christian morality implies, he conceives of honor in a very different way. As we saw in Chapter 5, Machiavelli's rhetorical invocation of certain strains of classical thinking, especially that of Xenophon, is meant in part to liberate the worldly pragmatism of classical statecraft from the overlay of excessive Christian otherworldliness. In this respect he is not unlike some of his contemporaries including Guicciardini. At bottom, however, Machiavelli distorts the classics more fundamentally than do his contemporaries, because unlike the other humanists, he strips the classics of their own considerable transcendentalist and transmundane leanings, a dimension of the classics that made it plausible for the great theologians including Augustine and Thomas to attempt to assimilate them to Christian revelation in the first place. Machiavelli's praise of the ancient Romans for their methodical ruthlessness and unbridled imperialism is meant to extol "the ancients" – that is, their real-world politics – at the expense of ancient political philosophy. Like physicians who can cure a disease the more readily the sooner they diagnose it, "the Romans did . . . what all wise princes should do. . . . Seeing inconveniences from afar, they always found remedies for them and never allowed them to continue so as to escape a war, because they knew that war may not be avoided but is deferred to the advantage of others" (*The Prince* chapter 3).

HOW ORIGINAL IS MACHIAVELLI? THE RELATIONSHIP OF VIRTUE AND FORTUNA

Before turning to Machiavelli's engagement with revelation, let us consider further how he differs from his humanist contemporaries. Machiavelli's understanding of virtue and fortune, as we have seen, is central to his originality as a political philosopher, but the degree and character of that originality is a much-debated question. In one influential interpretation, Quentin Skinner (1980) argues that the context of Machiavelli's discussion of virtue and fortune is provided by the Italian humanists of the fourteenth and fifteenth centuries.[1] Augustinian Christianity, Skinner argues, had viewed fortune as a lawlike force of divine necessity that left little or no room for human freedom. According to Skinner, the humanists by contrast reverted to the "classical belief that

---

1 Skinner (1980). Consider also Tarcov (1982, 2000) and Zuckert (2002).

the human predicament is best seen as a struggle between man's will and fortune's willfulness." In this view, Skinner claims, fortune is no longer seen as the "inexorable force of providence" but as a "capricious power" of irrational happenstance. By exerting the "creative powers" of his will against this flux, man is "able to shape" and "control his own destiny," "mould his own fate," and "remake his social world to fit his own desires." Understanding the humanists' revival of this classical theme compels us, Skinner believes, to abandon the "textbook" view that Machiavelli's argument is entirely sui generis. However, this will also enable us to see Machiavelli's originality more clearly, as when, for example, he departs from the "more orthodox defenders of republican liberty" by rejecting the "conventional Christian" meaning of virtue.[2]

I question this interpretation of the classical, Christian, and humanist understandings of virtue and fortune, and, as a consequence, the light they shed on Machiavelli's comparative originality. The "creative" view of virtue as able to master the world's disorder and "remake" it (to use Skinner's terms) is certainly to be found in Machiavelli. The conquerors and statesmen of "outstanding virtue" described in *The Prince* receive no assistance from fortune in successfully founding new modes and orders, and the belief that a supervening order of causes grounds man's hopes for peace and justice is squarely repudiated. In my view, however, this conception of virtue is difficult if not impossible to reconcile with the classical view of the relation between human virtue and the transhuman world. I would argue that there is scant suggestion among Greek and Roman thinkers that virtue can be understood as the creative will to overcome a capricious fortune so as to shape it to human needs. Moreover, unlike Machiavelli, these ancient authors do not equate fortune with the entire world external to or in opposition to man, but treat it as a subsidiary dimension within the complex of relations making up the order of causes. Because the classical writers believed the world to be rationally ordered – and hence the very opposite of a "capricious" or "willful" happenstance – they had a rather different way of conceiving of the problem of human freedom versus the objective constraints placed upon it. I would argue that the humanists cited by Skinner in his discussion of the relationship between

2 Skinner (1980) pp. 94–98, 129–131, 182.

virtue and fortune have a view of fortune that is also hard to reconcile with the creative one. Instead, they counsel a kind of forbearance
against the reverses of fortune by accommodating oneself to the divine
order of the universe, a blend of Christian precepts with the classical
understanding.

Skinner does not wish to drive too large a wedge between Christianity and humanism and assures the reader that Petrarch and his
successors among the humanists were "unequivocally Christian" – as
well as classical – in their espousal of such traditional virtues as justice, liberality, faith, and love. He does, however, wish to distinguish
their variant of Christian faith, which he believes made room for the
"creative" view of virtue, from "conventional" or "orthodox" writers
who shared the Augustinian assumption that man should not attempt
to resist the dictates of providence. Unquestionably there were many
variants and shadings in Christian belief and in humanism during this
period. On the particular theme of virtue and fortune, however, I do
not believe that Skinner adduces sufficient evidence for his way of distinguishing the conventional outlook from the "new attitude" he finds
in Petrarch, Salutati, and their followers.[3] If I am correct in my reading
of the classical, Christian, and humanist conceptions of virtue and fortune, for the humanists to conceive of virtue as man's creative power
to "mould his own fate," they must already have parted ways with any
attachment to the traditional virtues, whether classical or Christian.
For the traditional virtues presuppose man's subordination to a natural
or divine hierarchy of ends that prescribe his substantive duties and
fulfillment. In this view, the world external to man cannot be seen as
"capricious," and it is neither possible nor desirable to conceive of man
as being able to stand apart from the world and impose his own "will"
on it. The creative view of virtue cannot, in my view, be added to the
traditional one, which it contradicts at every level. I would argue that
the humanists in general accepted both the traditional account of virtue
and the traditional view of man's place in the world, suitably adapted
to Christianity. Whereas Skinner tends to range the humanists alongside the classics in opposition to orthodox, Augustinian Christianity, I
would suggest that the humanists he sees as bearers of the "new attitude" about virtue were in fact much closer to the conventional view of

3 Skinner (1980) pp. 92, 97.

it. What emerges from this reconsideration of Machiavelli's context, I suggest, is a Machiavelli who conceives of virtue and fortune in a radically different way from either classical, Christian, or other humanist writers, a new synthesis that is, indeed, entirely sui generis.[4]

In Greek and Roman philosophy, man's responsibility to choose virtue over vice is examined in the light of the obstacles posed by objective reality to his freedom of action. This transhuman reality is distinguished according to its various aspects of fortune or accident, necessity, and fate. Plato's *Republic* and *Laws*, for example, explore the possibility of reconciling man's freedom to choose virtue over vice within the overarching rationality of a cosmic order that provides the objects of virtuous striving (*Republic* 377a–383c, 476a–480a, 484a–486d; *Laws* 840, 893, 904, 907). It might be argued that Plato's endorsement of ethical responsibility is, at bottom, irreconcilable with the determinism of his metaphysics and theology.[5] For if, as the protreptic dialogues hold, virtue is knowledge and vice the equivalent of an error about one's own advantage, there seems to be no need for the specifically ethical education of character that makes us choose virtue for its own sake or for the honor it bestows on loyal and law-abiding citizens. As we saw in Chapter 3, Aristotle responds to this dilemma by trying to preserve ethical and political praxis from the dictates of the apodictic science of royal rule sometimes endorsed by Plato. Statesmen and citizens are responsible for grappling with the variable particulars of everyday politics, guided by a prudence developed through experience rather than by direct philosophic knowledge. It may still be wondered, of course, whether Aristotle is more successful than Plato in preserving man's freedom and responsibility for his actions within a rationally ordered cosmos. His attempt to distinguish precisely among the types of causes and his notion that final cause actualizes an immanent potentiality for growth within natural beings can be seen as an attempt to close, or at least narrow, the Platonic chasm between absolute Being and nature's self-movement (*Physics* 194a25–195a10; *Magna Moralia* 1182b5–1183b20). Ultimately, however, it appears that Aristotle cannot find a

---

4 Hulliung trenchantly formulates the distance between Machiavelli and the Stoic and Christian political morality of his predecessors. He sees the humanists as being "Christian despite their admiration of pagan antiquity." Hulliung (1983) x–xi, pp. 216–217.
5 Consider Guthrie (1984) pp. 139–142.

place within this cosmology for fortune or accident as a genuinely spontaneous occurrence – an effect without a cause (*Physics* 195b30–198b10; *Metaphysics* 1026a35–1026b30, 1065a30–1065b5). His uneasiness about the place of spontaneity in nature extends to politics as well, where, as we saw in Chapter 3, he waffles between endorsing republican self-government in which citizens are responsible for their actions and an absolute monarchy that rules according to reason and leaves no scope whatever for citizen participation. The classical account of freedom altogether arguably has almost no trace of anything akin to impulse, creativity, or spontaneity – it is no more than the freedom to become happy by choosing to actualize those virtues that are always already the best and only choice for you to make.

Because it is sometimes argued that Cicero is more immediately important than Plato and Aristotle for furnishing the context of the humanists, we should consider how he examines this dilemma of freedom and necessity. Two of his dialogues – *On the Nature of the Gods* and *On Fate* – are crucial for our understanding of how the Stoic, Epicurean, Peripatetic, and Academic schools of philosophy had developed the problem beyond its Platonic and Aristotelian formulations. *On the Nature of the Gods* considers whether the gods are not completely indifferent to, or powerless to influence, human life – in which case it makes no sense to worship them or to live virtuously and piously, echoing a disturbing possibility explored by Plato in the *Laws* and the *Republic*. The opposing view is that the world is entirely "governed by the will and wisdom of the gods," which appears to leave no room for human freedom (Cicero [1907] pp. 2–3). The Peripatetic Cotta attacks Epicureanism as representative of the first view, and Stoicism as representative of the second. The Epicureans, Cotta claims, are really atheists who mount an appearance of belief in gods "for the sake of avoiding unpopularity or punishment" (Cicero [1907] p. 106). But in reality, he demands of them, "what reason is there for your saying that men ought to worship the gods when the gods [in the Epicurean view] not only do not regard men but are entirely careless of everything and do absolutely nothing at all?" (Cicero [1907] p. 41). As for the Stoics, Cotta argues, "the prosperity of the wicked destroys the idea of divine providence," for how could omnipotent, omniscient gods tolerate this? On the other hand, although good men "sometimes" succeed, this cannot be proven conclusively to depend on the aid of the gods, as opposed to their own talent and effort (Cicero [1907] p. 137). The Stoic Balbus declines to refute Cotta's lengthy dissection of his philosophy, but simply observes that the falsity of Stoicism would mean the falsity of all religion and piety, which "defend Rome better than she is defended by her ramparts." Although the Epicurean Velleius is won over by Cotta's demolition of both positions, Cicero depicts himself in the dialogue as deciding that Stoicism possesses "the greater probability" (Cicero [1907] p. 140).

St. Augustine's interpretation of this dialogue in *The City of God* is of great interest for understanding how the terms of the classical debate about freedom and necessity were absorbed and altered by Christianity. If, as Skinner maintains, Augustinian Christianity was the main opponent of the humanist revival of the classical conception of virtue and fortune, it should help to clarify the relationships among all three bodies of belief. Not surprisingly, St. Augustine prefers Stoicism among the ancient schools to the Epicurean principle of pleasure. The Stoics believed the world to be governed by the rationality of the supreme being. Man brings himself more closely into accordance with this divine rationality by living virtuously. In interpreting Cicero's place in the debate, St. Augustine reasons as follows: if, as the Stoics correctly believed, God is "the Cause of all causes," he must also have foreknowledge of the future. Cicero, however, believed that man cannot be free if God has this foreknowledge. For if everything we do it predestined, there is no point in holding people responsible for choosing virtue over vice. The laws, education, and political morality meant to encourage this choice would all be in vain. According to Augustine, this is why Cicero, in his treatise *On Divination*, denies that there can be knowledge of the future. For St. Augustine, this is tantamount to atheism: "Thus, to make men free, he made them give up God." Why, then, does Cicero incline toward the Stoic view in *On the Nature of the Gods*? For Augustine, this can only be explained as Cicero's fear of being seen too openly to embrace the impious view he actually holds (rather as Cotta says of the Epicureans in the dialogue). Instead, St. Augustine argues, Cicero places his real views in the mouth of Cotta (Augustine [1958] pp. 102–105).

Augustine's interpretation is arresting, but it assumes that Cicero shared Augustine's view that the "order of causes" necessarily implies the foreknowledge of an interventionary supreme deity. Cicero did not see the matter in quite these terms, however, as can be confirmed by examining another of his treatises, *On Fate*. Cicero uses the term "fate" (*fatum*) when he wishes to discuss the problem posed by rational causality for human freedom as a philosophical one strictly speaking, as opposed to what he regarded as the deplorable superstitions frequently associated with Fortuna and other Roman cults. Here, he is explicitly concerned with finding a middle ground between the Stoic view, which can lead to a determinism in which human freedom and responsibility are impossible, and Epicureanism, which secures freedom at the expense of belief in the gods, or at least in gods willing and able to intervene justly in human affairs. Seemingly dry epistemological and cosmological debates prove, as Cicero analyzes them, to have important consequences for freedom and morality. The Stoic Chrysippus, for example, is presented as maintaining that every proposition must be true or false. Without this unambiguous correspondence between thought and truth, "it will be impossible to prove that everything is done in consequence of fate, and of the eternal causes of all future events." Epicurus, by contrast, denies this rather than "admit that everything happens through fate." For if propositions are true and false "from all eternity," human freedom is extinguished by the "necessity of fate" governing every possible occurrence. According to Cicero, Epicurus believed that his doctrine of the atoms avoided the determinism of this supervening rational necessity. The "fortuitous" clashing of the atoms, Cicero says, amounts to "an effect without a cause" (pronounced, we recall, an absurdity by Aristotle in the *Physics*). This is especially true, we may note, of the notorious "swerve" by which the atoms inexplicably cease being carried perpendicularly downward by gravity and, through a miraculous little ontological cha-cha, clash to generate visible phenomena (Lucretius *De Rerum Natura* 2:216–294). In Cicero's presentation, Epicurus believed that to grant that these combinations of atoms are foreordained by "natural and necessary" causality would be "to deprive man of his liberty" (Cicero [1907] p. 273). If the atoms are not free to move spontaneously and generate new combinations, in other words, neither are we.

At this point, Cicero sides with Epicurus as against Chrysippus, seeming to prove St. Augustine's view of him as an atheist (Cicero [1907] p. 272). But Cicero is careful to say that he agrees with Epicurus *only* rather than "grant that fate governs all things." As the treatise goes on, it is clear that Cicero will not allow himself to be trapped between a notion of rational causality that makes freedom of choice impossible by rendering all acts predestined and a notion that we can be free only if the world has emerged from an accidental concatenation of atoms. Finally, he sides with Chrysippus, finding him to be "an honorary arbiter" who "holds the middle course" between these extremes. Following Chrysippus, he argues as follows: "(R)eason itself" does oblige us, after all, to grant "that there are things true from all eternity," and therefore that every proposition is either true or false (Cicero [1907] p. 279). It does not follow from this, however, that all things are "bound to eternal causes of necessity." Man's freedom is compatible with the "doctrine of fate" so long as fate is not *synonymous* with necessity (Cicero [1907] p. 280). Some things are indeed caused by "necessary and compulsory causes," but human perceptions, for example, have a more proximal cause, which explains their precise content. An object "strikes our sense and conveys its image to our soul" – this is causal necessity. "Yet it leaves us free to form our specific sentiment concerning it." The proximal cause of these sentiments rests with man: "we have the moulding of their effects in our own power" (Cicero [1907] p. 281).

The preceding is not so important because it adequately resolves the problem of freedom versus necessity as for the light it sheds on Augustine's critique of Cicero. It appears that for Augustine, there can be no "middle course" of the kind sought by Cicero between Epicureanism and the more deterministic version of Stoicism. Because Cicero clearly means to preserve man's freedom from divine necessity, St. Augustine concludes that he could not really have believed in the order of causes in *any* sense and was therefore driven to dissimulate his views. As we have seen, however, not only does Cicero refuse to be bound by this dichotomy, but his middle course does not require grounding in an omnipotent, interventionary deity who stands beyond nature. The distinction between fated and necessary causes is all that the Ciceronian solution requires. The absence of this activist Abrahamic deity from Cicero's understanding of a reasonably ordered universe explains, I would argue, St. Augustine's inability to enter the debate on Cicero's own terms, or on classical terms in general. For to the Christian theologian, no resolution of the problem is thinkable apart from such a supreme personal deity.

This difference points to how much Christian theology altered classical thought about man's place within the order of the world even while adapting many of its categories and problematics. In Aristotle's *Physics*, for example, all natural movements are solicited into motion by a final cause that is itself unmoved. The final cause is therefore not a willing agency of any kind, which Aristotle would place under the heading of efficient cause. It is, rather, a perfection that solicits movement toward itself through efficient, material, and formal causes (Aristotle *Physics* 194b–195a, 258b10–259b20; *Metaphysics* 1071b10–1073a15). For St. Augustine, by contrast, final cause is conflated with the efficient cause of an interventionary deity whose will creates and sustains all things.[6] In keeping with this elevation of God's will over all other kinds of causality, St. Augustine's own solution to the problem of freedom versus necessity is to assimilate both "fate" and "necessity" to God's direct and constant supervision of the universe. As for fortune, chance, or accident, he simply denies that, strictly speaking, they exist at all, especially in human affairs. "As for the causes which are called fortuitous," they merely appear so to our limited understanding; they, too, are "latent" in the will of God. How is human freedom compatible with a deity who wills all and knows all? St. Augustine's answer is that God gives us the power to choose good over evil, and the choices we freely make reenter the chain of causes foreknown by God. In other words, as the efficient cause of the universe including human voluntarism, God wills our wills: "In His will is the supreme power which helps the good choices of created spirits . . . (our) wills have no power save what He gave them" (Augustine [1958] pp. 107–108).

Several contrasts emerge from the preceding analysis between the Christian and classical conceptions of virtue and fortune. For the Greek and Roman thinkers, the problem posed by the order of causes for human freedom admits of a number of more or less provisional solutions. We can summarize their general sense as follows: There is an

---

6 Compare St. Thomas, who represents Aristotelian causality not in its original sense as perspectives on a thing but as successive stages of the divine artisan's operations on material reality. Whereas Aristotle treats natural causality as *analogous* to art – in other words, like art in some respects, unlike it in others – Thomas is confident in his commentary on Aristotle's *Physics* that "nature is *nothing but* a certain kind of art, that is, the divine art, impressed upon things, by which these things are moved to a determinate end." Thomas (1963) p. 124; my emphasis.

eternal order of rational causality, but it does not fully determine every human thought and action. The play of nature's self-movement – and, therefore, of accident and contingency – leaves a wide latitude for sensible improvisation, as Aristotle had already argued with respect to prudence. There may be gods which provide an objective grounding for virtue, but this does not mean they constantly and reliably intervene in human affairs on behalf of the good, at least not without a matching effort by man (as Plato's *Timaeus* puts it, the god of the cosmos is "apathetic," without impulse or feeling, while according to the *Republic*, the gods do not change shape or assume human form; *Timaeus* 28–34; *Republic* 379a–381e). In sum, the classical thinkers try to find a place for fortune (albeit a severely circumscribed one) within the order of causes. For St. Augustine, on the other hand, fortune simply vanishes into the will of the Creator, or, expressed passively as His dispensation, into Providence. (As we consider at greater length subsequently, the fundamental theological conundrum as to whether God ought primarily to be understood as "making" or as "revealing" will prove central to Machiavelli's revaluation of virtue and fortune.)

However, if the classical understanding of the relation between virtue and fortune is different from the Christian one, still less does it resemble the idea of virtue described by Skinner as man's creative will exerting itself over a capricious fortune so as to shape it to human desires, a concept that, I am arguing, is distinctively modern and inaugurated by Machiavelli. For the Greek and Roman thinkers, virtue is a conditioning of the soul that brings one into closer proximity to eternal being. Cicero never questions that the objects of the virtues are prescribed for man by a rationally ordered cosmos; he works within this assumption even while resisting its more deterministic interpretation. Accordingly, the classical notion of virtue has no connotation of mastering fortune in the external world. Rather, by cultivating the virtues, one lessens one's desires, and therefore one's dependence on external goods. Because to be a slave of external goods is to be a slave of what is perishable, accidental, or less real, in this sense virtue can make one less vulnerable to the reverses of fortune. But this way of coping with unpredictable or unmerited suffering is more passive than masterful, grounded in our reconciliation to our natural place within the Great Chain of Being. If the reverses occur anyway, so the reasoning went, one can draw on the steadfastness, dignity, and self-control achieved through the cultivation of virtue to sustain or console oneself against them. Plutarch, for example, is full of homilies to this effect. In chronicling the lives of great statesmen and generals, he wants his readers to understand "how far a noble nature, an honorable ancestry and a virtuous upbringing can fortify men against grief, and that although fate may defeat the efforts of virtue to avert misfortune, it cannot deprive us of the power to endure it with equanimity... (A) virtue which a man embraces on principle and which is genuinely a part of his nature can never be transformed into its opposite by any mere stroke of fortune... " (Plutarch [1968] pp. 193, 204). This gray-bearded eat your peas prescription for noble resignation in the face of fortune's reverses could not possibly be further from Machiavelli's praise in chapter 25 of *The Prince* of hot-blooded youth's power to wrestle Fortuna to the ground and take her.

By the same token, the classical thinkers do not identify the various objective constraints on man's freedom with Fortuna in Machiavelli's sense of an overwhelming and singular power of irrational happenstance. Plato and Aristotle, for example, understand the world as being ordered by the intelligence that also provides human nature with its telos (Plato *Laws* 892–900; Aristotle *Physics* 256b20–258b10; *Nicomachean Ethics* 1142a25–30, 1143b1–5). Within this way of seeing things, fortune or accident is relegated to the secondary role of meaning the decline of perishable things from being into nonbeing. In keeping with this primacy of rationality over accident, the effects of sheer irrational happenstance – the whole gamut of natural disasters and human impulse – are relegated to a secondary role in politics and morality. This distrust of spontaneous impulse is reflected in the frequently noted lack of "realism" in classical political philosophy: the emphasis on transcending desire rather than acquiring the power to satisfy it; the emphasis on a stable internal politics and military self-defense rather than on a dynamic foreign policy of imperial expansion. As we have seen, what primarily concerned the philosophical schools of antiquity was, instead, how this concept of a rationally ordered cosmos affected the prospects for human freedom of choice. Does the order of causes leave man responsible for developing his moral and intellectual excellence through the pursuit of virtue? Because the telos is eternally prescribed from a transhuman source, is there any room for man's distinctive contribution? Far from being – as in Skinner's interpretation – too willful or capricious, too apt to spoil expectations of regularity and order, the world surrounding man may be entirely *too* rational, orderly, and good.

If we turn to the understanding of virtue and fortune among the humanists of the trecento and quattrocento with the classical and Augustinian perspectives in mind, two features emerge. First, as Skinner observes, they are indeed preoccupied with the power of fortune over human affairs. However, rather than reverting to "the classical image of man's predicament," as Skinner argues, it seems to me that they greatly heighten this sense of man's vulnerability to fortune's reverses. Despite this, however, the conception of virtue that the humanists invoke to deal with fortune's sway remains almost entirely classical in the sense I have discussed here. It places far more emphasis on the need to submit and reconcile oneself to the divine or rational order that rules the universe than on man's capacity to "mould his fate" and to be "the architect... of his own character." This can be confirmed by examining the authors cited by Skinner as being important for furnishing the "ideological" context for Machiavelli's republicanism. These include the followers of Salutati – Bruno, Poggio, and Vergerio – who in turn influenced Alberti, Mannetti, Valla, and Palmieri. Skinner also argues for the importance of Petrarchan humanism as helping to give rise to quattrocento humanism. Skinner sees Petrarchan and civic humanism as entering a distinct stream from that of "Augustinian Christianity," flowing into the republican ideology that flowered in the early sixteenth century when Machiavelli began to write.[7]

According to Skinner, Petrarch – in a theme on which Alberti, Manetti, and Pico della Mirandola made later elaborations – denies that fortune is the "inexorable force of providence," seeing it rather as "nothing more than a capricious power." Reverting to the classical view that "Augustine had tried to obliterate," Skinner argues, Petrarch no longer emphasizes the view of man as "the possessor of an immortal soul" but as able to "control his own destiny." In keeping with this, Skinner claims that Petrarch's admiration for Cicero was not merely as a contemplative sage but as a model for the life of action. However, as we have seen from our analysis of the classical view in general and Cicero's in particular, the fact that man can possess a free will and – as

---

7 Skinner (1980) pp. 96–98, 69, 71.

Pico della Mirandola writes, "many operations of intelligence" – is not sufficient to establish Skinner's thesis that virtue is now viewed as man's "creative powers" to "remake his social world to fit his own desires."[8] Certainly, as we have considered in previous chapters of this book, the classical thinkers attributed moral and intellectual qualities to man that made him fit for a life of civic responsibility. However, the strength of character to be a good citizen or ruler was thought to come from the transcendence of tyrannical and ungoverned desire – from avoiding, to the degree humanly possible, the pursuit of boundless power and prestige. Thus, it does not follow from the classical thinkers' attribution to human beings of free will and various kinds of talent that people are able, as Skinner infers, to reshape the world as they see fit to serve their own desires. Instead, the problem as the classical thinkers saw it was whether the freedom and intelligence with which man was endowed in order to pursue virtue were overwhelmed or rendered superfluous by the supervening order of causes. As we saw in Chapter 1, for Plato it was crucial to appeal to the passions on behalf of the intellect through myths and images that sublimated man's freedom to pursue honor and glory but did not try to assimilate it altogether to the study of the impersonal, unchanging One. Some scope for action had to be opened up between unbridled tyrannical impulse and the satiation of erotic longing by the pure light of the truth. The aim was neither to remain bound to the shadows of the Cave, nor to flee them forever and live in perfect detachment from human affairs like Socrates hanging in his basket in *The Clouds*, but to remain engaged in the affairs of the Cave guided by the light of philosophic enlightenment streaming into it from above.

The difficulty with Skinner's interpretation is evident in his characterization of Petrarch's dialogue *On the Remedies of Good and Bad Fortune* as exemplifying the beginnings of the "new attitude" about virtue and fortune (Petrarca [1967]).[9] An examination of the dialogue reveals that Petrarch is very far from encouraging a bold and masterful

---

8 Skinner (1980) pp. 87, 94, 98. Baron takes a different view. Although Petrarch admired Cicero as a philosopher, Baron argues, "Cicero's civic spirit was to him nothing but an offense against all the traditions of the Middle Ages." Baron (1938) pp. 72–97. As described by Hulliung, Machiavelli's opinion of Cicero is the precise opposite of this. Hulliung (1983) p. 132.
9 Skinner (1980) p. 97.

stance toward fortune's caprices. On the contrary, Petrarch depicts Reason as delivering a withering admonition to the youthful exuberance and optimism of Joy and Hope. In celebrating the ascendant powers of youth, Reason warns: "You put your trust in a most treacherous thing. This ascendancy of which you speak is in reality a decline. This brief life is furtively, between play and dreams, soon dissolved by unstable time. Would that God would permit us to realize (this) in the beginning. . . . Nothing is closer to life than death" (Petrarca [1967] pp. 4–5). The young should therefore abandon their hopes and follow "the straight and narrow path of virtue" before it is too late. Following this path requires a mixture of Christian and classical precepts: "The wise man will love God . . . he will love his neighbour, he will love virtue, his country, his parents, his brothers, his friends, and if he is really wise, he will also love his enemies – not for themselves . . . but for the sake of Him who wishes us to do so" (Petrarca [1967] p. 16).

According to Petrarch, the key to this way of life is to "learn once and for all" to "love" and "think of . . . eternal things," turning away from "that which is transitory:" "If you love nothing but what is visible, you can love nothing that is great" (Petrarca [1967] p. 14). One should overcome the love of beautiful bodies, for example, for the love of beautiful souls (Petrarca [1967] p. 10). Cicero and Plato are cited to adduce the familiar classical notion that bodily love makes one dependent on transitory goods that cannot last and desires that cannot be satisfied. By loving the eternal, we rise above such "anxiety . . . coarse desires, sighs and . . . burning thoughts" (Petrarca [1967] p. 17). As we can see from this, contrary to Skinner's interpretation, Petrarch places a great deal of emphasis on man's possession of an immortal soul. Of particular significance for our discussion of virtue and fortune is Petrarch's most un-Machiavellian argument that a wise man's love for eternal things also frees him from the passion for fame, which is likewise a transient thing – not true virtue, but its "shadow." According to Petrarch, in the form of praise for acquiring virtue, fame may help to educate a "generous and modest soul." But pursued for its own sake, it "casts down foolish and presumptuous souls," transforming prematurely celebrated young men into "unknown old men" (Petrarca [1967] p. 22). The exceptional fame of great statesmen and generals praised through the ages is, according to Petrarch, especially to be avoided, calling into question Skinner's claim that Petrarch admired Cicero's interest in worldly politics. Alexander the Great, Julius Caesar, and Augustus Caesar, he writes, may have been "very fortunate," yet "they nevertheless lived constantly in disquiet; they were constantly involved in turbulence and, therefore, never happy. Besides, death [often] came to them prematurely" on the battlefield (Petrarca [1967] pp. 23–24). Only those who acquire virtue by turning away from such "transient and uncertain" goods are truly happy (Petrarca [1967] p. 25). They are also less vulnerable to fortune's reverses, because they have no high station from which to fall and will not be conquered or betrayed by their rivals.

It is difficult to imagine anything further than this from Machiavelli's view that fortune can be mastered by *virtu* of the kind displayed by Caesar, Alexander, and Cyrus. Old Man Reason's finger-wagging at the "joy and hope" of youth's ascendancy in Petrarch's dialogue is the perfect foil for Machiavelli's encouragement of the hot-blooded new prince. It certainly does not support Skinner's argument that whereas Augustinian Christianity commended the pursuit of blessedness and moral virtue, "Petrarch and his successors" understood virtue as the acquisition of "the greatest possible amount of honor, glory and worldly fame."[10] Rather, Petrarch's emphasis is on the classical notion of virtue discussed earlier, filtrated through Christian otherworldliness – the correct education of the soul in accordance with virtues prescribed by a rationally ordered cosmos. The aim is not to subdue fortune in the service of desire but to transcend desire altogether – desire being the chief way in which fortune undermines us. Thus, one can minimize the reverses of fortune not by trying to master the world but precisely by *resisting* the passion to master it. Petrarch thoroughly dampens the youthful impetuosity that Machiavelli was later to praise as the best disposition for overcoming Fortuna. In his dismissal of the fame won by the ancient statesmen and generals as a delusion compared with man's inescapable mortality, in his emphasis on the need to orient oneself by the eternal and invisible rather than by the perishable and worldly, Petrarch's tone owes even more to Augustinian Christianity than it does to classical philosophy.[11] Plato's images of the soul, the realm of metaxy

---

10 Skinner (1980) p. 100.
11 As Nachod observes: "As a faithful son of the Church, [Petrarch] was fully satisfied with her teachings and did not need another guide in the labyrinth of this life, in

between the human and the divine where passion is sublimated by reason through the eros for honor, is utterly jettisoned, exposed as cheap
tinsel, and stripped of its allure as it is "dissolved by unstable time."

Although they can draw on more Greek and Roman texts for illustrations and arguments, the quattrocento humanists do not appear to be
any closer than Petrarch to advancing the conception of virtue described
by Skinner as man's power to reshape the world. In Manetti, Albertus,
and Pico della Mirandola – three figures whom Skinner links with the
Petrarchan view of virtue – we encounter the same mixture of Christian
theology with classical moral philosophy and metaphysics. For example, Manetti's *On the Dignity and Excellence of Man* does not suggest,
as Skinner argues, a commendation of man's creative powers to grap-
ple with the world and subdue it to his needs.[12] Instead, according to
Manetti, the dignity and happiness proper to men are conferred on those
who fully understand that the soul is immortal and of divine origin. By
pursuing virtue, Manetti argues, we can approximate that transmundane purity more closely in our earthly lives. Kings and princes, far
from being urged to use their talents for worldly success, prestige, and
stability, are adjured to submit themselves to the divine order: "Your
duties, as regards understanding and acting, you have in common with
omnipotent God; consequently, by acquiring and cultivating virtue, you
may attain the beatitude of a tranquil immortality" (Manetti [1967]
pp. 83–84, 100).

Similarly, Pico della Mirandola's *Oration on the Dignity of Man*
cannot really be said, as Skinner would have it, to posses as "a central
theme...the individual's free and creative powers."[13] The teleology
that Pico describes is incompatible with the primacy and freedom of the
individual. According to it, God endows human beings with a hierarchy
of "potentialities." At the bottom are those who live for their appetites
and so resemble "plants" and "brutes." At the top is the philosopher – a

this respect particularly under the spell of his great model Augustine." Nachod (1948)
p. 241. See also Kristeller, who points out that Augustinian Christianity was very much
a part of Petrarch's rediscovery of classical literature – not, as Skinner implies, a foil
for it. Kristeller (1969) pp. 361–363. On the general importance for the humanists of
neo-Platonism as it was filtered through Augustinian theology, see Cassirer, Kristeller,
and Randall (1948) pp. 6–7.
12 Skinner (1980) p. 97.
13 Skinner (1980) p. 97.

type who, having risen above his animal desires, is "a creature of heaven and not of earth" (Pico [1967] pp. 144–145). Statesmanship and other kinds of worldly political success do not even figure in this hierarchy, distinguishing it from its classical antecedents such as Aristotle's *Nicomachean Ethics* and reflecting the Augustinian devaluation of civic virtue. The "frenzies" of an ancient philosopher like Socrates to escape this fallen and impure world can, according to Pico, meet with far more certain success in Christian philosophy. This will "enable us to reach such ecstasy that our intellect and our very being become one with God" (Pico [1967] p. 152). Those who seek knowledge to be practically employed for the sake of worldly gain or success, rather than purely for its own sake, are roundly condemned (Pico [1967] p. 156).[14]

Clearest of all in this regard is Albertus's dialogue on *Fate and Fortune*. As Skinner observes, fortune is presented here as a power engulfing human affairs, anticipating Machiavelli's imagery in chapter 25 of *The Prince* about damming and redirecting a swollen river (Alberti [1967] pp. 35–38).[15] Albertus depicts fortune allegorically as a river carrying people along on its current, some of whom drown while others make it to shore. In the terms of the allegory, those who cling to "blown and pompous" skins to stay afloat are characterized by such vices as perfidiousness, shamelessness, cruelty, avarice, calculation, and gluttony. Those who "trusting to their own strength ... swim the whole course of Life" on their own fare much better. This appears to confirm Skinner's interpretation of the humanists' espousal of energetic self-reliance and willpower. Two points must be balanced against this, however. First, it is not the river current representing fortune but "the gods" who have the final influence on how people fare in the allegory. Moreover, it is not the swimmers whom the gods think most highly of and are therefore most likely to reward with good fortune. In Albertus's depiction, the self-reliant people have to pause to regain their strength for swimming by clinging to "little boats." These boats carry along in perfect

14 Pocock regards Pico's *Oration* as an example of neo-Platonism that forsook the *virtu* needed for civic community in favor of "an illumined communion with the cosmos." Pico's failure to find a bridge between philosophy and the requirements of political life helps to explain, in Pocock's view, his attraction to the "holy community" preached by Savanarola. Pocock (1975) pp. 98–99.

15 Skinner (1980) p. 96.

290

safety the most virtuous people of all. These are the "just, wise (and) honest," who "never cease thinking worthy thoughts." They "do good to others by offering a helping hand to those who are in difficulty." Moreover, "(n)one among men who are struggling in the river is more welcome by the immortal gods than those who, in the little boats, look to faith, to simplicity and to virtue" (Alberti [1967] p. 36). There is no elevation here of Skinner's interpretation of virtue as the Promethean capacity of man to "control his own destiny." Although the energetic and self-reliant people are given their fair due of commendation, they are clearly depicted as dependent on, and morally inferior to, those surpassingly good people in their modest little boats. On no level of the allegory does Albertus suggest that the mighty power of the river could be tamed and rechanneled to serve man's needs, as in chapter 25 of *The Prince*. Everyone must submit to its current, perhaps as to Providence, but the virtuous are able to make safe boats for themselves to avoid its dangers as they are borne along.

Turning to the other humanists cited by Skinner, we find further variations on the conception of virtue as a conditioning of the soul that brings one into closer proximity to eternal truth and being. Castiglione maintains that virtue can overcome fortune – but by virtue he means the moderation of the Golden Mean and insists that power should never be pursued for its own sake or for selfish and merely practical ends (Castiglione [1959] pp. 14–15, 323–324).[16] Valla illustrates especially clearly how close the humanists often were to orthodox Christian formulations of virtue and fortune when he observes that Fortune or "the divine will ... condemns some and saves others" without our knowing why (Valla [1967] pp. 63–64). In contrast to Skinner's view of how the humanists understood virtue, Valla argues that the appropriate response to this dilemma is not to rebel and assert our wills against fortune but to submit *even more thoroughly* to its dictates. We should not "request a guarantee" from Christ but hold onto "faith, hope and love." Here, the classical notion of virtue as a source of dignity and strength of soul amidst fortune's reverses is radicalized into the Christian's total faith in providence and disavowal of any need to account for God's ways. Aristotle's ambition for comprehensive knowledge of the order of the universe is accordingly dismissed as "proud and foolish," echoing an

16 Consider also Woodhouse (1978) pp. 65–67, 150–160.

Augustinian characterization of philosophy when it is unilluminated by and not subordinated to divine revelation. "Nothing is more becoming to the Christian," Valla concludes, "than humility."[17]

As we began by observing, Skinner links the humanists with what he takes to be the classical conception of virtue as man's exertion of will against Fortune's willfulness, as opposed to the Augustinian view that man cannot and should not resist providence. Our exegesis leads to a rather different conclusion. Augustine does represent a radicalization of the classical analysis of the several kinds of limitations on human freedom into a single, all-encompassing divine necessity grounded in the will of God. As I argue later in this chapter, Machiavelli's own conflation of every force external to man as the overwhelming singularity of Fortuna is in a way prepared for by Augustine's radicalization of the transhuman order into a single overwhelming force of providence. But the classical conception of the limitations placed by the cosmos on man's freedom is still very much one of objective and eternal rational causality, and not, as Skinner would have it, a "capricious power." Moreover, while the classical conception of virtue certainly provides more latitude than the Christian one for independent political judgment and improvisation, it is in no sense "creative" or able to "control destiny," as Skinner argues; instead it has its place within the order of causes. By contrast, Augustine would subordinate the order of causes to the will of God, while Machiavelli would subordinate it to the will of the prince. We saw that the humanists, although perhaps more preoccupied with the problem of fortune than their classical predecessors, shared their view of virtue as having its place within the order of causes. By reading into the other humanists what is in truth a uniquely Machiavellian conception of virtue that is difficult to reconcile not only with Greek and Roman thought but with humanism as well, it seems to me that Skinner exaggerates the differences between Augustinian Christianity on the one hand and classicism and humanism on the other, while misconstruing the terms of the real differences among these three on the question of virtue and fortune.

---

17 Valla was highly skeptical of prospects for the synthesis of classical learning with Christian revelation. See Trinkaus (1948) p. 149.

As we have seen, the classical thinkers were not primarily concerned with the problem of accident or fortuitous happenstance as an impediment to human freedom. They tended to identify accident with nonbeing, the failure of a thing to attain its end. Instead, they were concerned with how to account for man's freedom and responsibility to choose virtue over vice, given this rational order of causes. As Cicero's *On Fate* demonstrates, thoughtful Greeks and Romans had various teachings to choose among that gave more or less scope to man's freedom of choice and action within this order. Christianity took over the classical conception of an ordered but heterogenous cosmos and interpreted it as the laws through which God's singular and almighty will operates on mundane reality. This led to a narrowing of the classical debate. What had before been more of an open question, typified by dialogues such as Cicero's, now hardens into orthodoxy. God's will explains everything, and although worldly virtues are not unimportant, they are of far less significance than faith in and reliance on divine providence.

It is perhaps because the rigidity of the Christian doctrine seemed so inadequate to explain the tribulations of Italian politics that the humanists felt so much at the mercy of random circumstance. If God's will embodied reason, then the world around them, where God's will manifestly had not established peace and justice, was obviously an unreasonable place. Nevertheless, given what may be this increased feeling of vulnerability to the blows of fortune, the striking thing is that the humanists largely retained the classical conception of virtue rather than elaborate a coherent stance of rebellion and mastery in the face of fortune's "malignity." The transcendentalist metaphysics of the classics were taken to presage the final revelation of Christianity, but their comparatively more pragmatic statecraft might also offer Christian citizens and statesmen more latitude for strictly political considerations than Augustinian orthodoxy. Erasmus, for example, while certainly stressing the centrality of religious education to forming the character of a good prince, sees no contradiction between that priority and an exposure to the noble deeds of the ancients.[18] Nonetheless, that more pragmatic

---

18 "The deeds of famous men fire the minds of noble youths, but the opinions with which they become imbued is a matter of greater importance.... A prince who is about to

political teaching still remained firmly within the order of nature, never suggesting that nature could be mastered. Accordingly, while the humanists could not part ways with the classical understanding of virtue as man's reconciliation with the order of nature, they could not entirely part ways with the orthodox Christian conception of virtue either, for the Augustinian and other Christian views drew on the classical tradition just as they did. Skinner, it seems to me, underrates the tenets that the humanists held in common with more conventional religious opinion, despite the greater erudition and suppleness of their argumentation. He writes as if only Augustinian Christianity subsumed fortune under a lawlike, divine necessity, whereas the humanists understood virtue in terms of spontaneous freedom of choice. But this overlooks the large element of the classical view that flowed into both the humanistic and Christian understandings. All three shared the view of virtue as a conditioning of the soul that brings one into closer proximity to eternal truth and being.[19]

What Christianity and humanism shared in common with the classics makes us aware of how very different was Machiavelli's conception of virtue and fortune, a difference surpassing, in my view, any differences among the other three. For only here do we find the consistently elaborated view of fortune as an irrational flux that can be mastered by an anthropocentric purposive and calculating will. Plato and Aristotle saw the virtuous soul as embodying the rationality that orders the world as a whole. Machiavelli, however, treats man and Fortuna as opponents. He never examines fortune under its traditional rubrics as a subsidiary dimension of the order of causes, but rather equates it with all conditions external to the human will. The classical distinctions among necessity, accident, chance, coincidence, and fate are thus collapsed into a single protean force of happenstance. The world does

---

assume control of the state must be advised at once that the main hope of a state lies in the proper education of its youth. This Xenophon wisely taught in his *Cyropaedia*. Pliable youth is amenable to any system of training." Erasmus, *The Education of a Christian Prince*, quoted in Newell (2001) pp. 212–214.

19 By contrast, Felix Gilbert observes: "Machiavelli did not merely refute the idealist enterprise in politics in general but ... wrote with the conscious aim of discrediting the idealized conception of the prince as contained in the (humanists') catalogue of the virtues" (1939) pp. 478–480. In Hulliung's view, Machiavelli inhabits the form of the humanistic mirror of princes genre the more effectively to undermine its Christian and Stoic substance (1983) pp. 11–19, 24–25, 245.

not supply man with his rationality and end. Instead, princely men impose "new modes and orders" on the world. In this way, the terms of the debate about the relation of virtue to fortune undergo a profound ontological alteration. The classical view had been that the cultivation of virtue, by aiming at the rational and eternal, enabled man to overcome the power of chance. Pedagogically, psychologically, and morally this meant that overcoming tyrannical desires made a human being less dependent on perishable and external things. Machiavelli, however, wishes to expose the belief in an ordered universe, with its reflections in the utopian "republics" of Greek and Roman thought, along with Augustine's Republic of God, as a delusion. After reducing these (what he takes to be) imaginary standards to random chance, he opposes to it a conception of virtue as anthropocentric will that has no transcendental relation to the nonhuman world. Virtue can overcome fortune not by transcending chance through transcending desire, a prescription common to classics, Christians, and humanists alike. On the contrary, by yielding to our desires for glory, wealth, and power, as princes or as citizens of vigorous expansionist republics, we orient ourselves by the vital disorder that is at the heart of all existence.

I have been arguing in this book that Machiavelli's originality lies in this paradoxical reliance on disorder. He is not merely arguing that fortune is unreliable, but that fortune's hindrances are in a strange way actually to be welcomed and are constitutive of sound psychology and statecraft. Machiavelli's use, for example, of the Polybian cycle of the rise and decline of states in the *Discourses*, which we consider at length in the next chapter, omits Polybius's concern with transcending this temporal cycle in the direction of the eternal.[20] As Machiavelli puts it, "chance" and "the aid of events" can "perfect" republics without any assistance from such transcendental sources. Because there is no *nunc stans* or eternality of true being – because "everything is in perpetual movement" – "disunity" is a more reliable source of a republic's power and freedom than a unity that is doomed by the flow of events.[21]

---

20 See, for example, Pocock (1975) p. 189.

21 See Mansfield, who draws a connection between Machiavelli's use of the term "first cause" to describe the disorder underlying Rome's freedom and his use of the term "humors" (that is, bodily conditions) to describe the factions in Roman politics. I take him to mean that Machiavelli here converts the classical meaning of "first cause" into its opposite – into subrational chance – and that, in keeping with this reversal, political

Moreover, the challenge of founding or reforming a state in which people and conditions are unremittingly corrupt or hostile adds glory to the ruler's eventual success. A "wise prince," seeing that overcoming fortune's hostility increases one's prestige, will imitate fortune by, for example, deliberately cultivating hostilities among his subjects and then stamping them out (*The Prince* chapter 20). The correct employment of the lion and the fox – the belligerent and calculating aspects of human selfishness – depends on recognizing that disorder is indeed "the order of things." By being "impetuous" – that is, by letting this disorder fuel one's conduct – the prince can preempt the impetuosity of Fortuna. By being willful in this new kind of way, Machiavelli suggests, we can tap fortune's willfulness into our own calculations. We can be on guard against fortune's caprices because we have liberated that capriciousness through our own selfish impulses. That new stance, as we now consider more closely, is not comprised simply of a repudiation of Augustinian otherworldliness, but by a secularization of it.

SUNDERING DIOTIMA'S LADDER: THE CITY OF MAN, THE CITY OF GOD, AND MACHIAVELLI'S NEW SYNTHESIS

Many interpretations of Machiavelli stress either the relationship of his thought to classical political philosophy or to the classical teachings as they were transmitted by humanist writers on princely and republican statesmanship. Most scholars also agree that Machiavelli undertakes a refutation of both ancient political philosophy and of many of its humanist devotees for being insufficiently realistic and offering little practical advice for grappling with the problem of political instability and unrest.[22] As Machiavelli puts it in a passage that simultaneously recalls the optimal *politeia* of pagan philosophy and the Christian *civitas* of St. Augustine:

Since my intent is to write something useful to whoever understands it, it has appeared to me more fitting to go directly to the effectual truth of the thing than to the imagination of it. And many have imagined republics and

discourse in the Aristotelian sense is to be converted from the rational deliberation on ends grounded in the first cause of the visible cosmos into the random clash of impulse or interests. Mansfield (2001) pp. 42–43.

22 For a good general discussion of Machiavelli's uses of classical thought, see Gilbert (1984) pp. 179–200.

principalities that have never been seen or known to exist in truth; for it is so far from how one lives to how one should live that he who lets go what is done for what should be done learns his ruin rather than his preservation. (*The Prince* chapter 15)

I broadly agree with these interpretations, and my main purpose in this book has been to use my readings of Plato, Aristotle, and Xenophon as foils for illuminating some of the original tenets of Machiavelli's statecraft. However, I am also arguing that more attention should be paid to Machiavelli's relationship to Christianity – not simply as an obstacle to combat but as an opponent whose categories influence Machiavelli's thinking even as he attempts to repudiate them. I am trying to show that Machiavelli owes a kind of negative debt to Christianity that helps us to understand why his thought cannot be viewed simply as a return to the greater latitude for worldly statesmanship afforded by pagan philosophy in comparison with Christianity. There are two main facets to this negative debt. I will sketch them schematically, and then show how they come together in the discussion of the prince's relationship to Fortuna, famously (and notoriously) personified in chapter 25 of *The Prince*. In the next and final chapter, I try to show, through a reading of the discussion of the origins of republics in the *Discourses*, how Machiavelli's departure from the classical approach to the theme of the founding weaves together with his negative debt to certain tenets of Christianity to establish an entirely novel synthesis and a dynamic new prescription for political freedom.

The first element in Machiavelli's debt to Christianity concerns the altered meaning of causality effected by Christian theology. For Plato, causality is chiefly a matter of solicitation, not effectuation. In Aristotelian terms, final cause takes ontological priority over efficient cause. Phenomena are summoned toward their respective completions by the Good. The Good causes the fullness and fruition of their growth toward the stable form that perfects each class of beings. The Image of the Sun in Book 6 of the *Republic* best conveys this solicitative causality (506–509). As the Sun summons each natural being toward its growth, this solicitation sets in motion its natural power and energy for development. In other words, the form toward which each being naturally tends entails effectuation and structure. The same is true of the soul. For Plato the soul is naturally drawn toward the repose and stability offered by the prospect of union with the Good. Diotima's Ladder in the

Symposium is a sketch of how the Good solicits the soul's movements through the Beautiful toward itself, a summons that energizes the soul's volition and desires in the proper direction. When Socrates abstracts from eros in discussing the soul in the *Republic*, he stresses the energetic struggle that one must undergo in order to turn the soul away from its baser attachments – and its deluded identification of mere opinion with the truth – toward the light of transcendence. The prisoner in the Cave needs "someone" to turn him around through benevolently aggressive dialectical investigation and refutation (514–519). Yet this is not the same thing as arguing that one can strive for transcendence by willing oneself to overcome the limitations imposed by nature on our freedom, a hallmark of modern ethics begun by Machiavelli and perfected by Kant. For Plato, the energies that effectuate the soul's ascent are all along solicited and directed by the natural objects of erotic longing. Effectuation, in other words, is housed within the natural continuum of desire and the objects of desire linking the primordial and the transcendental. As Diotima puts it, eros is the "great spirit" linking man to the subhuman and the transhuman, between becoming and being, the source of both prudence and correct opinion. An exertion of human will cannot achieve this ascent on its own. Even when stressing the harsh, refutational path to transcendence – the turning around toward the light from the bonds of the Cave, a jarring transition that is first imposed on the prisoner by rough hands – Socrates is wont to compare it to a natural process (birth pains [*Theaetetus* 150–151], a kind of medical treatment [*Gorgias* 479–480], or gymnastic exercises [the *Lovers*] the soul must undergo for it to develop into a fit condition to receive the light and begin to be borne up toward it).

I do not of course mean to argue that efficient cause has no independent place in Platonic cosmology. The dialogues sometimes describe a god who "makes" (*poiein*) things – the demiurge of the *Republic* and *Timaeus*; the god in Book 10 of the *Laws* who sets up the cosmos in such a way that human beings can participate in the victory of order over disorder by becoming allies of *nous* (almost a nonhistoricist version of Hegel's *Phenomenology of Spirit* [*Laws* 897, 904–906]). Even when Plato describes a god who fabricates, however, it is not in the sense of the God of revealed religion who literally creates something out of nothing, including (in Thomism) the very matter out of which things are shaped, and whose creations are not constrained by a preexisting – or, depending on the theology, even a posterior – pattern of natural order and regularity. This difference is underscored by the fact that, because every noun in Attic Greek has an article, one cannot unambiguously express the concept of God – it is always *the* god (*ho theos*), which indicates the supervening whole within which we find it, including the possible existence of gods other than this one. The Platonic god of the *Timaeus* creates things in accordance with already established patterns of rationality and coherence. The demiurge is an agent of a cosmic rationality already present for him to actualize. There is a very great difficulty in reconciling this subordination of effectuation to an eternally preexistent cosmology with the God of revealed religion. Socrates depicts the gods as disembodied paradigms of objective clarity that do not intervene in human affairs, do not perform miracles or answer prayers, but uphold the eidetic stability of the world and thereby support human efforts to inculcate that repose within the soul through the cultivation of the virtues, even and including the best regime itself, a "pattern in the sky" that can be housed in an individual's soul as a moral compass for the inferior regime in which he lives. As Book 2 of the *Republic* puts it, the gods do not change their respective *eide* like wizards; they have no personal qualities whatsoever (380d).

By contrast, the Christian God as depicted in Thomistic, and even more clearly in Augustinian theology, conflates final cause with the efficient cause of an interventionary deity whose will creates and sustains all things. As St. Augustine puts it in criticizing Cicero and other pagan philosophers for identifying the highest being with an impersonal, objective rationality, "the only efficient causes of all things are voluntary causes, that is to say, causes of the same nature as the spirit or breath of life.... The Spirit of Life, which gives life to all and is the Creator of all matter and of every created spirit is God, a Spirit indeed, but uncreated." The difficulty of reconciling the Platonic, or more generally the classical account of causality with the Christian doctrine of creation is clear, to take but one example, from the objections made to Thomism by Christian critics who believed that even it too greatly constrained the creative power of God with the causal categories of pagan metaphysics, despite the fact that Thomas is quite clear that the latter are merely the means through which God effects his creative will and are entirely subsequent to God's creation of the world. Even matter, according to Thomas, not only the form imposed on it, must be seen as created out of nothing by God, lest even in its inert preexisting condition it somehow latently conditioned or shaped what God could fashion from it. Thomas argued that although God was free to create the world in whatever way he saw fit, once he had established its rational plan (*ratio*), phenomena would occur according to recurrent natural causes unless God intervened miraculously to alter his own laws. Short of these miraculous incursions, as a favor to us and our human need for regularity, He would leave the natural laws by which he had originally ordered the universe to operate on their own.

For more conservative theologians, however, during the period of debate over Thomism before his eventual canonization, even this attempt to subordinate pagan metaphysics to divine creation restricted God too much by implying that creation would ordinarily adhere to a settled natural pattern, mediating between God's will and our experience of phenomena. In this more fundamentalist, resolutely antipagan theology – which often viewed itself as cleaving to St. Augustine and which would reemerge with Luther – God constantly, endlessly, and directly supervises every event in the universe at every moment in time, sustaining it all through his active will. Otherwise, it would fall into the disarray and decay that is the essence of all natural matter. According to the Augustinian formulation, as the efficient cause of the entire universe including human voluntarism, God also continuously wills the wills of all humans. The pursuit of no mere natural object of aspiration, however noble or just it may appear, can ever enable us to live as we should – indeed, this will only drag us down. God so conceived is the great artificer who stands beyond all natural limitations and determinations, because he is their originator. He does not create in accordance with form; he creates form and imposes it on nature. Nature by itself is mere matter in motion, as Hobbes would later put it. Left to itself, it would fall into disarray. Its only potential for order and structure comes from the forms God continuously imposes on it. In this reading, modern physics, far from being a repudiation of Christian cosmology, flows directly from it, shorn of God's sustaining will, now to be replaced by Machiavelli's prince who creates "new modes and orders," Bacon's scientist who converts nature into power "for the relief of man's estate," and Hobbes's human artificer of the social contract.[23] Insofar as reason is assimilated to the human will, not only can princes be the source of their own prudence, but the thinkers who provide the new desacralized physics of chance are themselves princes of thought because they make the exertion of the human will over nature theoretically possible.

Therefore, one of the keys to understanding the originality of Machiavelli's political thought is to see how it transfers to human rulers this conception of a creative willpower to overcome natural limitations. In this way, while repudiating the moral restrictions placed by Christianity on successful statesmanship, Machiavelli makes use of a central tenet of Christian theology and, by misapplying it, opens up a scope for princely action going far beyond anything envisioned by even the most tough-minded and pragmatic writers on history and politics in the past. This is most trenchantly put in chapter 6 of *The Prince* in discussing the greatest founders, those of "outstanding" virtue, and the formation there is worth repeating: "As one examine their actions and lives, one does not see that they had anything from fortune other than the opportunity, which gave them the matter enabling them to introduce any form they pleased." From nature, in other words, the prince receives nothing but a chance to assert himself and gain power. As we see later in this discussion, for Machiavelli neither the world at large nor one's own natural character offers any teleological potential for development into an approximation of transcendence through civic and intellectual virtue. Christianity, especially in its quasi-Manichean Augustinian variation, had already drained nature of teleology and reduced it to matter. Machiavelli in effect removes God from this causal equation, leaving the statesman to face the same dismal environment and subdue it rather than allowing its random reversals to subdue him. Into this purposeless stuff, this sheer necessitousness that so often ruins human hopes, princes of *virtu* have the power to endow nature with the purpose it intrinsically lacks. They can, through sufficient persuasion and terror, create entirely new modes and orders, not merely serve or revive old ones. The concept of a creative will that can introduce into matter whatever form it pleases cannot, strictly speaking, be derived from Platonic or, more generally, classical metaphysics. Human beings are certainly never

---

23 A detailed discussion of these connections between Machiavelli and his successors is undertaken in the Conclusion.

attributed the power to reshape the world by classical thought; as we observed in Chapter 2, even the dissident strain of the pre-Socratics and Sophists, despite their embrace of political expedience, do not go to this length. For the classics, our only prospect for minimizing the reverses of fortune is to transcend our vulnerability to fortune through the desires by subordinating our desires to the natural and reasonable order of the cosmos. The fewer externals we consume, the less vulnerable we are to being knocked down by their chance destruction. The Platonic gods, to reiterate, are not attributed any such power of *creatio ex nihilo*. Their *poiesis* is not the creation of whatever they please, but their fashioning and rendering forth of phenomena according to the preexisting structures of *nous*. Only the God of revealed religion literally "introduces" a "form" of his own "pleasing" into matter. As we observed earlier, Machiavelli's language here is recognizably scholastic as it transfers this power to the human prince.[24]

24 The issue of creation out of nothing is at the heart of the contrast between reason and revelation. As Strauss argues in the essay *Progress or Return?*, classical philosophy and revelation can travel a certain distance along the same road together, inasmuch as both recognize the centrality of justice to human existence. At a certain point, however, they reach a fork in that road, and it is over the ultimate status of reality – for revelation, the creation of the world out of nothing; for classical reason, the eternity of the universe. These two cannot be reconciled. Strauss (1989). See also Newell (2010).

The *Timaeus*, used in medieval Christendom to show how Platonic philosophy anticipated Christian revelation, is one of the closer points of contact between the Abrahamic Creator God and Platonic cosmology. Yet the teaching of the *Timaeus* about the demiurge is not ultimately compatible with the Creator ex nihilo of Christianity. The demiurge fashions the world in accordance with a preexistent cosmic Good and Mind that in effect reduces divine agency to a subordinate partner in bringing things into being according to rational criteria that exist from all eternity – another version of the eternity of the universe, the principle that according to Strauss decisively separates reason and revelation. Timaeus says that everything depends on our choosing between two alternatives – 1) that the whole sprung into being spontaneously from nothing or 2) that it comes into being regulated by this preexisting orderliness (*Timaeus* 1235b–1236a). It is number two that is being urged on us. For classical philosophy as a whole, it is impossible to conceive of the Creator God or revelation without recasting it as chance or fortune (*tuche*). Revelation amounts to a cause without an antecedent cause (or as Augustine puts it, a Creator who is not created), which, as Aristotle puts it, is unintelligible, literally "without logos," because it would see the world as issuing out of sheer happenstance (*Physics* 196a25–196b).

In the history of Christian theology, the debate over creation took the form early on of two alternatives: God created the world out of nothing or He created it from preexisting matter, a view of God as an "arranger" more easily in harmony with pagan natural philosophy as exemplified by the passage from Plato cited in chapter 6 (*Republic* 596d). Borrowing from Platonism, Origen argued that matter was preexistent with

The transfer to human princes of a potentially godlike power for the transformation of human nature and the natural environment understandably leads to Machiavelli's implicit sanctioning of a degree of political violence and terror of biblical proportions. He only reveals this by degrees as he leads the reader from their veneration for the great

God as he created the world. However, Ireneus, wishing to expel Greek philosophy altogether, argued that there was no preexistent matter. To this, Tertullian added the argument that God also created the matter out of nothing from which the rest of the world was then created. Thomas also held that God created matter out of nothing before imposing form on it. As Colin Gunton puts it, "God is not to be likened to ... a potter who makes a pot from the clay which is to hand; he is, rather, like one who makes both the clay and the pot." Gunton (2001) p. 17. See also Copan (1996) and the exhaustive discussion in Pangle (2003).

Thomas Aquinas addresses the issue in the *Summa Theologica*, in the discussion of eternal and natural law. He asks: Is God's creation of the world consistent with the existence of a preexistent *ratio*, that is to say, a preexistent form, mind, or good (ST I. Q 44, 93)? The answer for Christians must clearly be no, for the reasons sketched earlier. Nothing restrains, guides or limits God's power to create out of nothing. That is why it is a *mysterium* – it can only be expressed as paradoxes. Thomas's solution to reconciling Aristotelianism with Christian theology goes no further than this: it is a gift of God that the world God creates out of nothing operates, after He creates it, according to Aristotelian natural law. Not because it must do so. God could make it operate any way He wants, could change it any or every nanosecond. The reason He makes it operate this way is out of compassion for *us*, so that we will have reliable benchmarks and regularity in making sense of the world. In sum, the Aristotelian natural law is operative only after the creation, and only because God makes it so. See also Thomas, *The Principles of Natural Science* Book 2, lecture 14, no. 268.

It should be stressed that even that compromise, which so clearly subordinated Aristotelian natural reason to Christian revelation, was not enough for Thomas's critics like the Bishop of Paris, Etienne Tempier, who suspected that Thomas was trying to sneak too much pagan philosophy into the faith and that even this endorsement of Aristotelian natural law as operative only after the creation still placed too many restrictions on God's constant, unpredictable power for miraculous interventions and power to sustain every single thing in the universe for every second of its existence by the sheer force of His will, unconditioned and unmediated by any natural causality. Etienne Tempier, *Condemnation of 219 Propositions*. In Lerner and Mahdi (1963) pp. 337–354.

To be clear, I am arguing that, in his secularization of creation ex nihilo, Machiavelli does not argue that, in mastering Fortuna, the prince can actually create matter out of nothing. Rather, he can "introduce" whatever "form" he chooses *into* preexistent matter. In this respect, he is somewhat closer to the neo-Platonic creationism of early Church fathers such as Origen, which held that matter preexisted with God, than to what emerged as the mainstream view of Irenaeus, Tertullian, and Thomas, according to which God created both matter and form out of nothing. This is borne out, as I discuss in Chapter 7, by Machiavelli's ruminations on the insuperable limitations placed on man's will by the underlying generational substratum of nature (reflections adapted in part from Lucretius's materialism).

names of antiquity to a clearer insight into the methods they must have employed in creating entirely new "modes and orders." At the end of chapter 6, having introduced us to his pantheon of outstandingly virtuous princes (Moses, Cyrus, Romulus, and Theseus), Machiavelli briefly mentions Hiero of Syracuse as a "lesser example" than the greatest princes but still one that "will have some proportion with the others" and can "suffice for all other similar cases." In other words, Hiero of Syracuse did not attain the level of great civilizational founders like Moses or Cyrus, but his methods illustrate on a lower level what those greater men might also have done. For the present in chapter 6, we are merely told that Hiero eliminated the old military and established a new one. Shortly thereafter, in chapter 8, we are given the example of another ancient tyrant, Agathocles of Syracuse, through which Machiavelli prepares us preliminarily and by stages for the new understanding of virtue, in which crimes can be virtuous. Agathocles summoned the Senate and the great men and had them slaughtered by the soldiers, thereby becoming tyrant (not, as Machiavelli says, "king"). He then takes us through three stages of reflection: 1) Because this slaughter removed all opposition and dependence on others at one blow, Agathocles owed little or nothing to fortune and is therefore virtuous according to the new definition of *virtu* in chapter 6. But: 2) Murder, betrayal, and fraud cannot be spoken well of or called virtue. However: 3) Cruelty can be "well or badly used." Well-used cruelty ("if," he writes, it is permissible to speak well of evil, implying now that it may not necessarily not be) is "done at a stroke, out of the necessity to secure oneself and is not persisted in but turned to as much utility for the subjects as one can. Badly used cruelty, by contrast, grows with time." Therefore: 4) Because Agathocles used cruelty well, the final judgment is that such rulers can "remedy...their state with God and man." In chapter 16, having softened the reader up for his new concept of virtue by his introduction in chapter 8 of the distinction between well-used and badly used cruelty, Machiavelli is now more explicit than he had been at the end of chapter 6 that Hiero did not merely eliminate the old army but had it "cut to pieces." The lesson of chapter 16 is that one should not rely on mercenary troops, as do so many Italian states, but on one's own arms. He then quite openly places the murderous Hiero on a level with David, God's anointed, and arguably a prince of "outstanding" virtue, using David's refusal of King Saul's gift of arms in fighting Goliath as a metaphor for relying on your own arms rather than those of another man (as Cesare Borgia relied on his father the pope). Machiavelli also endows David with a knife, not found in the biblical account, presumably because a sling is too distant from action at close quarters and therefore too reliant on Fortune (and God). Machiavelli can be *very* Machiavellian, old Nick himself!

To resume our main theme: the prospect of this seemingly superhuman power over nature, once the exclusive preserve of God, is now dangled by Machiavelli in front of secular rulers, a Nietzschean and millenarian dimension to his thinking that will require a new physics and a new kind of training. It may perhaps even imply historical progress as the retarding influences of the old morality are gradually drained away through enlightenment and newer generations of potential princes are ever more directly introduced to the new science of politics without a Christian or classical competitor. We sift some of these lineages issuing from Machiavelli in the Conclusion. In Machiavelli's view, the founder of new modes and orders need not possess a naturally moderate character nor the good fortune to have associated with a wise legislator in order to successfully establish his world. Plato's equivocations and circumspection about employing tyranny to found a just regime, as well as the elaborate pedagogy required to turn the soul away from its tyrannical longings, can be swept away. Because Machiavelli reduces the "virtue" of the prince to what is already the prince's own unprompted and spontaneous urgings for power and glory at the expense of his competitors, there is no need for a "pattern in the sky" to convert the potential tyrant into a benevolent statesman or citizen friendly to philosophy.

To be sure, as we see in this chapter and the next, the new prince cannot *act* spontaneously on his spontaneous longings. He needs training and direction. That training is not a kind of *paideia*, however, through which those spontaneous longings are sublimated and directed toward the Good. Instead, the prince needs a *method* for acting on his impulses that will bring about their own selfish agenda. Method differs from character formation, the essential meaning of *paideia*. That is, while Plato dwells on rehabilitating the passions by directing them toward their own highest ends, achieving both the governance of reason and emotional satisfaction for the soul, for Machiavelli, precisely because the passions contain no such potentiality for transcendence, they can only be manipulated externally by the prince's will within himself – the internalization within the Prince of the pure formalism of God's will over the random spontaneity of the now-secularized fallen realm of nature. Because reason is now fully immanentized within a desacralized irrational nature, even reason must be depicted somatically, as a "fox," that is, another kind of animal to control the "lion." The method of the fox is not so much reason as what we moderns might term "rationality," a distinction grounded in Machiavelli's *Realpolitik* and still a feature of contemporary political analysis in international relations. For example, to say that Vladimir Putin is a "rational actor" does not mean that he is *reasonable*, only that he will use any method necessary, including the threat of force, actual force where he can deploy it without fear of defeat, and the suspension of rights in order to maximize Russia's and his own power, but only if it does not entail a serious risk of Russia's and his own destruction, while at the same time he is not motivated by any millenarian or utopian fantasy of redemption through mass annihilation, including one's own, like Hitler or Ahmadinejad. We make some further broad comparisons of this kind in the Conclusion to this book.

Because there is no need for *paideia*, there is also no need, from Machiavelli's viewpoint, for Plato's and Aristotle's circumspection, detailed in previous chapters, about the brutal facts of how successful and stable regimes are originally set up. Whereas exploring the constructive uses of tyranny amounts, as we have seen, to a filigree within the classical treatment of the best regime and sound statecraft, Machiavelli reverses these proportions entirely: the internal just ordering of the republic becomes a filigree rarely spotted throughout his massive concentration on achieving power, and even when "good laws" are discussed for a few lines in *The Prince*, we quickly learn that they cannot exist without the prior establishment of "good arms," so better to concentrate on that. Understanding Machiavelli's appropriation and distortion of the concept of the will to overcome nature helps clarify these departures from the classical approach. Because he accepts Christianity's assimilation of formal cause to efficient cause and assimilates the latter to a purely secular or immanentized statecraft, Machiavellian politics are a politics of pure effectuation, an anticipation of what Heidegger means by "technology" and what George Grant, in characterizing the dynamic of technology within modernity, describes as "the

will to will."[25] Let the reader note that I say "anticipate." I am arguing that something akin to Nietzsche's will to power, something akin to
what Heidegger means by global technology, are possibilities that dwell
within Machiavelli's new thinking as harbingers of what Horkheimer
terms the "dark" side of modernity. Later on, however, I will be careful
to argue that Machiavelli *does* recognize limits on man's power over
nature and that certain facets of his thinking are also antecedents of the
more benign liberalism of Spinoza and Locke. Indeed, how and whether
these dangerous and benign strains can be reconciled in Machiavelli's
own thought is an excellent way of beginning to pose that question
about modernity as a whole.

As Machiavelli writes in chapter 15 of *The Prince*, he is not concerned
with imagined republics where men live as they ought, but the "effectual
truth" truth of how they do live and are to be governed. The act of the
founding becomes the cause of all stability; the ambition of the prince
becomes the cause of a successful founding. By collapsing the ends of
statesmanship into the genesis of power, Machiavelli is able to overturn
the Platonic formulation of the relationship of power to wisdom, so
that the "wise counsel" of the prince must now originate in his own
"prudence," not in someone else's. Machiavelli is as much aware as
Plato that all political constitutions decline with time, even the best
ones, just as he recognizes that some aspiring tyrants will turn out to be
brutal, rapacious thugs and nothing greater. His stress on the prince's
need for disciplined method and self-control concedes precisely this
observable fact. However, because Machiavelli 1) agrees with a certain
strain of Christianity that nature strictly speaking has no independent
inner capacity for order and regularity and 2) rejects the limitations
placed on human ambition by both the classics and Christianity, he
is able to arrive at the prospect that a prince can, godlike, re-create
corrupt political "bodies" and "humors" so that they become healthy
ones through vigorous acts of reconstruction. Indeed, whereas for Plato
the decline of good constitutions into corrupt ones in Book 8 of the
Republic is a lamentable but unavoidable necessity of time's passing –
of the fact that *physis* grows toward the permanence of Being but never
permanently attains it, falling back into becoming and decay (546) – for

25 Grant (2005) p. 679.

Machiavelli, a prince should *welcome* a corrupt and vicious society because it offers more scope for the reforms that can be effected by his will:

And truly, if a prince be anxious for glory and the good opinion of the world, he should rather wish to possess a corrupt city, not to ruin it wholly like Caesar, but to reorganise it like Romulus. For certainly the heavens cannot afford a man a greater opportunity for glory, nor could he desire a better one.... (W)here corruption has penetrated the people, the best laws are of no avail, unless they are administered by a man of such supreme power that he may cause the laws to be observed until the mass has been restored to a healthy condition. (*Discourses* 1.10.6)

This brings me to my second main point about Machiavelli's connection to the way in which Christianity altered the relationship between human virtue and nature, and how Machiavelli is able to utilize this transformation in such a way as to criticize both the classical and Christian approaches to politics and statecraft. Christianity tended to divide the natural realm from the divine realm, and to see the natural realm as fallen, shot through with sinfulness, and dependent on the will of God. This is particularly true of Augustinian Christianity, which, as is widely noted, never entirely lost its Manichean tincture.[26] There is no longer, as in Diotima's Ladder, a continuum from bodily hedonism to the love of the noble, but instead a chasm between fleshly drives and a perfection now seen to reside beyond nature altogether, attainable only through salvation. The Ladder of Love is broken into two pieces, the City of Man and the City of God.

This sundering has the further effect of reducing politics from the Platonic concern with the possibility of human nature attaining at least a degree of perfection within a well-ordered political community to a politics of the merely naturalistic – the management of natural human impulses that, left to their own workings, are uniformly sinful and exploitative. For Augustine, eros could not be the key to human transcendence – it could never be directed from its lower to its higher objects – because eros is at the core of human sinfulness. Eros has no inner potential for redirection but is indistinguishable from compulsive lust: "Nature, which the first human being harmed, is

---

26 Van den Berg (2010).

miserable.... Who can control this when its appetite is aroused?" ([1974] 6.25). The *summum bonum*, the proper object of erotic longing in Platonic ontology, is drained out of political life and transposed to an afterlife of incorporeal beatitude, while desire loses its rank order and sinks to the level of indiscriminate concupiscence. According to Christianity, perfection cannot be properly aimed for, let alone achieved, within the political sphere alone. Whereas for the pagans, piety and civic virtue were mutually reinforcing and could not exist without one another, for Augustine, the most one can say in favor of political life is that Christians, by being unconcerned with its honors and riches and devoted entirely to salvation, happen to possess secondarily the moral qualities requisite for good citizenship as well, so long as they are divorced from imperialism and other kinds of false grandeur.

The chasm in Augustine's thought between political success and the highest good means that there is indeed a family resemblance between Augustine and Plato, and it is not difficult to see why Augustine would prefer Plato over the other pagan thinkers.[27] Plato's distinction between

---

27 See his discussion of Socrates and Plato in Augustine (1958) pp. 146–150 Many historians have argued that as Greco-Roman antiquity unfolded, the transcendentalist dimension of neo-Platonic philosophy and the longing for a single, spiritually pure god in place of the frivolous anthropomorphic gods of the Olympian pantheon intensified, preparing a way for Christian monotheism. Marcus Aurelius's *Meditations* posits a division between the fallen world of bodily necessity and an inward realm of pure soul that alone is truly free that is almost Manichean or proto-Augustinian in its intensity. Indeed, if we were unaware of his identity, we could almost be reading Augustine or Meister Eckhart: "Of human life the time is a point, and the substance is in a flux and the perception dull, and the composition of the whole body subject to putrefaction, and the soul a whirl, and fortune hard to divine, and fame a thing devoid of judgement. And, to say all in a word, everything which belongs to the body is a stream, and what belongs to the soul is a dream and vapor, and life is a warfare and a stranger's sojourn, and after-fame is oblivion. What then is that which is able to conduct a man? One thing and only one" (quoted in Newell [2001] p. 166). For Marcus, it is philosophy, but it could as likely be faith. For the Stoic, all a man can do is bear up with integrity in the whirlwind of flux, but for the Christian, repose awaits in the world to come, although worldly fame is oblivion just as it is for Marcus.

In the *City of God*, Augustine poses a contrast between two irreconcilable ways of life, the city of the flesh and the city of the spirit. A life devoted to worldly ambition is vain, exploitive, arrogant, and restless. A life devoted to God is moderate, modest, peaceable, and allows a man to be at peace with himself: "Let us imagine two individuals.... Of these two men, let us suppose that one is poor, or better, in moderate circumstances; the other extremely wealthy. But our wealthy man is haunted by fear, heavy with cares, feverish with greed, never secure, always restless, breathless from endless quarrels with his enemies. By these miseries, he adds to possessions beyond measure,

the Idea of the Good and the realm of mere becoming, and his arguments for the superiority of philosophy and the purity of the soul over the satisfactions of ordinary politics, are indeed at times akin, especially in proto-Stoic dialogues such as the *Gorgias*, to the dualism of Augustine, especially when contrasted with Aristotle's attempt to locate the prospects for virtue more squarely within ordinary politics (a preference for the middle realm of what is "first for us" that is understandably more congenial to Thomism, which, broadly speaking, tries to modify the dualism of Augustine in a manner analogous to Aristotle's modification of the "divine madness" of Plato). Nevertheless, this broad similarity between Augustine and certain aspects of Plato is trumped by a more essential difference. For Plato, however wide may be the gap between conventional political honor and philosophical transcendence, that highest way of life can only be ascended to *by way of* the virtues of the *best* regime, the regime that is best not only according to nature but according to *logos*, guided by the soul's erotic ascent through political nobility toward the Idea of the Good as the perfection of nature. At bottom, the metaxy of Diotima's Ladder is more representative of Platonic philosophy than its occasional excursions into dualism. Augustine cannot follow Plato along this road, for the divine *logos* of Christian revelation altogether surpasses nature, even entails its obliteration or crucifixion.

For Augustine, the virtue that comes from obedience to God cannot be understood in any sense as an erotic pleasure, however sublime. As Augustine presents it, politics at best has a police function. It can discourage the grosser manifestations of sinfulness for the sake of public order. A Christian government's first duty is to protect the Church as an outpost of the City of God within the fallen purview of the City of Man.

but he also piles up for himself a mountain of distressing worries. The man of modest means is content with a small compact patrimony. He is loved by his own, enjoys the sweetness of peace in his relations with kindred, neighbour and friends, is religious and pious, of kindly disposition ... chaste in morals and at peace with his conscience. I wonder if there is anyone so senseless as to hesitate over which of the two to prefer." In general terms, this theme is a familiar one from Plato, in, say, Socrates' contrast between the philosopher's and the tyrant's ways of life in Book 9 of the *Republic*, or his claim that Callicles is a "double man" because he cannot reconcile natural happiness with a lust for political power. Although there are reaches of Plato in which the division between the body and soul is pushed to a proto-Stoic extreme, the crucial difference is that, for Plato, the happiness of the soul *is* available within the natural world of the here and now and most definitely by way of worldly civic virtue.

On its own, considered apart from the useful work it can do to prepare Christians for their salvation by protecting Christian institutions, politics can only aim at domination. For even the justice that regulates mundane political affairs does not originate within the natural realm and the limits of mortal reasoning. It is rather a gift of God conferred through the natural law whose content is specified by the Decalogue and the superordinate revelation of the New Testament. On its own, secular authority cannot achieve justice even of the secular variety, and "in the absence of justice," Augustine asks, "what is sovereignty but organized brigandage?" ([1958] p. 88). The classics would have made a distinction between regimes organized according to a virtuous principle such as aristocracy and those organized around the maximization of self-interest, which could take the form of venal "garden variety" tyrannies or collectively selfish and defective regimes like oligarchy, or imperialistic "tyrant" cities such as Athens as it was described in Thucydides. Yet Augustine, much like Machiavelli was to do later (as we consider in detail in the next chapter), collapses the distinction between good and bad regimes and reduces them all to being defective. Whereas Augustine does this to purify virtue by removing it from the natural realm, Machiavelli does it to purify politics by removing it from the transcendental realm. Augustine goes on, with what sounds like a slap at Romulus's founding of Rome:

For what are bands of brigands but petty kingdoms? They are also groups of men, under the rule of a leader, bound together by a common agreement, dividing their booty according to a single principle. If this band of criminals, recruiting more criminals, acquires enough power to occupy regions, to capture cities, and to subdue whole populations, then it can with fuller right assume the title of kingdom, which in the public estimation is conferred upon it, not by the renunciation of greed, but by the increase of impunity. ([1958] p. 88)

According to St. Augustine, this is what the Roman Empire over the course of time achieved. However:

The reward of the saints is altogether different.... (Their) city is eternal. There reigns that true and perfect happiness which is not a goddess, but a gift of God – toward whose beauty we can but sigh in our pilgrimage on earth, though we hold the pledge of it by faith. ([1958] p. 112)

Here is yet another anticipation of Machiavelli's negative debt to Christian revelation. In describing the evolution of Rome from a gang of thieves on the Tiber into the greatest empire the world had ever known, Augustine is sharply contrasting the brutal and avaricious *reality* of pagan political conduct with the empire's lofty pretensions to have institutionalized the noble philosophical doctrines of the Stoics and other great thinkers. While for Augustine, even those philosophers' claims to transcendence are hollow in contrast with the revealed truth of Christianity, the reality of pagan politics was in utter contradiction to even those professed and dubious moral values of the pagan philosophers. In his praise of the evolution of Rome in the *Discourses*, the theme of the next chapter, Machiavelli also sharply contrasts the *reality* behind its success with the moral virtues extolled by the ancient philosophers that could only condemn those practices. Yet whereas Augustine is using this contradiction to discredit political life, Machiavelli, employing Augustine's own depiction of politics as dominion, is using this contradiction to free politics altogether from that transcendental standard. Instead of Rome standing shamed (as it does in Augustine's judgment) by the contradiction between its profession of pagan piety and the reality of its vices, Machiavelli's Romans use the appearance of piety as a useful tool of social control as they gratify their vices full bore. We should realize from Machiavelli's revaluation of the Augustinian dichotomy – his embrace of the City of Man while jettisoning the City of God – that, again, it is not simply a question of Machiavelli opposing the realism of his politics to the idealism of the classics and Christians but of collapsing the ideal *into* the real, or the high into the low. The real is all that it should be, already the core insight of historicism beginning with Spinoza.

Plato had criticized some of the Sophists for depicting political communities if not as large-scale gangs of thieves, then as large-scale gangs of would-be thieves who forgo their opportunities for open-ended crime so as to maximize their long-term net gain in security and self-interest. In other words, justice for the Sophists had no more than an instrumental value and could never be choice-worthy for its own sake. The view that Plato stigmatized as characteristic of those who did not believe the political community was capable of encouraging virtue for its own sake, St. Augustine characterizes as the reality of *all* political communities that believe they can achieve virtue within the limits of nature. By arguing that dominion is the sole aim of a politics guided by nature, Augustine in effect restores the Sophists' low view of the city for the sake of elevating revelation above its taint. For classical political philosophy, the question of which constitution one lives under is crucial for a happy life because the prospects for actualizing the soul's potentiality for excellence is inextricably linked to the laws and the civic morality they enhance: it very much matters, for example, whether it is an aristocracy or an oligarchy. For Augustine, however, the whole traditional subject matter of the best regime, and how actual constitutions measure up to it, although not unimportant as a preliminary guidepost to virtuous living, pales into insignificance when we consider the vanity and frailty of all merely human prudence. Thus, although St. Augustine defends Christianity to its remaining pagan critics partly on the grounds that the moral rigor enjoined on Christians by their faith also makes them decent citizens of the City of Man, when he addresses the expectations one may properly form of political life in its own right, his tone is world-weary and despairing:

When it is considered how short is the span of human life, does it really matter to a man whose days are numbered what government he must obey, so long as he is not compelled to act against God or his conscience? . . . Is it reasonable and wise to glory in the extent and greatness of the Empire when you can in no way prove that there is any real happiness in men perpetually living amid the horrors of war, perpetually wading in blood? Does it matter whether it is the blood of their fellow citizens or the blood of their enemies? . . . And even though a crooked world came to admit that men should be honored only according to merit, even human honor would be of no great value. It is smoke that weighs nothing. ([1958] p. 113)

The erotic unity explored in the *Symposium* between duty and pleasure is irrevocably dichotomized here into a realm of nature, in which the drive for sensual gratification leads to the pursuit of power over others, and the divine as the transcendence of nature and desire. No peace and justice of any kind is truly to be found on earth; all lasting peace and justice are transposed to the other world beyond this mortal life. Given that all politics are fallen, what does it really matter what kind of regime we live under? A brief comparison with Plato illustrates how thoroughly this transforms the meaning of politics. In Book 1 of the *Republic*, Socrates dumbfounds Polemarchus by showing how, if justice is viewed on the analogy of the arts, then the city can do no harm, meaning that it can never go to war or punish malefactors, because the arts only benefit but never harm what they work upon. Moreover, because justice is meant to do good to friends and harm to enemies, it is impossible to necessarily identify those who deserve our friendship according to their natural merit with those who happen to be our fellow citizens. The direct application of philosophy to politics, then, leads to the disappearance of the city. Thrasymachus's angry interjection is meant to restore the centrality of the regime and its varieties, and although they agree on little else, Socrates thereafter accepts that justice must be found within the confines of a city-state that will also, at least defensively, have to go to war as well as police aberrant passions internally. For the classics, in other words, whatever justice and peace man can find must take place within the limitations of a community that cannot always be at peace. For Augustine, however, peace is taken out of the natural realm of politics altogether and found in its purity only in the heavenly afterlife, leaving the city itself as nothing but a field for conflict. In contrast with the classics, there is no necessary or intrinsic connection between success in achieving political dominion and an eternal order that might ennoble those worldly talents. To repeat: Diotima's Ladder is broken in two: the City of God and the City of Man.

For Plato, *physis* is a growth from *arche* toward *eidos*, a continuum between necessity and transcendence – in human terms, between the baser compulsions of animal desire and the fulfillment of our noble longings for completion through civic virtue and philosophy. The "nature" of man, in other words, is not a biological substratum to which the distinctively human traits of the will, personality, or mind have been added. It is a cyclical development out of necessity toward fulfillment and back. For St. Augustine, by contrast, just as nature is irrational disarray, the natural side of human life is synonymous with the basest compulsions of passion. Human nature evinces no potentiality for transcendence in its own right, either as an ascent from desire to fulfillment as in Diotima's Ladder or as an economy and harmony of the affects as in the psychology of the *Republic* or the famous images of the soul like the Chariot in the *Phaedrus*. Faith in God is the only source of stability and goodness in a mortal's life. Thus, although he grudgingly prefers the moderation of Stoicism over the hedonism of the Epicureans among the successors to Socrates, for St. Augustine, the Stoics' belief in the natural human capacity for virtue and wisdom is at bottom as vain as the Epicureans' more openly and self-consciously shameless belief that the individual's pleasure is all that matters ([1958] pp. 115–116). As he puts it in a characteristic if charmless passage, whereas the Epicureans openly make virtue into a whore, for the Stoics she is superficially more ladylike but still has a shady reputation. Indeed, the profession of virtue among pagan teachings is a more dangerous snare of Satan than those that are openly licentious, for whereas hedonism works openly as a streetwalker, Stoicism, which is every bit as much a slut for tempting us to believe we can be virtuous without God's help as hedonism is in telling us to embrace fleshly pleasures, is harder to spot because she is, as Frank Sinatra might put it, a classier broad. If we do achieve a degree of decency and restraint in this world, Augustine stresses, this is due "solely to God" – solely to His grace and mercy when we acknowledge our utter dependence and open ourselves to him ([1958] p. 116), Being good is not an occasion for pride, as it is for Plato and Aristotle, because it is literally not something we have achieved on our own through cultivating an inner natural potentiality.

In the *Symposium*, Socrates presents the seeress Diotima as the source of his understanding of eros as a way of mitigating the "manly," agonistic kind of eros bent on conquest in the pursuit of private and public pleasures – the error about ends that has led Callicles to confuse his eros to possess the boy Demos with possessing the Athenian Demos, seeking in both cases a one-sided gratification through victory, but that in fact will reduce him, Socrates foresees, to being at the beck and call of both fickle beloveds. Diotima is a fleshing out of that feminized "Madame Philosophy" ("philosophy" being a feminine noun, *he philosophia*) who, Socrates claims to Callicles, speaks through him the truth that it is better to suffer injustice than to do it (*Gorgias* 482b). From Socrates down to the neo-Platonists, philosophy was often depicted as a goddess – a being who offered the sweet prospect of natural perfection through the pursuit of wisdom and virtue. Yet as we have seen in the passage from *The City of God* quoted earlier, for St. Augustine the object of man's need is "not a goddess" – not a being of natural beauty and nobility, however perfect-seeming. Although St. Augustine respects to a degree the moral teachings of Socrates and the Stoics as precursors of the revelation of Christ, he believes that their trust in the unaided intellect to understand the truth undermines their own commendable desire to promote justice and the other virtues.

When Augustine refers in his critique of Rome quoted above to "a goddess" ([1958] p. 112), he most likely primarily means the Fortune of Rome, sometimes personified for worship as a goddess as part of the imperial cult. Given that Augustine has also stripped Fortuna of her Stoic garb to stand exposed as just another pagan shady lady, however, it is hard not to think simultaneously back to Diotima, one of a number of divine females in the pagan tradition like Athena who guide men toward virtue through their love of honor, and forward to Machiavelli's advice that Fortuna is not be worshipped but mastered. Given Augustine's distrust of the natural human condition, the goal of natural happiness whether through pleasure or through virtue takes on the aspect of a whore. The reduction of natural happiness from a noble goddess to a shady lady is not in itself tantamount to Machiavelli's notorious encouragement, in chapter 25 of *The Prince*, of a relationship between princely *virtu* and Fortuna akin to rape. On the contrary, the point of Augustinian theology is to repress natural longings for victory, pleasure, and power to the utmost degree possible for fallen humans. However, the Augustinian reductionism concerning the worth of human nature and its unaided capacity for virtue lends itself to Machiavelli's own undermining of the classical teachings. By denying any continuous connection between natural desire and transcendence, between eros and the good, in the interest of making obedience to God the sole path to virtue, Augustine unwittingly prepares the way for Machiavelli. Because of the dichotomy between nature and goodness already propounded by Christian thinkers in their critique of pagan philosophy, the object of princely virtue in Machiavelli's thought is no longer an eternal Beauty that assimilates, sublimates, and uplifts the tyrannical passions but is instead an alien Other, severed from all claims to nobility and eternal worth, an object of conquest to be taken as brutally as necessary. Augustine transposes the highest good to a world beyond nature and so deflates the moral claims of worldly politics. Machiavelli accepts the removal of the highest good from nature in order to liberate worldly politics from those moral claims.

Moreover, I would argue that Machiavelli's secularization of the Augustinian City of Man as the basis for his understanding of power politics and acquisitive human nature helps explain the tendency in his works to take what for the classics was a highly variegated and multifarious concept – that of Fortuna – and reify it into a single, unitary, and overwhelmingly hostile and irrational force governing the entire nonhuman world in opposition to man. For the ancients, Fortuna was a phenomenon that could manifest itself in numerous ways – sometimes hostile, sometimes unpredictable, but also as a benevolent, fecund force of pleasure and prosperity. We considered some of the philosophical nuances in our discussion of Cicero earlier in this chapter. A famous Roman statue of Fortuna conflates her with the archaic figure of Mother Earth, covered with the fruits of agriculture and dozens of life-giving breasts and potent testicles. The Fortune of the Roman People was worshipped throughout the empire as the benevolent guiding spirit of Rome's great success, peace, and virtue. All of these qualifications and shades of meaning Machiavelli casts aside, reducing fortune to an overpowering and empty singularity that goads man into fighting back. The counterpoise to Machiavelli's secularized Augustinian landscape of politics as sheer dominion and acquisition is the reification of the place formerly occupied in it by the saving will of the One God into the overwhelmingly adverse power of Fortune, the Single Other, whose power can also be utilized within ourselves so as to free ourselves of our dependence on her, a kind of secular salvation. (I discuss the stages of this process in the next section of this chapter.)

Machiavelli's identification of Fortune as the Single Other provides some insight into Leo Strauss's intriguing remark that Machiavelli's presentation of Fortuna "reminds one in some respects of the Biblical God" ([1969] p. 214). He continues: "She takes the place of the Biblical God. She is indeed not a creator and she concentrates entirely on the government of men." Strauss's formulation implies that, in terms of the theological paradox attempting to express God as that which "reveals" in distinction to that which "makes," Machiavelli attributes to Fortuna the role of revelation. For, as Strauss goes on, it would appear that Fortuna had established and "elected" the Roman people to greatness because of its justice, meaning that "Fortuna is guardian or source of justice." The proof is that Fortuna punishes cities less the more they are "filled with virtue, religion." Yet "she is indeed not a creator." I surmise from this formulation that, as Strauss sees it, while Fortuna provides Rome with the revelatory dimension of guardianship and election, the

role of the "maker" in the dyad of making/revealing is presumably transferred to the prince, or, as we consider in the next chapter, to republican
statesmen who, through their willpower and disciplined vigor, render
Fortuna's revelatory dispensation into actual political and imperial success by reshaping the "occasion" Fortuna gives them. Of course that
constructivist dimension, the will of the statesman or the prince, must
also be enfolded within Fortuna's sway, that is, wholly immanentized
within the life-world we call Fortuna. Fortuna's sway points to no transcendence strictly speaking in either the classical or Christian sense,
no soul with a connection to the *nunc stans* beyond the currents of
time. Because Fortuna (as Strauss puts it) "concentrates entirely on the
government of men," nothing strictly speaking transcends "the government of men." Nothing transcends the actualities of politics, society,
and power. Anticipating Spinoza and Hegel, Machiavelli appears to collapse God into existence, to equate God with the world, such that the Is
equals the Ought. Finally, with Heidegger, Fortuna sheerly reveals, and
"making" is stigmatized as a corrosive and intrusive force, technology,
divided from Being as revelatory origination.

To take a Hegelian perspective, the Augustinian dichotomy between,
on the one hand, human nature conceived of largely in terms of dominion and, on the other, a transcendence that stands beyond nature is
crucial for understanding much of modern thought, even or perhaps
especially thought that superficially appears to be markedly secular and
anti-Christian in character. Hegel argued that modernity as a whole
is a post-Christian phenomenon inasmuch as modern subjectivism can
only be understood as a development of the radical self-alienation from
nature prefigured in the God of the Absolute Religion – a divinity who,
having created nature from without, reenters it as Christ and suffers a
mortal death. This complete immanentization of the ideal within the
real, the kernel of historicism, begins, I suggest in the next chapter, in
Machiavelli's *Discourses*, although for reasons I discuss in the Conclusion, it does not strictly speaking anticipate the full-blown Philosophy
of History, which must await the crucial ingredient of Rousseau, himself
an idiosyncratic admirer of the Florentine. For now we can make the
broad observation that, for Hegel, modern autonomy is unintelligible
without the intervening concept of the Abrahamic God's freedom from
nature and cannot be seen as a mere derivation from classical philosophical notions of the soul like those of Plato and Aristotle, much as

these may have been a seed bed for a more universalistic politics to be brought about by stages by the progress of history. This is why, in the *Phenomenology of Spirit*, Hegel distinguishes between the "independence" (*Selbstandigkeit*) honored by the aristocratic morality of pagan antiquity and the "freedom" (*Freiheit*) acknowledged as the goal of humanity in the modern age. "Independence" is a kind of "lordship" and self-sufficiency thought to be possible through the cultivation of a naturally superior character, the model of "the best man" so important in the *Republic, Gorgias*, and other Platonic dialogues, as well as in Aristotle's understanding of *phronesis*. The ancients, in Hegel's view, saw this aristocratic character as a reflection of the substantive hierarchy of ranked ends that characterized nature as a whole, as when Aristotle, for example, bases his justification of natural mastery on the notion that nature as a whole is characterized by pairs of ruling and ruled parts. Callicles' erotic longing for completion through political preeminence and Socrates' attempts to educate it toward a properly natural fruition – moderate politics in the service of the common good guided by a philosophically grounded cosmology of friendship – would be seen by Hegel as an instance of the classical belief that independence could be achieved through a harmony with "Immediate Being," the supposition of an orderly cosmos within which human perfection finds its permanent place. "Freedom," by contrast, is the specifically modern consciousness of a capacity to overcome the limitations placed on us by nature, including apparently natural, substantive and fore-ordained differences between ranks of human beings, through an exertion of will. It is born of a sense of opposition between human satisfaction and nature – not, as for the ancients, from the prospect of a harmony between human nature and the cosmos. It owes its origin to the religious concept of a divine will that stands beyond all natural determinations, thereby reducing nature to empirical necessity.

Hegel believed that the progress of history was resolving this contradiction between the "substantive" Being of the ancient world and the "subjective" spirit of the modern, post-Christian will to freedom. My concern is not to pursue that large issue here, but to consider how the Hegelian distinction between ancients and moderns might enable us to clarify Machiavelli's relationship to modernity as a whole, particularly to the question of how *techne* becomes the engine for the conquest of nature, rather than, as for Platonismn, a key to self-forgetting and transcendence, an adumbration of the patterned orderliness of the Ideas radiating from the Idea of the Good. Machiavelli, I have argued, accepts the Augustinian valuation of politics and statecraft as dominion, while dispensing with Christianity's encouragement of shame over this natural fact deriving from its otherworldly standard of goodness. Thus, when Machiavelli observes in chapter 15 of *The Prince* that no one can possess all the virtues or be consistently virtuous "because human conditions do not permit it," there is a double irony. On one level, Machiavelli is using a characteristically Augustinian formulation in order to subvert the conventional Christian sentiment by altering its inner meaning. Augustine reminds us of the insufficiency of human nature to sustain virtue in order to remind us of our need for God's grace and mercy to carry through our own frail efforts and to save us from the sinful pride of believing that the nature of any created being could attain self-sufficiency and happiness on its own. Machiavelli uses the same kind of formulation to excuse us from even trying to practice these virtues, because the conditions of existence can make practicing them the very ruin of a prince or citizen. On another level, however, he agrees with Augustine: considered apart from the sustaining will of a Creator, nature is indeed nothing but random motion and perishable disarray, a realm whose disorderliness erupts in the compulsion of individuals and states to seek survival and power at the expense of others.[28]

28 As Wolin puts it, Machiavelli consigns the whole of political existence and human life altogether to the recesses of Plato's Cave, cut off from the sunlight of eternal truth, a world of "fleeting sense impressions and phenomenal flux" (2006) pp. 211–212. Consider also the essay by Kennedy, which argues that Machiavelli's politics amount to Augustine's City of Man stripped of the City of God (2000). For Kennedy, it is bootless to speculate whether Machiavelli (or later Hobbes) were believers. If they were, the fact that they hid this proves their theories were entirely secularized: "Machiavelli would agree with Augustine about the prevalence of evil in the *saeculum*, where men were bereft of faith, especially faith in one another. But Machiavelli was to offer no city of God as an alternative, or his faith in such a city was weakened by what he saw in the church's involvement in Roman, Florentine, and Italian politics in general, providing him with examples for *The Prince*. The earthly city, it would seem, was all man had and he should make the best of it, modelling it somewhat on the ancient polis, which would try to control chance, or Fortune. Machiavelli may have been a believer, as indeed may have been Thomas Hobbes (with whom he is often linked because of his power-based political philosophy). But the extent to which he hides it is itself a sign of secularism." Kennedy believes that this adaptation of Augustine's City of Man as all that we can aspire to must make us see Machiavelli as more of a pessimist and less as the founder of modern political science and the modern political era. But if we emphasize

Because nature offers no inner potential for the transcendence of those compulsions but is itself reducible to necessity, it makes no sense for a statesman to aim at a consistent standard of goodness: "It is necessary to a prince, if he wants to maintain himself, to learn to be able not to be good, and to use this and not use it according to necessity" (*The Prince* chapter 15).

Machiavelli further observes that for the prince to be able to alternate between what are conventionally perceived as virtues and vices according to what the circumstances call for, he must have "a spirit so built that (he is) able to know how to change to the contrary" (chapter 18). The prescribed mutability of the prince, we might say, is another secularized strain of Christian ontology. For what religion more than Christianity, in which God becomes man and man God – in which, as Luther's hymn put it, "God is dead" owing to the crucifixion before being resurrected – shows the capacity to "change to the contrary"? The psychological power of Christianity was arguably something new in the world. Its capacity to "change to the contrary" means that sight, the hallmark of classical metaphysics, is more vulgar and treacherous than touch, in the same measure as the visible world is a lure for the credulous and less reliable than our interior drives. Machiavelli's new methodologist who battles fortune within himself before mastering her outwardly, or, as later with Bacon, "vexes" and woos her, also takes his bearing from touch. As Machiavelli sums it up in chapter 18:

It is not necessary for a prince to have all the above-mentioned qualities in fact, but it is indeed necessary to appear to have them. . . . By having them and always observing them, they are harmful, and by appearing to have them, they are useful, as it is to appear merciful, faithful, humane, honest and religious, and to be so; but to remain with a spirit built so that, if you need not to be those things, you are able to know how to change to the contrary. . . . A prince should thus take great care that nothing escape his mouth that is not full of the above-mentioned five qualities. . . . He should appear all mercy, all faith, all honesty, all humanity, all religion. And nothing is more necessary

not merely the view of the saeculum that Machiavelli adapts from Augustine but also his focus on transferring the constructivist power of God's will to secular rulers, then his debt to Christianity is compatible with the view of his political theory as dynamic, future-oriented, and ultimately optimistic about man's capacity to improve his lot in the world. For another perspective on "Machiavelli's anthropology as a secularized version of Augustine on original sin," see Cosh (1999).

to appear to have than this last quality. Men in general judge more by their eyes than by their hands, because seeing is given to everyone, touching to few. Everyone sees how you appear, few touch what you are.

In general, then, by accepting the Augustinian characterization of human nature while rejecting the transnatural standard in light of which, for Augustine, our natures are a source of shame and proof of our need for God, Machiavelli is in effect exempting our natures from any blame for being appetitive and dominating. By truncating from Christian theology one of the key differences between Christianity and classical thought – its reductionist account of nature and human nature – Machiavelli is able both to repudiate Christianity's otherworldly morality and use a residue of Christian ontology to deny the Platonic contention that human nature in itself, without recourse to divine intercession or fortune, contains the immanent potentiality for its own development from base appetite to the noble pleasures of civic virtue and philosophy. For Machiavelli, human nature cannot be blamed for being unable to practice the virtues because it contains no such potentiality. The ill effects on peace and stability of the open clash of appetites are to be remedied not by civic *paideia* but by more efficient techniques of rule, or harnessed to provide energy for dynamic and prosperous republics and principalities. In this respect, Machiavelli is very close to Marlowe's stage Machiavel, who famously observes that the only real sin is ignorance. Machiavelli himself puts it this way in chapter 12 of *The Prince*, with a sideswipe at the monk Savanarola, who tried to rule Florence through sermons and ended up being burned alive over the Piazza della Popolo:

And he who said that our sins were the cause of it spoke the truth. But the sins were surely not those he believed, but the ones I have told of, and because these were the sins of princes, they too have suffered the punishment for them.

The consequences of faulty statecraft are not to be blamed on the moral failings of the people. Correcting those consequences is the goal of the art of ruling. For, as we have already observed, giving into one's passions for the acquisition of glory in the right way at the right time requires method. If one is to achieve *virtu*, acting on one's spontaneous desires cannot be done spontaneously, if only because the power of the "imagined republics" over the imagination is so strong. The "desire to acquire" comes naturally, according to Machiavelli, but the successful execution of this subrational urging requires a certain kind of rationality. One must "learn to be able not to be good" – it does not come automatically. Hobbes comes close to the same insight when he writes: "the fault is not in men as they are the matter, but as they are the makers of the commonwealth" ([1971] p. 363). As "matter," man is driven by the compulsion to survive at the expense of one's competitors for survival. Regulating these compulsions the better to achieve their natural goal is the task of a princely willpower that has freed itself from the delusions of classical and Christian transcendence through "learning" how and when to allow those compulsions their sway and when to choke them back. Machiavelli's new pedagogy will be indispensable for enabling princes to be themselves. His silent claim to be a prince of thought, which we discussed in Chapter 5 in connection with his own power to "make" matter into whatever form he chooses in his depiction of Cyrus and other great princes, is further evidenced by his stance in the Dedicatory Letter to *The Prince*. Ostensibly supplicating, it is actually patronizing toward its alleged addressee. While disavowing that a man from a low station could discuss the affairs of the high, by comparing his advice to that of a landscape artist, he implies that, just as they know the nature of high and low places, he knows the natures of both princes and peoples. Another way of putting it is that, as a prince of thought, Machiavelli knows both natures.

In a way, of course, Machiavelli does encourage a return to the comparative pragmatism of pagan political philosophy as opposed to Augustinian Christianity and the more pious recesses of Christian humanism. Machiavelli certainly tried to rehabilitate the pragmatic dimension of classical statecraft that had embarrassed the faith of the less worldly of the humanists like Petrarch. To see Machiavelli as doing only this, however, misses the deeper transformation. For although he rejects the City of God and its putative transcendence of appetitive human nature, Machiavelli does not urge a return to the Platonic or more generally classical view that politics can develop a potentiality of the soul for happiness through the practice of civic virtue. In this respect, he stands between Plato and Aristotle – who are able to evoke the full-bloodedness of political ambition so as to redirect its passions toward the Good while preserving a civic role for its vigor – and Hobbes, who takes Machiavelli's imposition of methodical rationality on the passion to rule to the extreme of trying to extirpate that passion entirely from human nature. As we consider in the Conclusion to this book, much as Hobbes is often seen as one of Machiavelli's lineal descendants, we have to go from Hobbes to English Republicans like Harrington to recapture Machiavelli's more fully rounded phenomenology of politics. Harrington's Atlanticist republicanism, which invokes Machiavelli as its preceptor, is richer than Hobbes's bureaucratic Leviathan – Sir Francis Drake as opposed to Kafka's *The Castle* – although Hobbes's is the superior mind. In sum, Machiavelli attempts to *liberate* the City of Man from the City of God on the grounds that because human nature is indeed driven by desire and dominion, statecraft must work with those necessities, free of either Christian or classical hopes for peace and repose. The world of Machiavelli's worldliness is not the classical view of the world but the Augustinian world stripped of God.

As Machiavelli describes princes of the most outstanding virtue in chapter 6 of *The Prince*, the external world provides no mediating link between the soul's inner potential and cosmically grounded objects of noble longing. It provides only the bare "occasion" for a prince's self-assertion and usually a negative inducement, an obstacle on which to focus and expend his power: "Such opportunities therefore made these men successful, and their excellent virtue enabled the opportunity to be recognized; hence their fatherlands were ennobled by it and became very prosperous." We recall from our comparison of Machiavelli and Plato in Chapter 2 that, in the *Laws*, the Athenian Stranger dwells briefly on the impediments that fortune can place in the way of states-manship, only to deny that we should feel overwhelmed by a sense of frailty before these forces and doubt our capacity to achieve virtue in cooperation with the *nous* that supervenes over chance disorder. The Platonic teaching altogether stresses that the only way in which a person can achieve independence and dignity is to rise above the passions operative on human nature through *tuche*; otherwise, as in the Chariot Image of the Soul, these passions will drag us down into the maelstrom of motion. By contrast, Machiavelli encourages us to dwell on, even run to embrace, the impediments thrown up by fortune – to see the world straight on as a place full of hostile forces – so as to encourage us to fight back and master it. We must come to see that, as chapter 6 puts it, statesmen "need" to encounter opposition, oppression, disorder, and corruption. These forces "make" them successful by compelling them to struggle, and thereby give them the opportunity to make their countries prosperous. They must experience a life-and-death struggle. Only if faced with the prospect that nature might overpower them will they be galvanized to assert their mastery.

THE THREE STAGES OF MASTERING FORTUNA

I now want to suggest more schematically that, as Machiavelli presents it, the process of mastering Fortuna has three main stages.

1. The prince or would-be prince must distance himself from the world. He must distrust it. He must not believe that human hopes for peace, happiness, and justice are grounded in the order of the world itself. He must not trust the looks of the world, the superficial appearance of stability and calm that Plato argues offers an intimation of a cosmic orderliness that supervenes over chance and perishability. As against the eidetic reasoning of classical thought, which encourages us to follow the eyes because sight glimpses in the looks of ordinary things the structures that transcend and ground all phenomena, Machiavelli advises us to turn inward, arming ourselves against this false appearance of stability. Eidetic reasoning is in fact the reasoning of the credulous many, for to repeat an earlier maxim: "Men in general judge more by their eyes than by their hands, because seeing is given to everyone, touching to few."

In this emphasis on inwardness, self-consciousness, and receptivity to "touch" as opposed to allowing oneself to be led astray by the looks of the world, one grasps another negative debt of Machiavelli's to Christianity – to the distrust of the world that St. Augustine evinces in his most Manichean moments. This Augustinian tenet was later crystallized in Luther's theses from the Heidelberg Disputation that "he is not worthy to be called a theologian who sees the invisible things of God as understood through the things that are made" (19) and "that wisdom which sees the invisible things of God as understood through His works altogether puffs up, blinds and hardens" (22). Machiavelli in effect secularizes this Augustinian theological tenet, newly emergent through Luther, when he argues that the traditional "writers" on statesmanship misidentify the visible outcome of princely virtue for its invisible cause, when in truth the visible stability and prosperity are caused by the primordial passions of the prince for power and glory. The writers, in other words, reify the "things that are made" by a prince of sufficient *virtu* into the preexistent and eternal causes for which virtue comes into being.[29]

2. Having separated himself from the world, the prince or would-be prince must "imitate" Fortuna by letting Fortuna's impetuosity empower him through his passions. For example, Machiavelli says, fortune likes to build things up in order to to knock them down. In the political realm, a prince can imitate this dimension of fortune's behavior by triumphing over adversity, which always compels admiration from subjects or adversaries. Someone who has attuned himself deeply to fortune's unseen rhythms can imitate fortune by anticipating

---

29 Blanchard (1996) discusses the importance of the distinction between touching and seeing as a way of reflecting on how Machiavelli's epistemology, and therefore his statecraft, differs from that of Plato. However, for Blanchard, instead of viewing Machiavelli as diametrically opposed to Plato, we should see in his statecraft "modifications of the Platonic approach (rather) than . . . a complete rejection of Plato." As he sums up this modification: "Whereas Plato resolves the problematic [about man's dependence on chance] by founding the soul on that which is, and which is better than and prior to man, Machiavelli supposes that man, starting from scratch, can construct his own foundations." Surely, though, this is all the difference in the world, not a mere modification. For if man is primarily defined in terms of a soul that is higher than and anterior to man, then that cannot be the *same* man who might start from scratch and construct his own foundations. The repudiation of Platonic cosmology inevitably entails an alteration in how we conceive of "man" as a political actor. If the Good is always already given, as it is for Plato, then man can never "start from scratch." Similarly, if art is not contained within the order of nature, as in Platonic cosmology, but can be employed by man to "construct" new foundations entirely on his own, then the world must *already* be reenvisioned in such a way as to make it capable of being reconstructed, and man's technical capacity to do so must now be understood as standing outside of nature, rather than, as for Plato, enfolded within it. Thus, although Blanchard is right to argue that Machiavelli's encounter with Plato is a genuine dialogue – as evidenced, for instance, by the fact that Machiavelli's discussion of the limits placed by chance on human affairs, and how human reason, virtue, and art might overcome those restrictions, parallels the discussion in Book 4 of the *Laws* – and although Blanchard is also correct to observe that both Plato and Machiavelli begin by appearing to concede that the sway of chance is overwhelming only to conclude that it can be overcome to a large degree, I would argue that Machiavelli's view that a prince can aspire to master nature and assimilate reason to the will, thereby making himself the source of his own prudence, is not only a modification of Plato's view but a profound reversal, which changes the meanings of all the cognate terms in the parallel as well. That is, just as Machiavelli overturns Plato's belief that man must find his place within nature, so do the meanings of fortune, knowledge, virtue, art, and prudence all undergo a complete reversal of meaning.

this particular tendency and consciously manipulating it to increase his authority. Thus, a prince might deliberately encourage conspiracies among his foes so as to have the opportunity to stamp them out. By building up his own enemies in order to knock them down, rather than sitting idly by while fortune builds them up – as will happen in the course of political affairs in any event – the prince preempts fortune's hostility while tapping "her" power and converting it to the service of his will (*The Prince* chapter 20).[30]

Thus, by first extricating himself from the world and renouncing all hopes of a connection between human happiness and the order of the cosmos, the prince lets the world empower his passions as disorder. Because he is conscious of this alienation between his will as the source of order and the world's disorder flooding through him, however, he will not be swept away or overpowered. For Plato, one could overcome fortune to some degree by aiming at transcendence. This meant pursuing virtue and thereby approximating through the governance of intellect over passion in the soul the predominance of harmony and stability over disorder that prevails in the world at large. For Machiavelli, however, this is tantamount to allowing oneself to be swept away by a powerful delusion, the root cause of being psychologically "unarmed" rather than armed, and of "relying on Fortuna and the arms of others" rather than on "virtue and one's own arms" (*The Prince* chapters 1, 6, 7).

---

30 This passage, recommending that a prince cultivate conspiracies so as to stamp them out, illustrates the active/passive dyad of the interior interaction between Fortuna and the prince. In chapter 6, fortune provided the bare (and hostile and dangerous) "occasion" for potential princes to imprint their will on "matter," a blank slate to be filled with their virtue. Here, the situation is turned around, and Fortune is reified into a weirdly benevolent goddess who actively contrives to put such occasions in the prince's path. Fortune, Machiavelli says, "wishes" to make a new prince great. The new prince does not have a hereditary position, which means he is already not reliant on the arms and the fortune of others (as was, for example, Cesare Borgia). Therefore, Fortuna "makes" enemies and obstacles for him so that, by crushing them, he can "climb higher" through an enhanced reputation for victory entirely through his own efforts. Understanding the weird favor Fortuna has done for him by throwing every possible threat and obstacle at him, a "wise" prince, having established his power through overcoming the initial impediments she created, will imitate her by deliberately encouraging conspiracies to form so that he can continue to "increase his greatness" by crushing them. In other words, what Fortuna does to the prince spontaneously, the prince will imitate methodically. This is the difference between "relying" on fortune, as do those who rest content with the status they have inherited or been given, and those who master Fortuna by channeling her spontaneity.

Machiavelli's prescription is an act of methodical self-abandonment. You allow the disorder of the world to enflame the passions and fuel the will precisely and only to the extent necessary to exert control over the limiting conditions on one's will. Thus, whereas Plato presents the relationship of the longing for virtue to the objects of virtue as an ascent through the visible hierarchy of human goods guided by an eros progressively enlightened as to its true satisfaction, Machiavelli presents the prince as alternating with dispassionate efficiency between the mode of the lion and the mode of the fox – to let himself be carried away by anger, rage, and belligerence or not to let himself be so carried away, depending on what maximizes power in the given circumstances (chapter 18).

The alternation between the violence of the lion and the cunning of the fox arguably parallels the alternation between force and fraud in the *Discourses* discussed in Chapter 5. Although Cicero is not discussed by name in either context, Machiavelli's pairings of force/lion with fraud/fox directly echo a similar discussion by Cicero in chapter 14 of the *Offices* (1955), where Cicero introduces the lion and the fox, pairing the lion with force and the fox with fraud. However, Cicero's judgment of these forces is the exact opposite of Machiavelli's. Injustice, Cicero says, can be committed in two ways: by "force, the property of a lion" or by "fraud, the property of a fox." He continues: "Both are utterly repugnant to society, but fraud is the more detestable." He concludes: "But in the whole system of villainy, none is more capital than that of the men who, when they most deceive, so manage as that they may seem to be virtuous men." It is hard to imagine two more diametrically opposed views than those of Cicero and Machiavelli on these traits. For Cicero, force and fraud are both "utterly repugnant" because, as the similes of lion and fox imply, they reduce us to the level of animals, forgetting about our souls and virtue. Fraud is "more detestable" because it involves sly, sneaky deceit rather than brute open force, which is at least honest in its directness. Machiavelli, as we have seen, is equally at home with the use of either force or fraud, depending on the circumstances, but in general favors fraud – for Cicero, the more despicable of the two – over force, because the lion lacks the subtlety of the fox. Moreover, whereas Cicero deplores the fact that the use of force or fraud reduces a man to the bestial, Machiavelli segues from the half man/half beast Chiron to the lion and the fox, endorsing the complete bestialization of the human character and the animalization of even its mind, traditionally thought to be the soul's closest connection to eternity. Finally, echoing Plato's discussion of the two ways of life in the *Republic*, virtue (including civic virtue) and vice (culminating in the extreme of tyranny), and how (as Glaucon maintains) the tyrant at his most successful can disguise his unjust actions as just, whereas the truly just man is taken to be unjust and is persecuted, Cicero writes that the lowest depth of moral depravity is that of men who deceive in order to take advantage of others but don the appearance of being just. Machiavelli, by contrast, tells the prince that there is nothing more useful for him than to cultivate the appearance of possessing the traditional virtues as a reputational smokescreen behind which he can gain and preserve power, involving, if necessary, any degree of fraud or violence required, the practice of those virtues for their own sake leading to political suicide. Could there be a more resounding demonstration of the fact that Machiavelli is completely opposed to Cicero's political teaching, rather than being, as some in the contextualist school would have it, his successor?[31]

Cold-bloodedly to allow oneself to be overwhelmed by passion is plainly a matter requiring the greatest dexterity, acuity, and subtlety, the political equivalent of windsurfing in which too little or too much release or control – too much impetuosity or too much caution – can submerge one's craft. Thus, it may be, as Hannah Pitkin suggests, that Machiavelli chooses to reify Fortuna as a woman so that the prince does not feel completely overwhelmed by the randomness and hostility of the forces he combats but has a recognizable and desirable foe to subdue.[32] Yet the

---

31 A similar argument is made by Ball (1984) pp. 73–76.
32 Pitkin (1999). Zuckert (1996) argues, based on Machiavelli's *Clizia* and the presentation of Sofronia, that Machiavelli attributes the capacity for *virtu* equally to men and women (Sofronia is a play on the Greek word for prudence, *sophrosune*). At the same time, she observes, Machiavelli does not mean by prudence what the classical thinkers meant. It is not a virtue that is fully actualized through political community but is on the contrary based squarely on one's own self-interest and property. Zuckert's essay is part of a wide-ranging debate, well sampled in this volume, over the status of Fortuna and of Woman for Machiavelli. Zuckert's argument is meant as something of a corrective to Pitkin, who argued that Machiavelli failed to live up to his political theory's aspirations for greater freedom and prosperity for mankind because of his root and branch misogyny, crystallized by his advice on the need to use force to subdue Fortuna, which she characterizes as a proto-fascistic conception of *virtu* as sheer machismo. Pitkin's most telling observation is that it may be necessary for Machiavelli's prince to personify

prince can only subdue Fortuna if he "imitates" her. For the ancients, the imitation of nature meant the attempt to inculcate the orderliness of the world in one's own character and habits, what the Stoics called *integritas*. For Plato, philosophy and its ordered view of the whole must be the supervisor and guide for correct poetic "imitation," such that Homer must be purged of his Dionysian sweetness, leaving only examples of virtuous living, the philosophic images that will replace the tragic poets' and Sophists' shadow show cast on the wall at the rear of the Cave. For Machiavelli, however, the imitation of nature means allowing the multifarious, unpredictable, subtle, treacherous, and malignant currents and moods of fortune to course through oneself; sampling them, savoring them, but never being swept away by their current; instead, turning their power outward in one's manipulation of others, especially in one's manipulation of how the credulous many see one's external reputation for virtue. We see again how Machiavelli conflates the roles of philosopher and poet. The hierarchy of philosophy over poetic imitation is replaced by the alternation between control and release.

Thus, there is an interesting ambivalence in Machiavelli's depiction of manliness. On the one hand, he encourages a crude masculinity and brute exertion of power:

Fortune is a woman, and it is necessary, if one wants to hold her down, to beat her and strike her down. And one sees that she lets herself be won more by the impetuous than by those who proceed coldly. And so always, like a woman, she is a friend of the young, because they are less cautious, more ferocious, and command her with more audacity. (*The Prince* chapter 25)

Even among the ancient exponents of tyranny, of the superiority of the "manly men" (*andres*) who live for victory in the contest for distinction,

the hostile and unpredictable forces of the external world as Fortuna – as a woman – because those forces will be less terrifying to the extent that the prince can reify them as one single foe who must be subdued. My own position is something of a middle ground between these two. Because I present the relationship of the prince to Fortuna as a kind of dance between his psychic interior and the generative matrix of nature, a dance in which the prince must tap into nature's own spontaneity and capacity for force, I agree with Zuckert that Machiavelli is arguing for a certain kind of mutuality and reciprocity between the masculine and the feminine, grounding the belief that, based on self-interest, women could be prudent as well as men, a basis for "liberal feminism." At the same time, though, I believe Pitkin is correct to see the prince's dyad with Fortuna as a potentially dark and terrifying fracas, and that although caution is sometimes to be preferred to impetuosity, in general the hot-blooded virility of the young is a better bet for bringing Fortuna under control.

it is hard to match the unvarnished crudeness of this portrait. Perhaps Callicles comes close in his extolling of the "natural master," identified with the archaic superhuman and wandering marauder Hercules (*Gorgias* 484). Yet even the Sophists argued that the art of rhetoric and the worldliness acquired from a foray into philosophy were necessary accoutrements of manly prudence – one could not prevail against the many by physical strength alone, for they would always win the contest through sheer force of numbers. As Werner Jaeger points out, the Sophists billed themselves as a replacement for the old aristocratic code of honor reaching back beyond Marathon.[33] With Machiavelli's likening of *virtu* to rapine, we seem closer to Nietzsche's blonde beast, or Heidegger's declaration that "the young" have already given themselves over to the destiny of the people, so that, having made the existential decision to follow the Fuhrer, they no longer need philosophy or the life of the mind.

Stoic and Christian gentlemen down to and including the Renaissance humanists were taught to recoil from this naked sort of belligerence as the coarse indelicacy of a slavish character who has no control over his bodily passions, the very epitome of the tyrant.[34] One need only think of Castiglione, who smoothly adapts Diotima's Ladder to a creed of courtly love in which chasteness and delicacy alone make one worthy of the beloved's love. As the would-be rapist of Fortuna, Machiavelli's prince is thus a good deal more "macho," as one used to say. On the other hand, although capable of a directness leading to bold, even crude actions, Machiavelli's prince will not be reliably open and honest in his dealings with others – unlike, say, Aristotle's great-souled man, who will not stoop to deceive or dissimulate because that would suggest a shameful preference for popularity among his inferiors over telling the truth (*Nicomachean Ethics* 1124b13, 1125a3). Machiavelli's prince

---

33 Jaeger (1965) pp. 289–296.
34 Erasmus illustrates well how the classical denunciation of the tyrant as a monster of excessive passions was assimilated to Christian statecraft: The tyrant is "a frightful, loathsome beast, formed of a dragon, wolf, lion, viper, bear and like creatures.... Never sleeping, but always threatening the fortunes and lives of all men; dangerous to everyone, especially to the good; a sort of fatal scourge to the whole world, on which everyone who has the interests of the state at heart pores out execration and hatred, because its maliciousness is hedged about with armed forces and wealth. This is the picture of a tyrant.... Monsters of this sort were Claudius and Caligula." Quoted in Newell (2001) p. 275. For a discussion of classical and courtly love, see Newell (2003) pp. 12–27.

will cultivate a reputation for honesty to the extent useful, but he will always manipulate it from behind the scenes, capable of the slyest deceits and most shameless reversals. In a way, therefore, Machiavelli's prince, although on one level excessively masculine in contrast with the classical model of the gentleman, is on another level more "feminine" in the sense that he takes on some of the qualities of fickleness, treachery, and evasiveness attributed by Machiavelli to personified Fortuna herself.[35]

This alternation between the bold and the deceitful, the forthright and the sly, undulates throughout the new psychology of the lion and fox. For example, when he praises the "inhuman cruelty" of Hannibal (*The Prince* chapter 17), Machiavelli is providing what he regards as the unvarnished truth about the kind of firmness in governing that the ancient authors also admired while flinching from identifying its actual psychological source. However, Machiavelli also praises treachery and deceit as routine methods for maintaining authority. In discussing "well-used" cruelty, for instance, he cites the examples of Agathocles of Syracuse and Oliveretto of Fermo. Whereas Agathocles convened the People and Senate of Syracuse and had his enemies among them slaughtered in the open, Oliverotto prepared to seize power first by luring the opposition to a "most secret" chamber and killing them out of sight. Reflecting on this contrast between ancient and contemporary examples, one wonders: Has the incredible psychological hold of the "imagined republics," epitomized by the Church that is at once a world government and militarily powerless, yet can sway powerful men through their piety to serve its own interests, introduced into the world a contradiction between appearance and reality that is much sharper than anything known to the ancients? That is to say, it may be more difficult, given the enormous psychological hold of the illusory imagined republics, to kill one's enemies openly, because such pragmatism is considered sinful, but less difficult to deceive them and kill them in secret because Christian *naivete*

---

35 In this connection, the summation by Lord (1979) of the relationship between the *Mandragola* and Machiavelli's larger political philosophy appears to be apt: to the extent that man might aspire to overcome Fortuna, and if the proper mode for success in doing so is akin to a hot-blooded youth's wooing of a tempestuous woman rather than to a cautious man's trust in the rationality of the cosmos, then Machiavelli's thought, although neither precisely comedic nor tragic (certainly not tragic, inasmuch as will and reason can plot a clear method for man's triumph over necessity and chance), bears a closer affinity to comedy, "if one understands by comedy the archetypical celebration of the triumph of youth and desire over age, authority and duty."

has made men more credulous in general and more inclined to accept a profession of virtue as its reality. One is reminded of how Shakespeare's characters so frequently alter their identities, from a woman playing a man playing a woman, from a wastrel to a king. If one wants to appreciate the full force of Machiavelli's wit, one need only think through his remark to the addressee of *The Prince* about what gifts a prince like Lorenzo would most enjoy receiving and the means through which Cesare Borgia lured the Orsini to Sinigaglia.[36]

The Machiavellian prince is profoundly interiorized and detached from the visible world with its established customs and distinctions, in this sense sharing the Augustinian soul's alienation from the world. He is as much Iago as Hannibal, as much an expert in the invisible levers of power as in its ferocious open exercise, as much if not more fox than lion, and both masculine and feminine by turns. All see him, but few "touch" what he is. The abstraction of the self from any concrete object of erotic longing in the world – a prerequisite for the mastery of self and others – calls for a plasticity and mutability of character whose feline slipperiness would have been excoriated as much by Callicles as by Socrates. The exchange of traits between the "virtuous" prince and the "malignant" goddess Fortuna is crystallized in a writing by Bacon, who credited Machiavelli with having understood that the purpose of knowledge is "the relief of man's estate" through the extraction of power from nature. Indeed, the methodological skepticism toward received opinion and tradition that formed the basis of the new natural science is arguably grounded in the Machiavellian ontology of alienation from, and imitation of, Fortuna. Bacon describes the scientist as someone who woos nature, who taps into nature's inscrutable rhythms, and to this extent imitates her and begins to merge with her. Yet this empathy exists only for the sake of subverting nature's power so as to empower human projects, torturing nature through experimental

36 In this connection, consider Dietz (1986), who argues that Machiavelli's advice to Lorenzo in *The Prince* is meant to hasten his overthrow and restore the liberty of Florence. To which one must respond, it could be true. However, it does not "[return] *The Prince* to its specific historical context" if this is seen as something at odds with his later legacy. After all, one can observe that Shakespeare's plays are at once veiled criticisms of the Tudors based on his own personal experience and observation and ascend to universal truths that speak to the ages. There is no need to choose between the "historical context" and the transhistorical experience, for the latter emerges out of the former and is transmuted by ongoing acts of interpretation.

science so as to reconstruct nature's parts (Bacon[1960] p. 25; [1857] I.iii). To do this, the scientist must rigorously puncture the pleasing images, what Bacon calls the "idols of the mind," that previous philosophy generated through its heavenly illusions; the scientist must forsake the surface and probe the interior. This indicates another connection between Machiavelli's meditations on Fortune and biblical revelation: As Leon Kass has argued, there is a profound kinship between the distrust of the visible world found in revealed Abrahamic religion and modern physics.[37]

3. The methodical alternation of self-release and self-control, grounded in a subjectivity constituted by the reflection that the world is a field of hostile forces, allows one to master Fortuna. By doubting the world, man can begin striving to locate himself outside it as a source of order. In this way, the will to impose form on matter traditionally attributed to God might be practiced by princes. It leads to a new paradigm for knowing. For Plato, *techne* provided an intimation of the substantive order and harmony that governed the whole. Precisely because he wants Callicles to realize that he cannot achieve whatever he pleases, Socrates compels him to subject his longings to the clarification afforded by the analogy of prudence to expertise, which leads to a view of the cosmos as governed by geometric proportionality and friendliness, and thereby helps to dampen tyrannical ambition. For Machiavelli, by contrast, art reflects nothing about the nonhuman world, lacking even that "small part" of it (rhetoric) that (as I hold) the pre-Socratics and Sophists argued was connected to *physis*. Art is the imposition of form by man on an otherwise recalcitrant and hostile nature. Just as it can combat Fortuna in the literal, outward sense by damming up rivers before they flood, so can princely rigor purge the social order of its malign "humors." It apes the form that the Divine Artificer imposes on the inchoate stuff of matter in Augustinian and Thomistic theology. Far from limiting tyrannical ambition, as it does for Plato, art is now its consummation, an expression of power so perfect that it ranges far beyond mere personal triumph to the imposition of epoch-making "new modes and orders," unprecedented in nature or history, on the currents of time. In this way, *techne* starts to become technology. There is a path from Machiavelli's art of princely rule to

37 Kass (2003).

Hobbes's contention that statecraft can imitate God understood as the artificer of the universe. Just as God is held to have originally created nature, *homo faber* can improve on it, specifically by making a political state that will remedy those innocent faults that proceed from unreconstructed human nature in its spontaneous pursuit of survival and dominion (Hobbes [1971] pp. 81–83, 188, 196, 202). Nevertheless, this path from Machiavelli is not the only one leading out of his thinking. For, as we consider in the next chapter, the interaction of the rhythms of Fortuna through the rise and fall of states with human *virtu* points to an ontology of history whose currents elude complete predictability and control.

As we have observed, for Machiavelli, mastering nature does not mean only, or even primarily, the power to literally impose one's will on external conditions. Before projects of literally reconstructing the natural environment or the state can be firmly undertaken, they must be grounded in the rooting out of that part of one's own nature vulnerable to the belief in the utopian morality of ancient thought and Christianity. Even so ruthlessly "virtuous" a prince as Cesare Borgia, after all, showed himself vulnerable to morality when he allowed an enemy to become pope, hoping that Julius II's gratitude would wipe out his desire for vengeance: "And whoever believes that among great personages new benefits will make old injuries be forgotten deceives himself" (*The Prince* chapter 7).[38] In order to resist the traditional moral teaching that service to the common good is preferable to "princely" (that is, tyrannical) power, Machiavelli argues, we must resist *believing* in the traditional characterization of tyranny, even if we are planning to choose it over virtue. In other words, it is not enough to choose tyranny and reject the common good. In the final analysis, Machiavelli is not urging an acceptance of the view argued by Callicles and some of the Sophists, that the best way of life is to become master of the city so as to

---

38 In criticizing Louis XII in chapter 3 for ceding the Romagna to Pope Alexander because he was under an obligation to him owing to the resolution of his marriage, Machiavelli observes that there is nothing "miraculous" about the fact that, by disobeying the Romans' rules for taking provinces, he failed. Because modern Christian rulers and states are taught to want peace above all else and view success such as the ancients achieved as vice, they cede the maximum of control over their own affairs, thereby making themselves maximally vulnerable to the reversals of fortune, hence making politics seem like a field of "miraculous" and equally accidental triumphs and defeats.

be able to gratify one's own pleasures to the utmost. For, Machiavelli implies, in choosing a life of political mastery defined in terms of erotic excess, we make ourselves vulnerable to the Platonic critique. We are already part of the way to accepting the traditional account of the tyrant as someone whose excesses leave him wretchedly unhappy compared with the happiness of contemplation or beatitude.

The classical thinkers do encourage the release of the passions in a certain sense. Because Plato believed that the good life must entail both happiness and justice, he did not see any sense in simply preaching abstinence and self-restraint. Socrates' exaggerated emphasis in the *Gorgias* on an emptily geometrical cosmic order, leaving Callicles' eros across a gulf untouched and unrepentant, is compensated for by the *Symposium*, in which eros itself, properly clarified, leads the soul on a simultaneously emotional and intellectual ascent to the Good. To take another example of Plato's awareness that virtue must entail the satisfaction of the affects, the Athenian Stranger criticizes Kleinias for thinking that the passions can simply be made war on (repressed or punished) without regard for the soul's inner satisfaction. The gloomy doubts of spirited young men who believe that the gods do not exist or do not care for them must be assuaged with a psychologically satisfying account of the whole (*Laws* 886–888, 899–901). Plato offers a wide-ranging evocation of tyrannical ambition, hedonism, and the pursuit of honor through a political career and then tries to show how these ambitions, properly understood, contain principles of orderly development that would bring the passions to fruition by enlisting them in the service of truly noble ends, rather than allowing them to drag the soul down into mere random lusts or spasms of anger and belligerence. The goal, in other words, is not merely to repress the desires but to show that their fullest satisfaction lies in the direction of the common good and contemplation rather than in tyranny.

Thus, Plato presents Achilles as a man whose indiscriminate urges make him explode in anger at every opposition because the world presents so many impediments to his unconstrained passions. He is heroic but mad, as capable of attacking a river as fighting his country's bravest foe, or, conversely, paralyzed by his ruminations over the meaninglessness of life. In Plato's presentation, his passionate anger, although left to itself destructive of political order, contains the seed of its own rehabilitation, for it expresses in an inchoate way the longing for a world in which one's needs are recognized and granted some grounding beyond oneself. Achilles is right, in other words, that the world should answer in some way to his own needs. The key to reforming such ambitious types is to educate their needs so that they come to experience the equilibrium between the development of their own best qualities and the harmoniousness characteristic of the most real dimensions of the cosmos. Such men will then turn their anger inward against their own aberrant impulses or restrict its outward exercise to enemies of justice and decency, like the Auxiliaries in the *Republic*, whose steadfast and moderate manliness is Plato's replacement for the doomed and brooding Achilles. They will no longer howl with anguish like Achilles at their inability to achieve everything they desire, or, as Socrates puts it in Book 10, cry like a small boy holding the place where it hurts until someone kisses it better, because the noble harmony of the world as they have been educated to apprehend it will suffuse their passions and harmonize them within the soul (*Republic* 386a–388b, 390e–391c, 604d).

For Machiavelli, by contrast, it is necessary to release one's passions *without* being seduced by the longing they produce for some such ultimate satisfaction in the world. Before one can hope to master nature and the natures of one's subjects, one must first win the battle against the seductive inner promptings of nature in oneself. One must let one's will be empowered by the longing for might, satisfaction, and honor while refusing to allow those passions to weave imaginary republics of repose and harmony that captivate these longings and sap their primordial strength. For Fortuna in Machiavelli's depiction, as we have observed, loves to build something up so that she can knock it down, and in Machiavelli's estimation, there is no more of a tragic catharsis in this nemesis than there is in being hit by a bus; there is nothing redemptive about failure and suffering. This is why Machiavelli is much more given to depicting princely virtue in terms of belligerence, violence, deceit, and cold-hearted glory rather than as the fruition of eros. Pleasure and happiness as ends in themselves, as the achievement of repose and tranquillity, are virtually absent from his prescription for princely rule. Although opposed to the Stoic model of steadfast self-control, even less does he want to return to the ancient philosophical school of hedonism, the main successor in the dissident strain opposing the classical natural right of Plato and Aristotle, which argued that the pleasures properly cultivated led to an inner harmony of the soul best achieved in private life and away from politics. The use of rape as a metaphor for the prince's relation to Fortuna is meant above all to forestall any sentiment on the prince's part that there is a link between the world and his own better qualities of self-restraint and admiration for nobility and beauty.

Machiavelli does not attempt to link the tyrant's longing for public preeminence with ultimate personal satisfaction akin to a successful love affair, rejecting not only the Platonic attempt to rehabilitate the longing of a Callicles but Callicles' erotic longing itself. To avoid the Platonic cure, Machiavelli throws out the Platonic diagnosis of the disease. Not only the Platonic therapy for tyranny but the very diagnosis of it as the disorder of a potentially orderly eros must be expelled with a pitchfork, and the expulsion of Augustinian transcendence while retaining its reduction of virtue to dominion greatly aids Machiavelli in this project. The objectification of nature as the treacherous goddess Fortuna is meant, in other words, to entirely forestall the Platonic starting point for the diagnosis and rehabilitation of the erotic longing for wholeness manifested by ambitious public men like Alcibiades and Callicles. In depicting the personality of Callicles, Plato gives us to understand that his kind of confusion of public and private erotic longings was the source of the tyrant's ambition to possess the city like a lover, but also contained the potential for its rehabilitation and education toward virtue. For Machiavelli, on the other hand, this confusion of public and private erotic longings is precisely what gets in the way of the clear-headed, single-minded pursuit of power undistracted by the concerns of the hedonist, whether reformed or not.

Thus, whereas Plato wants to curb eros for the sake of civic virtue and philosophy, Machiavelli wants to curb it for the sake of an "effectual" politics. Machiavelli does not object merely to the Platonic reform of the ambition to rule but to the description of it even in its basest spontaneous erotic manifestations – a diagnosis that already implies the reform. Whereas Plato argues for the assimilation of erotic unruliness into the harmony of the Good, Machiavelli argues that the delusions of eros get in the way of the dynamism of the primordial impulse toward mastery. On the whole, as we consider at greater length in the next chapter, Machiavelli prefers the fox to the lion, prefers calculation to aggression: "One needs to be a fox to recognize snares and a lion to frighten the wolves. Those who stay simply with the lion do not understand this" (*The Prince* chapter 18). At the same time, on the whole, he prefers impetuosity to caution. Within classical thinking, this combination would be a contradiction. If a wise calculation rules the soul, the aggressiveness of ambition will be tamed. If spirited impetuosity rebels against calculation, the cool-headedness of caution cannot prevail. For Machiavelli, however, there is nothing contradictory about this combination of opposites. The lionlike side of passion, left to itself, tends to get carried away and make its possessor forget why he allows himself to roar. Someone who manipulates his own rage by remote control, with the coolness of the fox, is more likely to bring off successfully those impetuous assaults on enemies and hostile "occasions" that Machiavelli thinks are likelier to put one in control of one's fate than waiting cautiously for favorable circumstances to arise. Because only if channeled efficiently – channeled away from the distraction of erotic longing, even an eros for honor and mastery – can the power of the passions be methodically focused against Fortuna.

Thus, to expand on an earlier motif, there is a larger meaning than is sometimes supposed to Machiavelli's advice that it is better for a prince to be guided by fear rather than by love in his dealings with his subjects. It does not merely mean that a prince should inspire fear rather than be kind. This hardheaded tactic is only one consequence of the more general implication that a prince should not practice the virtues in order to become an object of love to his subjects. He should resist the delusion that they can have friendly feelings for him based on their admiration for his superior qualities of character.[39] This is the kind of civic *philia* between citizens and statesmen sketched by Socrates for Callicles and elaborated by Diotima. In resisting this temptation, the prince will resist

---

39 Tolstoy's *War and Peace* provides a vivid illustration of the erotic longing for honor that may be stirred in a subject by his absorption in the nobility and beauty that he sees in the prince when Tolstoy describes a review by the czar of his troops, as well as the young nobleman Nikolai Rostoff's transport of martial and patriotic ecstasy as he imagines dying in battle for the splendid and kindly young emperor. The emperor's outward splendor perfectly mirrors the noble nature Rostoff attributes to him and toward which he is irresistibly drawn: "The handsome young Emperor Alexander in his Horseguards' uniform and three-cornered hat worn point forward, with his pleasant face and clear but not loud voice, was the cynosure of all eyes . . . 'My God! What would happen to me, if the sovereign were to address me!' thought Rostoff. 'I should die of happiness! . . . Oh, to die, to die for him! . . . My God! How happy I should be if he would only bid me to dash instantly into the fire!" Quoted in Newell (2001) pp. 352–354.

falling in love with his own reputation as magnified by his subjects' love. Otherwise, a prince-statesman can forget the levers of his power and float away in rapture with his own reputation, until this infatuation with the reified image of his own nobility makes him lose his "touch" for sensing subterranean threats to his power from the discontented or from secret plotters among his colleagues. Thus, whereas Socrates wishes to help men like Callicles understand that their eros cannot be satisfied by political achievement alone, Machiavelli wishes to help them understand that eros is a distraction from political achievement.

That statesmen avoid believing their own achievements are actually summoned into being by a preexisting objective hierarchy of noble fulfilment is good not only for princes but for popular regimes as well. As we saw in Chapter 5, according to Machiavelli, a republican statesman like Manlius had a character of such natural savagery that he was cruel to everyone without distinction, so that his rigor to enforce the laws was quite disinterested. This made him very much to be preferred to statesmen like Valerius Corvinus and Scipio who, by trying to make the people love them, thereby confused a private erotic relationship with the maintenance of the republic. They subverted the impartial rigor of the law by showering favors on their admirers and clients, threatening to replace republican equality with the personal authority of a monarch over his household. Thus, whereas Plato presents thumotic savagery as capable of being tamed by *paideia* (in the *Republic*) or assimilated by an eros for political nobility (in the *Symposium*) as two alternative routes to serving the public good, Machiavelli truncates them. Thumotic savagery and an eros for honor are not two perspectives on routes to the unity and health of the soul, with eros taking the leading role, but two kinds of ambition – the more savage one helpful to republics, the gentler one subversive of them. Manlius Torquatus is pure thumotic indignation bereft of a Platonic education in the harmonious beauty of the cosmos. Scipio's eros for fame and the admiring love of his fellow citizens, the kind of longing thought by Plato to be a basis for public service, is for Machiavelli the germ of the Roman Republic's corruption into an "eastern" despotism sapped of its manly rigor.

We recall that the love of a prince's subjects, according to Machiavelli, is a voluntary obligation. The prince relies on them to incur this obligation so long as he cultivates the virtues of soul recommended by the traditional writers. In terms of Diotima's Ladder, subjects see their prince as participating in the beneficent harmony that characterizes the beauty and goodness of the cosmos. They are drawn toward him in admiration because he supplies an object for their own love properly educated. For Machiavelli, however, the belief in this evanescent bond between lover and beloved in public life is a particularly disastrous example of relying on fortune – relying on the morality according to which people are capable of feeling an obligation to a virtuous ruler and of honoring him. By alienating himself from the hope of participating in this beautiful ladder of transcendence, the prince begins to master fortune in himself. By reducing his subjects to their consciousness that they depend on him for survival, either because he protects them or because he has the power to destroy them, the prince snaps this evanescent bond purporting to unite him and his subjects in their common love of the beautiful and good. Their obedience is now necessary, rather than voluntary; in the prince's control rather than dependent on their sense of obligation, in this way reversing the maxim of Aristotle's *Nicomachean Ethics* that a virtue practiced by choice is nobler than one practiced from compulsion (1110a–1112a). (As we see in the next chapter, Machiavelli consistently reverses Aristotle's maxim so as to make necessity the very basis of freedom.) Rather than relying on the visible image of his reputation to elicit love and respect, the prince will "touch" directly on the invisible compulsions that motivate his subjects to preserve their lives and possessions. He will rely more on their self-consciousness rooted in insecurity and desire than on their capacity for self-forgetting in their absorption in the object of their admiration. In elevating fear over love as the basis for the prince's reliance on the people, Machiavelli secularizes Augustine's dichotomy between the City of God and the City of Man, radicalizing the Christian theologian's truncation of Diotima's Ladder by replacing God's sustaining will over nature with the will of the prince.

By removing these hopes for transcendence from his relations with his subjects, by appealing to them primarily through fear and their desire for self-preservation, Machiavelli's new prince chastens the relation of their passions to his will just as he has chastened this relation within himself. Thus, the prince, having learned from the necessitous perils of Fortuna to purge himself of hopes for erotic transcendence in order to fight back and establish his mastery, imparts the same lesson to his subjects. His rule institutionalizes the malignant power of Fortuna, but for politically constructive purposes rather than caprice. By teaching his subjects to be guided by self-preservation rather than hope and ambition, his "state" replicates on the political level the more general lesson that life teaches us when we understand fortune. What Fortuna does to humans unconsciously and spontaneously, the prince can do consciously and methodically to – and for – his subjects, just as in the next chapter we see how Machiavelli argues that the successful unfolding of the Roman republic into an empire, having unfolded by chance, can now be consciously reenacted through method.

Statecraft can preempt the dangers of Fortuna to us all by channeling "her" power to inspire dread through the prince so as to stimulate the people to labor and achieve prosperity – a prosperity that this cold-blooded and self-disciplined prince will not despoil but protect. As Hobbes was to systematize this insight in chapter 14 of the *Leviathan*, without the fear of violent death imposed on us by nature, whether directly or through the invasive passions of our competitors, the social contract is but a bundle of unenforceable words. The Sovereign can replicate this terror and thus periodically compel his subjects to give up dangerous political ambitions and prosper in private. He can remind his subjects of their good fortune in escaping the state of nature by occasionally reproducing its terrors. Or as Hegel puts it in describing Nature's immediate threat to life that the Master wields mediately over the Slave, "fear of the Lord is the beginning of wisdom." Thus, whereas Plato thought the common good could be served by a certain kind of education of eros, Machiavelli thinks it is best served by the extirpation of eros from the subject matter of statesmanship, a path already laid in part by Augustine for completely opposite reasons. If they follow his advice, princes – whether real-world rulers, potential princes, or princes of thought – must uproot from themselves all vestiges of reliance on the world as characterized by Platonic friendship and harmony. Here we encounter the beginning of the impersonal authority, of the deeroticization of the sovereign, closely linked to modern terror and technological domination, but also to the beginning of the benign idea that governments should get out of the way of their subjects' desires to prosper and, as long as they do not harm one another or raise their hand against the state, let them live as they please. Machiavelli's advice that the prince should not plunder his subjects' possessions and should encourage them to prosper anticipates the modern conception of the state as the impersonal arbiter and umpire of contract law (*The Prince* chapters 9, 17, 22; Hobbes [1971] pp. 196, 202). Rule as denatured management begins to replace rule emerging from character development and civic pedagogy. Manlius is savage, but he has no distinct personality; he gives no inkling of suppressed wants, pleasures, or hidden complexities like those of Alcibiades and Callicles that make them so ripe for Socrates' erotic therapy. He is like a natural force erupting directly into the political order as an engine of enforcement. As we see in the next chapter, Machiavelli believes this force can be institutionalized as a part of the constitutional balance of powers.

In concluding this chapter, and by way of transition to the next, I want to reiterate that I am not attributing to Machiavelli the belief that nature can literally and in every way be brought under the sway of human mastery. I have suggested throughout that Machiavelli goes further than any classical thinker in promising the possibility of a hitherto unprecedented human power to stand outside of nature and achieve greater control over it, and that this possibility emerges from the regrounding of political existence in a post-Christian ontology that has no precise analogue in the classical approach. However, as we will see in turning to the *Discourses*, there is a side of Machiavelli that, in its ultimate recognition of the limitations placed on human freedom by the cycles of nature, historical events, and the shortcomings of human psychology, does share in the moderation of the ancients. It is a slender tendril of a connection, and one that, in Machiavelli's treatment, is drained of just about all the teleological content of the classics' understanding of nature aside from its insuperable objectivity. But it is a connection nevertheless. That point made, I still believe it is fair to say that Machiavelli encourages the liberation of the project for mastering Fortuna to an extraordinarily greater degree than any of the classics, such that his political science cannot be adequately comprehended as a modification of the classics or indeed even as their simple and complete reversal.

There is a side of Machiavelli's thinking, most boldly formulated in chapters 6 and 25 of *The Prince*, that promises the conquest of nature at its most radical; that seems to anticipate an ideal, to be progressively realized, of the pure mastery of nature by an exertion of will – a sense, in other words, in which Machiavelli anticipates Bacon, Kant, or even

Ficthe, that thinker who goes furthest in casting nature as nothing but sheer fodder for an endless dynamic for the assertion of human freedom, "the material of our moral duty rendered sensuous." There is another side of Machiavelli's thinking, however, most evident in the *Discourses*, that bounds the capacity for the exertion of human willpower within the surrounding contexts of time, circumstance, accident, human folly, and the rise and fall of regimes. In other words, the radically voluntaristic, proto-Baconian and proto-Ficthean side of Machiavelli is conjoined with a more immanentist, organicist approach to the unfolding of history and the recurrent cycles of events. In this way, Machiavelli might be seen as anticipating Hegel's attempt to reconcile the search in history for both freedom and community ("the unity of subject and substance"), with the very significant difference that Machiavelli does not propound a unifying synthesis between these two dimensions at the end of history.

VII

THE REPUBLIC IN
MOTION

Machiavelli's Vision of the New Rome

In this chapter, bringing to a conclusion my focus on the conquest of nature as the unifying ontological premise of Machiavelli's political philosophy, I try to show how Machiavelli's point of departure from the ancients over the relationship of virtue to fortune leads him to radically reorient the classical account of the founding of regimes and the prescription for the best regime. Although appearing to follow classical typologies like those of Aristotle and Polybius, at the end of the day, in endorsing the Roman Republic's dynamic imperial expansionism, Machiavelli turns virtually every premise of classical political philosophy on its head, from the pragmatic and psychological to the metaphysical. For, while the classics had maintained that a regime might be perfected insofar as its politics transcended chance and spontaneity in the direction of the permanent unity informing the whole, Machiavelli argues on the contrary that the history of Rome shows how a republic can be perfected by "chance" and "the aid of events." In Machiavelli's depiction of the progressive historical evolution of the Roman Republic, moreover, we find a prescription that combines what Plato and Aristotle had firmly maintained was not combinable – republican virtue as the basis for imperial aggrandizement.

Some scholars see a sharp distinction between *The Prince* as a pragmatic guidebook for princes (a job application, in effect, submitted by Machiavelli to a not terribly prepossessing ruler: *Tyranny for Dummies: A Guide to Oppression for the Rest of Us!*) and the *Discourses* as containing his deeper and more heartfelt republican convictions, as well as more openly philosophical speculation about fortune and the cycle of human affairs. If that were strictly true, it might appear as if my theme of tyranny should confine itself to *The Prince* and leave republics aside. There is something to this distinction. But I am going to try to show that the subject matter and intrinsic political teachings of the two books converge to a very large degree, bearing in mind that just as an individual prince can be a tyrant, so, too, can a republic or any self-governing community that is also imperialistic. As we observed in Chapter 4 in this regard, Thucydides presents Pericles as reminding the Athenians that, while they are a self-governing democracy internally, they are a "tyrant city" in the eyes of their allies and victims abroad.

As we consider in this chapter, Machiavelli integrates the discussion of the "new prince" in *The Prince* with the founders of republics in the *Discourses*. Moses, Romulus, and Theseus, who appear as new princes in *The Prince*, also appear as the founders of republics in the *Discourses*. In other words, qualities that might be deemed tyrannical in an individual ruler seeking his own power and glory might, viewed in another context, be identical to those needed to establish healthy and vigorous republics.[1] So it is essential to discuss Machiavelli's republicanism to see when and how he blurs these categories and also to round out our understanding of his new teaching on tyranny. In this respect, although differing profoundly from Plato and Aristotle in his conclusions, Machiavelli does share one of their own points of departure in viewing the founding of republics as necessarily entailing a consideration of tyranny. For, as we recall, Plato discusses in the *Laws* how a tyrant might found a republic, and Aristotle in the *Politics* concedes that a despot might conceivably make the best ruler. However, as I argue in this chapter, although beginning with these traditional rubrics, Machiavelli completely transforms their content. He conflates what the classics maintained must be conceived of as separate kinds of authority – the public realm of the city and the individualistic realm of the household. His encouragement of individualism extends to both princes and to their peoples. Everyone is encouraged to maximize their pursuit of security and well-being. Tyrannical foundings and refoundings are periodically necessary to keep republics vigorous and in fighting trim.

As we have seen in previous chapters, for the classics going back to Plato and Aristotle, imperial or despotic authority was an extension of

---

[1] As Mansfield observes, Rome could be viewed as having been founded by a foreigner, Aeneas, or by the native Romulus. It does not matter whether a republic is well founded or unified by internal founding or by external possession. Mansfield (2001) p. 32.

the art of household management. It could foster peace and prosperity, even on a multinational level, as captured by Xenophon's idealization of Cyrus the Great. Republican virtue, by contrast, was possible only within a small, self-governing, nonexpansionist polis where material wealth took second place to civic virtue. You can have a rational monarchy or a virtuous republic, the classics argue, but not both. Machiavelli, in sharp contrast, argues through the case of Rome that hardy republican virtue and liberty can be the *basis* for acquiring honor, prosperity, and stability through imperial expansion. Far from being uncombinable, Machiavelli argues, the merits of both household and polis can be "mixed" within a dynamic, mutating, ever-expanding imperial republic. I conclude this chapter by drawing some connections between Machiavelli's prescription for a "mixed" republic bent on imperial expansion and certain strains in the American Founding.

THE CLASSICAL UNDERSTANDING OF IMPERIALISM AS A MODE OF TYRANNY

Before turning to the *Discourses*, let me underscore with some general observations the classical approach to empire as a foil for the "untrodden path" Machiavelli claims he is opening up (1, preface). The classical political thinkers did not have a separate category for "imperialism" in their political analysis. As we recall from earlier chapters, for both Plato and Aristotle, what we would term an "empire" was an application of *despotike* – the rule of a master over subjects who are akin to slaves inasmuch as they are not called upon or considered equipped by nature to deliberate as citizens, a form of household management that could be extended over a vast extent of territory and peoples. Sometimes, as we see from the example from Thucydides, a polis could be referred to as a collective tyranny. Aristotle makes a similar observation in the *Politics* when he argues that "most people" view *all* politics as the pursuit of "mastery," either by individuals or nations (*Politics* 1324b20–40). Our term "empire" derives specifically from the Roman term *imperium*, originally the consuls' power over life and death in their capacity as the military commanders of the Republic's armies, later exclusively attached to Augustus and his successors as the title Imperator, that is, a field commander acclaimed by his troops, hence our term "emperor." Further to my previous observation, then, in viewing imperialism as a theme continuous with princely or despotic rule, Machiavelli is in this respect firmly planted in the classical tradition.

What we call an empire, and which the ancients would have regarded as a variety of tyranny, despotism, or universal monarchy (*pambasileia*) – or, in the Roman tradition, the hated title of *regnum*, kingship, which is why Augustus so carefully chose his new title of "emperor" (commander) – was well known to the classical political philosophers both in theory and practice. As we have seen, Plato and Aristotle were well aware of the alternative to the Greek city-state presented by the Persian Empire and, in Aristotle's case, the Alexandrian Empire. Cicero defended the idea of the *res publica* against the emerging imperial ambitions of Pompey, Caesar, and Octavius, already bent on replacing the aristocratic government of the original Roman polis with a Hellenistic-style monarchy, open or concealed. Moreover, classical political philosophy was not simply hostile to the concept of empire. As we observed in earlier chapters, both the Platonic and Xenophontic Socrates used the Persian Empire as a foil for the polis, sometimes to the detriment of the latter. For Xenophon, an idealized Persian empire under Cyrus the Great provided an alternative version of the best regime to that of Plato's idealized polis, the *Republic*. Aristotle is ambivalent as to whether a republican aristocracy or a monarchy patterned on *oikonomia* – the art of household management – is the best form of rule, and in the latter case explicitly extends the concept of monarchy to a multinational authority over many "cities and peoples" (*Politics* 1285b30–35).[2]

For all that, however, it cannot be denied that classical political philosophy as a whole has a preference for the small, self-governing republic. Even Xenophon arrives at the conclusion that the Persian republic from which the young Cyrus emerged – a blend of real-life Sparta and something akin to Plato's best regime – is in some ways superior to the vast multinational household that he establishes through his conquests. Plato's best regime is of course a polis, and Aristotle ends the *Politics* by endorsing his own version of the neighborly homogeneous republic. What explains this republican preference? Plato, Xenophon, and Aristotle all identify empire with the elevation of the art of household management – the production of material goods and the division of labor – over the cultivation of the moral and intellectual virtues solicited

---

[2] Consider also Plato *Alcibiades* I 121–124. See also Newell (1983).

by civic deliberation about the common good. Whereas republics foster the common good, empires allow individuals to maximize their individual security and gain. Whatever their merits, therefore, empires fall short of the highest human excellence. This is implicit, for example, in Aristotle's remark that, if economics were the chief end of politics, all cities could be united in a single state, as happens with multinational trade agreements (*Politics* 1280a35–40). Just as important, even in their relative approbation for empire, the ancient thinkers do not stress the conquest, bloodshed, and power seeking necessary to establish it so much as the unity of the finished product. For Xenophon, Cyrus's perfected empire embodies the art of household management that his Socrates establishes as a path to the Good, the conception of an ordered whole.

Much the same is true of Cicero with respect to the imperial dynasts and of Tacitus with respect to the Augustan principate: if it is necessary to accept that the republic has been superseded by the empire, one must endorse the empire only insofar as it guarantees the settled peace and the rule of law. Although Cicero never forsook his dream of the republic, he recognized that Caesar's dictatorship, a monarchy in disguise, provided stability and security, especially for the plebs, welcome after many years of civil war, and conceded that the continuing strife between the dynasts Antony and Octavius might well portend the likelihood that the old republic would never be restored. Virgil endows Rome's founder Aeneas with Stoic qualities of duty and perseverance that he then transfers to Augustus, divinely appointed to carry out Rome's divine destiny of bringing peace to the world. Ronald Syme (2002) notes that many of Augustus's apologists airbrushed, so to speak, Julius Caesar and especially his dictatorship out of the prehistory of the "restored" republic as an unseemly precursor due to Caesar's deliberate subversion of the old regime. The new Augustan regime wanted to emphasize its final embodiment as the guarantor of peace on earth, not the bloody and revolutionary means it had employed to get there. Tacitus grudgingly concedes that the principate was necessary to bring peace after the civil war years and that it was popular, especially in the provinces.

All the classical thinkers are at one in downplaying and severely criticizing the kind of dynamic, violent, and expansionist foreign policy that is needed to establish the path to imperial rule. Bearing this in mind will enable us better to appreciate what is novel about the specifically modern conception of empire that I argue is first theoretically elaborated by Machiavelli in his *Discourses*. That novelty has two main components that I hope to bring out through a reading of the opening chapters of Book 1 dealing with the crucial theme of how cities are founded and ordered. First, Machiavelli denies the classical contention that the pursuit of wealth and power rank beneath the pursuit of moral and intellectual virtue on the scale of human excellence. On the contrary, he maintains that the honor of success in the pursuit of wealth and power is constitutive of human excellence itself, as well as beneficial to all. Second, Machiavelli's endorsement of empire is not limited to its end state of established peace and law. On the contrary, he focuses on and praises the dynamic rise of republic to imperial power through an expansionist foreign policy that enriches all classes. For the classics, such approbation as could be extended to empire was based on the degree to which it might mirror the settled orderliness of the cosmos. For Machiavelli, on the other hand, it is the dynamism of the rise to empire – embodied in the career of Rome – in response to "chance" and "the occurrence of accidents" (*Discourses* 1.2) that achieves whatever perfection politics can sustain by imitating the flux of *Fortuna* in its clash of interests and pursuit of mastery. Little wonder that Machiavelli could say of his own new science of politics, with a well-nigh millenarian fervor, that "although the envious nature of men has always made it no less dangerous to find new modes and orders than to seek unknown waters and lands ... I have decided to take a path as yet untrodden by anyone" so as to "bring common benefit to everyone" (*Discourses* Preface 1).

According to the classics, one must choose between the communal honor of a republic and the individual security and well-being fostered under an orderly empire. According to Machiavelli, by contrast, the ambitious energies bred by the laws of an honor-loving republic can be harnessed to a project of imperial expansion resulting in individual security and well-being. This combination of what the classics regarded as difficult or even impossible to combine is what makes it plausible to term Machiavelli's vision a *liberal* empire, an empire in which republican virtue is the basis for the liberty of the individual. The challenge to statesmanship is not, as it would have been for the classics, to encourage the rise of empire to arrive as soon as possible at the peace and orderliness of its end state but, rather, to embody in the very institutions of the regime the vitality and ambition of its rise; to unleash recurrently the power seeking of individuals in all classes as the mainstay of the regime's stability. For Machiavelli, a way must be found of consciously reenacting the rise of republic to empire that Rome achieved spontaneously and unpredictably, so that the new empire to come, a discovery, he suggests, even greater than that of the new world across the seas that would become its future home, might be methodically established.[3]

VIRTUE, NECESSITY, AND CHOICE IN THE FOUNDING OF CITIES

The alternation between modes of princely rule conveyed by the metaphor of the lion and the fox that we explored in the last chapter also extends, as we now consider, to Machiavelli's discussion of republican constitutions in the *Discourses*. The methodical alternation between the lion and the fox implies that there is no substantive satisfaction available for the princely character in terms of the wholeness sought through union with the beautiful and the good in Diotima's Ladder and other Platonic images of the soul. The world contains no "middle way" of unity and peace but is governed by the clash of "bodies" that wells up into the clash of political bodies in the struggle to survive, aggrandize, or die (1.7). The prince must let himself be governed selectively by these chaotic forces, operative through his *virtu*, so that he can tap these forces to fuel his own ambitions rather than be swept away by them. So, too, as we explore in this chapter, must republics let themselves be governed by chance. They must set aside hopes for the "middle way" extolled by Aristotle and let their affairs be energized by desire, motion, and time: "the aim of the republic is to enervate and weaken all other bodies so as to increase its own body" (2.2). As we will see, this leads to a new basis for conceiving of the republican constitution as a dynamic equilibrium between two contending and acquisitive classes – nobles and people – whose energies are directed outward in a foreign policy

---

[3] See the valuable study by Hornqvist (2004), who argues that the revival of Republican Rome, with its emphasis on glory and liberality, was at the heart of Machiavelli's project, more important than the independence of Florence or the liberation of Italy. This constitutes further evidence, along with works by Rahe (2005, 2009) and Sullivan (1996, 2004), of a solid intrinsic connection between Machiavelli's own view of statecraft and the influence later traceable to him over English republicanism, as opposed to a mere retroactive appropriation or adaptation of his ideas.

of preemptive aggression and imperial growth. The same alternation of release and control – following the metaphor of the lion and fox – that princes are instructed in *The Prince* to maintain is carried out in the republican prescription of the *Discourses* by the common people and the senatorial ruling class. Thus, although the differences between *The Prince* and the *Discourses* are important, these works do not fundamentally contradict each other. Rather, Machiavelli's new ontology of denatured and deeroticized statecraft generates the different modalities of both principalities and republics.

Whereas Plato and Aristotle stress the telos – the substantive idea of virtue and the civic education needed to breed the disposition suitable to it – that each constitution embodies and downplay both its material preconditions and the threats to it from external aggressors, Machiavelli dwells exclusively on the origins of the state in necessity and adversity. He launches the Ship of State rudderless on the shifting seas of time and invites us to consider where it may head. He goes much further than merely providing a more realistic fleshing out of the disorderly preconditions out of which, in the classical conception, the constitution emerges, as one of his likely sources Polybius had done. As we saw in previous chapters, Plato and Aristotle, although circumspect about the role played by violence and coercion in the founding, as well as the occasional need to supplement an educational appeal to a noble character with law, force, and punishment, did not flinch before these facts. Machiavelli, however, is not merely arguing that virtue cannot be practiced successfully unless states pay more attention to these adversities, but that adverse necessity is actually *constitutive* of virtue. Concerns with survival, household management, and the entanglements of foreign policy that the ancients thought might, if properly guided and restrained, provide the wherewithal or the appropriate milieu for the pursuit of virtue are now set forth as the very genesis of virtue itself. It is not so much that, to cite the famous tag about Machiavelli, the ends justify the means as that the classical means *become* the modern ends, unified and given new direction by the project for the conquest of nature.

We recall from *The Prince* that, in the case of the greatest founders, those princes of "outstanding virtue," the "occasions" provided by fortune for them to exercise their talents are in fact terrible instances of adversity and disorder. Here, too, in the *Discourses*, using two examples

(Aeneas and Moses) of which one (Moses) is also in chapter 6 of *The Prince*, Machiavelli writes that the founders of cities become "independent" when are they "obliged" to flee some disaster, as Aeneas and Moses were forced to flee their birthplaces (1.1). The kind of adversity (wholesale peril, violence, and economic scarcity) that Aristotle would have concluded made it unlikely that any constitution might emerge in which virtue could be fully pursued – where at most survival and rudimentary order might be maintained in lieu of a higher fulfillment of man's nature as a political, deliberative animal – Machiavelli sets forth as the very *best* circumstances for the exercise of virtue either by a prince or a republic. Generalizing this point, he argues: "Virtue has more sway when labor is the result of necessity rather than choice." We recall from Aristotle that, in classical thought, *prohaeresis*, or choice, is what makes us capable of a distinctively human excellence. The need for material goods and the need to reproduce fall into that realm where human beings are determined by the same necessities, the same tissue drives, as we might now put it, that govern all living organisms. The art of household management provides these necessities so as to equip human beings with the wherewithal to cultivate virtues that we are free either to choose or avoid (in order to gratify our passions) and whose choice therefore confers the greatest merit. For Machiavelli, by contrast, the possibility of choice is the beginning of the "effeminization" of virtue. The hostility of the world forces us to fight back by laboring to survive, and so, in a perverse way, we have "the malignity of Fortuna" to thank for compelling us to stay in fighting trim.[4]

This contrast enables us to understand how Machiavelli radically reformulates what on the face of it is a traditional question with a pedigree stretching back to Book 7 of Aristotle's *Politics*: What is the best natural environment for the founding of a good constitution? Machiavelli poses the choice between a sterile site for a city and a fertile one. Aristotle had argued that it would be best to have a site that is neither

---

[4] Gilbert notes the paradoxically liberating aspect of Machiavelli's emphasis on necessity as the cause of virtue through labor: "In Machiavelli's view, Necessita is not just a hostile force which makes man's actions purely automatic. Necessita may coerce men to take action which reason demands. Necessita may create opportunities.... Thus, according to Machiavelli, rarely is there a situation which ought to be regarded as entirely desperate.... As long as man uses all the capacities with which nature has endowed him he is not helpless in the face of external pressures." Gilbert (1984) p. 193.

sterile nor bounteous, so that the city would neither be absorbed in struggling for survival nor corrupted by luxury. He chooses the middle way – a moderately fertile environment reflective of the orderly balance at the core of the world. For Machiavelli, by contrast, nature oscillates between extremes of sterility and fertility, necessity and dissolution. Of these two extremes, Machiavelli takes the sterile mode to be closer to the truth about nature as a whole because, although nature does sometimes generate bounteousness, its bounty cannot be relied on. Viewing nature as "soft" and bounteous is the beginning of a deluded trust in the world that leads one to rely on peace and stability as the normal state of affairs, themselves reflective of even more perfect and stable "imagined republics." The consequent love of ease in a bounteous environment that begins by corrupting the bodily strength and vigor of citizens eventually corrupts their minds as well and leads them to fancy that the repose at the heart of the world is the prior cause and reward of their virtue.

Machiavelli thinks it is better for founders and republics to imitate the necessitous side of nature, to let its hostility goad you into constantly fighting back. Both princes and republics must, in other words, recognize that their human passions are bestial, that they contain no potentiality for divine or immortal transcendence. There is no longer a contrast, as there was for Plato, Aristotle, and the Stoics, between the bestial and virtuous sides of the soul, but a series of more-or-less subtle animal characteristics – from the beast-man Chiron, whose connection with the primordial force of subhuman vigor made him fit to teach princes, to the completely bestial modes within the prince of the lion and fox. By being severed from teleological substance, reason is both contentless and completely somatic or immanentized within temporal existence. By embracing their bestial character, princes and republics can release these passions selectively to empower their struggles without being deluded. Again, we see how Machiavelli's thought prefigures the dichotomy between nature and freedom central to German Idealism: we achieve independence through a consciousness of nature's hostility. One might almost say, anticipating Heidegger, that for Machiavelli, the insubstantial happenstance, the nothingness, of Fortuna is the ground of the presence of nature's visible bounty; that being comes to presence through the battle to appropriate nature to which fortune constantly subjects our existence, but that, once settled, these presences can bewitch us, carry us adrift in the pursuit of their stable perfection, causing us to forget the burden of time on human existence from which they issued in their original vigor: "For time brings out everything, the good and the bad" (*The Prince* chapter 3).

Because necessity and struggle are paramount, Machiavelli concludes, it may be best to choose deliberately a sterile region where necessity will "compel" people to be industrious, "therefore less given to idleness... more united and less exposed by the poverty of the country to occasions for discord." On the face of it, the praise of industriousness and the disparagement of idleness sounds in accord with both elements of the Great Tradition in the West, Judeo-Christian revelation and the pagan classics. Yet to make industriousness the *ground* of virtue in the absence of other virtues takes what for the tradition was regarded as a comparatively low virtue and elevates it into one of the highest. The Christian and classical traditions did not approve of laziness, but they did not praise industriousness to any great degree either, and certainly not as the basis of political order and unity. One need only consider Plato's and Aristotle's strictures on excessive commerce and the unlimited sway of *oikonomia*, echoed by Thomas Aquinas. Laziness is bad not primarily because it is unproductive but because it is a sign of a character falling beneath itself at the most rudimentary level of mastering one's passions, antecedent to higher virtues involving deliberative choice rather than mere self-repression.[5]

For Machiavelli, on the other hand, civic disunity or discord stem altogether from "idleness," from a condition that, according to the tradition, properly directed, made contemplation possible. What Machiavelli calls "idleness" includes the leisure (*skole*) that, according to Aristotle, enables us to dwell on what most unifies us, philosophy and deliberative citizenship (*Nicomachean Ethics* 1176b–1178b). Indeed, Machiavelli collapses Aristotle's distinction between mere relaxation and leisure into idleness. For Aristotle, idleness might, if properly cultivated, become the leisure that is indispensable for the actualization of civic virtue through a full-time devotion to public affairs and, at the highest level, cultivating the contemplative virtues. Far from preferring labor to idleness (properly improved as leisure), Aristotle argues that

---

[5] Consider, for example, Plato *Republic* 419a–422a; Aristotle *Politics* 1252b–1253b, 1255b–1256a; Thomas *Commentary on Aristotle's Politics* 13, 31, 38.

the correct employment of idleness as leisure requires that we not have to labor for survival. Those who must labor for a living are not capable of the fullest citizen virtues (Aristotle *Politics* 1278a20–27). Idleness is acceptable to the extent that it provides us with the opportunity to pursue those civic and philosophic ends that are the surest source of friendship and unity among humans in the city. For Machiavelli, by contrast, this drifting away into the contemplation of "imagined republics" (*The Prince* chapter 15) afforded by idleness is precisely what is most likely to undermine a republic's unity, discipline, and energy.

While both the classics and Christian revelation focus on the ends for which leisure (perhaps more accurately rendered on the Christian side as devotion) is to be employed – contemplating the higher world – for Machiavelli, leisure to contemplate the higher world is what distracts us from *virtu*. Labor compelled by necessity overcomes poverty as a source of discord. In contrast to Machiavelli making the conquest of poverty one of the chief aims of politics, all Aristotle could do to ameliorate the harmful effects of poverty on the common good was to suggest the "mixed" regime (polity) as a way of mitigating the worst effects of excessive wealth and poverty while encouraging public virtue (*Politics* 1293b22–1297b35). For Machiavelli, collective labor itself forges the unity of the city. Aristotle assumes that the material wherewithal for the practice of virtue, and the founding of the city to ensure minimal order, are already largely taken care of when he turns to the prescription for the best regime (*Politics* 1258a20–30). Machiavelli uncovers these preconditions and makes their achievement – and continuing reachievement – the sole and sufficient basis for the common good. For the classics, the necessity for physical survival, the realm of *oikonomia*, is, because it necessarily individuates, the least likely basis for the common good. Once the material wherewithal is achieved, we can turn toward civic virtue and wisdom, which transcend individuation and therefore unite us in the actualization of our virtues of soul. For Machiavelli, by contrast, the necessity for material survival that individuates, for the very reason that its dangers cannot be avoided, drives us to labor in common with others and so create a bulwark of prosperity and order.

The first stage of Machiavelli's argument about how to found a republic, then, is to suggest that a body of citizens working hard together can convert a sterile spot into one that yields the basic necessities for everyone, roughly analogous to the City of Sows in Plato's *Republic*.

Unfortunately, Machiavelli goes on, not all men are content with a modicum of prosperity but want an abundance and also "desire to exercise command." Because there are those who want to dominate, a people cannot rest content with the internal security achieved by a moderate degree of wealth wrested by collective labor from a sterile site. They need to become "powerful," but this requires settling in a region "where the fertility of the soil affords the means of becoming great, and of acquiring strength to repel all who might attack it, or oppose the development of its power." From first favoring the extreme of sterility, then, Machiavelli goes to the opposite extreme of favoring a "most fertile" environment, again avoiding the Aristotelian mean.[6]

The first stage of the argument, and the objection that Machiavelli then raises to it, reminds us of Glaucon's objection to the City of Sows – that there are some people who are not content with security and the basic necessities of life. Their "feverish" passions for wealth and mastery require a city not only to protect itself from external aggression but to become an aggressor itself. Whereas Plato and Aristotle respond to this complexity in human nature by prescribing an internal ordering of the constitution and an education aimed primarily at helping such people transcend the passions that lead to tyranny and imperialism, Machiavelli instead proposes to think through what type of constitution those passions would require if no attempt were made to educate and sublimate them toward civic and philosophical moderation. He aims to conjoin the "feverish" soul with a stable republican constitution and loyalty to the common good, a project that the ancients thought impossible.

With respect to Plato specifically, this requires a major reorientation of political psychology. In the pedagogical thought experiment of the *Republic*, in which Socrates tries to draw Glaucon away from tyrannical temptation by getting him to think about founding a just regime, Socrates uses Glaucon's objection to the City of Sows to introduce an unrestrained eros for multiple pleasures, the seed of the tyrant's disordered personality. However, having introduced eros to necessitate

---

[6] As Mansfield observes, choice and necessity are grounded in an underlying primordial strife: "Instead of blaming necessity for the limits to human (and thus political) choice, Machiavelli traces both choice of site and ordering of laws to an apparently unnecessary human wish to seek to master others.... Thus Machiavelli avoids giving the political lesson that could be shown in the conflict of choice and necessity" (2001) p. 31.

the introduction of a class of warriors to launch the newly feverish city's wars of acquisition, Socrates immediately drives eros out of the discussion, arguing that the courage and self-control required of these soldiers is most plausibly rooted in thumos, with its capacity for courageous and honorable loyalty to the common good. Socrates, in other words, introduces eros briefly so as to expand the scope of the soul from mere desire for material survival to the grander passions of pride and glory seeking, but then expels eros from that scope and attempts to ground civic *paideia* largely in the thumotic part of the soul, eventually subordinating that part of the soul, and the honor-seeking type of man, to rule by philosophers who themselves are erotically motivated. Viewed in this perspective, Machiavelli can be understood as expelling eros altogether, implying that the passion for honor is sufficient in itself for explaining the transition from the City of Sows to the imperial city, and that the thumotic capacity for self-overcoming and the mastery of random inclinations can be liberated from the governance of philosophy within the city and the soul and allowed to expand free of all such philosophical restrictions, launching the virtuous small republic on the path to empire. To recall the argument of Chapter 6, I would reemphasize that the draining away of erotic transcendence from political virtue to leave only cold-hearted dominion already effected by Augustinian theology greatly aids Machiavelli in this truncation of honor seeking from an openness to a love of the beautiful and good.

Machiavelli's argument here also anticipates Hobbes, especially his argument in chapter 15 of the *Leviathan* that the difficulties of surviving in a natural environment of scarcity and danger incline most people to pursue the arts of peace and productivity, content to renounce their natural power to invade the lives and possessions of others in exchange for a modicum of well-being and security from the invasiveness of others. The "vainglorious," however, desire "mastery" for its own sake, and because they seek power beyond what is necessary for a modicum, they compel everyone else, including their intended victims, to strive for the power to dominate as well (in other words, kill or be killed). The difference is that, whereas Machiavelli turns these "vainglorious" types outward as the vanguard of the expansionist republic's wealth and power, Hobbes thinks they must be crushed and psychologically rehabituated to protect the state's internal stability. Again, Machiavelli leads to Sir Francis Drake, Hobbes to *A Clockwork Orange*. Machiavelli of course recognizes the danger that the masterful types may turn their ambitions toward internal political affairs and provoke usurpation and civil war. But he believes that glory seeking can be turned outward by a policy of republican imperialism in which such thrusting men will take the lead, thereby carrying their people to new heights of grandeur and wealth, protecting them from external aggression and finding in that duty a justification for their own relentless ambition.

Whereas the psychology of tyranny is largely driven underground by Hobbes as a theme for extensive and nuanced consideration, Machiavelli encourages those whom Callicles termed the "natural masters" and brings to life their many varieties through his meditations on history. Indeed, it might be said that while the Platonic Socrates sifts dialectically through opinions within the city about the Good, Machiavelli sifts dialectically through the historical patterns of cities in conflict with one another to clarify the "effectual truth" about politics. This is one reason Machiavelli's writings are a source of much richer speculation about the nature of tyranny and leadership than anything to be found in Hobbes – a richer historical phenomenology of how states and their internal parts are subject to the stimulus of external motions forced on them by competing states. Machiavelli already foresees that his "new path" will require "unknown lands" comparable to the one discovered by Columbus, and the founding of a New Rome required by the international and multinational scope of Machiavelli's republican prescription. Hobbes's philosophy, by contrast, envisions politics as nothing but a mechanism for internal order and control, one in principle capable of limitless extension but bereft of the full-blooded patriotism, love of the earthly fatherland, and the exhilarating scope of imperial conquest and Elizabethan swashbuckling to which Machiavelli gives rise. This is why, as we consider in more detail in the Conclusion, a visionary of Atlanticist, Protestant republicanism like James Harrington – a project for commercial imperialism already underway in Tudor and Stuart mercantilism and exploding in the New World – could extol Machiavelli's republicanism while decrying Hobbes as an apologist for absolute monarchy without any sense of contradiction. Hobbes is a successor of Machiavelli, but only of a narrow version of his thought.

To resume: The danger of a fertile site is that its "pleasures and softness" will "make men idle and unfit for the exercise of valor." Or, as Machiavell amplifies the point in 2.25, "the dissensions in republics are generally the result of idleness and peace, while apprehension and war are productive of union." Again, the achievement of the peace and leisure that, for Plato and Aristotle, provide the milieu for subtler ethical choices and an interest in philosophy, for Machiavelli represents the gravest threat to "virtue." Machiavelli's solution is not to attempt to moderate these feverish passions through education (as Plato and Aristotle advise) but to incorporate into a fertile natural environment an artificial replica of the necessity that nature imposes on people in a sterile environment. The replica is "law." Law takes the place of nature's direct compulsion provided by scarcity in a sterile environment. Laws "offset the pleasures and softness" of a fertile environment with the "rigors of a strict discipline." Properly executed, these laws, by imitating the dire truth about nature – that it is, at bottom, hostile necessity – not only prevent citizens living in a bounteous environment from being corrupted, but produce "better warriors than what nature produces in the harshest climates and most sterile countries." We might recall in this context Machiavelli's preference, considered earlier in connection with his treatment of Xenophon's *Education of Cyrus* as a mirror of princes, for the disinterested harshness of Manlius Torquatus (more suitable for republics) in contrast with the generosity and mercy of Scipio (more suitable for monarchy). As in *The Prince*, by imitating nature in political life, we can master nature – improve on our natural condition by gaining the power to restructure it for our own survival, aggrandizement, and glory. This requires a new understanding of law. For Aristotle, law is subordinate to the *politeia*, which embodies a division of offices based on a partial account of justice and virtue. The content of the law depends on the distinct regime (*Politics* 1287b15–20, 1280a7–21, 1276b34–1277b16). For Machiavelli, because nature is uniformly indifferent to human purpose and supplies no such teleological ordering, law becomes the abstract regulator of nature as field of forces or happenstance. Through the "strict discipline" imposed on their citizens by law, republics can imitate nature's hostility while distancing themselves from a reliance on nature's bounty.

In a fertile environment, the disorderly side of Fortuna flourishes. Laws enable a republic to replicate consciously the severity that necessity unconsciously produces when nature's reversals and fluctuations force a people to fight back through labor and industriousness. "Skilful and sagacious legislators" can provide, through laws, a corrective to nature's bounteous, beneficent dimension – a bounteousness against which we must be psychologically armed, and ready to combat pre-emptively, lest we be devastated by its inevitable reversal. The severity of the legislator cuts back this bounty, tapping its power while preventing it from dissipating republican vigor in the enjoyment of ease and pleasure. In a striking passage from the second chapter of Book 3, Machiavelli formulates the statecraft of his heroes, the Romans, as a kind of human horticulture: "For the Romans wished to act according to the usage of the good cultivator who, for a plant to thicken and be able to produce and mature its fruits, cuts off the first branches it puts forth, so that they can with time arise there greener and more fruitful, since the virtue remains in the stem of the plant." Looking ahead to Machiavelli's impact on the Elizabethans, one can hardly avoid thinking of the allegorical figure of the Gardener in Shakespeare's *Richard II* (act 3, scene 4), whose maxims provide a backdrop for the rise of the Machiavellian new prince Henry Bolingbroke and the fall of the flawed Christian monarch Richard: "All must be even in our government... We at time of year do wound the bark, the skin of our fruit-trees, lest, being over-proud in sap and blood, with too much richness it confound itself.... Superfluous branches we lop away, that bearing boughs may live."[7]

"One prudent orderer," Machiavelli writes, can provide a corrective to too much bounty from nature. The severity of such founders cuts back nature's fecundity, tapping its power for vigorous labor while keeping it from dissipating in ease and pleasure. Even though the achievement of power and pleasure are the goals of virtue, to give in to the enjoyment of those goals undermines the self-control and fighting prowess needed to maintain that power. For the most urgent practical reasons, then, a republic must avoid relying on the delusion of nature's teleological beneficence. In general in the *Discourses*, "the people" are especially vulnerable to the delusions that come from nature's bounteous side. Left to themselves, they tend to turn from the rigors of citizenship in a

---

[7] Machiavelli's horticultural simile in the *Discourses* is analogous to his description of the Romans in chapter 3 of *The Prince* who, in going to war preemptively to avoid a worse war later, are like "physicians" who treat a disease in its early stages before it reaches the incurable stage. Do the similes of horticulture and medicine parallel, respectively, the communal emphasis of the *Discourses* as opposed to the princely emphasis of *The Prince*?

dynamic expansionist republic to the enjoyment of their achieved luxury and adornment. They would like to see in the prosperity and stability achieved by the force and fraud employed by earlier generations of the republic the reflection of a higher order of permanent peace, justice, mercy, and concord, and convince themselves that by cultivating the qualities of ease, repose, and moderation, they are cultivating the virtues that bring them the tangible benefits of the republic's power – when it is in fact the republic's pristine and original power seeking that has achieved over long years of struggle the tangible benefits that now make it possible to indulge in such idleness and speculation. For these reasons, the people are especially attracted to men who seem to embody the soft qualities of peaceableness, mildness, and generosity and who promise them an end to harsh discipline and struggle. They are always on the verge of elevating a Scipio, Catiline, or Caesar from leading citizen to monarch because they see in the predominance of such a monarch the triumph of the soft virtues that make their own lives easier.

By contrast, a leading citizen who understands Fortune's recurring incursion into the apparent calm and stability of the republic's every-day existence – a bracing jolt of an underlying but more fundamental disorder, the perilous necessity from which stable power eventually emerged because people wrested it from her through their struggle – can save the republic from corruption. "For it never or rarely happens that a republic or monarchy is well constituted, or its old institutions entirely reformed, unless it is done by only one individual" (1.9.2). This masterful leader restores vigor by overturning these settled appearances, restoring primitive discipline, crushing monarchical or demagogical pre-tensions, returning the republic to the pristine anxiety of its origins on the brink of survival. Machiavelli specifically refers to these refounders as "princes" (1.18.4), thereby further eroding the apparent distinction between the subject matter of the *Discourses* and *The Prince*.[8] For

---

[8] 1.18 discusses the grave difficulties of refounding corrupt republics and why princely natures are needed to do so. Because someone can become the "prince" in a corrupt republic only by wicked and violent means, you either need that rare good man who is willing to use wicked means to achieve a good end or hope that a bad man, having achieved power, will somehow decide to labor for good ends: "From these causes arise the difficulty or impossibility of maintaining liberty in a republic that has become corrupt." In such circumstances, the republic may need to be transformed into a monarchy where one man will crush the turbulence of the many. In 3.1, Machiavelli returns to the importance of refounding, employing unusually scientific/alchemical language: "Nothing is more true"

Machiavelli, Rome is the paradigm of how to combine fertility and prosperity (with the attendant danger of relying on the spurious and merely apparent beneficence of nature) with law-bred severity, with the result that "they maintained it full of as much virtue as has ever adorned any other city or republic." The Senate uses the people to fight its wars and buys them off with land and booty. The people and nobles of the conquered areas join the Roman people and nobles and press outward to an ever-expanding perimeter. Like a cell dividing and redividing, the republic becomes a cosmopolitan empire containing (to borrow a phrase from chapter 17 of *The Prince*) "men of all nations."

THE CYCLE OF REGIMES

The theme of the origin of cities in *Discourses* 1.1 leads to the theme of the founder, the constitution, and the best regime in 1.2, a transition that Machiavelli endows with a subversive new content: how the alternation we have just considered between prosperity and law-bred severity can be institutionalized within a single regime.

Some republics, Machiavelli observes, are founded by one man and never undergo danger because of his prudence. The most illustrious case, Sparta, founded by Lycurgus, lasted for eight hundred years. The Spartans had "the great good fortune" to be given "all the laws they need" in a "single act" at the outset of a prudent and skillful legislator. Others, most notably Rome, "become perfect" through "the occurrence of accidents." Their growth is always accompanied by danger, because only danger convinces people of the necessity to change.

Does this suggest that a statesman might want to imitate "the occurrence of accidents" by introducing seemingly chance stimuli such as the threat of a foreign aggressor (or the claim that one exists) in order to keep the danger fresh? As we observed in Chapter 6, Machiavelli does

---

than that everything, including republics, has a limited existence. However, only those whose "bodies" do not become disorganized will run the full limit of their existence. In "mixed bodies" like republics and religious sects, the aim should be to "bring them back to their original principles." Better still if they have institutional means for frequently renewing themselves, or do so in response to "extrinsic accidents" such as war or the threat of conquest. "It is a truth clearer than light that, without such renovation, these bodies cannot continue to exist... " The inclusion of religious sects arguably supports the interpretation of Machiavelli as calling for a pristine, patriotic Christianity, not its complete abolition.

suggest in *The Prince* that a ruler might want to allow domestic conspiracies to reach a certain point – thereby deliberately encouraging to
a degree the disorder that Fortuna will try to reap in his affairs in any
event – so that he can then exercise his virtue by cutting them down,
mastering Fortuna by encouraging and then preempting her hostility.
Would the republican version of this policy be to seek out possible
foreign foes, let the danger they pose grow for a time or even goad
them into hostility, so as to galvanize the citizenry into going to war?
However this may be, the main thing to notice in this section of the
Discourses is how Machiavelli supplements the Platonic teaching on
founding. Plato had argued in the *Laws* that a well-founded regime
might require the good fortune of an ambitious tyrant coinciding with
a wise counsellor. Machiavelli concedes that good fortune might provide such a founder all on her own, while shearing away the role of the
philosophic counsellor. In other words, Lycurgus was presumably the
source of his own prudence, as Machiavelli advises in chapter 17 of *The
Prince*, not dependent for his prudence on another. Even more strikingly, Machiavelli suggests that "chance" itself might perfect a republic
bereft of any such genius founder. Indeed, a republic like Rome that perfects itself by tapping into the forces of Fortuna will more successfully
surmount Fortuna's reverses than a regime like Sparta whose internal
strength is the gift of the great good fortune of a single brilliant founder.
Institutions that have evolved over time to shunt, channel, and focus
Fortuna may preempt the role of the uniquely gifted legislator.

In contrast to the security and stability provided by a constitution
like Sparta's set in place in the beginning without need of change, this
second course is "never effected without danger," because "the majority of men never willingly adopt any new law tending to change the
constitution of the state, unless the necessity of change is clearly demonstrated." A republic "perfected" in this way may therefore have to court
destruction before its citizens recognize clearly the need to change. Of
course this may actually lead to its destruction before the improvements
can take root, as happened, Machiavelli believes, to the Florentine
republic. But we will not be surprised to learn that this is the course that
Machiavelli prefers, successfully exemplified by the Roman republic.
We have already seen that, in his view, although "great good fortune"
of the kind allegedly demonstrated by the emergence of Lycurgus is
not to be spurned, even greater power and prosperity will result when

men of virtue receive nothing from fortune but a barren, even adverse "occasion" against which to struggle. We know from *The Prince* that what princes achieve in these circumstances is entirely the result of their own prowess. Their power remains more surely their own than that of princes who receive even a portion of their authority from good fortune, as with Cesare Borgia's good fortune in having Pope Alexander VI as his natural father. Here, we are given the republican parallel of Machiavelli's advice to princes. Sparta, with the great good fortune of her founding, is an admirable example for republics to emulate, but Rome is even more admirable. Because she started out with nothing but bare "chance," sheer adverse happenstance, the power she achieved by fighting back against adversity became more surely rooted over time. Sparta was complete from the beginning, hence inflexible and prone to shatter when a truly hard blow from fortune finally came. Rome evolved in an ad hoc manner, incorporating fortune's unpredictable impetuosity within her own institutions. By taking the risky course of dynamic innovation through imperial expansion, Rome deliberately exposed her institutions to that same dangerous necessity that, when we are subjected to it by the natural environment, compels us, both princes and peoples, to fight back by laboring for survival and power. Moreover, as in *The Prince*, leaders need not wait for fortune to throw up the danger that will convince the people of the inescapable need for change. By inspiring terror in the people, thereby tapping into fortune's capacity to inspire the fear needed for change by acting consciously as its agent, leaders can expedite the needed reforms. (Although Machiavelli depicts Lycurgus as a founder who sprang directly from "great good fortune," we are of course entitled to wonder, based on Machiavelli's own guidelines that we considered in Chapter 5 in connection with the life of Cyrus, to what extent he shaped the Spartans' generational memory of him.)

In classical political thought, the purpose of a good constitution and the civic education it reinforces is to transcend, to the degree possible within the limitations of human nature, the ravages of "chance" – not in the sense of fighting nature and mastering it by accumulating power, but in the sense of immunizing oneself from vulnerability to the temptations provided by perishable goods, and hence to the inevitable reverses of fortune, by educating the soul to moderation. To the extent that the soul's potentiality for transcendence is actualized through an education in good citizenship that stresses deliberation upon the issues of domestic self-government and avoids warfare and imperial adventures, a political community can insulate itself from the primordial motions that assault the individual through the passions and assault the city through the temptation to imperialism, assaults that in turn call for the elevation of belligerent, tyrannically inclined leaders. (Such a city, Aristotle observes, might internalize the stability of the Unmoved Mover [*Politics* 1325b23–33].) Such perfection, then, as politics can achieve is a measure of its success in excluding the realm of chance from determining the goals of statesmanship through spasms of unruly passion. For Machiavelli to argue that a republic can actually "perfect" itself by opening itself up to this realm of chance therefore constitutes a breathtaking reversal of every tenet of classical morality and metaphysics. It lets in the pulse of history, hardheaded experience, imperialism, and the strife between the haves and have-nots. The classical thinkers had seen the primordial realm as a falling away from transcendence into perishability and disarray. In human terms, as in Plato's Chariot image, embracing the primordial realm meant the decline of the soul from virtue's approximation of the stability that characterizes true being into the chaotic disarray of the passions. In diametric contrast, Machiavelli lets the primordial flood in. For Machiavelli, chance does not constitute a decline from the realm of form, stability and unity, but on the contrary, energizes and sustains this realm by placing it on a new ontological basis. This new relationship between the primordial and the transcendental realms of political existence is mirrored in Machiavelli's ensuing discussion of the traditional rubric of the types of constitutions and how they change over time.

Alluding to unnamed "writers on politics" believed by "many" to be wise (and generally assumed to include Polybius and Aristotle), Machiavelli begins with the classical typology of constitutions – three good kinds of government (monarchy, aristocracy, and popular) that degenerate respectively into tyranny, oligarchy, and licentiousness:

So that a legislator who gives to a state which he founds, either of these three forms of government, constitutes it but for a brief time; for no precautions can prevent either one of the three that are reputed good from degenerating into its opposite kind; so great are in these the attractions and resemblances between the good and the evil.

Up until the last words of this formulation ("so great are the attractions and resemblances between the good and the evil"), Machiavelli remains within the horizon of both classical and Christian teachings on government. It is the classical political philosophies themselves that emphasize how unlikely it is that the right circumstances – the right locale, virtuous citizens, prudent statesmen framing good laws – will come together to form a good constitution. In setting forth his picture of an optimal aristocracy in Book 7 of the *Politics*, Aristotle uses a verb meaning "to pray" when detailing what conditions would have to be present for virtue to flourish, for however brief a time, in a political community (1330a34–1330b8). As we have seen, Plato in the *Laws* regards the conditions for a good founding as tantamount to the gift of a god, while in the *Republic* he regards the best regime, next to impossible to come about in the first place, to be foredoomed to decay and collapse (546a–547a). No one is more aware than Plato or Aristotle of the fragility of even minimally virtuous constitutional arrangements, of even mere constitutional truces between aggrieved parties that might allow public life to rise a little above the level of constant wrangling for power and distrust between rich and poor. So, in stressing the "brief time" for which all such arrangements last, Machiavelli does not tell us anything for which there is not abundant acknowledgment in the classical sources. No one is more informative than Plato and Aristotle on any specific issue of everyday political circumstance – the difficulty of getting different parties to agree even on relatively negotiable economic disputes, let alone larger issues of justice; the danger that the need to defend one's country from aggressors will distract energy from domestic political life and summon forth tyrannically minded men who will use national security as an excuse for subverting the rule of law at home; the temptation to become the imperialistic aggressor oneself and end the uncertainty about economic scarcity. They are anything but optimists or dewy-eyed idealists. As we have observed, they are well aware that education and noble rhetoric need the backing of force. The revenge of Strepsiades against Socrates in the *Clouds* is a sign that the Sophists do not understand that passions of anger based on the love of one's own cannot always be neutralized by rhetoric. The Platonic Socrates, however, knows this lesson, just as his companion Xenophon, in his real-life military campaigns, understood the need for harsh discipline, unlike Proxenus, a follower of Gorgias, who could not rule nongentlemen because he relied on rhetorical persuasion alone.[9]

As we considered in the previous chapter, and must amplify here in the context of Machiavelli's teaching on republics, the Augustinian strain of Christianity achieved a greatly heightened sense of the disproportion between how it would be best for human beings to live and the manifest failings and fragility of observable human efforts to do so. To the extent that Christianity severed the immediate connection between human nature and its capacity to participate in transcendence through the political realm posited by ancient political philosophy, Christianity drove an even more radical wedge between the *nunc stans*, the eternal "now" of true being, and the merely "secular" time – the cycles of decay and desire – to which man was subjected because of his fleshly limitations and sinfulness. For the ancients, it was possible, in rare and brief periods, for human nature to rise, with the assistance of a good constitution, civic education and statesmanship, toward a substantive participation in this eternal now, the "divine spark" in the human soul that linked it through the cultivation of the moral and intellectual virtues to the divine intelligence and perfection knitting the cosmos together. Machiavelli, in my view, is able to exploit the strain of Christianity that most heightens the chasm between the secular and the divine by retaining its view of fallen human nature and the subversion of all merely human aspirations to happiness by the incorrigible ravages of time, while stripping away and discarding its concept of the relationship of human nature to the divine. Machiavelli uses the former (the premise that human nature is fallen) as a weapon against the concern with the soul's perfection that Christianity shared with classical philosophy.

St. Augustine had stressed that all merely human attempts to achieve political justice were worn down and exposed as vain by the flesh-bound currents of time. Yet although Augustine sometimes wrote as if the paltriness of human virtue made it unimportant even to distinguish between good and bad constitutions on earth, he would never have allowed this to lead to Machiavelli's conclusion that this proves how "great are the attractions and resemblances between the good and the evil," such that "no remedy can be applied there to prevent it to slipping into its contrary because of the likeness that the virtue and the vice have." For

---

[9] See Strauss (1989) p. 131.

St. Augustine, the insufficiency of human virtue in secular time hardly permits one to collapse good and evil into mere modalities by which constitutions pass into one another as Machiavelli does here. For Augustine, man's incapacity to be virtuous and overcome vice without God's mercy and aid hardly entitles one to conclude that virtue and vice share a "likeness" that leads one to collapse into the other. The distinction between the frailty of merely human virtue and the transcendence residing with the divine that Christianity had radicalized in order to heighten our awareness of the contrast between good and evil, Machiavelli exploits in order to obliterate this contrast altogether within the realm of human and political affairs. Because Machiavelli denies that there is a "middle way" – denies that there is a telos, a stable order of substantive being in which time participates – he allows all moral distinctions to collapse into the coming to be and passing away of time. This profane cycle of merely apparent, shaky and transitory stability collapsing repeatedly into a more fundamental nothingness may be described as how the *saeculum* manifests itself after the Christian path from it to transcendence has been excised. This secularization of Christian profundity, of its preference for the hidden depth to the gleaming surface of life (the preference for "touch" over sight that we considered earlier), enables Machiavelli to imply that the ancients were naive in their treatment of the cycle of regimes. In remarking that the traditional "writers" on regimes (led by Aristotle) were "wiser according to the opinion of the many," Machiavelli may be suggesting again that "the many" lean to the spurious moral distinction between good and bad regimes, and that classical political philosophy panders to the prejudice of the mob, anticipating Nietzsche's description of Christianity as Platonism for the people.

In these ways, Machiavelli uses certain strains of Christianity to deepen our sense of the fragility of human efforts to found good constitutions, already amply demonstrated by ancient thought itself. By further undermining the possibility of the classical prescription for the fulfillment of human nature within the best regime by means of a post-Christian ontology of time-bound decay, while at the same time ignoring Christianity's account of how the prospect of salvation makes us capable of a *degree* of goodness in secular life, Machiavelli thoroughly demolishes the traditional basis for coping with the fragility of good constitutions. With that, he begins to set forth what is truly original about his own approach to this traditional theme: "Chance has given birth to these different kinds of governments among men." Such an assertion would be unfathomable from within the horizons of either classical thought or Christian theology. Whatever the insufficiency of human nature to achieve virtue on its own in Christian theology, it is nonetheless true that God, the divine author, has endowed man with conscience. If we turn from Augustine to Thomas, there we find a pronounced narrowing of the Augustinian chasm between the secular and the divine: much of the content of Aristotle's teaching about man's natural proclivity to political community – as well as the distinction between good and bad regimes – supplemented by conscience and the moral content of the Decalogue, is subsumed within the final revelation of Christianity. Although human nature in and of itself leads only to lust, vanity, and the pursuit of dominion, God has written on that nature a moral code that the intellect, more akin to the Creator than the passions, can awaken in the soul by receiving the commandments of the Old Testament completed by the certain faith of salvation promised by the New Testament. For Christian theology, in sum, earthly constitutions are fragile efforts to instantiate God's governance of the universe because they are merely human, but they are certainly not "born" from "chance." On the contrary, to the extent that a constitution is a distinctly good kind, preferably a monarchy ruled by a devoutly Christian king, this is because, in Augustinian and Thomistic theology, it has held fast to that portion of the divine *ratio* with which the Creator endows the mere random generational stuff of nature, imparting purpose and reason to it and thereby sustaining it. For Thomas, the natural law is unable to stand on its own without the divine law, but the natural law is nonetheless binding on our conduct. As for the ancient thinkers, it could never be said that the *kinds* of constitution are born out of chance, as opposed to their primitive starting points. As Aristotle argues in Book 1 of the *Politics*, one can explain the city as genesis, as coming into being over time, only when one examines it under the aspect of necessity. Only to the extent that the city is concerned with self-preservation and economics can it be seen as a genesis from the most primitive associations of *oikos* and mastery into more complex clan associations and finally into a polis. But the city "becomes" only for mere life. It "is" for the sake of the good life. Its telos is to be a deliberative association of citizens whose chief purpose is to discuss and debate the meaning of justice in public affairs. This higher and prior cause always already summons into being the lower and more primitive economic and familial elements that develop into the polis. The "kinds" of constitutions, embodying as they do permanently valid distinctions between justice and injustice, as opposed to their mere generational substratum, are given under the aspect of eternity.

When Machiavelli argues that "chance" is the sole origin of the visible forms of constitutions, we might recognize an element from the pre-Socratic argument that Plato and Aristotle were concerned to refute, according to which, as the Athenian Stranger summarizes it, the apparent stable reality of the world around us is in fact the transitory appearance of a more profound, underlying series of "great motions... out of necessity, according to chance." The Heracleitean belief that permanence was a mere shell or husk temporarily masking a more profound mutability led, in Plato's and Aristotle's judgment, to the belief that the passions are the part of human life corresponding to the great motions that underlie and generate the visible world and that their limitless gratification constitutes the only natural way to live. Not surprisingly, Machiavelli does return in part to this pre-Socratic and Sophistical view. But he does not merely return to it. The pre-Socratics and Sophists had argued that this primordialist ontology rendered pointless any attempt to account for intrinsic ethical or rational distinctions among the visible, completed forms of constitutions. As Thrasymachus puts it in his general definition of government, behind the facade of the various constitutions, the ruling element pursues its own advantage and designates this as just, gulling the ruled into going along with it. "Justice" is universally "the advantage of the stronger": the specific regime principles themselves are mere accidental local coloration and custom. At bottom, the pre-Socratics and Sophists think, the natural life of "getting the better" can be lived without any intrinsic connection to the kind of constitution. One can get along in a democracy, oligarchy, monarchy, or what have you by aping the local conventions and taking advantage of others where one can safely get away with it. The only political way of life that is in complete harmony with nature is that of the tyrant, which for Plato and Aristotle amounts to the destruction of all politics as shared rule or as rule with an ethical responsibility toward the souls of the ruled. As a kind of antipolitics, tyranny is simply the nature of man as it was understood by the Sophists showing itself openly in its pure individuated selfishness.

It is important to note that the Sophists' indifference to the distinctions among regimes is not Machiavelli's view. Although he does not account for distinctions among kinds of governments on the same basis as Plato or Aristotle, he is far from regarding those distinctions as unimportant. Whereas the Sophists avoided this type of debate over the classification of regimes on the grounds that they were all merely conventional, and therefore equally arbitrary, Machiavelli immerses himself in it as fully as Plato, Aristotle, or Polybius. He regards certain kinds of constitutions as being very much preferable to others, for he does not believe it is possible for human nature to achieve "virtue" in his much modified sense of the term in pure isolation from other people in a political association. Machiavelli is in this sense very much a "classical" thinker and not at all a "pre-Socratic." He does not dispense with the classical rubrics about distinctions among regime principles, but attempts to place them on a new basis that he thinks more adequately explains what Plato and Aristotle thought they were explaining, and points the way to more effective solutions to the political ills of instability, factional strife, and violence with which Plato and Aristotle had also concerned themselves.

To recall our earlier discussion, Machiavelli's project for the conquest of fortune assimilates the meaning of virtue to the will. I would argue that, as a consequence, from Machiavelli's viewpoint, Socrates was correct when he argued to Gorgias that, far from being a mere kaleidoscope of arbitrary local conventions and a trick-bag of rhetorical manipulations, *politike* was a genuine science to which rhetoric was merely subordinate (*Gorgias* 463). The residue of this Platonic elevation of the art of ruling to rigorous knowledge lurks in Machiavelli's conversion of statecraft to the effective and methodical deployment of the will. Whereas Plato saw in the claims of *politike* to genuine knowledge an intimation of the objectively enduring cosmic mind that linked the soul to the wider world, Machiavelli converts statesmanship into a rational project for the imposition of order, organization, and control on a refractory nature. Rightly from Machiavelli's perspective, Plato and Aristotle had argued that the Sophists could not address the sources of disorder in political life because they identified human excellence with isolated self-preservation and pleasure, abstracting human nature from the whole welter of relations among citizens and between ruler and ruled. Machiavelli would agree with the classics that the pre-Socratics strayed too far from observable political reality, that they set up too simplistic a dichotomy between nature and convention, when in truth – as Socrates tried to convince Callicles – human nature is so constituted as to find its own prospect for satisfaction in and through convention, through cooperation with others; that indeed the specific *politiea* under which a man lives, or aspires to live, will be mirrored in his very soul (*Gorgias* 513). It is not the scope and subject matter of ancient thought that Machiavelli rejects, but rather its specific philosophical and meta-physical content. In his own genealogy of regimes, he does not simply banish the distinctiveness and integrity of the respective constitutions by reducing their various forms to their origins in the undertow of chance. Rather, he tries to demonstrate how the distinct forms emerge phenomenologically through history, action, psychology, and experi-ence. He conjoins the problem of the form of the constitution with the problem of its origins in chance and necessity, a synthesis that neither pre-Socratics nor Socrates would have thought tenable – the emergence of political form or reason *out of* chance. What follows is a genealogy of how regimes rise and decline in a world drained of both classical and Christian transcendence, a world in which time does not participate in the eternal, leaving a profane cycle of tenuous stability and more funda-mental decay. No longer are we to see regimes as solicited into existence by the final cause or purpose toward which they partially and imper-fectly arise. The causal priority of the end is replaced by the generative source in historical happenstance. "These variations of governments," as Machiavelli puts it, "arise by chance among men." The variations do matter, however, especially when we come to the history of Rome.

Phase One of Machiavelli's genealogy of regimes resembles arguments made by Sophists like Protagoras to the effect that human beings lived at first "like beasts" in a primitive and dispersed condition, coming together in rudimentary associations for the sake of survival. They placed whoever was "more robust and of greater heart" at their head and obeyed him in exchange for protection. At this point, when a crude despotism has provided enough organization to stave off extinction by natural disaster or external attack, sentiments of justice and injustice, virtue and vice, first arise. With the emergence of these first moral sen-timents, people look for a ruler who is wise and just rather than merely courageous. When this monarchy becomes hereditary, however, the rulers are no longer necessarily the best men but come to "surpass others in sumptuousness and lasciviousness and every other kind of license." The hatred these arrogant libertines provoke in the people leads the rulers in turn to become more tyrannical. Finally, certain citizens who surpass the others "in generosity, greatness of spirit, riches and nobility who were unable to endure the dishonest life of that prince" establish an aristocratic republic in which "they governed themselves according to the laws ordered by them, placing the common utility before their own advantage."

Now we are at the transition to Phase Two, the transition from the primitive origin of authority in the prepolitical state of nature to the cycle of regimes as we know them now, and similar to the typologies of Plato and Aristotle. The difference is that whereas for Plato and Aristotle the regimes are present at any time in principle, for Machiavelli they are first historically created by those possessing "greatness of spirit." In effect, the Platonic and Aristotelian typologies are engendered historically out of the prepolitical state of nature and the primitive compact. Somewhat as in Book 8 of the *Republic*, decline sets in after the original high point of an aristocratic regime devoted to the common good. However, for Machiavelli, the high point is the regime Socrates describes as "timocracy" – for Machiavelli, those possessing "greatness of spirit." Socrates' own version of "aristocracy," the regime ruled by philosopher-kings, is absent. Just as Socrates depicts the decline of regimes as a series of rebellions by less virtuous sons against their fathers, Machiavelli observes that the children of the aristocracy (his version of aristocracy, the men possessing generosity, greatness of spirit, riches, and nobility) succeeded the fathers and turned to "avarice, to ambition [and] to usurpation of women," causing the aristocratic government to degenerate into oligarchical oppression. The people rebel against the oligarchy and institute a popular government. However, echoing Plato's strictures against the hedonism and selfishness of popular government, Machiavelli observes, "it came at once to license, where neither private men nor public were in fear, and each living in his own mode, a thousand injuries were done every day." To escape from anarchy, they returned to the government of a prince, starting the cycle over again.

How does Machiavelli reconcile these accounts? The Sophists usually stopped at the emergence of laws and government from the dangers of the prepolitical state of nature. They had little apparent interest in cataloguing the specific characteristics and institutional arrangements of various regimes (unlike Aristotle, who collected constitutions) because all were alike in imposing conventional restraints on our selfish natures, constraints we only obey because we are more afraid of what others would do to us if these constraints were removed than we are hopeful about what we could achieve for ourselves by harming others. By contrast, the Platonic and Aristotelian accounts assume first and foremost that the defining characteristic of a constitution is the specific end and conception of justice around which its laws, offices, and mores are organized, and that human nature cannot fulfill itself entirely unless it is a part of some political community. To understand Machiavelli's new synthesis, we must be attentive to the new content with which he tries to endow these traditional questions.

First of all, in explaining the decline from aristocracy to oligarchy, democracy, and tyranny, Machiavelli puts more emphasis on violent usurpation and revolution than did Plato. In Book 8 of the *Republic*, it is the dissatisfaction of the sons with the intrinsic motives of their fathers for practicing virtue that leads to newer and increasingly more lax definitions of virtue. The sons of the timocrats, for example, rebel against their fathers' austerity because they believe that they need a certain degree of wealth to protect their honor from insult and injury, especially from the many. They begin simply by relaxing some of the restrictions on private property that Socrates had prescribed for the best regime; only gradually do they degenerate from this to an exclusive concern with wealth accumulation. By contrast, Machiavelli stresses that it is the fact that the sons of the aristocrats have never faced the terrible dangers that their fathers faced in overthrowing the preconstitutional tyranny that allows them to degenerate into idle luxury and softness. In this way, the dire necessity and peril of the first account of the development of primitive authority out of the state of nature is carried over into the ostensibly more Platonic discussion of the distinct ends of government. The primordial passions operative in a grosser way in the first, more genetic account (the establishment of a "robust" monarchy to secure survival and safety from random oppression) become the basis for the changes in the form of the constitution analyzed in the second, more eidetic account (the genealogy of distinct regimes). In this way, Machiavelli develops the maxim from the previous chapter of the *Discourses* about the need for a bracing dose of peril to restore peoples to the vigor of their virtue. We can surmise in advance that Machiavelli's diagnosis of the very best kind of constitution will find a way of deliberately introducing a healthy dose of fear and peril to each succeeding generation, so that "changes of fortune" and "reverses" will prevent the sons of the aristocrats from degenerating into libertinage and disorder.

Similarly, whereas Plato chronicles the decline from oligarchy to democracy as the extension of the oligarchs' concerns with moneymaking to the wider populace, who in turn want to start spending that money on luxuries and enjoying themselves, Machiavelli depicts this change as a revolution of the people, who are outraged and disgusted at the overbearing power and arrogance of the moneymaking elite: "This disposition soon produced an avenger, who was sufficiently well seconded to destroy them." Again, Machiavelli does not search for the causes of decline primarily in dissatisfaction with the intrinsic way of life under one kind of regime as opposed to another. Instead, he reaches back into the more primitive emotions of fear and outrage against despotic oppression that characterized the initial development of order out of the primitive origins, and shows how these continue to be operative social forces during much later stages of development. We also observe here the strong and weak sides of "the people" in Machiavelli's view. At their worst, they want libertinage and luxury. At their best, led by savage and commanding men, they react with anger against privilege and oppression, and so lend the power of their numbers to a restoration of the law-bred austerity and severe order that replicate within the state the adverse necessities that nature imposes on us prior to the emergence of the state, thus stimulating *virtu*. Primordial origins continue to generate political development.

We should note a final echo of the Platonic understanding in Machiavelli's genealogy, in order to see how, beginning with similar observations about political phenomena, he proceeds in a new and radically different direction in addressing the problem of the best regime. The transition from the genetic account of Phase One, which explains the evolution of rudimentary political order into a patriarchal monarchy that tries to extend the natural pattern of family life to a larger clan, to the typology of constitutions properly speaking in Phase Two is, as we have observed, signaled by the emergence of a minority of men characterized by "grandeur of soul." They are the ones who lead the revolution against the first primitive tyranny and establish the virtuous republic. In their greatness of soul, wealth, courage, and refusal to be ruled by despots, they contrast with the "feeble and timid," presumably the majority who, without the inspiration and leadership of these rare men, would have continued to knuckle under, hating the tyrant but preferring to live under him than to risk their lives in rebellion. It is "under such powerful leaders" that "the masses armed themselves." There is a return here to one of the crucial arguments with which Socrates sought to persuade Callicles and Glaucon of the inadequacy of the Sophists' account of justice as a compact made by naturally selfish individuals. Unlike Antiphon and some of the Sophists who, like Hobbes later, believed that all people are motivated by self-preservation, Callicles and Glaucon (like other of the Sophists and their followers) tended to supplement this unedifying version of the social contract by stressing an important exception to it. They focus on the few "real men" (*andres*) who would never have agreed to it in the first place, preferring always to rule than be ruled and willing to court the consequent dangers (*Gorgias* 483; *Republic* 359a–c). We have observed in earlier chapters that the Sophists were hampered in giving a fully persuasive account of the qualities of soul that would characterize such a person, the natural master who is noble by nature rather than by convention. Because of their dichotomous distinction between human nature as motivated by prepolitical drives for survival, power and pleasure, and convention as uniformly artificial and unconnected with any natural need, the Sophists had little basis on which to account for the observable qualities and psychological subtleties of superior statesmanship in the world around them. They admired power, but they tended to depict it in crude subpolitical terms: in Callicles' speech, the natural master is rather like a petty thief, a stealer of cattle, except that he carries off his thefts on a grand scale. Only an understanding of everyday observable politics – its laws, its customs, its education, and the kinds of human character its principle of justice solicits – can explain how this crude Herculean master could evolve into a subtle and sophisticated ruler like Pericles.

By making the city prior to the individual and by arguing that, contrary to the Sophists, we cannot understand the nature of the individual until we understand the soul "writ large" as the city, Socrates can provide this psychological account of leadership in a far more compelling way than can the Sophists. Callicles and Glaucon are both drawn to tyranny, certainly to being the leading statesman. But they want such political mastery to entail the noble and admirable qualities of a fully developed and civilized character – skill at governing, generosity to friends, a degree of philosophical cultivation, an exposure to the fine arts, cultivated conversation, and the merited admiration of their fellow citizens or subjects for doing large and good things for their country. This erotic longing to find a naturally satisfying way of life *within* fully evolved conventional political existence, a way of life that unifies and consummates the talents and virtues solicited by conventional political life, is what Socrates plays upon. He wants to convince them that, instead of seeing convention as an antonym for nature, a realm of primitive passions and conflict standing across a gulf from an evolved city, they should join Socrates in searching for a specific set of conventions that, in contrast with defective sets, allows human nature to fulfill itself *within* the *politiea* in a way that it never could in the subpolitical state of nature.

A part of this argument is for Socrates to reject the very premise of the Sophists' genetic account of nature. The Sophists presented tyranny as a crude natural force, emerging spontaneously from the "great motions" issuing from nature construed as necessity and chance, a primordial strife that is covered over by the unnatural constraints of conventional equality, piety, and law-abidingness. In the *Republic*, Socrates gets Glaucon and Adeimantus to agree that, even in its most primitive origins devoted to bodily self-preservation, the city is never merely a compact among individuals but is from the outset organized by a division of labor based on the objective validity of *techne* (369a–371a). In this way, Socrates makes genesis coeval with *eidos* because the stability and architectonic ranking of the arts already foreshadow the clarity and stability of the Ideas toward which all generated phenomena are drawn in fulfilling their ends. Having introduced a reasonably organized community into even the most primitive origins of political life, Socrates proceeds to goad Glaucon into objecting that life in this City of Sows would lack the urbane grandeur of the erotic passions (372a–373d). In this way, he encourages Glaucon's implicit dissatisfaction with the Sophists' impoverished psychology while compelling Glaucon to express his erotic longings within an already agreed-on principle for distinguishing the passions as clearly as possible from one another (the division of eros from thumos and desire in the tripartite structure of the soul) and educating them to find their place within an ordered community. In sum, Socrates tries to convince Glaucon that his instinct about tyranny and the greatest passions is correct: they do not come to light in a primitive prepolitical situation, as the Sophists argued, but in fact develop rather late, when the political community and its need for order and rank and its eros for nobility are already fully in place. This means, however, that in order to clarify his erotic longings, Glaucon must accept the need for them to be sublimated politically and, if Socrates is successful, channeled into the service of the common good. Eros and justice are often enemies, but if Socrates is right, they arise ("naturally grow") together enmeshed with *nomos* (372e).

Machiavelli agrees that only with the emergence of "grandeur of soul" do we leave the primitive origins and enter the world of developed political life, statesmanship, and constitutionalism. He also thereby agrees that grandeur of soul is only inadequately satisfied by the rudimentary authority based on physical survival and security that characterizes the state of nature. Again we see that Machiavelli is aiming for much higher stakes than merely reverting to the arguments of ancient Sophistry and materialism. He wants to sketch a new theory of constitutional authority that is complex and refined enough to solicit and satisfy the fullest political talents and the most subtle sagacity in statecraft, but without following the Platonic and Aristotelian route whereby the original, purely political grandeur of this soul, its pristine vitality and fecundity as it first emerges from the primitive demands of the primordial origins into the dawning possibilities of consummate might and achievement, is lured away from these dynamic origins and rich potentiality by philosophy and moderation. This is why Machiavelli runs together the constitutions that Plato distinguishes as aristocratic and timocratic – the rule of philosophers and the rule of the spirited class of warriors – into his own version of an aristocracy that promotes the common good. With this he implies that justice and the common good are better served by an overweening sense of honor and martial prowess than by a moderation instilled by philosophy or by an education – like that of the Auxiliaries – that provides a pale imitation of philosophy. Precisely the vigor, even the belligerence, of the warriors is needed to combat the corruption and libertinage toward which the people, if left to their own devices, are disposed.

Socrates himself concedes this when he makes *thumos* the engine of civic morality and the governor of low desires in the best regime, but, from Machiavelli's perspective, he shies away from the consequences. This is another reason from Machiavelli's viewpoint for rooting the eidetic account of the forms of the constitution *in* the genetic, historical account. If, as Plato argues, the ends of virtue are eternally present, if peace and stability are the norm, so that people are living according to nature when they turn away from the perils of war and empire to cultivate the soul through an absorption in domestic politics, then it is plausible to crown a typology of regimes with the constitution that embodies the greatest stability and repose possible for politics: rule by philosophers. If, however, as Machiavelli contends, the aspiration to virtue is always underlain by and sharpened by these dangers, then the best constitution must be one that can recurrently and in its very structure surmount the perils constantly besetting it, preferably by using them to its own advantage. For Plato and Aristotle, a well-ordered political community will assimilate the unruliness of the passions while granting them their necessary leeway. The polis will circumscribe the *oikos*, allowing it to supply gratification for the desires within set limits. For Machiavelli, by contrast, the very unity of a republic is guaranteed by the dynamic struggle between passion and order. The goal is not to sublimate the passions, to draw them off in the service of the telos, but to find an equilibrium between passion and order – between the lion and the fox. Whereas for Aristotle, as we saw in Chapter 3, the art of ruling assists the parts of the city in fulfilling their natural development, for Machiavelli the art of ruling is a technique that stands outside of natural forces and manages their combinations in whatever way is most productive of stability, power, and prosperity.

In connection with these issues, we can see more clearly the importance of history for Machiavelli as the medium through which to convey his teaching. In earlier chapters, I have stressed that the pre-Socratics' and Sophists' account of nature as motion, although emphatically sub-political and unable to sustain the elaborately nuanced political psychologies of Plato and Aristotle, nonetheless differed from the modern physics of matter in motion by accounting for a general kind of human nobility, grandeur, and justice existing by nature as opposed to convention, demonstrated by the "natural master" whose life of "force" and "getting the better" mirrored the "great motions" of nature itself as genesis. In contrast with the pre-Socratic ontology of motion, the modern physics of matter in motion, because it is a secularized version of the Augustinian account of nature as mere random forces drained of any account of nobility, could account for political virtue as nothing but an inchoate impulse to dominion. As a consequence, modern thinkers such as Hobbes, building on Baconian physics, could not follow the pre-Socratics or Sophists in arguing for a way of life that was noble and just by nature – all such distinctions are purely conventional, created by the social contract. By contrast, as we have seen, Gorgias in one of his fragments grants courage and prudence the status of natural virtues.

In this chapter, I am arguing that Machiavelli, although partial to the pre-Socratics' and Sophists' stress on *pleonexia* as the best way of life, would concur with Plato's judgment about the psychological poverty of their teachings. Machiavelli wants a much more detailed, subtle, and robust psychology of leadership than the vague nobility based on brute force ascribed by Callicles to the natural master. Like Socrates, Machiavelli does not see the naturally best way of life as standing across a chasm from convention, but wants to present it as integrated with and articulated by life in the various kinds of political communities. At the same time, however, he rejects the Platonic understanding of where true human satisfaction resides – the longing for union with the eternally beautiful and good. He embraces and secularizes the Augustinian account of human nature as reducible to the pursuit of dominion, a reductionism even more severe than the pre-Socratics' and Sophists' account of nobility and justice by nature. By the same token, however, Machiavelli does not want to take the narrow path from this synthesis that was later taken by Hobbes, a project for the pure managerial control of human nature drained of all natural nobility, grandeur, and honor. How, then, to account for that nobility without embracing classical teleology and while resisting the psychological barrenness of both the pre-Socratic and Augustinian accounts of political life? Only through history itself. It is through the dynamic unfolding of events out of chance that the phenomenological richness of scope of Platonic political psychology re-emerges – or at least Machiavelli's attempt to recapture that scope – but now firmly rooted in *pleonexia* itself, thereby wholly altering its content.

To crystallize these contrasts, let us revisit one of our core themes, the harmonious ordering of the passions prescribed by classical political philosophy that we first considered in Chapter 1. For Socrates, as we observed in Chapters 1 and 2, the place of *thumos* in the city is highly problematic. He encourages its prominence in Book 2 of the *Republic* as the psychological mainstay of the citizenry even as he points to the need for its sublimation or even eclipse through a civic education grounded in an orderly and moderate cosmos. *Thumos* has to be restrained from serving eros directly – lest it become the means employed by the imperial ambitions of the "feverish" city of excessive longing – but it cannot serve philosophy directly either, because its own motivation is not philosophic, and, unlike eros, it cannot be pointed directly toward philosophy. Thumos has to be driven by a love of honor, but must prefer moderation over ambition and avoid too much severity on behalf of justice. Again, however, thumos cannot grasp the requirements of this ordering of the soul and city directly on theoretical grounds but only through habituation to Socrates' new cosmology of divine orderliness. Socrates finally admits, in Book 8 of the *Republic*, through his depiction of the rebellion of the Auxiliaries against the Guardians, that the attempt to rehabilitate the bellicose energies of thumos very likely will not succeed, certainly not reliably or for long.

For Machiavelli, by contrast, thumos *can* be liberated. That is because, for Machiavelli, order is the *consequence* of thumos compelled to fight by Fortuna and kept in fighting trim by the enactment of severely repressive laws at home and the discipline imposed on it by the pursuit of imperialism abroad. Socrates had early on in Book 2 almost given up the quest for the best regime when he reflected that, if the soul was to be capable of justice, each part of it must perform only one job, while thumos was required to perform two jobs, being gentle to fellow citizens and savage to the city's enemies. Education, including the reform of poetry and belief in the gods, was hypothesized as the way of ameliorating this conflict, but the results in the *Republic* are ambiguous at best. Machiavelli's solution is to liberate the conflict at the heart of thumos by methodically alternating between its savage and restrained modes, not subordinating the former to the latter. So whereas Socrates stigmatizes timocracy in Book 8 of the *Republic* as the beginning of the decline from the common good into self-interest – kicked off by the honor seeking of the timocrats – Machiavelli identifies precisely this type of constitution as the one that best serves the common good. It will be made up of the aggressive men of "grandeur of soul," the type whom

Callicles and Glaucon admire *before* they are subjected to the Socratic elenchus and its attempt to implant an education in moderation in their characters. For Plato, restraint can come only to the extent that the savagery of thumos is tamed by civic education or by an eros ultimately devoted to philosophy. For Machiavelli, restraint is maintained by the general necessity, the overwhelming peril, at the heart of existence, which can be replicated by severe laws that admit of no exception to their discipline. In this way, moderation becomes lawfulness, a deeroticized kind of control. It is not, as in Platonic statecraft, the orderliness that the pursuit of substantive satisfaction confers on the soul as its passions are drawn off from grosser objects of satisfaction toward higher, more lasting ones, but the general necessity imposed on the passions by the overwhelmingly powerful primordial genesis in which the passions themselves are rooted, the Godlike singularity of Fortuna.

Moreover, to recall our general thesis about Machiavelli first broached in Chapter 1, to the extent that Machiavelli fully liberates thumos as a passion, he presupposes its rigorous subjection to the imposition of order on nature by the will. Whereas Plato attempts to restrain thumos within the harmony of the affects ordered by reason so that its openness to honor and the divine might flourish, Machiavelli liberates it only after entirely bestializing it.

THE REPUBLIC PERFECTED BY CHANCE

Because republics are "destined" to go through this cycle repeatedly, Machiavelli concludes, "all kinds of government are defective." He then proceeds to propose that instead of looking for a single constitutional principle such as monarchy, oligarchy, or democracy with which to order the political community, the best solution to the cycle of decline may lie in a "mixed" constitution:

Thus prudent legislators, knowing the vices of each of these modes of government by themselves, have chosen one that should partake of all of them, judging that to be the most stable and solid. In fact, when there is combined under the same constitution a prince, a nobility, and the power of the people, then these three powers will watch and keep each other reciprocally in check.

On the face of it, Machiavelli is taking us back to the famous Aristotelian prescription for the mixed constitution. As we saw in Chapter 3, this is the constitution that can best achieve the minimal requirements for a stable political association, ameliorating the explosive tensions between rich and poor that tend to cause the greatest civil unrest. By mixing the principles of two defective constitutions, oligarchy and democracy, Aristotle sketches a constitution that combines the inclusiveness of the democratic claim to authority with the meritocracy of the oligarchical claim, while weakening the one-sidedness of each party's claim (for, although democrats are right to say men are equal, they are not equal in all respects, and although oligarchs are right to say they are unequal, they are not unequal in all respects, nor is superiority in wealth tantamount to superiority in all virtue). A moderate middle class of the least rich and the least poor will elect magistrates based on merit with perhaps a small property qualification, leading to a deliberative governing body that may in the course of time deserve to be called aristocratic (*Politics* 1294a35–b14). Aristotle identifies this particular constitution by the generic term "constitution" (*politeia*) because it is the pattern for reform that most existing cities have a chance of actually implementing. It takes care of stability by reducing class conflict and allows a relatively high degree of public virtue to emerge. Machiavelli's remark that "all kinds of government are defective" is a direct gloss on Aristotle's introduction to the discussion of the mixed constitution in Books 3 and 4 of the *Politics*, for Aristotle observes that each of the six archetypal constitutions, even the good ones, tends to define authority too sharply and exclusively, limiting it too narrowly to one portion of the body politic and thus provoking indignation and a feeling of being exploited in those who do not share in it. From the viewpoint of including as many people of sufficient virtue (if not the highest degree of virtue) for self-government as possible, "all such constitutions," Aristotle also concludes, "are defective" (1283a23–29).

Once again, Machiavelli's employment of a traditional rubric of statecraft is a carapace under which he radically alters its content. For it must be stressed that Machiavelli's illustration of a successful mixed constitution is not Aristotle's "polity," but Lycurgus's constitution for Sparta, a constitution that Aristotle criticizes as being on the whole wrong-headed (*Politics* 1270a29–1271b20, 1324b5–15, 1333b5–20). When Aristotle recommends mixing and blending antagonistic political forces, this is because he believes the debate between democrats and oligarchs implies, even at its most heatedly partisan, an implicit possibility of agreement, because human beings at their best fulfill their natures through participating in such debates guided by *logos*. For both parties, as he says, "lay hold" on a "part" of the meaning of justice, bending the principle of equal treatment for equals and unequal treatment for the unequal to serve their own self-interest and justify their indignation at the prospect of being ruled over by the other. For Aristotle, as we saw in Chapter 3, justice in politics is a distribution of offices in accordance with the respects in which people are equal to each other through the virtues they contribute to the political community but also in accordance with the respects in which some are superior to others. Aristotle believes that if authority can be spread around to the most moderate and sensible elements of both parties in such a way as to make each side cease feeling that it is threatened with domination or expropriation by the other, it will be possible, as the most compulsive kind of self-interest thereby calms down, for the citizens and their magistrates to rise to the deliberative freedom to sift fairly among the different claims to equality and inequality in reasoned debate (the chief task, he says, of "political philosophy" [1280a7–21;1282b14–23]).

Machiavelli, by contrast, does not believe that the clash between hostile parties implies any such supervening discursive unity or common good to be actualized through reasoned deliberation. The goal of politics is to maximize security and well-being for both princes and peoples. Even the survival of the constitutional order is secondary to this goal. So much is this the case that he can even recommend that a republic perpetually racked by partisan strife might be better off by becoming "subject after a while to some neighbouring state that is better organized than itself." Aristotle, much as he is against a political community becoming imperialistic, would never argue that it could actually benefit by being absorbed by a more powerful foe itself, which is in any case an endorsement of imperialism from another perspective. The only exception to the prohibition against waging a war that is not in self-defense is a just war aimed at freeing an unjustly oppressed people. But that would preclude absorbing it into one's own domain (*Politics* 1333a30–35, 133b37–1334a11; *Nicomachean Ethics* 1177b9–11). Among the classics, only Xenophon in the *Education of Cyrus* comes close to Machiavelli's proposition, when he has the young Cyrus wax indignant at the follies of neighboring countries and their governments and claim that conquering and absorbing them would improve them.

For Aristotle, only a small and neighborly polis, independent of foreign domination, eschewing empire, and self-sufficient enough to look inward, can approximate the wholeness that orders the cosmos. A multinational state, however prosperous and powerful it may become, cannot do this. Its size, diversity, and the absence of civic deliberation shared among a self-governing citizenry prevent it from being a whole within the whole. Indeed, as we observed in Chapter 4, for Aristotle such an empire would not really form a political community at all. Generally devoted to maximizing the material goods produced by the art of household management, it would more closely resemble a contractual commercial relationship like trade alliance. By contrast, Machiavelli is concerned above all with how political "bodies" can survive, regenerate, and expand their power. If this is better achieved by a multinational empire that, like Rome, absorbs its former foes and adds them to the forces it turns outward on the next enemy, that is all to the good. To be the secure and prosperous ally or even province of such an empire might be preferable to an impoverished and constantly imperiled independence. It is in this ironic sense that Machiavelli discusses what he terms the "mixed principality" in chapter 3 of *The Prince*. Despite the superficial nod to Aristotle in the chapter title, he extols the success of the Roman republic in making republican self-sufficiency of the Aristotelian kind impossible for all she came into contact with, absorbing them like a cell that continually divides itself and grows so as to absorb further nourishment. Even in the contemporary parallel, in which Machiavelli usually contrasts *faineant* contemporary rulers with the ever-successful Romans, King Charles XII of France is described as aiming to create a "mixed" principality by annexing parts of Italy.

Machiavelli gives his qualified endorsement to Lycurgus's constitution for exactly the same reasons on which Aristotle based his critique of it: instead of attempting to mix the three powers of government in the service of the common good, according to Aristotle, Lycurgus let them clash, each retarding the other precisely through the vigor of its ambition, but forced to cooperate to the degree necessary to keep their helot population under control and to stave off their external enemies. Aristotle concedes that this clash and check of powers held Sparta together. But in the case of each of its institutions, he criticizes Lycurgus for allowing its partisans to pursue their own ambition and self-interest and for thereby abandoning from the outset any hope that these contending factions could be educated to transcend their passions so that they could deliberate in common according to *logos* about the meaning of the just and unjust, thus fulfilling their natures as political animals:

And because the [ephorate] was too powerful, and equal to a tyranny, the kings were also compelled to cultivate popular favor, so that in this way too the constitution was jointly injured, for out of an aristocracy came to be evolved a democracy. (1270b6–17)

In other words, for Aristotle, pitting several conflicting principles against each other within a regime is not the same thing as mixing them to promote their common ground. For Machiavelli, however, the fact that the ephors or the representatives of the other two powers might be motivated by selfish ambition or love of money and luxury is not objectionable in itself. The clash of these powers will prevent any one of them from winning out and bringing the struggle to an end, and the perils of the clash will keep each power in fighting trim, unable to relax its guard and sink into effeminacy. For Aristotle, on the other hand, it is precisely Lycurgus's belief that it makes no sense to try to educate statesmen to moderate these passions that is so objectionable.

[The] lawgiver clearly does the same here as in the rest of the constitution: he makes the citizens ambitious and has used this for the election of the elders, for nobody would ask for office if he were not ambitious; yet surely ambition and love of money are the motives that bring about almost the greatest part of wrongdoing that takes place among mankind . . . (It) would be advantageous that kings should not be appointed as they are now, but chosen in each case with a regard to their own life and conduct. But it is clear that even the lawgiver himself does not suppose that he can make the kings men of high character: at all events he distrusts them as not being persons of sufficient worth. (1271a9–26)

What Aristotle deplores about Lycurgus, Machiavelli extols. At bottom, the fact that Lycurgus does not trust human nature enough to believe it capable of being educated to moderation, so that he premises his constitution on conflict, is rooted in the fact that Sparta's whole reason for existing is to sharpen the aggressive passions and turn them outward against external foes and inward against the helots. "The entire system of laws," Aristotle observes, "is directed toward one part of

virtue only, military power, because this is serviceable for conquest."
For Machiavelli, the internal clash of powers, checks, and balances criticized by Aristotle is precisely what is admirable about Sparta, earning
Lycurgus "the highest praise" for providing Sparta with "over eight
hundred years (of) the most perfect tranquility." We recognize, of
course, an anticipation of the modern constitutional theory of checks
and balances in the mode of such students of Machiavelli as Montesquieu, arguably the chief philosophical influence on the American
constitution, one of whose framers endorsed it for enabling "ambition
to counter-act ambition."[10]

The constitution of Lycurgus, Machiavelli goes on, was in every
way superior to Athens, which ran through the entire cycle of regimes
because it tried to set up a distinct regime each time, as if imitating "the
writers on republics" who maintain that regimes must serially embody
the specific claims of monarchy, aristocracy, and democracy rather
than, like Sparta, containing them all within one regime and allowing
them to clash and check. Athens behaved as if what the traditional
authorities on statecraft had argued was true: that each constitution is
distinct from another, because each constitution is to be ranked according to how successfully and in what way, given the limitations of human
nature and circumstance, it instantiates the orderliness and repose at
the heart of the cosmos. Because Athens tried to set up one distinct
constitution each time – popular, tyrannical, oligarchical, and so forth –
those who were excluded from authority bided their time until they
could overthrow it. This was because the original laws drawn up for the

---

[10] I substantially agree with Sullivan's argument (2004) that Machiavelli's prescription for
institutional checks and balances within a republic so as to preserve the liberties of both
the common people and the great, while harnessing their competitive energies for the
mutual aggrandizement of all, is central both to the English Republicanism of the seventeenth century and to more explicitly liberal thinkers like Locke. For reasons I discuss
at greater length in the Conclusion, I have a more difficult time reconciling Hobbes with
either stream, especially the republican one, because his theory of absolute sovereignty
would rob political life of the republican dynamism Harrington and others admired
in Machiavelli's view of Rome, while his defense of individualism on the grounds of
mere self-preservation eschews any need for a self-governing commonwealth, the brunt
of Locke's critique. As Mansfield observes with respect to Machiavelli's republicanism,
but in a way that could also anticipate the proceduralism of the prescription for the
American founding, "The business of government is not so much positive legislation to
benefit the people as the negative exchange of accusations that entertains the people.
While making use of ambitious princes, republics must take care to appease the popular
fear and dislike of ambition." Mansfield in Machiavelli (1996) p. xxix.

Athenians by Solon were unable to "temper the power" of the people, the prince, or the nobles and chasten their "insolence" and "license." Thus, Athens was doomed to suffer what Aristotle himself observed was the bad consequence of distinguishing too rigidly among the regime principles – provoking the anger and rebellion of those excluded from a share of offices. For Aristotle, however, as we saw in Chapter 3, this bad consequence stemmed from a failure to appreciate how the goal of establishing a unified and homogeneous magistracy must bend and compromise with the necessities of ordinary political tension. The unity of virtue and of the best regime extolled by Plato must, according to Aristotle, be diluted by the heterogeneous and composite nature of cities as we really find them. When the most rigorous standards of virtue and public service were diluted sufficiently to make the citizen body large enough that a majority would not feel excluded, the political community would have a better prospect for achieving whatever deliberative harmony it could without destabilizing the very basis of all civil order. The goal of "polity," in other words, was still the common good – Aristotle was simply willing to loosen the standards relatively speaking. For Machiavelli, however, it is the pursuit of Aristotle's goal, whether rigorous or diluted, that necessarily undermines order and results in civil strife. Solon was unable to curb the insolence and power seeking of the hostile strata of the populace precisely because he tried, through his laws, to inculcate in the Athenians a virtuous disposition. Only if, like Lycurgus, he had allowed the insolence and power seeking of those strata to clash with and neutralize each other might his laws have stood some chance of preventing these traits from reaching the extreme point where they destroyed public order.

"But let us come to Rome" (1.2.7). With this, Machiavelli breaks through the traditional rubrics and reveals just how much he has revolutionized their content. Rome is even better than Sparta because Rome let in the full sweep of chance. Rome became a "perfect republic" through "disunion." This constitutes a complete reversal of classical metaphysics and the grounding it provided for classical political philosophy, whereby perfection comes from the degree to which the regime participates in unity and rest (the inward-looking deliberation on domestic public affairs) and avoids disunity and motion (the outward-looking tyranny over other peoples enflamed by selfish passions at home [Aristotle *Politics* 1325a15–1325b30]). As Machiavelli observes of Rome, "so many accidents arose in it through the dis-union between the plebs and the Senate that what an orderer had not done, chance did." A founder can be great, but the power of chance, the pulse of Fortuna, is even greater when harnessed to energize the republic's institutions. Lycurgus institutionalized conflict, but only to maintain inner stability and resist further evolution. Unlike Sparta, on the one hand, Rome developed historically. "Fortune was so favor-able to Rome" because she opened herself up to the shifts of history. Unlike Athens, on the other hand, Rome did not change regimes serially from one principle to another but let the claims of people, nobles, and monarchy clash and check.

Altogether, therefore, Rome's historical success defied those "who have written on republics" by combining what they decreed could not be combined: a mixed regime capable of imperial expansion. Dynamic, dialectical, and flexible, Rome retained whatever was useful from the regime's previous evolution and incorporated it in a new response to necessity. The cycle of regimes in Phase Two that we discussed earlier is now shown to be contained within *one* evolving mega-regime, a pro-gression in which one regime principle is never entirely superseded by the next. The monarchs became the consuls answerable to the Senate, while the Senate's arrogance was restrained by the tribunes of the peo-ple. Remaining class conflicts were submerged in the joint project of imperial expansion, which gave scope for honor and brought land and wealth to all strata.

For Machiavelli, the career of Rome is the unique case of how a regime can deliberately open itself to Fortuna so as to let Fortuna pro-voke the necessary new modes of statecraft. The law-bred internal sever-ity praised in the initial discussion of foundings can be supplemented, we now learn, by the regime's recurrent self-exposure to the prospect of conquering or being conquered. The ensuing chapters illustrate this premise through a discussion of the conflict between the Senate and People. Machiavelli begins by observing that men are only "good" – by which he means orderly and disciplined, and therefore able to acquire power – through being subjected to some external compulsion (neces-sity, fear, danger, the hostility of Fortuna [1.3]). Freedom without the stimulus of compulsion degenerates into the disorder and confusion produced by too much ease, comfort, and the relaxation of vigor. This brings us to what is possibly the central and most difficult paradox of Machiavelli's new political science: the republic's achieved goal of power, wealth, and security through its rise to empire is precisely what at length causes it to unravel into effeminacy and laziness. Its *virtu* is its own gravedigger.

Rome provides the best model for statecraft to date because during her rise to empire, the ceaseless struggle between the People and the Senate imposed necessity on each, keeping each strong and orderly through mutual opposition and thereby preventing degeneration. This enabled each to get what it wanted as the regime expanded outward. Rome, however, by Machiavelli's own admission, did undermine the vigor of its original virtue by the enjoyment of its material results. The empire's achievement of unprecedented wealth, security, and peace sapped the capacity for honor seeking and ambition, destroyed all local traditions of national independence, and at length generated a spiritual longing for a permanent kingdom of peace on earth, the seed bed of Christianity.[11] Much as he praises the ruthless dexterity of Rome's leaders, that praise is conspicuously absent when it comes to Julius Caesar and Octavian, who began the transition to a permanent peace and therefore the effemination of virtue.[12] Is there a way around this seemingly

[11] Brilliantly analyzed by Cantor (1976) in his treatment of Shakespeare's Roman plays, particularly *Antony and Cleopatra*.

[12] There are two references to Octavian, later Augustus Caesar, in the *Discourses*, both of which clearly connect him to Rome's eradication of the spirit of republican liberty as she grew into an empire, and with that "effemination" of Roman virtue that set in with "the long peace that was born into the world under Octavian" (I.I.3), a metaphor that reminds us of the prediction made in Virgil, and later widely associated with Christ, that during the reign of Augustus a child would be born who would bring peace to mankind. The second reference, at 1.52.3 is more explicitly hostile. Here, Machiavelli recalls how "Tully" (Cicero) convinced the Senate to back the young Octavian so as to undermine the soldiers' support for Mark Antony, owing to the power of the name "Caesar" that Octavian now claimed. It all came to nothing, however, for Octavian went over to Antony, and "this affair was the destruction of the party of the aristocrats," that is, tantamount to the death of the old republic. The fault was Cicero's for having deluded himself that "that name" Caesar could bolster the republican cause when in truth, it should not "have been believed that, either from his (Caesar's) heirs or his agents anything could ever be had that would conform to the name of freedom." There could hardly be a more withering summing up of the failures of the ancient "writers." Ironically, in trying to conscript the ruthlessly ambitious young Octavian against Antony, Cicero was behaving in a superficially "Machiavellian" way, choosing as an ally the younger, apparently less formidable foe of the republic over the more established one, a lesser of evils choice in which the greater evil (Antony) would be neutralized and the lesser one (Octavian) coopted. At bottom, however, Cicero remained vulnerable to the allure of Caesar's name and reputation for "glory," believing it could

inevitable decline? While Machiavelli extols a republic's pursuit of prosperity, his endorsement of this aim is not unqualified, especially when balanced against his praise of honor seeking. Machiavelli often makes clear his ranking of honor and austerity over commercial expansionism and wealth, a priority that was relaxed by authors later influenced by him like Montesquieu. He praises the Germans for their lack of commerce with other countries, their self-sufficiency and eschewal of

be harnessed to the "aristocrats'" cause, when in truth it represented the unvarnished and irreversible triumph of tyranny over the republic. Given Cicero's portrait of Scipio the Younger as prizing the life of the mind over even civic honor, Machiavelli would appear to be implying that, just as Cicero was deluded in believing that monarchical virtues like those displayed by Scipio and his namesake the elder Scipio, follower of Xenophon's Cyrus, could ever be compatible with republican equality before the law, so in real life Cicero delusionally saw in the young Octavian a real-life Scipio whom he, like the philosophic counsellor to the young tyrant with an eros for the city described in Book 4 of the *Laws*, would guide away from any lurking tyrannical ambitions to becoming the servant of the republic, under Cicero's wise guidance. The example shows how Machiavelli's allegedly amoral teaching could arguably be viewed as both a more principled and a more clear-headed defense of republican liberty than that of Cicero.

Machiavelli's strictures on Julius Caesar (1.10, 1.37.2) are also quite severe. Do not believe in Caesar's "glory," he warns us, because he either bribed those who wrote about him or they were afraid of him. The scorn heaped on Catiline by Cicero and Sallust reveals what they would have said about Caesar himself if they had not been afraid. Hypocritically, they excoriated after the fact the man who had merely attempted to become tyrant, while whitewashing or omitting to censor the "much more detestable Caesar," who actually succeeded. Even the widespread praise of Brutus was somewhat insincere, "as though, unable to blame Caesar because of his power, they celebrate his enemy." The truth is, "Caesar was the first tyrant in Rome, such that never again was that city free." Given that the Romans lost their liberty under the empire founded by the Caesars, Machiavelli argues that, comparatively speaking, their best government thereafter took place under the "Good Emperors," from Antoninus Pius to Marcus Aurelius, who held office through election rather than by hereditary descent. During the Antonine period, Rome experienced "a secure peace in the midst of secure citizens, and the world full of peace and justice" (he omits to say liberty). On either side of that era, first the Julio-Claudians who ruled by hereditary descent and after the return to hereditary descent with the accession of Commodus, Rome is "all rancor, all license, corruption, and ambition eliminated." Whereas many historians might view the Antonine era as the developed and institutionalized perfection of the original Augustan principate begun by Caesar's heir Octavian, to be followed by a dark age of autocrats like Severus, Machiavelli lumps together the era before and the era after the Antonines as the joint consequence of Caesar's original tyranny, treating the period of the good emperors as a fortunate but temporary interlude in the despotic and corrupting despotism founded by Caesar. Someone surveying this entire history, therefore, "will then know very well how many obligations Rome, Italy and the world owe to Caesar." Caesar's overthrow of the republic, and his heir's creation of the empire, were one enormous ghastly mistake which should have been avoided and that the founders of the new Rome must at all costs avoid: "Truly, if a prince seeks the glory of the world, he ought to desire to possess imported goods: "Thus they have been prevented from adopting either French, Spanish or Italian customs, and these nations are the great

a corrupt city – not to spoil it entirely as did Caesar but to reorder it as did Romulus." True glory comes from reshaping and reinvigorating the fallen matter of nature. However, as long as princes long for the glory of the "imagined republics," of "the writers" like Xenophon and his depiction of Cyrus, they will choose the path of Caesar and corrupt the people. What era could be more corrupt, on Machiavelli's arguments, than Machiavelli's own, the nadir of effemination? The new prince will have his work cut out for him but also a perhaps unprecedented prospect for achieving "the glory of the world."

In chapter 19 of *The Prince*, there is a parallel discussion to the one in the *Discourses* of the good emperors. Whereas in the *Discourses* he stresses that the Antonines were good rulers compared with the fallen period before and after them inaugurated by Caesar, in this context, in which the focus is more on the virtue of the singular prince than on republican statesmen, he is less critical of their successors, especially Septimius Severus, whom he praises for astutely embodying the qualities of the lion and the fox. Severus was able to keep the soldiers, the nobles, and the people in line through a judicious mixture of terror and rewards, leaving them "astonished and stupefied," similar to the words ("satisfied and stupefied") he used to describe Cesare Borgia's effect on the Romagna by using Remiro d'Orco to crush disorder and then executing him and leaving his dismembered body in the public square, thereby terrifying the people through an intermediary and satisfying their hatred of that intermediary by killing him (as Stalin did with successive secret police chiefs). Moreover, Severus recognized that, if forced to choose between satisfying the soldiers and the people, one must choose the soldiers, because one needs their power more, whereas today (in Machiavelli's own era) rulers must please the people because they are more powerful than the soldiers, who are often mercenaries. It might appear from this praise of Severus that Machiavelli is qualifying his remark in the *Discourses* that the people form the soundest basis for rule: "As regards prudence, I say that the people are more prudent and stable, and have better judgement than a prince; and it is not without good reason that it is said, 'the voice of the people is the voice of God'" (1.58). However, we must bear in mind that, in that particular context in the *Discourses*, he is offering a prescription for a healthy republic like early Rome. Here in *The Prince*, by contrast, he is talking about a ruler's need to be cruel when "the body which you choose to maintain you ... is corrupt." Corrupt republics and principalities both need founders or refounders who can reinvigorate them through a jolt of harshness and terror. Hence, in the context of the corrupt period after the end of the Antonines, a terrifying ruler like Severus was best. The main foil for the cruel and cunning Severus in this chapter is the gentle Marcus Aurelius, who, because he came at the end of a comparatively uncorrupt era, was able to satisfy the people, nobles, and soldiers without such harsh measures.

Putting the discussion of the Antonines in *The Prince* and the *Discourses* together, then, we arrive at the following rank order: the ancient Roman Republic was the least corrupt of the Roman regimes, the principate founded by Caesar and Augustus the most corrupt, and the Antonine emperors an interval of relatively less corruption – more corrupt than the republic, but less corrupt than Caesar's principate – after which the Caesarian era's corruption resumed and required much harsher measures.

In a moment of wry humor in chapter 19 of *The Prince*, Machiavelli refers to Marcus Aurelius as "Marcus the Philosopher." When we recall that Marcus broke the chain of corrupters of the world" (1.55.2–3). Similarly, in 2.19, he writes: "Acquisition sometimes proves most injurious even to a well-regulated republic, when they consist either in a city or a province that has been enervated by pleasures and luxury, for these indulgences and habits become contagious." How might the new Rome keep republican virtue keen and prevent it from degenerating into the longing for peace, ease and enjoyment? We return to this conundrum of too much success at the end of this chapter.

Machiavelli is aware that the traditional writers on politics tended to look askance at the "extraordinary and almost wild" means by which Rome gained her empire in comparison with the standards set by the best regimes of Plato, Aristotle, and their followers. He entertains this viewpoint but quickly abandons it: "One should blame the Roman government more sparingly," for its internal tumults are "frightening only to those who merely read of them" as opposed to the men of action who achieved Rome's success (1.4). Thought and action may not have a common end. But could Rome have achieved its greatness *without* the ongoing dissension between Senate and People? To consider this fully, Machiavelli argues, we have to return to the two alternatives posed by Rome and Sparta. By implication, the traditional typology of regimes discussed initially in 1.2 has now been disposed of, superseded by these two archetypes that combine all regime principles within themselves – people, nobles, monarch – as powers that "watch and keep each other reciprocally in check" (1.2.5).

By summarizing his discussion of the genealogy of regimes with a gloss on Aristotle's remark about the defectiveness of all the archetypal constitutions, Machiavelli signifies his agreement about the seriousness of a problem analyzed by classical political philosophy. He also signifies his judgment that the solutions to this problem available within the horizon of classical thought and experience could never be fully actualized – both the Athenian attempt to institute one distinct constitution after another and the attempt of Lycurgus to institutionalize within

---

elected emperors that Machiavelli saw as the Antonine age's finest feature and returned to the Julio-Claudian practice of hereditary emperors, destroying the interval of peace and security by allowing his own worthless son Commodus to inherit the throne, we realize that even a philosopher is not capable of doing what the ancients always say we should do, that is, placing the good of the political community over the love of one's own, especially love of family.

one system the hostilities that the good regimes in Aristotle's typology sought to transcend. Of the two approaches, however, Machiavelli prefers Sparta, for "Athens lived a very short time in respect to Sparta" (1.2). Aristotle had judged the Spartan constitution to be worthwhile only at a relatively low level of human merit. In the *Nicomachean Ethics*, courage, Sparta's chief virtue, is one of the two lowest-ranked virtues of character (along with bodily continence), because courage stems from the compulsion to survive when faced with the threat of death and so cannot *not* be chosen, whereas higher virtues lacking in Sparta such as liberality are not compelled by self-interest and involve a greater degree of choice as to how they are actualized (*Nicomachean Ethics* 1119a20–b13, 1111b1–1112a11). For Aristotle, Sparta's longevity and stability certainly entitled it to a measure of commendation, if rather sparse. Characteristically, what for the ancients represented the lowest level of political virtue that they could admit into the discussion of the proper aims of government represents for Machiavelli the *only* element of their pragmatism that is worth salvaging. Hence Lycurgus merits discussion and high praise in Machiavelli's consideration of the various regime principles, whereas Aristotle is not even mentioned by name.

Machiavelli's preferred solution to the defectiveness of all the regime principles lies in a new direction, a combination that could not be envisioned by the classical tradition regardless of whether it was talking of high standards or low ones: "The disunion which existed between the Senate and the people produced such extraordinary events that chance did for her what the founder had failed to do" (1.2.7). Rome was perfected by "her" disunity. The very forces of change and strife, the struggle for power, prestige, and wealth, that the ancients had thought made political unity (to say nothing of perfection) difficult if not impossible become, in Machiavelli's prescription, their only sure basis. Unlike Sparta, the Roman constitution developed over time, so that it was not cut off from the shifts of fortune. Unlike Athens, Rome did not fruitlessly substitute one type of constitution for another. It retained whatever proved useful from past experience and incorporated it into the new forms that necessity prompted. Thus, to expand on an ealier observation, after the monarchy was overthrown, "those who expelled it immediately appointed two consuls in place of the king." This prevented the senatorial class from wielding absolute power. Similarly, the people extracted from the aristocracy the creation of the office of the tribunes: "The nobility, to save a portion of their power, were forced to yield a share of it." The tribunes could veto acts of the Senate, thus providing a check against the overweening arrogance of the patriciate, but they could not initiate laws themselves nor usurp the executive and military functions of the consuls. The Roman constitution, then, was dynamic and dialectical in its response to adverse circumstances. Its negations of past forms were, to use a Hegelian term, "determinate negations" that preserved a residue of what they had superseded – monarchy, as Machiavelli observes, was "never entirely abolished," and the nobles were "never entirely deprived" of their authority over the common people. One distinct form of constitution need not succeed another. Instead, unity can result from diversity; being can be maintained by difference and becoming.[13]

Rome thus shows how the Spartan internal prescription for "powers in check" can be combined with an expansionist, imperialistic foreign policy. For the ancient thinkers, the cycles of rise and decline that Machiavelli set forth in the previous chapter, a cycle disastrously illustrated by the history of Athens, showed that only to the degree that a constitution could embody the stability of the *nunc stans*, of the eternality of true being approximated in the soul by the pursuit of moral and intellectual virtue, might one transcend, in some degree and for some period of time, this cycle of disarray. For Machiavelli, by contrast, Rome's dazzling success demonstrates how a *single* constitution can contain this whole cycle of changes traditionally thought to result in the decline of good constitutions or limit their prospects for success. There is no need to hope for breaking out of this cycle by transcending the primordial passions and the base material and bodily necessities they entail. On the contrary, by opening itself up to these primordial underpinnings, the generative power out of which the distinct constitutional forms come

---

[13] For example, the Romans turned the Tarquinian kingship of pre-Republican times into the purely ceremonial "king of the sacrifices," so that the people would not have to miss the old rituals. Republics should preserve a semblance of traditional forms even when their content has changed, "so that it may seem to the people that there has been no change in the institutions, even though in fact they are different. For the great majority of mankind are satisfied with appearances, as though they were realities, and are often even more influenced by the things that seem than by those that are" (1.25). The phraseology recalls the maxim from chapter 18 of *The Prince*: "Everyone sees how you appear, few touch what you are." On the character of the Hegelian historical dialectic, see Newell (2009a).

into being and back into which they pass away, a republic like Rome can survive its own dissolution again and again, gaining new strength each time. For the primordial underpinnings out of which these legal and institutional forms emerge and into which they eventually collapse is the life force of the acquisitive, expansionist republic itself. By tapping into the disorder at the heart of existence, by letting itself be energized by the clash of natural and political bodies, such a republic cannot be undone by a reliance on any permanent form. Rather than attempt to approximate the stable unity of the whole, such a constitution leaps into the void of its own untutored impulses, developing itself in response to perilous necessity by continual self-division and supersession. It opens itself up to Fortuna, lets Fortuna provoke it to develop new techniques and institutions: "Fortune favored her" because Rome's virtues always arose fresh from the crucible of the direst necessity. In this sense Rome took the same stance toward Fortuna collectively that, as we discussed in Chapter 6, Machiavelli prescribes for the individual prince.

Aristotle had criticized Lycurgus for assuming that people were incapable of voluntary goodness. Machiavelli now states that one must always "start with assuming that all men are bad and ever ready to display their vicious nature." In this way, the Christian doctrine of original sin, one of whose consequences is that perfection cannot be aimed for through participating in political life, is now secularized so that, once drained of its otherworldly orientation, it can be used as human material for a new kind of political perfection, not through the teleological flowering of the soul but, on the contrary, through its suppression. "People are good," as Machiavelli has told us, "only upon compulsion." The freedom to choose without compulsion – for Aristotle, what chiefly distinguishes the human telos from that of other biological organisms (*Nicomachean Ethics* 1097b25–1098a15) – always leads to "confusion and disorder." Summing up his earlier advice, Machiavelli reminds us that, where the hostility of nature manifested by "poverty and hunger" does not directly force men to become industrious, "the law immediately becomes necessary" to replicate artificially nature's spontaneous severity. The division and clash of powers within the Roman Republic kept the law's capacity to compel virtuous behavior constantly fresh and vigorous. The Senate and the People, the one constantly vying to dominate and the other constantly struggling not to be dominated, imposed necessity on each other recurrently through their ongoing struggles. Each thus kept the other strong and orderly, preventing either one from lapsing into luxury, enervation, and laxity, and thereby kept each other's passions keen. Disciplined repeatedly by this internal battle, the ambitions of each class expended themselves on foreign conquest, not on each other. The Senate led the people into war, recompensing them with a share of land and riches, albeit frequently extracted from the aristocracy by the people under threat of insurrection or desertion. Swollen with new allies and tributaries, the Republic's increased numbers pressed outward to a new perimeter of expansion, vitality maintained by the ongoing domestic class struggle.

Machiavelli is emphatic that he does not make these arguments because he is in favor of mindless, widespread violence and bloodshed for their own sake. On the contrary, he observes that during the three hundred years in which the nobles and people fashioned the division of powers among Senate, consuls, and tribunes in a series of truces in their struggles for predominance, only a handful of people were exiled or put to death. In Machiavelli's view, letting ambitions contend with one another is the likeliest way of preventing them from destroying the republic. They check each other's success internally and bring power, stability, and prosperity to the weaker states that are absorbed. The chaos, violence, and partisan hatred is much worse, he maintains, in states like Athens precisely because each party believes that the constitutional ordering it wants represents an approximation of the final, unchanging truth about the universe. It therefore places an intolerable burden on the self-interest and honor of those whom it excludes, and in the course of time on the repressed ambitions of the ruling class itself (as we saw so vividly illustrated by the rebellion of the young aristocrats in Xenophon's *Education of Cyrus*).

As we have observed, Machiavelli notes that the traditional writers on government have always criticized the example of Rome for its "turbulence and disorder," claiming that only "extreme good fortune" prevented these defects from destroying her. Machiavelli suspects that "all these things can only alarm those who read of them" – that what really scandalizes the traditional-minded critics of Rome is not the violence of the republic's actual history, which was minimal, but the way in which the actual basis for Rome's success so manifestly contradicts their belief that political life must reflect the stability and repose divined in the order of the cosmos by philosophy and philosophical morality. Machiavelli agrees with the ancients that a republic needs "good education," which depends, in turn, on "good laws." Good laws, he continues, spring in turn "from those agitations which have been so inconsiderately condemned by many," rather than, as the ancient philosophers would have prescribed, mirroring the eternal orderliness and moderation of the cosmos. In truth, he concludes, "every free state ought to afford the people the opportunity of giving vent, so to say, to their ambition." For "the demands of a free people are rarely pernicious to their liberty." Whereas the ancients hoped an education in virtue would teach people to transcend to some degree the necessities operative on human nature through the passions, Machiavelli believes that the best education for statecraft is an experience of how the passions clash and how these clashes might be harnessed to maximize security and prosperity for the state.

Still, however much Machiavelli might appeal to hard-headed common sense and an experience of the real world, this rhetorical stance should not lead us to overlook the fact that a *kind* of theoretical guidance and character formation for princes and statesmen is as crucial to Machiavelli's new science of politics as it was to that of the classics, albeit with a radical transvaluation of content from ends toward means, or from the teleological fulfillment of nature to its methodical control. As we have previously seen at some length in Machiavelli's diagnosis of the ills of politics, people in fact are often more spontaneously inclined to the deluded belief in the "imagined republics" of classical and religious morality than they are to a clear-headed assessment of how to achieve their own self-interest. Before Machiavelli's successors can appeal to *Realpolitik*, or to the "real world" as opposed to the mere "ideals" of justice and community extolled by the ancients, the real world first has to be completely altered in how it is perceived by statesmen and citizens. Machiavelli is a "writer" who aims to undo the spell of the traditional "writers." "Reality," the observable world, has to be theoretically reconstructed so as to yield the proper theory of politics from observation. Otherwise, the siren song of Platonic eros and Christian otherworldliness will continue to beckon, which to its adherents is every bit as much observable from experience as is the reality of self-interest. Here we can anticipate a famous conundrum of early modern rationality: does Bacon derive his project for the mastery of nature from his observations about nature, or does he arrange his observations about nature to justify and render possible our mastery of it? Does Hobbes derive his teaching on power and the social contract from the new physics of matter in motion? Or does he append the new physics as a preface so as to ground in natural philosophy an approach to politics primarily derived from observation and history but further buttressed by this theoretical reconstruction of observable reality? We explore these issues in the Conclusion to this book.

To recall Machiavelli's question: Would it have been possible for the Romans to have established a government that, following the classical prescription, put an end to this constant struggle between nobles and people? Machiavelli explores this question in order to sum up the results of his cumulative undermining of the traditional rubrics of political philosophy. Again we are presented with the two alternatives of Sparta and Rome. As Machiavelli presents Sparta here, it embodies the closest historical approximation of the classical prescription for the best constitution that both Plato and Aristotle advanced: She was strong enough to defend herself, but not so powerful as to provoke her neighbors. Her laws discouraged commerce and encouraged an austere equality, which helped make her unattractive to foreign aggressors seeking riches, in turn keeping the internal temptation to war and glory-seeking at bay. If, he writes, such as state

remains quiet within her borders, and experience shows that she entertains no ambitious projects, the fear of her power will never prompt anyone to attack her; and this would even be more certainly the case if her constitution and laws prohibited all aggrandizement.

Machiavelli fully understands the appeal of such a model – unified and homogeneous, free from violent disturbances, at peace and at rest:

And I certainly think that if she could be kept in this equilibrium, it would be the best political existence, and would insure to any city real tranquility.

Life, however, does not permit us this degree of tranquility, however eagerly we can imagine it:

But as all human things are kept in a perpetual movement, and can never remain stable, cities naturally either rise or decline, and necessity compels them to many acts to which reason will not influence them . . . (1.6.4).

As the use of Sparta as his example reveals, Machiavelli will not even grant that the ancient thinkers were able to grasp what kind of republic would in actual practice embody their own prescription, untenable as it was. For, although Plato and Aristotle criticize Sparta for falling far short of the best regime, Machiavelli sees it as the closest any state could come in reality to what these philosophers admired. Sparta was stable; her laws discouraged the acquisition and the enjoyment of luxury. But the only notably successful instance of this type of constitution in history came about, Machiavelli argues, for reasons the very opposite of those endorsed by the classical writers. Spartan economic austerity stemmed from the law-bred severity that Machiavelli recommends for replicating fortune's hostility within political life. Its stability resulted chiefly from the fact that its monarchs restrained the nobles in order to preserve their own power, which thus made the common people their allies – the essence of the advice Machiavelli gives to princes who wish to found their power on the people at the expense of the nobles in chapter 9 of *The Prince*. Both princes and peoples are likelier to achieve stability through an alliance with one another than by relying on the aristocracy, on whom Plato and Aristotle pinned their chief hopes. Hence, a "tranquil" republic, the "best" republic, does not result from the pursuit of the moral and intellectual virtues, as the ancients held – the cultivation of our natural telos through deliberation and statecraft. Instead, it is generated by the repression of human nature by laws that imitate the harsh necessity with which Fortuna in her hostility tries to overwhelm us.

Sparta and Rome appear to embody respectively the alternative modes of approaching Fortuna prescribed in chapter 25 of *The Prince* – caution and daring. As he puts it in *Discourses* 3:9: "Whoever desires constant success must change his conduct with the times." The constancy lies in one's resolve, not in the objects of one's pursuit. Furthermore, as we also know from *The Prince*, although caution and daring can both succeed in certain circumstances, where one is uncertain and the situation perilous, it is better to be daring. Both modes are useful, but impetuosity more closely mirrors the inner dynamism of Fortuna herself.[14] Rome could have taken the cautious path of Sparta, Machiavelli concedes. She could have avoided foreign entanglements

---

[14] Sometimes, though, caution is better. Whenever any extrinsic or intrinsic danger to a republic arises, according to Machiavelli, it may be better to temporize rather than attempt to extirpate it lest one only increase its power. Most such dangers arise not from external threats, but are intrinsic, such as the rise of a "noble youth" of extraordinary merits who becomes the cynosure of all men's eyes, so that they raise him so high that

and conquests, limiting herself to self-defense or at most a secure perimeter of allies, on the grounds that, as Sparta thought, to arm the masses and to add new peoples to one's constitution will necessarily lead to popular upheavals at home and destabilize the republic's internal order. However – and for Machiavelli this is the heart of the matter – she would never have become immortally great:

If (Rome) had been more tranquil, it would necessarily have resulted that she would have been more feeble, and that she would have lost with her energy also the ability of achieving that high degree of greatness to which she attained; so that to have removed the cause of trouble from Rome would have been to deprive her of her power of expansion. (1.6.3)

To draw these points together, let us look at Machiavelli's comparative assessment of the merits of each regime. Sparta with its equality of poverty and martial rigor is the perfection of that law-bred severity and institutionalized necessity set forth in the modes of founding in *Discourses* 1.1. This is not the equality of citizens who, as Aristotle prescribes, rule and are ruled in turn, engaging in a common deliberation about justice and injustice that solicits the cultivation of our moral and intellectual virtues through open discourse and the leisure to reflect. Machiavelli prefers the taciturn Spartans to the chatty Athenians, who lived out the Aristotelian typology in their fruitless lurching from one exclusive regime type to another in a ceaseless din of public disputation. Sparta instead embodies as a regime type the repression of our natural longing for happiness, and therefore degeneration, by an abstract general necessity. Antagonism and repression galvanize the lawfulness that holds the forces and clashing bodies of nature in a dynamic equilibrium. The monarchy restrains the nobles on behalf of the people. The citizens are few in number in order to maintain neighborly cohesion. To reiterate, for Machiavelli, Sparta is the only possible real-world version of what Plato and Aristotle idealize but render fanciful by adding their own superfluous and dangerous concerns with ethical choice and public deliberation. There is no "middle way." You cannot combine a small, austere, self-governing republic with "grandeur of soul." As suggested in chapter 16 of *The Prince*, you can have an austere and orderly

when they regret their error it will be too late to bring him down (1.33). This could be a description of Xenophon's Cyrus.

small republic or an empire that provides the scope and wherewithal for grander virtues of pride and liberality. It is impossible to combine the cultivation of liberality with a moderate political order that eschews imperialism, because it is only by conquering other peoples that a prince can gain the wherewithal to be generous toward his own. Therefore, one must choose between, on the one hand, internal stability with fiscal austerity or, on the other hand, imperialism with liberality. The middle way or golden mean of Aristotle, in which the grander virtues can be exercised within a small orderly polis, does not exist.

At bottom, then, one must decide between Rome and Sparta. Rome could not have been great without the disorder, class conflict, and selfish ambitions that the classics regarded as political vices. Moreover, there is no infallible choice as between Sparta and Rome, only the least bad choice under the circumstances. One or the other may best suit the times. Regimes such as Sparta (or the Venice of Machiavelli's day as he views it) are undermined by the external shock of war and the compulsion to conquer or be conquered, because war invites masterful personalities to assert themselves at the expense of republican equality and unravels collective discipline and social cohesion through the prospect of greater riches and power. Yet as we know from chapter 1 of the *Discourses*, the rise to empire cannot be avoided: Even if you choose a sterile environment in order to breed toughness through labor, the world will crash in on your orderly small republic in the form of external aggressors. Sparta is the best example of a regime that resisted the compulsion to empire, and it is, to repeat, the real-life version of the "best regime" of the classics: Machiavelli cannot even endorse its partial virtues without reformulating it and dispensing with the classical original. A regime such as Sparta is neither too weak nor too strong. It does not threaten others and therefore avoids to the degree possible being menaced by others. It remains quiet at home and the laws forbid expansion abroad.

Such "balance," Machiavelli grants, would be the best political way of life, but it cannot last, because "one cannot balance . . . this thing nor maintain this middle way exactly" (1.6.4). The only fundamental alternatives are rise or decline. Necessity compels a republic – even an inward-looking one like Sparta or Venice – either to expand or go under. Reason has no influence on this cycle. It cannot be transcended by choice, leisure, deliberation, contemplation, or prayer. A republic must recurrently undermine its own constitutional foundations by imperial expansion in order to survive and prosper, as did Rome. If a small republic remains at peace for a long time, this can only be because "heaven" is "so kind that it did not have to make war." To rely on this peace to last forever is to rely on Fortuna in the bad sense of disarming oneself literally and psychologically. Hence the fervor of Machiavelli's mission: he wants everyone to "know how much more (the Romans') virtue could do than fortune in acquiring that empire" (2.1). Even when a regime is so fortunate as to enjoy long-lasting peace, it commonly leads to internal dissension and is "effeminating": we recall from Book 1, chapter 1 of the *Discourses* that the flourishing side of nature in a fertile spot makes men soft, vain, and unruly (the beginning of Aristotelian leisure is the end of public virtue). In another parallel to his advice in chapter 25 of *The Prince* that, in a pinch, impetuosity is to be preferred to caution, Machiavelli here concludes that because there is no exact "middle way" between the archetypes embodied by Sparta and Rome, one must choose "the more honorable part," the course of imperial expansion, wealth, and glory enacted by Rome. Sometimes rest or moderation is better than motion or impetuosity, but rest is only the temporary pause in an underlying and ongoing motion, so when unsure, leap boldly toward honor. We are reminded of those men possessing "greatness of spirit," the prepolitical great men of the state of nature, who began the cycle of regimes. Rome was the one regime that might constantly breed and employ them. In this way, Machiavelli, as it were, encourages the decoupling of prudence from contemplation.

This brings us to the core of Machiavelli's critique of the ancients. A small, neighborly and austere republic may be stable, but it cannot achieve a "high degree of greatness." As we saw in the earlier chapters of this book, the whole premise of the classical therapy for tyranny rests on this: there is an optimal ordering of the political community that mirrors and instantiates the harmony and moderation characteristic of the cosmos. In serving this kind of community, and actualizing the virtues of character that civic life requires, a person achieves such a degree of satisfaction, honor, and repose that tyranny is no longer attractive. Socrates deliberately encourages Callicles and Glaucon to dwell on their most intoxicating expectations from political eminence. He goads them into exploring their dissatisfaction with mere bodily hedonism and encourages their yearning for a political order that would call for and honor their best talents of enterprise and command, a city whose love would be worth possessing and whose nobility would be worth loving. Having stimulated an erotic longing for union with the beautiful and good through political eminence, Socrates then attempts to convince them that only a moderate political order mirroring the cosmic order glimpsed by philosophy will offer their eros an approximation of the repose and dignity for which it yearns – a public *philia* complementing the moderation of private friendship, a reciprocal bond between honorable equals rather than the all-consuming passion of the tyrant to possess one's country as a triumphant lover would possess his beloved. In the very best instance, these lovers of the city will be led by their eros for the beautiful and good through civic virtue toward the philosophic life itself, the noblest of all.

It is precisely the instinct for "grandeur" characteristic of men like Callicles and Glaucon that Machiavelli denies can ever be conjoined with such a moderate political ordering. As we have seen, however, the root of the problem lies in the potential for misunderstanding this grandeur that exists in the "princely" type of men themselves. Because it is human nature to seek satisfaction and tranquility, to follow the erotic longing for completion, it is all too easy to persuade oneself that the world has already provided such a safe haven; that one must only moderate one's passions and bring one's own behavior into accordance with this eternally preexisting unity and harmony in order to be successful and happy. The princely men must therefore be taught not to let themselves be taught about this promised ascent from bodily desires to noble pleasures, a hierarchy of goods mirroring the order of the world. They need method rather than eros; self-consciousness rather than the elaborate civic pedagogy suggested by the *Republic, Nicomachean Ethics*, and other traditional writings. They must reach deeper into the primordial underpinnings of their first, unmediated impulses for success and glory. They must learn that this vital potentiality for grandeur springs from the dynamism and the creativity of disorder, not from the enervation of a delusory success, and so come to see that their best prospect for achieving it is conjoined with an imperial republic whose achievements are constantly fueled and invigorated by its capacity to tap into the disorder of nature through its institutionalized strife. That is why "the greatness of its empire could not corrupt it for many centuries, and (Rome's lawgivers) maintained it full of as much virtue as has ever adorned any other city or republic" (1.1.5), including, of course, the City of God and the *Republic* of Plato.

Because there is no prospect for lasting equilibrium and tranquility, no potential for unity through shared deliberation, politics becomes a matter of making a decision for the least bad alternative. But on the whole, it is better for a republic to be like Rome than Sparta, just as it is better on the whole for princes – who for Machiavelli can double as founders or refounders of republics – to be daring than cautious. Even if necessity, operative through foreign aggression, does not compel an austere republic to expand (a prospect so unlikely that Machiavelli characterizes it as a favor from heaven), her very success in remaining stable would undermine her. Because people are "good" only when acting under compulsion, "continued tranquility would enervate her, or provoke internal dissensions." Just as in his teaching about princes, for Machiavelli it is better for republics to imitate the deeper, underlying hostility of the world than to rely on fortune's occasional beneficent intervals, which make us soft and unruly. In sum, because the best constitution of the ancients is existentially impossible, Machiavelli encourages, as it were, the revolt of the Auxiliaries in Plato's *Republic* and their conversion to a new historical project. Whereas the philosophic truth of the Idea of the Good had to be concealed from these warriors through a mediating education in correct opinion, Machiavelli's war on nature can be offered to them openly and directly as a project worthy of their own ambitious energy. He severs the delicate connection traced by Aristotle between the prudence of practical statesmanship and the contemplative virtues. *Phronesis* as a link between *praxis* and *nous* by way of an architectonic art of statesmanship collapses into the will to master nature.

THE RISE AND FALL OF THE NEW ROME

For Machiavelli, a prudent founder can provide a corrective to too much bounty from nature, turning statecraft, as I suggested earlier, into a kind of human horticulture that cuts back nature's fecundity so as to reinvigorate its roots. Even though power is the goal, to give in to the enjoyment of the rewards of power undermines the vigor and self-control needed to acquire and maintain that power. We must therefore avoid the illusion of the world's beneficence. Here we might detect a connection between what came to be known as the "worldly asceticism" of the bourgeois virtues – the deferral of gratification – and the inwardness and self-denial sought by the Reformation's repudiation of "the theology of glory" (Luther's derogatory term for Thomism), a synthesis arguably indispensable for the emergence of modern liberal democracy.[15] In revolving the comparative merits of a sterile and fertile environment for the founding, Machiavelli is arguing that although nature can be either sterile or bounteous, the sterility is more fundamental. Chance and disorder are the substance, he is arguing, peace and bounty are the accidents, reversing classical metaphysics. To imitate the bounteous side alone must lead to the teleology of the "imagined republics" and the delusion that the passions possess an immanent potentiality for virtue leading us to peace, the eternal, the divine, and their instantiation in a just republic. Therefore, it is more prudent to imitate the hostile and necessitous side. As in his advice to princes in *The Prince*, so, too, in republics, he counsels, founders and statesmen must let the hostility of Fortuna fuel their actions so as to be able to turn the tables on "her" treacherous reversals and fight back. Recognizing that the passions are not a mixture of beast and soul, but all beast, lion and fox, will enable a leader to alternate methodically between their release and control for the sake of maximizing security and well-being.

The classical search for the middle way reflects the orderliness and moderation supposed to be at the core of the world. For Machiavelli, by contrast, nature as Fortuna oscillates between sterility and fertility, necessity and dissolution. Sterility is closer to the truth, which is that the fertility cannot be relied on. We achieve freedom through our consciousness of nature's hostility, which engenders in us the will to fight back. We imitate nature's hostility by distancing ourselves from a reliance on nature. This denaturing or abstraction of self from nature is necessary for mastery. Law, accordingly, far from being subordinate to the regime as it was for Aristotle, supersedes the regime as the core of statecraft. Constitutions are the most useful and efficacious arrangements of political "bodies" subject to the uniformity of law as the controller of hostile chance or, on the other hand, its deliberate reinjection

---

[15] Consider Tawney (1950) and Grant (1991). The complex debate about the meaning or existence of Machiavelli's religiosity is discussed in the Interlude at the end of this chapter.

into the body politic to jolt it out of the enervation and complacency of too long a period of success. In this way, the regime becomes a local historical modality of the law, and the distinction between good and bad regimes is replaced by the criterion of legitimacy.

To collapse the distinction between good and bad regimes as Machiavelli does might seem to restore ancient conventionalism. Although there are similarities between Machiavelli's argument and ancient conventionalism, there are, as we have seen, more important differences, and as we reach the conclusion of this book, it will be useful to summarize them schematically.

According to the Sophists, one can react to the meaning of nature as chance by 1) private vice and the manipulation of convention through rhetoric to create a public appearance of virtue, 2) the defense of convention as a bulwark against the chaos of the state of nature, or 3) embracing tyranny as the most natural way of life. But because the Sophists tend to see nature as the upsurge of spontaneous motions, they doubt that it can be methodically controlled on the political level. Those who claim that it can run into difficulties. Hence, for example, Thraysmachus's search for a *techne* of injustice is frustrated by Socrates' demonstration that *techne* is self-forgetting, not self-aggrandizing, and leads to order, harmony, and beneficence. Protagoras, more insightful, doubts that statecraft is rigorous knowledge at all, seeing it as more akin to a local "way," like picking up a language, analogous perhaps to Burkean "prejudice."

Machiavelli is after much bigger stakes than any of these varieties of ancient conventionalism. In his new science of politics, the disorder of nature is the *source* of political power, stability, and rationality. It can be tapped and channeled by correctly designed institutions. By imitating the impetuosity of Fortuna, we can gain methodical control over "her" reverses by anticipating them, preempting them and fighting back. It is the belief in fixed conventions – in political order – that leads to decay, chaos, and weakness and does not, as Protagoras maintained, act as a bulwark against them. So chance (*tuche*) does not have to be fenced off or concealed under a rhetorical guise that preserves *nomos*. Instead, Machiavelli says: Let chance in; let selective spurts of chaos invigorate and set in motion the levers of power. Statecraft will be more methodical and more consistent if we allow politics to be empowered by disorder. We need not be helpless in the face of the rise and decline of regimes because we will undertake no mistaken search for permanence in the first place whose inevitable failure could disillusion us or catch us off guard. This calls for a new notion of *techne* – not, as it is for Socrates, an intimation of, and path toward, the *taxis* and *sunounia* of the cosmos, a harmony of proportions that grounds subject and object, lover and beloved, citizen and citizen, polis and cosmos (Plato *Gorgias* 506d–e). Instead, *techne* is to be seen as the imposition by man of form on matter, the conquest of nature for the sake of power, the act of resolve whereby a prince, like God, can "introduce into matter whatever form he pleases" (*The Prince* chapter 6). Had Thrasymachus and the other Sophists possessed this concept, they could not have been defeated by the Socratic *elenchus* based on the craft analogy.

I would like speculatively to suggest that Machiavelli's revaluation of the relation between virtue and nature has three main stages:

1. Nature is viewed as hostile and alien to man. Reason is seen as anthropocentric with no immanent link to nature.

2. Having alienated yourself from the world, you must also let the disorder of the world empower your desires while remaining conscious of how the intoxication of those passions can undermine your self-mastery. In the terms of *The Prince*, you must know how to alternate methodically between the lion (allowing the world to empower you) and the fox (reasserting your alienation from the world and from your own passions).

3. A certain strain of Christianity – more Augustinian than Thomistic, arguably more Protestant than Catholic – has paved the way in several senses:

i. It supplies the concept of a radically pure will that is able to create out of nothing and oppose itself to all natural limitations. This power to alienate the will entirely from nature so as to aim at its complete mastery is transferred from the Abrahamic God to the secular prince.

ii. The Abrahamic God's ability to uproot Himself from nature, once transferred to human agency, fortifies man's ability to assert freedom and mastery over nature by treating it as an alien other, as a foe. Classical philosophy could not provide this fortification even if the claims of philosophy were dismantled from its defense of civic virtue because classical philosophy, strictly speaking, has no conception of a pure anti-natural will that parallels that of the Abrahamic faiths. For the ancients, virtuous acts derive from (while bolstering) the proper ordering and

balancing of passions like eros and thumos, while vicious and tyrannical acts stem from (while aggravating) their disharmony. Both virtuous
and vicious acts take place within the boundaries of nature. You can be
educated to pursue eros toward its highest objects, civic virtue and philosophy, thereby directing eros away from tyrannical excesses, but you
cannot extirpate it or step outside of nature. Thumos can be kept at bay
through laws and education, but not overcome or jettisoned. The thumotic man of Platonic psychology is angry, moralistic, self-righteous,
and prone to religious zealotry. For Machiavelli, therefore, he is not
cold-blooded and focused enough; too much lion, not enough fox. He
requires, not *paideia*, but the correct method.

iii. By draining the natural world of transcendental purpose and placing it in the otherworldly Beyond, a certain strain of Christianity already
reduces nature to Fortuna. Once we part ways with our loyalty to that
otherworldly kingdom, we can allow the natural world of purposeless
happenstance already drained of teleological purpose by Christianity
itself to empower us with its sheer force and impulse. These passions
contain no immanent potential for transcendence. Not only can we aim
to control the external world, but we can treat our own inner passions
as pure other, pure foe, or energy to be imprisoned until needed.

In these ways, then, Machiavelli prepares a new synthesis. Reason
can and should still govern the city, just as Plato and Aristotle maintain. Viewing nature as genesis does not require us to view politics as
tragic in the sense that chance and necessity must doom the reason of
the statesman, as in *Oedipus Tyrannus*. The assimilation of reason to
willpower promises to free man altogether from nature, or at least to an
extraordinarily greater degree than anything envisioned by the classics.
The rational clarity of the Platonic Ideas becomes the goal to be imposed
on nature by the willpower of the Abrahamic God's efficient cause, the
power to create ex nihilo, transferred to the secular prince. Because
Machiavelli is not simply seeking to restore classical wisdom, even
its strictly pragmatic political wisdom in contradistinction to its transcendentalist leanings, but is calling for a wholesale transformation of
human and political life and how we understand them, he cannot in my
view be strictly termed an Averroist. More on this later in the chapter.[16]

---

[16] Lukes (1984) makes the simple but telling observation that, despite his admiration for
Roman courage as opposed to modern pacificity, and for the Romans' always being

The foregoing discussion of the *Discourses* scarcely constitutes a full appreciation of Machiavelli's teaching, but it does, I hope, uncover enough of its basic premises so that we can make some broader observations about the theme of empire with which we began this chapter. Machiavelli claims that his *Discourses* open "a path as yet untrodden by anyone," paralleling the exploration of "unknown waters and lands," very likely an allusion to the discovery of the new world. It is an eerie and prophetic parallel because it can certainly be argued that the greatest imperial republic since Rome emerged in the new world and enacted many of Machiavelli's prescriptions. America was indeed a regime founded on the checks and balances among branches of government that deliberately harnessed and played off against one another the power of the people (House of Representatives), the notables (Senate), and the chief executive (Presidency). Its pedigree through Montesquieu, Locke, and Harrington back to the original "Machiavellian moment" (as Pocock termed it) is well documented. The American republic, from its origins, and in keeping with Machiavelli's account of Rome, harnessed the ambition of the common people for a better life and projected it outward so as to forestall internal class strife and a popular assault on the remnants of Old World gentry (the original Whig-Federalist ruling class) while furthering the interests of that class as well. The first object for expansion was the American continent itself through the displacement of the aboriginals and the development of agriculture and commerce through successive waves of immigrants (recalling Machiavelli's description of Hannibal's and Cyrus the Great's capacity to unite "men of all nations"). With the nineteenth and twentieth centuries came the projection of economic and military power throughout the world, accompanied by the crusade to extend the individual's liberty to achieve a better life to all peoples on earth.[17] In all these ways, America embodied Machiavelli's claim that one need not

---

ready to go to war as opposed to his contemporaries' avoidance of it, Machiavelli nevertheless does, in *The Art of War*, endorse the invention of modern artillery as an improvement over ancient and even Roman warfare. Just as he is not against all forms of Christian-era warfare, Lukes argues, he is not necessarily against all usages of Christianity. More generally, I would argue that the project for the mastery of nature guarantees progress in military technology among many new modes of power, and in this sense outstrips the guidance of either pagan political practice or philosophy.

[17] Consider the discussion in Newell (2009) part II.

choose, as the classics had maintained one must, between a virtuous self-governing republic and imperial *oikonomia*; that, on the contrary, the ambitious energies of the people and their love of liberty could be the vehicle for a republic's expansion into an empire in which all classes would benefit.

Whether and to what degree one would assess the American crusade to extend its version of republican liberty to the rest of the world as idealistic, as a justification for power, or some blend of the two is beyond the scope of this book. Clearly it has been all three in varying proportions from one event to another. My task is to offer a judgment about whether and to what degree it is a Machiavellian crusade. The central paradox of the *Discourses*, illustrated by the career of Rome and already implicit in the segments of Book 1 we have considered, is that eventually the expansionist republic has nowhere left to expand, at which point those cravings to enjoy the settled peace sap the vigor of the empire, leading to a disenchantment with honor and war and a longing for the otherworldly peace. Christianity thus emerged as the spiritualization of the universal safety promised by the Augustan principate at its zenith in the Antonine age. It is not clear to me that Machiavelli believed he had found a way whereby even his prescription for a consciously reenacted duplication of Rome's "chance" career could in the long run avoid this inner degeneration and the longing for a counterfactual utopia of permanent peace and safety.[18]

I offer the following inferences in support of this assertion. In the preface to Book 2 of the *Discourses*, Machiavelli depicts the world's virtues as first arising in Assyria, then migrating to Media and Persia, then to Italy and Rome. Greece, the home of philosophy, is omitted, as is Jerusalem.[19] However, after the Roman Empire and its fall, this complete set of virtues finds no new home. We find only fragments of them scattered among France, the Ottoman Sultanate, Germany, and the Saracens. Something about the Roman Empire's rise and fall prevents all the virtues from migrating intact to a new empire. What is that something? It can only be Christianity, a religion that developed

[18] For a thoughtful discussion of the paradox whereby Rome engenders its own subversion, consider Coby (1999).
[19] As Strauss comments, the omission of Jerusalem reveals the rhetorical quality of Machiavelli's reverence for antiquity, because the "Mosaic laws and orders" are arguably "of the most ancient antiquity." Strauss (1969) p. 93.

under the empire and inhabited its dead husk when it fell, replicating its universal political order as a universal eccleisiastical order (*The Prince* chapter 12). In *Discourses* 2.2, Machiavelli begins by making a sharp distinction between the pagan religion of Rome and "our" religion: the Roman religion promotes glory, whereas our religion promotes humility. (He had earlier observed in 1.11 that "whoever reads Roman history attentively will see in how great a degree religion served in the command of the armies, in uniting the people and keeping them well conducted, and in covering the wicked with shame.") He qualifies the contrast between Rome's religion and "ours" by going on to suggest that it is a false interpretation of Christianity to conclude that it must inevitably make us effeminate and unable to defend our country: "And although the world appears to be made effeminate and heaven disarmed, it arises without doubt more from the cowardice of the men who have interpreted our religion according to idleness and not according to virtue" (2.2.2). He then suggests another reason for this effeminization, which shows that there is a link between Rome and the humility-saturated version of Christianity he decries. Through her conquests, Rome extinguished republican liberty everywhere ("eliminated all republics and all civil ways of life"). By extinguishing the spirit of liberty everywhere, the Roman Empire effeminated itself and prevented the world's virtue from finding a new imperial homeland. Finally, in *Discourses* 3.1, Machiavelli remarks that all religious republics will decay with time unless returned periodically to the vigor of the original rise by recurrent refoundings. Although the notion of a religious republic might seem to refer exclusively to modern Christian states, Rome, too, was a religious republic – religion was essential to its success, according to Machiavelli – and the examples he uses to illustrate the need for re-founding are drawn from Rome as well as from modern times. In 3.17, in remarking that officials could commit outrages even during the early republic when Rome "was still uncorrupt," he concludes that "it is impossible to order a perpetual republic because its ruin is caused through a thousand unexpected ways." Although everything possible should be done to return a republic to the vigor of its origins, there is nothing more true than that "all the things of this world have a limit to their existence" (3.1).

Altogether, then, Machiavelli appears to concede that all republics will eventually wane. Even the best-founded republic of all, Rome, whose religion was subordinate to, and a means toward, civic vigor and patriotism, eventually succumbed to its own inner decay. How likely is it, then, that any virtuous republic founded now, in a world already under the sway of Christianity, which for Machiavelli not only does not support citizen virtue and patriotism but actively undermines it, could avoid this eventual decay, if indeed it could ever be founded in the first place?

Machiavelli's writings do contain one possible response to this dilemma, an adaptation of certain strains of Christian political theory and especially that of the emerging Reformation. Machiavelli's strictures against Christianity are abundant and well known: it has effeminated man, subverted his loyalty to the earthly fatherland in favor of the heavenly beyond, and extolled unarmed prophets who fail instead of armed ones who succeed. Yet clearly Christianity was in some sense "armed." As an institutional religion, it had been a great success. As Machiavelli sardonically notes in chapter 11 of *The Prince*, only ecclesiastical authorities "have states and do not defend them; have subjects and do not govern them; and the states, though ungoverned, do not care." Yet rule they did. Christ's teaching might have been "unarmed," and thus brought the unarmed prophet Savanarola to ruin, but could one really characterize it altogether as a political failure, given its enormous authority over the centuries as the civilizational conglomerate of Christendom? In *The Prince*, Machiavelli diagnoses the rise of institutionalized Christendom as the church slowly replaced the decaying husk of the Roman world state with a spiritual world state of its own, primarily based on moral authority but nonetheless equipped with some worldly force.

The crucial element in the Christian spiritual world state's power was its psychological hold over the faithful. This insulated it against many of the dangers of its otherwise feckless pursuit of worldly power and allowed ruthless popes like Alexander VI – arguably one of the most successful statesmen of Machiavelli's era, the master pulling the strings of his son Cesare – to operate free of censure or a candid grasp by others of what they really were. Christianity's psychological hold also undermined the effectiveness of men like Cesare, who would have been capable in the ancient world of any iniquity, yet whose capacity for "well-used" cruelty was rendered fickle and inconsistent by his residual vulnerability to a belief in Christian morality. Similarly, the King of

France failed to consummate a successful invasion of Italy because he needed a divorce, his half-measures as a conqueror accruing to the pope's strategic advantage.

So, in envisioning a new Rome on the rise, it is tempting to see Machiavelli as looking for a new psychological teaching that will compete with Christianity's inner hold on the psyche while maximizing rather than minimizing the new creed's hold on worldly power and success. Might one find a new universal political teaching that was spiritually rigorous but also psychologically "armed"? The very notion of the "modern," a contraction of the Latin phrase meaning "the way of today" (*modus hodiernus*), already gaining currency in the Renaissance, was that one belonged to a party of the like-minded that crossed borders, an emerging new world order based on a belief system in parts both secular and religious bent on transforming Christendom from within, just as Christendom had once transformed the Roman Empire from within. Looking ahead to the unfolding of the Renaissance into the Reformation and the Age of Reason, we might detect here a further conjunction between Machiavelli's own psychology of the inward mastery of nature, and especially of eros, with the rising Protestant demand for a purified, interiorized faith not reliant on the appearances of the world (the "theology of glory") but on God's direct entry into the innermost recesses of the self, paralleling Machiavelli's preference for "touch" over "sight." Aided by the influence of Luther, the self-professed devotee of Augustine in the battle with Thomism, Machiavelli can further draw on the Augustinian extremism of the divide between the City of Man and the City of God, which as we have seen is conceptually so crucial for his new science of politics. In the conjunction between Machiavelli's secular psychology of interior self-mastery through the conquest of eros and the interiorized religious psychology of emergent Protestantism, we can see the outline of the coming alliance between the forces of Protestant reform and the forces of secular modernity (not always clearly distinguishable from one another), launching, as one scholar has suggested, the religious wars of the sixteenth and seventeenth centuries as essentially wars on behalf of Machiavelli and Bacon by their Puritan Republican allies to rid first England and then all of Europe of "kings and priestcraft."[20]

---

[20] Impressively chronicled and analyzed by Rahe (2008).

A new psychology of self-repression for the sake of future gain, the deferral of gratification, is the new spiritual teaching to replace the universality of the original Christian world culture. A part of the genius of modernity is that it is both a concept of the state – the social contract – and a new stateless psychology of individualism that is universal, the product of enlightenment. On the basis of our discussion of Machiavelli's new method for internal self-mastery, we are entitled to call this blend of secular and religious inwardness that first emerges with the Reformation a spiritual or psychological teaching, because it is not reducible to mere appetitive hedonism or materialism. It requires an inner deepening and internalization of the encounter between Fortuna and the will purified of its illusions. The "methodism" implicit in Machiavelli's prescription for the internal mastery of eros is therefore arguably not unrelated to the "methodism" of Puritan meditative exercises for purging the soul of its reliance on the world of fleshly appearances – a fateful conjunction that explains the birth of political modernity coevally with the spread of the Reformation.

In sum, the conquest of one's own inward nature, the conquest of eros, was common to both Machiavelli's new science of politics and to the Reformation, albeit for radically different motivations – in the first case, to maximize worldly power and wealth, in the second case, to maximize our abstention from such worldly goods, including the celebration of nature in its God-infused teleological richness crowned by the *Imitatio Christi*.[21] Historically, however, as has been widely observed, the withdrawal from the world that had originally motivated Protestant spirituality became in time a method for mastering it through commerce. Just as in Machiavelli's psychology, the first step to mastering the world around one was to radically alienate oneself from it and its snares of delusion about the world's natural beneficence. The "bourgeois" virtues of thrift, probity, hard work, and the deferral of gratification, extolled on religious grounds because they might confirm one's position among the chosen or the elect, also happened to be exactly those character

---

[21] According to Tinsley, Luther "became convinced that the 'imitation' of Christ conflicted with the essence of the Christian gospel as he had come to interpret it. He found himself unable to reconcile the presuppositions of the practice of the imitation of Christ with his doctrine of justification by faith. The imitation of Christ he believed must inevitably involve a denial of grace and conceal an incipient doctrine of works." Tinsley (1972) pp. 45–67.

traits most required by a market economy. Hence Tawney's summation of those traits as "worldly asceticism." Although commercial enterprise was not the whole or even the most important of Machiavelli's aims for political life in comparison with the pursuit of honor and liberty, it certainly was one of his aims, and a source of honor in itself.

Still, whatever hopes Machiavelli might have entertained for this new spiritual teaching as the creed for citizens of republics, it would appear to be trumped by his own more fundamental observation, clearly applicable to all places and times, that "all the things of this world have a limit to their existence." We might further observe in this connection that Machiavelli appears to adopt Lucretius's teaching (without its apolitical corollaries) that countless worlds have emerged from the atoms and passed away, worlds stretching infinitely into the past and future that will never be known to us, just as our world will disappear unremembered.[22] Although the eternal substratum of the atoms is so thin and empty of structure or content as to be almost nonexistent, and for this very reason capable of generating an infinite variety of worlds – thereby directly contradicting Aristotle's teaching about the eternity of the completed, visible cosmos just as we now experience it – that substratum is a limit, however evanescent, on man's complete power to re-create the world. As I have argued in this chapter, Christian theology had recognized that even the most minimalistic account of a substratum of unshaped matter still placed too great a set of limiting conditions on God's untrammeled power of creation ex nihilo: although mere inert fodder, it was still something given prior to God's action on it. Therefore, Thomas Aquinas concluded, we must believe that God created unformed matter out of nothing as well, before shaping it in specific ways. In contrast to this teaching about the limitless creative power of God, Machiavelli's endorsement of Lucretius's cosmology of the

---

[22] For a discussion of the influence of Lucretius on Machiavelli and other Florentine thinkers, see Brown (2010). Brown shows how Lucretius's materialistic philosophy was of assistance in criticizing religious superstition and a belief in the afterlife. She also connects what she see as his pre-Darwinian theory of evolution to a dynamic history of the rise of states, and relates the Florentine thinkers' praise of free will to Lucretius's view that the world came about by chance – the same paradoxical relationship I have explored between the prince's freedom to reshape Fortuna by tapping into "her" spontaneity. Still, we must bear in mind that Lucretius's atomism led to a profoundly apolitical stance toward life, whereas his modern followers use the materialistic theory he originated as the basis for political engagement, an enormous transvaluation of values.

underlying atomic structure, and how the clash of atoms generates infinite, utterly irreconcilable worlds, introduces an undertow of insuperable necessity and limitation to his view of the world and an insuperable limit on man's power to master Fortuna absolutely, however much he might radically reshape it. The new prince may indeed be able to introduce form into matter, but not create or re-create matter itself. He may be able, through the introduction of "new modes and orders," to transform the conditions of political existence right down to the ground, but not of existence per se.

Returning to the relationship between Machiavelli's republican prescription and America, might it not be the case at present that, as America extends its power, influence, and economic might to the furthest reaches of the globe, two challenges are emerging to the empire's sway that Machiavelli would immediately recognize? On the margins of the empire, hardier and angrier peoples who have either not tasted the promised material benefits or despise them are stoking the fires of communal honor and a fear of being overwhelmed. These are motives that, as we have seen, Machiavelli certainly appreciates as preconditions for the continued rise of healthy and vigorous republics into a greater historical sphere. More significantly, within the population of the imperial heartland itself, there is arguably growing an ever more powerful counterfactual longing for a global peace, a universal society "beyond" politics with its unedifying compromises and clash of interests – the parallel of that "effemination" that Machiavelli was obliged to concede was inevitable even for Rome. Within today's imperial republic, during the apparently endless sunny noon of its Antonine age, with the legions securing the borders and unprecedented wealth and relaxation enjoyed within them, the citizens grow ever more bored with the republican hardhihood of their origins, ever more enervated through their hedonistic satiation, and ever more attracted to the dream of that coming global paradise when all conflict will end forever.

So there is a sense in which Machiavelli not only showed the route to the new Rome but foresaw its downward spiral. Machiavelli thought that Rome had contained "as much virtue as has ever adorned any other city or republic" and hoped that the rise to such greatness could begin again. However, he knew that even Rome would have to atrophy due to her very success and that even the methodical and conscious imitation of her spontaneous career would carry the danger of this same long-term inner decay. Although Machiavelli argues that the mastery of Fortuna is possible to an extraordinarily greater degree than anything entertained by the classics, he also appreciates that it is ultimately limited and that all things, including the peaks of human greatness, must pass. Life is so structured as to provoke endless desires that are largely foredoomed to dissatisfaction. As he observes in the *Discourses* in a characteristically pseudo-Augustinian tone that nevertheless bespeaks his true conviction, "as human desires are insatiable (because their nature is to have and do everything while fortune limits their possessions and capacity of enjoyment), this gives rise to a constant discontent in the human mind and a weariness of the things they possess."[23] Insofar as he recognizes that all human excellence is impermanent, he remains at one with the classics and offers a sobering reminder that, whatever may be the comparative merits of empire and republic, human or even political perfection is not available on this earth.

INTERLUDE: MACHIAVELLI AND RELIGION

The diversity of perspectives on Machiavelli's stance toward religion deserves its own discussion. Let us begin with what might be taken as examples of Machiavelli's deeply blasphemous impiety.

In *Discourses* 1.25–26, he argues that when a republic reforms itself, the semblance of the old institutions should be maintained, but when one ruler aims at absolute power, "such as the ancient writers called a tyranny," he must "change everything," using modes that are "very cruel." This is in keeping with the godlike scope to create new modes and orders attributed to the most outstanding princes in chapter 6 of *The Prince*. Because Machiavelli has already in the *Discourses* identified such founders (Moses, Romulus) as the founders of republics as well as principalities – indeed, one could say that the republic of the Romans grew out of the principality of Romulus – by implication, they may found republics through the same godlike transformations, in contrast with already-established republics reforming themselves gradually and preserving the old forms. As Mansfield observes about Machiavelli's

---

[23] Compare Augustine's description of the man who is totally immersed in the City of Man as opposed to the man who lives on earth preparing for the City of God (1958) pp. 87–88.

conflation of the prince with the prophet of godlike will with respect to his discussion of the "one prudent orderer" exemplified by Lycurgus: "If Machiavelli had not specified one *man* so prudent, he could have been speaking of a divine beginning at one stroke" ([2001] p. 33).

Such a "prince" (the ancients may have called him a tyrant, but Machiavelli will not) like David or Philip of Macedon (a typical Machiavellian equation of a divinely anointed ruler with a pagan one) will raze everything and build everything anew, make the poor rich and the rich poor, and resettle populations like a herdsman moving his flocks. The biblical quote Machiavelli uses to describe David is actually a description of God himself: "(He) filled the hungry with good things and sent the rich away hungry" (Luke 1.53). This appears both to confirm the godlike scope of the most virtuous prince and to imply that God himself is a tyrant. Whoever does not have the stomach for ruling in this godlike and "very cruel" way, Machiavelli recommends, should remain a citizen reliant on the rule of law and established institutions. Few are wise enough to do so, however, becoming either ineffectual tyrants or lukewarm citizens, because "men generally decide upon a middle course, which is most hazardous, for they know neither how to be entirely good nor entirely bad." This choice between civic virtue and tyranny reminds us of the contrast between Sparta's caution and Rome's boldness, the only true alternatives in contrast with the illusion of the "middle way." If the citizen as described here might parallel Sparta in the earlier discussion, might the godlike tyrant parallel the Roman Republic? For although good to its own people and those taken on as allies, did not Rome, in addition to being founded by just such a tyrant, in conquering others perform many of the same acts of destruction, resettlement, and the transfer of wealth attributed here to David and Phillip of Macedon?

As another instance of almost cavalier blasphemy, let us take Cesare Borgia's use, praised by Machiavelli in chapter 7 of *The Prince*, of his brutal lieutenant Remiro d'Orca. After employing Remiro to suppress civil disorder, allowing Remiro to attract the people's hatred while insulating himself from it, Cesare, peace having been restored, acts as the people's avenger against his own enforcer: "He had (Remiro) placed one morning in the piazza...in two pieces, with a piece of wood and a bloody knife beside him. The ferocity of this spectacle left the people at once satisfied and stupefied." Is a bizarre pantomime of

Christianity implied here? That is, God, the source of so many woes and disappointments for his people, distances himself from them through an intermediary who then dies for "their" sins, but tacitly satisfies the people by allowing them to take revenge on him through the crucifixion of his intermediary.

But we cannot leave it at pronouncing Machiavelli an atheist and blasphemer, for there is still the question about whether and to what extent he recognizes an important role for religion in political life. Moreover, as we have seen throughout this book, Machiavelli's critique of Christianity is shadowed at all times by his revaluation of aspects of its own ontology. Not only is the founder presented in a prophetlike, millenarian light, but so are what I have termed the princes of thought, best exemplified by Machiavelli himself. The divinization of politics is not the equivalent of out and out atheism because it battens off the experience of revelation and recognizes and attempts to fashion a simulacrum of its psychological power.

The preface to part 2 of the *Discourses* gives us a further sense of what it would mean to call Machiavelli a prince of thought. Employing his rhetorical invocation of antiquity, Machiavelli writes that he will "boldly and openly" (perhaps like the Columbus of thought treading an as yet untrodden path in the preface to part 1) compare the virtuous past with the inadequate present, so as to "excite in the minds of young men" the desire to imitate the ancient virtues whenever "fortune presents them with the occasion." In other words, Machiavelli will "excite" the "desire" of potential young statesmen and princes to restore ancient virtue (but not ancient philosophy). He will replace the intermediary role of "the writers" with his own new way of writing, in which historical events take the place of dialectic. In this way, he will prepare them for whatever "occasion" that fortune will present them with, just as he says in chapter 6 of *The Prince* that princes of "outstanding virtue" make use of the occasion Fortuna offers them. It could seem as if, whereas Plato argues that the Idea of the Good, suitably interpreted by his Socrates, might excite the erotic longing of potential statesmen, Machiavelli is arguing that he *himself* will be the source of their excitation, the fashioner of their image of nobility, drawing upon not ancient philosophy but the direct unvarnished experience of ancient nobility. This of course inevitably entails an act of reflection and the projection of something new upon the ancient past, for we cannot actually enter into how the ancients understood themselves and their virtues if we fully jettison their concern with philosophy. Moreover, because Christianity is arguably a valid continuation of aspects of ancient philosophical transcendentalism, and even of the pagan religious longing in late antiquity for the One God, Christianity can claim as readily as Machiavelli's image of ancient virtue to have preserved something fundamentally important from the ancient world and its heritage. Insofar as Machiavelli makes himself a more direct source of inspiration to the young than the ancient writers and reshapes their access to the ancient past, is not his role vis-à-vis these potential new rulers and statesmen not more interventionary, more Godlike, in the Abrahamic sense, than Plato's role as a medium through whose writings the immortally and changelessly true might be glimpsed? Is he not a new kind of prophet? However this may be, whereas Plato and especially Aristotle try to draw young men toward maturity by means of the cultivation of their initially spontaneous longings for nobility, Machiavelli offers to help them directly, as they are right now; to further enflame them with the glories of the past. (The counterpart to his advice in *The Prince* that Fortuna prefers a hot-blooded young wooer.) This willingness to excite the passions of young men to restore ancient virtue stands in sharp contrast with Hobbes, who particularly fears the effects on young men both of ancient authors like Aristotle and of the ancient exemplars of virtue, who in his view flatter their vain conceit that they are fit by nature to rule, only one instance of the narrowing of Machiavelli that Hobbes undertakes in his pursuit of pure political method.

Several representative passages from the *Discourses* further illustrate the complexity of interpreting Machiavelli's stance toward religion. Let us consider them by stages.

1. In the preface to Book 1, he writes: Despite "the general respect for antiquity," it (antiquity) is often "more admired than imitated, or so much neglected that not the least trace of this ancient virtue remains." Readers take pleasure in reading about the ancients, he argues, but do not try to imitate their "noble actions" because they are believed "impossible, as though heaven, the sun, the elements and men had changed . . . and were different from what they were in ancient times." But for Christians, of course, they *had* changed (particularly "heaven" and "men," inasmuch as God had become a man and through his

death and resurrection saved all men from death). Thus, Machiavelli's appeal to reverence for the ancients (including at 2.5.1 a not disparaging reference to Aristotle's view about the eternity of the visible universe while indicating his own preference for Lucretius) masks an attack on Christianity's claims to have transformed man from an honor seeker into a peace lover worshiping the Creator God and Savior.

2. *Discourses* 2.2 discusses the difference between the ancients' education and religion and ours, issuing in a withering critique of ours. Machiavelli writes that ours "causes us to attach less value to the honors and possessions of this world, while the pagans, esteeming those things as the highest good, were more energetic and ferocious in their actions." This is the counterpoint to the preface to Book 1, where Machiavelli argued that we can imitate the ancients because nature has not changed. For as he writes here, what "our religion teaches as the truth and the true way of life" is a mere addition or overlay to a more constant underlying natural leaning toward honor and possessions, a leaning distorted by ancient philosophy as well. The fact that such a teaching can hold us in its grip despite our underlying and constant natural disposition toward honor and gain points to the enormous power of man to re-create appearances, to the point of almost blotting out nature, through the "imagined republics." Machiavelli continues in the same withering vein: "The pagan religion glorified only men who had achieved great glory, such as commanders of armies and chiefs of republics, while ours glorifies more the humble and contemplative men than the men of action. Our religion . . . places the supreme happiness in humility, lowliness and a contempt for worldly objects, while the other . . . places the supreme good in grandeur of soul and body, and all such other qualities as render men formidable; and if our religion claims of us fortitude of soul, it is more to enable us to suffer than to achieve great deeds."

3. Reading on, however, we learn that our religion is but a distortion of the original and true Christian teaching, a seemingly more virile and worldly Christianity that perhaps dovetails with the Reformation's invocation of the pristine origins of the faith (on which more below): "Although it would seem that the world has become effeminate and Heaven disarmed, yet this arises from the baseness of men, who have interpreted our religion according to the promptings of indolence rather than virtue."

4. So far, then, we have been presented with the view that Christianity has irreparably distorted the ancient love of honor, although that love of honor is still underlyingly true about human nature, supplemented by the view that a more honor seeking and patriotic core of the original Christianity might be salvaged, its current distortion owing only to human baseness. Another passage from 2.30.5 completes the dynamic. Here, Machiavelli observes that, owing to the difference between today's republics and ancient republics, we now career between extraordinary defeats and extraordinary victories with no consistency of purpose, because "where men have little virtue, Fortune more signally displays her power." Then the language becomes millenarian. These fluctuations in events will continue until "some ruler shall arise who is so great an admirer of antiquity" that when he rules, Fortune will not be able "to display her influence and power . . . with every revolution of the sun." Precisely because Fortuna is so mutable and unpredictable, she cannot even be relied upon to thwart the return of ancient valor. Indeed, the new prince may "arise" from her very fluctuations and, armed with Machiavelli's teaching, tap into her power and force her into equilibrium. First, Machiavelli argued that we should restore the ancient and enduring natural love of honor as against the wild distortions introduced into human conduct by Christianity. Then he argued that we might salvage a pristine Christianity closer to that natural and enduring stalk, to fortify us against these wild fluctuations. Now he is arguing that the wildness of those fluctuations might occasion the rise of a prince who would transform nature *again*, but this time in a healthy way. (His preference for Lucretian cosmology over Aristotelian may stem from Lucretius's belief that innumerable entirely different worlds have existed in the past and will exist in the future.)

Putting together these passages, then, we arrive at the following stages of Machiavelli's argument: 1) Today's men, however much dominated by Christianity, are wrong to think they cannot restore ancient virtue, because nature has not changed. He silently avoids the fact that, for any believing Christian, nature has been fundamentally changed by the death and resurrection of God. 2) Failing this restoration of ancient virtue, they could at least restore a manlier version of "our" religion. 3) The fluctuations of Fortuna restore on a secular level the transformative dynamic of Christianity by which the death and rebirth of God did change nature, so that Machiavelli can now openly argue that a new prince may emerge who will *further* transform nature for the sake of man's security and well-being. The stages show how Machiavelli's rhetorical appeal to antiquity, initially couched in the view that nature has not changed, gradually drops its mask to reveal a new scope for the transformation of nature prefigured by revelation itself (cosmologically, Aristotle gives way to Augustine, with the place of the Creator God taken by the new prince).

Bearing these permutations in mind, as well as our whole consideration of Machiavelli's relationship to Christianity throughout this book, let us turn to some major interpretative rubrics, including the question regarding Machiavelli's endorsement of the political use of religion.

I agree with Sullivan's view (1996) that Machiavelli criticizes Christianity for sapping worldly patriotism on behalf of otherworldliness. I also agree with her insight that, for Machiavelli, the problem with Rome was that it eventually led to the Caesars, the craving for permanent peace and, therefore, to Christianity. However, I see Machiavelli's prescription for the new Rome of the future rather differently. Sullivan thinks it will avoid religion altogether. As I suggested in this chapter, I think it will provide a new psychological teaching based on the conquest of nature and human nature that will be "armed" where Christianity was "unarmed," but also take advantage of the world-scale politics created by Christendom rather than return to the polis that was the original Roman republic. Certainly Machiavelli does fear that the rise of republic into empire may make a universal state inevitable, and therefore some degree of effemination. But for a republic *not* to rise to empire would consign it to being stagnant like Sparta. So the new Rome will have to rise to empire, but equipped with a new teaching about the self, to a degree coeval with the spiritual interiority promoted by the Reformation, that will stave off effemination. In the long run, though, decline is probably unavoidable for any future Rome, for the reasons I have observed in the conclusion to this chapter.

In contrast with Sullivan, Viroli (2010) argues that Machiavelli promotes a virile Christianity that supports patriotism and worldly success. Many scholars see a connection between this side of Machiavelli and the blend of enhanced secular state power with a purified and individualistic Christianity espoused by the Reformation, such that one could view

Oliver Cromwell, for instance, as both a Machiavellian patriot and a Lutheran man of God (a "godly republican," to use Rahe's term [2008] p. 207). Carty (2006, 2010) sees a connection between Machiavelli and Luther in that both attack the Church and defend the autonomy of the secular state (for very different reasons, of course). Is Machiavelli interested in reforming Christianity? Is he looking for a new, more civically robust version of the faith? My avenue into this debate is Machiavelli's emphasis on psychological interiority and the exercise of the will, desacralized versions of themes so prominent in Augustine. Augustine was, of course, central to Luther and the Reformation altogether in its rejection of Thomism's Aristotelianism-saturated worldly teleology.

Aristotle's political philosophy had become a major force in Europe in the late Middle Ages. It took the form of Thomas Aquinas' adaptation of Aristotle's natural philosophy to Christian revelation, to which it was meant to be seen as squarely subordinate. But it also took a more controversial form as the "Latin Averroism" thought to have influenced Marsilius of Padua, the transmission from Islamic philosophy of an unqualified preference for philosophy and reason over revelation and faith that led Marsilius to argue for an early version of the secular state. The degree to which Machiavelli partook of Latin Averroism is difficult to assess. While no doubt something of Marsilius's endorsement of secular political authority informs Machiavelli's stance, because of what I see as Machiavelli's emphasis on willpower and the conquest of nature – a concept of the will that is, in my view, unintelligible without the Abrahamic concept of God – I cannot view Machiavelli as an Averroist strictly speaking, because he is not simply advocating a return to ancient rationalism. Given what I see as Machiavelli's adaptation of Augustine's view of political existence as dominion (while rejecting his concern with the City of God), combined with his call for the liberation of the human will from the constraints of nature, I do not believe it can be argued that Machiavelli would have settled for the purely worldly, pragmatic side of ancient political rationality even if its most transcendentalist, proto-Christian side could be jettisoned. For even that pragmatic teaching would, from Machiavelli's perspective, still be too confined by the teleological order of nature. Schram (1987) provides a useful discussion of how Strauss and Voegelin lined up on this issue: Strauss argued that the Averroist strain in Machiavelli cast doubt on Voegelin's association of

Machiavelli with Joachism, whereas Voegelin believed Averroism itself, by sundering reason from faith, paved the way for modern totalitarianism along with the gnosticism he sometimes located in Machiavelli.

In his interesting book, Parel (1992) argues that we should see Machiavelli less as a founder of modern political science and more as a follower of the astrological cosmology of the Renaissance, as evidenced by his belief in the "occult" forces of humors. According to Parel, this premodern astrological cosmology was more important for Machiavelli than either the classical or Christian worldviews. For Parel, the determinism of astrological cosmology also affects Machiavelli's view of virtue and fortune. Because this astrology has no place for a cosmic mind like that of classical cosmology or for a sovereign God, humans are free to pursue their desires for riches and glory through their own resolve. Machiavelli's political anthropology, according to Parel, is influenced by the idea that a person's character is fundamentally shaped by bodily "humors," a composite of passion-driven autonomy and spiritual rationality that can be extended from the individual to the larger political bodies of republics, principalities, and empires.

Parel makes many sound points about Machiavelli's anthropology, particularly about the importance of "humors," which combine body, mind, and will in an organic immanentized whole, and therefore constitute, in my terms, a primordialist rather than a transcendentalist conception of nature. However, I do not see how this proves that Machiavelli's anthropology was therefore premodern. For would not many scholars argue that Renaissance astrology was itself a forbear in part of modern natural science? During the Renaissance, arguably, a form of "scientific astrology" began to develop in which court astrologers would blend their forecasts based on horoscopes with actual empirical discoveries about nature. Thus, figures such as Galileo, Tycho Brahe, and Johannes Kepler, credited with having overthrown the old order of astrology and Aristotelian cosmology, were practicing astrologers and scientists at the same time.

Roger Masters (1996) covers similar territory as Parel with his argument that Machiavelli was influenced by Leonardo's ideas about the use of science and technology to benefit human life, but he draws from it the opposite conclusion – that Machiavelli's political science, and that of his successors, is deeply connected with the evolution of modern science and its study of nature. Just as one might observe about Parel that some of his exemplars like Galileo were to some degree already scientific moderns, one might observe about Masters that Leonardo was to some degree still a premodern in his study of astrology and alchemy. My own view is that, although Machiavelli's understanding of nature probably does owe something to Renaissance astrology, and especially to the ancient medical concept of "humors," whether one regards these bodies of knowledge as premodern or (as I am inclined to think) protomodern, his own political ontology is not wholly reducible to any of these influences, but is, in its desacralized Augustinian view of politics as dominion and his emphasis on the will to master nature formerly attributed to God, a unique new synthesis of ancient and modern themes and of reason and revelation.

In an interesting variation on these quandaries, Lukes (1984), although rejecting as self-evidently ridiculous the idea that Machiavelli was a conventionally believing Christian, also argues that the spiritual power of Christianity was one that Machiavelli wished to enlist in his own cause, and not merely reject, which meant that, much as he might have admired the pagan civil religion of the Romans, he neither could nor wished entirely to return to it. Lukes sees in *The Mandragola* a formula by which religious leaders could assist political rulers in spreading the new political science while, precisely because they are religious leaders, they could assist the prince in this way without being "accused of temporal aggrandizement when secretly promoting the aims of the armed politician through careful manipulation of church doctrine. . . . Savanarola's mistake is not that he remains unarmed, but that he does not form a secret alliance with a capable prince." In other words, precisely the apparent otherworldly focus and detachment from power politics of the Christian spiritual leader could be a powerful weapon in promoting the new politics, in contrast with the blatant politicality of the Romans' civil religion. This very much comports with my own view of how Machiavelli wants to make use of the universalism of Christianity while endowing it with new content. If Lukes is correct (and I think he is), then there is a more direct and fungible connection than is sometimes apprehended between Machiavelli and Hobbes's later, more forthright attempt to assimilate the authority of the Church and its teachings to the Sovereign's needs in maintaining the social compact. Of course one should add in the case of Savanarola that, were he to form a secret alliance with a capable prince, the content of his own teaching would have to change as well, presumably in a more Lutheran direction according to which the secular political sphere could be accommodated rather than thundered against for its moral turpitude.

Going to the core of Machiavelli's probable intention, Germino (1966) takes issue with Strauss's interpretation of Machiavelli as a covert "blasphemer," although he does not deny that Machiavelli preferred to focus on the concrete world of the here and now rather than on the world of the hereafter. He relies to an extent on Machiavelli's *Exhortation to Penitence*, an admittedly anomalous work in that it takes the form of a sermon. Now, of course, if one viewed Machiavelli as sensing a possible congruence between his own new science of politics and the side of the rising Reformation that stressed the renunciation of worldly teleology, the enhancement of secular political authority and called for inner self-mastery and the purification of the will, he might well have believed it salutary to associate himself rhetorically with calls for the Church in Italy to reform. His argument in the *Exhortation* that the Church has encouraged "sloth" is certainly in keeping with his praise of labor and strictures against sloth in the *Discourses*, which, as I suggested earlier, although superficially endorsing traditional morality, arguably undermines faith rather than bolsters it by making the labor for material survival more important either than classical contemplation or religious devotion. As for Machiavelli's reminder in the *Exhortation* that nothing in this human realm is lasting – which Germino stresses in order to suggest that Machiavelli is not a rank atheist or blasphemer – that, too, is a theme sounded throughout the *Discourses* and is one that is compatible with any number of secular or pagan philosophies ranging from Plato to Lucretius, as well as with elements of Christianity.

There is certainly a valid debate as to whether Machiavelli is rejecting all forms of religious faith altogether (especially that of his own era), calling for the restoration of a Roman-style civil religion, or calling instead for a return to the spiritual purity of Christianity in its earliest form, deemed by Viroli not to be incompatible with worldly patriotism. Pellerin (2006) provides an interesting twist on Machiavelli's qualified receptiveness to some versions of Christianity with his argument that Pope Alexander VI is favored by Machiavelli as the kind of religious leader who might reunite Italy. My own view is that Machiavelli is attempting to provide a new, psychologically "armed" teaching to replace the "unarmed" teaching of Christianity, based on the inward and outward struggle to master nature. It is a teaching that possesses the universality of Christianity while eschewing its unworldliness and pacifism and is at the same time compatible with the spread of commercial materialism and self-interest, the liberation of the secular state from ecclesiastical interference, and with the emerging trend of the Reformation to seek to purify Christianity by turning away from worldly teleology and its celebration of the visible splendors of nature crowned by the *Imitatio Christi* and returning to the inwardness often associated with Augustine. The conjunction between Machiavelli's secular promotion of inwardness and Luther's spiritual promotion of it is, as a long and varied literature testifies, a watershed moment in which the growth of secular political power, the expansion of market societies, and of religious Protestantism unfolded in tandem, captured by Tawney's phrase "worldly asceticism." Two recent, somewhat but not entirely complementary books have contributed fresh perspectives on this debate. Gillespie (2009) takes the view that modernity did not seek to eradicate religion but to evolve a new understanding of its place in society. Although he makes this case with respect to Ockham, Petrarch, Erasmus, Luther, Descartes, and Hobbes, I believe it could be made with respect to Machiavelli as well, in the qualified sense I am arguing here. Beiner (2010) takes the more familiar view that modernity regarded revealed religion warily, as a source of zealotry and intolerance, but also recognized its value for a civil religion and code of culture that would ground liberal individualism and elevate it above mere material self-interest.

I have no quarrel with de Grazia's argument (1994) that religiously derived motifs run throughout Machiavelli's writings. Machiavelli certainly does present a speculative cosmology within which are ranged the forces of fortune, virtue, the rise and fall of states, the limitations placed by time and fortune on human aspiration, and the meaning of virtue and vice. I have argued specifically that Machiavelli adapts and reconfigures Augustinian conceptions of dominion and will. But the point is that they are religiously *derived*, not religious in their intrinsic content. If I am right that Machiavelli's political science is based essentially on Augustine's City of Man bereft of the City of God, then it would not be surprising that he shadows the theologian in multiple ways. This is not tantamount to Machiavelli himself writing from the stance of religious revelation, however. Moreover, some of his cosmo-logical speculations draw much more forthrightly from pagan thinkers such as Lucretius than from any element of recognized Christian theology. I agree entirely with Nederman (1999) who, in adding to the line of argument begun by de Grazia, emphasizes Machiavelli's focus on freedom of will as a religiously derived theme. Again, though, I would argue that Machiavelli extracts the power of the will from the Augustinian conception of God so as to transfer it to the secular prince in a way that no form of religious belief or earlier theology could have advocated.

Finally, turning to the issue of the specific connection between Machiavelli and Luther, Maddox (2002) argues: "From quite different motives, both set out to deconstruct the political authority of the Church of Rome and both adopted an appeal to antiquity over the head, as it were, of the medieval Christian establishment." A similar position is taken by Figgis (1960), who, in Maddox's words, saw in Luther "an accomplice to Machiavelli's aggrandizement of the secular prince." Although Luther was appealing to the pure origins of Christianity and Machiavelli was appealing to the pure origins of ancient republicanism, they could make common cause in their critique of the contemporary Church. Was this a conscious alliance? Carty (2006, 2010) believes that, although we can be fairly certain Machiavelli knew about the Lutherans, there is no explicit evidence that Luther knew about Machiavelli. Guicciardini, Machiavelli's contemporary, wrote sympathetically about Luther, symptomatic of Florentine anticlericalism. Viroli (2010) believes that Machiavelli "knew about Luther and the Lutherans" but that he was not interested in their specific program for reforming the Church, wanting instead "a God who would help the men of his own time, and those of times still to come, to rediscover their love of liberty and the inner strength demanded by a free way of life." Many scholars, of course, would see the Reformation as more fertile ground than the Church of Rome for this new view of Christianity as an ally of the love of liberty, and I share that leaning. I am not primarily dwelling in this book on the detailed connections between Machiavelli's and Luther's respective defenses of the autonomy of the secular state (for Luther's side, see Carty op. cit.), but instead on this psychology of "inner strength" that both extol.

Gilbert ([1984] p. 193) makes an intriguing observation about the kind of modern leadership "elect" envisioned by Machiavelli. Whereas the traditional view of Fortuna, he writes, was that she chose her favorites capriciously and that nothing could alter her choice, "in contrast to the static quality inherent in the belief in the existence of Fortuna's elect, Machiavelli's formulation presumed the dynamism of a constantly changing scene in which sudden action can bring about the existence of Fortuna." This would also be an important way in which Machiavelli's "elect" of princes or would-be princes successful in imposing their will on nature would differ from the "elect" of Lutheranism or Calvinism, a preordained conferral of grace that no worldly action can alter, although, as Tawney observed, in the sheer vacuum opened up by the Reformation between the sole individual and a distant God, with the world in between drained of Thomistic teleology and natural order, in practice those who were successful, particularly in commerce, came to view that as some kind of marker for their presumed membership in the Elect. I add some further observations about Machiavelli's envisioned leadership Elect in the general Conclusion.

CONCLUSION

Tyranny Ancient and Modern

THE MANY FACES OF MACHIAVELLI

As we have considered throughout this book, Machiavelli has many faces, and attempting to detect the true or truest one has generated a highly stimulating interpretive literature. An early response to Machiavelli saw him as a teacher of evil, lending Satan the name "Old Nick" for "Niccolo," while the stage Machiavel became a familiar figure in the dramas of Marlowe and Shakespeare, whose Iago says he will follow and improve upon "Machiavel's murd'rous intent." From the outset, however, the evaluation of Machiavelli was mixed. Francis Digby, in his 1685 translation of the *Education of Cyrus*, recommended Xenophon by stressing his resemblance to "Machiavel" and the wisdom of his "Florentine Prince." In other words, he reversed the trend we noted in Chapter 5 with regard to Machiavelli himself: whereas Machiavelli lent his own cause respectability by invoking the ancient Socratic, Digby praises the ancient thinker on the basis of his resemblance to the Renaissance modern. As we earlier observed, Bacon and Spinoza admired Machiavelli's political realism and the benefits this worldly approach might confer. James Harrington in *Oceana* extolled Machiavelli's preference for republican liberty in contrast with Hobbes's endorsement of an absolute monarchy indistinguishable from tyranny, which calls into question the tendency to see Hobbes as Machiavelli's direct and most systematic successor. By the same token, state-building despots ranging from Henry VIII (whose future *eminence grise*, Thomas Cromwell, was said to have discovered Machiavelli's *Prince* while living in Europe) to Hitler and Stalin have all been alleged (probably apocryphally) to have kept Machiavelli's handbook for tyrants close by for consultation.

Given his range of influences, one scholar has understandably been prompted to ask: Will the real Machiavelli please stand up?[1] Throughout *The Prince* and the *Discourses*, we find Machiavelli extolling both principalities and republics; exhorting Florence to reassert her ancient republican love of liberty; urging other states to do the same, frequently at one another's expense; advising foreign princes how Italy might be reunited through conquest; and criticizing the French invader Louis XII for his mistakes in attempting to do so, as if to suggest someone else should have another go at it. He advises tyrants on how to crush their opponents and republics on how to avoid or overthrow tyrants. He presents the same men under one aspect as the founders of principalities and from another perspective as the founders of republics. He also suggests that republics, following the model of Rome, might institutionalize periodic refoundings by princely personalities in the garb of leading statesmen so as to restore republican vigor and combat effemination. If security and well-being are the aims of all statecraft, the means to achieve them can be many and various – princely or republican; through self-liberation or liberation from without. What matters above all is that politics be this-worldly. Hence Machiavelli's invocation of the love of the fatherland meant to encourage an attachment to the earth, to the love of one's own, as the prerequisite for any successful version of statecraft, whether its outcome is republican, princely, or imperialistic. *The Prince* and the *Discourses* examine different modalities embodying this same underlying purpose.

Reconciling these various dimensions of Machiavelli's new science of politics shows, in my view, why political theorists should perhaps pay more attention to the ontological underpinning of an argument, rather than assessing it purely in terms of its positive, pragmatic advice – that is to say, to trace these dimensions back to an underlying ground, a fundamental characterization of reality, beyond which or behind which there is no antecedent premise. In this book, I have suggested that Machiavelli's political ontology has at its core the proposition that Fortuna might be mastered. As we have also seen, this capacity of a secular prince to strive to stand outside of nature entails, paradoxically, the complete immanentization of sound statecraft within nature as a

---

[1] Matteo (2007) p. 245. For a detailed discussion of Machiavelli's reception through his earliest translators, see Anglo (2005).

time-bound process of existence. For once nature has been drained of teleological transcendence, first by the more Manichean strain of Augustinian (as opposed to Thomistic) Christianity, and then in purely worldly terms by Machiavelli, all that remains is temporal existence. In this sense the "new prince" can be seen as incarnated in nature and launched on a project to bring power, prosperity, and liberty to the world, reanimating what Machiavelli hopes is the declining world state of Christendom just as Christianity had originally reanimated the world state of Rome.

There is a paradox here that bears a family resemblance to theology. Machiavelli is arguing that the prince must strive to stand outside of nature so as to master it. But insofar as there is no transcendental ordering of the whole, everything, including the will of the prince, falls within time-bound existence. The will of the prince is meant to master the primordial realm of origination by means of methodical rationality, yet will and reason are entirely immanentized within the primordial realm of genesis, chance, and motion. This paradox is akin to the difficulty of distinguishing between the notions that God "creates" and "reveals." In the first case, God stands outside of the world and fabricates it. In the second case, something issues through God or from God. From the second perspective, applied to Machiavelli, one might say that the entire world, human and nonhuman, including the will of the prince in its interior dance with time, is Fortuna, which may shed some further light on the intriguing remark of Leo Strauss discussed in Chapter 6 that Fortuna "reminds one in some respects of the Biblical God." We might already detect how Machiavelli's successors try to resolve this theological paradox in exclusively this-worldly terms by embracing and intensifying one side or the other of it: Hobbes's radical bifurcation between will as fabrication and nature as purposeless spontaneity, on the one hand, and, on the other, Spinoza's view of nature evolving continuously into a life-world that contains will and reason within its temporal fold.

If, to reiterate, the aim of Machiavelli's new political science is security and well-being for both princes and peoples, that aim can involve any or all of the apparently contradictory means and policies that can be attributed to Machiavelli. More fundamentally, just as the ontology of the Platonic-Aristotelian tradition – the priority of rest over motion – can radiate in many directions (the best regime as monarchy or aristocracy, an education in civic virtue, a private life of well-ordered pleasure, happiness through philosophizing), Machiavelli's reversal of it into the priority of motion over rest (whereby political "perfection" can be achieved through "chance" and "the aid of events") can radiate in many directions as well. The difference is that, in Machiavelli's political ontology in contrast with that of the ancients, there is no overarching transcendent unity – the One or the Good. As a consequence, each modality of statecraft must stand side by side with the others in its own existential space. Machiavelli's ontology is, so to speak, horizontal rather than hierarchical. Not until Rousseau, when the modern ontology of motion is conjoined *with* the pursuit of erotic fulfillment, is there a similarly rich flowering of alternatives out of the same fundamental vision.

Hence, there is no single "real" Machiavelli whom we can expect to stand up. Machiavelli is at once the Florentine patriot and the champion of Italian unification, but also the amoral advisor to whoever seeks power, including a foreign conqueror. Machiavelli is the champion of republican self-government – the antecedent for the vision of an expansionist, Atlanticist commercial republic – and first formulated the theory of checks and balances later transmitted by Montesquieu to the American Founders. But he is also the defender of the social contract between an absolute princely ruler and the ruled based on self-interest and the protection of property, anticipating the doctrine of the Sovereign in Hobbes's *Leviathan*. At the same time, Machiavelli's view that everyone, the common people included, has a natural desire for survival and prosperity leads away from Hobbesian-style political absolutism and toward the notion that governments can be representative, based on an appeal to voluntary assent by citizens to ensure their own well-being as individuals, the classical liberalism of Locke. However, a dark corridor also runs from Machiavelli's endorsement of force and fraud in the act of founding new modes and orders to Hobbes's Sovereign with his capacity to inflict terror and on from there to Rousseau's Legislator, and thereby in a sense to modern totalitarianism, inasmuch as human nature must be thoroughly transformed and provided with entirely new ways of life at the expense of all previous loyalties. Still, for reasons I will explore in this Conclusion in due course, although totalitarianism does partake of an element of Machiavelli's summons to the conquest of nature and human nature, no truly millenarian and utopian vision of revolution of the kind necessary to explain the Jacobins, Bolsheviks, and Nazis appears until Rousseau. Or, as we might put it, Machiavelli is open to brutality, but not to sentimental brutality. His more direct heirs among the tribe of despots are not revolutionary fantasists like Robespierre, Hitler, or Stalin, ushering in by means of genocide the global nirvana of absolute equality and collectivism, but modernizing despots like Kemal Ataturk, the last shah of Iran, or Vladimir Putin – Hobbesian Sovereigns in practice.

For Machiavelli, then, it depends on the situation whether security and well-being can best be maximized by republican liberty, princely control, an expansionist empire, or even by conquest and unification from without.[2] Any of these are preferable to the effeminacy and instability created by Christianity and the Church, the only institutions Machiavelli consistently criticizes in every context, although, as we observed in Chapter 7, the universal (albeit psychologically "unarmed") state created by Christianity does up the ante for the scope of

---

[2] Machiavelli does not always favor republics over principalities, or the overthrow of principalities in order to establish republics. Although some republics like Rome were for a time capable of being restored to liberty from an interval of corruption ("losing the head while the trunk was still sound"), some peoples under princely rule have been so thoroughly corrupted that it would be better for the current prince to be replaced by another prince than for them to try to live as a republic (*Discourses* 1.17). As Gilbert observed in a still valuable work (1954), quoting Ranke, it is arguable that Machiavelli thought Italy's condition to be so desperate that even conquest and unification from without was an acceptable cure. A good example of Machiavelli's indifference as to whether Italy is unified by a prince or a republic is chapter 4 of *The Prince*, in which Machiavelli segues from Pope "Alessandro" in chapter 3, patron of Cesare and a master manipulator, to "Alessandro" (the Great's) conquest of Asia. Unification faces two challenges: centralized states like that of Darius or the Ottoman Sultan that, although hard to conquer, pass intact into your hands and are easy to maintain, and decentralized states like France, which are easy to conquer but, owing to their many feudal statelets, and hence their memory of independence, are hard to hold until the local noble bloodlines are extinguished, as the Romans demonstrated. Machiavelli's Italy is both decentralized because of its many small states (like France) and centralized owing to the Church's authority (like "Asia" or "the Turk"). A new "Alessandro" will have to find a way of combining both modes of occupation – perhaps by being less of an otherworldly ruler like the pope and more of a worldly one like the sultan, who combines secular and religious authority, an expansion of secular state power that was already emerging in the sixteenth century owing to Luther and the Reformation and was to some extent a return to the Caesaropapism of the early Christian and Orthodox emperors.

Machiavelli's own envisioned new modes and orders. The "desire to acquire," guided by a psychology of internalized method for the mastery of nature, most easily combinable with the interiority of Protestantism as opposed to the celebration of nature crowned by the *Imitatio Christi* found in much of Catholicism (and we may recall that, in parting with Thomism's "theology of glory," Luther saw himself as returning to the ascetic purity of Augustine), may generate a new teaching that is both spiritual inasmuch as it spreads through the influence of modern ideas and, psychologically speaking, is not "unarmed" because it is free of the delusions that lead us to relying on Fortuna.

That all said, however, I believe that, among these various alternative modes of rule, there is a definite preference on Machiavelli's part for a vigorous republic that is able to resist encroachment from without by being able to expand and absorb other regime principles in a flexible, dynamic mixture of powers, the model of which is Rome, the city that contained "more virtues than any other republic," including, of course, the republic of Plato and the republic of God. "Rome" comes closest to combining, within its dynamic evolution, all of Machiavelli's other endorsements of princely, republican (in the small-scale Spartan sense), and imperial rule, whereas no single one of those other modes can likewise be said to embrace all the others. The teaching on republics in the *Discourses* is, accordingly, more comprehensive than the teaching on princes in *The Prince*, because the teaching on republics can comprehend the teaching on princes – they are in the best instance the founders or refounders of republics, while their vigor can resurface in leading citizens like Manlius Torquatus defending the rigor of the law – whereas the reverse is not the case, although this does not mean that in certain circumstances a lone prince who can establish internal order would not be the preferable alternative to a republic less adroit or more corrupt than Rome. Altogether, because princely personalities emerge periodically in republics as refounders, the *Discourses* has, as it were, the best of both worlds, the comprehensive teaching on both republics and princes. Moreover, because it is more comprehensive, the *Discourses* is in my view a more overtly philosophical work than *The Prince*, and, as we have earlier observed, contains speculations about fortune, human nature, and time in more explicitly philosophical terms than does the shorter work. It is also more speculative because, whereas *The Prince* is addressed (at least ostensibly) to an established ruler, the *Discourses* is addressed to potential princes, the two young men to whom it is dedicated. ("I . . . do not address myself to such as are princes, but to those who by their infinite good qualities are worthy to be such").[3]

Having made these general observations about how, in my view, the many influences of Machiavelli flow from a core ontological stance, I now want to consider some of those individual pathways. Let us begin with the best known and the most accessible, the tradition of the "stage Machiavel." It is most directly identifiable in Marlowe's *The Jew of Malta*, where Old Nick himself opens the play with the remark: "I count religion but a childish toy/And hold there is no sin but ignorance." Although the first line is an oversimplification – Machiavelli regarded the psychological hold of religion as truly formidable, not a childish toy – the frankness with which it portrays Machiavelli as an atheist must point to a widely held view of him some sixty years after his death. The second line, "there is no sin but ignorance," which implies an antithesis between wisdom and religious faith, is more interesting. For the reverse would be "there is no virtue but wisdom," which is to that faith is not a virtue; that wisdom can be achieved without faith. As I observed in Chapter 6, the line is arguably a gloss on Machiavelli's remark in chapter 12 of *The Prince* where, alluding to the preaching of Savanarola to the effect that Italy was easily invaded by the King of France because of its sins, he sardonically writes: "He who told us that our sins were the cause of it told the truth, but they were not the

[3] Strauss's judgment about the comparative merits of *The Prince* and the *Discourses* is nuanced. He begins by arguing that it is "prudent" to assume that Machiavelli's "teaching in either *The Prince* or the *Discourses* is all-comprehensive." However, he qualifies this by observing that whereas *The Prince* is a "call to action" to liberate Italy, the *Discourses* is "leisurely" because it is aimed at the development of "potential princes," particularly through a meditation on "the spirit of antiquity." Leisure is the precondition for philosophy, and, in this sense like the *Republic*, the *Discourses* is aimed toward potential leaders, not actual ones. In this regard, therefore, its scope would appear to be both broader and more contemplative than that of *The Prince*. Finally, as Strauss observes, although "we find in the *Discourses* a number of statements to the effect that republics are superior to principalities, we do not find in *The Prince* a single statement to the effect that principalities are superior to republics." This would comport with my view that the teaching of the *Discourses* is both more philosophical and more republican. Finally: "Princes are superior to peoples as regards the founding of states, peoples are superior to princes as regards the preservation of states." Assuming that preservation (which includes refounding) is even more important than founding, this would put the *Discourses* ahead of *The Prince*. Strauss (1969) pp. 22, 25.

sins he imagined, but those which I have related. And as they were the sins of princes, it is the princes who have also suffered the penalty." In other words, the sin of princes is ignorance about the "effectual truth" of statecraft, specifically of the chapter's general maxim that, because there cannot be good laws without the enforcing power of good arms, we should omit the discussion of good laws entirely and focus only on how to acquire the arms. This maxim constitutes another reversal of the classics, for whom military policy, if discussed at all, should only be a subordinate factor in a city's just constitution because focusing on it too prominently might elevate the aims of foreign policy, warfare, and conquest over those of internal self-government.

Living in the wake of the Enlightenment, where we might view the maxim of Marlowe's Machiavelli ("there is no sin but ignorance") as a droll drawing room quip savoring of Metternich or Kissinger, we need to reimagine how shocking many people would still find it in early modernity. In stark contrast with classical philosophy, which held that wisdom was the highest human aim, the Abrahamic faiths uniformly proclaimed it the height of pride and folly to suppose that the study of nature by the unaided human intellect could achieve wisdom in the absence of divine authority. Indeed, human observation and learning on their own were likelier to compound one's ignorance, like one who mistakes a stick bent by its reflection in the water for the real thing. As the Ecclesiast wrote in a sentiment that might be admired by pious Jews, Christians, and Muslims alike: "My son, be admonished: of making many books there is no end, and much study is a weariness of the flesh. This is the end of the matter; all hath been heard: fear God, and keep his commandments; for this is the whole duty of man." For the biblical faiths, reliance on any merely human wisdom about nature virtually summed up the meaning of sin, whereas a disavowal or avoidance of such knowledge, far from being (as Marlowe's Machiavelli would have it) the *only* sin, reflected a humility appropriate to man's fallen condition in contrast with the vainglorious pursuit of knowledge without obedience to God. Hence, the maxim placed by Marlowe on Machiavelli's lips would truly have been a Count Floyd moment for many theater-goers – very scary! Its shocking quality becomes clearer when we recall that man was expelled from Eden for wanting to eat from the tree of knowledge. In this acute sense, from a religious perspective, ignorance, or at least ignorance about philosophy, far from being the only sin, is arguably the only virtue, and the pursuit of knowledge absent a submission to God the only vice. Of course, we must bear in mind at the same time that the Marlowe Machiavelli's implicit defense of wisdom over ignorance is of the *new* wisdom of man's capacity to master nature, in this respect as alien to the classical understanding of wisdom as it is to the biblical faiths.

Machiavelli is mentioned by name in several of Shakespeare plays ("Am I politic? Am I subtle? Am I a Machavel?" asks the Host in *The Merry Wives of Windsor*), perhaps most notably when Richard III claims that, in his capacity for deceiving others, he can outdo Machiavelli himself ("set the murderous Machiavelli to school"). Richard's ability to "frame (his) face for all occasions," to "add colours to the chameleon" and change "shapes with Proteus," certainly does recall Machiavelli's maxim in *The Prince* that one must appear to cultivate all the virtues for their own sake while not actually doing so, because "all see you, few touch what you are." Still, the capacity for deception, ruthlessness, treachery, and murder does not in itself add anything fundamentally new to our understanding of human behavior that is not found either in the Bible or the classics. People were well aware of this side of human behavior before Machiavelli appeared to openly endorse it, and aspiring tyrants and glory seekers had always acted on it and were known to have done so. In my view, the deeper and more distinctively Machiavellian portrayal of the new prince in Shakespeare's plays is not Richard III but Henry Bolingbroke in *Richard II*. This play captures as perhaps no other of Shakespeare's plays does so clearly the passing away of the old politics of the classical/Christian conglomerate and the emergence of the new prince called for by Machiavelli, even though that transition is set anachronistically in the fourteenth century (not the only time Shakespeare uses the past as a way of commenting on the Tudor and Elizabethan present). Old John of Gaunt depicts the classical/Christian conglomerate rooted in the soil of the island kingdom: "This seat of Mars/This other Eden, demi-paradise, this fortress built by Nature for herself . . . This nurse, this teeming womb of royal kings" (2.1). Nature is beneficent, orderly, and self-regulating, producing kings by hereditary descent whose Christian legitimacy prevents corruption and usurpers from arising. We might recall Machiavelli's brief depiction of hereditary principalities in chapter 2 of *The Prince* – one emerges much like the last, like one brick being laid upon another in a wall.

Richard II, by contrast, is a prime example of Machiavelli's observation in the *Discourses* that men in general "do not know how to be either altogether wicked or altogether good," preferring to "take certain middle ways that are very harmful" (1.26). Richard is neither entirely good nor entirely bad, and this ambivalence invites his overthrow. He insists on his divine right and the absolute obedience to which it obliges his subjects. Yet by ordering the Duke of Gloucester's death and stripping Henry Bolingbroke of his inheritance because he fears that Bolingbroke aims to expose his guilt for this political murder, Richard undermines his own legitimacy and the principle of hereditary right. It is Richard himself who subverts the beneficent teleological order eulogized by John of Gaunt, sealing his own doom. As the Duke of York laments, when a king undermines the just treatment of subjects and the hereditary principle he is pledged to uphold, all authority is thereby subverted from the crown on down (2.1.195–200). From Machiavelli's perspective, we might say that Richard is riven by the same vacillation and inconsistency as Cesare Borgia – while capable of ruthlessness, he at the same time clings to the very morality he has undermined. Like Richard specifically, Cesare as depicted by Machiavelli uses deception and violence against opponents yet relies on hereditary descent, in this case his peculiar legitimacy as the natural son of Pope Alexander. He is thus, in Machiavelli's depiction, an unsuccessful halfway house in contrast with Hiero of Syracuse's "well-used" cruelty in slaughtering the entire nobility at one go. Richard, too, from Machiavelli's perspective, should either have ruled justly – for the reputation for justice, we recall, can be a source of power – or have been much more consistent in his use of force and fraud, throwing off the veneer of divine right and the feudal obligations to primogeniture until his power was absolutely established, at which time he could have history rewritten so as to reinstate his legitimacy in terms of the traditional virtues. Instead, he is "Machiavellian" only in the superficial sense that he has parted with a sense of shame over political murder and treachery, but has not parted with his reliance on Fortuna as the source of his throne by hereditary descent. He is half evil: the Duke of York complains that Richard is addicted to "fashions in proud Italy/Whose manners still our tardy-apish nation/Limps after in base imitation," a slightly anachronistic reference given that the play is set in 1327, but for its Elizabethan audience with its still awakening exposure to the Renaissance, perhaps a suggestion that Richard's addiction to this more sophisticated foreign culture has helped corrupt him and rob him of the stalwart decency of old England.

It is Bolingbroke who grasps Machiavelli's new princely methodology of the lion and fox, the cold-blooded alternation between force and fraud. Even before he sends Bolingbroke into exile, Richard voices the suspicion that he has been courting the common people. When Bolingbroke returns to lead a rebellion that has already broken out, his advance is relentless and silent, like a shark speeding beneath the water. He claims that he only wants his inheritance restored, but we know that others like Northumberland already see him as a future king. Initially, he neither encourages nor discourages them in this expectation. Soon after, however, he begins referring to himself as a "prince" whose bloodline is as legitimate as that of Richard, upping his claim from mere nobility to royal competitor. While professing that he has returned to *rescue* Richard from the rebels, perhaps with some implication of a new entente between crown and nobility, he executes Richard's captured ministers as if he were already king himself. He maintains this outward ambivalence about whether he will restore Richard or depose him until the very end, when, having methodically stripped Richard of his allies, he is in a position to depose him without opposition or risk, a perfect example of Machiavelli's recipe for the alternation between the lion (in this case, an outward profession of loyalty to a just cause, the "rescue" of Richard) and the fox (an inner calculation of pure self-interest). As Bolingbroke makes his steady headway, Richard careens between overconfidence and despair. He relies on Fortuna in the form of the armies and allies he deludedly believes are coming to save him, then is absolutely crushed when Fortuna betrays him in the form of their desertion to Bolingbroke, driven at length to the mad excess of believing that he can summon a host of angels to his rescue. As his power slips away, he is increasingly captive to the delusion of the "imagined republics," specifically the divine right of kings that he himself has subverted, a phantasm of principle that is entirely, to use Machiavelli's term, "unarmed."

Especially striking is the contrast between Bolingbroke and Richard in the use of speech and rhetoric. Bolingbroke is terse in issuing orders and taking counsel, saying only what is necessary to advance his cause. Although he will justify himself in public to his followers, he indulges in no lengthy private soliloquies about the meaning of his life, emotions, and beliefs. In this, I believe he is a more profoundly Machiavellian portrayal by Shakespeare than those superficially more recognizable and widely regarded as such, including Iago and Edmund, both of whom revel privately at length in their treachery and cynicism, and relish the revenges they are plotting against the mighty. Bolingbroke best exemplifies Machiavelli's new prince because he will not allow himself to become enthralled by the spell of his own rhetoric, to fall in love with claims about the justice of his cause, or to blind himself with moral zealotry over the evil of his opponent. Cold at the core, he projects his rhetorical effects to his followers like a movie on a screen. As Machiavelli advises, the prudent prince will not fall prey to believing in the nobility and beauty of his own claim to rule: he understands the need to purge from his inner motives this erotic longing for the kind of immortality through a noble reputation extolled by moral philosophers. The victor can write his own history later.

Richard, by contrast, who is neither perfectly good nor bad, becomes ever more loquacious, ruminative, and introspective as his royal power drains away, ever more saintly as his only remaining prop is the whim of Fortuna, which he misinterprets as the invisible support of God. Shakespeare employs Richard's utter folly and delusion about what it really takes to be a prince as the source of some of the most beautiful poetry in any of his plays, with a marked Augustinian resonance in its emphasis on the frailty of man in his worldly pomp when confronted with the ravages of mortality and time (3.2):

"For within the hollow crown
that rounds the mortal temples of a king
keeps Death his court and there the antic sits
scoffing his state and grinning at his pomp
allowing him a breath, a little scene
to monarchize, be feared and kill with looks,
infusing him with self and vain conceit
as if this flesh which walls about our life
were brass impregnable and humored thus
Comes at the last, and with a little pin
bores thorough his castle wall, and farewell king!"

The consolation of mystical insight for the foolish loss of worldly power is an irony that Machiavelli might well appreciate.

The bookend to John of Gaunt's vision of the teleological beneficence of England under the classical/Christian conglomerate, a symbol
of the old politics, is the Gardener's speech (3.4), the symbol of the
new Machiavellian politics embodied by Bolingbroke, now Henry IV.
Whereas Gaunt praised nature for her teeming bounty, including the
steady breeding of legitimate hereditary kings, the Gardener stresses
that nature must be controlled through pruning and cutting back – similar to language that, as we noted in Chapter 7, Machiavelli employs in
the *Discourses* in reference to the Romans, those surgeons and horticulturalists of power. The defender of the old order was a royal duke, but
the avatar of Bolingbroke's regime is a lowly person, an artisan. This
reflects Bolingbroke's alliance with the common people at the expense
of the nobles, whose arrogance and love of honor make them, as Machiavelli advises in chapter 9 of *The Prince*, less reliable than the common
people's humble expectations, and who therefore must be purged. As
the Gardener concludes about his horticultural techniques in the little
fiefdom of his garden, "all must be even in our commonwealth." Bolingbroke's own method parallels that of the Gardener when he refers
to Richard's swaggering entourage as "the caterpillars of the commonwealth, which I have sworn to weed and pluck away."

THE TWO CORRIDORS TO MODERNITY (DARK AND LIGHT)

Now that we have considered the impact of the stage Machiavel on
the early modern imagination, let us proceed to the consequences and
implications of Machiavelli's new political science more strictly in terms
of political philosophy. I have argued that from the core of Machiavelli's
new ontology of tyranny – the summons to conquer fortune or chance
and the immanentization of political existence as a completely time-
bound process – many paths radiate. By way of concluding this study, I
want to trace two main corridors that open up into the development of
political modernity, corridors to some extent separate from one another,
but sometimes intertwining. I begin with an overview, then look more
closely at some of the major components.

What Machiavelli in chapter 3 of *The Prince* terms "the natural
desire to acquire" material goods and prosperity opens the way to a
politics based on a social contract designed to maximize every individual's prospects for survival and commodious living, entailing the

overthrow of the old feudal-theocratic politics of economic monopoly and frozen social mobility and advancement. Accompanying this project for a politics of individual opportunity and prosperity was the new physics of Bacon, explicitly designed to create power over nature for "the relief of man's estate" (Bacon [1937] p. 214). In this sense, Bacon's call for the mastery of nature through scientific experimentation represents a narrowing of Machiavelli's more general and variegated ontological summons to the conquest of Fortuna by the new *virtu*. Hobbes continues this narrowing by building his teaching about the social contract on the physics of matter in motion inaugurated by Bacon, transferring to human agency – as Machiavelli had envisioned – the power of "artificer" over nature formerly reserved for God.

In keeping with the Tudor and Elizabethan opening up of the New World, and later against the backdrop of the civil wars in seventeenth-century England which were to some degree a battle between the old and new politics as well as between the Church of Rome and the Reformation, the Machiavellian prescription based on the evolution of Rome from republic to empire is increasingly identified with the English vision of a commercial Atlanticist republic whose destiny lies to the west, the future site of those scientific marvels for mankind's benefit envisioned by Bacon's island utopia, the *New Atlantis*. The new world of Shakespeare's *The Tempest*, the island of Bermuda, is followed by Harrington's island republic *Oceana*. Harrington, although intellectually not on a level with Hobbes, does return behind Hobbes's reduction of Machiavelli's new science of politics to a model for absolute monarchy to the more full-blooded republicanism of the *Discourses*, on whose account of the evolution of Rome *Oceana* is partly based. Harrington is every bit as much a materialist as Hobbes, and he shares both Hobbes's appeal to individual self-interest and his distrust of the classical prescriptions for an education in virtuous character. At the same time, however, Harrington rejects Hobbes's exclusive endorsement of monarchy and, more like Machiavelli, envisions an expansionist republic of checks and balances, "bent on increase" and driven by the tension between its agrarian commoners and a martially inclined nobility. He is also more inclined than Hobbes – and in this, again, truer to Machiavelli – toward treating honor seeking as an independent variable in political motivation, not reducing it like Hobbes to a distorted understanding of a more fundamentally natural and rational desire for self-preservation and a fear of violent death. Like Machiavelli, Harrington often drapes his anticlassicism in, as Paul Rahe (2008) puts it, the rhetorical "toga" of veneration for the pragmatic political practice of the ancients, as opposed to the transcendentalism of their philosophy.

We recall from Chapter 1 that Hobbes is silent about the motivation of the absolute ruler of the *Leviathan* – the one glory seeker who is needed to crush all the other glory seekers – because to explore this psychology would call into question the alleged universality of the desire for self-preservation according to which glory seeking is degraded into mere irrational "vainglory." Harrington, by contrast, and again more like Machiavelli, is prone to recognize the rare type of men who want supreme prestige for its own sake. The founder of Oceana, the Lord Archon – a stand-in for the Lord General Oliver Cromwell and an idealization of what Harrington would wish him to be – is said to establish Oceana out of a love of glory. Moreover, whereas Hobbes's chief concern was with the state's inner order and security, Harrington and the other English republicans understand, like Machiavelli, the potentially universal appeal of the spirit of republican liberty. As Rahe has argued, long before the French Revolution, the English republicans (Puritans and Machiavellians alike) dreamed of liberating all Europe from kingship and priestcraft, further confirming the early connection we have discussed, already visible in Machiavelli, between the spiritual individualism and interiority of Protestantism and the worldly individualism of what would come to be regarded as the Protestant "work ethic."[4]

Meanwhile, as this tableaux of westward expansion unfolded, philosophers not explicitly concerned with fomenting a commercial expansionist republic but more concerned with a prescription for internal self-government, such as Spinoza and Locke, worked to humanize and rehabilitate the harshly reductionist materialism and authoritarianism of Hobbes, arguing that individualism was not wholly at odds with

---

[4] In addition to his overall superb scholarship and rare ability to relate theoretical principles to the flow of events and personalities, I am specifically reliant on Rahe's reading of Harrington, how he compares and contrasts with Hobbes, and, in my own assessment of what I term the many faces of Machiavelli, Rahe's argument that the English republican experiment conducted between 1649 and 1660 was already aiming, Puritans and Machiavellians alike, more than a century ahead of the Jacobins, to spread the revolution against traditional divine right monarchy and "priestcraft" throughout all of Europe. Rahe (2008).

a larger sense of historical community and could serve nobler values of tolerance and educational enlightenment beyond mere self-enrichment, and, most important in Locke's case, that self-interested individuals were capable of voluntarily establishing their own institutions of representative self-government, avoiding the need for the odious Hobbesian prescription for a monarch who in truth would be indistinguishable from a tyrant. In this respect, Locke wrote the script for the Glorious Revolution of 1689, while his Whig successor Edmund Burke continued Locke's work by grafting liberalism onto the unfolding of English history since Magna Carta, ostensibly reconciling the radicalism of the new science of politics with stalwart English traditions of the rule of law, a hierarchy of classes, and the sanctity of property.

The English Revolution continued to unfold into the American Revolution (as Michael Barone [2007] has suggested, they were two installments of the same dynamic), a Lockean prescription leavened by Montesquieu, who like Harrington had revived and extended Machiavelli's interest in Rome, which Montesquieu used as one of the bases for his model of a mixed regime premised upon enlightened self-interest and a respect for commerce and its concomitants of religious tolerance and rationality, as against the superstitious priest-ridden world of feudal Europe. These several streams came together in the New Rome, America, whose founders often saw their work as the reenactment of ancient republican virtue mediated by the Enlightenment, propertied and liberally educated men of substance who identified with Brutus and liberty as against Caesar, Catiline, and demagoguery, promoting a regime of internal checks and balances combined with a nascent continental empire to be opened up through agriculture and commerce. Jefferson's Palladian masterpiece Monticello embodied these overlapping motifs – it was adorned with Greek and Roman antiquities but also had a portrait of Locke prominently displayed.[5]

---

5 I very much agree with Rahe (2005), as against the Cambridge school, that the American founders, however much they may have admired classical antiquity, were not primarily influenced by classical political philosophy but by the new science of politics, as Hamilton regarded it, filtered to them, on the one hand from Montesquieu, and on the other from the English republicanism of Harrington and Locke, stretching back to their common stalk, Machiavelli. See my own discussion of the Founders' and especially Hamilton's dislike of the ancient Greek polis and his belief that the new science of politics had remedied the defects of classical republicanism. Newell (2009) pp. 129–206.

One corridor to modernity, then, runs from Machiavelli to the relatively sunny uplands of Lockean liberalism, science at the service of the common man, prosperity, and representative government.[6] However, another, darker corridor runs from the same source, and because our theme is tyranny, that darker corridor concerns us foremost in what remains of this Conclusion. That darker side entails the extension in principle of Machiavelli's summons to the conquest of nature to the tyrannical reshaping of human nature in the apocalyptic creation of "new modes and orders" by rulers of godlike scope and power. Hobbes's Sovereign is equipped to liquify his subjects in fear by replicating, through his own acts of terror, that terror inflicted directly on us

---

[6] An interesting variation on the issue of the narrowing and reinterpretation of Machiavelli's new science of politics can be found in the bracing book by John McCormick (2011). McCormick argues that the Cambridge School (exemplified by Pocock and Skinner) have turned Machiavelli into the precursor of modern American republicanism, which the author views as egregiously elitist, plutocratic, and undemocratic. He attempts to rescue Machiavelli from this cooptation by stressing that Machiavelli finds in Rome a prescription for populist democracy, not elitist and capitalistic republicanism. He accuses the Cambridge School of smoothly integrating Machiavelli's teaching into the stance of ancient thinkers such as Cicero, ignoring the fact that they were defenders of oligarchy and patrician privilege and therefore antithetical to Machiavelli's defense of the common people and their justified need to "patrol" the upper classes and keep their greed and power seeking in check. I am partly sympathetic to this interpretation. I have argued in this book that Machiavelli's political teaching is radically opposed to that of even the most pragmatic among the ancients such as Cicero, which is why Machiavelli's discussion of Cicero is scant and far from completely approving, but not primarily because they represented an elitist viewpoint, but rather because they mistook the reality of princely and republican power seeking and were too heavily mortgaged to the classical orientation on the eternal truth about the cosmos. I also agree that there is a certain kind of populism in Machiavelli's diagnosis, accompanied by an ironic debunking of oligarchical claims to superiority (for instance, in chapter 9 of *The Prince*). Nonetheless, I believe McCormick goes too far in seeing in Machiavelli's approval of class conflict a consistent recipe for populist curtailment of elites. Surely that class conflict is a dynamic by which both "the people" and "the nobles" aggrandize their power and wealth – there is both a populist and a plutocratic dimension. Furthermore, although Machiavelli does praise institutions such as the tribunate for curbing the arrogance of the patricians, he surely also values the consulship as well as the Senate for its aristocratic contribution to deflecting the many from overthrowing them by turning their energies outward in conquest. That all said, I do sympathize with McCormick's implication that we should not view Machiavelli wholly in terms of the commercial republicanism of his successors like Montesquieu and the American Founders. Although Machiavelli valued economic expansion and success, these were to serve or demonstrate the more authentic aims of honor and glory. The commercial republicanism of Montesquieu and the English republicans is a valid but somewhat reductive reading of Machiavelli's more full-blooded endorsement of patriotic fervor and collective honor.

in the state of nature through the war of all against all. The Sovereign's power to terrorize is an institutionalized salutary reminder that we are always better off obeying the contract, and the importation of Machiavelli's more general prescription for the use of law to replicate the severity of nature through periodic acts of republican refounding into a more narrowly focused technique for autocratic repression.

Rule by institutionalized terror was probably not Hobbes's preferred path to consolidate the social contract, but modernizers in a hurry were to seize on it. We are very far now from the benign utopianism of Bacon or even Harrington's exuberant republicanism, although for reasons we will consider, Hobbes is at the juncture of both corridors, the light and the dark. For now, suffice it to say that the Hobbesian Sovereign at his most fear-inspiring as the methodical crusher of all human impulses not reducible to conformity to the social contract leads directly along the dark corridor to Rousseau's Legislator, who "re-creates" human nature with a godlike determination, and from there to the "incorruptible" Robespierre, a prime example of the "secular saint" who destroys thousands, without personal malice, for the sake of the collective. It leads finally to ascetic police state mass murderers including Dzerzhinsky and Himmler, for whom the cleansing of class and race enemies in order to create a perfect community of interchangeable human integers is a duty requiring all sentiments of pity, or even of personal anger, to be overcome for the sake of the ideal. Here is the most extreme working-out of Machiavelli's designs for the deeroticization of tyranny.

Awful prospects. Yet it is fair to say that, as moderns, we remain ambivalent in our assessment of the tyrannical founder – an ambivalence, moreover, in the history of political ideas that, as we have seen in this book, goes all the way back to Plato's *Laws*. For, although I have distinguished for purposes of analysis between a light and a dark corridor to modernity, it would be more precise to say that, in the warp and woof of political history from which these motifs are abstracted, the dark corridor has at least two shafts and is not always or entirely separable from the more benign face of modernization. Nationalist modernizing revolutions have often been accompanied by autocrats. In this sense, Kemal Ataturk or the last Shah of Iran could be classified as Hobbesian Sovereigns, attempting to bring their peoples into the world of secular liberalism and materialism from above, postponing or forbidding democratic self-government until the new modern character type has been sufficiently habituated to part ways with premodern sectarian and religious animosities. Although these modernizing autocrats have no aim beyond the pragmatic – the creation of secular regimes with productive economies and technological progress – sometimes more radical, out and out millenarian revolutions bent on bringing about utopia through the extermination of whole classes or races are accompanied by this more pragmatic agenda for modernization in the here and now. In this respect, Stalin, Hitler, and Mao, although bent on utopian genocide to create a new world of pure community, also hastened the modernization of their respective nations, not in the sense of promoting democratic values or the rights of the individual, but in the sense of achieving rapid economic, military, and industrial development. Even today, some Chinese still regard Mao as a great patriotic founder, even as they press for full political liberty. Russians can feel similarly conflicted about Stalin, who made their country into a modern industrial economy and superpower seemingly overnight while systematically exterminating millions of "class enemies."

Again and again, I would argue, we are drawn back to Hobbes – and his narrowing of Machiavelli's new science of politics – at the juncture of the opposed tendencies within modernity. For Machiavelli, honor is always at the forefront of political existence, summoned forth by the pursuit of princely might or communal liberty through a life and death struggle as republics and empires continually rise and fall. Hobbes, by contrast, abstracts entirely from foreign policy as a constituent of internal self-government, the outside pressure of events that, in Machiavelli's view, requires republics to act boldly to expand their sphere of power and brings men of "grandeur of spirit" to the helm of affairs. By abstracting the method for constructing and maintaining the social contract from the historical cycles of foreign policy, Hobbes is able to almost completely expel honor seeking and a republican sense of the communal "we" that Machiavelli, despite other profound differences between them, does share with the classical republican thinkers. In contrast with Machiavelli's robust and tumultuous republican Rome with its vital, clashing classes, Hobbes's *Leviathan* is a world of isolated monads ruled absolutely by another monad.[7] Honor seeking as an

---

[7] Especially in *Taming The Prince* (1993), Mansfield begins with the classical understanding of the relationship between tyranny and monarchy in Aristotle, and the qualified

independent variable in human motivation remains only as the lacuna in the Hobbesian Sovereign's own hidden and unacknowledgable eros for glory. It is an impulse which, when it crops up in any other member of the social contract, is hurled aside with contempt by Hobbes as "the fool who hath said in his heart, 'there is no justice,'" based solely on the assumption that, given the almost complete certainty of being defeated, disgraced, and violently killed, those who attempt to usurp authority because they are driven by glory seeking are irrational to the point of madness (Hobbes [1971] p. 203). Yet Hobbes's own design for the social contract requires at least one of these madmen to act as umpire over the pedestrian desires for survival and comfort of all the others, to silently work the levers of power while crushing within himself the impulse to flaunt his power through invading and despoiling his subjects or lavishly rewarding his favorites. One must combine the abstemiousness of a monk with the cruelty of a Caligula.

Aside from this psychological lacuna of the hidden tyrant, the Hobbesian social contract is a bloodless, rootless mechanism, with no connection to history, tradition, or patriotism – a despotic algorithm for internal peace that can be imposed anywhere, or indeed, everywhere,

---

endorsement of a form of monarchy guided by reason that might well resemble a tyranny in its absolutism and eradication of citizen participation. He then examines Machiavelli's unvarnished endorsement of princely coercion, including large-scale violence, and poses the question of how we might explain the "banalization" of the Machiavellian prince in the institutions of the modern liberal constitutional polity such as the "executive power" and "war powers" of the American presidency. How, he asks, does this banalization or "taming" occur? "The answer is that the history of Machiavellism is chiefly a process of domestication, whereby Machiavelli's thought was appropriated and absorbed by liberal constitutionalism so that it could be regularized and legitimated" (p. xxiii). This comports with my suggestion that the Hobbesian Sovereign, already a narrowing of the Machiavellian prince to a mechanism for sheer control and umpirage of the social contract, could as efficiently or more efficiently be deployed as a completely impersonal constitutional mechanism for checks and balances exemplified by the American Constitution. The essence of the superiority of what Hamilton regards as the new science of politics over that of the ancients is this reliance on impersonal institutions in contrast with the vagaries of personal rule. I would only add that there is a competing stream in modern political philosophy, what I have termed the light path exemplified by Spinoza and Locke, in contrast to the dark corridor that leads to the more unvarnished endorsement of executive power, that helps mitigate the potential in the modern executive power for spilling over into dictatorship. I wholly agree with Mansfield that both Skinner and Pocock, by beginning with an already tame Machiavelli, occlude our understanding of why he *needed* to be tamed. The side of liberalism that dispenses with Machiavelli's harsher prescriptions does not come from Machiavelli himself as much as from the modification of his view of the relationship of man to nature undertaken by the holism of Spinoza.

a precursor of Kojeve's universal homogeneous state. In the European aesthetic consciousness, it becomes the nightmare of the faceless, omnipresent bureaucratic state of Kafka's *The Castle*, or, to use Weber's bleak phrase for modern life, "technicians without vision" ruling over "voluptuaries without heart." This pedigree proceeds straight down to Anthony Burgess's *A Clockwork Orange*, in which Alcibiadean ambition can find no outlet in a dreary welfare state dystopia except base criminality, and whose psyche must be rejigged in the correct Hobbesian direction through torture, behavior modification, and regular visits from a social worker. In its sheer impersonality, the faceless and rootless mechanism of the Hobbesian Sovereign is already "technological" in its essence, in the sense meant by Heidegger (1993) – that prior to the literal creation of modern machine technology, nature must be ontologically reconceived as that "calculable coherence of forces" mapped by modern physics over which total mastery can be projected. Indeed, Hobbes's project for the reconstruction of reality, not only political but economic and cultural, through the imposition of the will to fabrication on the physics of matter in motion, is the closest match among political philosophers to what Heidegger means by technology – a project that aims to surmount even those limitations placed on the human will by chance evoked by Machiavelli, to say nothing of Plato and Aristotle. The Hobbesian prescription, fully developed, could be a super-efficient technology of robotic surveillance like the science fiction dystopia of *The Matrix*, or, in real life, the increasingly relentless digitized surveillance of daily existence in England. To think through another implication: as that matchless Hobbesian and Marxist materialist C. B. Macpherson (1972) once opined – in an unusually optimistic interlude – the threat of universal annihilation through violent death posed by nuclear weapons technology might function as the ultimate Hobbesian Sovereign, bringing peace to the world by terrorizing all mankind into an awareness of the need for survival and reconciliation under a world authority securing it.

The paradox of modernity, already foreseen by Machiavelli, is that although it liberates desire, thereby understanding itself to be more realistic and hard-headed than the ancient philosophers' "imagined republics," that success in the liberation of desire leads in the long run to "effemination" and the unrealistic longing (far more unrealistic than anything envisioned by the ancient thinkers) for permanent peace.

Much as Machiavelli admires the dynamic evolution of Rome from republic to empire, he deplores the full-blown imperial outcome, which destroyed the spirit of liberty as it crushed every remaining local republic, and, by making the subjects of its world-state soft, prosperous and insulated from the dangers that had prompted the republic's original rise, opened up a craving for universal peace and its religion, Christianity. As we observed in Chapter 7, a striking instance of Machiavelli's ambivalence about Rome's rise to empire is his evaluation of Augustus Caesar. Although Augustus was arguably one of the most Machiavellian rulers in all history, with his cold determination, bottomless mendacity, and inhuman self-control as he strode over mountains of corpses from a young putschist and generalissimo to become the benign and revered master of the world – a man so alienated from himself and his inner feelings that his dying words were to jokingly ask for a tip like a stage actor who has turned in a good performance – Machiavelli has not a word of praise for him, because he destroyed the republic for good.

In an analogous way, Hobbes, in his initial diagnosis of human nature, is realistic and hardheaded about people's unvarnished ambition for power, honor, and wealth and their willingness to tyrannize whenever they can get away it with. However, he is realistic about these facets of human nature precisely because he believes that, having been identified without flinching or squeamishness, they can now be methodically controlled and even eradicated. Yet whereas Machiavelli is troubled by the universal pacification that is the outcome of an "effectual" politics and regrets what is arguably its inevitability, Hobbes is an unqualified proponent of it – another symptom of his narrowing of Machiavelli's vibrant phenomenology of political existence to a mere set of authoritarian techniques. Hobbes is confident that men can be changed by his new psychology of power seeking, brought to trade in their dangerous ambitions for honor and glory in exchange for a guaranteed net gain in security and material well-being. Although the Sovereign holds in reserve the emergency capacity to terrorize the contumacious, this is probably not (to amplify an earlier observation) Hobbes's preferred solution. Indeed, the need for its constant use might prove that vainglorious ambition was not eradicable, calling into question Hobbes's core contention that the pursuit of honor is not strictly speaking or intrinsically a facet of human fulfillment at all, in contrast with what the classical political thinkers would have maintained. For

Hobbes, the solid and lasting change in human conduct will come not primarily through terror and direct coercion, but through the steady and peaceable spread of "right reason," of enlightenment. Under the influence of the new psychology of appetitive desire, man will come to set aside martial strife and pride and, as Voltaire urged, to cultivate his garden. When James Madison argues that the new American republic's checks and balances will allow "ambition to counter-act ambition," the Machiavellian surface of this observation is underlain by the Hobbesian premise that ambition will already have been largely channeled into the competition for success through the peaceful arts of commerce. It is not that a Cato will counteract a Catiline but that a Bill Gates will counteract a Warren Buffet.

As I stress that a potential project for "permanent revolution" – the project for the endless reengineering of the human soul through terror – is, although a dark possibility lurking in Hobbes's political science, likely not his preferred prescription, I want to reemphasize my view that modern revolutionary terror is at best no more than *partially* explained by aspects of early modern political theories like those of Machiavelli and Hobbes even at their most ominous. For reasons I discuss presently, the meaning and scope of modern tyranny changes drastically with Rousseau, his detestation for bourgeois liberalism, his rejection of early modern natural right (especially of Hobbes's view of the state of nature and the social contract), and his romanticization of "the people," a shift in the ontology of tyranny that carries us beyond the thematic limits of this study. Before turning to a sketch of that boundary transformation, however, let me continue with this broad overview from within the premises of my focus in this book on the conquest of nature and of eros characteristic of early modern political thought.

As the modern age and the Enlightenment unfolded, people certainly continued to *know* about the dangers of tyranny as set forth by the classics, but the rising belief in the progress of history led to the conclusion that the dangers of tyranny were being steadily overcome as well. For Hegel, history begins in the "slaughter-bench" of the pursuit of mastery, but it will end in peace and the brotherhood of man. The *Phenomenology of Spirit* begins historically with the master-slave dialectic and ends with a verse from Schiller's *Ode to Joy*. For Marx, even more than for Hegel, history to date has been one unending, blood-soaked struggle for tyrannical mastery by one ruler or class over all the rest, but it will end in the disappearance of all such conflict, indeed of politics as such.[8]

In the totalitarian revolutions beginning with the Jacobins and continuing with the Bolsheviks and Nazis, the use of terror and genocide in the present is justified because it will bring about a new world of lasting peace, joy, community, and equality. In the aftershock of these terrible experiments in utopian genocide, culminating in the apocalyptic war of the Nazi and Bolshevik *Weltanschauungen* in the East in World War II, students of politics began to wake up from the slumber of the Enlightenment's residual belief in the progress of history. Figures as diverse as Leo Strauss, Eric Voegelin, Seymour Martin Lipset, Max Horkheimer, Aaron Wildaavsky, Theodore Adorno, and Hannah Arendt all became keenly aware that tyranny was still with us in the twentieth century and could be again in the future. Still, as I will elaborate later in this Conclusion, the Hobbesian underlay of the social sciences remained for many an almost insuperable obstacle to complete clarity about the recurrent reality of tyranny and of the psychology peculiar to it. The Hobbesian realism of the social sciences could be drawn on to identify tyrannical ambition when it reared its head, but it cast that ambition psychologically in such a way as to persevere in the optimistic belief that tyrannical and ideological violence might fade away if modern progress and prosperity continued to take root, an article of faith ringingly reaffirmed as recently as President Barack Obama's speech during his first run for the White House, "The War on Terror We Need to Win." In order to reflect on why modern social science has been unable fully to grasp the reality and the ongoing danger of tyranny, we must look further into the narrowing of Machiavelli's new science of politics by Bacon and Hobbes.

THE TORTURE OF NATURE?

When I argue that the narrowing of Machiavelli's new science of politics proceeds by way of Bacon and Hobbes, I am not necessarily implying a negative judgment as to the worth of their philosophies, only the need for an appreciation of Machiavelli's scope so as to more adequately unfold his more broad-reaching premise. As Beland (2010) puts it in

---

[8] Consider Hegel (1997). See the discussion in Newell (2009a); (1994) pp. 107–122.

describing Richard Kennington's assessment of Bacon's contribution to the origins of modernity, "Bacon's philosophy radicalizes the thought of Machiavelli in extending to the natural world the reflections that the latter restricted to the human world. Disease, famine and death: those are, in the eyes of Bacon, the true reverses of fortune against which man must protect himself." My only reservation about this formulation is that, in my view, it is Bacon's new natural science that restricts the scope of Machiavelli's phenomenology of political existence because Machiavelli's project for the conquest of nature so as to maximize security and well-being for peoples and princes already entails and anticipates Bacon's modification of it as a model for the study of nature. In other words, it is not Bacon who escapes Machiavelli's restrictions but Bacon who restricts Machiavelli's range, which was never limited to the human world alone but always grounded the human in a new ontology of nature.

We have already considered Bacon's complimentary gloss on chapter 15 of *The Prince*, arguing that philosophers should forsake "imaginary commonwealths" and focus on the world as it is. The purpose of natural science, as Bacon famously put it, should be to acquire power "for the relief of man's estate." As with Machiavelli himself, who as we observed in Chapter 6 conceals his project for a radical reorientation toward nature as a mere realist's scrupulous attention to observable fact, what amounts in Bacon's thought to a new and revolutionary assertion of the power to reconstruct nature through an act of will presents itself on first inspection and at the most superficial level as the mere patient observation and accumulation of factual data. Thus, Bacon writes in further praise of Machiavelli, he chose a sound method for his study of government: "Namely, discourse upon histories or examples, for knowledge drawn freshly, and in our view, out of particulars, findeth its way best to particulars again; and it hath much greater life in practice when the discourse attendeth upon the example than when the example attendeth upon the discourse" (Bacon [1869] p. 99). In other words, Bacon claims, Machiavelli arrived at his general theory of government through the observation of particulars, instead of, like the ancients, twisting the particulars to fit their already-held cosmologies. Or as he puts it about his own work: "Men have sought to make a world from their own conception and to draw from their minds all the material which they employed, but if, instead of doing so, they had consulted experience and observation, they would have the facts and not opinion to reason about, and might have ultimately arrived at the knowledge of the laws which govern the material world" (Bacon [1854] pp. 343–371).

Like Machiavelli as he depicts him here, Bacon appears to be exhorting us to set aside improbable cosmologies like those of the ancients, based on factually unverifiable myths such as the Platonic Forms or the Aristotelian Unmoved Mover, in favor of the patient accumulation of facts about the world as it is, not as it ought to be. This corresponds to Machiavelli's claim that he is setting aside the pretensions of the "imagined republics" of the ancients so as to focus on the "effectual truth" – the real world, as we might say, rather than the ideal. Yet just as Machiavelli presents this appeal to observable experience as the gateway to a Promethean assault on nature, the possibility of which is not exclusively derivable from observable experience itself, Bacon, too, reveals that the allegedly empirical observation of nature can only proceed once nature has already been intellectually assaulted and subdued by an act of will in the mind of the scientist. Like Machiavelli's emphasis on the will, the radical voluntarism of Bacon's scientific method wholly outstrips any precedent to be found in ancient materialism, the pre-Socratics, or the Sophists, the "Homeric-Heracleitean doctrine" that evolved a view of nature as cycles of motion out of an already existing poetic emphasis on the tragic limitations placed on human action and reason by necessity and chance.[9]

9 Richard Kennington (2004), following what he takes to be Strauss's understanding of Machiavelli, perhaps comes closest to the view that Bacon envisioned nature ahead of time in such a way as to make possible the project for its mastery, not that he derived the project for mastery from the empirical observation of nature. This pursuit of "mastery" Kennington traces to its source in Machiavelli's call for the conquest of Fortune. As a commentator on Kennington has put it about Kennington's view of Bacon, "he [Bacon] achieves this [the synthesis of science and mastery] through a fusion of Epicurean materialism and Platonic mathematics as resulting in a non-metaphysical or methodological materialism. This fusion is based on the principle that the first grounds of knowledge are human constructs, or that we know only what we make. Philosophy, formerly the attempt to grasp the eternal, becomes without residue the mastery of chance or fortune." Velkley (2002). I have somewhat analogously characterized Machiavelli's project for the mastery of Fortuna as a synthesis of Platonic rationalism and the view of nature as motion. In other words, man will impose on the flux of nature the rationalism of the Platonic forms, now seen as a purely anthropocentric agenda for reshaping nature, an empty formalism drained of its teleological content and connection with the world. However, I do not believe Machiavelli goes as far as Kennington's Bacon in believing this agenda for mastery can anticipate complete success. For Machiavelli, fortune will to some

Time and again, Bacon's characterization of the natural scientist's correct methodological stance toward nature recalls Machiavelli's adjuration that Fortuna must be subdued and mastered by force. He takes what Machiavelli presents as a poetic, metaphorical, and existential stance toward nature and, abstracting it from the ebb and flow of historical events, the rise and clash and decline of entire political bodies caught in the cycles of history and time, refines it into a conceptual framework for scientific experimentation. It is already rationalism presupposing existentialism, the dilemma of Max Weber. Personifying nature as a woman in the *New Organon* exactly as had Machiavelli in *The Prince*, Bacon maintains (contrary to his erstwhile pose as the modest empirical observer) that we learn more not when nature is "left to her own course" but when she is "under constraint and vexed; that is to say, when by art and the hand of man she is forced out of her natural state and squeezed and molded" (Bacon [1960] p. 25). Just as for Machiavelli, for Bacon, nature cannot be trusted in her outward, visible manifestations – the interior matrix of origination is what matters. At times, he comes as close as Machiavelli had to characterizing, in metaphors close to obscene, the proper stance toward nature as akin to rape: "I invite all such to join themselves, as true sons of knowledge, with me, that passing by the outer courts of nature, where numbers have trodden, we may find a way at length into her inner chambers" (Bacon [1960] p. 36). This appeal to the "sons" stresses both the newness of the moderns in choosing "the way of today" over the classical-Christian yesterday and also the lustiness of "the young," whom Machiavelli also regarded as most likely to win over Fortuna owing to her preference

---

extent always elude the grip of human mastery, partly for reasons based on Machiavelli's view of Lucretian materialism itself. Thus, it is not true for Machiavelli strictly speaking or in every instance that we can "only know what we make," for we can know that fortune will always limit man to some degree, and our own desires will never remain stable or contented; we will not be able to devise any solutions for these impediments that reach right down to the bottom of the world's existence so as to uproot and transform it entirely. Not every Bacon scholar agrees, however, with Kennington's interpretation of Bacon, which makes Baconian mastery seem almost to anticipate Fichte's voluntarism or Nietzsche's will to power, or, indeed, Kuhn's quasi-Nietzschean view of science as a paradigm shift. Travis Smith (2009), for example, thinks Bacon's promise of mastery for the relief of man's estate is partly a rhetorical means for gaining broader popular support for a scientific project whose tangible benefits will remain in doubt for some time to come. Rousseau famously regarded Bacon as the very archetype of the philosopher motivated by a pure love of the truth.

for hot-blooded youth over cautious old age. However, it is hard not to detect in Bacon's words a transition from the comparative *delicatezza* of Machiavelli's multifaceted and balletic wooing of Fortuna to something more akin to the cloddishness of a methodological soccer club. Perhaps Swift had this rape of nature in mind when he named his parody of Bacon's Royal Society – an island of scientific technocrats flying over the inherited traditions of the Old World like the islands of the new world beckoning to the west – Laputa, the whore, nature whored.[10]

Just as Machiavelli counsels the prince to expel erotic longing from his own character and replace it with methodical discipline, Bacon says that the scientist must probe nature with a "chaste and severe course of inquiry" (Bacon [1960] p. 28). Just as Machiavelli urged this inner process of deeroticization so that one might guard oneself against the allures of the imagined republics, the psychological key to our reliance on Fortuna, leading to the rejection of the Great Tradition in its entirely, Bacon argues that "the entire work of the intellect (must) be commenced afresh, and the mind itself be from the very outset not left to take its own course but guided at every step" (Bacon [1960] p. 34). Just as, for Machiavelli, seeing nature as it really is must be preceded by one's inward-turning alienation from its bewitching outward sheen of beneficence encouraging the belief that nature upholds peace and justice, for Bacon as well, rigorous science requires that the mind be reshaped in abstraction from all received experience and tradition "and the business done as if by machinery" (Bacon [1960] p. 34).

For Bacon, before we can conquer nature, we must purge our minds of her influence over us through the seductive traditions of the past or the apparently beautiful patterns of the visible world. This inner self-purgation corresponds with a preference for breaking nature down into her constituent parts and forsaking the allure of the surface harmony, a discipline that Machiavelli had urged princes to practice on themselves and in their relationship with their subjects (for "all see you, but few touch what you are"). For Bacon just as for Machiavelli, in other words, the study of nature is grounded in a secularized Augustinian distrust of

---

[10] The ungallant description of "her" outer chambers as places where "numbers have trodden" suggests she has been pretty undiscriminating in her earlier admission of wooers. More brutal and deeper penetration is apparently required to get past this antechamber of aging Aristotelian ponces.

the looks of the world, the visible flourishing of phenomena that led Plato and the ancients to reason upward through those orderly appearances toward the perfect archetypes of the Forms. For Machiavelli and Bacon, whatever order the world possesses will be fashioned by the sustaining will of the prince, or the prince of science, transferred from God to man.

I suggested in Chapters 5 and 6 that Machiavelli's fully rounded view of the proper approach of the prince to Fortuna is more complex than mere hot-blooded subjugation, however stirring that metaphor in chapter 25 of *The Prince* may be to ambitious young men. Instead, it is an inner dyad alternating between the unseen recesses of the prince's character and the unseen spontaneous forces of Fortuna herself. Fortuna as the unseen source of origination bonds with the prince's inner character, a primordial as opposed to a transcendental link between man and the world. The prince must imitate fortune's impetuosity in order to channel and tap into her power. Paradoxically, complete mastery comes by way of complete submission. Only by renouncing our hopes from nature can we gain freedom from her, which is also freedom over her.[11] In this sense, for Machiavelli, the knowledge of nature is assimilated by the will to subdue her through imitating her own lack of intrinsic teleological purpose. So, too, does Bacon argue that "human knowledge and human power meet in one." If we do not know the cause, its "effect cannot be produced." Most important, "nature to be commanded must be obeyed." When we understand nature, we can harness and replicate her spontaneous effects so as to maximize man's power over her: "That which in contemplation is as the cause is in operation as the rule" (Bacon [1857] I.iii). To know something is to be able to make it, but this mastery of nature through technique is preceded by submission to nature's sheer power of genesis.

We considered in earlier chapters how, according to Machiavelli, the centuries-old conglomerate of the classical and Christian "imagined

---

[11] Pesic (1999) makes the interesting argument that the Baconian scientist's stance toward nature should not be seen exclusively as "torture" but as more akin to a wrestling match. This comports with my view of the Machiavellian prince's relationship with Fortuna as a kind of dance or dyad in which the prince mush channel fortune in order to subdue her, and while I see the Baconian stance as more straightforwardly dominating, Pesic has a point that the scientist must also internalize the flow of nature – in effect, to woo and not merely conquer.

republics" had produced an overwhelmingly beguiling and authoritative medium for the refraction and distortion of our expectations from the world, a psychological grip so powerful that even the most ruthless of contemporary rulers such as Cesare Borgia could not consistently emulate the "well-used" cruelty of ancient tyrants like Hiero – and above all, those matchless surgeons of political force the Romans – always falling prey at the crucial moment to some residual attachment to the old morality. We also noted that Machiavelli frequently characterizes "the writers" of the Great Tradition as appealing to the prejudices of "the many," as if to imply that, in attributing the success of statesmen to the pursuit of the moral and intellectual virtues for their own sake, they were playing to a vulgar, childish, and sentimental desire of the many to view their rulers as kind and good, as in a fairy tale. (There is perhaps in Machiavelli's critique an echo of Callicles' charge that Socrates, in arguing his excessively namby-pamby view that it is better to suffer injustice than to do it, is "playing the demagogue," that is, playing to the credulous moralism of the many [*Gorgias* 482].)

Altogether, a remarkable transformation is implied in this judgment about the vulgarity of the Great Tradition, what we might term the replacement of the aristocratic political morality of the classics with the elitist leadership style of modernity. The political morality of the classics is centered around the prescription for a balance in the soul between mind and desire that allows the passions themselves to be fulfilled in the service of civic nobility and the philosophical longing for immortality. This prescription could be participated in, to varying degrees, by all strata of society in normal circumstances absent the crises of war or insurrection, excluding only the most vicious or desperate. Certainly for Plato and Aristotle, the class of gentlemen is best favored to devote itself to political deliberation and philosophy. However, as Aristotle argues in his discussion of polity, even the decent middle-class majority can approach an aristocratic degree of virtue, while Plato and Aristotle would agree that most people, irrespective of their rank, can be shaped by correct opinion about virtue even if they lack the leisure for a full-time devotion to politics or philosophy. Socrates concedes in the *Republic*, for instance, that even the lowest class of the best regime, the Artisans, must to *some* degree be capable of sharing in the moderation of the Auxillaries (421c–422a). With Machiavelli and Bacon, in sharp contrast, we encounter a new deeroticized cadre of political methodologists, for whom the harmony of the soul is irrelevant in comparison to their disciplined minds, and who, like the "projectors" on Swift's flying island of Laputa, stand outside of all other social groups in their dedication to pure technique. Their minds have no objective correlate in the structure of the cosmos, no "divine spark," as Aristotle put it, connecting the human intellect to the Unmoved Mover. For the new elite of methodologists, nature is an alien Other to be subdued and rendered orderly.

As we have seen many times throughout this book, Plato and Aristotle promote the appeal of philosophy primarily through an appeal to the "beautiful and good ones," the gentlemen. Plato's primary therapy for curing the leaning of excessive eros toward tyranny is through an appeal to eros itself and its longing for the beautiful or noble. As depicted in the *Republic*, tyrannical eros is shameless, vulgar, and demagogic, an extension of the vices of democracy, the regime most disdained by the gentleman. The rehabilitation of eros toward the pursuit of civic virtue and contemplation attempts to wed an aristocratic standard for personal integrity and public service to a respect for philosophy as the steadfast guardian of the truth, as in Cicero's *Dream of Scipio*. As Aristotle presents his hierarchy of virtues, the moderate traits of character most desirable in citizens are also required by philosophy, and through studying the eternal truth, philosophy shelters the gentleman's code from the passions of the day and ties it to the teleological order of the cosmos, granting it permanent validity in its properly subordinate role. The man of superlative virtue is himself a kind of way station to the philosophic life (the candor of the great-souled man, for example, resembles that of the philosopher), although his virtue is noble and self-sufficient in its own right. Prudence, the highest of the political virtues, is itself in the sphere of the virtues of the intellect, second only to *sophia*, the very highest of the virtues, and not strictly speaking in the subordinate sphere of the virtues of character (*Nicomachean Ethics* 1139b11–1142a27). Although good citizens on the whole need only follow correct opinion about the virtues of character, the very best citizens and statesmen must share to a lesser but real degree in the theoretical orientation of the philosopher toward the eternal truth.

Machiavelli seeks utterly to disrupt this teleological ascent from civic virtue through the highest political prudence toward the contemplative life. In effect, he treats the alliance between philosophy and aristocratic morality forged by the classics as part and parcel of the delusions of the many, making them subject to the pretensions of what Hobbes would come to call the "vainglorious." A part of Machiavelli's populism is evident in his belief that, although the people want only to survive and enjoy their property, the *nobiles* always want to displace the prince, and so are the chief fomenters of instability. Contrary to what Aristotle argued, there is no distinction in principle between aristocracy and oligarchy. Whatever they may call themselves, their motives are venal (*The Prince* chapter 9). In the fluid world of the rise and fall of states, self-described aristocrats are oligarchs plotting to become tyrants. What Plato and Aristotle regarded as the better sort of men, the gentlemen, whose innate or inherited nobility might incline them toward the nobility of philosophic independence from the sway of base passion, are lumped together by Machiavelli with countless other varieties of deluded hopes, ambition, and self-indulgence. Standing over against all of these moralizers – the people, the so-called nobles and their flatterers, the philosophers of old – is Machiavelli's new prince, an amalgam of a ruler and a thinker, whose reason is assimilated to his will and the mark of whose excellence is his inner austerity, his rigorous self-purgation of the delusions of the old conglomerate. One might well ask at the end of the day who has a better opinion of the people, Machiavelli or the classics? Plato and Aristotle believe that the common people, although not best equipped or situated to actualize their virtue, can be educated or habituated to do so to some extent by rising above base desires. Machiavelli, by contrast, encourages the people to pursue their base desires in an alliance with the prince by liberating them from the sway of belief in ancient moral philosophy and its intertwining with Christian revelation – a liberation that will require the methodical reshaping of their natures by a cadre of leaders so as to save them from their own attachment to the Great Tradition. When Machiavelli, in urging the prince to forsake the nobles for the people, remarks that "who builds on the people builds on mud," we realize that a mud foundation is a very strong one and at the same time a simile for lowness of character.

There are many parallels with Machiavelli in Bacon's thought for the need to purge both natural science and political morality of its joint delusions about the teleological beneficence of nature: what Machiavelli termed "imagined republics," Bacon terms "the idols of the tribe."

Moreover, in the distinction Bacon makes between followers of the old Aristotelian physics – where "numbers have trodden" but never found their way past nature's outer chambers to her interior – and his vigorous new band of the "sons of knowledge" who will probe her all the way, we sense a contempt for the numerous credulous dodderers of the past, pandering to the idols of the many, and their coming displacement by a bold new elite of methodologists. As Descartes and Hobbes were both to argue, the idols of the tribe must be demolished through rigorous self-emptying, alienation from history and tradition, and introspection. ("Everything is to be doubted.") The interior of what we now might term the "unencumbered" self becomes the criterion for judging reality, not the soul that participates in the Idea of the Good, sped in its longing for wholeness by eros as the demonic link between the human and the divine. Comparing the power of these idols to an "assault" on the mind that recalls Machiavelli's warnings about the hostility of Fortuna, Bacon writes:

The idols and false notions which are now in possession of the human understanding and have taken deep root therein, not only so best men's minds that truth can hardly find entrance, but even after entrance is obtained, they will again in the very instauration of the sciences meet and trouble us, unless men being forewarned of the danger, fortify themselves as far as may be against their assaults. (Bacon [1857] I xxxviii)

In a way that is analogous to Machiavelli's teaching on the need for refoundings, Bacon warns that extirpating these idols will require ceaseless vigilance stretching into the future, because "the human understanding is of its own nature prone to suppose the existence of more order and regularity in the world than it finds" (Bacon [1857] 1.xlv). The mind tends to interpret what it encounters in the light of received opinion: "The human understanding when it has once adopted an opinion . . . draws all things else to support and agree with it" (Bacon [1857] 1.xlvii). The grip on the mind and emotions of the Idols of the Tribe must be continually overcome by the "severe law and overruling authority" of Bacon's new method. In this, we might see the internalization by the new natural scientist of Machiavelli's more general teaching about the need for severe law in the founding of healthy republics. We recall from the *Discourses* that Machiavelli believed republics were more vigorously founded when the open hostility of nature forced on them the necessity to labor. However, when the severity of nature was remedied by manmade prosperity, there ensued the danger that men would read into nature the bounty they had achieved through their own labor and let down their guard. This danger could be remedied by fashioning harsh laws that continuously reimposed the austerity of the founding situation, thereby purging illusion and restoring vigor. Tapping into nature's power to oppress us through the artificial simulacrum of the law might keep citizens in a continuously virtuous condition. Bacon is in effect importing Machiavelli's prescription for the refounding of republics into the mind itself, internalizing his teaching on republics as a methodological prescription for the continuous refounding of the necessity to labor against nature through the purgation of mental sloth.

Taken together, these references help us past the initial, superficially modest pose of the empirical observer to the truly revolutionary, millenarian stance of Bacon's new science, a project for the endless, dynamic transformation of nature for the benefit of man, what Heidegger will later term "technology." To use Kuhnian terms, Bacon's own language often lifts the coverlet of "ordinary science," ostensibly limited to the patient accumulation of data, to reveal the underlying and more fundamental "paradigm shift" of modernity. Echoing Machiavelli's comparison of himself in the first pages of the *Discourses* to a Columbus of statecraft opening up an "as yet untrodden path," Bacon proclaims that his object is "to open a new way for the understanding, a way by [others] untried and unknown." The parallel to Machiavelli is even more explicit when he writes:

(I)t is fit that I publish and set forth these conjectures of mine which make hope in these matters reasonable, just as Columbus did, before that wonderful voyage of his across the Atlantic, when he gave the reasons for his conviction that new lands and continents might be discovered besides those which were known before; which reasons, though rejected at first, were afterwards made good by experience, and were the causes and beginnings of great events. (Bacon [1857] 1.xcii)

As the comparisons in this passage suggest, Columbus was the seafaring equivalent of Bacon's *Novum Organum*, searching for the New Atlantis. In Bacon's depiction, Columbus began with his "conviction" that a new world existed, and then he went out to find it – analogous to Bacon's call to probe nature's inner chambers by an act of will in order to unlock her powers, with the empirical verification to follow. Columbus's reasons for his confidence were at first rejected by followers of the Idols of the Tribe, but through his boldness Columbus overcame them by afterward providing the evidence, and now a great new canvas awaits for the creation of mankind's future. Bacon envisions his scientific voyage in analogous terms. The consistent metaphorical depiction of modernity as being akin to seafaring is striking. Beginning with Machiavelli's self-alignment with Columbus, recurring in different ways and with varying relationships to the Classical/Christian conglomerate, in More's *Utopia* (an island commonwealth in which the common man's material needs are met), Shakespeare's *The Tempest* (where a deposed duke, natural philosopher and alchemist, banished from Milan to Bermuda, uses his wisdom to create astonishing new marvels of power and finally takes back his dukedom), Bacon's own *New Atlantis* with its robots and clinics and later Harrington's *Oceana*, a seafaring republic of prosperous farmers, merchants, and a martial nobility, this new world of the modern finds, by progressive degrees, its field of action westward toward the Americas, first in the imagination and eventually in reality.[12]

---

[12] Tuck (1993) sees in Bacon's project a synthesis of Judaism and Protestantism. This certainly comports with the view of Rahe (2005, 2008) and Sullivan [1996, 2004]) that English republicanism was a synthesis between Puritans and Republicans, meaning to say between the Reformation and modern secular political thought. It also comports with the earlier linkage between Machiavelli and Luther, especially given that the Reformation early on identified with the ancient Hebrews. Others, however (Lampert in Bacon [2000]; Kennington [2004]) see Bacon as entirely antireligious and purely rational, such that Bacon's new science sparked, in Lampert's words, "the actual holy war fought in Europe . . . the warfare of science against religion that tamed sovereign religion." We can never resolve with certainty or complete transparency the degree to which those wars were carried out by rationalists wishing to overthrow Christianity or by Protestants wishing to overthrow the Church of Rome, or to what degree the actors viewed themselves as one, the other, or both (for example, Milton, Protestant theologian and the defender of freedom of speech). Both sides, Protestant and modern rationalist, were united in their wish to jettison classical teleology, the buttress both of classical philosophy and Thomism, the latter of which sanctioned both the sovereignty of the Church in religious matters and of divinely anointed monarchy over republicanism. A part of the antiteleological temperament of the Reformation, and of English Protestants, was their self-identification with the ancient Hebrews, owing among other things to the Hebrews' monotheism, comporting with the Protestant trend against Trinitarian consubstantiation and toward an elevation of God the Father at the expense of the Son, excluding altogether the Mother of God as a polytheistic abomination. In another vein altogether, Leon Kass (2003) has identified the Jewish God's radical distance from nature – leading to a distrust of the looks of the world, and in direct contrast with Platonic philosophy

However disturbing may be the resemblances of Bacon's new scientific methodology to the torture and rape of nature, he sets his face
forward toward this brave new world. He foresees a future in which new
technical marvels wrested from the inner power of nature will improve
life for everyone, dispelling the fear, oppression, misery, superstition,
and intolerance of the past. It is important to note that, for Bacon,
the scientist's tyranny over nature to extract this bounty need not be
extended to tyranny over human beings themselves, at least not in an
overt political sense, as opposed to their liberation through the spread
of the new reason from the delusions of tradition. Nor will ordinary
people, as opposed to the elite of methodologists, have to be purged
of their pedestrian comforts and pleasures. On the contrary, because
nature can be reshaped, ordinary people will enjoy as never before
the peaceful and commodious existence Machiavelli had feared as the
source of the republic's rot and decline, an important departure on
Bacon's part from "the Florentine's" own republican prescription and
where he joins forces with the more benign liberalism of Locke.[13] With
Hobbes, however, we encounter an altogether more brazen prescription for the conquest of human nature itself, with far darker political
prognostications including the open endorsement of tyranny, ostensibly
based on the new Baconian physics.

In the opening of the *Leviathan*, Hobbes argues that nature is like a
machine designed by God. By imitating nature so conceived, man can
create an artificial man, the Commonwealth, and so remedy the natural
defects of our passions that, unchecked, lead to the war of all against all.
Man might replace God the artificer, with reason assimilated to the will
to reconstruct nature. As in Bacon, for Hobbes, the knowledge of nature

in which the visible world crowned by the Sun is seen as the paradigm for knowledge –
with the distrust shown by modern Baconian science toward teleology (an "idol of the
mind") and a corresponding emphasis on the will to master the knowledge of nature
by standing outside of nature. There are many paths, in other words, to the notion of
Bacon's thought as a synthesis of modern rationalism with the Reformation and with
Judaism.

[13] In this connection, see Clarke (2008) who plausibly argues that Bacon distinguishes
himself from Machiavelli by signaling "his rejection of an imperial model based on
violent conquest. . . . In its place, he erects a new imperial model dedicated in principle
to humanity, prosperity and cosmopolitanism."

is also the power to refabricate it (Hobbes [1971] p. 115). Moreover, following Machiavelli's adaptation of the Augustinian and Thomistic reversal of Aristotelian causality, whereby efficient cause located in God is given priority over formal and final cause as the imposition of will on matter, Hobbes's artificer of the Commonwealth (like Machiavelli's prince of "outstanding virtue" who can "introduce into matter whatever form he chooses") prospectively takes the place of God as the fashioner of nature and human nature (Hobbes [1971] pp. 82–83).

However, lest this master artificer be confused with the classical account of superlative virtue and prudence in statesmen, Hobbes couples his elevation of technical willpower with a frontal assault on Aristotle's maxim that man is by nature a political animal. In constructing a sound commonwealth, Hobbes tells us, we should introspect about human nature, comparable to Descartes' call on the self to divest itself of all received tradition in seeking clear knowledge derived from sense-data and observable experience. Our guide, Hobbes argues, should not be the objects of the passions, but the "similitude" of the passions themselves, which reduce down to the simplest impulses for survival ("which are the same in all men, desire, fear, hope, etc."). What Hobbes terms the objects of the passions ("the things desired, feared, hoped, etc.") correspond to the opinions regarding how to live about which, in Aristotle's definition of human nature, citizens deliberate – the debate about the meaning of the just, the noble, and the advantageous for the city. Because, according to Hobbes, these clashing opinions are inherently unstable, divisive, and controversial, they make peaceful consensus impossible: Aristotle's definition of the fulfillment of human nature, if acted on, leads inevitably to civil strife, insurrection, and the war of all against all. Moreover, we ourselves, being systems of matter in motion, even if we could agree on one day about the meaning of justice and the other virtues, our shifting passions might incite us to reverse ourselves the next as we are struck by new desires. The passions, in contrast with the objects of the passions, though purely impulsive, are paradoxically more rational in the sense of being universal, yielding the kind of "political arithmetic" (as R. H. Tawney [1950] put it) on which a solidly crafted social contract can be constructed, with the logical necessity of a geometric proof. Stripped of their objects in the world at large – different substantive understandings of justice, happiness, nobility, and truth – the passions possess the "similitude" of their emptiness, at once abstract and irrational. Opinions vary, but the passions themselves are common to all.

Hobbes's reversal of Aristotle's definition of the purpose of human nature means that human nature is fulfilled – because its only natural impulse is self-preservation – by *avoiding* the full debate over ends that Aristotle maintains actualizes our telos. Politics is only about securing the means to self-preservation, not the seditious issues of who is right about justice, virtue, and the entitlement to rule. This reversal enables Hobbes to parody Aristotle's *Politics* at every turn. He derides Aristotle for arguing that some are by nature "more worthy to command" because they favored his philosophy, "as if Master and Servant were not introduced by consent of men, but by differences of wit" (Hobbes [1971] p. 211). If human nature is solely and entirely fulfilled through the pursuit of self-preservation, then an argument for the existence of superlative virtue cannot be grounded in nature, as Aristotle would have it, but only by whatever conventions happen to currently prevail due to "consent." The Hobbesian Sovereign does not rule because he has a superior character ("more worthy to command" due to "differences of wit") but because he employs the correct method. He is the neutral umpire of the social contract, protecting everyone else from their own and others' aberrant natural impulses, thereby maximizing the net gain of every individual in security and well-being. Aristotle's much-vaunted prudence, the hallmark of the natural monarch and leading aristocrat, is in Hobbes's reduction nothing but the accumulated experience of staying alive, common to all animals and men. Worthiness to command is not grounded in nature at all, but is a purely conventional claim that serves merely to justify one's own preferences stemming from self-interest and vanity. Young men like to read ancient thinkers such as Aristotle on the naturally superlative ruler because they flatter themselves that they fit the bill (Hobbes [1971] p. 162).

In the most blatant parody of all, Hobbes claims that in Aristotle's view, creatures such as "bees and ants" are "numbered amongst political creatures" (Hobbes [1971] p. 225). But, Hobbes's reasoning runs, if Aristotle believes that human beings are capable of living in harmony like bees and ants, why, one might ask of him, is it so manifestly the case from all known history and observable experience that they in fact cannot? In contrast with what Hobbes presents as Aristotle's naive assumption about human beings' proclivity to communal cooperation, Hobbes's answer is that mens' "continual competition for honor and glory" leads to "envy and hatred," for man's chief joy is in establishing himself as preeminent over other men. In other words, whereas Aristotelians naively believe that men in political communities might be effortlessly gregarious and cooperative like bees and other "political creatures" working harmoniously away, the worldly wise Hobbes knows that their competition for prestige makes voluntary political associations impossible in the absence of an absolute monarch to enforce the peace.

But of course Aristotle never argues that men are naturally gregarious: on the contrary, he defines the nature of man as "political" in direct *contrast* with the nature of gregarious creatures like bees and ants (1253a7–10). A careful exegete like Hobbes must have known that he was attributing to Aristotle the very opposite of what Aristotle in fact argues, and so constructing a fake debate between himself and Aristotle, likely to slide by the casual Aristotelian reader, over a position Aristotle never held. For according to Aristotle, in fulfilling his nature through civic deliberation, the actualization of man's end is inherently controversial, attended by the permanent danger that heated debate may boil over into civil strife. What Hobbes does not want to acknowledge is that Aristotle himself provides for this danger by encouraging the development of a high level of civic virtue through education, through civic institutions that moderate excessive greed and promote inclusiveness, and by relying on the inherent authority of reason itself to illuminate the correct path to the common good, supplemented by laws and coercion where needed. Rather than introduce these complexities into his reduction of human nature from Aristotle's definition of man as a political animal to the barren "similitude of the passions," Hobbes simply burlesques Aristotle as having his head in the clouds. Because Aristotle's reasoned distinction between superlative virtue in one or a few statesmen and tyranny has been excluded except as a matter for snide parody, Hobbes is free to drive home his conclusion that any attempt to distinguish between one ruler as a virtuous monarch and another as a tyrant depends solely on whose ox is being gored. As long as the law is enforced by a neutral umpire, protecting individuals from each other's unchecked natural passions for exploitation and mastery, and enabling people freely to buy and sell their labor to survive and prosper, this distinction is insignificant.

The need to obviate an Aristotelian riposte to his new political science through a parody of Aristotle's actual teaching points, in my view, to the irreparable incoherence of Hobbes's point of departure. The central paradox of Hobbes's thought is that he wants to ruthlessly expose the hidden ambitions of men – to tear away from our eyes the comforting veil of Aristotelianism and Christianity that teaches us that man has the potential (whether based on reason or revelation) to be good – in order to eradicate those ambitions permanently. Whereas the classics began by taking it as a given that men would always seek honor, and in the worst case tyranny, so as to think about how to lead them toward civic virtue and a friendliness for philosophy, Hobbes begins by severing any possible connection between honor seeking and this prospect for transcendence. Apart from Augustine, no profound thinker about political existence so thoroughly drains honor of its connection to the erotic longing for wholeness at the heart of classical and especially Platonic pedagogy – with the very great difference, of course, that whereas Augustine does this in order to purify man of his natural longings in light of a higher supernatural standard, Hobbes does so in order to sever honor seeking from any connection to a higher natural standard in light of which its good and bad versions might be assessed. By denying the capacity of all varieties of honor seeking for moral or philosophical transcendence, Hobbes might at first blush appear to be more realistic than the ancients, given what we know from history and experience about how people really act when they claim to be motivated by honor – amply demonstrated, as Hobbes believed, by Thucydides' history of ancient Greece and by the political strife of his own England. Yet Hobbes's reductionist account of honor seeking is for the ultimate purpose of suppressing or even eradicating honor seeking altogether. The notion that political ambition of the kind leading to empire and immortal glory could be extirpated from human beings arguably makes Hobbes ultimately much *more* optimistic than the ancients about the prospects for permanent peace – optimistic to the point of being delusional himself, based on how people and states have actually acted since Hobbes's efforts to enlighten them about their own motive of self-preservation.

Hobbes's social contract requires that one honor-seeking man – the Sovereign – discipline his pleasures so as to crush methodically all the other proud ones. He can then allow the peaceable majority to prosper and live as they please in private life as long as they do not contest the Sovereign's absolute authority. The price this Sovereign must pay is that, to the extent that he dedicates himself to Hobbes's method for ruling, he must give up his own full scope for glory seeking and for exploiting his subjects wantonly. It is not that he must go from being a Nero to a Marcus Aurelius, the kind of transition from an exploitive tyrant to a benevolent monarch the classics would have urged (a distinction based, in Hobbes's language, on "differences in wit"), but that he must go from being a Nero *or* a Marcus Aurelius to being a kind of detached and invisible manager. Indeed, his method of ruling could arguably be best carried out by an impersonal mechanism – say a constitution that, through checks and balances, retarded political ambition by sluicing the people's passions into three mutually impeding branches of government – rather than a flesh-and-blood human being at all, with all his potential for inconstancy and whim.

Broadly speaking, then, the potential of Hobbes's political philosophy for the future runs in two different directions: totalitarianism and enlightenment. On one level, as we have observed, the Sovereign must have the capacity to inspire terror, especially in the vainglorious; to replicate the terror that would spontaneously be experienced when we revert from the social contract to the state of nature with its war of all against all, thereby schooling those foolishly tempted to do so to change their course of action. By replicating this terror institutionally, the Sovereign saves us from ourselves through a salutary dose of fear, anticipating Hegel's depiction of the slave as being liquefied by the fear inspired in him by the master. In this sense, Stalin was one of history's most consistent Hobbesians. He used terror in a relentless campaign to re-create human nature as empty integers interchangeable with one another, stripped of ambition, living in enforced harmony. Hitler employed the same methods for the purification of the *Volk*. Still, as I have already stressed, no dimension of early-modern political theory, even in its darkest potential, fully explains the potential for totalitarian and millenarian revolution or terrorism like that of the Bolsheviks or Nazis. That further radicalization of the exercise of the will to reshape human nature can only be thought through by way of Rousseau's romanticization of the "people." More on this later.

Moreover, we must recall again that Hobbes's own preferred solution to the problem of ambition was not this constant, institutionalized use of terror, which would be a kind of concession that the nature of the vainglorious was irrepressible and ineradicable. Instead, Hobbes hoped and believed that his new psychology of pedestrian appetitiveness, to be taught "in the universities" ([1971] p. 728) in the place of "Aristotelity," would over time genuinely convince people that they should understand all their passions, including honor seeking, as deriving from a desire for comfortable self-preservation and fear of violent death, thereby realizing the irrationality of honor seeking and especially tyrannical ambition. The universality of the scientific method imported from Bacon leads to the "political arithmetic" of the "similitude of the passions" – the reduction of human nature per se, and without exception, from an absorption in the objects of men's ambitions in the wider world to a baseline of sheer survival, echoing Machiavelli's endorsement of fear over love as the basis for sound statecraft, or, alternatively put, for what "touches" man inwardly as opposed to his bedazzlement by the looks of the world. Hobbes will not admit of an exception to this reduction of honor seeking to self-preservation in anyone guided by a true understanding of nature (as opposed to the spontaneous and misguided impulse for mastery characteristic of some in the state of nature), making his view of the state of nature different from that of the Sophists, who had maintained that there was a just and noble life by nature as opposed to convention; that while the just and noble life by convention was indeed the morality of equality and contract, based on pedestrian appetites and the fear of being tyrannized over, there would always be certain naturally noble "masters" who would never submit. Gorgias, Callicles, and the other Sophists would never have agreed with Hobbes that the distinction between master and servant existed solely by "consent" and not in nature. Unlike Hobbes, the Sophists would not have disagreed with Aristotle that the distinction between the superior and inferior man existed by nature. Their disagreement would have been over what the nature of that superiority, including the most satisfying way of life, really is.

Hobbes believes that this kind of man, the alleged master by nature idolized by Callicles, can eventually be brought to understand that he is not truly independent or set apart from the many who are concerned with mere survival and comfort. He argues in chapter 15 of the *Leviathan* that aspiring tyrants who believe they can get away with achieving dominion simply have not thought through how the dangers of failure, including being crushed by the authority they want to usurp, must always outweigh through fear any merely prospective gains they could make by continuing to struggle for predominance. But this, after all, one might object, is a mere assertion or expression of hope on Hobbes's part, because people then and now manifestly do continue to take the risk. However that may be, this side of Hobbes's argument, in my view his preferred outcome, leads not to totalitarianism but to enlightenment – the belief that the new psychology of pedestrian appetitiveness will by degrees work its way into the human character, leading man to shed aggression and intolerance in exchange for the right to comfortable self-preservation.

The same paradox we have identified in Hobbes – an ostensibly more realistic presentation of human nature than that of the premodern tradition in order to usher in a far more optimistic set of expectations about the complete withering away of tyrannical aggression and oppression than anything the premodern tradition would have envisioned – becomes an in-built feature of much of modern political thought. Spinoza is a case in point. Like Machiavelli, whose wisdom he acknowledges, Spinoza gives a realistic, pragmatic, this-worldly account of Moses in order to deflate the claims of revelation that Moses was a divinely guided prophet. In Spinoza's depiction, Moses used force judiciously and created a religious faith so as to unite his people. In the first instance, this real-world account appears to bring power politics to the fore as against concerns about divine revelation and the life of faith. As Wildavsky (2005) puts it concerning this secular approach to interpreting Moses' authority, by stripping Moses of his "sacerdotal" character, we can better appreciate his genius, courage, prudence and ingenuity as a ruler, including how he sometimes verged on "despotism." However, insofar as Spinoza's long-term goal is this-worldly peace, tolerance, harmony and stability, the realistic side of politics exemplified by Moses' leadership will eventually give way to a spiritualized liberal democracy where the hard-headed realism of the founder can be dispensed with. On reflection, therefore, we realize that the fundamental aim of Spinoza (presaged by Machiavelli in presenting the realistic Moses, the secular leader or, to use Machiavelli's more poetic language, "armed prophet") was to *tame* Mosaic politics by separating them from the nonnegotiable zeal and righteousness sustained by a faith in God and God's justice. This tension between unsentimental realism about politics in the present for the sake of a peaceful, bounteous, tolerant, nonaggressive future undulates, as we consider in the next section, throughout the Enlightenment. Even later rebellions from the fascist right against what it regarded as liberal weakness and pacifism were unable to escape its contradictions. Carl Schmitt tried to derive the primacy of the friend-enemy distinction from Hobbes's warlike state of nature as a weapon against what he saw as the creeping and despiritualizing bourgeois materialism of Europe. He could not, however, successfully derive a more robust code of political strife from Hobbes's view of the state of nature because the most consistent long-term outcome of Hobbes's initially unvarnished presentation of honor seeking – domination and strife as man's spontaneous natural condition – is, through the construction of the social compact, precisely that bourgeois hamster wheel that Schmitt and many other fascists and National Socialists so loathed.[14]

Let us restate the central paradox of early modern political theory in its approach to tyrannical honor seeking as it originates in the thought of Hobbes. Political realism is advanced against what is caricatured as classical and Christian idealism or unworldliness so as to promote a project for political and social peace beyond anything ever thought possible by the allegedly unrealistic ancients. The principled rebellion against this emerging bourgeois world, and against early modern natural right, begins with Rousseau and Hegel, who recognize the superficiality and naivete of liberalism's hopes and so strive to reintroduce more full-blooded notions of honor, civic virtue, the warrior's code, and manly patriotism, often invoking the heroic republicanism of the ancient world. Yet in many ways these critics of the Enlightenment remain in the thrall of its paradox. Hegel's philosophy of history begins in the master–slave encounter, his strident celebration of history as a "slaughter bench" in which selfish passion alone can advance justice, and his broadsides against Kantian naivete for thinking that political

---

[14] On Schmitt and Hobbes, see Strauss (1995). On Moses as a political leader, consider Wildavsky (2005).

ambition could ever be "disinterested." It culminates, however, in the view of a coming world of forgiveness and reconciliation, with the last shock of tyrannical violence, the French Revolution and Napoleonic Wars, being but the darkest hour before the dawn, the final birth-pang of a new world of brotherhood and harmony.

We can extend these reflections much closer to the present. The approach to the phenomenon of tyranny taken by contemporary political science, fed by these deeper intellectual sources, remains in the thrall of the paradox we have identified. It begins with hardheaded realism about self-interest as the driving force of all political actors and ends in strikingly optimistic prognoses about the coming "new global civil society" of lasting peace, community, and equality in "a world without borders." Starting with the theories of Hegel and Marx, and continuing today with the alleged revolutionary power of economic globalization, the historical process itself becomes the tyrant that will once and for all free us from tyranny. Once the final avatar of violent transformation (the oppressive and destructive values of the Enlightenment, global capitalism, the bourgeoisie, today increasingly identified with the United States) needed to bring about nirvana is itself finally eclipsed, along with all oppressive nationalisms and competitiveness, world peace will reign. As the hope for a coming world of peace and the end of conflict always inherent in liberal political philosophy has unfolded, one might argue that its extravagant idealism has steadily eroded its underlying and original realism. In John Rawls's still-influential *A Theory of Justice* (1971), we find a world already completely transformed into a Hobbesian bourgeois social contract where we all prospectively have a "plan of life" and the economic means to carry it out, but completely abstracted from the Hobbesian state of nature. Whereas Hobbes's state of nature at least evoked the inherently belligerent side of human nature in order to remind us of the woes we would face without the social contract, and to remind us as well that human wolves will continue to roam the dark margins beyond the artificially constructed safety zone of the contractual state, Rawls's world abstracts entirely from those dark margins of war, imperialism, religious and national sectarianism, and fanaticism. Shorn of its moorings in a realistic assessment of man's belligerent side, liberalism, its original dynamism fueled by being conflicted, being torn, between hardheaded appraisals of the present and utopian expectations for the future, has increasingly passed in its intellectual classes to the utopian expectations alone, the coming postmodernist nirvana. Yet if the history of the great antiliberal revolutions from the Jacobins down through Bolshevism, National Socialism, Maoism, the Khmer Rouge, and the International Jihad are any guide, we can confidently predict that in any coming revolution on behalf of the "new global civil society," the pacifists and reformists will be swept aside by the more methodical and committed totalitarians.

THE PHENOMENOLOGY OF TYRANNY

My argument about the central paradox of early modern natural right regarding the status of tyranny and honor seeking has so far been deliberately rather general, abstracted, as it were, from the warp and woof of historical events. Now I would like to reintegrate some of that historical texture for a more rounded phenomenology of tyranny and its relationship to contemporary political science.

Political ideas, it is well to bear in mind, do not cause events in a lockstep way, but can be abstracted from them to illuminate an important dimension of events. In this book, although I have been arguing that, at a very general level of theoretical abstraction in the history of political thought, the understanding of tyranny changes from the erotic to the impersonal, and that the identity of modern tyranny is in some measure obscured by being adopted as an instrument for radical political and social change, I mean nothing so superficial as to suggest either that tyranny of the kind originally diagnosed by the classics actually disappeared from the world or that people ceased identifying and understanding tyranny in ways still heavily reliant on the classics, which remained at the heart of liberal education as it was conceived of by the Enlightenment.

For example, the American founders, steeped in the classics including Plato, Aristotle, Sallust, and Cicero, carefully pondered the permissible limits of ambition and the danger, discussed at length throughout this book, of would-be tyrants posing as liberators. Modern conquerors like Napoleon were certainly recognized by their contemporaries, including Emerson and Guizot, as attempting to imitate the glories of ancient rulers like Julius Caesar or Alexander the Great. Hegel, as already noted, extolled the need for ambition and a lust for prestige as an engine for the achievement of justice and derided the Kantian notion of a purely "disinterested" morality, while at the same time arguing that modern mass man needed the counterweight of classical learning to combat materialism and frivolity more than any previous epoch. Whereas Tocqueville worried that grand martial and political ambition might disappear in America because of its overwhelming interest in bourgeois commerce, the young Abraham Lincoln took the view that, on the contrary, ambition characteristic of "the tribe of the lion" including Alexander, Caesar, and Napoleon would always emerge, in America as much as anywhere else. The danger was not that grand ambition would fade away, but that it would find democratic politics too paltry to furnish such leonine men with a sense of honor from serving the common good.[15] For these Alcibiadean strivers, Lincoln worried, there might be more glory in overthrowing the republic than in saving it.

Distinguished historians and statesman including Gibbon, Macaulay, Churchill, and Charles de Gaulle all recognized the important role of honor seeking in political life and the need to distinguish between permissible and impermissible varieties of ambition and pride. Moreover, they were very much alive to the problem first observed by Sophocles, Plato, and Aristotle that some of the same dark or bellicose qualities present in tyrants might also fuel the vigor of the leading statesman. As Emerson memorably put it about Napoleon: "Here was an experiment, under the most favorable conditions, of the powers of intellect without conscience. Never was such a leader so endowed and so weaponed; never leader found such aids and followers."[16] In some ways, then, modern historians and men of affairs did not succumb to Hobbesian reductionism about the place of honor seeking in political life. Grand ambition still had a role, for good or ill. To quote de Gaulle:

When faced with the challenge of events, the man of character has recourse to himself. His instinctive response is to leave his mark on action, to take responsibility for it, to make it *his own business*.[17]

At the same time, however, beginning with the Age of Reason and the Enlightenment, we also find a tendency to believe that, with however many fits and starts and occasional relapses, the history of the West

---

[15] For a full discussion of Tocqueville on the danger posed to grand ambition by democracy and Lincoln's differing view in the "Lyceum Speech," see Newell (2009) part 2.

[16] Quoted in Newell (2001) p. 279.

[17] Quoted in Newell (2001) p. 297.

was progressing toward ever greater prosperity, freedom, justice, peace, equality, and tolerance and that this process could not be reversed. Figures as various as Gibbon, Tocqueville, and Marx all believed this, albeit with very different expectations for the final outcome. Hegel among others recognized that Napoleon was not merely the recrudescence of some ancient conqueror, but spread the rationality of the Enlightenment through his conquests. He was, in effect, a liberalizing tyrant who, because he introduced the modern conception of the nation-state and the social contract to the backward remnants of the ancien regime in Europe, would conceivably make conquests and imperial glory seeking like his own unnecessary in the future, when the peaceful individualism and commercialism promoted by Hobbes, Locke, Montesquieu, and Voltaire would reign supreme.

This belief in the progress of history had to qualify the extent to which thinkers and historians believed that tyranny of the kind diagnosed by the ancients had survived in pure form or would survive long into the future. For must it not fade away as men became more enlightened, even if, as Hegel argued, the twenty years or more of revolution, terror, and war between 1789 and 1807 was the necessary final spasm of violence needed to bring about the rule of reason? But then, finally, we reach the supreme paradox that the twentieth century, when one might have imagined that the beneficent progress of history was nearing its end state, produced tyrannies unprecedented in scale, destructive power, and fiendishness, suggesting that not only had the modern belief in progress arguably been naive, but that the ancients themselves, for all their belief that tyrants will always be with us, would have been confounded by the likes of Stalin and Hitler. Something new had been added to our experience and understanding of tyranny, it could be argued, not only from the classical viewpoint, but from the liberal progressivist one as well. By way of concluding these studies, let us try to unravel the layers of this enigma in turn. As I have already suggested, the attempt at a full explanation of the distinctive totalitarian tyrannies of the twentieth century, including their more recent Islamist variant, is beyond the scope of this study. For they cannot be explained solely within this book's theme of the deeroticization of tyranny or the conquest of nature alone. At the same time, however, totalitarian tyrannies do, I am suggesting, share in these strains of the first transition to modernity inaugurated by Machiavelli. In this way, I hope to substantiate, on the basis of everything we have considered throughout this book, my suggestion in the Introduction that tyranny cannot be understood as a constant in the history of political ideas, psychology, or, indeed, political experience.

I have described the classical approach to tyranny as trying to determine in a given context just where the untutored passion for distinction can be sublimated and reformed into a sense of honor that comes from benefiting one's fellow citizens; where an egotism and belligerence that might in one setting lead to tyranny can in another be the fuel to excel in public service. To reiterate: this classical temperament for evaluating the relationship between tyranny and statesmanship did not go away as modernity took root. Quite the contrary: the general love of classical learning consequent upon the Renaissance, and that even Machiavelli contributed to inspiring despite his radical repudiation and modification of it, was renewed during the Age of Reason and the Enlightenment. Even a strictly religious humanist like Erasmus, in his prescription for a Christian King, although disapproving of the moral slipperiness of the Machiavellian Prince, regards honor and glory as perfectly legitimate rewards for just rule, a manly satisfaction in its own sphere that need not bow to Christian humility in the undiluted way required of the clergy, in this sense marrying Aristotle' great-souled man to the vision of a Christian commonwealth.

To take a later and even more forthright example of a political realism at least partially classical while modulated by a more modern, Machiavellian temperament, Edward Gibbon's description of the future emperor Constantine as a young man expresses well how traits unattractive or overbearing in themselves and in private relationships may be necessary (a point made repeatedly, as we have seen, by the classics) for the development of a ruler's character, a sap that strengthens the fully developed plant even as it is submerged in and shaped by it:

He was dexterous in all his exercises, intrepid in war, affable in peace; in his whole conduct, the active spirit of youth was tempered by habitual prudence; and while his mind was engrossed by ambition, he appeared cold and insensible to the allurements of pleasure. (Gibbon [1900] vol.1, p. 470)

This could be a description of Xenophon's Cyrus.

Separated from the context in and for which these character traits were developed, what type of person is this? An intense but outwardly reserved man, unlikely to be too free with his thoughts or feelings, relentless in the pursuit of distinction and reproaching, by his very presence, the ordinary pleasures of those around him. Not a pleasant dinner companion or a suitable talk-show host. In the wider context of which Gibbon writes, though, the restorer of the Roman state after one of its starker passages of decline.

As another example, let us take Lord Charnwood's biography of Abraham Lincoln. Written in 1912, it is considerably closer to home for us in time and spirit, yet has a genuinely Aristotelian flavor in its judicious balance of admiration for a statesman who dedicated himself to his country's highest principles of justice with a shrewd insight into how strong were Lincoln's longings for success and fame. "Very soon," Charnwood observes after describing Lincoln's first emergence as a national politician after eight years in the Illinois state house, "the question of whether a proposal or even a sentiment was timely or premature came to bulk too large in the deliberations of Lincoln's friends. The reader will perhaps wonder later whether such considerations did not bulk too largely in Lincoln's own mind." Charnwood then formulates the problem that ambitious servants of the common good such as Lincoln presents to the student of politics:

Was there in his statesmanship, even in later days when he had great work to do, an element of that opportunism which, if not actually base, is at least cheap? Or did he come as near as a man with many human weaknesses can to the wise and nobly calculated opportunism which is not merely the most beneficial statesmanship, but demands a heroic self-mastery? (Charnwood [1917] p. 74)

This is an updated version of the question first posed, as we saw in Chapter 4, by the chorus in *Oedipus Tyrannus*: Where do political opportunism and personal ambition leave off and great statesmanship begin? Might they be combined in the same persons? Indeed, as we have already observed, it is Lincoln himself in the Lyceum Speech who mused on the choice between a life devoted to serving the republic and one, perhaps more glorious, devoted to bringing it down. In contrast with Charnwood's nuanced and mature evaluation of political ambition, still plausible to readers on the eve of World War I, our own categories usually require us to choose between, or at least lean toward, one of two equally implausible notions: that political actors are motivated either by a purely disinterested devotion to universal morality, or by a desire for power, wealth, and status regardless of whatever rhetorical cant they may employ in public. Charnwood's middle ground of a "wise and nobly calculated opportunism" is still evident in certain leaders in practice, but has all but vanished as a psychological category among political analysts and commentators.

The earlier literature stretching back to the Renaissance of which Charnwood's biography is a late but fine example, a compendium of classical, Christian, and modern learning, understood that to achieve good for people through politics, one needed to achieve political power, which will inevitably entail a degree of ethical compromise and even unscrupulousness. The goal of this literature was not merely to describe ambition, but to distinguish its permissible varieties from the tyrannical ones so as to encourage the former and discourage the latter. The respective descriptions were meant to entail the condemnation or commendation, as in, say, Plato's description of the tyrant versus his description of the just man. However, as Charnwood observes, sometimes these two aims were at cross-purposes. Some of the classically or religiously inspired accounts are so eager to condemn tyrannically or venally motivated honor seeking that they bury the more complicated blend of personal ambition and public service typical of the greatest statesmen in bromides about how one should never under any circumstances be ambitious or seek honor. Against this excessively moralistic stance Charnwood, perhaps with a view to the Calvinistic morality of the particular nation whose hero he was praising, observes with respect to Lincoln:

We must accept without reserve Herndon's reiterated assertion that Lincoln was intensely ambitious; and if ambition means the eager desire for great opportunities, the depreciation of it, which has long been a commonplace of literature, and which may be traced back to the Epicureans, is a piece of cant which ought to be withdrawn from currency, and ambition, commensurate with the powers which each man can discover in himself, should be frankly recognized as a part of Christian duty. (Charnwood [1917] p. 260)

Altogether, then, despite the massive shift in ontological orientation between the classical and modern understandings of tyranny beginning with Machiavelli, a rich trove of ambiguities about the character and desirability of political ambition, compounded of classical, Christian, and modern sources, continued to flourish. Nevertheless, the growing conviction that modernity, with its emphasis on equal rights, individual self-interest, and a preference for the peaceful arts of commerce over aristocratic pride and martial glory, was being progressively revealed as the direction in which all previous human history was inexorably tending, did have the long-run consequence of dulling the perception that tyranny every bit as monstrous as, or more so than, the worst previous examples might continue as a recurrent and unavoidable feature of political life. Gibbon himself, a matchless psychologist of ambition when examining the Roman past, believes at the same time that historical progress will steadily dissipate the possibility of tyrannical violence and conquest in the future, as the new psychology of enlightened self-interest originated by Hobbes and other modern thinkers continued to spread:

We cannot determine to what height the human species may aspire in their future advance toward perfection; but it may safely be presumed that no people . . . will relapse into their original barbarism. . . . The benefits of law and policy, of trade and manufactures, of arts and sciences, are more solid and permanent.

After Auschwitz and the Gulag, not to mention Chairman Mao, the Khmer Rouge, and the Taliban, it is difficult, to say the least, to believe in our "advance toward perfection." Surveying the tumult of twentieth century politics in his 1960 classic *Political Man*, Seymour Martin Lipset acknowledged and drew upon the regime types first elaborated by Plato and Aristotle, including tyranny, despotism, oligarchy, democracy, and the danger posed to popular government by "the appeal of irresponsible demagogues." There was ample evidence for reconsidering Aristotle's contention in the *Politics* that the desire to tyrannize was not reducible to the desire for pedestrian material gratification – that a man did not become a tyrant "in order to get in out of the cold" (1267a2–17). The Enlightenment had believed that someone's desire to dominate and oppress others derived from the frustration of his desires for security from harm and for material pleasures that are in themselves harmless. The solution lay in removing the frustration needlessly caused by religious and moral restrictions on self-interest and private pleasure, thereby dissipating the sources of war and hatred. After the unprecedented devastation of World Wars I and II and the superpower conflict of the Cold War, however, it was perhaps actually easier to agree with Plato and Aristotle than it had been for Gibbon and other earlier moderns in the salad days of the belief in historical progress that certain people intrinsically want to tyrannize over others, whether out of greed, conviction, a love of mastery, or all three – and find that the glory and exhilaration of doing so far outweigh the risks to one's security and comfort that this kind of ambition may entail.

The twentieth century was the era when the goals of the Enlightenment, one might have claimed, had been most thoroughly actualized in North America and Europe. The scientific wonders fantasized about by Bacon in *The House of Solomon* and viciously lampooned by Swift (for example, a machine for extracting sunbeams from cucumbers) in *Gulliver's Travels* had all come to pass. It was assumed by Voltaire, Becarria, and the other preceptors of the Enlightenment that when individual self-interest, liberated from feudal and theological restrictions on commercial enterprise and aided by science, held sway everywhere, people would lose their hatreds and intolerance because, once the impediments to their survival, comfort and self-fulfillment vanished, so would the motives for aggressive conduct. The steady spread and success of this worldview led nineteenth-century Europe to see all of history as advancing toward an impending future of perfect democracy, prosperity, individual freedom, rationality, and peace. War would be outmoded, either for the idealistic reason that people would finally shed the last lingering prejudices of religion, race, class, or caste that prevented mutual respect, or for the utilitarian reason that the material cost and devastation of war were demonstrably too high in an era that depended on uninterrupted economic growth to facilitate social advancement. On the eve of World War I, and in a strange way making people welcome it, the belief was widespread that this was the "war to end all wars"; that for something so retrograde and barbaric to happen at the opening of the twentieth century could only mean that it was the apocalyptic prelude to the final achievement of the emerging new era of lasting peace; that its horrors would finally teach us our lesson and impel us to abandon militarism for good. Yet, as we know, 1914 was instead the prelude to a series of tyrannies, revolutions, and wars unparalleled in all of history for their levels of carnage and destruction, their efficiency in murder and torture, and the depths of depravity sunk to by the oppressors and of despair by their victims.

These things were not supposed to happen. In the century when liberalism was to be triumphant everywhere, not only did tyranny and wars of conquest not vanish, but they achieved levels of destruction and cruelty that made the "tyrants" decried by eighteenth- and nineteenth-century revolutionaries look like comic opera martinets by comparison. The psychology of liberalism and the Victorian belief in cumulative material and moral progress could not account for such leaders or movements often erupting in the very countries where the Enlightenment's political and economic agendas were most advanced. The spread of prosperity and rights, by dispelling ignorance and removing the bases for prejudice and belligerence, should have made tyranny too dangerous, irrational, and indecent a goal for any sensible person to pursue or support. It should likewise have robbed anyone aberrant enough still to want it of credulous, backward masses to obey him. As Gibbon's work reveals, the modern age had preserved an appreciation for the richness of classical political psychology out of its general respect for learning and desire to foster it. Yet precisely Gibbon, as we have seen, did not believe that modern Europe's progress could regress into barbarism like that of Rome's decline into the Dark Ages, let alone something worse.

Here is where we reach the most difficult issue in the ontology of tyranny, one that I initially raised in the Introduction to this book: Is it enough to recognize the danger of modern tyranny by reverting to the classical perspective, thereby freeing oneself from the delusions of historical progress and Hobbesian reductionism? For even that classical psychology, never entirely lost sight of in the West, with its detailed exploration and condemnation of the tyrannical character and regime, might well appear to be inadequate to account for the most monstrous of our own era's tyrants like Hitler, Stalin, Mao, or Pol Pot. As we have observed, the Hobbesian and Kantian strains in contemporary political morality tend to dismiss political ambition and honor seeking altogether as either camouflage for a more basic impulse to exploit others for material gain, or as an unworthy, extraneous motive for performing our duty. The classical thinkers were more receptive, both descriptively and prescriptively, to entertaining such motives because they saw the ambition for honor and rule as partially condemnable but also partially redeemable facets of human behavior. Rather than dismissing the pursuit of honor on a priori grounds, their moral aim was to enlist honor seeking in the service of a self-governing community under the rule of law. They sought to convince the ambitious, tyrannically inclined man that the pursuit of tyranny, as opposed to civic virtue guided by philosophy and the life of the mind, could lead only to a dishonorable, despised, degradingly self-indulgent, paranoid, and bestial existence.

The bizarre quality of modern totalitarian regimes is that their tyrants (if, indeed, this is even the best term for them) have not been self-indulgent in the gargantuanly hedonistic sense condemned by Plato and Aristotle. Moreover, the honor they desire is of an arguably different character than the strictly personal type of recognition that the classical thinkers saw a tyrant as gaining from his subjects and from which, they conceded, the tyrant could take a certain satisfaction (recalling Xenophon's portrait of Hiero), albeit a misguided one, as the "lover" or "owner" of his people. For, in contrast with the vivid and urbane tyrants of the ancient world, our contemporary totalitarian tyrants have at once a public aspect that is titanic, omnipresent and beyond personal human scale (reflected in the mechanized mass genocide and the architectural brutalism of Stalin and Hitler) and in their personal lives a kind of self-effacement, crankishness, banality, or awkwardness. Whereas the lives of the ancient tyrants are seamlessly interwoven with the personalistic, patrimonial character of their regimes, so that their political predominance is conflated with the possessiveness but also at times the generosity, charm, or flamboyance of a lover (think of Alcibiades or Julius Caesar), we are astounded at the kind of "gray blur" (to use Trotsky's famous description of Stalin) who stands behind the levers of the totalitarians state's superhuman power. While having millions killed, Hitler showed an elaborate Austrian courtesy toward his secretaries, like that of a bourgeois banker, teasing them that they were fattening him up with too much cake. Himmler suffered from chronic stomach pains and, while supervising the Holocaust, thoughtfully remembered his secretaries' birthdays. These rulers do not seem to seek public honor, at least not in the traditionally recognizable splendor of past emperors and kings. They often spurn elaborate ceremonials, regalia, and other marks of high office for "a plain field tunic," avoiding the public for years at a time in their bunkers or walled compounds. Stalin's quarters in the Kremlin have been compared in size to those of an Oxford don; Hitler's summer retreat to that of a relatively prosperous businessman. Osama bin Laden, once the aspiring revolutionary leader of the Muslim world, was killed in a near-empty bedroom. The point is not that these leaders were actually incorruptible or did not have secret vices and purloined wealth. The point is that their personal lives were entirely sundered from their monumental public image, whereas past despots lived on a scale and in a way (think of Nero's Golden House or Louis XIV's Versailles) that merged their capacity for luxury, adornment, and refinement with their public identities as rulers.

Reclusive in their "Spartan quarters," modern totalitarian tyrants purge and recreate human existence on a vast scale, through the destruction and transportation of millions of people, in the service of doctrines that proclaim an ideal, beyond compromise, of equality, virtue, classlessness, and communal or racial purity. Although capable of setting in motion prodigies of terror that in the past one can find only in descriptions of the most vengeful deities – and which the Enlightenment believed would vanish with the end of Europe's religious wars – in person our tyrants tend to be gray, mild, lacking in vanity of dress or manner, studious, gluttonous, and fussy. Many witnesses testify to Hitler's shyness and tentativeness in private, in contrast with his thundering public performances, while Stalin's speaking style even in public was tediously dry and pedantic, reflective of his early seminary training. Sometimes they are histrionic in the manner of an overwrought professor or café intellectual, eager to lay out their crankish opinions on all facets of life from the cycles of empire to music, diet, and grooming (such unendurable monologues were common to Stalin, Hitler, and Castro). As Flaubert sums up his character Senecal in *L'Education sentimentale*, the would-be Jacobin of 1848 who ends up as the police agent of Napoleon III, they "smell of the pedagogue and the priest."[18] We wonder what secret of our age would finally explain the connection between such unprepossessing individuals and the titanic scale of their destructiveness.

A brief example from the ancient and modern literature will crystallize this contrast. In Aristotle's description, the tyrant at his worst is a monster of desires who outrages his subjects by plundering or ravishing them (*Politics* 1312b17–38, 1313b32–1315a40). Citizens are driven to tyrannicide by the need to rid society of this bloated exploiter. This powerful condemnation, repeated and embellished by humanist

---

[18] See the discussion of eros and revolution in Flaubert's novel in Newell (1995).

commentators both religious and secular, still animates many contemporary denunciations of oppressive regimes, like the 2011 uprisings in Tunisia, Egypt, and Syria against corrupt kleptocrats and their idle, spoiled families and hangers-on. In striking contrast, however, as Sergey Nechaev writes in a classic modern statement of the terrorist's creed, *Catechism of the Revolutionist*, the terrorist's violence is aimed at the purgation of society's *own* bloated desires and corruption.[19] Tyrannical methods are used for ascetic ends by ascetics who want to force everyone else to be ascetics. Nechaev's very use of the term "catechism" suggests that terrorism aims to create a politicized, secularized version of a community of religious penitents with its absolute monastic discipline, forced to renounce their pleasures and luxuries for the sake of the collective. Even pity for the oppressed themselves, the poor and disadvantaged, cannot stand in the way of striking at those among them who, through foolishness or venality, prop up the established order. The majority of the guillotine's victims under Robespierre were from the middle and lower orders. Ostensibly the intended beneficiaries of the French Revolution, in practice they often clung most staunchly to their religious faith and loyalty to the monarchy. The terrorist's creed calls, as it were, for an idealistic and disinterested tyrant, murderous and pure of spirit, a paradox that points to the limitations of the Aristotelian categories for characterizing this peculiarly modern kind of coercion. "Hard toward himself," Nechaev writes in language at once ruthless and principled, "he must be hard toward others also.... He must not be what the promptings of his personal inclinations would have him be, but what the general interest of the revolution prescribes." This new psychology of the ascetic terrorist is one attenuated outcome of what I have argued is the ontological shift, inaugurated by Machiavelli, from the classical emphasis on the character of the ruler grounded in the harmony between the intellect and the passions and the modern impersonal method of rule requiring the conquest of eros.

Just as these actual or aspiring terroristic tyrants promote the image that they are not hedonistic, vain, splendid, or flamboyant in their desire for public adulation, they do not attract their following because, as Plato and Aristotle had tended to argue, tyrants pander to the masses' own hedonism and moral laxness, such that tyranny for Plato emerges

[19] Nechaev (1987) pp. 68–72.

seamlessly from the basest traits of democracy. On the contrary, where they do not terrify their followers, these leaders often elicit a kind of selfless zeal on their part as well. The followers participate in the leader's sense of having a "historic mission" whose scope and intensity of destruction were formerly approached only by the most savage of religious wars and persecutions, a mission that requires of its participants that they renounce not only an easy life of pleasure and relaxation but the luxury of ordinary moral scruples and decent sentiments of compassion and tolerance. In this connection, we can think of Himmler's infamous speech at Posen in 1943 to a secret gathering of SS leaders describing the glory of the Holocaust as a "secret page" of history that they alone would share, or of Bukharin's effusions about the "difficult tasks" faced by the Cheka during the Soviet Union's campaigns of forced collectivization and the liquidation of the kulaks. Both points of view share in common the idea that what distinguishes these revolutionary movements from the selfish interests of both bourgeois democratic and traditional throne-and-alter conservative politics is precisely the lack of venality or personal passion that characterizes the elite cadres who carry out the surgical reconstruction of society through genocide. The "greatness" of these revolutionaries stems in their own minds from their ability to feel nothing toward their victims, not even an ugly spasm of envy, cruelty, or triumph. They aspire to a purely disinterested murderousness.

The classical thinkers begin with this ugly spasm – with such passions as anger, envy, and hatred (as in Aristotle's *Rhetoric*) – on the assumption that, even at their basest, these passions harbor a potentiality for rising above selfish desires and exploitation, so that, shaped by education and rhetorical exhortation, their energies might be converted to exertion on behalf of the common good. Although, left to themselves, such spasms may result only in the domination and conquest of one's competitors, they can, when properly educated, be redirected toward the honor derived from public service. Arrogance, cruelty, and hatred can be sublimated by – while providing the transmuted emotional energy for – the merited pride of a leading citizen.

Our terroristic tyrants, by contrast, appear to elude the classical starting point altogether. They measure their own success by their striving not to manifest any of the traditional signs of a corrupt character – vanity, lust, dissipation, greed, vengefulness – and so are more disturbing, because their self-restraint is not on behalf of reason or justice at the expense of tyranny, but to enhance their tyrannical focus at the expense of all pleasures and sentiments. They aspire to practice a weird idealism calling for the repression and purgation of ordinary passions for the sake of maximum efficiency, undistracted by hatred, in pursuing hatred's goals. If anyone is to be pitied (Bukharin and Himmler both express this view), it is the executioners themselves, for the psychic toll which their self-discipline takes in requiring them to give up the luxury of ordinary anger or greed, let alone compassion for or misgivings over the fate of their victims. The ideal is to achieve a pure will to annihilate, to be denatured in the service of the cause. Striving for this ideal of impersonal destruction protects the purity of the revolutionary movement not only from blandishments based on traditional and customary notions of shame, compassion, and decency but from the temptation to perform one's duty to kill out of any sense of personal gratification. For to hate or envy the victim on a personal level implies the possibility that you could be mistaken about the desirability of the possession you envy them for, about whether they actually possess it, and about whether they have really done or said the things you hate them for. Changing one's views about the object of one's hatred might lead to forgiveness and reconciliation. If, however, one wills the destruction of another *regardless* of one's personal opinion or feelings about their blameworthiness, there is no danger that murderous passions might be led by gentler sentiments and better reasoning and information to convert themselves into acceptance and friendship.

The point is not that the murderers actually or even frequently attained this state of inner purity, but that the movements understood and presented themselves this way as an ideal to which they should aspire. Himmler was appalled at any instance of unorganized violence or sadism toward the victims of the Holocaust that might taint the purity of the will to annihilate the Jews with corrupt personal motives, and he was scandalized by, and sought to punish, the widespread theft of the victims' belongings by the camp guards and officers. The German *Volk* must take everything from the conquered with a clean conscience, but the SS man must aim for a higher standard: to liquidate the German people's enemies without personal greed or malice toward individuals. The capacity of such movements to inflict death on millions in a technologically routinized manner appears to comprise a new kind of tyranny, a de-natured, impersonal ideal of rule that can make all traditional understandings of honor and virtue appear irrelevant. For they are led by rulers who not only disprove the assumptions of liberal psychology that equality and prosperity will dissipate the sources of aggression, but also seem to fall outside the classical assumption that aggression can be sublimated by a love of honor that elevates and enlists the passions by promising honor from one's fellow citizens in exchange for public service, possible at bottom because the eros for exclusive prestige and tyranny is a misguided version of the longing for the beautiful and the good that contains the kernel of its own self-transcendence. When we look back to the eve of World War I and reflect on the catastrophes to come, Charnwood, writing in 1912 about Lincoln's love of honor through serving justice and the common good, might as well have really been writing in Aristotle's time.

Considering what I have termed the impersonal, deeroticized character of modern rule leads us to the question of technology itself and how it has arguably assimilated the drive to tyrannize, an issue I first broached in the Introduction. Some important contemporary thinkers, above all Heidegger, have identified technology as the defining essence of modernity altogether, fully manifest in the destiny of the West only in the last century, and therefore establishing a fateful break between our era and all previous ones. Given the permanent terror in which the world has been held by nuclear weapons technology – a terror that, because it is daily and mostly unseen, is not identifiable as terror in the usual sense of that word as an extreme emergency, but is taken to be the height of normality – and given the more mundane ways in which our lives are increasingly organized and surveyed by machinery including cybernetic technology, it might well be asked whether the masters that rule our fates are primarily people at all, or rather an autonomous network of interlocking electronic forces. The problem of technology is especially dramatic in the case of totalitarian tyrants such as Hitler or Stalin, for the technology of the modern police state enables such rulers to launch destruction on a scale unavailable to past despots. As I write these words in the summer of 2012, the ever more pervasive power of global communications technology is both a source among dissidents of potential liberation from oppressive regimes such as China or Syria but also of the state's extension of its own capacity for monitoring or shutting down all communications among citizens. In a strange way, it might actually be reassuring if one could assume that modern tyranny equaled something like ancient tyranny plus technology – "Genghis Khan with electricity" as Stalin was once termed. For if this were true, it might mitigate the bleak picture just sketched. It would suggest that we could after all understand modern tyrants according to the traditional categories or as some derivation from them. Technology would be a mere instrument that, although terrible in the hands of a tyrant, could in principle be treated separately from tyranny and deployed solely for humane purposes.

The problem, however, may go deeper than this. On a descriptive level, as we have just seen, there are reasons for doubting that modern tyranny at its most extreme can be characterized in terms even similar to those of classical political psychology, as (to vary the metaphor) a sort of Hiero of Syracuse on Twitter. More fundamentally, the same machine and cybernetic technology which makes the police state possible also makes possible the prosperity of the liberal democracies and is grounded in a human and spiritual revolution stretching back to the Enlightenment. The transformation of the premodern politics of classical/Christian communality into the new politics of autonomous, self-interested individuals linked together by the artificial instrumentality of the social contract always entailed, as we have considered throughout this book, the conquest of nature in the material sense, the *scientia propter potentiam* envisioned by Bacon. Yet the conquest of nature in the outward, material sense also entails, and must continually reaffirm, that man is by nature inwardly this isolated, individual rights-bearing producer and consumer of commodities, grounded in the self-introspecting subject of Cartesian epistemology. The full sense of technology, then, is not only the productive apparatus of the modern economy but, more profoundly, the new ontological stance toward the world originating in Machiavelli, Bacon, and Hobbes in which such unprecedented productivity is grounded. For if man forgets that he is alienated and dissociated by the state of nature, he may slip back into the reliance on priests and kings, on theology and teleology, that once restrained individual self-interest and commercial enterprise in the name of a higher social wholeness. Technology is the pregnant term for this transformation of man's relation to the world, in which man is ripped out of the communal, pedagogical, and theological contexts provided by the old politics of the classical-Christian conglomerate and cast alone into a hostile world that must be fought with and subdued before it can be made to yield the material balms that will make aggression disappear. Running counterpoint, one might say, to the optimistic strain of the Enlightenment with its hopes for a peaceful and prosperous future for all is this ongoing project for the reconstruction of human nature as individualistic, spurred by the existential anxiety of one's solitariness and vulnerability. For Hobbes, only ceaseless anxiety in the face of our finitude will keep our desire keen to embrace the benefits of the social contract and live as long and as well as we can. Here is where the light and dark corridors radiating out of Machiavelli's project through Hobbes may most closely intersect.

Tempting as it may be, however, to follow Heidegger in equating modernity altogether with technology (indeed, for Heidegger, its origins run back to the ancients themselves, to Plato's metaphysics), we must beware of so doing, because it involves a massive distancing of oneself from the world of observable political experience, a world in which, however much they may need to be supplemented or qualified, the fundamental premises of classical political philosophy are still operative – at least as an earlier level of the archaeology of tyranny added to by Machiavelli and the moderns – and provide a starting point for diagnosing tyranny in our own era, even if it is not the whole story. For to assimilate modernity entirely to technology, as Heidegger does, is to obliterate any proximal distinctions – based on our own experience, historical memory, and learning – between more or less just or unjust, more or less legitimate or illegitimate, regimes.

As Heidegger famously wrote in *An Introduction to Metaphysics* (1959), viewed from the perspective of the unstoppable juggernaut of global technology, summing up the entire destiny of the West from Anaximander to Fordism, it makes no difference whether one lives under Franklin Roosevelt's America or Stalin's Russia: As the two superpower variants of global technology's relentless unfolding, they are "metaphysically the same." Yet all of our experiences, the lessons we draw from history, our capacity for discriminating judgment, and our whole heritage of political philosophy both ancient and modern, tell us that this is not so: it *does* make a difference. Tyranny may come to us in the guise of invisible or impersonal technology, with its threat of annihilation or total control. But it also still announces itself, as it always has, in the open manner of cynical and murderous pirates like

Saddam Hussein with his rogue's gallery of blood-sucking relatives and hangers-on, or of murderous religious extremists like the Taliban, to say nothing of more ordinary, shambling garden variety Mafia-style klepto-crats like Mubarak, or nationalistic, would-be Great Power militarists of the nineteenth-century Bismarckian *Reatpolitik* variety like Putin.

Perhaps none of these varieties is precisely identical with tyranny as it was practiced and understood in the ancient past. But they are at least intelligible, as a point of departure, in terms of the traditional categories of political philosophy, both ancient and modern. Modern totalitarian tyrants, although different from any ancient counterparts in the utopian and millenarian aim of their destruction, do display some of their psychological traits, such as the capacity diagnosed by Plato of spontaneous thumos for righteous zeal, anger, bellicosity, jealousy of rivals, and possessiveness. On the lowest level of base conniving thug-gery, the rise of a Saddam Hussein through treachery and murder could come out of the annals of past tyrants and political adventurers includ-ing Hiero of Syracuse or Cesare Borgia. That said, we admittedly still face the central hermeneutical conundrum that I sketched in the Intro-duction to this book: If the character of modern tyranny is in some crucial respects fundamentally different from, and unanticipated by, the classical account, does this mean that human nature itself and how it experiences and evaluates political life has been historically altered by the project for the conquest of Fortuna?

Leo Strauss once characterized the social sciences, in a reference to the famous scene of the Emperor Nero, as "fiddling while Rome burns," a remark that did not endear him to those disciplines.[20] Although not referring to tyranny in that particular context, he made it clear in other works that a major part of this fiddling was that the social sciences could not recognize tyranny, including its contemporary manifestation as totalitarianism, for what it was. This obfuscation he regarded as one of the central contrasts between ancient and modern political sci-ence, to the discredit of the latter. Although the behavioral revolution long ago abated, overtaken by the postbehaviorists and postmodernists, the obfuscation Strauss identified as a hallmark of the social sciences is still widespread. It is still fundamentally rooted in Hobbes and the

[20] In Storing (1962).

assumption that aggressive behavior is not an independent variable in political motivation rooted in honor, patriotism or moral conviction, but a distorted psychology stemming from the desire for self-preservation. Once the fear of death is mollified by peaceful and commodious living, it is still widely maintained, the sources of aggression will dissipate.

This assumption began as a core value of the Enlightenment, and, in regimes like the United States, Canada, and those of Western Europe, gradually became a self-fulfilling prophecy buttressed by procedural democracy and a long process of character formation stressing tolerance and the debate over means rather than ends.[21] But it has never been true of much of the rest of the world, then or now. In much of the rest of the world, many of the core premodern and nonliberal values that required three centuries of steady erosion in Europe and North America to dissolve remain vigorous and even self-renewing. Much of the world still believes (or is constrained to believe) in the primacy of the household over the civic community, of clan and patrimonial authority over the rights of the individual, whether locally or writ large as entire regimes ruled by "strong men" like Putin or collectivist oligarchies like China. Much of the world's politics is motivated by clan and sectarian rivalries and hostilities based on ethnicity and religious conviction. Frequently, the rival factions do not hesitate in acting on those disagreements violently. Frequently, the victors will seek to erect a tyrannical authority over their rivals based on revenge, greed, the passion for mastery, religious or ideological conviction, or all of these together. Large parts of the world, in short, are in Hobbes's state of nature or on the brink of it. People of course do not want to be terrorized or tyrannized over, but unfortunately many do want to do this to others, and even where it is possible to agree that peace benefits everyone, a good many believe there are aims in life that are more important, dignified,

---

[21] In this connection, consider Berlin's characterization of Machiavelli's protoliberalism. He makes an interesting link between Machiavelli's shattering of the "unity" provided by the Platonic notion that there is only one Good for all human beings and the tolerance that results from realizing that, because there are numerous incompatible goods, the debate about politics should concern only means, not ultimate ends. Men had always been aware of the need to "make agonizing choices between incompatible alternatives," but Machiavelli "converted its expression from a paradox into something approaching a commonplace. . . . His achievement is of the first order." Berlin (2000) p. 79.

and satisfying than peace, because they involve passionate conviction, nonnegotiable justice, and righteous anger.

In the real world of politics, and especially of international relations, political actors and observers in the West are often faced with the difficult, and ethically queasy, task of distinguishing between better and worse versions of nondemocratic government. Should we always support democratically motivated revolutions against dictatorships and one-party states, like the brave struggles of the Arab Spring in Egypt, Tunisia, Libya, and Syria? Or are we sometimes faced with balancing the support for democracy against other important pragmatic and moral concerns – for example, the fact that Hosni Mubarak maintained Egypt's peace with Israel and opposed radical Islamism, while we do not yet know how his successors will treat those issues.

Does democracy simply equal the absence or removal of tyranny, absolute monarchy, or dictatorship? Or does a people's spontaneous and understandable desire for liberation from a tyrannical oppressor require a long period of character shaping before they can become the rights-bearing individuals of a fully developed liberal democracy – a process of secularization, the replacement of debates over nonnegotiable ends with debates over means toward the same ends of economic security and well-being, and the inculcation of the values of tolerance, freedom of speech, and freedom of worship? Might overthrowing a despot lead to something even worse following in its stead? This has happened in successive revolutions including the French, Russian, Maoist, Cuban, and Iranian, in each of which a fitfully modernizing authoritarian regime was replaced by more radical reformers who were themselves rapidly swept away by totalitarian collectivists. Quandaries of this kind were difficult enough for the classical political theorists, as we saw in our examinations of Plato and Aristotle on the possibility of benign despotism and a role for tyrannical founders in establishing just or at least stable regimes, an examination shrouded in circumspection and caution in order not to undermine their foreground preference for republican self-government. Although modern political science beginning with Machiavelli and Hobbes started out, by contrast, with a seemingly franker, bolder, and more realistic assessment of these moral gray zones in distinguishing openly between relatively constructive and unconstructive tyrannies and endorsing the former, oddly enough, the original pragmatism of modern political theory has in the long run been undermined by its extravagant counterfactual longing for a future world free of all oppression, violence, and injustice. Today, as a consequence, political science is frequently ill equipped to embark on the disturbing but necessary discussion of the greater and lesser evils among nondemocratic regimes.

Throughout this book, I have argued that the drive toward an impersonal paradigm of authority launched by Machiavelli and radicalized by Hobbes, entailing the severing of the connection between the spontaneous longing for tyrannical mastery and the potentially rehabilitative erotic longing for the beautiful and the good first elaborated by Plato, is the source of what is arguably modern political science's psychological deficit when it comes to understanding the varieties of regime types and leadership types, including the varieties of tyranny and of honor-seeking ambition across the spectrum from out and out tyranny to a robust service of the common good and all the shades of gray in between. Although Machiavelli's new science of politics remains in an interstitial zone between the modern drive toward pure method and the more rounded and heterogeneous account of political existence characteristic of the ancient philosophers and historians, Hobbes's political theory, aided by Baconian science, aims to achieve the complete draining of eros from political ambition and the reduction of honor seeking to the empty, abstract impulse to seek power for the sake of mere self-preservation. Thus, the deeroticization of tyranny went hand in hand with the triumph of Hobbesian method in the behavioral social sciences.

THE TRANSITION TO TOTALITARIANISM AND THE WILL OF THE PEOPLE: THE LIMITS OF THIS STUDY

I have argued that modern political science beginning with Hobbes starts by being more pessimistic than the ancients about the motivations for political ambition and ends up being more optimistic about the prospects for a future in which tyrannical aggression disappears than anything to be found in the ancients. In other words, the pessimistic undertow of Hobbes's state of nature, in which ambition is presented as the unvarnished drive for the exploitation and mastery of others and stripped of any Platonic capacity for transcendence, is in the long run consumed by the rational superstructure of the social contract erected over it. Prompted by the danger posed by the state of nature, the construction of the social contract comes to be seen as eradicating that danger altogether.

For Plato, there are "great natures" like Alcibiades capable of the worst and the best behavior. The aim of *politike* is to encourage the eros of a man like Alcibiades away from tyranny and toward moderate politics and a friendliness for philosophy. Modern political science begins by denying as a matter of principle that a man like Alcibiades is capable of any drive other than tyranny, but maintains that, through the proper construction of the social contract and the psychology of enlightened self-interest, such men will gradually "wither away," as Marx forecast about politics altogether (which he also identified with sheer domination). For Plato and the classics, Alcibiades is a type of man who will always be with us, dangerous but capable of rehabilitation, a threat to the political community, but whose vigor must sometimes be placed at its service. For Hobbes and modern political science, Alcibiades has always been with us so far, has always been dangerous and incapable of rehabilitation, is of no use at all to the service of sound government, but need not be with us in the future.

If these reflections have any merit, it becomes especially important to emphasize the continuing relevance of classical political science as a counterweight to the unrealism of modern political science and a matchless resource for our need to continually identify tyranny in the world around us. Nevertheless, I still do not believe that it is possible simply to restore or return to classical political science without a supplementary account of what is distinctive about the modern version of tyranny. I have argued throughout this book that, despite the continuing relevance of the classics, one cannot treat modern tyranny entirely as a continuation of or variation on the classical typologies. I would now like to sum up this argument by way of conclusion, as well as to suggest that what is distinctive about modern tyranny in its most radical, totalitarian, and chiliastic manifestations lies outside the boundaries of both classical political philosophy *and* early modern political philosophy as inaugurated by Machiavelli, despite drawing on some characteristics of the latter, and is therefore beyond the boundaries of this study in its concentration on the mastery of Fortuna.

Let me return to our central motif in contrasting the ancient and modern understanding of tyranny – the conquest of eros. Whereas the classics understood the passion of eros as both the source of tyranny

and as containing the potential for its rehabilitation, modern totalitarian tyranny, I would argue, is aimed at the extirpation and suppression
of eros altogether in both ruler and ruled. Thus, modern tyrannies like
those of Stalin and Hitler must be understood not primarily in erotic
terms, or even as deformed versions of eros, but as the radicalization
of the will to master nature that includes the repression of human
nature, most especially as it is characterized by an erotic longing for
the beautiful and the good and the longing for an immortal reputation
through noble deeds. The characteristically modern tyrant has therefore
much less in common with exemplars of depraved or excessive eros like
Alcibiades or (depending on your judgment) Julius Caesar and more in
common with Torquemada. The modern totalitarian tyrant is a secularized fanatic, what Konrad Heiden called "the man in the plain field
tunic" who is abstemious and ascetic, or at least not prone to public
displays of luxurious personal grandeur, ornamentation, architectural
splendor, and robes of state characteristic of traditional monarchs all
the way back to Cyrus the Great. This turn from erotic excess to secularized fanaticism is anticipated, as we earlier observed, in the rise of the
terrorist in nineteenth-century Europe and vividly depicted in Flaubert's
portrait of the 1848 revolutionary Senecal, as well as Turgenev's portrait of the nihilist Bazarov, and later on in Solzhenitsyn's fictionalized
account of Lenin in Zurich.

I have referred to Hegel's discussion of the French Revolution and
Terror a number of times throughout this book as an interesting benchmark for what distinguishes ancient from modern tyranny as a theme
in the history of political philosophy. It is true that, strictly speaking,
Hegel is locating this change in a particular historical event, the Jacobin
Terror of 1793. Even so, for Hegel, the attempt of the Jacobins to master
nature and human nature through the imposition of "absolute freedom
and terror" in 1793 is the result of a long dynamic in human history
as a whole, that aspect of the historical process driven by the will to
master nature in the pursuit of freedom ("the labor of the negative").
This aspect of history is one that Hegel squarely locates as a dominating
characteristic of modernity, beginning with the Reformation, the Age
of Reason, and the Enlightenment, an emphasis on the will to master
nature that can only be derived from the concept of the Abrahamic
God and that is not derivable from the ancient Greek world or ancient

Greek philosophy. So Hegel may not accord Machiavelli the centrality that I do in the transition from ancient to modern political thought, but he does believe there is something distinctive about the modern focus on freedom from and over nature (as opposed to the ancient focus on the virtues of character within the natural order), with its concomitant danger of reaching an excessive extreme of the will to master nature and human nature, a danger that comes to fruition in revolutionary movements like the Jacobins. Hegel is also an important benchmark because his view of freedom in history continued to inform debates about modern rule including Alexandre Kojeve's famous left-Hegelian emphasis on man's ongoing pursuit of mastery over nature in the furtherance of his freedom.

In considering Hegel's analysis of Jacobin terror as the distinctive hallmark of modern political extremism, one might ask of my approach in this book: Because modern natural science and its technological applications, as well as modern ideological movements and regimes, postdate Machiavelli by a considerable distance in time, can one explain what is distinctive about modern tyranny without taking account of these post-Machiavellian factors? I would answer: No, but the shift inaugurated by Machiavelli from the ancient focus on the education of character to the modern focus on impersonal method is one absolutely central and massive dimension of the transition from ancient to modern tyranny that is this book's theme. Moreover, I have also tried to sketch some of the paths from Machiavelli's originary project for the mastery of nature to those later technological and ideological consequences. Questions that arise for further consideration as we reach the boundary of our consideration of the transition from the classical account of *politike* to the new science of politics of the modern age and the Enlightenment, and the concomitant shift from personal to impersonal or "representative" canons of authority, include the following: How might the existence of what are arguably completely impersonal agencies for modern tyranny and terror, including nuclear weaponry, environmental devastation, and the World Wide Web – with the danger it poses for the global surveillance and coordination of all human affairs simultaneously with the hopes it encourages for further human emancipation – be considered as extensions of the project for the mastery of Fortuna first broached by Machiavelli, Bacon, and Hobbes? Is Heidegger correct that all varieties of modern authority, regardless of whether we might try to classify them as legitimate or illegitimate according to premodern concepts of justice and ethics, are indistinguishably assimilated into the ceaseless dynamic of global technology, the Baconian and Hobbesian project for the imposition of instrumental rationality on the rest of existence?

At this point, I want again to make it emphatically clear that I do not believe that Heidegger's technology discourse explains all versions of modern tyranny (let alone liberal democracy). The existence of global technology, in my view, does not fully explain National Socialism, Stalinism, or their leaders, and, to reiterate my earlier argument, the power of global technology does not prevent us or excuse us from making proximal distinctions between more just and less just regimes; between tyranny and republican self-government, or between more and less humane understandings of government. I also want to reemphasize that I am not arguing that Hitler and Stalin and their fellow political mass murderers including Mao Tse-tung are direct equivalents of Machiavelli's new prince. We can certainly explore them as starting points from more recent history for reflecting on a change in the meaning of authority which I have argued is inaugurated by Machiavelli. The emphasis on the power of the human will to master nature is certainly manifest in both Bolshevik and Nazi ideology, and that is one strain of Machiavelli's influence. But to arrive at a full elaboration of the totalitarian ideologies and movements of the twentieth century and their contemporary progeny, we need to add to this emphasis on the power of the will to negate and transform nature a political romanticism that extols the supreme value of "the people," a romanticization of the collective that begins with Rousseau. Although I am confident that it is enough for one book to uncover the dimensions of modernity that emphasize the conquest of nature, by way of summing up, I do want to bring my analysis to the cusp of the issues surrounding political romanticism and existentialism, and suggest in very broad strokes that, having uncovered the dynamic of the conquest of nature through power politics and science characteristic of early modern political thought, we might now be in a better position to turn to the "folkish" dimension of contemporary totalitarian revolutions and movements that first crystallizes in Rousseau and in aspects of German Idealism. The full exposition must await the planned sequel to this volume.

I will formulate the difference as broadly as I can for now. For Machiavelli, the "humors" or passions of the people can be constructive (when directed toward imperial expansion, for example, or expressed in the division of clashing powers within a republic), but they also have to be purged periodically so that they do not undermine public order. It is not a matter of educating them to pursue higher ends, but, to recall Machiavelli's horticultural imagery, pruning them back to the roots. Those humors themselves, therefore, cannot be the source of goodness or wholeness in the Platonic sense. Hence, Machiavelli's statecraft, notwithstanding a millenarian dimension, is based on intelligent or rational self-seeking – the mastery of the passions so as better to achieve their own long-term goals of security and well-being. Although Machiavelli does differ from some of his successors including Hobbes in insisting on the importance of honor seeking as an independent incentive to further this rational politics, he harbors no expectation that honor can bring one happiness in the transcendental sense of Platonic psychology: it is an energy to be methodically deployed for gain. It must wait for Rousseau to transform the modern understanding of human nature from Hobbesian perpetual anxiety over the fear of violent death to "the sweet sentiment of existence," a spontaneous instinct for wholeness which, when collectivized, leads to a republicanism not merely efficiently and rationally deployed for the sake of security and material well-being and a worldly patriotism entirely consistent with individual self-interest (as in the early-modern republican prescriptions of Machiavelli, Harrington, and Montesquieu), but that promises transcendence and happiness on a sheerly spontaneous, immanent level. With Rousseau, then, modernity opens up into its second major paradigm. The first paradigm, Machiavelli's exhortation to the prince to exert his will over nature, narrowed by Bacon and Hobbes into the scientific and methodical reconstruction of nature, leads at its most extreme to a hypertrophic rationalism and an agenda for the complete technological mastery of the world at the service of utility, pedestrian hedonism, and soulless materialism. The second paradigm, inaugurated by Rousseau in zealous, heartfelt opposition to the first, leads eventually to romantic tribal nationalism, political existentialism and Volkish collectivism. Rousseau shares Machiavelli's preference for the earthly fatherland over the heavenly beyond. But whereas

Machiavelli's republican Romans, like those of Montesquieu, are cool calculators of commerce and gain, Rousseau's are heroic extremists.[22] While Machiavelli's Romans are like surgeons and horticulturalists of power, Rousseau's are sincere, passionate, and committed unreservedly to the collective.

To put this shift in sharper focus, let us revisit some of our main themes concerning the ways in which nature can be characterized and their relationship to different views of statecraft. At the outset of this book, I suggested that the classical understanding of tyranny, and the possibility of forestalling or reforming it, presupposed a view of the cosmos in which the primordial, time-bound origins of existence were solicited toward their teleological fulfillment within an ordered, harmonious, and beneficent whole. A well-educated soul could instantiate in itself, through the cultivation of the civic and intellectual virtues, this cosmic balance and repose. Eros, as the longing for the beautiful and the good and the desire to possess it forever, was for Plato the passion that, if left untutored, could derail into the excesses of tyrannical violence, corruption, and depravity, but which, properly educated, could lead the soul in the ascent from the primordial to the transcendental limned in Diotima's Ladder – the erotic longing for immortality best satisfied by philosophy, but entailing, at the second level of ascent, the virtues that served the city and family as well.

We have seen that, beginning with Machiavelli, the shift from the classical to the modern diagnosis of tyranny begins by demolishing this classical cosmology. Nature is now viewed as Fortuna, a field of sheer origination and happenstance, typically indifferent if not outright hostile to human hopes for peace, prosperity, justice, and repose. Instead of reason mirroring and instantiating the order of the cosmos linking the erotic longing of the soul to the immortally beautiful and good, reason is drained out of the world and transformed into a purely anthropocentric, instrumental faculty. Reason is assimilated to the assertion of will, borrowed from the Abrahamic God, by which princes and statesmen of outstanding virtue can strive to overcome nature and reshape it to serve human purposes – a new politics of security and well-being to replace the old politics of virtue and community. Drained of its teleological substance and its link to the whole, reason is narrowed down to the

---

[22] See the discussion in Yack (1992).

methodical rationality with which rulers impose their will on nature and human nature.

This early-modern project, whether it travels the darker corridor from Hobbes to Rousseau's Legislator toward totalitarianism, or the more benign path through Locke and Montesquieu toward liberal democracy, shares the assumption that nature is indeed indifferent or hostile to human purposes and that, whatever security and justice is to be achieved by man, it must come from subduing and reshaping this irrational force, both through the power of Baconian natural science over nature and through the suppression of our own natural human proclivity to violence and exploitation. The social contract must constrain the natural passions of each individual for the good of each individual. For each individual to act on his passions, grounded in the impulse for survival and domination, would lead to the war of all against all, thereby contradicting the fundamental aim of human nature – self-preservation and the avoidance of violent death. On this view, it is self-evidently irrational and contrary to "right reason" to want to live naturally without the restraint of the contract.

With Rousseau, however, comes a new watershed, equal in profundity, radicalism, and impact to that of Machiavelli, which carries us beyond the scope of this study into another phase of tyranny, the collective tyranny of *le peuple* and *das Volk*, a collectivist aggressiveness and fervor without which the great antiliberal revolutionary movements beginning with the Jacobin Terror and proceeding through Bolshevism, National Socialism, the Khmer Rouge, and al-Qaeda cannot be fully understood. For, although these revolutionary movements do also partake of the Machiavellian project for the imposition of man's will on nature and human nature – their rejection of liberal democracy and individual rights is seen as being in no way incompatible with embracing modern military or police state technology or economic might – it is for the sake of a new set of aims, not merely security and prosperity or even enforced uniformity, but the blissful return to the Arcadian origins of the golden age, what the Jacobins termed the return to "the year one." Starting with the Jacobins, and in stark contradiction to the great liberal revolutions of 1689 and 1776, these revolutions are simultaneously both atavistic and futuristic – they want to rapidly accelerate modernization, but for the sake of returning to a lost age of collectivist harmony and purity.

This transformation can only come about because, owing to Rousseau, the state of nature is no longer viewed as dangerous and hostile, as it was for Machiavelli and the early moderns, but as, on the contrary, the only condition in which human beings once knew wholeness and happiness. The aim of politics is therefore not merely to repress and control nature as self-evidently destructive, unreliable, or malign, but to liberate us from all restraints, both premodern and modern, that alienate us from our original happiness in the primordial origins. Machiavelli's political philosophy had drained eros from nature, following Augustine in snapping the Diotiman link between eros and transcendence, so as to liberate the primordial realm of chance, accident, and impulse and then enable us to master it, equipped with reason assimilated to willpower as our weapon. Rousseau, by contrast, transposes the erotic longing for wholeness from the transcendental cosmos of the classics to the realm of the primordial itself, such that reason now stands in the way of our happiness because of its project for the conquest of nature. This is a synthesis unknown either to the early moderns (for whom satisfaction came through conquering nature) or to the classics (for whom happiness culminated in the fulfillment of our capacity for reason within the natural order). The erotic wholeness that Plato believed only the best could achieve through the lifetime cultivation of moral and intellectual virtue, and which Machiavelli disparaged as imaginary, Rousseau transforms into the spontaneous and effortless possession of all mankind, alienated from us by the political and social order, whether this is seen in terms either of classical or modern political philosophy, such that the aim of revolution becomes to shatter entirely the rule of all convention, premodern and modern alike, and restore "the people" to their spontaneous collective happiness. Accordingly, while I have broadly compared Hobbes's Sovereign to Rousseau's Legislator with their power to instill terror and re-make human nature, and although Rousseau's Legislator does in some measure batten off of the Hobbesian Sovereign's scope, their aims ultimately differ profoundly. The purpose of the Hobbesian Sovereign is to restrain our natural individualism so as to enable individual self-interest to flourish, whereas the purpose of Rousseau's Legislator is to force those who have already begun to lose the "sweet sentiment of existence" in the pristine state of nature due to individual self-interest to recover their lost wholeness through the forging of the General Will. That Rousseau lionizes the ancient republics of Sparta and Rome in lieu of classical political philosophy affirms this transition. Although in this sense he follows Machiavelli in preferring ancient republican practice to ancient republican theory, he does it for contrary reasons. Whereas Machiavelli wanted modern man to reenact Rome's ascent toward imperial republican prosperity, grandeur, and power, Rousseau longs nostalgically for a Rome that will never evolve beyond its most austere and bucolic rootedness.

German Idealism springs from this new Rousseauan paradigm and, by transposing Rousseau's lost golden age of sheer immanent communality from the beginning of history to its end, allows us to believe that revolutionary struggle is bringing us closer to that final transpolitical nirvana. The long and rich debate begun by Hegel and continued by Marx, Nietzsche, and Heidegger revolves around whether the progress of history is in fact bringing us closer to this release, or, reverting to the underlying Rousseauan critique of modernity, is in fact continuing to alienate us from it by ratifying the status quo of the established order. With Heidegger, we reach the limit of this debate. By returning behind and beneath the settled outcome of history proclaimed by Hegel and other nineteenth-century progressivists so as to reopen Rousseau's original vision of existence as a sheer matrix of spontaneous possibility and fullness, Heidegger dismantles all doctrines of the teleological progress of history and urges that "the people" return to the pristine vigor of its origins, his particular contribution to the *Volkish* worldview of National Socialism. Only now, that spontaneous wholeness which for Rousseau emerges from its green shoots in a permanent underlying nature is entirely temporalized as the unfathomable and bottomless "presencing" and "destining" of Being.

Moreover, instead of accepting the distinction we have pursued from the beginning of this book between the classical view of the cosmos in which man is subordinate to nature and the modern view according to which man is impelled to conquer nature, Heidegger argues that the modern conquest of nature through technology is already fully implicit in classical metaphysics itself; that technology is the centuries-long "working out" of classical metaphysics in its fully evolved present dispensation. For Heidegger, modern global technology is rooted in Plato's attempt to erect "the tyranny of the forms" over the sheer originary matrix of Being, thereby chaining its revitalizing powers of genesis and our authentic communal existence within the gray confines of alienating materialism, instrumental rationality, and pedestrian self-interest. Whereas Plato had argued that the metaphysics of the Forms, as the guide for philosophic and civic education, provided the best prospect for the rehabilitation of tyrannical aggression, Heidegger is arguing that the metaphysics of the Forms is *itself* the consummate attempt to tyrannize over the rest of existence, including human freedom. Whereas the classics believed that the tyrannical impulse was the ultimate departure from the life of reason, whose only therapy lay in redirecting it toward the guidance of reason, Heidegger argues that reason itself, originating with Plato and actualized as global technology, is the worst and most complete tyranny ever experienced, and that the only escape from it is to return headlong into the primordial origins of chance, chaos, accident, motion, and impulse. Far from acting as the philosophic charioteer in Plato's image of the soul in the *Phaedrus*, steering and redirecting the passions under the guidance of nous, Heidegger in effect seizes the reins and deliberately goads the steeds of eros and thumos into plunging downward into the maelstrom.[23]

Thus, we have come from Machiavelli urging the conquest of Fortuna to Heidegger arguing that our only salvation lies in our complete self-abandonment to Fortuna, to the "overpowering power" of Being. Far from wanting to master Fortuna by letting her selectively empower our wills, as Machiavelli argued, we must, Heidegger proclaims, let her overwhelm us entirely so as to sweep away the superstructure of will, reason, and method and fill us with a new and "ecstatic" sense of possibility, potency, and freedom. Rousseau's vision of the prepolitical state of nature as the source of our happiness, his transposition of Platonic eros as the longing for the transcendental end to Machiavelli's Fortuna as the longing for the primordial origins, culminates in Heidegger's ominous rune: "Now only a god can save us." We must abandon reason, will, and virtue and wait for the primordial to envelop us and take us where it will. As a consequence, the whole topic of the best regime becomes meaningless and naive. The early moderns had not lost sight of the distinctions among regimes or the distinction between just and unjust, legitimate and illegitimate government, even as they severely criticized the classical approach to these distinctions and placed them

---

[23] On the relationship between German Idealism, and particularly the thought of Heidegger, and totalitarianism, see Newell (1984, 1988a, 1988b, 1988c).

on the new basis of the mastery of nature for a politics of prosperity and power. It was still possible for the early moderns to entertain the distinction between tyranny and legitimate authority, as witness Harrington's and Locke's stout rejections of Hobbesian absolute monarchy, without repudiating the maximization of security and material well-being. For Heidegger, however, all such distinctions among regimes, or between just and unjust regimes, whether classical or from the modern social contract school, along with any attempt to expound a rational teleology of historical progress, are but ancillary instruments in the juggernaut of global technology, such that the attempt to distinguish between America and the Soviet Union is baseless, because they are "metaphysically the same," twin "pincers" of the debased materialism threatening "the people's" recommitment to the primordial destiny of its origins in Being.

Readers who have made it this far may wonder why in this study I have not discussed at length the sense in which religious institutions or movements can be tyrannical. Of course, it has been implicit all along as I have dwelled on Machiavelli's sustained critique of the Church and of what he takes to be Christianity's deleterious consequences for patriotism and its attempt to dominate political life through its institutions and theology, and as I have speculated on what psycho-spiritual teaching he might have envisioned to guide the new Rome of the future. I have, however, omitted a discussion of the sense in which the millenarianism of the Joachites, or the search for a pure Christian community bereft of priesthood or Church typified by the Cathars or Anabaptists, could be seen as prototypes for later revolutionary millenarianism, as discussed, say, by Cohn (1970) and more recently by Landes (2011). Voegelin, moreover, saw Joachite millenarianism as an antecedent for Machiavelli's own version of an apocalyptic prince in his creation of "new modes and orders."

The reason is as follows. In limiting myself to the contribution of early modern political thought, headed by Machiavelli and Hobbes, to the understanding and practice of tyranny, I have centered on their emphasis on willpower and the reduction of political life to dominion which they import, in a secularized version, from the Augustinian strain of Christianity. As they seek to elbow out their mainstream competitors, the Church and Christian theology, the early moderns take a mainly negative view of faith as what Hobbes termed "the Kingdom of

Darkness," religious superstition bound up with "Aristotelity," and the overall belief in "imagined republics" that the new science of politics must regulate and perhaps replace or whose content it might dictate to make it serve the social contract.

In my view, it is not until the totalitarian revolutionary populism of the twentieth century, the Bolsheviks and National Socialists, already anticipated by the Jacobins, that we see a recrudescence not of mainstream Christianity, its institutions, and its theology – all of which, indeed, these revolutionary movements viewed as a mortal enemy – but of that dissident strain of alienated millenarianism including the Anabaptists and Cathars. In the anarchistic populism of the early Bolsheviks and Nazis, in other words, we might detect a secularized version of the search for the direct and unmediated immanentization of the divine presence in a purely collectivized political community. However, that transfer of an aspect of religious millenarianism to revolutionary politics must, in my view, await Rousseau's reversal of the meaning of Fortuna from a hostile force meant to be mastered through the social contract, science and commerce into a positive force of sheer possibility, enchantment, love, harmony, and richness, a dynamic of sheer spontaneous origination that can be immanentized in the life-world of "the people."

Only when the world is viewed as historical through and through – such that Being can be evoked, as does Hegel, as a "self-originating wealth of shapes" – can the political community take on some of the aspects of the dissident religious tradition of apocalyptic millenarianism. Not until the rise of historicism, in other words, do we witness the phenomenon of politics being thoroughly divinized, or of the state being, as Karl Lowith put it about the Nazis and Heidegger's philosophical justification of the Third Reich, the incarnation of God. Here, then, I would depart from Voegelin, who sees a continuous development from that earlier religious millenarianism toward modern totalitarianism. I do not disagree with Voegelin's view that Machiavelli's new prince may share in a strain of Joachite apocalypticism, and I have already suggested that modern totalitarianism does partake of some aspects of Machiavelli's call to master nature. In the main, though, Machiavelli's emphasis on the mastery of nature cannot take us directly to modern totalitarianism, which proceeds by way of Rousseau's worship of the origins, or, as I have put it, his transfer of eros and the prospects for erotic wholeness from the telos to Fortuna. To that extent as well, the religious millenarianism that we might see as secularized in modern revolutionary totalitarianism does not proceed directly by way of Machiavelli and the early moderns. Instead, these modern revolutionary movements including the Jacobins, Bolsheviks, and Nazis reach back *behind* the early moderns in an atavisitc longing for the lost golden age of the distant past, before the rise of bourgeois materialism, when the people were whole and as one. To my mind, the early modern period is mainly characterized by the attempt to control, even crush, or at least tame and coopt religious faith into the liberal separation of church and state. It may be socially useful in bolstering liberal values, but it must be kept strictly within its boundaries of personal freedom of worship. Not until Rousseau's transposition of eros to the origins does the prospect for the divinization of the people and the state emerge.

EPILOGUE

The Hermeneutical Problem of Tyranny

Throughout this book, I have tried to show that there are fundamental differences in the understanding of tyranny between classical and modern political philosophy, mirrored in the historical reality of modern tyranny itself, especially at its most radical totalitarian extreme. In arguing this, do I necessarily commit myself to the view that human nature in general has actually changed? Let me end with a few speculative remarks on this basic but enormously complex hermeneutical problem.

I will begin by posing some fairly blunt alternatives. Is nuclear weaponry, for example, no more than the outcome of the long evolution of the human capacity to inflict destruction stretching back to the Roman catapult? This is conceivable. On the other hand, did man's ability to split the atom, which presupposes modern natural science and its refutation of ancient cosmology, introduce an entirely new force into human history – the capacity to destroy human civilization? If so, the destructive reach of tyrannical power has arguably been fundamentally transformed from what it was before the twentieth century. In the human realm, are Hitler and Stalin merely recognizable tyrants from the classical typology equipped with military and technological power that did not exist in the ancient past? Or (as I am inclined to believe) did their secular millenarianism and projects for the futuristic reconstruction of the world and the creation of a "new man" through genocide introduce a fundamentally new element not comprehendible within the ancient categories, perhaps closer to religious millenarianism and fanaticism?

If we are asking whether tyranny has fundamentally altered its character, it would seem that we are led inevitably to the broader question of whether history, human nature, and our understanding of them have also fundamentally changed. If they have not – if modern tyranny is but a modification, however far-reaching, of the enduring archetypes – then was Plato basically right, or closest to being right, about human existence per se, with all later philosophy, as Emerson remarked, being merely commentary or motivated by a vain desire to be original? If this is so, then would it follow that the philosophic life, which Plato argues is present at all times in principle for man regardless of historical circumstances inside the "cave" of the here and now, has actually been fully and completely experienced only once, at the very beginning? This would be to argue for a kind of reverse historicism of decline or "fall" from the origins, implying that human existence was open to the truth only once during the pristine origins of ancient Greece and has added nothing fundamentally new since then, or has even drifted away from that original pristine experience of access to the truth into the delusions of modernity. It is certainly possible to argue that the modern theory and practice of tyranny, however deep a modification of classical political science, is at bottom no more than that – a modification of categories already sufficiently established by, say, Plato, and merely added on to an underlying conception of human nature and psychology that remains constant. Again, Genghis Khan on Twitter. The mirror image opposite of this argument for the constancy of the classical understanding of human nature and regime principles is the view that the truth was only discovered in modern times, correcting the delusions of the classics – the view that modernity constitutes an advance over the ancient world that is still a hallmark of much contemporary education. In both cases, however, it is posited that human nature has changed in the course of history, because the one side argues that human nature possessed unmediated access to the truth only at the beginning, then declined, perhaps irrecoverably, from that golden age, while the other side argues that human nature was not in possession of the truth about nature and human nature until modernity, when mankind was transformed by possessing it for the first time. So the very attempt to maintain the existence of the permanent truth – whether it has been true all along or discovered only by modernity – tends to undermine itself by making our access to the truth historically conditioned in both versions. Although the question of the difference between ancient and modern tyranny is a gateway to this dilemma, it is fortunately not my burden here to attempt to resolve it, only to sketch some of its contours as they flow from the theme of this book.

Readers will recall from the Introduction that I questioned the tenability of Leo Strauss's view in apparently maintaining that, although there is a fundamental break between ancients and moderns over the meaning of tyranny and statecraft in general, the underlying truths about human nature and classical political philosophy remain constant and are preferable to the available modern alternatives. As he puts it in a formulation characteristically rich in ambiguity: "Once we have learned again from the classics what tyranny is," we will have taken "the first step toward an exact analysis of present-day tyranny, for present-day tyranny is fundamentally different from the tyranny analyzed by the classics" (Strauss [1968] p. 189). But I myself, of course, am partly guided in my own analysis of the differences between ancient and modern tyranny by Strauss's conception of such a break, which in both Strauss's case and my own is implicitly critical of Heidegger's view of tyranny as the tyranny of the Platonic forms, Platonic metaphysics "completing itself" as technology (1954). So my attempt to distinguish modern tyranny from ancient tyranny does invite the question as to whether and to what extent the ambiguities about human nature and historical change sketched here are characteristic of Strauss himself, and how the theme of tyranny might point to and illuminate some broader issues in Strauss's hermeneutic and his relationship to historicist thinkers such as Heidegger.

Let me begin by restating the fundamental alternatives. If ancient and modern tyranny (along with the other dimensions of statecraft) are underlyingly identical, then arguably nothing of fundamental importance for political philosophy has been done or thought about since the classics. If, by contrast (and as I lean toward), ancient and modern tyranny are fundamentally distinct from one another, then arguably there may be nothing permanent about human nature and political life. To the extent that Strauss embraces (as he appears at times to do) the view that there is something fundamentally distinct about modern tyranny, he might indeed be seen as embracing a historicist view. The difficulty cannot be avoided by arguing (bluntly and for the purposes of brevity and clarity) that the classics got it basically right, whereas all modernity from Machiavelli through Hegel to Nietzsche, Heidegger, and their epigones has been a compendium of various kinds of distortions in which philosophy, in Strauss's memorable phrase, not only avoided leaving the Cave but set about to dig us deeper into its lower recesses. Because that would mean, again, that philosophy, which is supposedly present for human beings as an alternative at all times in principle, has in fact not been properly grasped for at least the past five hundred years, maybe longer. Could something permanently natural and accessible – moreover the highest way of life – be lost for so much of human history, including to its greatest minds? To say that the classics got it basically right is arguably only another, reverse kind of historicism, replacing modernity and the Enlightenment's claims to have surpassed the ancients with the claim that ancient Greece was some kind of uniquely privileged historical situation in which philosophy could emerge. That would make philosophy at bottom a "Greek" phenomenon – that is, a historically rooted and historically limited phenomenon.

As I understand Strauss's thinking (and I do not claim to understand it fully), the dynamism of his work came from its constant revolving around these paradoxes. For example, the essay *Progress or Return?* (1989) seems to suggest that Abrahamic Revelation, by going down the same road as classical philosophy to a certain extent over the centrality of justice, might provide a permanent prephilosophic explanation for the emergence of philosophy that would itself be enduring and not tied to "the Greeks" or to any specific historical epoch. Even in making this argument, however, Strauss appears to concede that it might be necessary to explain the need for the emergence of philosophy on the basis of some set of prephilosophic experiences, problems, or a sense of wonder – and hence again, in this sense, philosophy itself might be grounded in some kind of historical, existential, psychological, or revelatory context and not able to explain or justify itself entirely on its own terms. Hence, there is arguably a degree of affinity between Strauss and Heidegger over their shared interest in this prephilosophic horizon. What links them as well is their shared view that we must clear away centuries of sedimented, intervening interpretations and doctrines in order to recover the pristine emergence of ancient philosophy in all its radicalness. But then we are back to the same difficulty: Does this mean that the greatness of philosophy owes itself to the robustness and vigor of its historical origins? Finally, one would have to consider Strauss's ambivalent relationship not only to Heidegger but to German Idealism as a whole. I believe he found promising its search for a holism that would overcome the dualism of the modern Cartesian subject, and hence in some measure restore the holism of the classics. Yet by making history the basis for that wholeness, historicism in another way ventured even further from classical rationality than the admittedly truncated version of it retained by Hobbes and other moderns. (I elaborate on this theme in my essay, *Did Plato Believe in His Own Metaphysics? And Did Strauss?* [2010].)

These issues certainly do bear on the provenance of tyranny. In maintaining that modern tyranny does differ from ancient, I open myself to the contention that I am taking a historical approach to the issue and downplaying the underlying constants in human nature. As I see it, however, and as I suggested in the Introduction and have tried to demonstrate throughout, we can only think through the possibility of such underlying constants in human nature and political philosophy if we first pose the differences between ancients and moderns in their most extreme dimensions, for me summed up by the deeroticization characteristic of modern tyranny. Strauss himself famously argued the paradox that we need "historical studies" precisely in order to overcome doctrinal historicism and reawaken the possibility that the classics might be true. I do hold open the possibility, briefly alluded to in the Introduction, that there may be some underlying constants in the ancient and modern approaches to tyranny and statecraft, perhaps centering on thumos and a reconceiving of it under the aegis of modernity and the will, some of which I have tried to do in this book. More generally, there might be some elastic and broadly characterized human leanings toward honor, justice, nobility, and happiness sufficiently underdetermined as to prevent an absolute dichotomy between the ancient and modern approaches to statecraft. We might, for instance, read Aristotle's characterization of human nature as a civic animal with its capacity for virtue, deliberation, and honor more as a series of *leanings* or *probabilities* than as fixed, fully determined categories, introducing an elasticity into *politike* that I tried to articulate in Chapter 3 with respect to whether a monarchy or a republic was the best regime. This prospect of recurrent but underdetermined human experiences that orient us to a sense of wonder about life and the possibility of its further illumination by the search for the truth can arguably be explored without falling prey to the extreme of pronouncing that either the ancients or the moderns are in the main completely right about everything or the extreme of denying that there is anything distinctive about the modern approach at all.

As best as I can understand, Strauss may have been exploring this alternative: a set of recurrent human concerns that are not sufficiently laden with content as to rest exclusively with one philosophy or another or be tied historically to one age or another. This search is conveyed by his use of a term like the "problem" of Justice (as opposed to the more strictly Platonic debate about the "Idea" of justice with its implied metaphysical moorings) or "the fundamental problems " as pretheoretical intimations of what eventually emerge as fully articulated, varying, and even contradictory philosophical schools. ("The possibility of philosophy does not require more than that the fundamental problems are always the same..." [1974] p. 35.) I maintain what I first argued in the Introduction: better an unresolved and possibly unresolvable tension among fundamental alternatives than the rush to submerge them in the illusion that, from Plato to Heidegger, all the great ones have been in open or secret agreement. In other words, could we find a set of recurrent prephilosophical leanings that would show how philosophy is an enduring human concern while also showing how the full philosophical elaboration of those concerns can differ so markedly between ancients and moderns, among thinkers such as Plato, Machiavelli, Hegel, and Heidegger? (Paul Ricoeur's *Fallible Man* and Gadamer's "fusion of horizons" also explore this notion.) In this sense, Strauss's long engagement with the apparently resolutely unmetaphysical Socratic Xenophon might have been his way of evoking a prephilosophic world, perhaps analogous to Heidegger's exploration of the "anthropology of Dasein," in which the Question of Being emerges from a "preontological" experience of the everyday world with its experiences, challenges, and concerns.

BIBLIOGRAPHY

Ahrensdorf, Peter. *Greek Tragedy and Political Philosophy.* Cambridge: Cambridge University Press, 2009.

Alberti, Leon Battista. "Three Dialogues." *Renaissance Philosophy. Vol. 1: The Italian Philosophers.* Fallico and Shapiro eds. and trans. New York: The Modern Library, 1967.

Anderson, J. K. *Xenophon.* London: Duckworth, 1974.

Anglo, Sydney. *Machiavelli – The First Century: Studies in Enthusiasm, Hostility and Irrelevance.* Oxford: Oxford University Press, 2005.

Annas, Julia. *An Introduction to Plato's Republic.* Oxford: Oxford University Press, 1981.

Arendt, Hannah. *The Human Condition.* Chicago: University of Chicago Press, 1996.

Aristotle. *Magna Moralia.* Tredennick trans. Cambridge: Harvard University Press, 1977.

———. *Metaphysics.* 2 vols. Tredennick trans. Cambridge: Harvard University Press, 1980, 1977.

———. *Nicomachean Ethics.* Rackham trans. London: Loeb Classical Library, 1977.

———. *On the Soul.* London: Loeb Classical Library, 1957.

———. *Physics.* 2 vols. Wickstead trans. Cambridge: Harvard University Press, 1980, 1968.

———. *Politics.* Rackham trans. London: Loeb Classical Library, 1967.

———. *The Politics of Aristotle.* Newman ed. 3 vols. Oxford: Clarendon Press, 1950.

Athenaeus. *Deipnosophists.* Gulick trans. Boston: Heinemann, 2009.

Augustine St. *The City of God.* Walsh trans. Bourke ed. Garden City: Image Books, 1958.

———. *Imperfectum Contra Julianum.* Zelzer ed. Vienna: Hoelder-Pichler-Tempsky, 1974.

Aulus Gellius. *Attic Nights.* Rolfe trans. Boston: Heinemann, 1961.

Bacon, Francis. *The Advancement of Learning.* Oxford: The Clarendon Press, 1869.

_____. *An Advertisement Touching A Holy War.* Lampert ed. and comm. Long Grove: Waveland Press, 2000.

_____. *Essays, Advancement of Learning, New Atlantis and Other Pieces.* Foster Jones ed. New York: Odyssey Press, 1937.

_____. *The New Organon.* New York: Library of Liberal Arts, 1960.

_____. *Novum Organum.* 3 vols. Montague ed. and trans. Philadelphia: Perry and MacMillan, 1854.

_____. *The Works of Francis Bacon.* London: Longman and Company, 1857.

Ball, Terence. "The Picaresque Prince: Reflections on Machiavelli and Moral Change." *Political Theory* 12:4 (1984).

Balot, Ryan. *Greed and Injustice in Classical Athens.* Princeton: Princeton University Press, 2001.

_____. *Greek Political Thought.* London: Wiley-Blackwell, 2006.

Barker, Ernest. *Greek Political Theory.* London: Methuen, 1951.

Baron, Hans. "Cicero and the Roman Civic Spirit in the Middle Ages." *The John Rylands Library Bulletin* 22 (1938).

_____. *Humanistic and Political Literature in Florence and Venice at the Beginning of the Quattrocento.* Cambridge: Harvard University Press, 1955.

Barone, Michael. *Our First Revolution: The Remarkable British Upheaval That Inspired America's Founding Fathers.* New York: Crown Books, 2007.

Beiner, Ronald. *Civil Religion: A Dialogue in the History of Political Philosophy.* Cambridge: Cambridge University Press, 2010.

_____. *Political Judgement.* Chicago: University of Chicago Press, 1983.

Beland, Felice. "The Enigma of Modern Science." American Liberal Arts Blog. Intercollegiate Studies Institute. July 5, 2010.

Berlin, Isaiah. "The Originality of Machiavelli." In *Against the Current.* New York: Viking Press, 2000.

Blanchard, Kenneth. "Being, Seeing and Touching in Machiavelli's Modification of Platonic Epistemology." *Review of Metaphysics* 49 (March 1996).

Blitz, Marc. *Plato's Political Philosophy.* Baltimore: Johns Hopkins, 2010.

Breebart, A. B. "From Victory to Peace: Some Aspects of Cyrus' State in Xenophon's *Cyropaedia.*" *Mnemosyne* 36 (1983).

Breitenbach, H. R. *Xenophon von Athen.* Stuttgart: Alfred Druckenmuller, 1966.

Brown, Alison. *The Return of Lucretius to Renaissance Florence.* Cambridge: Harvard University Press, 2010.

Bruell, Christopher. "Socratic Politics and Self-Knowledge: An Interpretation of Plato's *Charmides.*" *Interpretation* 6 (1977).

Bruni d'Arezzo, L. "Concerning the Study of Literature." *Vittorino da Feltre and Other Humanist Educators.* Woodward ed. Cambridge: Cambridge University Press, 1897.

Burger, Rona. *Aristotle's Dialogue with Socrates.* Chicago: University of Chicago Press, 2008.

Butterfield, H. *The Statecraft of Machiavelli.* London: G. Bell, 1940.

Cantor, Paul. *Shakespeare's Rome.* Ithaca: Cornell University Press, 1976.

Carcopino, Jerome. *Daily Life in Ancient Rome.* Lorimer trans. New York: Penguin, 1960.

Carty, Jarrett. *Machiavelli, Luther and the Reformation of Politics.* Unpublished doctoral dissertation. Political Science. University of Notre Dame, 2006.

———. "Martin Luther's Restoration of Temporal Government." *Interpretation* 37:2 (2010).

Cassirer, Ernst, Kristeller, Paul Oskar, and Randall, John Herman. *The Renaissance Philosophy of Man.* Chicago: University of Chicago Press, 1948.

Castiglione, Baldesar. *The Book of the Courtier.* Singleton trans. New York: Anchor Books, 1959.

Charnwood, Lord. *Abraham Lincoln.* New York: Garden City Publishers, 1917.

Cicero. *Offices.* Warrington trans. London: Dent, 1955.

———. *On the Nature of the Gods; On Divination; On Fate; On the Republic; On the Laws.* Yonge trans. London: George Bell and Sons, 1907.

———. *On the Republic.* Keyes trans. Cambridge: Harvard University Press, 1966.

———. *Tusculan Disputations.* King trans. Cambridge: Harvard University Press, 1971.

Clark, Stephen. *Aristotle's Man.* Oxford: Clarendon Press, 1975.

Clarke, Michelle T. "Uprooting Nebuchadnezzar's Tree: Francis Bacon's Critique of Machiavellian Imperialism." *Political Research Quarterly* 61:3 (2008).

Coby, Patrick J. *Machiavelli's Romans.* Lanham: Lexington Books, 1999.

Cohn, Norman. *The Pursuit of the Millenium.* Oxford: Oxford University Press, 1970.

Copan, Paul. "Is *Creatio Ex Nihilo* a Post-Biblical Invention?" *Trinity Journal* 17:1 (Spring 1996).

Cornoldi, Giovanni S. J. *The Physical System of Saint Thomas*. New York: London and Leamington, 1893.

Cosh, Marcia L. "Republicanism, Religion, and Machiavelli's Savanarolan Moment." *Journal of the History of Ideas* 60:4 (1999).

Craig, Leon. *The War Lover: A Study of Plato's Republic*. Toronto: University of Toronto Press, 1994.

Cropsey, Joseph. *Plato's World: Man's Place in the Cosmos*. Chicago: University of Chicago Press, 1995.

Davis, Michael. *The Soul of the Greeks*. Chicago: University of Chicago Press, 2011.

de Grazia, Sebastian. *Machiavelli in Hell*. Princeton: Princeton University Press, 1994.

Delebecque, Edouard. *Essai sur la vie de Xenophon*. Paris: Librairie C. Klincksieck, 1957.

Dietz, Mary. "Trapping the Prince: Machiavelli and the Politics of Deception." *American Political Science Review* 80:3 (1986).

Dodds, E. R. *The Greeks and the Irrational*. Berkeley: University of Chicago Press, 1984.

Eliade, Mircea. *A History of Religious Ideas*. Vol. 1. Chicago: University of Chicago Press, 1978.

Euben, J. Peter. *Platonic Noise*. Princeton: Princeton University Press, 2003.

———. *The Tragedy of Political Theory*. Princeton: Princeton University Press, 1990.

Everitt, Anthony. *Cicero: The Life and Times of Rome's Greatest Politician*. New York: Random House, 2003.

Ferrari, G. R. F. *The City and Soul in Plato's Republic*. Chicago: University of Chicago Press, 2003.

Figgis, John Neville. *Political Thought from Gerson to Grotius*. New York: Harper and Sons, 1960.

Forde, G. *On Being a Theologian of the Cross: Reflections on Luther's Heidelberg Disputations*. Grand Rapids: Eerdmans, 1977.

Fortenbraugh, W. W. "Aristotle on Slaves and Women." In *Articles on Aristotle*. Schofield and Sorabji eds. London: Duckworth, 1977.

Foster, Edith. *Thucydides, Pericles and Periclean Imperialism*. Cambridge: Cambridge University Press, 2010.

Freeman, Kathleen. *Ancilla to the Pre-Socratic Philosophers*. Oxford: Basil Blackwell, 1948.

Friedlander, Paul. *Plato: An Introduction*. Princeton: Princeton University Press, 1973.

Fukuyama, Francis. *The Origins of Political Order*. New York: Farrar, Strauss & Giroux, 2011.

Gadamer, Hans-Georg. *Dialogue and Dialectic*. Smith trans. New Haven: Yale University Press, 1980.

———. "On the Scope and Function of Hermeneutic Reflection." *Philosophical Hermeneutics*. Linge ed. and trans. Berkeley: University of California Press, 1976.

———. *Reason in the Age of Science*. Lawrence trans. Cambridge: MIT Press, 1983.

———. *Truth and Method*. London: Continuum, 1975.

Gallet-Guerne, Danielle. *Vasque de Lucene et la Cyropedie a la Cour de Bourgogne (1470)*. Geneve: Librairie Droz, 1974.

Galstone, William. *Justice and the Human Good*. Chicago: University of Chicago Press, 1980.

Germino, Dante. "Second Thoughts on Leo Strauss's Machiavelli." *Journal of Politics* 28 (1966).

Gibbon, Edward. *The Decline and Fall of the Roman Empire*. New York: Fenelon, Collier and Son, 1900.

Gilbert, Allan. *Machiavelli's Prince and Its Forerunners*. Durham: Duke University Press, 1938.

Gilbert, Felix. "The Concept of Nationalism in Machiavelli's *Prince*." *Studies in the Renaissance I*, 1954.

———. "The Humanist Concept of the Prince and *The Prince*." *The Journal of Modern History* December (1939).

———. *Machiavelli and Guicciardini: Politics and History in Sixteenth Century Florence*. New York: W. W. Norton, 1984.

Gillespie, Michael Allen. *The Theological Origins of Modernity*. Chicago: University of Chicago Press, 2009.

Grant, George P. *Collected Works*. 4 vols. Davis, Roper, Grant, Emberley eds. Toronto: University of Toronto Press, 2005.

———. "In Defense of North America." In *Technology and Empire*. Toronto: Anansi, 1991.

Griswold, Charles. "*Politike Episteme* in Plato's *Statesman*." In *Essays in Ancient Greek Philosophy*. Vol. 3. Anton and Preuss eds. Albany: State University of New York Press, 1989.

———. *Self-Knowledge in Plato's Phaedrus*. New Haven: Yale University Press, 1986.

Gunton, Colin. *The Christian Faith*. London: Wiley-Blackwell, 2001.

Guthrie, W. K. C. *Socrates*. Cambridge: Cambridge University Press, 1984.

———. *The Sophists*. Cambridge: Cambridge University Press, 1983.

Habermas, Jurgen. *Theory and Practice*. Boston: Beacon Press, 1973.

Hadot, Pierre. *Philosophy as a Way of Life*. London: Wiley-Blackwell, 1995.

Hall, Robert. "*Psyche* as Differentiated Unity in the Philosophy of Plato." *Phronesis* 8 (1963).

Halloran, J. Warren. *The Synoptic Gethsemane*. Analectic Gregoriana 191. Rome: Gregorian University, 1973.

Hankins, James. *Plato in the Italian Renaissance*. London: Brill, 1990.

Harrington, James. *The Commonwealth of Oceana*. Charleston: Nabu Press, 2010.

Hegel, G. W. F. *Early Theological Writings*. Knox trans. Philadelphia: University of Philadelphia Press, 1948.

_____. *Hegel on Tragedy*. Paolucci ed. New York: Doubleday, 1962.

_____. *Phenomenology of Spirit*. Miller trans. Oxford: Oxford University Press, 1979.

_____. *Reason in History*. Hartman trans. Upper Saddle River: Prentice-Hall, 1997.

Heidegger, Martin. *Early Greek Thinking*. Krell trans. Chicago: Harper and Row, 1984.

_____. *An Introduction to Metaphysics*. Mannheim trans. New Haven: Yale University Press, 1959.

_____. "Plato's Doctrine of Truth." In *Pathmarks*. McNeill ed. Cambridge: Cambridge University Press, 1998.

_____. "The Question Concerning Technology" and "The Letter on Humanism." In *Basic Writings*. Krell ed. San Francisco: Harper Collins, 1993.

_____. "Uberwindung der Metaphysik." In *Vortrage und Aufsatze*. Pfullingen: Gunter Neske, 1954.

Hermardinquer, M. *La Cyropedie: Essai sur les idees morales et politiques de Xenophon*. Paris: Ernest Thorin, 1872.

Herodotus. *The History of Herodotus*. Grene trans. Chicago: University of Chicago Press, 1988.

Higgins, W. E. *Xenophon the Athenian: The Problem of the Individual and the Society of the Polis*. Albany: State University of New York Press, 1977.

Hobbes, Thomas. *The Citizen: Philosophical Rudiments Concerning Government and Society*. In *Man and Citizen*. Gert ed. Garden City: Anchor 1972.

_____. *Leviathan*. Macpherson ed. Baltimore: Penguin Books, 1971.

Homer. *The Iliad of Homer*. Lattimore trans. Chicago: University of Chicago Press, 1973.

_____. *The Odyssey of Homer*. Lattimore trans. New York: Harper and Row, 1968.

Horkheimer, Max. "Beginnings of the Bourgeois Philosophy of History." In *Between Philosophy and Social Science: Selected Early Writings*. Hunter trans. Boston: MIT Press, 1995.

Horkheimer, Max, and Adorno, Theodor. *Dialectic of Enlightenment*. Stanford: Stanford University Press, 2007.

Hornqvist, Michael. *Machiavelli and Empire*. Cambridge: Cambridge University Press, 2004.

Hulliung, Mark. *Citizen Machiavelli*. Princeton: Princeton University Press, 1983.

Hyland, Drew. "Plato's Three Waves and the Question of Utopia." *Intepretation* 18:1 (1990).

———. *The Virtue of Philosophy*. Athens: Ohio University Press, 1981.

Irwin, Terence. *Plato's Moral Theory*. Oxford: Clarendon Press, 1977.

Jaeger, Werner. *Paideia*. Vol. 1. Highet trans. New York: Oxford University Press, 1965.

Kagan, Donald. *The Peloponnesian War*. New York: Viking, 2003.

Kant, Immanuel. *The Critique of Practical Reason*. Beck trans. Indianapolis: Bobbs-Merrill, 1956.

Kass, Leon. *The Beginning of Wisdom: Reading Genesis*. New York: The Free Press, 2003.

Kennedy, E. "The Tangled History of Secularism." *The Modern Age* 42:1 (2000).

Kennington, Richard. *On Modern Origins*. Kraus ed. Lanham: Lexington Books, 2004.

Kerford, G. B. *The Sophistic Movement*. Cambridge: Cambridge University Press, 1981.

Kleinhaus, Emile A. "Piety, Universality and History: Leo Strauss on Thucydides." *Humanitas* XIV:1 (2001).

Klosko, George. "The Insufficiency of Reason in Plato's *Gorgias*." *Western Political Quarterly* 36 (1983).

Koziak, Barbara. *Retrieving Political Emotion: Thumos, Aristotle and Gender*. University Park: Pennsylvania State University Press, 2000.

Kraut, Richard. "Egoism, Love and Political Office in Plato." *Philosophical Review* 82:3 (1973).

Kristeller, Paul Oskar. *Studies in Renaissance Thought and Letters*. Roma: Edizioni di Storia e Letteratura, 1969.

Lacqueur, Walter, and Alexander, Yonah, eds. *The Terrorism Reader*. New York: Meridian, 1987.

Lampert, Lawrence. *How Philosophy Became Socratic*. Chicago: University of Chicago Press, 2010.

Landes, Richard. *Heaven on Earth: The Varieties of the Millenial Experience.* Oxford: Oxford University Press, 2011.

Lerner, Ralph, and Mahdi, Mushin eds. *Medieval Political Philosophy: A Sourcebook.* Ithaca: Cornell University Press, 1963.

Lilla, Mark. *The Reckless Mind: Intellectuals in Politics.* New York: New York Review of Books, 2001.

Lipset, Seymour M. *Political Man.* Baltimore: Johns Hopkins, 1981.

Lord, Carnes. *Education and Culture in the Political Thought of Aristotle.* Ithaca: Cornell University Press, 1982.

———. "On Machiavelli's *Mandragola.*" *The Journal of Politics* 41:3 (1979).

Luccioni, Jean. *Hieron: Texte et traduction avec une introduction et un commentaire.* Paris: Ophrys, 1947.

Lucretius. *De Rerum Natura.* Rouse trans. Cambridge: Harvard University Press, 1975.

Ludwig, Paul. 2006. *Eros and Polis.* Cambridge: Cambridge University Press, 2006.

Lukes, Timothy. "To Bamboozle with Goodness: The Political Advantages of Christianity in the Thought of Machiavelli." *Renaissance and Reformation* 20:4 (1984).

Machiavelli, Niccolo. *The Art of War.* Lynch trans. Chicago: University of Chicago Press, 2003.

———. *Discourses on Livy.* Mansfield and Tarcov trans. Chicago: University of Chicago Press, 1996.

———. *Mandragola.* Flaumenhaft trans. Prospect Heights: Waveland Press, 1981.

———. *Opere di Niccolo Machiavelli.* Raimundi ed. Milan: U. Mursia, 1976.

———. *The Prince.* De Alvarez trans. Irving: University of Dallas Press, 1980.

———. *The Prince.* Mansfield trans. Chicago: University of Chicago Press, 1998.

———. *Tutte le Opere.* Martelli ed. Florence: Sansoni, 1971.

MacIntyre, Alasdair. *After Virtue: A Study in Moral Theory.* London: Duckworth, 1981.

Macpherson, C. B. *The Real World of Democracy.* Toronto: Anansi, 1972.

Maddox, Graham. "The Secular Reformation and the Influence of Machiavelli." *The Journal of Religion* 82:4 (2002).

Manent, Pierre. *Modern Liberty and Its Discontents.* Mahoney and Seaton trans. and eds. New York: Rowman and Littlefield, 1995.

Manetti, Gianozzo. "On the Dignity and Excellence of Man." *Renaissance Philosophy. Vol. 1: The Italian Philosophers.* Fallico and Shapiro eds. and trans. New York: The Modern Library, 1967.

Mansfield, Harvey C. "Hobbes and the Science of Indirect Government." *The American Political Science Review* 65:1 (1971).

———. *Machiavelli's New Modes and Orders: A Study of the Discourses on Livy*. Ithaca: Cornell University Press, 2001.

———. *Machiavelli's Virtue*. Chicago: University of Chicago Press, 1998.

———. *Taming the Prince: The Ambivalence of Modern Executive Power*. New York: The Free Press, 1993.

Masters, Roger D. *Machiavelli, Leonardo and the Science of Power*. Notre Dame: University of Notre Dame Press, 1996.

Matteo, Sante. "Will the Real Machiavelli Please Stand Up?" In *Seeking Real Truths: Multidisciplinary Perspectives on Machiavelli*. Vilches ed. London: Brill, 2007.

McCormack, John P. "Machiavelli against Republicanism." *Political Theory* 31:5 (2003).

———. *Machiavellian Democracy*. Cambridge: Cambridge University Press, 2011.

Meier, Christian. *Caesar: A Biography*. New York: Basic Books, 1997.

Montaigne. *The Essays*. Cotton trans. Chicago: Enclyclopedia Britannica, 1952.

Montefiore, Simon Sebag. *Stalin: The Court of the Red Czar*. New York: Vintage, 2005.

Mulgan, R. G. *Aristotle's Political Theory*. Oxford: Oxford University Press, 1977.

Munscher, Karl. *Xenophon in der griechische-romischen Literatur*. Leipzig: Dietrich, 1920.

Nachod, Hans. "Francesco Petrarca: Introduction." *The Renaissance Philosophy of Man*. Cassirer, Kristeller, Randall eds. Chicago: University of Chicago Press, 1948.

Nadon, Christopher. *Xenophon's Prince: Republic and Empire in The Cyropaedia*. Berkeley: University of California Press, 2001.

Nechaev, Sergey. "Catechism of the Revolutionist." In Lacqueur ed. *The Terrorism Reader*. New York: Meridian, 1987.

Nederman, Cary J. "Amazing Grace: Fortune, God and Free Will in Machiavelli's Thought." *Journal of the History of Ideas* 60:4 (1999).

Nelson, Lowry. "Alcibiades' Intrusion in Plato's *Symposium*." *Sewannee Review* 94 (1986).

Newell, Waller R. "Aristotle's Ambivalent Assessment of Oligarchy." In Koivukoski, Tabachnick eds. *Oligarchy*. Toronto: University of Toronto Press, 2011.

———. *Bankrupt Education: The Decline of Liberal Education in Canada*. With Peter C. Emberley. Toronto: University of Toronto Press, 1994.

———. *The Code of Man: Love, Courage, Pride, Family, Country.* New York: HarperCollins, 2003.

———. "Democracy in the Age of Globalization." In Koivukoski, Tabachnick eds. *Globalization, Technology and Democracy.* Albany: State University of New York Press, 2004.

———. "Did Plato Believe in His Own Metaphysics?" In Burns ed. *Recovering Reason: Essays in Honor of Thomas L. Pangle.* Lanham: Lexington Books, 2010.

———. "The Distant Command of the Greeks: Thoughts on Heidegger's Rectoral Address." *Proceedings.* Annual Meeting of the American Political Science Association. Ann Arbor: University Microfilms International, 1988c.

———. "Eros and Revolution: On Flaubert's *Sentimental Education.*" In Palmer and Pangle eds. *Political Philosophy and the Human Soul: Essays in Memory of Allan Bloom.* Lanham: Rowman and Littlefield, 1995.

———. "Heidegger on Freedom and Community: Some Political Implications of His Early Thought." *The American Political Science Review* 78:3 (1984).

———. "How Original Is Machiavelli? A Consideration of Skinner's Interpretation of Virtue and Fortune." *Political Theory* 15:4 (1987).

———. "Is There an Ontology of Tyranny?" In Koivukoski, Tabachnick eds. *Confronting Tyranny: Ancient Lessons for Global Politics.* Lanham: Rowman and Littlefield, 2006b.

———. "Machiavelli and Xenophon on Princely Rule: A Double-Edged Encounter." *The Journal of Politics* 50:1 (1988).

———. "Machiavelli and Xenophon's Cyrus: Searching for the Modern Conception of Monarchy." In Mitchell ed. *Every Inch a King: Comparative Studies on Kings and Kingship in the Ancient and Medieval Worlds.* Leiden: Brill, forthcoming.

———. "Machiavelli's Model for a Liberal Empire: The Evolution of Rome." In Tabachnick ed. *Empire.* Toronto: University of Toronto Press, 2009.

———. "Origins of Enchantment: Conceptual Continuities in the Ontology of Political Wholeness." In Ranasinghe ed. *Logos and Eros: Essays Honoring Stanley Rosen.* South Bend: St. Augustine Press, 2006.

———. "Philosophy and the Perils of Commitment: A Comparison of Lukacs and Heidegger." *History of European Ideas* 9:3 (1988a).

———. "Politics and Progress in Heidegger's Philosophy of History." In Day and Beiner eds. *Democratic Theory and Technological Society.* London: M.E. Sharpe, 1988b.

————. "Redeeming Modernity: The Ascent of Eros and Wisdom in Hegel's *Phenomenology*." *Intepretation* 37:1 (2009a).

————. *Ruling Passion: The Erotics of Statecraft in Platonic Political Philosophy*. New York: Rowman and Littlefield, 2000.

————. *The Soul of a Leader: Character, Conviction and Ten Lessons in Political Greatness*. New York: HarperCollins, 2009.

————. "Superlative Virtue and the Problem of Monarchy in Aristotle's Politics." *The Western Political Quarterly* 40:1 (1987).

————. "Tyranny and the Science of Ruling in Xenophon's *Education of Cyrus*." *The Journal of Politics* 45:4 (1983).

————. *What Is a Man? 3,000 Years of Wisdom on the Art of Manly Virtue*. Edited with an interpretive essay and commentary by Waller R. Newell. Revised and abridged for paperback. New York: HarperCollins, 2001.

Nicholls, M. P. "The Good Life, Slavery and Acquisition: Aristotle's Introduction to Politics." *Intepretation* 11 (1983).

Nicholls, Mary. *Socrates and the Political Community*. Albany: State University of New York Press, 1983a.

Nussbaum, Martha. *The Fragility of Goodness*. Cambridge: Cambridge University Press, 1983.

Ober, Josiah. *Political Dissent in Democratic Athens*. Princeton: Princeton University Press, 1998.

Orwin, Clifford. *The Humanity of Thucydides*. Princeton: Princeton University Press, 1994.

————. "Machiavelli's Unchristian Charity." *American Political Science Review* 72 (1978).

Palmer, Michael. *Love of Glory and the Common Good*. Lanham: Rowman and Littlefield, 1992.

Pangle, Lorraine. *Aristotle and the Philosophy of Friendship*. Cambridge: Cambridge University Press, 2000.

Pangle, Thomas. *Political Philosophy and the God of Abraham*. Baltimore: Johns Hopkins University Press, 2003.

————. "The Political Psychology of Religion in Plato's *Laws*." *The American Political Science Review* 70:4 (1976).

————. Introduction. *Studies in Platonic Political Philosophy*. Chicago: University of Chicago Press, 1985.

Parel, Anthony. *The Machiavellian Cosmos*. New Haven: Yale University Press, 1992.

Pellerin, Daniel. "Machiavelli's Best Friend." *History of Political Thought* 27:3 (2006).

Pesic, Peter. "Wrestling with Proteus: Francis Bacon and the 'Torture' of Nature." *History of Science* 90:1 (1999).

Petrarca, Francesco. "On the Remedies of Good and Bad Fortune." *Renaissance Philosophy. Vol. 1: The Italian Philosophers*. Fallico and Shapiro eds. and trans. New York: The Modern Library, 1967.

Pico della Mirandola, Giovanni. "Oration on the Dignity of Man." *Renaissance Philosophy. Vol. 1: The Italian Philosophers*. Fallico and Shapiro eds. and trans. New York: The Modern Library, 1967.

Pitkin, Hannah. *Fortune Is a Woman*. Chicago: University of Chicago Press, 1999.

Plato. *Gorgias*. Dodds ed. Oxford: Oxford University Press, 1979.

———. *The Laws of Plato*. Pangle trans. New York: Basic Books, 1980.

———. *Platonis Opera*. Burnet ed. 5 vols. Oxford: Clarendon Press, 1902.

———. *Plato's Theaetetus*. Benardete trans. Chicago: University of Chicago Press, 1984,

———. *The Republic of Plato*. Adam ed. 2 vols. Cambridge: Cambridge University Press, 1920.

———. *The Republic of Plato*. Bloom trans. New York: Basic Books, 1968.

———. *The Statesman*. Skemp trans. London: Routledge and Kegan Paul, 1961.

———. *The Symposium of Plato*. Bury ed. Cambridge: Cambridge University Press, 1932.

———. *Timaeus*. Zeyle trans. Indianapolis: Hackett, 2000.

Plutarch. *Makers of Rome*. Scott-Kilvert trans. Baltimore: Penguin Books, 1968.

Pocock, J. G. A. *The Machiavellian Moment*. Princeton: Princeton University Press, 1975.

Popper, Karl. *The Open Society and Its Enemies*. Vol. 1. Princeton: Princeton University Press, 1971.

Rahe, Paul A. *Against Throne and Altar: Machiavelli and Political Theory under the English Republic*. Cambridge: Cambridge University Press, 2008.

———. *Machiavelli's Liberal Republican Legacy*. Cambridge: Cambridge University Press, 2005.

———. *Republics Ancient and Modern: Classical Republicanism and the American Revolution*. Chapel Hill: University of North Carolina Press, 1992.

Ranasinghe, Nalin. *Socrates in the Underworld: On Plato's Gorgias*. South Bend: St. Augustine's Press, 2009.

———. *The Soul of Socrates*. Ithaca: Cornell University Press, 2000.

Randall, J. H. *Aristotle*. New York: Columbia University Press, 1968.

Rasmussen, Paul. *Excellence Unleashed: Machiavelli's Critique of Xenophon and the Moral Foundations of Politics*. Lanham: Lexington Books, 2009.

Rawls, John. *A Theory of Justice*. Boston: Harvard University Press, 1971.

Ricoeur, Paul. *Fallible Man*. Kelbley trans. Chicago: Henry Regnery, 1965.

Roochnick, David. *Beautiful City: The Dialectical Character of Plato's Republic*. Ithaca: Cornell University Press, 2006.

Rosen, Stanley. *Plato's Republic: A Study*. New Haven: Yale University Press, 2005.

Ross, Sir David. *Aristotle*. London: Methuen, 1960.

Ruffo-Fiore, Silvia. "Upon Eagle's Wings: The Sacral Nature of Machiavelli's New Prince." *Rivista di Studi Italiani* 3 (1985).

Salutati, Coluccio. "De Tyranno." *Humanism and Tyranny: Studies in the Italian Trecento*. Emerton ed. Cambridge: Cambridge University Press, 1925.

Saxonhouse, Arlene. "Comedy in the *Callipolis*." *The American Political Science Review* 72:3 (1978).

Schlatter, Richard. *Hobbes' Thucydides*. Camden: Rutgers University Press, 1975.

Schram, Glenn. "Strauss and Voegelin on Machiavelli and Modernity." *The Modern Age* Summer/Fall (1987).

Shakespeare, William. *The Tragedy of King Richard the Second*. Muir ed. New York: New American Library, 1963.

Shell, Susan M. *The Embodiment of Reason*. Chicago: University of Chicago Press, 1996.

Shorey, Paul. *What Plato Said*. Chicago: University of Chicago Press, 1968.

Skemp, J. B. "Causes of Decadence in Plato's *Republic*." *Government and Opposition* 17 (Winter 1982).

Skinner, Quentin. *The Foundations of Modern Political Thought*. Vol. 1. Cambridge: Cambridge University Press, 1980.

Smith, N. D. "Aristotle's Theory of Natural Slavery." *Phoenix* 37 (1983).

Smith, Travis. "Being Altogether Bad, Becoming Altogether Good." In *The Arts of Rule*. Krause ed. Lanham: Lexington Books, 2009.

Sophocles. *Oedipus the King*. In Sophocles I. Greene trans. Chicago: University of Chicago Press, 1973.

Speer, Albert. *Inside the Third Reich*. New York: Avon Books, 1997.

Spinoza, Baruch. *Tractatus Theologico-Politicus*. Shirley trans. London: Brill, 1997.

Stauffer, Devin. *The Unity of Plato's Gorgias*. Cambridge: Cambridge University Press, 2006.

Storing, Herbert ed. *Essays on the Scientific Study of Politics*. New York: Holt, Rhinehart and Winston, 1962.

Sullivan, Vickie. *Machiavelli, Hobbes and the Formation of a Liberal Republicanism in England*. Cambridge: Cambridge University Press, 2004.

———. *Machiavelli's Three Romes*. DeKalb: Northern Illinois University Press, 1996.

Strauss, Barry. *The Battle of Salamis: The Naval Encounter That Saved Greece – and Western Civilization*. New York: Simon and Shuster, 2004.

Strauss, Leo. *The City and Man*. Chicago: University of Chicago Press, 1977.

———. *Natural Right and History*. Chicago: University of Chicago Press, 1974.

———. "Notes on Carl Schmitt's *The Concept of the Political*." In Meier, Heinrich. *Carl Schmitt and Leo Strauss: The Hidden Dialogue*. Chicago: University of Chicago Press, 1995.

———. *On Plato's Symposium*. Chicago: University of Chicago Press, 2001.

———. *On Tyranny*. Ithaca: Cornell University Press, 1968.

———. "Plato's *Apology of Socrates* and *Crito*." In *Studies in Platonic Political Philosophy*. Pangle ed. Chicago: University of Chicago Press, 1983.

———. *The Political Philosophy of Hobbes*. Chicago: University of Chicago Press, 1952.

———. "Progress or Return?" In *The Rebirth of Classical Political Rationalism*. Pangle ed. and intro. Chicago: University of Chicago Press, 1989.

———. "The Problem of Socrates." In *The Rebirth of Classical Political Rationalism*. Pangle ed. and intro. Chicago: University of Chicago Press, 1989.

———. *Thoughts on Machiavelli*. Seattle: University of Washington Press, 1969.

———. *Xenophon's Socratic Discourse: An Interpretation of the Oeconomicus*. Ithaca: Cornell University Press, 1970.

Syme, Ronald. *The Roman Revolution*. Oxford: Oxford University Press, 2002.

Tacitus. *The Annals and the Histories*. Church trans. New York: Modern Library, 2003.

Tarcov, Nathan. "Machiavelli and the Foundations of Modernity: A Reading of Chapter 3 of *The Prince*." In *Educating the Prince: Essays in Honor of Harvey Mansfield*. Blitz and Kristol eds. New York: Rowman and Littlefield, 2000.

———. "Quentin Skinner's Method and Machiavelli's *Prince*." *Ethics* 92 (1982).

Tarnopolsky, Christina. *Prudes, Perverts and Tyrants: Plato's Gorgias and the Politics of Shame*. Princeton: Princeton University Press, 2010.

Tatum, James. *Xenophon's Imperial Fiction: On the Education of Cyrus*. Princeton: Princeton University Press, 1989.

Tawney, R. H. "Religion and the Rise of Capitalism." London: Peter Smith, 1950.

Thomas Aquinas. *Aquinas on Matter, Form and the Elements: A Translation and Interpretation of De Principiis Naturae and De Mixtione Elementorum*. Bobik trans. South Bend: University of Notre Dame Press, 1998.

———. *Commentary on Aristotle's Physics*. Blackwell and Spath trans. New Haven: Yale University Press, 1963.

———. *Commentary on Aristotle's Politics*. Regan trans. Indianapolis: Hackett, 2007.

———. *Summa Theologica*. Fathers of the English Dominican Province trans. London: Christian Classics, 1981.

Thompson, Norma. *Herodotus and the Origins of the Political Community: Arion's Leap*. New Haven: Yale University Press, 1996.

Thucydides. *The Peloponnesian War*. Crawley trans. New York: The Modern Library, 1951.

Tinsley, E. J. "Some Principles for Reconstructing a Doctrine of the Imitation of Christ." *Scottish Journal of Theology* 25 (1972).

Trinkaus, Charles Edward. "Lorenzo Valla: An Introduction." *The Renaissance Philosophy of Man*. Cassirer, Kristeller, Randall eds. Chicago: University of Chicago Press, 1948.

Tuck, Richard. *Philosophy and Government 1572–1651*. Cambridge: Cambridge University Press, 1993.

Valla, Lorenzo. "On Free Will." *Renaissance Philosophy. Vol. 1: The Italian Philosophers*. Fallico and Shapiro eds. and trans. New York: The Modern Library, 1967.

Van den Berg, Jacob. *In Search of Truth: Augustine, Manicheaism and Other Gnosticisms*. London: Brill, 2010.

Vatter, Miguel. *Between Form and Event: Machiavelli's Theory of Political Freedom*. Dordrecht: Kluwer Academic Publishers, 2000.

Velkley, Richard. "Masks of Mastery: Richard Kennington on Modern Origins." *Political Science Reviewer* 31:1 (2002).

Vergerio, Pier Paolo. "Concerning Liberal Studies." *Vittorino da Feltre and Other Humanist Educators*. Woodward ed. Cambridge: Cambridge University Press, 1897.

Villa, Dana. *Socratic Citizenship*. Princeton: Princeton University Press, 2001.

Viroli, Maurizio. *Machiavelli's God*. Shugar trans. Princeton: Princeton University Press, 2010.

———. *Niccolo's Smile: A Biography of Machiavelli*. New York: Farrar, Strauss & Giroux, 2000.

Vlastos, Gregory. "The Individual as Object of Love in Plato." *Platonic Studies*. Princeton: Princeton University Press, 1981.

Voegelin, Eric. "Machiavelli's Prince: Background and Formation." *Review of Politics* 13 (1951).

———. *The New Science of Politics*. Chicago: University of Chicago Press, 1952.

———. *Order in History*. Vol. 3. Columbia: University of Missouri Press, 1999.

———. "Review of *On Tyranny* by Leo Strauss." *The Review of Politics* 11 (1949).

Walzer, Michael. *The Revolution of the Saints*. Boston: Harvard University Press, 1982.

Weiss, Roslyn. *Virtue in the Cave: Moral Inquiry in Plato's Meno*. Oxford: Oxford University Press, 2001.

Whelan, Frederick. *Hume and Machiavelli: Political Realism and Liberal Thought*. Lanham: Lexington, 2004.

Wildavsky, Aaron. *Moses as Political Leader*. Jerusalem: Shalem Press, 2005.

Wolin, Sheldon. *Politics and Vison: Continuity and Innovation in Western Political Thought*. Boston: Little and Brown, 2006.

Wood, Neal. "Xenophon's Theory of Leadership." *Classica et Mediaevelia* 25 (1964).

Woodhouse, J. B. *Baldesar Castiglione: A Reassessment of "The Courtier."* Edinburgh: Edinburgh University Press, 1978.

Xenophon. *Cyropaedia*. 2 vols. Miller trans. London: Loeb Classical Library, 1968a.

———. *The Cyropaedia or Institution of Cyrus*. "Bibliographical Notice of Xenophon." Watson trans. London: George Bell, 1880.

———. *Kurou paideia, or, The Institution and Life of Cyrus the Great*. Digby trans. Beinecke Rare Book Room and Library, Yale University, 1685. Preface.

———. *Memorabilia, Oecnonomicus, Symposium, Apology*. Miller trans. London: Loeb Classical Library, 1968.

Yack, Bernard. "Community and Conflict in Aristotle's Political Philosophy." *Review of Politics* 47 (1984).

———. *The Longing for Total Revolution*. Berkeley: University of California Press, 1992.

Zeigler, Gregory. "Plato's *Gorgias* and Psychological Egoism." *The Personalist* 60 (1979).

Zuckert, Catherine. "Fortune Is a Woman – But So Is Prudence: Machiavelli's *Clizia*." In *Finding a New Feminism: Rethinking the Woman Question* for *Liberal Democracy*. Jensen ed. New York: Rowman and Littlefield, 1996.

―――. *Plato's Philosophers: The Coherence of the Dialogues*. Chicago: University of Chicago Press, 2009.

―――. *Understanding the Political Spirit*. Zuckert ed. New Haven: Yale University Press, 1988.

Zuckert, Michael. "Appropriation and Understanding in the History of Political Philosophy: On Quentin Skinner's Method." In *Launching Liberalism*. Lawrence: University Press of Kansas, 2002.

INDEX

Xenophon (*cont.*)
  on Cyrus the Great, 189–190, 194,
    196–209, 260–261
  Cyrus the Great as an idealized
    Alcibiades, 200, 225–226
  Education of Cyrus (work), 193–194,
    197–198, 199–209, 232, 238–241,
    243–244, 247–248, 256–260,
    265–266
  on eros and thumos, 200, 203, 207–208
  esoteric teaching concerning fraud and
    violence, 238–240, 258–260
  Hiero (work), 13, 191–196
  Memorabilia (work), 194, 197
  on monarchy and the art of household
    management, 195, 204–205
  Oeconomicus (work), 196–199, 209
  preference for monarchy over republics,
    188–189
  relationship to Aristotle, 190–191, 195,
    199–200, 202, 224–225
  relationship to Herodotus, 47, 205,
    235–236, 237, 240, 242,
    247
  relationship to Plato, 102–103,
    188–191, 199–200, 224–225
  relationship to the mirror of princes
    genre, 228, 239, 244, 257
  relationship to Thucydides, 212
  on the philosophic life and political
    excellence, 189–190
  on the reform of tyranny, 200
  on virtue, fortune, and nature,
    208–209
  on what it means to be a gentleman,
    196–197, 209

Zuckert C., 18, 35, 48, 51, 102